The Blue Guides

Albania

Austria Austria
Vienna

Belgium and Luxembourg
China
Cyprus
Czech and Slovak Republics
Denmark
Egypt

France France
Paris and Versailles
Burgundy
Loire Valley
Midi-Pyrénées
Normandy
South West France
Corsica

Germany Berlin and eastern Germany
Western Germany

Greece Greece
Athens and environs
Crete
Rhodes and the Dodecanese

Holland Holland
Amsterdam

Hungary Hungary
Budapest

Southern India
Ireland

Italy Northern Italy
Southern Italy
Florence
Rome
Venice
Tuscany
Umbria
Sicily

Jerusalem
Jordan
Malaysia and Singapore
Malta and Gozo
Mexico
Morocco
Moscow and St Petersburg
Poland
Portugal

Spain Spain
Barcelona
Madrid

Sweden
Switzerland
Thailand
Tunisia

Turkey Turkey
Istanbul

UK England
Scotland
Wales
Channel Islands
London
Oxford and Cambridge
Country Houses of England
Victorian Architecture in
  Britain
Churches and Chapels of
  Northern England
Churches and Chapels of
  Southern England

USA New York
Museums and Galleries of
  New York
Boston and Cambridge

Rome

by Alta Macadam

Maps and plans by John Flower

BLUE GUIDE

A&C Black • London
WW Norton • New York

Sixth edition 1998

Published by A & C Black (Publishers) Limited
35 Bedford Row, London WC1R 4JH

A CIP catalogue record of this book is available from the British Library.

ISBN 0–7136–4669–1

Published in the United States of America by
WW Norton and Company, Inc
500 Fifth Avenue, New York, NY 10110

Published simultaneously in Canada by
Penguin Books Canada Limited
10 Alcorn Avenue, Toronto
Ontario M4V 3B2

ISBN 0–393–31804–4 USA

The author and the publishers have done their best to ensure the accuracy of all the information in Blue Guide Rome; however, they can accept no responsibility for any loss, injury or inconvenience sustained by any traveller as a result of information or advice contained in the guide.

Alta Macadam has been a writer of Blue Guides since 1970. She lives in Florence with her family (the painter Francesco Colacicchi, and their children Giovanni and Lelia). Combined with work on writing the guide she has also been associated with the Bargello Museum, the Alinari photo archive, and Havard University at the Villa I Tatti in Florence. As author of the Blue Guides to Northern Italy, Rome, Venice, Sicily, Florence, Tuscany and Umbria she travels extensively in Italy every year to revise new editions of the books.

Cover picture: detail of Ganges, one of the rivers represented on Bernini's *Fontana dei Quattro Fiumi* in Piazza Navona.
Title page illustration: Arch of Titus in the Roman Forum.

Printed in Great Britain by William Clowes Ltd. Beccles and London.

Contents

Practical Information

Background Information

The Guide

Maps and Plans

Introduction

Rome is one of the most celebrated cities of the world, and ever since her greatest days as the centre of the Roman Empire, and later as the home of the Roman Catholic Church, the city has had a role of the first importance in European history. The Eternal City was the Caput Mundi ('Head of the World') in the Roman era, and from it law and the liberal arts and sciences radiated to the confines of its vast empire, which covered the whole of the known western world. The ancient Roman city, with a population of over one million, was built over the famous seven hills on the left bank of the Tiber. The walls built to defend it by the Emperor Aurelian in the 3C still defined the urban limits of the city in the late 19C, and it was only in the 1940s that the population of the city begin to reach (and supersede) that of ancient Rome.

The city today, the capital of Italy, preserves numerous magnificent Roman buildings side by side with palaces and churches from later centuries. Some of these are very well preserved such as the Pantheon and Colosseum, together with commemorative columns and triumphal arches, while others are picturesque ruins in the very centre of the city. The Vatican, in part of the area of the city which from the 9C onwards became the stronghold of the popes, has, since 1929, been the smallest independent state in the world. Splendid basilicas and churches and beautiful palaces were built in Rome over the centuries by numerous popes, and the city has particularly fine Baroque churches and fountains, including masterpieces by Bernini and Borromini. No fewer than 15 ancient Egyptian obelisks (only five survive in Egypt itself), brought to the city by the ancient Romans, decorate its delightful squares.

The large parks in the centre of Rome are a special feature of the city. Rome also has numerous fashionable shops, mostly in the elegant pedestrian streets which converge on Piazza di Spagna. The great museums in the city include superb collections of ancient Greek and Roman sculpture, while the Vatican collections are famous for their classical sculpture as well as their frescoes by Michelangelo and Raphael, and there are still some fine private patrician collections of paintings in the city.

For centuries Rome has been visited by pilgrims and travellers, but now mass tourism threatens the enjoyment of the individual visitor to Rome (over three-million people see the Sistine Chapel every year, with up to 20,000 in a single day). Thirty million visitors are expected for the Holy Year in the year 2000. Traffic congestion has in part been solved since the 1970s by the closing of much of the historic centre to private cars, but there is still a lot to be done to cut down the volume of traffic in Rome, since the suburbs have become more congested than ever and the air pollution has reached unacceptable levels. The important decision to close the Via Appia Antica to traffic on Sundays was finally taken in 1997.

Since the last edition of the guide the Museo Nazionale Romano has been partially opened in Palazzo Massimo, the Galleria Borghese has been reopened after 14 years of restoration, the Museo Nazionale d'Arte Moderna is now entirely open, the paintings in the Galleria Doria Pamphilj have been rehung, the Etruscan Museum in the Vatican has been rearranged, the Museo Nazionale d'Arte Orientale, Museo Napoleonico and the Palatine Antiquarium have reopened, and a selection of the objects in the Antiquarium Comunale is now exhibited on the Celian Hill. However, many important monuments and museums have been closed or partially closed for decades (including the Museo Nazionale d'Arte Antica in Palazzo Barberini, the Domus Aurea, the Museo Nuovo and Braccio Nuovo in the Musei Capitolini, and the Museo di Roma, although many promises are being made that they will reopen in time for the Holy Year. In this sixth edition more detailed practical information has been provided to ensure the visitor has all the information necessary for a visit to the city.

Acknowledgements

For the revision of this sixth edition of the guide, I am particularly grateful to **Jon Eldan** who did much of the footwork in Rome, checking the descriptions of museums and churches, finding out about opening times, and ensuring that all the details in the text were accurate. Carla Lionello also helped gather information. John Law was kind enough to assist me on some historical questions. I am most grateful to Vittorio Guida for granting us permission to use his photographs as sources for some of the illustrations.

I would also like to thank Dottoressa Marina Sapelli of the Museo Nazionale Romano, Dottoressa Lucina Vattuone of the Vatican, and Principe Jonathan Doria Pamphilj for their kind assistance.

How to Use this Guide

The guide is divided into 30 **chapters**, 27 of them devoted to walks within the city, each of them designed to be accomplished in no more than a day (with the help of public transport for those routes outside the historic centre of the city). The last three chapters cover the immediate environs of Rome, which can be reached easily in a day by public transport from the centre of the city.

Each important monument in the city is given a **reference** in the text (Pl. 1; 1) referring to the 15-page **atlas** at the back of the book, which has been gridded with numbered squares. The first figure denotes the page of the atlas, and the second denotes the grid square. Ground plan references are given in the text as a bracketed single figure or letter.

Opening times of the museums and monuments in force in 1997 are given in the text and in the timetable on pp 37–9. Telephone numbers have also been given, since opening times change frequently, and it is always best to check locally. Prices, which vary greatly (and can sometimes be unjustifiably high at private museums) have also been listed. Opening times of most churches have been given within the text.

Telephone numbers throughout the text appear without the prefix for Rome (06), which has to be used if you are calling from outside the city.

The **most important monuments** or **works of art** in Rome have been highlighted in bold throughout the text, and **asterisks** are used to indicate works of art which are particularly beautiful or interesting. The **highlights** section on p 10 singles out the major monuments of each period which should not be missed.

All **churches** are taken as being orientated, with the entrance at the west end and the altar at the east end, the south aisle on the right and the north aisle on the left. Although many churches in Rome are not, in fact, orientated, this has seemed the simplest way of providing a standard description of church interiors, beginning at the entrance and following the right side up to the sanctuary and then returning down the left side to the entrance.

An exhaustive section at the beginning of the book lists all the **practical information** you are likely to need during a visit to Rome. A small selection of **hotels** (see pp 16–20) has been given, listed according to location and category (which indicates the price range). They have been keyed in the list with plan references which refer to the 15-page atlas section at the back of the book (eg, Pl. 4; 1 is page 4, square 1 of the atlas). A small selection of **restaurants** (see pp 24–9)has been given, listed according to price range and area (and their telephone numbers supplied so that you can check they are open, and, if necessary, book a table).

Numerous people, including popes and emperors, appear throughout the text: their dates have not been repeated at every reference, but can easily be found in the lists of **Roman emperors** (p 53) and **list of Popes** on p 415. Artists' dates are given in the **index to artists** (p 422). Architectural terms, etc. are explained in the **glossary** on p 411.

Abbreviations used in the guide

EPT	Ente Provinciale per il Turismo (the Provincial Tourist board)
ATAC	Azienda Tramvie e Autobus del Comune di Roma (the bus company which serves the city of Rome)
COTRAL	Consorzio Trasporti Pubblici Lazio (the bus company which serves Lazio)
fest. festa,	festival (i.e. holiday)
Pl.	plan reference to the atlas at the back of the book
km	kilometre(s)
m	metre(s)
C	century
FS	ferrovie dello Stato (Italian State Railways)

The 24-hour clock is used for all opening times, etc. (eg 8.15–19)

For Glossary, see p 411

The Highlights of Rome

Ancient Rome. The best place to start a visit to Rome is on the Capitol Hill, the historic centre of the ancient city, with splendid views of the Forum and Palatine and, in the other direction, of the modern city, with St Peter's on the skyline. In the piazza, designed by Michelangelo, are the Capitoline museums, with very fine collections of Roman sculpture.

The Forum and Palatine, with their remarkable ruined temples, palaces, triumphal arches, basilicas, etc, evoke the spirit of the Roman Republic and Empire as nowhere else, and symbolize the grandeur of the ancient city. On the peaceful Palatine Hill the great monuments survive amid luxuriant vegetation.

The Colosseum, a huge amphitheatre, is the most famous monument of ancient Rome. The Pantheon, with its extraordinary dome, is the best preserved Roman building. The monumental Baths of Caracalla and the exquisitely carved Ara Pacis also represent some of the highest achievements of Roman architecture and sculpture (and are among the least visited). The commemorative columns of Trajan and Marcus Aurelius are still important features of the city, even though the very fine sculptured reliefs on them are difficult to appreciate with the naked eye. Beyond the impressive Circus of Maxentius and the Tomb of Cecilia Metella, the Via Appia still preserves its appearance as an important consular highway leading out of the city (best visited on Sundays when closed to traffic).

Districts of Rome which are particularly attractive and typical of the city include Piazza di Spagna (and the neighbouring elegant streets of Via Condotti, Via Frattina, Via del Babuino, Via Margutta), Piazza Navona, the area around the Pantheon, Campo dei Fiori and its vicinity (including Piazza Farnese), and Trastevere (with Piazza di Santa Maria in Trastevere).

St Peter's and the Vatican Museums are of the highest interest. The huge 16C basilica of St Peter's, with its dome by Michelangelo, and its works by Bernini, is the most famous church in Christendom. The Vatican Museums include extensive collections covering all periods, especially notable for their superb Greek and Roman sculpture, as well as for the Sistine Chapel frescoed by Michelangelo, and the Stanze frescoed by Raphael.

Churches. After St Peter's, the historic basilicas of Santa Maria Maggiore, San Giovanni in Laterano, and San Paolo fuori le Mura, are the most important churches in Rome. Among smaller basilicas which have particularly attractive interiors are Santa Sabina and Santa Maria in Trastevere. Other churches which should not be missed include Santa Maria della Pace (closed at the time of writing), Santa Maria del Popolo, San Giorgio in Velabro, Santa Maria in Cosmedin, Santo Stefano Rotondo, San Giovanni a Porta Latina and San Clemente.

Museums. Apart from the Vatican collections and the Capitoline Museums, the most important museums include the Museo Nazionale Romano, with ancient

Roman works (but only partially open); the beautifully restored Museo and Galleria Borghese (for works by Bernini and Caravaggio); the Galleria Doria Pamphilj (a private Roman patrician collection); the Galleria Nazionale d'Arte Antica (13C–18C paintings) in Palazzo Barberini and Palazzo Corsini (Baroque paintings); the Museo Barracco (ancient sculpture); the Museo Nazionale Etrusco di Villa Giulia (Etruscan works); the Museo di Palazzo Venezia (decorative arts); Galleria Spada (17C and 18C works); and Castel Sant'Angelo. Specialised collections include a fine museum of musical instruments.

Rome has a wealth of beautiful **gardens and parks**. The largest parks include the extensive Villa Borghese and Pincio in the centre of the city, and the Villa Doria Pamphilj on the southern outskirts. The Farnese gardens on the Palatine Hill are famous. For other gardens, see p 40.

The city is particularly famous for its **Baroque** buildings. Among the Baroque churches are the Gesù, Sant'Andrea della Valle, Sant'Agnese in Agone and Sant'Ignazio. **Bernini**, the most important Baroque artist who worked in Rome, designed the splendid Piazza in front of St Peter's (as well as the *baldacchino* and *tribuna* inside the church) and the church of Sant'Andrea al Quirinale. His sculptures can be seen in the churches of Santa Maria della Vittoria, Santa Bibiana, and San Francesco a Ripa, as well as in the Museo Borghese. His delightful fountains include the Fontana del Tritone, and Fontana dei Quattro Fiumi in Piazza Navona. **Borromini** was the architect of San Carlo alle Quattro Fontane, Sant'Agnese in Agone, and the courtyard of the Palazzo della Sapienza (with the church of Sant'Ivo).

Beautiful Renaissance palaces include Palazzo della Cancelleria, Palazzo Farnese and the Villa Farnesina.

Artists who worked in Rome, and who are particularly well represented here, include Raphael, Michelangelo, and Caravaggio. The remarkable frescoes in the Stanze in the Vatican are **Raphael's** masterpiece (and there are paintings by him in the Vatican picture gallery). Other works by him are to be found in Santa Maria del Popolo, Santa Maria della Pace and Sant'Agostino. **Michelangelo** designed the dome of St Peter's, Piazza del Campidoglio, and part of Palazzo Farnese; there are sculptures by him in St Peter's (the Pietà), San Pietro in Vincoli (Moses) and Santa Maria sopra Minerva; and his greatest works are the beautiful frescoes in the Sistine Chapel. **Caravaggio** left works in San Luigi dei Francesi, Sant'Agostino, and Santa Maria del Popolo, and there are paintings by him in the collections of the Pinacoteca Capitolina, Galleria Borghese, Palazzo Corsini, Palazzo Barberini, and Galleria Doria Pamphilj.

There are many churches with lovely **mosaics** all over Rome: Santa Costanza and Santa Pudenziana (4C), Santa Maria Maggiore (5C and 13C), Baptistery of San Giovanni (5C and 7C), San Marco, Santa Cecilia in Trastevere, Santa Prassede and Santa Maria in Domnica (9C), San Clemente, Santa Maria Nova and Santa Maria in Trastevere (12C).

The **fountains** of Rome are a special feature of the city as Rome has an abundant water supply. The most famous fountains are the Fontana di Trevi, and the Fontana dei Quattro Fiumi in Piazza Navona, but there are numerous others in nearly every piazza. The **Tiber** can best be seen from the picturesque little Isola Tiberina, or from Bernini's Ponte Sant'Angelo.

The **catacombs**, the extensive underground cemeteries of the early Christians, are fascinating sights: the most important ones are St Calixtus and San Sebastiano on the Via Appia; St Domitilla on Via delle Sette Chiese; St Agnes on Via Nomentana; and Priscilla on the Via Salaria.

The **environs of Rome** include the excavations of the important Roman city of Ostia Antica, and the magnificent ruins of Hadrian's Villa outside Tivoli, set in a beautifully planted and peaceful site. Famous gardens include the Villa d'Este at Tivoli.

The most recent changes
Please note the following changes that took place during the final stages of production of this edition and which we were unable to include in the main text.

The Palatine (p 95). Admission 9–2 hours before sunset; Sun 9–13.

Palatine Antiquarium (p 95) reopened after 13 years' restoration. The fine collection of material from palaces on the hill includes wall decorations and frescoes, stucco, marble intarsia, and sculptures. The painted terracotta panels were found near the Temple of Apollo, and the frescoes of Homeric subjects and marble intarsia pavements in the Domus Transitoria of Nero.

Colosseum (p 115). Upper level 9–2 hours before sunset; Sun and Wed 9–13, ☎ 699 0110. Lire 10,000. The upper storeys remain closed.

Pantheon (p 118). Admission 9–18.30; Sun 9–13.

Casina delle Civette (p 266). The delightful little Art Nouveau **Casina delle Civette** has been restored and was reopened as the **Museo della Vetrata** (9–17, exc Mon; Lire 5000. Designed by Vincenzo Fasolo, it has interesting stained glass by Cesare Picchiarini (1916–19) and the museum also contains stained glass by Duilio Cambellotti and others. Several neo-Gothic garden buildings of 1840 by Giuseppe Japelli are to be restored.

Loggia of Cupid and Psyche (p 279) opened after a lengthy restoration.

Museo Nazionale di Castel Sant'Angelo (p 287) open 9–19; closed second and fourth Tues of the month.

Practical Information

Getting to Rome

When to Go. The climate of Rome is exceptionally good except in the height of summer and periodically in the winter. The best months to visit the city are October and November or March (the most crowded periods, to be avoided if at all possible, are Easter, May and June, September, and Christmas).

Passports are necessary for all British and American travellers entering Italy. A lost or stolen passport can be replaced with little trouble by the relevant embassy in Rome.

Embassies

Australia: 25/c C. Trieste, ☎ 8522721. Open Mon–Thurs, 9–12 and 13.30–17; Fri 9–12.
Canada: 30 Via Zara, ☎ 445981. Open weekdays 8.30–12.30 and 13.30–16.
Republic of Ireland: 3 Piazza Campitelli, ☎ 697 9121. Open weekdays 10–12.30 and 15–16.30.
New Zealand: 28 Via Zara, ☎ 440 2928. Open weekdays 8.30–12.45 and 13.45–17.
South Africa: 14 Via Tanaro, ☎ 8522541. Open weekdays 8.30–12.
United Kingdom: 80/A Via XX Settembre, ☎ 482 5441. Open weekdays 9.30–13.30.
United States of America: 121 Via Veneto, ☎ 46741. Open weekdays 8.30–12.

Italian Tourist Boards. General information can be obtained abroad from the Italian State Tourist Office (ENIT, *Ente Nazionale Italiano per il Turismo*), who distribute free an invaluable *Traveller's Handbook* (usually revised every year) and an annual list of hotels in Rome.
Canada: 1 Place Ville Marie, Suite 1914, Montreal, ☎ (514) 886 7667, fax (514) 392 1429.
Netherlands: Stadhoudestrade 2, 1054 ES Amsterdam, ☎ 6168246, fax 6188515.
UK: 1 Princes Street, WIR 8AY, ☎ 0171 408 1254, 0171 493 6695.
USA. New York: 630 Fifth Avenue, Suite 1665, NY 10111, ☎ 245 4822, fax 586 9249. Chicago: 401 North Michigan Avenue, Suite 3030, ☎ 644 0996, fax 644 3019. Los Angeles: 12400 Wilshire Blvd, Suite 550, ☎ 820 1898, fax 820 6357.

In Rome the official tourist office for Rome and its province (*Ente Provinciale per il Turismo di Roma*), known as the EPT, has an information office at 5 Via Parigi (☎ 488 99253 or 488 99255), open Mon–Fri 8.15–19; Sat 8.15–13.45; closed Sun. It also has offices at the main railway station of Termini and at Fiumicino airport (with information on hotel vacancies); opening hours are 8.15–19; Termini, ☎ 487 1270, fax 482 4078; airport branches, ☎ 659 56074, fax 659 54471. EPT offices supply a list of hotels in Rome, a map, a brief guide to the city, and up-to-date opening times.

Among the numerous **tour operators** which offer package holidays to Rome from the UK are: *Crystal Holidays* (☎ 0181 241 4000; fax 0181 390 6378); *International Chapters* (☎ 0171 722 9560), *Magic of Italy* (☎ 0181 748 7575; 0181 748 3731), *Prospect Music and Art Tours* (☎ 0181 995 2163; fax 0181 742 1969), *Martin Randall Travel* (☎ 0181 742 3355; fax 0181 742 1066), *Thomson City Breaks* (☎ 0990 502555),

Accommodation services from the UK are offered by *Accommodation Line Ltd* (☎ 0171 409 1343; fax 0171 409 2606); *Hotel Connect* (☎ 0181 906 2686; fax 0181 906 262); *The Italian Connection* (☎ 0171 486 6890; fax 0171 486 6891) who can arrange accommodation in hotels, pensions, and self-catering apartments; *Room Service* (☎ 0171 636 6888; fax 0171 636 6002) can also help with flights, car hire, and insurance.

Getting to Rome by air. Direct air services between London and Rome are operated by *British Airways* (☎ 0181 897 4000), *Alitalia* (☎ 0171 602 7111 or 0181 745 8200), and *British Midland Airways UK* (☎ 0345 554554). Details of charter flights can be obtained through travel agents or in newspapers, especially the Sunday newspapers and the London *Evening Standard*, and in *Time Out*. Scheduled services offer special fares which are available according to season; youth fares are available and fly-drive schemes can also be arranged.

Air Services from the USA include *Alitalia* (☎ 800 223 5730), which flies non-stop from New York, Boston, Chicago and Los Angeles; *Continental* (☎ 800 231 0856), New York to Rome; *Delta* (☎ 800 241 4141), New York to Rome; *TWA* (☎ 800 892 4141), New York to Rome; and *United* (☎ 800 538 2929), Washington DC to Rome. *British Airways, Air France, KLM,* and *Sabena* offer flights connecting through London, Paris, Amsterdam and Brussels, and these are often more economical than direct flights.

Getting to Rome by train. Rome can be reached by through train from Paris Lyon overnight (by sleeper); there are now frequent trains from London Waterloo through the Eurotunnel via Calais to Paris Nord (in c 3hrs). For more information, contact *European Rail Ltd* (☎ 0171 387 0444; fax 0171 387 0888). Italian State Railways are represented in the UK by *Citalia* (☎ 0181 686 0677; fax 0181 686 0328).

Getting to Rome by coach. For details of the coach services available from the UK to Rome, contact Eurolines (☎ 01582 404511) or a local National Express Agent. In Italy, the offices of SITA will be able to advise on international coach travel.

Arriving in Rome

Airports. Fiumicino (*Leonardo da Vinci*; ☎ 65 951), 26km southwest of Rome, is the airport for both international and domestic air services. Trains (FS) from Stazione Termini hourly (from about 7 to 21.15) in 30 minutes; and from Tiburtina station via Ostiense and Trastevere in 41 minutes (from about 5.00 to 23.00). Taxis have standard meter charges plus an airport supplement of Lire 10,000, or by agreement in advance. It is recommended that you take a taxi if you are arriving late at night.

Ciampino (☎ 794 941), 13km southeast of Rome, is a subsidiary airport used mainly for domestic flights and international charter flights. It can be reached by underground (line A) from Termini Station to Anagnina station, and from there by airport bus (COTRAL) every 30 minutes (from 6 to 22.00), but this journey is not very convenient and most visitors prefer to take a taxi.

Railway Stations. Stazione Termini (Pl. 5; 4), Piazza dei Cinquecento is the main station for all services of the State railways and for the underground railway. ☎ 147 888 088 (Lost Property, ☎ 473 066 82). The luggage deposit centre (☎ 483 062 75) is open 7–10. The DrugStore Termini, a mini supermarket, is open 24 hours a day; other shops here open normal business hours. Stazione Roma Tiburtina is used by some fast trains which do not stop at Stazione Termini. Less central than the main station, it is well served by buses, and is on Line B of the underground (*la metropolitana*), four stops from Termini. The stations of Ostiense and Trastevere are on the line to Fiumicino Airport. Subsidiary stations (of little interest to the tourist) include Roma Tuscolana, San Pietro and Prenestina.

Money and banks
The monetary unit is the Italian *lira* (plural, *lire*). Notes are issued for 2000, 5000, 10,000, 50,000, 100,000 and 500,000 lire. Coins are of 50, 100, 200, 500 and 1000 lire. There are currently three sizes of 50 and 100 lire coins. Travellers' cheques and Eurocheques are the safest way of carrying money when travelling, and most credit cards are now generally accepted in shops, hotels and restaurants (and at some petrol stations). In the centre of town there are numerous automatic teller machines (ATMs) called Bancomat, and also machines which change foreign bank notes.

Banks are usually open Monday–Friday 8.30–13.30, 14.45–15.45 (or 14.30–15.30); closed Saturday, Sunday and holidays. They close early (about 11) on days preceding national holidays. The commission on cashing travellers' cheques can be quite high. Money can also be changed at exchange offices (cambio), travel agencies, some post offices, and main railway stations. Some hotels, restaurants, and shops exchange money (but usually at a lower rate).

Accommodation
The **hotels** in Rome are all listed with their charges in the annual (free) publication of the EPT of Rome: *Esercizi Ricettivi di Roma e provincia* (available from EPT offices). It is essential to book well in advance at Easter and in September and October; you are usually asked to send a deposit (or leave a credit card number) to confirm the booking. Information about hotels in Rome can be obtained from Italian State Tourist Offices, and on arrival at the EPT information office at the railway station, or at the other information offices of the EPT. The **Hotel Reservation Service** provides free booking services with over 350 hotels from booths in Stazione Termini and Fiumicino Airport, or over the phone (☎ 699 1000), from 7.00–22.00.

The most pleasant areas to stay in the city include the streets around Piazza di Spagna, the Pantheon and Campo dei Fiori. The numerous hotels near Termini Station and on Via Veneto are in much less attractive districts and further away from the main monuments.

Every hotel has to declare its prices annually (and these are published in the EPT hotel list). The total charge for the room should be displayed on the back of the door of the hotel room. Prices change according to the season, and can be considerably less in off-peak periods. Breakfast (usually disappointing and costly) is by law an optional extra charge, although a lot of hotels try to include it in the price of the room. When booking a room, always specify if you want breakfast or not. It is usually well worthwhile going round the corner to the nearest bar for breakfast. Hotels are obliged by law (for tax purposes) to issue an official receipt to customers; you should not leave the premises without this document (*ricevuta fiscale*).

There are five official categories of hotels in Italy, from the luxury 5-star hotels to the most simple 1-star establishments. However, these categories are bound to disappoint many travellers: they are now established by the services offered (television in each room, private telephone, minibar, etc), and often do not reflect quality. 3-star and 4-star hotels in Rome are not always on a par with hotels with the same designation in the other large European cities. Rome has some 750 hotels and only a small selection has been given below; omission does not imply any derogatory judgement. The hotels have been listed according to category and location. The Pl. references (eg Pl. 4; 1) refer to the atlas section at the back of the book.

Hotels in Rome

Near Piazza di Spagna

5-STAR

Hassler Villa Medici (Pl. 4; 1), 6 Piazza Trinità dei Monti; ☎ 699 340; fax 678 9991. Famous hotel at the top of the Spanish Steps, elegantly furnished with antiques and crystal chandeliers. Stunning views from street-side rooms and the rooftop terrace/restaurant, and a well-earned reputation for first-rate service. Summer garden. Garage and restaurant.

4-STAR

De La Ville (Pl. 4; 3), 69 Via Sistina, 00187; ☎ 673 31; fax 678 4213. Along with the Hassler, one of the classiest and most luxurious hotels in town. Many rooms with frescoes and stucco decoration. Great views from top floor rooms. Garage and restaurant.

D'Inghilterra (Pl. 3; 4), 14 Bocca di Leone, 00187; ☎ 699 81; fax 699 22243. A small, elegant hotel at the heart of Rome's fashionable shopping streets. Rooms are decorated with turn-of-the-century English furniture. The charming breakfast room in the basement is entirely frescoed with Roman garden scenes. Restaurant.

Plaza (Pl. 3; 4), 126 Via del Corso, 00186; ☎ 699 2111; fax 699 41575. Large, busy hotel, popular with businessman and politicians, though its elegance is slightly worn around the edges. Rooms vary greatly in size and decor. Terrace and restaurant.

3-STAR

City Nova (Pl. 4; 3), 97 Via due Macelli, 00187; ☎ 679 7468; fax 679 7962. A solid, comfortable pensione on the street that runs between the Piazza di

Spagna and the Trevi Fountain. Helpful and professional staff.
Gregoriana (Pl. 4; 3), 18 Via Gregoriana, 00187; ☎ 679 4269; fax 678 4258.
A small, well-cared for hotel on one of the quietest streets in the area. Several
rooms with balconies. Breakfast served on the lovely terrace in summertime.
Internazionale (Pl. 4; 3), 79 Via Sistina, 00187; ☎ 679 3047; fax 678 4764.
Housed in a 16C convent, this 42 room hotel retains a pleasantly old-fashioned
atmosphere. Rooms on the fourth floor have balconies, and several rooms have
jacuzzi tubs, a rarity in Rome.
Locarno (Pl. 3; 2), 22 Via della Penna, 00186; ☎ 336 10841; fax 321 5249.
Located just off Piazza del Popolo, about 15 minutes' walk to Piazza di Spagna,
the Locarno is a lovely hotel decorated in Art Deco (Liberty) style. A pleasant
roof bar and complimentary bicycles are available on loan.
Scalinata di Spagna (Pl. 4; 3), 17 Piazza Trinità dei Monti, 00187; ☎ 699
40896; fax 699 40598. Some of the rooms are a bit small, but this quiet,
romantic hotel is right by the Spanish Steps, with a lovely roof garden.

2-STAR
Homs (Pl. 4; 3), 71 Via della Vite, 00187; ☎ 679 2976; fax 678 0482. A
simple, family-run hotel in the heart of Rome's fashionable shopping area, with
a beautiful terrace. Bathrooms and rooms are rather small.
Margutta (Pl. 4; 3), 34 Via Laurina, 00817; ☎ 322 3674; fax 482 4277.
Lovely pensione tucked away on a quiet street just off Piazza di Spagna. The 21
double rooms are furnished with iron beds and dark wooden furniture.
Suisse (Pl. 4; 3), 56 Via Gregoriana, 00817; ☎ 678 3649; fax 678 1258.
Spotless budget hotel in a prime location . Some of the 13 rooms have decorated
ceilings and antique furniture.

Near the Pantheon, Piazza Navona and Campo de' Fiori

5-STAR
Holiday Inn Crowne Plaza Minerva (Pl. 2; 6), 69 Piazza della Minerva,
00186; ☎ 699 41888; fax 679 4165. Right behind the Pantheon, a well-maintained 17C façade hides a dramatic, modern interior, designed by Paolo
Portoghesi, and full of marble and stained glass. The rooms are comfortable and
quiet; many have views onto the narrow streets below. Beautiful roof garden.

4-STAR
Sole al Pantheon (Pl. 3; 6), 63 Piazza della Rotonda, 00186; ☎ 678 0441; fax
699 40689. Just steps away from the Pantheon (several of the 25 rooms have
views), this hotel has been in business since the 15C. Rooms are cool and fresh,
with whitewashed walls and terracotta decorations; jacuzzi tubs are a modern
touch.

3-STAR
Del Senato (Pl. 3; 6), 73 Piazza della Rotonda, 00186; ☎ 679 3231; fax 699
40297. Many rooms look out onto the Pantheon, just a few steps from the hotel.
The lower floors and entrance have been renovated tastefully; the upper floors
remain a little dated.
Santa Chiara (Pl. 3; 6), 21 Via di Santa Chiara, 00186; ☎ 687 2979; fax 687
3144. An elegant, family-run hotel just behind the Pantheon. Well-appointed

rooms have solid wood furniture and marble bathrooms. Many rooms have pleasant views, a few with balconies.

Portoghesi (Pl. 3; 4), 1 Via dei Portoghesi, ☎ 686 4231; fax 687 6976. Unassuming hotel, well-located on a quiet street between the Tiber and Piazza Navona. Great view from the terrace, where breakfast is served in summertime.

2-STAR

Campo de' Fiori (Pl. 2; 8), 6 Via del Biscione, 00186; ☎ 688 06865; fax 687 6003. A well-maintained, reasonably priced hotel just off the piazza of the same name. The 27 rooms are cosy (those on the first floor have the best decor), but only nine have full bathrooms. Views of the lovely square from the two common terraces.

Sole (Pl. 3; 5), 76 Via del Biscione, 00186, ☎ 687 9446; fax 689 3787. This medium-sized, cosy hotel is one of the best deals in the area, although not all the rooms have bathrooms and there is no breakfast service. You can watch the sun set over the dome of the church of Sant'Andrea della Valle from the top terrace or relax in the inner garden. No credit cards.

Teatro di Pompeo (Pl. 3; 6), 8 Largo del Pallaro, 00186, ☎ 683 00170; fax 688 05531. Located in a quiet small square between Campo de' Fiori and Corso Vittorio Emanuele, this tranquil hotel sits on the remains of a Roman theatre, whose original 55 BC circular structure is still visible in the breakfast room. All the 13 attractive rooms (only one single available) feature old wooden ceilings.

On the Aventine Hill

3-STAR

Domus Aventina (Pl. 8; 5), 11b Via di Santa Prisca, 00153; ☎ 574 6135; fax 573 00044. Well-run and comfortable, this very popular hotel offers peace and comfort at a excellent price. Housed in an ex-convent, 26 spacious rooms, some with balconies, face onto a courtyard and the wall of a lovely church.

Sant'Anselmo (Pl. 8; 5), 2 Piazza Sant'Anselmo, 00153; ☎ 578 3214; fax 578 3604. Tucked into the peaceful residential neighbourhood atop the Aventine Hill, the 45 rooms are cheerfully decorated like a Venetian villa. Some rooms have balconies. Breakfast is served in a pretty garden.

Villa San Pio (Pl. 8; 5), 19 Via Sant'Anselmo, 00153; ☎ 574 5174; fax 578 3604. Under the same management as the Sant'Anselmo, with a slightly larger garden and only 19 rooms.

Via Veneto and the Parioli

5-STAR

Eden (Pl. 4; 1), 49 Via Ludovisi, 00187; ☎ 478 121; fax 482 1584. Totally renovated in 1994, the Eden is one of the finest hotels in Rome; very elegant with all the comforts and services of a first-rate hotel. The roof restaurant, with adjoining piano bar, has a panoramic view of the city and is among the best in town. Gymnasium.

Excelsior (Pl. 4; 1), 125 Via Vittorio Veneto, 00187; ☎ 47081; fax 482 6205. Opposite the American Embassy on the Via Veneto and one of Rome's most famous hotels, the Excelsior thrives on the glory days of old. Rooms were redone in 1990.

Lord Byron (Pl. 11; 5), 5 Via de Notaris, 00197; ☎ 322 0404; fax 322 0405.

This quiet, exclusive hotel built in a converted mansion in the Parioli area, with views onto the Villa Borghese, seems far removed from the chaos of the centre of town. First-rate restaurant on the ground floor. Excellent, attentive service.

4-STAR

Ambasciatori Palace (Pl. 4; 1), 70 Via Veneto, 00187; ☎ 474 93; fax 474 3601. An elegant, old-style hotel. The decor is rich with antiques and plush carpets. Courteous and attentive staff.

La Residenza (Pl. 4; 1), 22 Via Emilia, 00187; ☎ 488 0789; fax 485 721. A popular hotel which combines a central location with villa-style decor and large, comfortable rooms. Good service.

Vittoria (Pl. 4; 1), 41 Via Campania, 00187, ☎ 473 931; fax 487 1890. Just a block off the Via Veneto, this Swiss-run hotel offers excellent value: spacious, spotless rooms and friendly staff who attend to the smallest detail. Rooftop terrace with view onto the Villa Borghese across the street.

3-STAR

Villa Borghese (Pl. 4; 1), 31 Via Pinciana, 00198; ☎ 854 9648; 841 4100. A pleasant hotel just off the park of the same name. Rooms are small but well cared for. Breakfast is served on an ivy-covered patio.

2-STAR

Merano (Pl. 4; 1), 155 Via Veneto, 00187; ☎ 482 1808; fax 482 1810. A small pensione with dated decor, but a prime location.

Near the Vatican

4-STAR

Cicerone (Pl. 2; 3), 55/c Cicerone, 00193; ☎ 3576; fax 688 01383. Reasonably priced, modern hotel located near Castel Sant'Angelo in a side street off the busy Via Cola di Rienzo. The 237 rooms are comfortable but without character. Friendly, professional staff. Covered parking in the basement.

Farnese (Pl. 2; 3), 30 Via Alessandro Farnese, 00192; ☎ 321 2553; fax 321 55129. A recently renovated mansion offers comfortable and tastefully decorated rooms in the quiet, residential Prati quarter, not far from the shopping on Via Cola di Rienzo and just across the river from the *centro storico*.

Amalia (Pl. 1; 4), 66 Via Germanico, 00192; ☎ 397 23356; fax 397 23365. Popular with Italians, this super-clean modern hotel is convenient for the Vatican and the Ottaviano Metro stop. Friendly staff.

3-STAR

Columbus (Pl. 1; 6), 33 Via della Conciliazione, 00193; ☎ 686 5435; fax 686 4874. Two minutes' walk from St Peter's Square. A pleasant hotel with well-furnished rooms, beautiful common areas with wooden ceilings and a carved terrace full of green plants and flowers make this ex-convent an excellent choice.

Sant'Anna (Pl. 1; 4), 133–4 Borgo Pio, 00193; ☎ 688 01602; fax 683 08717. Small hotel decorated in Art Deco style. Ample rooms on the top floor have small terraces. Parking.

Via Nazionale, Stazione Termini and Santa Maria Maggiore
5-STAR

Le Grand Hotel (Pl. 4; 4), 3 Via Vittorio Emanuele Orlando, 00185; ☎ 47091; fax 474 7307. Old-fashioned, classy hotel near Stazione Termini has long been one of the city's finest. Marble baths and Murano chandeliers recall a day when no expense was spared to decorate top class hotels. Afternoon tea is still served in the richly decorated main salon.

4-STAR

Massimo d'Azeglio (Pl. 5; 6), 18 Via Cavour, 00184; ☎ 488 0646; fax 482 7386. Serviceable hotel just a few blocks from Stazione Termini which has been in business since 1875. It has a decidedly dated feel. The 203 spacious rooms have solid furniture in the classic style. Attentive staff.

3-STAR

Aberdeen (Pl. 5; 3), 48 Via Firenze, 00184; ☎ 482 3920; fax 482 1092. Pensione on two floors within a building on this street. Large buffet breakfast.
Ariston (Pl. 5; 6), 16 Via Turati, 00185; ☎ 446 5399; fax 446 5396. Unexciting but basic, quiet hotel near the station.
Impero (Pl. 5; 3), 19 Via Viminale, 00184; ☎ 482 0066; fax 483 762. Close to the Teatro dell'Opera, the Impero is graciously set in a 19C building. Spacious common areas alternate with cosy living rooms. The doors are painted with scenes from Ancient Rome, and the whole decor is done in Liberty style.
Patria (Pl. 5; 3), 36 Via Torino, 00184; ☎ 488 0756; fax 481 4872. Totally renovated in the last few years, with modern fixtures and anti-noise windows. 49 rooms on five floors, and a bar open 24 hours a day.
Villa delle Rose (Pl. 5; 4), 5 Via Vicenza, 00185; ☎ 445 1788; fax 445 1639. A quiet, friendly hotel housed in a villa with a garden near the station. The bar and lounge have original frescoes on the ceiling, in sharp contrast with the very simple decor of the 40 rooms, some of which are spacious enough to accommodate extra beds. The non-smoking breakfast area is a welcome surprise.

Capital, Campidoglio and Forum
4-STAR

Forum (Pl. 4; 5), 25 Via Tor dei Conti, 00184; ☎ 679 2446; fax 678 6479. The Imperial Fora are just a few steps from the front door of the hotel, and many of the rooms and the rooftop terrace (with restaurant and bar service) offer some of the best views in the city onto the ruins of ancient Rome. The 76 rooms are comfortable but not particularly attractive with varied decor that is a bit worn-out.

3-STAR

Edera (Pl. 9; 2), 75 Via Poliziano, 00184; ☎ 704 53888; fax 704 53769. Sober, medium-sized hotel with spacious doubles and an inner garden. On a quiet street, two minutes' walk from the Colosseum.

2-STAR

Casa Kolbe (Pl. 4; 7), 44 Via San Teodoro 00186; ☎ 679 4974, fax 699-41550. Located on a tranquil street an the edge of the Forum, the Kolbe offers great double rooms with bath at a reasonable price. Small garden. No credit cards.

Youth Hostels and Students' Hostels. The *Associazione Italiana Alberghi per la Gioventù* (Italian Youth Hostels Association) has its national headquarters at 44 Via Cavour (☎ 474 1256). The Rome Youth Hostel (and regional headquarters) is at the Ostello del Foro Italico, 61 Viale delle Olimpiadi (☎ 3242571 or 3242573). Girls' hostels include the YWCA, 4 Via Balbo (☎ 488 0460 or 488 3917), and Protezione della Giovane, 158 Via Urbana. The Salvation Army has a hostel at 39/42 Via degi Apuli. Religious organisations run some hostels for students and visitors.

Camping. The sites are listed in the annual EPT hotel list. Rates charged must be displayed at the camp site office. Full details of the sites in Italy are published annually by the Touring Club Italiano and Federcampeggio in *Campeggi e Villaggi turistici in Italia*. The Federazione Italiana del Campeggio have an information office and booking service at 11 Via Vittorio Emanuele, Calenzano, 50041 Florence (☎ 055-882 391). Among the sites on the outskirts of Rome open all year are: *Roma Camping*, 831 Via Aurelia (☎ 662 3018); *Capitol*, 195 Via Castelfusano, Ostia Antica (☎ 565 7344); *Seven Hills*, 1216 Via Cassia (☎ 303 10826), and *Nomentano*, 11 Via della Cesarina (corner of Via Nomentana), ☎ 414 00296. In Lazio there are sites at Anzio, Nettuno, Bracciano and Subiaco.

Eating in Rome

Food in Rome, as in the rest of Italy, is generally extremely good, despite the fact many Romans lament the disappearance in the last few decades of many typical Roman *trattorie* with their traditional food. There are still a great number of good restaurants although there tend to be fewer and fewer cheaper ones. Excellent pizzas are still made in numerous *pizzerie*. The least pretentious restaurant usually provides the best value. Most restaurants display a menu outside which gives you an idea of the prices. However, many simpler restaurants do not provide a menu, and here, although the choice is usually limited, the standard of the cuisine is often very high. Lunch is normally around 13.00, while dinner is around 20.00 or 21.00. Some restaurants still have a cover charge (*coperto*, shown separately on the menu) which is added to the bill (although this has officially been discontinued). Prices include service, unless otherwise stated on the menu. Tipping is therefore not necessary, but a few thousand lire can be left on the table to convey appreciation. Restaurants are now obliged by law (for tax purposes) to issue an official receipt to customers; you should not leave the premises without this document (*ricevuta fiscale*). It is always acceptable to order a first course only, or to skip the first course and order only a main course.

The menu

Some of the best items of traditional Roman cuisine often served in Roman restaurants and *trattorie* are listed below.

First Courses

Fresh **pasta** dishes (usually made on the premises) include *fettuccine*, ribbon noodles (often served with a meat sauce, or with porcini mushrooms), *tonnarelli*, and *bigoli*.

Spaghetti alla carbonara, has a light sauce of salt pork, beaten egg, pecorino cheese, and black pepper.

Penne all'arrabbiata is short pasta with a hot (piquant) tomato sauce.

Bucatini or *penne all'Amatriciana* is a thick hollow spaghetti or short pasta served in a light sauce of salt pork, tomatoes and pecorino cheese.

Pasta alla checca is pasta with diced mozzarella cheese, raw tomatoes and basil.

Pasta con broccoli is short pasta with broccoli, pine nuts, and garlic.

Timballo is a rich pasta dish cooked in the oven, usually with peas and ham and a cheese sauce.

Gnocchi alla Romana is another typical first course made from a dough of semolina flour, eggs and milk, covered in cheese and baked.

Gnocchi di patate alla Romana are potato dumplings served in a light meat and tomato sauce (traditionally made on Thursdays).

Agnolotti are ravioli filled with meat.

A **soup** often served in Rome is *stracciatella*, a meat broth with parmesan and a beaten egg.

Polenta, made from yellow maize flour, is usually served with meat stews in a tomato sauce, or grilled fish.

A summer **hors d'oeuvre** is *fichi* or *melone* with *prosciutto*, figs or melon, with Parma ham.

MAIN COURSES

The best known **meat** dish in Rome is *abbacchio arrosto* or *al forno*, roast suckling lamb. *Scottadito* are grilled ribs or chops of suckling lamb.

Saltimbocca alla Romana is veal escalope with ham and sage.

Involtini are thin rolled slices of meat in a sauce, and *stracotto* is beef cooked in a tomato sauce, or in red wine.

Pollo or *coniglio alla cacciatora* is chicken or rabbit cooked in a tomato sauce, with herbs and onions.

A number of traditional dishes using offal are served in numerous restaurants in Rome.

Coda alla vaccinara is oxtail in a celery and tomato sauce.

Pajata or *pagliata* is a dish made with the intestines of oxen and sheep (also often used as a sauce for pasta).

Coratella d'abbacchio is a stew of young lamb's liver, heart, etc.

Other dishes of this type are: *cervello* (brains); *rognoncini trifolati* (sliced kidneys sautéed with parsley); *animelle* (sweetbreads); and *trippa* (tripe).

FISH

This is usually the most expensive item on the menu, but can be extremely good in restaurants specialising in fish.

Pesce arrosto or *pesce alla griglia* is roast or grilled fish: among the most succulent (and expensive) fish usually cooked in this way are *dentice* (dentex), *orata* (bream) and *triglie* (red mullet).

A *fritto di pesce* or *fritto misto di mare*, various types of small fried fish (almost always including *calamari*, or squid, and *seppie* or cuttlefish) is usually the most inexpensive fish dish on the menu.

Seafood includes *cozze* (mussels) and *vongole* (clams), often served cooked in

white wine with garlic and parsley; and *gamberi* (prawns), usually grilled.
Anguilla (con piselli in umido) is eel (stewed with peas).
Filetti di baccalà fritti are fillets of salt cod fried in batter.
Zuppa di pesce is a rich fish stew made with a wide variety of fish.

VEGETARIAN DISHES
An expensive delicacy (only served in season, from October to December and
    around Easter) is *porcini*, large wild mushrooms (best grilled), also often used
    as a sauce for pasta.
In winter, there are rich warming dishes, such as *pasta e fagioli* or *pasta e ceci*
    (short pasta with white beans or with chick peas).
Scamorza al forno is cheese baked in the oven.
Another vegetarian main dish is *melanzane alla parmigiana*, aubergine cooked in
    the oven with a cheese and tomato sauce.

VEGETABLES
Numerous delicious fresh vegetables are served in season.
Artichokes (*carciofi*) are an important part of Roman cuisine, and are cooked in
    a great variety of ways. They are always young and small (and usually eaten
    whole). They are called *alla giudìa* when deep fried, or *alla Romana* when
    stuffed with wild mint and garlic, and then stewed in olive oil and water.
Courgettes (*zucchini*) are sometimes served *ripieni* (stuffed) or fried. *Fritto di fiori
    di zucca* are zucchini flowers stuffed with mozzarella cheese and salted
    anchovies, dipped in batter and fried.
Insalata di puntarelle is a typical Roman salad made from the shredded stalks of a
    locally-grown chicory, with anchovy dressing.
Particularly good cooked green vegetables found in Rome and Lazio include
    cicoria and *broccoletti*.

Cheese specialities include *pecorino*, a strong, hard cheese made from sheep
milk, and its fresh byproduct *ricotta*, delicious on its own; and *mozzarella di bufala*,
made from buffalo's milk (which can also be *'affumicata'*, smoked).

DESSERT
Italians usually prefer fresh fruit for dessert and sweets are considered the least
important part of the meal. In many simple restaurants and *trattorie* only fruit
is served at the end of the meal.
    The **fruit** available varies according to what is in season: strawberries (*fragole*)
are good served with fresh lemon juice or red wine (rather than with cream).
Fragole di bosco, tiny wild strawberries are also often served.
    In summer, water melon (*cocomero* or *anguria*) is particularly refreshing.
    Fruit salad (*macedonia*) is almost always made from fresh fruit in season.
    If the menu includes *crostata* (tart) this is also usually made with fresh fruit.
    Zuppa inglese, a rich trifle, and *tiramisù* are often available. The ice cream
(*gelato*) offered in restaurants is not always homemade.

Wines. Lazio used to be famous for its Vini dei Castelli, with their clear amber
tint, but these wines have deteriorated drastically in quality and it is now very
difficult to find a good bottled wine from this region. However, some restaurants

still buy their wine in demijohns directly from vineyards in the Alban Hills and it is often a good idea to try this 'vino della casa' before ordering a more expensive bottle. The house wine served in Rome is almost always white.

The few wines of Lazio still worth looking out for include the white from Capena, Colli Lanuvini, and Montefiascone; the red 'Cesanese' from Piglio; the strong red wine of Marino; and 'L'Aleatico', a red dessert wine from Gradoli near the Lago di Bolsena. It is no longer easy to find a good wine from Frascati or Velletri, but, as in other parts of Italy, the wine bottled by the local 'Cantina Sociale' is usually of an acceptable standard. Bottled wines of good quality (but not cheap) are available in most Roman restaurants: those from the Veneto, Puglia, Sardinia, Sicily and Tuscany are often the best.

Restaurants (Ristoranti, Trattorie)

It has become extremely difficult to recommend restaurants in Rome since they change hands frequently and the standard often deteriorates once they become well known. In the simplest *trattorie* the food is usually good, and considerably cheaper than in the well-known restaurants, though furnishings and surroundings can be a lot less comfortable.

The best guide (but only in Italian) to eating in Rome is *Roma: Ristoranti, trattorie* published annually by Gambero Rosso Editore.

A selection of a few restaurants grouped according to location is given below. They have been divided into four categories:

££££   over Lire 100,000
£££   Lire 65,000–100,000
££   Lire 30,00–65,000
£   under Lire 30,000

Pantheon, Piazza Navona and Campo dei Fiori
££££
Camponeschi, 50 Piazza Farnese, ☎ 687 4927. Open evenings; closed Sunday. Carefully prepared dishes (mostly fish) are presented with elegance in this old Roman restaurant, although the real attraction here is the opportunity to dine outside on one of Rome's great piazzas

La Rosetta, 8 Via della Rosetta, ☎ 683 08841. Closed Saturday lunchtime and Sunday. A handsome restaurant a few steps from the Pantheon, La Rosetta is widely held to be the top fish restaurant in Rome. Preparations are gracefully simple and accentuate rather than disguise the flavour of wonderfully fresh fish and seafood. Excellent list of wines and champagne.

Toulà, 29b Via della Lupa, ☎ 687 3498. Closed Saturday lunchtime and Sunday. Tastefully decorated with antiques and English prints, Toulà has an extensive menu which always includes several dishes from the Veneto region, where the Toulà group of restaurants originated. Excellent food and sure-handed service in a serene and classy atmosphere.

Papà Giovanni, 4/5 Via dei Sediari, ☎ 686 5308. Closed Sunday. One of the most original, and expensive, restaurants in Rome, famous for its fresh salads, truffles and Roman cuisine presented in the lightest possible manner. Intriguing wine list. One of the few restaurants in Rome with a non-smoking room.

£££

Il Convivio, 44 Via dell'Orso, ☎ 686 9432. Closed Sunday and Monday lunchtime. A good, small restaurant with anything but anonymous food. Cooking that begins with traditional ingredients and ends up decidedly modern, with a *menù degustazione*—a many course set menu—that changes weekly.

Vecchia Roma, 18 Piazza Campitelli, ☎ 686 4604. Closed Wednesday.. Still worthy of the attention that has made it a favourite of locals and tourists for decades, the tables outside on Piazza Campitelli are among the most pleasant in town. The menu is varied and the service crisp.

££

L'Eau Vive, 85 Via Montenerone, ☎ 688 01095. Closed Sunday. A long established restaurant inside a 15C palace. The French nuns that run the restaurant provide traditional French cuisine.

Al Pompiere, 38 Via Santa Maria dei Calderari, ☎ 686 8377. Closed Sunday. Only traditional Roman fare is served at this first floor restaurant in the heart of the Jewish ghetto. Potato *gnocchi* (dumplings) on Thursdays, *pasta e ceci* (chick pea soup) and salt cod on Fridays, fried *zucchini* flowers stuffed with anchovies, and spaghetti *cacio e pepe* (with pecorino cheese and plenty of freshly ground black pepper).

Bacaro, 27 Via degli Spagnoli, ☎ 686 4110. Open evenings only; closed Sunday. A tiny, bistro-like restaurant in the Piazza Navona neighbourhood with an ample choice of pasta dishes and imaginative second courses. Weather permitting, a couple of tables are set in the quiet alley outside.

La Carbonara, 3 Campo dei Fiori, ☎ 686 4783. Closed Tuesday. Pleasant dining out on Piazza Campo de' Fiori, and a menu with plenty of Roman and Italian standards to choose from.

£

Cul de Sac 1, 73 Piazza Pasquino, ☎ 688 01094. Closed lunchtime Sunday and Monday. The first wine bar in Rome. Long and narrow, warm and friendly, this place makes a pleasant change from pizza whenever an informal or frugal meal is required. Cheeses, cold meat, vegetable quiches, but also hearty lentil soup in wintertime. There are over 700 wine labels to choose from.

Anacleto Bleve, 9a/11 Via Santa Maria del Pianto, ☎ 686 5970. Open for lunch only; closed Sunday. In the heart of the Jewish ghetto, this old-style wine bar is perfect for a short rest. It offers a few hot dishes and a good selection of cheeses and cured pork meat from different Italian regions. The tables of the wine bar are surrounded by shelves of bottles of wine which you can buy to drink inside or take away.

Piazza di Spagna
£££–££

Al Moro, 13 Vicolo delle Bollette, ☎ 678 3495. Closed Sunday. Situated near the Trevi Fountain and very well known, Al Moro has the look of a restaurant but the feel of a trattoria. Service can be a little slow.

Dal Bolognese, 1/2 Piazza del Popolo, ☎ 361 1426. Closed Monday. One of the great dining spots in town, sited at the edge of Piazza del Popolo with a view up to the Pincio. As the name suggests, the cuisine is from Bologna, with excellent fresh pastas and a solid *bollito misto* (mixed plate of boiled meats served with chutney or *salsa verde*).

££

Porto di Ripetta, 250 Via di Ripetta, ☎ 361 2376. Closed Sunday. Close to Piazza del Popolo and popular with people who work in the area (there is a special business lunch menu). Chef Maria Romani provides innovative Italian cuisine based on traditional combinations. Good wine list.

Al 34, 34 Via Mario de' Fiori, ☎ 679 5091. Closed Monday. Well-prepared Roman food at reasonable prices, which is rare in this part of town. A long-standing favourite with tourists.

Lounge del Roman Garden, 14 Via Bocca di Leone, ☎ 69981. Open every day. The small, elegant restaurant of the Hotel d'Inghilterra makes a great lunch stop while shopping in the Piazza di Spagna area.

Via Veneto and the Parioli

££££

Sans Souci', 20 Via Sicilia, ☎ 482 1814. Open evenings only; closed Monday. This was the luxury restaurant of choice at the time of *La Dolce Vita* (late 1950s and 60s), and it is still doing well. The decor is an interesting combination of antique pieces and tacky details. Impeccable, elegant service. Very popular with American tourists and wealthy Romans in search of a very late meal.

La Terrazza dell'Hotel Eden, 49 Via Ludovisi, ☎ 478 121. Open every day. Having the best view in the city tends to distract attention from the food, but this is one of the finest restaurants in Rome. The modern interpretations of Italian classics are expertly prepared and beautifully presented.

Relais le Jardin, 5 Via G. de Notaris, ☎ 322 0404. Closed Sunday. The prestigious restaurant of the Hotel Byron. English silverware and crystal decanters do not glitter in the sunshine—the restaurant is located in the basement—but it is still one of the classiest places in town. More suitable for dinner than lunch.

£££–££

Al Ceppo, 2 Via Panama, ☎ 841 9696. Closed Monday. A favourite with locals in the quiet Parioli quarter, Al Ceppo has been here for more than 30 years. The menu always features specialities from the Marche region, and the grilled meats are especially good.

Colline Emiliane, 22 Via degli Avignonesi, ☎ 481 7538. Closed Friday. This is a friendly, family-run *trattoria* located between Via Veneto and the Trevi Fountain. It offers specialities from the Emilia region; an interesting selection of cured pork, home-made *fettucine*, pumpkin *ravioli* in wintertime, followed by a simple grilled beef fillet or *cololetta alla bolognese* (fried veal topped with ham and melted cheese) are always on the menu. Delicious home-made tarts for dessert.

Papà Baccus, 36 Via Toscana, ☎ 474 2808. Closed Sunday. A faily-priced restaurant not far from Via Veneto, serving light Italian food. Good selection of appetizers and home-made pasta. Professional yet warm and friendly service. Very good desserts accompanied by a remarkable selection of wines by the glass.

Trastevere

££££

Alberto Ciarla, 40 Piazza San Cosimato, ☎ 581 8668. Open evenings only; closed Sunday. Mostly fish on this menu, which is always well prepared and beautifully presented in the elegant, candle-lit dining room. Several set menus as well as à la carte dishes, and a good selection of wines.

££

Paris, 7a Piazza San Callisto, ☎ 581 5378. Closed Sunday evenings and Monday. A comfortable restaurant near Piazza Maria in Trastevere, Paris offers traditional Italian cooking with many good Roman dishes such as fried zucchini flowers stuffed with mozzarella and anchovies and *zuppa di arzilla* (fish soup with broccoli). Excellent wine list.

Peccati di Gola, 7a Piazza dei Ponziani, ☎ 581 4529. Open evenings only; closed Monday. The slightly over-priced menu always features some specialities from Calabria, and pasta dishes are well made. Located on a pleasant secluded little square (tables outside, of course) it is a particularly attractive option on a hot summer evening. One of the few restaurants in Rome that stays open throughout August.

Checco Er Carrettiere, 10 Via Benedetta, ☎ 580 0985. Closed Sunday evenings and Monday. An extremely popular and noisy restaurant in Trastevere, line with photographs of past customers (the famous as well as the unknown). It offers traditional Roman dishes, such as *coda all vaccinara* (oxtail stewed in a tomato and celery sauce), as well as lighter food, such as simple grilled fish. Home-made desserts.

Sora Lella, 16 Via di Ponte dei Quattro Capi, ☎ 686 1601. Closed Sunday. A small, neat, family-run *trattoria* located on the Tiberina island. Traditional Roman cooking, such as *amatriciana* (pasta in a tomato sauce with chunks of cured pork), *coda all vaccianara* (oxtail stewed in a tomato and celery sauce); when in season, artichokes stewed with mint (*alla romana*) or deep-fried (*all giudia*); home-made desserts.

Sabatini, 13 Piazza Santa Maria in Trastevere, ☎ 581 2026. Closed Wednesday. Outside dining room on one of Rome's great piazzas, opposite the wonderful church of Santa Maria in Trastevere. Customers come more for the view and atmosphere than the food.

£

Da Lucia, 2b Vicolo del Mattonato, ☎ 580 3601. Closed Monday. A basic, family-run *trattoria* in the heart of Trastevere, with tables outside on the narrow alleyway when the weather permits. Just a few dishes to choose from, but usually traditional Roman fare. No credit cards.

Testaccio

£££

Checchino dal 1887, 30 Via di Monte Testaccio, ☎ 574 6318. Literally carved out of Monte Testaccio and run by the same family for over a hundred years, Checchino serves the most traditional Roman cuisine. Simple decor and one of the best wine lists in the city.

££

Perilli, 39 Via Marmorata, ☎ 574 2145. Closed Wednesday. Possibly the most typical Roman trattoria of them all, still serving many traditional local dishes. Noisy and fun.

££–£

Da Felice, 29 Via Mastro Giorgio, ☎ 574 6800. Owner Signor Felice does it all: he shops at the nearby Testaccio market, cooks excellent Roman dishes, sets the tables with strings of sausages as centrepieces, and looks customers in the eyes before allowing them to sit down and taste his daily efforts. No credit cards.

Vatican
££
Girarrosto Toscano, 56 Via Germanico, ☎ 397 25717. Typically Tuscan food from a great family restaurant not far from the Vatican museums; a welcome oasis in a neighbourhood of bad restaurants. Grilled meats, particularly the *bistecca all fiorentina*, are wonderful. Outside dining.

Il Simposio, 16 Piazza Cavour, ☎ 321 1502. Closed Saturday lunchtime and Sunday. Close to Castel Sant' Angelo, this elegant wine bar has built its reputation on the sensational choice of first-quality cheeses (48 different kinds), smoked fish and cured meats. But for those who would rather have a full meal there is a real chef in the kitchen: soups, souffles, duck breasts and beef, followed by very good desserts are always in the menu. The wine shop in the basement deserves special attention.

Esquiline and Termini
££–£
Trimani, 37b Via Cernaia, ☎ 446 9630. Closed Sunday. Located near Stazione Termini, Trimani is one of the oldest wine shops in town. The friendly wine bar round the corner was renovated in 1991 and has a decidedly modern feel. The wine list is great. The menu includes a few hot dishes, such as soups, quiches, grilled beef and seasonal vegetables, as well as a tempting selection of cheeses, smoked fish and cured pork. Friendly service and good air-conditioning.

Pizzerie
Most pizzerias are open only for dinner, usually from 20.00 to 00.30 or even as late as 2.00 in summertime. The Roman version of pizza is plate-sized, very thin, and usually baked for a scant minute in a very hot wood burning oven. Classic pizzas include the margherita (tomato sauce and mozzarella cheese) and the napoletana (tomato sauce, mozzarella cheese and anchovies), but all pizzerias seem to have their own combinations on offer. Without drinks, the cost of a pizza ranges from Lire 6000 to Lire 16,000, depending on the toppings you choose. Italians typically wash down their pizza with beer or soft drinks, though most pizzerias also provide a small selection of inexpensive wines. *Bruschette* (toasted bread drizzled with olive oil and served with various toppings) are also available, as are other snacks such as *crostini* (similar to *bruschette*, but done in the oven), or deep-fried salt-cod fillets.

TRASTEVERE
Dar Poeta, 45 Vicolo del Bologna, ☎ 588 0516. Evenings only; closed Monday. Credit cards accepted.
Acchiappafantasmi, 66 Via dei Cappellari, ☎ 687 3462. Open evenings only; closed Tuesday. No credit cards.
Panattoni, 53 Viale Trastevere, ☎ 580 0919. Open evenings only; closed Wednesday. No credit cards.
ESQUILINE
Alle Carrette, 14 Vicolo delle Carrette, ☎ 679 2770. Open evenings only; closed Monday. No credit cards.

VATICAN
Il Bersagliere, 24 Via Candia, ☎ 397 42253. Open evenings only; closed Monday. No credit cards.
L'Isola della Pizza, 47 Via degli Scipioni, ☎ 397 33483. Open lunchtime and evenings; closed Wednesday. No credit cards.
PANTHEON
Montecarlo, 13 Vicolo Savelli, ☎ 686 1877. Open daily lunchtime and evenings. No credit cards.
PIAZZA DI SPAGNA
Leoncino, 28 Via del Lioncino, ☎ 687 6306. Open evenings and also for lunch during the week; closed Wednesday. No credit cards.
PARIOLI
Il Crilè, 44–46 Viale Maresciallo Pilsudski, ☎ 808 2690. Open evenings only; closed Sunday. No credit cards.
COLOSSEUM
Pizza Forum, 34–38 Via San Giovanni in Laterano, ☎ 700 2515. Open daily, evenings only. No credit cards.

Snacks. There are a number of self-service restaurants in the centre of the city (including **Il Delfino**, 67 Corso Vittorio Emanuele, Largo Argèntina). For pizzas and other good hot snacks go to a *rosticceria* or *tavola calda*; some of these have no seating accommodation and sell food to take away or eat on the spot. They often sell sliced *porchetta*, roast suckling pig, while other hot snacks include *supplì* (fried rice balls with mozzarella), *arancini* (fried rice balls with tomato), *calzoni*, a pizza 'roll' usually filled with ham and mozzarella, and *crocchette*, minced meat or potato croquettes.

Picnics. Excellent food for picnics can be bought at *pizzicherie* and *alimentari* (grocery shops), and *fornai* (bakeries). Sandwiches (*panini*) are made up on request, with ham, cheese, etc, and bakeries usually sell excellent individual pizzas, cakes, etc.
  Some of the most pleasant spots in the city to have a picnic include: the Palatine Hill, the Parco degli Aranci on the Aventine, the Borghese gardens, the Pincio, the Belvedere di Monte Tarpeo on the Capitol Hill, the Circus Maximus, the park of the Villa Doria Pamphilj, the public gardens off Via del Quirinale, the Parco Oppio, the Villa Celimontana on the Celian Hill, the Janiculum Hill, the Park of the Tomb of the Scipios (between Via di Porta Latina and Via di Porta San Sebastiano), and on the Via Appia (in the Circus Maxentius or beyond the tomb of Cecilia Metella).

Cafés (*bar*) are open all day. Most customers eat the excellent refreshments they serve standing up. You pay the cashier first, and show the receipt to the barman in order to get served. In almost all bars, if you sit at a table you are charged considerably more (at least double) and are given waiter service (you should not pay first).
  Well-known cafés in the city, all of which have tables (some outside), include: **Caffè Greco**, 86 Via Condotti (a famous café, see p 170); **Babington** (English tea rooms), Piazza di Spagna; **Rosati**, 4 Piazza del Popolo; **Tre Scalini**, 31 Piazza Navona, noted for its ices, including *tartufi* (truffles); **Giolitti**, 40 Uffici

dei Vicario (famous for its ice creams); **Camilloni a Sant'Eustachio**, Piazza Sant'Eustachio; and **Doney** and **Caffè de Paris**, 90 and 145 Via Veneto. **Pascucci**, Via di Torre Argentina, is justly famous for its fresh fruit milk-shakes. **La Casa del Caffè**, Via degli Orfani (near the Pantheon), serves particularly good coffee.

Travelling around Rome

By car. You are strongly advised not to use a car in Rome. The centre of the city is closed to private cars (without special permits) for a large part of the day, and there are many restricted streets and lanes. Car parking is extremely difficult anywhere in the city. Access is allowed for the disabled and visitors with a hotel reservation (some hotels have garages). Public transport has become more efficient in recent years.

There are very few large **car parks** in the city. The most central (with hourly tariffs, usually around Lire 2500 an hour, or around Lire 25,000 for a day) include: Viale Giulio Cesare (near the Vatican); Viale del Muro Torto (under the Villa Borghese gardens); Piazza Bocca della Verità; and Piazza dei Cinquecento (by Termini station).

Always lock your car when parked, and never leave anything of value inside it. It is forbidden to park in front of a gate or doorway marked with a 'passo carrabile' (blue and red) sign. Once a week street cleaning takes place at night, so cars have to be removed (or the owner may be fined and the vehicle towed away); ask locally for information. When driving in Rome, beware of motorcycles, mopeds and Vespas, the drivers of which seem to consider that they always have the right of way.

The principle **car-hire** firms (which include Maggiore, Hertz and Avis) have offices at Fiumicino Airport and Termini Station as well as in the centre of Rome.

Avis	☎ 470 1400	Budget	☎ 484 810
Europecar	☎ 167 014410	Hertz	☎ toll-free 167/234 679

Motoring organisations. Italian Automobile Club (ACI) head office, 8 Via Marsala (☎ 499 81); Automobile Club of Rome, 261 Via Cristoforo Colombo (☎ 514 971). For ACI breakdown service, ☎ 116.

By bus. Rome is well served by a fairly efficient bus and tram service, since most of the centre of the city has been closed to private traffic. The service (orange buses) is run by ATAC (for information, ☎ 167 431784; lost property office, ☎ 581 6040). A free map of principal routes is available from the ATAC information kiosk (open Mon–Sat 8–20) on Piazza dei Cinquecento in front of Stazione Termini. Tickets (Lire 1500 in 1997 valid for 75 minutes on any number of lines, and for one jouney on the metro) are sold at tobacconists, bars and newspaper kiosks, as well as ATAC booths, and automatic machines at many bus stops and in metro stations; they have to be stamped at automatic machines on board (at the rear of the bus).

It is usually well worth while purchasing a ticket pass (from ATAC booths, tobacconists, kiosks, etc) valid for one day (BIG: biglietto integrato giornaliero) which expires at midnight of the day it was purchased (Lire 6000 in 1997; this has to be stamped once on board). A seven-day ticket (CIS: carta integrata settimanale) expires at midnight of the seventh day (Lire 24,000 in 1997). Season tickets are also available valid for one calendar month (Lire 50,000 in 1997).

Town Buses

119 • An electric minibus which serves the centre of the city on a circular route.
Piazza Augusto
  Imperatore
Via della Ripetta
Via Monte Brianzo
Via della Dogana
  Vecchia
Pantheon
Via del Seminario
Piazza Colonna
Via del Tritone
Via Due Macelli
Piazza di Spagna
Via del Babuino
Piazza del Popolo
Via della Ripetta
Piazza Augusto
  Imperatore.

•

53 • (weekdays only)
Piazza San Silvestro
Largo Tritone
Piazza Barberini
Via Po (for the Galleria
  Borghese)
Via Salaria.

•

56 • Largo Argentina
Piazza Venezia
Via del Corso
Largo Tritone
Piazza Barberini
Via Veneto
Via Po (for Galleria
  Borghese)

60 • Piazza Sonnino
Largo Argentina
Piazza Venezia
Via del Corso
Largo del Tritone
Piazza Barberini
Via XX Settembre
Porta Pia
Via Nomentana

Piazza Sempione

•

64 • Stazione Termini
Via Nazionale
Piazza Venezia
Corso Vittorio Emanuele
San Pietro (for Vatican)

•

70 • Via Giolitti
Santa Maria Maggiore
Via Nazionale
Piazza Venezia
Largo Argentina
Corso Rinascimento
Ponte Cavour
Piazza Cavour
Viale delle Milizie
Piazzale Clodio

•

71 • Via Giolitti
Santa Maria Maggiore
Traforo Umberto I
Piazza San Silvestro

•

81 • Piazza del
  Risorgimento
Lungotevere in Augusta
Mausoleo di Augusto
Via del Corso
Piazza Venezia (returns
  via Largo Argentina)
Corso Rinascimento
Lungotevere Marzio

•

85 • Piazza San Silvestro
Piazza Venezia
Colosseum
San Giovanni in
  Laterano

•

87 • Piazza Cavour
Corso Rinascimento
Largo Argentina
Piazza Venezia
Via dei Fori Imperiali
Colosseum
San Giovanni in
  Laterano

90 • Piazza Venezia
Via del Teatro di Marcello
Terme di Caracalla
Porta Metronia
Piazza Zama

•

94 • Largo Argentina
Piazza Venezia
The Aventine
Via G.A. Sartorio

•

95 • Piazzale dei
  Partigiani
Piazzale Ostiense
Lungotevere Aventino
Piazza Bocca della Verità
Via del Teatro di
  Marcello
Piazza Venezia
Via del Corso
Via del Tritone
Via Vittorio Veneto
Villa Borghese
Piazzale Flaminio

•

218 • San Giovanni in
  Laterano
Piazza Epiro
Piazza Galeria
Via Appia Antica
Via Appia Pignatelli
Fosse Ardeatine

•

760 • (9–19 on
  Sundays)
Via del Circo Massimo
Terme di Caracalla
Via di Porta San
  Sebastiano
Via Appia Antica
Catacombs of San
  Sebastiano

•

Because of one-way streets, return journeys do not always follow the same route as the outward journey. As in other large cities, you should always beware of pickpockets on buses. There are no bus or underground services in Rome on 1 May or on the afternoon of Christmas Day (and there are limited services on other holidays). Night bus services operate from 00.10 to 5.30 and the numbers on these routes are followed by 'N'.

A small selection of the 238 bus routes and seven tram routes in the city is given below, and some of them are described only in part.

Trams

13 • Porta Maggiore
Piazza Santa Croce
San Giovanni in
    Laterano
Colosseum
Piazza di Porta Capena
Piazzale Ostiense
Ponte Sublicio
Viale di Trastevere

19 • Porta Maggiore
Piazzale Verano (San
    Lorenzo)
Viale Regina Elena
Viale Regina Margherita
Viale delle Belle Arti
Via Flaminia
Ponte Matteotti
Viale delle Milizie
Piazza Risorgimento

30b • Piazzale Ostiense
Viale Aventino
Colosseum
Porta San Giovanni
Porta Maggiore
Viale Regina Margherita
Viale delle Belle Arti
Piazza Thorwaldsen

Night Service

60N Piazza Sonnino
Piazza Venezia
Piazza Barberini
Via Nomentana
Corso Sempione

75N Piazza Venezia
Largo Argentina
Viale Trastevere
Monteverde

78N Piazzale Clodio
Piazzale Flaminio
Piazza Cavour
Corso Rinascimento
Piazza Venezia
Stazione Termini

By underground railway (metropolitana). There are two lines in Rome, although if you want to visit the centre of the city, you are almost always better off taking a bus. The only really useful parts of the system are from Termini station to Piazza di Spagna, and from Termini station to the Colosseum. The service begins at 5.30 and ends at 23.30.

Line A, opened in 1980, runs from near the Vatican (Via Ottaviano) via Piazzale Flaminio, Piazza di Spagna and Piazza Barberini, to Termini Station. From there it continues to San Giovanni in Laterano and traverses the southern suburbs of Rome along the Via Appia Nuova and Via Tuscolana to terminate beyond Cinecittà. It runs underground for the whole of its length (14km) except for the bridge across the Tiber. The intermediate stops are: Ottaviano, Lepanto, Flaminio, Spagna, Barberini, Repubblica, Termini, Vittorio, Manzoni, San Giovanni, Re di Roma, Ponte Lungo, Furio Camillo, Colli Albani, Arco di Travertino, Porta Furba, Numidio Quadrato, Lucio Sestio, Giulio Agricola, Subaugusta, Cinecittà and Anagnina.

Line B (the first part was opened in 1952). It runs southwest from Stazione Termini to Porta San Paolo, in Piazzale Ostiense, where it comes to the surface just beyond Ostiense Station, running from there alongside the Rome–Lido railway as far as Magliana, beyond the Basilica of San Paolo fuori le Mura. It then runs underground (northeast) to terminate at Tre Fontane (Laurentina). It has recently been extended northeast from Termini Station as far as Rebibbia. Intermediate stations at: Rebibbia, Ponte Mammolo, Santa Maria del Soccorso, Pietralata, Monti Tibertini, Quintiliani, Tiburtina, Bologna, Policlinico, Castro Pretorio, Termini, Via Cavour, Colosseo, Circo Massimo, Piramide (Porta San Paolo), Garbatella, San Paolo, Magliana and EUR. A service also runs from Porta San Paolo to Ostia Antica and Ostia Lido.

By taxi. Taxis (white or yellow in colour) are provided with taximeters; you should always make sure these are operational before hiring a taxi. The fare includes service, so tipping is not necessary. It is not advisable to accept rides from non-authorised taxis at the airports or train stations. Licensed taxis are hired from ranks; there are no cruising taxis. To call a taxi, ☎ 3570, 3875, 4994 or 88177 (you will be given the approximate arrival time and the number of the taxi). There are additional charges for night travel (22.00–7.00), on Sundays, and for each piece of luggage. Horse cabs are used exclusively by tourists, and you should agree the fare before starting the journey.

By bicycle and scooter. Bicycles can be hired at stands in Piazza del Popolo, Piazza San Silvestro, Piazza di Spagna and Piazza Augusto Imperatore (on Via del Corso). Rental firms for both bicycles and scooters: Scoot-a-long (302 Via Cavour, ☎ 678 0206), Scooters for Rent (84 Via della Purificazione, ☎ 488 5485), St Peter's Moto (43 Via di Porta Castello, ☎ 687 5714).

Sight-seeing tours of Rome are run by ATAC (see above). Bus No. 110 departs from Piazza dei Cinquecento daily in summer at 15.30 and in winter at 14.30. The itinerary lasts c 2hrs (there is no guide but a brochure is supplied). Booking and information at the ATAC information office beside Termini station.

Coach and train services in the environs. There is no central coach station in Rome; the coaches start from and return to various underground railway stations. The services (blue coaches) are run by COTRAL (Azienda Consortile Trasporti Lazio), 25 Via Portonaccio (information office open Mon–Fri, 7.45–16.40, ☎ 591 5551). For further details about transport in the environs, see the beginning of Chapters 28–30.

Disabled travellers

Italy is at last catching up with the rest of Europe in the provision of facilities for the disabled. All new public buildings are now obliged by law to provide access and specially designed facilities for the disabled. In the annual list of hotels in Rome published by the EPT, hotels which are able to provide hospitality for the disabled are indicated. Airports and railway stations in Italy provide assistance, and certain trains are equipped to transport wheelchairs. The seats at the front of city buses are reserved for the disabled, and there are free parking spaces for disabled drivers who display an official disc. In the list of current opening times of the Museums and Galleries in Rome available from the EPT, those which are accessible to wheelchairs are indicated. However, the historic centre of Rome remains a very difficult place to traverse in a wheelchair.

Disabled travellers can contact Co.In (Consorzio Cooperative Integrate)

☎ 232 67504, Mon to Fri 9.30–17. This organisation provides a guide to Rome for the disabled and lists hotels that are wheelchair accessible.

Personal Security

For all emergencies, ☎ 113. As in large towns all over the world, pickpocketing is a widespread problem in Rome; it is always advisable not to carry valuables in handbags, and to be particularly careful on public transport. Cash and documents, etc, can be left in hotel safes. It is a good idea to make photocopies of all important documents in case of loss. Help is given to British and American travellers who are in difficulty by the British and American embassies in Rome (see p 13). They will replace lost or stolen passports, and will give advice in emergencies.

Crime should be reported at once. There are three categories of **policemen** in Italy: *Vigili Urbani* (municipal police who wear blue uniform in winter and white during the summer and hats similar to London policemen); *Carabinieri* (military police who wear black uniform with a red stripe down the side of their trousers); and the *Polizia di Stato* (State police who wear dark blue jackets and light blue trousers). The central police station of the *Polizia di Stato* is at 15 Via San Vitale (☎ 4686). Office for Foreigners, 2 Via Genova (☎ 4686/2987). In emergencies the municipal police can be called on 67691, and the *Carabinieri* on 112. Railway police, ☎ 481 9561. A detailed statement has to be given in order to get an official document confirming loss or damage (essential for insurance claims). Interpreters are usually provided.

Emergencies

☎ 113. For first-aid and ambulance service, ☎ 118. Ambulance service run by the Red Cross, ☎ 5510. *San Giovanni*, in Piazza San Giovanni in Laterano, is the central hospital for road accidents and other emergencies (for first aid, ☎ 770 55297). The *American Hospital in Rome*, 69 Via Emilio Longoni, ☎ 225 5290, is a private English-speaking hospital which accepts most American insurance plans. The *International Medical Centre*—☎ 488 2371, nights and weekends ☎ 488 4051—will refer callers to English-speaking doctors.

Medical Services

British citizens, as members of the EU, have the right to claim health services in Italy if they have the E111 form (issued by the Department of Health). For additional cover, you might also want to take out your own private insurance policy. First Aid services ('Pronto Soccorso') are available at all hospitals, railway stations and airports.

Chemists or Pharmacies (**farmacie**) are usually open Mon–Sat 9–13, 16–19.30 or 20. Some are open 24 hours a day (including the one outside Stazione Termini on Piazza dei Cinquecento). A few are open on Sundays (and holidays), and at night (listed on the door of every chemist, and in the daily newspapers).

Public Toilets. There is a notable shortage of public toilets in Rome as in the rest of Italy. All bars (cafés) should have toilets available to the public (generally speaking the grander the bar, the better the facilities). Nearly all museums now have toilets. There are also toilets at the railway stations, and in Piazza di Spagna.

Telephones and Postal Information

There are numerous public telephones all over Rome in kiosks, bars, restaurants, etc. These are operated by coins or telephone cards (Lire 5000, 10,000 and 15,000), which can be purchased from tobacconists (displaying a blue 'T' sign), bars, news-stand kiosks, and post offices. Telephone numbers in Italy can have from four to eight numbers. The telephone code for Rome is 06. For calls out of Rome, begin with a zero and the area code (i.e. 055 for Florence). Placing a local call costs Lire 200. Directory assistance (in Italian) is available by dialling 12. Numbers that begin with 167, called *numero verde*, are tollfree, but require a deposit of at least 200 *lire*. Most cities in the world can now be dialled direct from Rome (and international telephone cards are now available). The telephone exchange at Termini station is open until midnight.

The head post office in Rome is in Piazza San Silvestro (Pl. 3; 4), open every day 9–18. Fermo Posta correspondence can be addressed here (and collected every day except Sunday). Stamps are sold at tobacconists (displaying a blue 'T' sign) as well as post offices. Letters and postcards for outside Rome should always be posted into red boxes, or the blue boxes in the centre of town. The Vatican postal service (with its own stamps which are not valid for the Italian state postal service) is usually thought to be more efficient than the Italian state service: it costs the same and there are post offices in Piazza San Pietro and the Vatican Museums, as well as in Trastevere in the courtyard of Palazzo San Calisto, 16 Piazza San Calisto (blue letterboxes).

Working Hours

Shops (clothes, books, hairdressers, etc) are generally open 9–13, 16–19.30, including Saturday, and for most of the year are closed on Monday morning. Food shops usually open 7.30 or 8–13, 17–19.30 or 20, and for most of the year are closed on Thursday afternoon. From mid-June to mid-September all shops are closed instead on Saturday afternoon. Hardware shops are closed on Saturdays. Government offices usually work Mon–Sat 8–13.30 or 14. For banking hours, see under 'Money and Banks' (p 15).

Public Holidays

The main holidays in Rome, when offices and shops are closed, are as follows:
In addition, the festival of the patron saints of Rome, Peter and Paul, is celebrated on 29 June as a local holiday in the city.

Museums are usually closed on 29 June, Easter Sunday and 15 August, and there is no public transport on 1 May and the afternoon of Christmas Day.

1 January (New Year's Day)	1 November (All Saints' Day)
25 April (Liberation Day)	8 December (Immaculate Conception)
Easter Monday	25 December (Christmas Day)
1 May (Labour Day)	26 December (St Stephen)
15 August (Assumption)	

Annual Festivals

5–6 January	Epiphany (Befana), celebrated at night in Piazza Navona
Shrove Tuesday	Carnival is celebrated in the streets and piazze
23–24 June	Festa di San Giovanni, at night, near the Porta San Giovanni

19 March	Festa di San Giuseppe, celebrated in the Trionfale district
First Sunday in June	Festa della Repubblica, a military parade in the Via dei Fori Imperiali
21 April	Anniversary of the birth of Rome, celebrated on the Campidoglio
1 May	open-air pop concert in Piazza San Giovanni in Lateran
July	Festa di Noantri, celebrations in Trastevere for several weeks

Shops

The smartest shops are in Via Frattina and Via Condotti (the Bond Street of Rome), which lead out of Piazza di Spagna, in the area between the Corso Piazza di Spagna and Piazza del Popolo. A good shopping area (less expensive) is in the area of the Pantheon and Campo Marzio. Another important shopping street in the city (even if in a less attractive area than the above) is Via Cola di Rienzo in the Prati distict between Piazza del Risorgimento and the Tiber.

Italy has notably few department stores: the best known in Rome (both open on Sunday) are *La Rinascente*, Via del Corso and Piazza Fiume, and *Coin*, Piazza San Giovanni. There are branches of the chain department stores called *Standa*, and *Upim* all over the city (they all have shoe repair departments, and also cut keys). Standa usually has a food supermarket in the basement. There is a mini-market open 24 hours a day in the Termini station.

English books are stocked at *The Lion Bookshop*, 33 Via dei Greci (just off Via del Corso), ☎ 326 54007; fax 326 50437; open 10–19.30 Mon to Fri, and 10–13 on Sat. The shop also has a reading room and tea and coffee are available. *The Anglo-American Bookstore*, 102 Via delle Vite (near Piazza di Spagna); ☎ 679 5222; closed Sun. *The Corner Bookshop*, 48 Via del Moro, ☎ 583 6942; closed Mon mornings. *The Economy Book and Video Center*, 136 Via Torino (near Via Nazionale), ☎ 474 6877; closed Sun. Via del Babuino, Via dei Coronari, Via dei Banchi Vecchi and Via Margutta are known for their antique shops. Via del Governo Vecchio has numerous thrift shops (second-hand clothes and 'junk').

Open-air markets are open Mon–Sat, 8–13.30. These include excellent food markets at Campo dei Fiori, Piazza Vittorio Emanuele II (with North African and Middle Eastern products), Via Andrea Doria, and Testaccio. New and second-hand clothes are sold in Via Sannio (Porta San Giovanni), and old prints and books at the Mercato delle Stampe, Largo della Fontanella di Borghese. Porta Portese is a huge chaotic general 'flea market' between Via Portuense and Viale Trastevere, open 7–13 on Sunday mornings.

Newspapers and magazines

The most widely read Italian newspapers in Rome are *La Repubblica*, *Corriere della Sera*, *Messaggero* (with a Tuesday supplement, called *Metrò* on events in the city), and *Il Tempo*. Some important British and American newspapers (including the *Financial Times*, *USA Today*, and the *International Herald Tribune)* arrive daily at many of the kiosks in the historic centre. The kiosk opposite Piazza Colonna (Pl. 3; 4) is open 24 hours. The *Ospite a Roma*, and *Where* are both promotional monthly magazines given away free at hotels, with up-to-date information on events in the city. *Roma c'è* is a weekly guide (issued on Thursday and available all week from news-stands) with comprehensive listings of everything going on in Rome (and an abbreviated section in English). *Wanted in Rome* is a useful English magazine published every fortnight (17 Via dei Delfini), on sale at the English bookshops (see above under 'Shops').

Museums, Collections and Monuments

Hours of admission to the various museums, galleries and monuments in Rome are given in the text and below. Opening times vary and often change without warning; those given below should therefore be accepted with reserve. An up-to-date list of opening times is always available at the EPT information office. To make certain the times are correct, it is worth telephoning first. All museums, etc are usually closed on the main public holidays in Rome: 29 June, Easter Sunday and 15 August, although they are sometimes open on other holidays such as 1 January, 25 April, 1 May and Christmas Day. On other holidays (see below) they open only in the morning (9.00–13.00). More and more museums are introducing longer opening hours, although Monday remains the most usual closing day for the State museums and those owned by the Comune. Most opening times change between summer and winter. The **entrance charges** are also given in the text. It has become much more expensive to visit museums in Italy in the last few years (entrance is free if no price is given in the list below). British citizens under the age of 18 and over the age of 60 are entitled to free admission to State-owned museums and monuments. Students with ID (or ISIC) cards are only given discounts at state and local museums if they come from countries with whom Italy has a reciprocal agreement (notably the Vatican).

Lecture tours of museums, villas, etc (sometimes otherwise closed to the public) are organised by various cultural associations. These are advertised in the local press. Guided visits to the Imperial Fora and Capitol Hill are usually held in late September and early October, information from Civita, 11 Piazza Venezia, ☎ 699 1191. Museum Week (Settimana dei Musei Italiani) has now become established as an annual event (usually in November). Entrance to most museums is free during the week, and some have longer opening hours; private collections may be specially opened.

The museums owned by the Comune of Rome have been marked 'C' in the Museum table below. The opening hours for Sundays usually apply also to holidays. Most museums close their doors 30 minutes before the official closing time.

Hours of Admission to Museums, Collections and Monuments

Accademia di San Luca; ☎ 679 8850; Mon, Wed, Fri and last Sun of the month, 10–13

Antiquarium del Celio (C); ☎ 700 1569; Lire 3750 ; 9–19; Sun 9–13.30; closed Mon

Antiquarium of the Forum; *see* Forum

Antiquarium of the Palatine; *see* Palatine

Ara Pacis (C); ☎ 671 1035 69; Lire 3750; 9–17; Sun 9–13; closed Mon

Auditorium of Maecenas (C); 9–19; Sun 9–13; closed Mon

Basilica of Porta Maggiore; closed indefinitely, *see* Note **a**

Baths of Caracalla; ☎ 575 8626; Lire 8000; 9–15; summer 9–18; Mon, Sun 9–13

Baths of Diocletian; *see* Museo Nazionale Romano

Calcografia Nazionale; 9–13 except Sun

Casino Pallavicini; first day of every month 10–12, 15–17

Castel Sant'Angelo; ☎ 687 5036; Lire 8000; summer 9–19; closed 2nd & 4th Tues of the month

Catacombs (*see* Note **b**); Lire 8000; normally 8.30–12 and 14.30 (or 15) to dusk

Priscilla; ☎ 862 06272; closed Mon, and in Jan

Sant'Agnese; ☎ 861 0840; 9–12, 16–18; Mon 9–12; Sun 16–18

San Callisto; ☎ 513 6725; closed Wed and in Feb

San Domitilla; ☎ 511 0342 closed Tues and in Jan

San Sebastiano; ☎ 788 7035; closed Thur and in Nov

Circus of Maxentius (C); summer: Tues–Sun 9–19; winter: Tues–Sun 9–17.30; Sun 9–13.30

Colosseum; ☎ 700 4262; Lire 10,000; for both the lower and upper level; 9–one hour before sunset; Sun, Wed 9–14

Domus Aurea closed indefinitely; *see* Note **a**

Forum (Roman) and Palatine; ☎ 699 0110; the Forum is free; entrance to the Palatine is Lire 12,000; 9–18; Sun 9–13

Forum of Augustus, Forum of Nerva (C); *see* Markets of Trajan

Forum of Caesar (C); closed indefinitely

Forum of Trajan; *see* Markets of Trajan

Gabinetto Comunale delle Stampe; ☎ 687 5880; 9–13 except Sun, Mon

Galleria Barberini (Galleria Nazionale d'Arte Antica); ☎ 481 4591; Lire 8000; 9–19, Sun 9–13; closed Mon

Galleria Borghese (Villa Borghese); ☎ 854 8577; Lire 4000; 9–14; Sun 9–13; closed Mon

Galleria Colonna; ☎ 679 4362; Lire 10,000; Sat 9–13; closed in Aug

Galleria Comunale d'Arte Moderna; ☎ 474 2848; Lire 10,000; 9–19; Sun 9–13.30; closed Mon;

Galleria Corsini (Galleria Nazionale d'Arte Antica); ☎ 688 02323; Lire 8000 9–14; Sun 9–13; closed Mon;

Galleria Doria-Pamphilj; ☎ 679 7323; Lire 12,000; Mon, Tue, Fri, Sat, Sun 10–17; closed Thur

Galleria Nazionale d'Arte; *see* Galleria Barberini and Galleria Antica Corsini

Galleria Nazionale d'Arte Moderna; ☎ 322 981; Lire 8000; 9–19; Sun 9–13; closed Mon

Galleria Spada; ☎ 686 1158; Lire 8000; 9–19; fest. 9–13; closed Mon

Gramophone Museum (Museo degli Strumneti di Riproduzione del Suono); 8.45–17; summer 8.45–13.45; closed Sun

Keats–Shelley Memorial House; ☎ 678 4235; Lire 5000; 9–13, 15–18; closed Sat, Sun

Mamertine Prison; 9–12, 14.30–18

Markets and Forum of Trajan; ☎ 679 0048; Lire 3750; daily 9–18.30; closed Mon

Mausoleum of Augustus; *see* Note **a**

Museo dell'Alto Medioevo; ☎ 592 5806; Lire 4000; 9–14; fest. 9–13

Museo dell'Arma del Genio; ☎ 372 5446 for appointment

Museo delle Arti e Tradizioni Popolari; ☎ 592 6148; Lire 4000 9–14; Sun 9–13

Museo Astronomico Copernicano; ☎ 353 47056; Wed & Sat 9–13

Museo Barracco (C); ☎ 688 06848; Lire 3750; 9–19; Sun 9–13; closed Mon

Museo Canonica (C); ☎ 884 2279; Lire 3750; 9–19; Sun 9–13; closed Mon

Musei Capitolini (C); ☎ 671 02071; Lire 10,000; daily 9–19; closed Mon

Museo della Civiltà Romana; ☎ 592 6041; Lire 5000; 9–19; Sun 9–13.30; closed Mon

Museo della Comunità Ebraica di Roma; ☎ 687 5051; Lire 8000; Mon–Thu 9.30–14, 15–17; Fri 9.30–14; Sun 9.30–12.30; closed Sat

Museo Criminologico; Tue, Wed, Fri, Sat 9–13; Tue & Thu 14.30–18.30; closed Sun & Mon

Museo del Folklore (C); closed at present

Museo Mario Praz; ☎ 6861089; Lire 4000; 9–13, 14.30–18.30 exc Mon morning

Museo delle Mura; ☎ 704 75284; Lire 3750; 9–19; winter 9–17.30; Sun 9–13.30; closed Mon

Museo Napoleonico (C); ☎ 688 06286; Lire 3750 9–19; Sun 9–13.30

Museo Nazionale d'Arte Orientale; ☎ 487 4218; Lire 8000; Mon, Wed & Fri 9–14; Tue & Thu 9–19; Sun 9–13

Museo Nazionale di Castel Sant'Angelo; *see* Castel Sant'Angelo

Museo Nazionale delle Paste Alimentari ☎ 699 1120 Lire 12,000 9.30–12.30, 16–19; Sun 9.30–12.30

Museo Nazionale Preistorico Etnografico 'Luigi Pigorini' ☎ 549521; Lire 8000; daily 9–14; Sun 9–12; closed Mon

Museo Nazionale Romano:

Terme di Diocleziano and Palazzo Massimo; ☎ 488 0530; Lire 12,000; 9–14; Sun 9–13; closed Mon

Aula Ottagonale; ☎ 4870690; 10–19

Museo Nazionale di Strumenti Musicali; ☎ 7014796; Lire 4000; 9–13.30 except Sun

Museo Nazionale di Villa Giulia; ☎ 320 1951; Lire 8000; 9–19; Sun 9–19; closed Mon

Museo Numismatico della Zecca; ☎ 476 13317; 9–13 except Sat & Sun

Museo delle Origini; by appointment only

Museo di Palazzo Venezia; ☎ 679 8865; Lire 8000; 9–14; Sun 9–13; closed Mon

Museo di Roma; closed

Museo Storico dei Bersaglieri; Tue & Thu 9–13

Museo Storico Nazionale dell'Arte Sanitaria; ☎ 683 52353; Mon, Wed, Fri 10–12

Museo Storico delle Poste e Telecomunicazioni; Lire 1000; 9–13; closed Sun

Museo Storico del Vaticano (Palazzo del Laterano); Lire 6000; first Sat & Sun of the month, 8.45–13

Museo della Via Ostiense ☎ 698 83333; Lire 4000; daily 9–14; also 14.30–16.30 on Tues & Thur; closed Mon, and second and fourth Sun of the month

Orto Botanico; ☎ 686 4193; Lire 4000; 9–18.30; winter 9–17.30; closed Sun

Palatine and Antiquarium of the Palatine; ☎ 699 0110; Lire 12,000; 9–1hr before sunset; Sun, Tue 9–13

Palazzo del Esposizioni; ☎ 482 8760; Lire 10,000; 10–21; closed Tues

Palazzo del Quirinale; first and third Sun of month; 8.30–12.30 (gardens on 2 June)

Palazzo Spada; *see* Galleria Spada
Pantheon; ☎ 683 00230; 9–16.30; Sun 9–13
Pinacoteca Capitolino; *see* Musei Capitolini
Roman Forum; *see* Forum
Teatro di Marcello; *see* note **a**
Tomba di Cecilia Metella; ☎ 780 2465; 9–18; winter 9–16; Sun & Mon 9–13
Tomba dei Scipioni; closed
Vatican Museums; *see* p 335
Villa Farnesina; ☎ 683 8831; Lire 6000; 9–13 except Sun
Villa Giulia; *see* Museo Nazionale di Villa Giulia
Villa Medici (Accademia di Francia); ☎ 676 11; Lire 4000 (gardens only); Sun
   10–12.30 (guided visits on the half hour)
Villa Torlonia; ☎ 686 1044; visits only by appointment and not in Aug; see p
   279
Zoo; ☎ 321 6564; Lire 10,000; 8–17 or 18
Notes
a can be visited by written request (giving your local telephone number and days
of availability) to the Ripartizione X del Comune di Rome, 29 Via Portico
d'Ottavia, 00100 Rome; fax 689 2115; ☎ (06) 671 03819.
b the other catacombs may be visited by special permission only (see p 43).

Parks and Gardens in Rome

Rome has many fine parks and gardens, most of which are well maintained.
Those described in the text (see the Index) include the following.

The largest public park in the centre of the city is the **Villa Borghese** (particularly attractive around the 'Giardino del Lago'), with the adjoining **Pincio**.
Another huge public park, southwest of the centre, is the **Villa Doria
Pamphilj**. Parts of the Janiculum and Oppian Hills are occupied by gardens.
Smaller parks, beautifully kept, include the Villa Celimontana, the Parco Savello
(on the Aventine), the park by the Tomb of the Scipios (between Via di Porta
Latina and Via di Porta San Sebastiano) and two parks off Via del Quirinale. The
Palatine Hill is covered with luxuriant vegetation and fine trees, and here are
the delightful Farnese gardens laid out in the 16C and still beautifully maintained.

To the north of the centre are the large public parks of **Villa Glori**, with fine
trees, and **Villa Ada**. The gardens of Villa Torlonia, with Neo-classical and neo-
Gothic buildings, and of the Villa Blanc, both on the Via Nomentana, are in an
abandoned state. The park of the Villa Torlonia (formerly Albani), on the Via
Salaria, with its umbrella pines, is still privately owned by the Torlonia. The Villa
Sciarra, on the Janiculum, is a public park (fine wistaria). The **Orto Botanico** is
one of the most important botanical gardens in Italy. There is a rose and iris
garden (May and June) in Via di Valle Murcia at the foot of the Aventine Hill
(above the Circus Maximus). The Spanish Steps are covered with a magnificent
display of azaleas at the beginning of May. On the borders of the lake in EUR are
a thousand Japanese cherry trees. A flower market is open on Tuesday mornings
(10.00–13.00) in Via Trionfale.

Villas and palaces which preserve their gardens (but can be visited only
with special permission) include the 17C formal garden around the Casino del
Bel Respiro, in the Villa Doria Pamphilj, and the Priorato di Malta on the

Aventine. Other gardens which can normally be seen during the opening hours of the palaces include those of the Villa Farnesina in Trastevere (although this is not at present open), Palazzo Pallavicini Rospigliosi, Palazzo Colonna (the garden can only be seen from the windows of the gallery), and the Villa Giulia. There is a formal garden behind the Palazzina Borghese in Villa Borghese. Perhaps the most beautiful villa garden which survives from the 16C is that of the **Villa Medici** (normally open for guided tours on Sundays; ☎ 67611). Tours can be taken of the (rather disappointing) Vatican gardens. The beautiful gardens behind the Quirinal palace are only open on rare occasions, and it is also difficult to see the hanging garden of the Villa Madama (used by the Foreign Office).

There are beautiful gardens in the environs at Tivoli (Villa d'Este).

Visiting Rome with Children

The **Roman remains** in the centre of the city cannot fail to fire the imagination of children of all ages: the Colosseum and Roman Forum and Palatine Hill provide an immediate picture of the splendour of the Empire. The place to begin a visit to Rome is the Capitol Hill with its views of the Forum. The Capitoline Museum here contains some of the masterpieces of Roman sculpture and is a particularly pleasant museum to visit. Another Roman monument which gives a clear idea of the scale of ancient Rome is the Baths of Caracalla, and the Via Appia, in the stretch around the Tomb of Cecilia Metella and the Circus of Maxentius, leaves an indelible impression. For children particularly interested in ancient Rome, the Museo della Civiltà Romana in EUR has a didactic chronological display (using casts) and a splendid scale model of the city in the 4C. You can walk along a stretch of the Aurelian walls in the Museo delle Mura. At least one of the vast underground **catacombs** on the Via Appia should be seen.

The **fountains** of Rome are particularly delightful. The element of surprise provided by the Trevi fountain, as well as its noise, are unforgettable. It is fascinating for children to discover how many different sculptural motifs were used in the decoration of the fountains all over the city: the boats in Piazza di Spagna and Piazza Santa Maria in Domnica; the grotesque masks in Via Giulia and Piazza Pietro d'Illiria on the Aventine; the tortoises in Piazza Mattei; the bees in Piazza Barberini; the tritons in Piazza Barberini and Piazza Navona, etc.

Piazza Navona and **Piazza di Spagna** (with the Spanish steps) are perhaps the two most lively places in the city, always fun to visit. The best place to see the **Tiber**, and some of its oldest bridges, is from the Isola Tiberina. A visit to the **Galleria Doria Pamphilj** gives a clear picture of how one of the great Roman patrician families lived, and the **Keats-Shelley Memorial** house, overlooking the Spanish steps, preserves the atmosphere of a 'pensione' in the last century. **Castel Sant'Angelo** is one of the most exciting museums for children to visit, and much of it is open for exploration—from the ramparts to the dungeons. One of the most curious sights in the city is the **policeman** who directs the traffic with great aplomb in Piazza Venezia at the head of the Corso. The exceptionally tall **Presidents' guards** at the Quirinal can usually be seen outside the palace, and the **Swiss guards** with their splendid uniforms stand at the entrance to the Vatican beside St Peter's.

When choosing a means of public transport, try to take a **tram** (more interesting than a bus); numbers 13 and 30B take an unusual route near the Colosseum.

The **Aventine Hill** is a particularly peaceful place to visit, with several little gardens and a delightful view of the dome of St Peter's through the keyhole of the Priorato di Malta. In Trastevere the small **Folklore Museum** (currently closed for restoration) has charming life-size tableaux showing scenes of life in Rome in days gone by A visit to the **Vatican** is exhausting for grown-ups and children alike, especially when it is crowded. Although a brief visit is obligatory, never attempt to stay too long or see too much. In St Peter's the dome is well worth climbing.

There are a number of 'didactic' museums grouped near each other in **EUR**; an ethnographical museum related to Italy (Museo Nazionale di Arti e Tradizioni Popolari) and an ethnographical collection from the Americas, Africa and Oceania (Museo Etnografico Luigi Pigorini), as well as the Museo della Civiltà Romana, described above. Also here is a museum illustrating postal history, and the development of the telegraph and telephone.

Among Rome's many splendid **parks**, the largest are the Villa Borghese (which also has a zoo) and the adjoining Pincio (where a band plays on Sunday morning in May and June). Open-air puppet shows are sometimes held in summer on the Janiculum Hill. The largest park of all is the Villa Doria Pamphilj. For all the other parks, see 'Parks and Gardens' above.

Breaks during a hard day's sightseeing should always be made at a *gelateria* which sell the best ice creams; for details about cafés, see 'Eating in Rome' above. Pizzas are generally excellent in Rome. For annual festivals, see below. Postcards and colourful interesting literature are now on sale in most museums.

In the **environs** the Roman remains of Ostia Antica and Hadrian's Villa are splendid places to spend a whole day with a picnic. The fountains of Villa d'Este in Tivoli are another memorable sight (especially pleasant on a hot day).

Churches and Church Ceremonies

St Peter's and the other three great basilicas are open all day (7–19; 7–18 in winter). Other churches are closed between 12 and 15.30, 16 or 17, but almost all of them open at 7. Some churches, including several of importance, are open only for a short time in the morning and evening (opening times have been given where possible in the text below, but might vary). Most churches now ask that sightseers do not visit the church during a service. If you are wearing shorts or have bare shoulders you can be stopped from entering some churches, especially at St Peter's. Closed chapels, crypts, etc are sometimes unlocked on request by the sacristan. Many pictures and frescoes are difficult to see without lights which are often coin operated (100 lire or 500 lire coins). When visiting churches it is always useful to carry a torch and a pair of binoculars. Churches in Rome are very often not orientated. In the text the terms north and south refer to the liturgical north (left) and south (right), taking the high altar as at the east end.

The Basilicas of Rome. The four great patriarchal basilicas are San Giovanni in Laterano (St John Lateran; the cathedral and mother church of the world), San Pietro in Vaticano (St Peter's), San Paolo fuori le Mura and Santa Maria Maggiore. These, with the three basilicas of San Lorenzo fuori le Mura, Santa Croce in Gerusalemme, and San Sebastiano, comprise the 'Seven Churches of Rome'. Among minor basilicas rank Sant'Agnese fuori le Mura, Santi Apostoli, Santa Cecilia, San Clemente and Santa Maria in Trastevere.

Roman Catholic Services. The ringing of the evening Ave Maria or Angelus bell at sunset is an important event in Rome, where it signifies the end of the day and the beginning of night. The hour varies according to the season. On Sunday and, in the principal churches, often on weekdays, Mass is celebrated up to 13 and from 17 until 20 hours. High Mass, with music, is celebrated in the basilicas (see above) on Sunday at 9.30 or 10.30 (10.30 in St Peter's). The choir of St Peter's sings on Sunday at Mass at 10.30, and vespers at 17. The Sistine Chapel choir sings in St Peter's on 29 June and whenever the Pope celebrates Mass.

Roman Catholic services in English take place in San Silvestro in Capite, St Thomas of Canterbury and Santa Susanna; in Irish at St Patrick's, Sant'Isidoro, San Clemente and Sant' Agata dei Goti. Confessions are heard in English in the four main basilicas and in the Gesù, Santa Maria sopra Minerva, Sant'Anselmo, Sant'Ignazio, and Santa Sabina.

Church Festivals. On saints' days Mass and vespers with music are celebrated in the churches dedicated to the saints concerned. The Octave of the Epiphany is held at Sant'Andrea della Valle. The Blessing of the Lambs takes place at Sant'Agnese Fuori le Mura on 21 January around 10.30. In the evening of 6 January there is a procession with the Santo Bambino at Santa Maria in Aracoeli (although the statue was stolen in 1994). The singing of the Te Deum annually on 31 December in the church of the Gesù is a magnificent traditional ceremony. In San Giovanni in Laterano a choral Mass is held on 24 June, in commemoration of the service held here on 24 June 1929 by Pius XI, and the Pope attends the Maundy Thursday celebrations in the basilica when he gives his benediction from the loggia on the façade. On 5 August the legend of the miraculous fall of snow is commemorated at Santa Maria Maggiore in a pontifical Mass in the Borghese Chapel. On Christmas morning in this basilica a procession is held in honour of the sacred relic of the Holy Crib. The church of Sant'Anselmo on the Aventine Hill is noted for its Gregorian chant at 9.30 on Sunday. Holy Week liturgy takes place on Wednesday, Thursday, and Friday in Holy Week, at St Peter's, St John Lateran, Santa Croce, and other churches.

Papal Audiences, see p 319.
Catholic services in English: Chiesa di San Francesco in Capite, Piazza San Silvestro, ☎ 679 7775.
All Saints (Anglican), 153 Via del Babuino, ☎ 679 4357.
St Paul's Within the Walls (American Episcopal), 58 Via Napoli, ☎ 488 3339.
St Andrew's (Scottish Presbyterian), 7 Via Venti Settembre.
Methodist, 38 Via Firenze; Christian Science Society, 42 Via dei Giardini.
Synagogue, Lungotevere dei Cenci, ☎ 686 4648.
Mosque, Centro di Cultura Islamica e Moschea, Via della Moschea (Parioli), ☎ 808 2167.

The Catacombs

The catacombs are fascinating early Christian underground cemeteries outside the walls of Rome (since burial within the walls was forbidden). For a full description, see p 264. The most famous catacombs (**San Callisto** and **San Sebastiano** on the Via Appia, and **San Domitilla** on Via delle Sette Chiese) all have guided tours in several languages and tend to be crowded with large tour groups, which can impair a visit if you are on your own. In some of them explanatory films are shown before the tour. Routes often vary and are shortened at the height of the tourist season. All the catacombs have some steep stairs and uneven narrow corridors (often poorly illuminated), making the visit not normally advisable if you have difficulty in walking. The two other catacombs open to the public (**Sant'Agnese** on Via Nomentana, and Priscilla on Via Salaria), of no less interest, are visited by far fewer people.

For the admission times to the above catacombs, see the relevant sections of the text. The other catacombs (listed below) are not open regularly to the public: for information enquire at the Pontificia Commissione di Archaeologia Sacra, Via Napoleone III, 00185 Rome, ☎ 446 56107, fax (06) 446 7625. Visits to the catacombs for research or study purposes can be arranged by writeen application—be sure to include requested dates and a contact number in Rome. Off Via Nomentana are the catacombs of Nicomedes (32 Via dei Villini), and of the Cimitero Maggiore (Via Asmara), with interesting frescoes. Near Via Salaria are the catacombs of Panfilo; of Sant'Ermete, with a large underground basilica, containing an 8C fresco which includes the earliest known representation of St Benedict; of Santa Felicità (or Massimo), with a small underground basilica; of the Giordani, the deepest catacombs in Rome, with five tiers of galleries, which contain a fine 4C mural of a woman in prayer; and of Via Anapo, with interesting frescoes of Old and New Testament scenes, dating from the 3C and 4C.

In Via delle Sette Chiese are the catacombs of Commodilla, and on the Via Appia Pignatelli, those of Praetextatus, with pagan burials above ground, and Christian sarcophagi below (including those of the martyred companions of St Cecilia), and 2C paintings. At No. 643 Via Casilina are the catacombs of Santi Pietro e Marcellino (3C–4C), which contain more wall paintings than any of the other catacombs. In the Parioli district are the catacombs of San Valentino, beside a basilica built by St Julius I (pope 337–52) over the tomb of the saint.

The **Jewish catacombs** on the Via Appia (No. 119A), excavated in 1857, have tombs in the form of loculi or niches dating from the 3C to the 6C. The symbols include the cornucopia (Plenty), the palm-leaf (Victory), and the seven-branched candlestick, and the epitaphs are mostly in Greek. They are open by request to the Soprintendenza di Archeologia di Roma, Piazza delle Finanze 1, Roma 00100, fax (06) 481 4125. Beneath the Villa Torlonia (closed to the public) on Via Nomentana, there are more Jewish catacombs (2C or 3C), which originally extended for over 9km, but are now mostly caved in.

Concerts and plays

Concerts, theatre performances, and exhibitions are advertised on wall posters throughout the city. Free up-to-date information (also in English) is available from the EPT, and in *Un Ospite a Roma*, a monthly promotional magazine available free at hotels and information offices. By far the best source of information is *Roma c'è*, which is published every Thursday. It costs Lire 1500 and is available from newsstands. The Italian listings are easily decipherable and there is a brief section in English at the back.

Opera takes place at the **Teatro dell'Opera** (Pl. 4; 4), Piazza Beniamino Gigli, off Via Nazionale; ☎ 481 60255 (free information line 167-016665; 9–13); ticket office open daily 9–20; closed Mon.

Ancient Rome ~ an introduction

By T.W. Potter

Few cities make quite so indelible an impression as Rome. Although in part brought about by the warm golden-brown hue of the soft volcanic *tufo* stone, and the cheerful, bustling *vivante* atmosphere, it is above all the sense of history that is so pervasive. Every street brings a fresh and exciting vista, sometimes graced by a classical building from the days of the Roman Empire, then an elegant Renaissance *palazzo* or a glorious church, next the imposing façade of a structure erected in the wake of Italy's reunification in 1870, when Rome once again became capital. History is writ large upon the streets and piazzas of Rome, and it is impossible for the visitor, however casual, not to engage with it.

Our archaeological and historical appreciation of Rome's ancient and medieval landscape has in fact advanced enormously over the past decade or so. In response to enlightened proposals put forward by the Archaeological Superintendent for Rome, Professor Adriano La Regina, in March 1981, Parliament voted to release substantial funds for the investigation and, above all, conservation of the city's monuments. As inspection following an earth tremor in 1979 had showed, pollution from car emissions and central heating fumes was having a devastating effect upon the marble and stone that face the monuments of the Eternal City. Visitors were to become all too familiar in the 1980s with the green gauze that draped many of Rome's most famous landmarks. But behind those screens were scholars and conservators, seizing the chance to study and preserve the past, in tandem with teams of archaeologists, Italian and foreign, who were opening new windows into earlier layers all over the city. Plans to close down and remove Mussolini's Via dei Fori Imperiali, which cuts across Rome's ancient centre, may not have come to pass, reflecting the modern dilemma between the conservation of the past and the needs of the present; but enormous strides have been made in our understanding of the evolution of one of the world's greatest cities.

Assimilating and interpreting all this new information is one of the challenges of the 1990s. Coupled with it is the fresh scrutiny of documents and artifacts from discoveries by earlier generations of investigators, like the indefatigable Italian engineer and archaeologist Giacomo Boni ('excavation' in museum storerooms, as it has become known). This is shedding much light on matters long considered settled. To know that the reliefs on Trajan's Column were almost certainly executed at the behest of his successor, Hadrian, is not a matter of dotting i's and crossing t's, but a fundamental advance in knowledge. It shows how Hadrian, by honouring his adoptive father's military achievements, sought to render more secure his own precarious political position: for the emperor Trajan, while bestowing upon Hadrian favours and high political office, had nevertheless not nominated him publicly as his successor. Countless rulers of Rome, whether consul, emperor, pope or president, have used architecture as symbolic statements of their power and prestige, a point that will not be lost upon those who gaze upon their monuments.

Rome's beginnings

Rome was to grow up at the one easy crossing point along the lower reaches of the River Tiber. Excavations at nearby Sant'Omobono show evidence of settlement from as early as about 1500 BC. By the early first millennium BC, villages of oval wooden houses were emerging on the Palatine and Capitoline hills, both natural strongholds, the contours of whose once steep cliffs have been softened over the passage of time. There were also cemeteries on the spurs of the Quirinal, Viminal and Esquiline, which stretch like the fingers of a hand towards the Tiber, as well as on the low-lying ground beneath the Capitol, where later the Roman Forum was to develop. The distinction between the settlements of the living, and the burial grounds of the dead, maintained throughout the ancient history of the city for all but the greatest, was thus established at a very early date.

Traditionally, of course, Rome was founded by Romulus and Remus, perhaps in 753 BC (although the ancients disagreed about the exact date). They are described as descendants of Aeneas who, as a fugitive from the Trojan Wars, settled at Lavinium, near the mouth of the Tiber; Roman historians thus provided their compatriots with a respectable ancestry, firmly locked into Greek mythology. It was one of the marvels of the early 1980s to see, emerging from the bottom of the great trench at the foot of the Palatine Hill, a high wall 1.4m in width, with a ditch in front. Datable to about 730–720 BC, on good archaeological evidence, it was rather convincingly proclaimed as the wall of Romulus, built to mark the *pomerium*, the sacred zone that surrounded the city. Archaeology and legend for once seem to cohere.

Six kings are supposed to have followed Romulus, and it is clear that some, including the last, Tarquinius Superbus, were Etruscans, from the region to the north of Rome. To Servius Tullius (578–535 BC) is attributed the building of a great wall around the city (as yet unconfirmed by archaeology), and it was the Etruscans who drained the site of the Forum. The first paving stones were laid around 625 BC over a huge deposit of made-up ground (not a village, as was once supposed), and it rapidly developed into the religious, political and commercial centre of what was beginning to be a proper city-state. Nearby was the Regia, the sanctuary of the *Rex Sacrorum*, who was responsible for the official sacrifices of the State; it was constructed on the site of the Temple of Vesta, where the sacred flame of the community had been housed. Of the Agora in Athens, Sir Mortimer Wheeler could write that 'here, in a real sense, is the initial focus of the European mind'; of the Forum Romanum in Rome we might observe that here lie the ground and monuments where the Romans inspired the creation of the first world state. It *does* require imagination to hear Caesar or Cicero speaking from the rostrum; but, by shutting out the noise of modern Rome, we know that it really did happen there.

The Romans establish control

But we are getting ahead of ourselves. It was therefore in the late 7C and 6C BC that Rome took on characteristics, such as public buildings, squares and fortifications, among others, that permit us to describe it as urbanised. To what extent Etruscan rulers were ultimately responsible is a matter of scholarly contention; but there is no doubt that, while it was already a cosmopolitan place, the language and culture were predominantly Latin. Thus in 510 BC the Romans, themselves Latini, expelled their Etruscan tyrant, Tarquinius Superbus and, despite the famous (but perhaps apocryphal) siege of Lars Porsenna of Etruscan *Clusium* (modern Chiusi, in Tuscany), abolished the monarchy (509 BC). As a Republic, authority now became vested in the hands of two magistrates (later consuls), who were elected annually and chosen only from the aristocratic patrician class. As time went on, however, this exclusive concentration of power caused ever increasing resentment among the impoverished *plebs*. An intense class war ensued, which was to linger on for some 250 years. The Twelve Tables (451–450 BC) were an early attempt to introduce some legislative order, and were followed by a succession of new laws. Ultimately the sovereignty of the People was recognised, at least in theory; thus, while a patricio-plebeian élite effectively continued to hold the strings of power, via the magistrates and Senate, democracy ostensibly prevailed. It was a typically Roman, pragmatic solution.

It was also during this period that, through wars and alliances, Rome gradually extended domination over Italy. By 275 BC control had been established all over the peninsula, leaving the way open for intervention overseas. Sicily (241 BC), Sardinia (238), Spain (206) and North Africa (146) all were to become provinces, and during the 2C BC and 1C BC, large parts of the East Mediterranean also came under the Roman yoke. From being a parochial, somewhat rustic town in the 6C BC, Rome was now the wealthy mistress of a great Empire.

The effect upon the city was to be profound. New fortifications had been built in the early 4C (still to be seen outside the Stazione Termini), following the sack of Rome in 390 BC by an army of Gauls. Enclosing about 400 hectares, they excluded the flattish ground of the Campus Martius, now Vecchia Roma in the bend of the Tiber, where the Roman youth received military training, and popular assemblies met. But the vast area within the walls is eloquent testimony to a fast-expanding population, as well as of a new sense of urban identity and purpose. Development was needed of the riverside dockyards and nearby cattle-market (Forum Boarium), to feed the populace and promote commerce; and to Appius Claudius Caecus is due the credit for piping in water by building the city's first aqueduct in 312 BC. It must have seemed a miraculous achievement in a chaotic, crowded, and, by Greek standards, still somewhat provincial Italo-Etruscan town.

It was contact through conquest, especially of the Greek world, that was to change this image. Huge profits were realised, not least through the sale of slaves, and Rome became an immediate beneficiary. Victorious generals were accorded triumphal processions into the city and, in return, often paid for the building of a temple, vowed in the midst of battle. This glorified both the city and their own name, and it was Greek deities that were frequently thus honoured. Likewise, Greek statues were brought back to grace the public places of the city, and paintings in the Greek style were commissioned to represent a military success. To the Roman, the Greek world, and its cities, appeared sophisticated and culturally illustrious. From the 2C BC in particular there was a conscious move to Hellenise the city of Rome, not least through literature, architecture and the arts. While moralist Romans like Cato (234–149 BC) denounced such developments, which seemed alien to the noble traditions of the strong farmer-soldier, most accepted them with fervour. The elegant Graeco-Roman temples of Portunus (a god of commerce) and Hercules Victor, both built in the later 2C BC in the Forum Boarium, are still-standing reminders of this.

Rome's population, ultimately to reach a million or more in the first century

AD, was by now very substantial. The aristocracy lived in favoured areas like the Palatine, where their mansions were designed with *atria*; here their supporters (*clientes*) might be received. The plebeians inhabited high, multi-storey squalid tenements, ever vulnerable to fire, and often cheek by jowl with great public monuments. Feeding and entertaining these poor classes became an important facet of public life. When the general Gaius Flaminius Nepos built a circus in the Campus Martius in 221 BC, he was to establish the area as a place of popular entertainment. Here Pompey provided the first stone theatre to be built in Rome, in 55 BC, and Caesar planned, and Augustus had constructed, the theatre of Marcellus, Augustus' nephew. Dedicated in 13 BC, it still remains a very imposing and impressive monument.

The building of Rome

The great generals of the first century BC, particularly Sulla, Pompey and Gaius Julius Caesar, all sought to increase their prestige by embellishing Rome. Caesar's schemes were the most grandiose. Of lasting significance was his forum, near the old Forum Romanum, and by the Curia (which he rebuilt), where the senate met. The forum was dominated by a high temple of his divine ancestress Venus Genetrix, and the whole complex must have appeared a fitting symbol of the power and pre-eminence of the Julian family. Caesar's murder, in 44 BC, brought his own high personal ambitions to an end; but his adoptive son and heir, Octavian, once he had seized the reins of power by defeating Antony and Cleopatra at Actium in 31 BC, was more than capable of resuscitating them. Bestowed with the title Augustus ('reverend') in 27 BC, he was to rule a largely peaceful empire for a further 41 years. Rome was particularly to benefit. His famous boast that he 'found a city made of brick and left it made of marble' was far from idle. The white marble quarries at Carrara, in northwestern Italy, were greatly developed at this time, and huge quantities were shipped down to Rome. The building programme was on an enormous scale. Immediately initiated was the Augustan forum. It lay close to Caesar's forum, and was crowned, (as it still is), by a temple of Mars Ultor, the Avenger of Caesar's murderers. Filled with statues of Roman heroes, not least those of the Julian clan, it became the monumental focus of Augustan Rome, where proper respect was paid to the city's ancestors, and the great were received. Old buildings of historical and religious significance were restored, among them the House of Romulus, close to which, so as to emphasise his illustriousness, Augustus built his own residence; deliberately modest, it was the beginning of a process that was to transform the Palatine into an area of exclusive Imperial palaces.

Augustus was much aided by his devoted ally, the hugely wealthy Marcus Vipsanius Agrippa. Builder of Rome's first major public baths, two aqueducts, and the Pantheon (which still bears his name, although it is a Hadrianic reconstruction), he, like Augustus, was concerned to turn Rome into a well-run and elegant city that was a worthy capital of a great empire. The Ara Pacis, altar of Peace, with its marvellous reliefs depicting legends concerning the foundation of Rome, and of Augustus and his family, symbolised the new stability. A food dole was provided for the needy, and Augustus' own mausoleum in the Campus Martius was a massive architectural statement of the legitimacy and authority of the empire's *princeps*, first citizen.

Many of the ancient standing buildings that one sees in Rome today are of

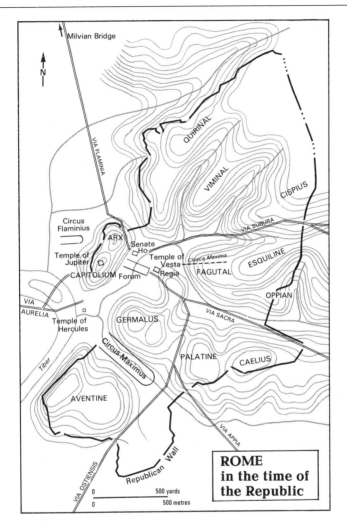

Milvian Bridge

N

VIA FLAMINIA

Circus
Flaminius

ARX

QUIRINAL

VIMINAL

CISPIUS

VIA SUBURA

Senate
Ho

Temple of
Jupiter

CAPITOLIUM

Temple of
Vesta

Forum

Regia

Temple of Vesta

Cloaca Maxima

FAGUTAL

ESQUILINE

VIA
AURELIA

Temple of
Hercules

GERMALUS

VIA SACRA

OPPIAN

Tiber

Circus Maximus

PALATINE

CAELIUS

AVENTINE

VIA APPIA

VIA OSTIENSIS

Republican Wall

**ROME
in the time of
the Republic**

0   500 yards

0   500 metres

course creations of the post-Augustan age. They are particularly characterised by the use of concrete faced with brick, an invention which seems to have taken place in Campania in the third century BC. It was, however, not until the days of Augustus' successor, Tiberius (AD 14–37), that the first large-scale building project using concrete was initiated in Rome: the construction of the Castra Praetoria, where the solders of the Praetorian Guard were housed. Set in the northeastern part of the city, between the Via Nomentana and the Via Tibertina, it was laid out like a legionary fortress. Troops had never before been based in Rome, for they potentially posed dangers for the unwary ruler. Indeed, when Claudius was proclaimed emperor in AD 41, it was the Praetorian Guard that did so.

Claudius, in AD 43 conqueror of Britain (an event which was commemorated with a triumphal arch), was to provide Rome with two new aqueducts to serve emerging residential areas on the Quirinal, Pincian and Aventine. He also built an all-weather harbour at Ostia, to facilitate importation of the vast supplies that the city needed: here was responsible civic management. Nero (AD 54–68), by contrast, invested many of his energies into creating a vast palace and pleasure gardens, known as the Domus Aurea, Golden House, between the end of the Forum Romanum and the Esquiline. The dark underground rooms, that one can soemtimes visit today, hardly convey the once sumptuous splendour of this extraordinary place, which covered some 50 hectares; but it was architecturally a visionary, if megalomaniac, project. It was later blotted out by the Colosseum (dedicated in AD 80; it may have taken its name from a colossal statue of Nero, set up nearby); the Baths of Titus (AD 79–81); and, in the early 2C, by the Baths of Trajan. The heart of the city was once more in the public domain.

Nero did rebuild many streets after the devastating fire of AD 64, including the Sacra Via which was provided with a great colonnade, like cities in the East. They were wider and straighter and, in combination with stringent new fire regulations, must have lent an altogether more organised impression to the city. The Flavian dynasty (AD 69–96), which under Vespasian seized power after a catastrophic civil war, were further to enhance that image. Thus Vespasian was to build a new forum, with as its centrepiece the Temple of Peace, echoing the message of Augustus's Altar of Peace. Although now largely buried, this once elegant architectural creation lay not far from the huge Flavian Colosseum, an amphitheatre where 50,000 people might relish the lavish, if often gruesome, entertainments provided mainly from the Emperor's pocket.

The last Flavian ruler, Domitian (AD 81–96), also built facilities for entertainment; not least was a stadium for athletic competitions, the shape of which is now fossilised by the Piazza Navona. He also started to lay out a new forum, which was completed by his successor, Nerva. However, his most striking achievement was the construction of a vast palace on the Palatine, overlooking the Circus Maximus. Known as the Domus Augustana, it was to become the residence for rulers over the next 300 years, a symbolic reminder with its innovative architecture, and lavish decoration, of the achievements and power of the Flavian family.

But times were changing. When Trajan became emperor in AD 98, he was to become the first provincial to take the throne. A Spaniard by birth, he nevertheless left his stamp on Rome in a remarkable way. His enormous forum stretched northeastwards from the Forum of Augustus, and included the Basilica Ulpia, 170m in length. His famous column, one of the mightiest monuments in Rome, lay just beyond the basilica, and was flanked by two libraries, one for Latin works, the other for Greek. Also still to be seen are his magnificent purpose-built market halls and shops, constructed beside his forum rather like a modern shopping centre; they underline how the fora had now become places of pomp and ceremony rather than humble commerce. Likewise, he attended to civic needs by building vast public baths, over Nero's Golden House. As much, or more, places for social concourse as for cleanliness, they further enhanced Rome's image as a truly great city.

Trajan paid for these works largely with booty won in two wars from the Dacians, in the lower Danube region. But he by no means emptied the state

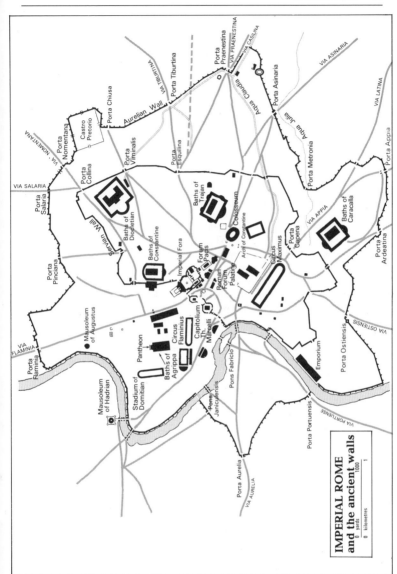

IMPERIAL ROME
and the ancient walls

coffers, and his successor Hadrian (AD 117–38), also of Spanish origin, had plenty of funds to realise his own projects. Among them were the rebuilding of the Pantheon, justly described as one of the masterpieces of Roman architecture; and his mausoleum, now Castel Sant'Angelo, which still dominates part of the skyline of Rome. But it was near Tivoli that he created his main residence, a huge villa whose buildings embodied the architectural ideals of the Greek and Eastern worlds that he so admired. Hadrian was above all a devoted philhellene, who ruled a united and largely harmonious empire. When Aelius Aristides delivered an encomium to Rome in AD 144, only six years after Hadrian's death, he could liken the empire to a single household, enjoying a perpetual holiday.

Yet the pre-eminence of the city of Rome was already beginning to wane. No more were there to be wars of conquest, bringing in fresh funds, and power was gradually slipping away to provinces like those of North Africa, which became ever more wealthy, especially through commerce. Septimius Severus, who ascended the throne in AD 193, was to be the first African emperor. His huge triumphal arch, dedicated in AD 203, is one of the more imposing monuments in the Forum Romanum today, and he also built a great, three-tiered façade to a new wing of the imperial palace. Called the Septizodium, it held statues of seven planetary deities with, at the centre, the Sun, symbolically facing Africa; it was, alas, demolished in 1588.

It was Severus's son, Caracalla, who built the enormous baths that still bear his name; covering some 20 hectares, they remain one of the most impressive sights of ancient Rome. But with the demise of the last Severan, Alexander, in AD 235, much of the empire was to be plunged into nearly 50 years of anarchy, warfare and chaos. It is to this period that the Aurelianic wall circuit belongs. Begun in the early 270s, it extends for 19km, and was so massively built that it remains as impressive today as in antiquity. Now Rome had become a stronghold in the new world of late antiquity and, when Diocletian (AD 284–305) restored order, the city lost its position as sole capital of the empire. Although he built his great baths (parts of which were converted in the church of Santa Maria degli Angeli by Michelangelo), he did not visit Rome until AD 303, and so disliked what he saw that he almost immediately departed. When Constantine founded his New Rome of Constantinople, modern Istanbul, dedicated in AD 330, a page of history was turned: after nearly a thousand years of pre-eminence Rome was no longer mistress of the world.

Constantine did of course endow Rome with many monuments, not least the churches of St Peter and St John Lateran, and his triumphal arch by the Colosseum; but we are here looking forward to the shaping of the medieval city, and away from its ancient past. Dark days were to lie ahead, especially in the fifth and sixth centuries as the population dwindled away; but so too was a distinguished and brilliant future as, under Charlemagne and the popes, a renaissance gradually took place from the early 9C. Rome and the Romans have always shown a remarkable capacity for innovation, and survival, over an immense period of time. There is no other city with so sustained a record of achievements, surely a remarkable tribute to the founding fathers, and their innumerable distinguished successors.

Further Reading

T. Ashby, *The aqueducts of ancient Rome* (Oxford 1935). M.T. Boatwright, *Hadrian and the City of Rome* (Princetown 1987). J. Carcopino, *Daily life in ancient Rome* (Harmondsworth, 1973 reprint). A. Claridge, *Hadrian's Column of Trajan*. Journal of Roman Archaeology volume 6 (1993), 5–22. F. Coarelli, *Il foro romano* (2 vols, Roma 1983,1985). M. Cristofani (ed.), *La grande Roma dei Tarquinii* (Rome 1990). F. Lepper and S.S. Frere, *Trajan's Column* (Gloucester 1988). R. Krautheimer, *Rome. Profile of a city 312–1308* (Princeton 1980). R. Meiggs, *Roman Ostia* (2nd ed., Oxford 1973). T.W. Potter, *Roman Italy* (2nd ed.,

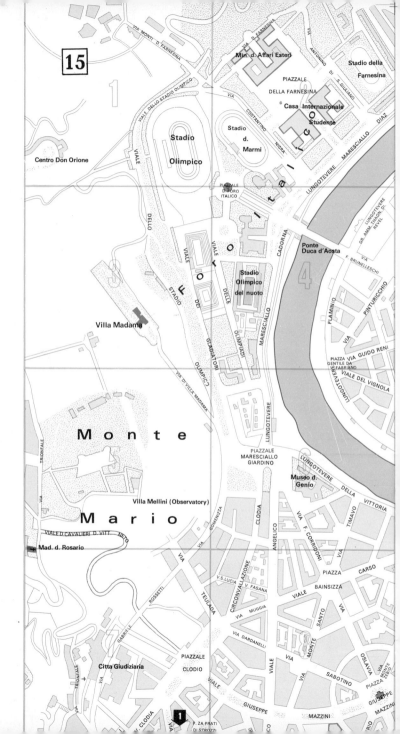

VIA MONTI D. FARNESINA

VIA D. FARNESINA

Min. d. Affari Esteri

PIAZZALE
DELLA FARNESINA

VIA ANTONINO DI S. GIULIANO

Stadio della
Farnesina

VIALE DELLO STADIO OLIMPICO

VIA

VIA COSTANTINO NIGRA

Casa Internazionale
Studente

Stadio
Olimpico

Stadio
d.
Marmi

Centro Don Orione

VIALE

VIALE

DELLO

VIA TITO LIVIO

LUNGOTEVERE MARESCIALLO DIAZ

PIAZZALE
DI FORO
ITALICO

LUNGOTEVERE GR. AMM. THAON DI REVEL DI

Ponte
Duca d'Aosta

F. BRUNELLESCHI

VIA

VIALE DEI GLADIATORI

VIALE DELLE OLIMPIADI

VIALE DELLO STADIO

Stadio
Olimpico
del nuoto

VIA CADORNA

MARESCIALLO

VIA FLAMINIO

VIA PINTURICCHIO

Villa Madama

VIA DI VILLA MADAMA

PIAZZA VIA GUIDO RENI
GENTILE DA
FABRIANO

LUNGOTEVERE

VIALE DEL VIGNOLA

VIA TRIONFALE

M o n t e

LUNGOTEVERE

PIAZZALE
MARESCIALLO
GIARDINO

LUNGOTEVERE DELLA VITTORIA

Museo d.
Genio

VIA

Villa Mellini (Observatory)

M a r i o

VIALE D. CAVALIERI D. VITT. VENETO

Mad. d. Rosario

VIA GOMENZZA

VIA CLODIA

VIA ANGELICO

VIA F. CORRIDONI

VIA TIMAVO

PIAZZA
CARSO

VIA ROSSETTI

VIA TEULADA

CIRCONVALLAZIONE

V. S. LUCIA
V. FASANA

VIA MUGGIA

VIALE

BAINSIZZA

VIA SANTO

VIA

VIA GABRIELE

VIA TRIONFALE

VIA DARDANELLI

VIA

VIALE

VIA MONTE SANTO

SABOTINO

VIA OSLAVIA

PIAZZA
GIUSEPPE

VIA MONTE NERO

PIAZZALE
CLODIO

Citta Giudiziaria

VIA CLODIA

VIALE

VIALE GIUSEPPE

MAZZINI

VIA

1

P. ZA PRATI
DI STROZZI

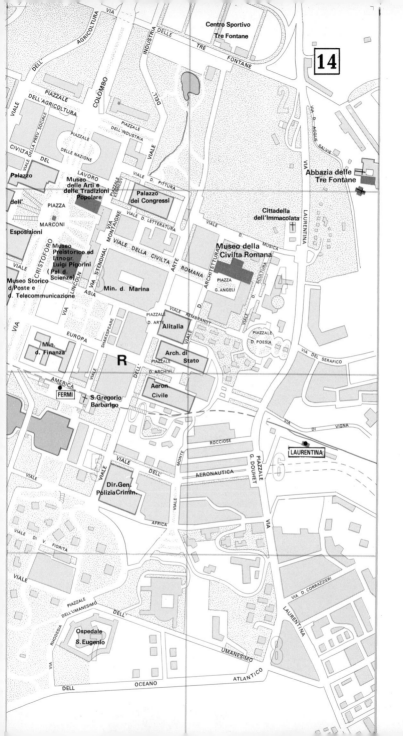

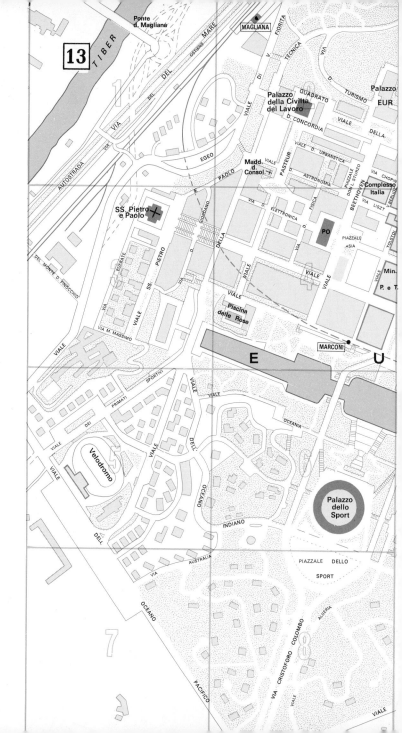

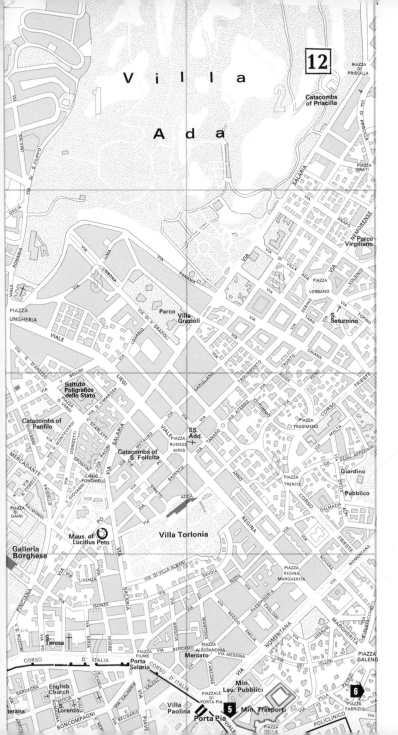

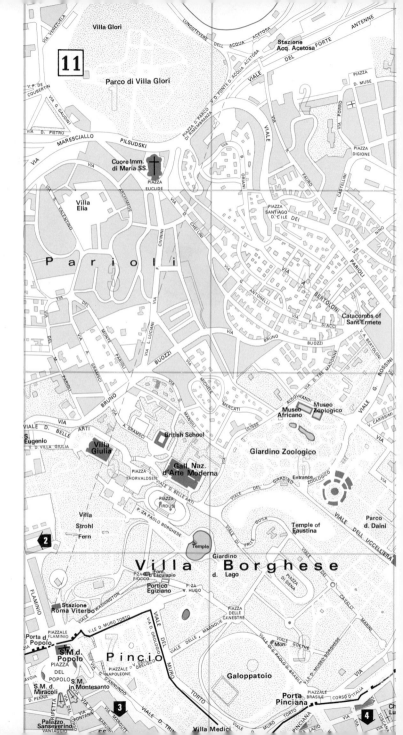

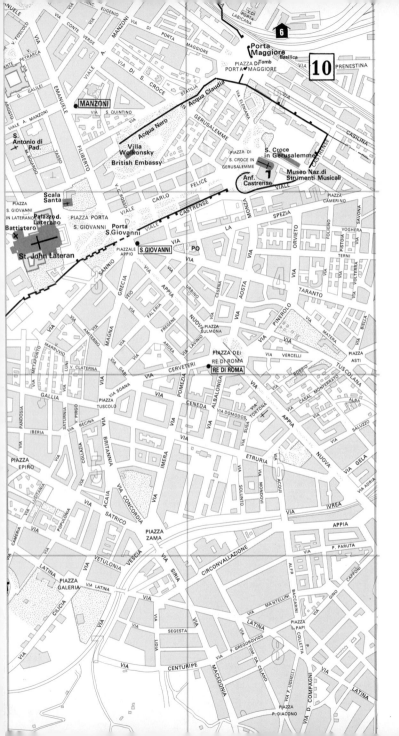

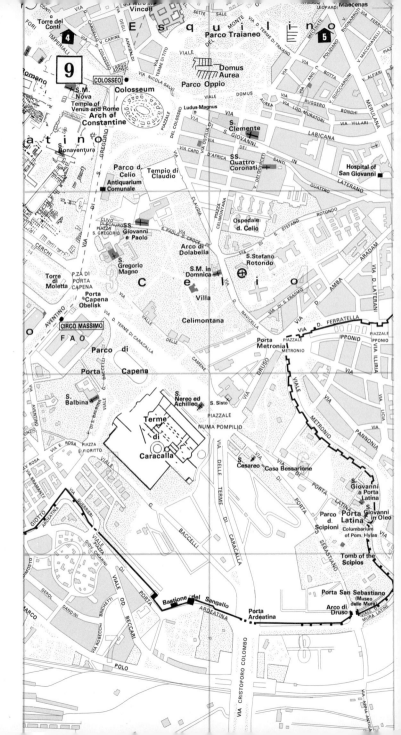

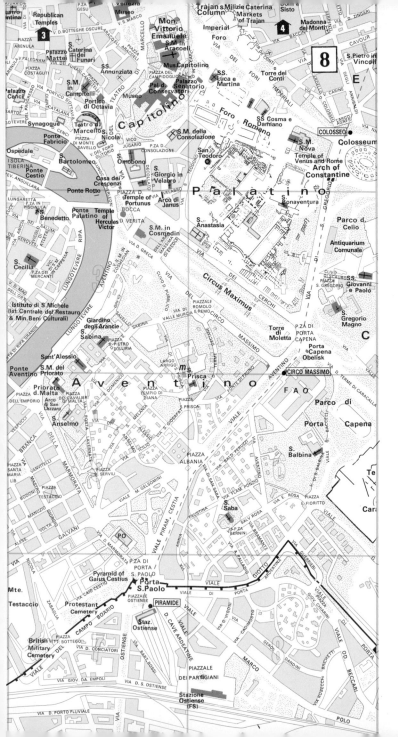

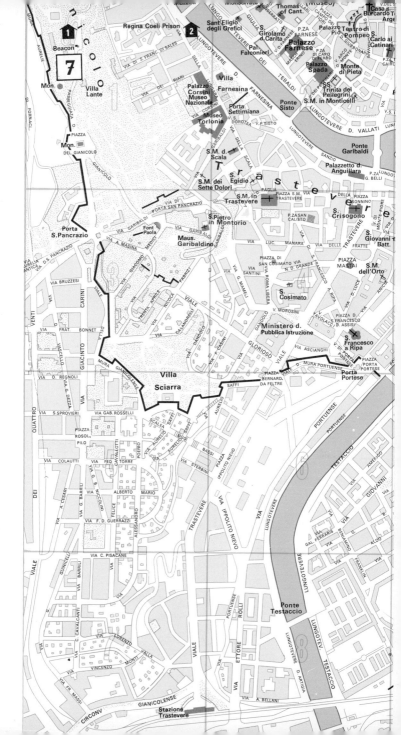

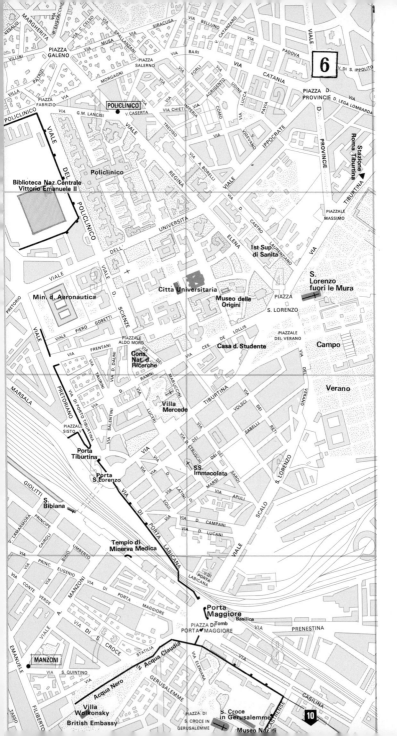

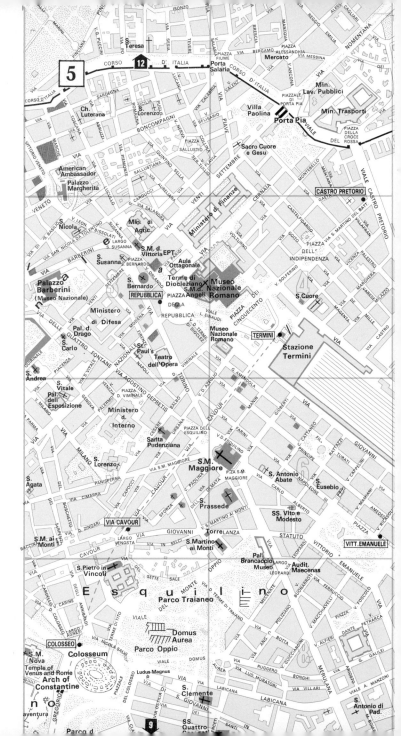

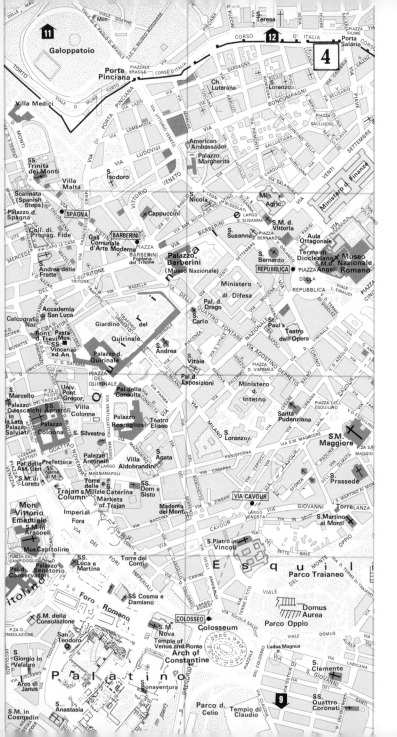

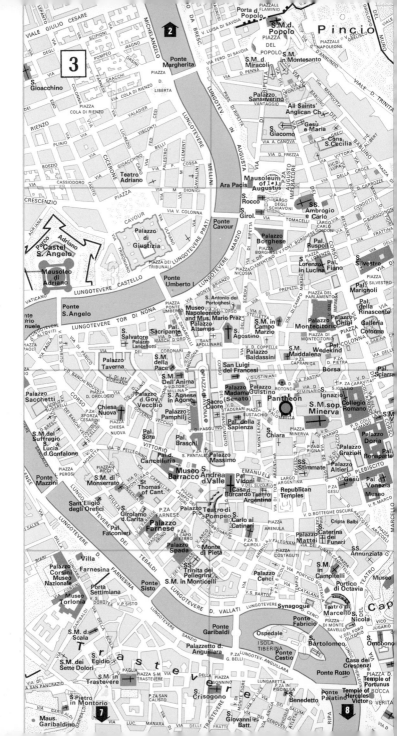

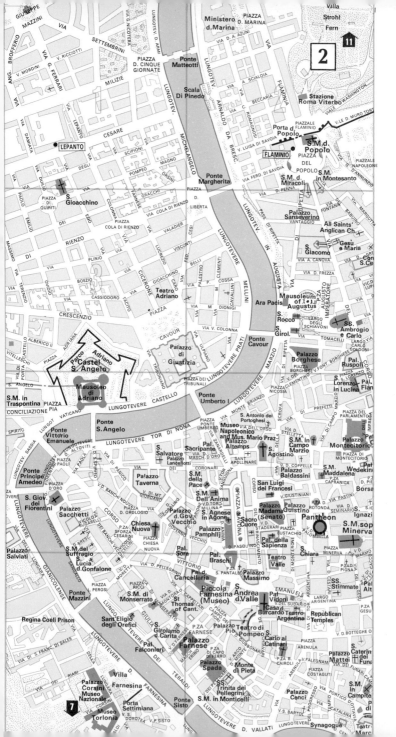

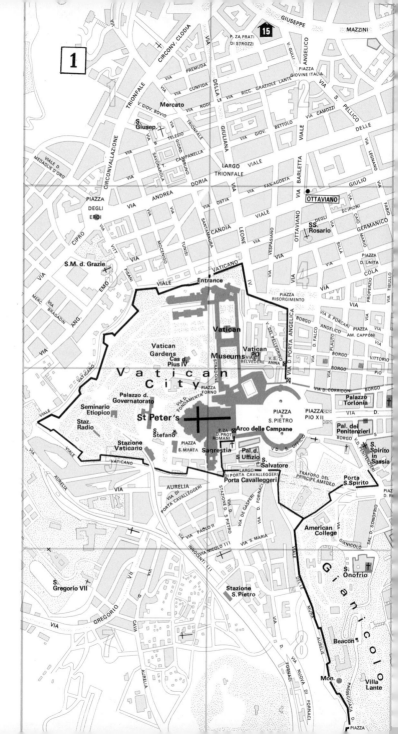

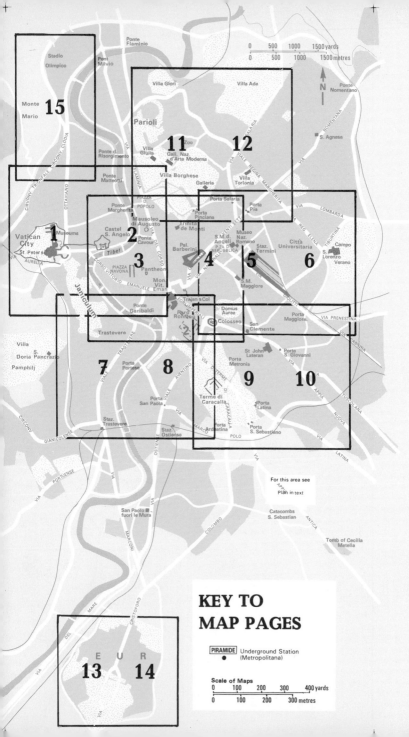

KEY TO MAP PAGES

PIRAMIDE	Underground Station (Metropolitana)

Scale of Maps

London 1992). M. Pallottino, *The Etruscans* (London 1975). L. Richardson, Jnr., *A new topographic dictionary of ancient Rome* (Baltimore and London 1992). J.E. Stambaugh, *The ancient Roman city* (Baltimore and London 1988). M. Todd, *The walls of Rome* (London 1978). J.B. Ward-Perkins, *Roman imperial architecture* (Harmondsworth 1981). P. Zanker, *The power of images in the age of Augustus* (Ann Arbor 1988).

Roman Emperors

27 BC–AD 14	Augustus
14–37	Tiberius
37–41	Caligula
41–54	Claudius
54–68	Nero
68–69	Galba
69	Otho
69	Vitellius

Flavians

69–79	Vespasian
79–81	Titus
81–96	Domitian
96–98	Nerva
98–117	Trajan

Antonines

117–38	Hadrian
138–61	Antoninus Pius
161–80	Marcus Aurelius
161–69	Lucius Verus
180–92	Commodus
193	Pertinax
193	Didius Julianus

Severians

193–211	Septimius Severus
211–17	Caracalla
211–12	Geta
217–18	Macrinus
218–22	Heliogabalus
222–35	Alexander Severus
235–38	Maximinus
238	Gordian I
	Gordian II
238	Pupienus
	Balbinus
238–44	Gordian III
244–49	Philip I
247–49	Philip II
249–51	Decius
251–53	Trebonianus Gallus
253	Aemilian
253–60	Valerian
253–68	Gallienus

268–70	Claudius II
270	Quintillus
270–75	Aurelian
275–76	Tacitus
276	Florian
276–82	Probus
282–83	Carus
282–85	Carinus
283–84	Numerian
285–305	Diocletian
286–305	Maximian
305–06	Constantius Chlorus
305–10	Galerius
308–24	Licinius
306–07	Flavius Severus
306–12	Maxentius
308–14	Maximinus
306–37	Constantine the Great
337–40	Constantine II
337–50	Constans
337–61	Constantinus II
350–53	Magnentius
361–63	Julian
363–64	Jovian
364–75	Valentinian I
364–78	Valens
367–83	Gratian
375–92	Valentinian II
378–95	Theodosius I

WESTERN EMPIRE

395–423	Honorius
425–55	Valentinian III
455	Petronius Maximus
455–56	Avitus
457–61	Majorian
461–65	Libius Severus
467–72	Anthemius
472	Olybrius
473	Glycerius
474–75	Julius Nepos
475–76	Romulus Augustulus

From the Fall of the Roman Empire to the Present Day

The Roman Church was not recognised until the reign of the Emperor Constantine when, by his famous Edict of Milan in 313, Christians throughout the Empire were granted liberty of worship. A primitive shrine had been built between AD 160 and 180 over the tomb of St Peter, and the first basilica of St Peter was consecrated in November 326. Other early Christian places of worship were the churches of Santa Pudenziana, San Sebastiano, San Lorenzo fuori le Mura and Santi Giovanni e Paolo. To Constantine is attributed the foundation of San Giovanni in Laterano and its baptistery, St Peter's and Santa Croce in Gerusalemme. Public pagan worship was forbidden in the city in 346 and ten years later temples were closed. Christianity became the state religion under Theodosius (died 395). The population of the city in the 4C estimated at about 500,000 was gradually to diminish in succeeding centuries until the city began to expand again in the 11C.

Rome was sacked by the Goths and Vandals repeatedly during the 5C. In 476 Odoacar, king of the Goths, compelled Romulus Augustulus to abdicate and so effectively put an end to the Western Roman Empire.

Medieval Rome
The supremacy of the bishop of Rome was gradually recognised by a Christianised western world, and the 'Donation of Constantine' was used to prove that the Papacy had inherited territory from the Emperor: it was not until the 15C that this document was discovered to be a 5C forgery. The papacy of St Gregory the Great (590–604) marked the foundation of medieval Rome, although not much is known about the city in this period since little archaeological evidence has survived. Rome, the possession of which was disputed in the 6C by Goths and Byzantines, passed at the beginning of the 7C under the temporal protection of the popes, and from then, right up until the 19C, the history of the papacy became intricately connected with the history of Rome.

When Pope Stephen III was threatened by the Lombards, he appealed for help to Pepin, king of the Franks, who defeated them and granted the Pope a portion of Lombard territory (AD 754). This marked the beginning of the temporal power of the popes over the States of the Church. On Christmas Day 800, Charlemagne, son of Pepin, was crowned by Leo III in St Peter's as Augustus and Emperor, and the Empire, known as the the 'Holy Roman Empire' from the 13C onwards, survived until the abdication of Francis II of Austria in 1806. The walls of the Leonine City, built to defend the Borgo and St Peter's, date from the 9C.

The strength of the papacy increased under Pope Nicholas I (858–67) but after his death the prestige of the popes declined and the German emperors took an active part in the papal elections thoughout the 10C and early 11C. Gregory VII (1073–85), with the help of some Roman noble families, reasserted papal authority, but was unable to prevent the Norman Robert Guiscard, who had conquered Sicily, from devastating the city in 1084. As in other large Italian

towns during the 12C the Commune of Rome strengthened its administrative position, and in 1188 it received official papal recognition. During the splendid pontificate of Innocent III (died 1216) Rome became the capital of the western Christian world, and the influence of the Empire in the Italian peninsula dwindled.

Boniface VIII proclaimed the first jubilee in 1300, which brought thousands of pilgrims to Rome from all over Europe, and provided a large income for the papal coffers. His Bull 'Unam Sanctam' asserted unequivocally the temporal power of the papacy. But in 1309 Pope Clement V removed the papacy from Rome to Avignon, where it remained under the protection of France for most of the 14C. Meanwhile Rome, and the surrounding countryside, was devasted by wars between rival Roman aristocratic families (including the Colonna, Caetani and Orsini), and the Commune of Rome, in the absence of the pope, gained in strength. In 1347 Cola di Rienzo was made 'tribune' of the 'Holy Roman Republic', but he failed in his patriotic but utopian attempt to revive the ancient power and glory of the Imperial city (and he was killed on the Capitol Hill in 1354). In 1378 Gregory XI was persuaded by St Catherine of Siena to return to Rome, and the Commune, while acknowledging the papal overlordship, at the same time attempted to retain its authority. Between 1378 and 1417, during the Great Schism, various popes fought over the chair of St Peter, while the city suffered both physically and socially and the population was reduced to some 20,000 inhabitants. The ruins of ancient Rome were used as pastureland, and plundered for use as building material or for lime.

The Renaissance period

Pope Martin V, a member of the important Roman Colonna family, began to restore the city in 1420, and the temporal power of the popes was gradually established in central Italy, where the Papal States now included Lazio, Umbria, the Marches and Romagna.

During the papacy of Nicholas V (1447–55) the supremacy of the pope over the Commune was finally recognised, and the city acknowledged its dependency on the papacy. Nicholas V not only carried out building work at St Peter's and the Vatican (where he established his residence) and strengthened the fortifications of Castel Sant'Angelo, but also restored the administrative offices of the Commune on the Capitol hill, and (under the guidance of Leon Battista Alberti) recognised the importance of preserving the buildings of ancient Rome, which, however, continued to be plundered for their stone and marble until the 16C.

Sixtus IV, a member of the Della Rovere family, was one of the richest patrons of his time. In 1471 he founded the oldest public collection in the world when he donated to the city the sculptures which now form the nucleus of the Capitoline Museum, and he considerably increased the holdings of the Vatican library and opened it to the public. He rebuilt the 'Sistine' Chapel (with is named after him) and constructed the Ponte Sisto across the Tiber. He also reorganised the streets of the city. The grandest of all the wealthy Cardinals' residences erected at this time in the city was the splendid Renaissance Palazzo della Cancelleria, commissioned by Sixtus's nephew Cardinal Raffaello Riario. At the end of the century, Nero's Domus Aurea was discovered beneath the Baths of Trojan and the painted decoration on its walls had a great influence on Renaissance artists, many of whom imitated these 'grotesques'.

At the beginning of the 16C Cardinal Giuliano Della Rovere was elected Pope Julius II: he spent untold riches on ambitious artistic projects designed to glorify the papacy as successor to the ancient Roman Empire. Rome became the centre of the High Renaissance while the three greatest artists of the age—Bramante, Raphael and Michelangelo were at work here. Using Bramante as architect, Julius took the audacious decision to rebuild St Peter's, and he enlarged the Vatican palace on a magnificent scale. He commissioned the frescoes on the vault of the Sistine Chapel from Michelangelo, and the frescoes in the 'Stanze' in the Vatican from Raphael. He planned the long and straight Via Giulia and Via della Lungara on either side of the Tiber. The Medici Pope Leo X appointed Raphael as commissioner responsible for the preservation of the ancient buildings of Rome.

After Clement VII took sides with Francis I of France against the Emperor Charles V, German mercenary troops captured Rome in the devastating Sack of Rome in 1527, when great damage was wrought to the city. It lost its prestige as a centre of Humanism, and its population fell to around 30,000 inhabitants. This humiliation for Clement VII (who had to take refuge in Castel Sant'Angelo) as well as the attacks on the papacy by Martin Luther (who visited Rome in 1511) preluded the period of the Counter-Reformation. The Farnese Pope Paul III introduced the idea of Rome as the 'Holy City', and many fine buildings were erected, including the splendid Palazzo Farnese, perhaps the most dignified and impressive palace in Rome. The very heart of the ancient city, Piazza del Campidoglio, was redesigned in 1538 by Michelangelo, and the ancient Roman statue of Marcus Aurelius was set up here. Paul III approved the founding of the Order of the Jesuits in 1540, and later in the century the great Jesuit church of the Gesù was built.

Pope Sixtus V (1585–90) did more than any of his predecessors to improve and adorn the city in celebration of the Catholic church. With the help of Domenico Fontana, he built new long and straight streets (including the 'Strada Felice', part of which is now called Via Sistin, over 3km long, which ran up and down four hills of the city) and set up obelisks to close the vistas at the end of them or as focal points in piazze. He also completed the dome of St Peter's, and enlarged the Vatican and Lateran palaces. He brought the water of the Acqua Felice by aqueduct from the Alban Hills into the centre of Rome. The district of the Borgo (between the Vatican and Castel Sant'Angelo), which had been the stronghold of the papacy since 850, was formally incorporated into the city of Rome in 1586. By now the population of the city was around 100,000 and Rome became the most cosmopolitan city of its time.

Baroque Rome

Paul V (1605–21) completed St Peter's (consecrated by Urban VIII in 1626), and reactivated an aqueduct from Lake Bracciano, built by Trajan, which ends on the Janiculum hill. The 'Aqua Paola' still supplies water to the Vatican and its fountain. It is to the 17C popes Urban VIII, Innocent X and Alexander VII that Rome owes its Baroque aspect of today. Urban VIII (1623–44) was the patron of Bernini, one of whose most remarkable works was the colonnade in Piazza San Pietro. He also designed numerous delightful fountains in the city, the most elaborate of which is in Piazza Navona. Borromini, the other great architect of this time, built the courtyard of Palazzo della Sapienza, San Carlo alle Quattro

Fontane, the church and dome of Sant'Ivo, Sant'Agnese in Agone, and the Oratorio dei Filippini.

The flamboyant staircase beneath the Trinità dei Monti, known as the Spanish Steps, dates from the 18C, as does the Trevi fountain. This was the century of the Grand Tour when numerous rich young men from Britian came to Rome on a leisurely visit to complete their education, admire Rome's classical remains, and, where possible, acquire some antiquities. The city came to be regarded as a centre of European culture at this time. In February 1798, the French entered Rome and proclaimed a republic: Pius VI was taken as a prisoner to France where he died in 1799. In 1809 Napoleon annexed the States of the Church, already diminished, to the French Empire: in 1810 the French Senate proclaimed Rome to be the second capital; and in 1811 Napoleon conferred the title of King of Rome on his newborn son. On the fall of Napoleon in 1815, Pius VII returned to Rome, to which were also restored almost all the works of art that had been removed by the emperor.

The Risorgimento

The city took an active part in the agitated period of the 'Risorgimento' or political renaissance of Italy, and shared with the rest of Europe the revolutionary ideas of 'liberty' and 'independence'. A republic was proclaimed by an elected assembly in Rome under the guidance of Mazzini and the Pope fled to Gaeta. When the French sent an army in support of the Pope in 1849, the defence of the city was entrusted to the able hands of Garibaldi who made a heroic stand against the foreigners of the Janiculum Hill. The inhabitants of Trastevere were particularly enthusiastic supporters of Mazzini and Garibaldi. In the first half of the 19C important restoration work was carrried out on the Colosseum and Pantheon.

In 1867 Garibaldi made another attempt to rouse the Romans against the papal government, with the help of the Cairoli brothers who were killed in the same year. In 1870 the French garrison, who had occupied Castel Sant'Angelo since 1849, withdrew from the city, and a month later the Italian army, under Raffaello Cadorna, entered Rome through a breach in the walls beside the Porta Pia. This brought an end to the papal rule of the city, although an agreement was made on the same day with the papacy that the Leonine City was excluded from the jurisdiction of the Italian troops. The city, still contained within the Aurelian walls, was proclaimed the capital of united Italy in 1871.

At the end of the 19C the ugly Via Nazionale, Via Cavour and Corso Vittorio Emanuele II were all built, and the embankments constructed along the Tiber. An obtrusive monument to the first king of Italy, Vittorio Emanuele II, was set up in the centre of the city in 1885–1911 (after the First World War it became also the burial place of Italy's Unknown Soldier). By 1911 the population of the city was around 500,000 inhabitants.

The Twentieth Century

After the First World War the movement known as 'Fascismo', the creation of Benito Mussolini, rapidly developed. He organised the 'March on Rome' on 28 October 1922, after which the king, Vittorio Emanuele III, invited Mussolini to form a government. In 1929 the Lateran Treaty (the 'Concordat') was signed, by which the Vatican City became an independent sovereign state. The classical

Roman period was glorified by Mussolini who attempted to imitate it through his building activities and his attempts to create a new foreign 'Empire'. Numerous disastrous interventions of 'urban planning' were perpetrated in the 1930s: the Capitol hill was flanked by two broad thoroughfares, both opened in 1933 (Via dei Fori Imperiali and Via del Teatro di Marcello). Beyond the Tiber, the old medieval district of the Borgo was transformed by the building of Via della Conciliazione (1937), which also altered irrevocably the dramatic effect of Bernini's Piazza in front of St Peter's. The district of EUR and the Foro Italico are typical of the grandiose conception of Fascist Rome.

Italy entered the Second World War on the German side on 10 June 1940; the Fascist regime was finally overthrown in 1943 (and Mussolini was killed by partisans in 1945). In 1944, 335 civilians were shot by Nazi troops at the Fosse Ardeatine near the Via Appia, as a reprisal for the killing of 32 German soldiers in Rome by members of the Italian Resistance movement. After the landings at Anzio and Nettuno in 1944, the American 5th Army entered the capital. In 1946 Vittorio Emanuele III abdicated, and less than a month later a general election, with a referendum on the form of government, was held. The referendum approved the establishment of a Republic, with an elected president. In 1947 the Constituent Assembly passed the new republican constitution.

In the 1950s the population of Rome grew from 1.6 million to 2.1 million inhabitants. The population is now around 2,777,800. The metropolitan area of the city is about ten times greater than it was in the 1950s, and most of the residents now live in the sprawling suburbs which have spread into the Roman Campagna in an uncontrolled way. The historic centre suffers from depopulation (it is estimated that only some 150,000 residents now live here), and many of the buildings are used as offices.

In 1978 Aldo Moro, President of the Christian Democrat Party, the largest political party in Italy at that time, was kidnapped and assassinated and his body abandoned in a street in the centre of the city. In the same year John Paul II was elected, the first non-Italian pope since 1522, and the only Polish pope in the church's history. In 1993 the mayor of Rome was for the first time elected directly by the inhabitants of the city.

Since the 1980s interesting excavations have been carried out in the Roman Forum and on the Palatine hill, and important restoration projects have been completed on numerous monuments and works of art (including Trajan's Column, the Arch of Constantine, the equestrian statue of Marcus Aurelius, the frescoes by Michelangelo in the Sistine chapel, and the frescoes by Raphael in the 'Stanze' in the Vatican). In the 1990s many church and palace façades, and fountains, blackened by the polluted air, have been carefully cleaned. Rome is now preparing to receive some 30 million visitors expected in the city for the Holy Year in 2000.

The Guide

1 · The Capitoline Hill and Piazza Venezia

PIAZZA VENEZIA (Pl. 4; 5), a huge and busy square, is the focus of the main traffic arteries of the city. Towards it converge Via del Corso from the north, Via del Plebiscito (the continuation of Corso Vittorio Emanuele) from the west (and St Peter's), Via Battisti (the continuation of Via Quattro Novembre) from the east (and the station), and, from the southeast and southwest respectively, Via dei Fori Imperiali and Via del Teatro di Marcello. The piazza was transformed at the end of the 19C when parts of the Renaissance city were demolished and the Capitoline Hill itself encroached upon to make way for the colossal Monument of Vittorio Emanuele II (see below) which is an unforgivable intrusion into the centre of the city. At the busiest times of the day a policeman regulates the traffic at the head of the Corso, which from the north side of the piazza runs straight for nearly 2km to Piazza del Popolo with its obelisk.

Dwarfed by the Monument, and to the right of it, is the Capitoline Hill. It is separated from Piazza d'Aracoeli (with a fountain of 1589 designed by Jacopo della Porta) by a wide, modern, traffic-ridden road (Via del Teatro di Marcello), one of the most difficult in the city to cross on foot, which runs south to the Tiber past the foot of the hill. Beside the Vittorio Emanuele II Monument here are the interesting ruins, discovered this century, of a Roman tenement house or 'insulae' built in the 2C AD and over four storeys high.

The **CAPITOLINE HILL** (in Italian, *Campidoglio*; 50m) is the smallest but most famous of the Seven Hills of Rome. Already inhabited in the Bronze Age, it was the political and religious centre of ancient Rome, and since the end of the 11C has been the seat of the civic government of the city. On its southern summit (the *Capitolium*) stood the Temple of Jupiter Optimus Maximus Capitolinus (remains of which still exist, see below), the most venerated temple in Rome, since Jupiter was regarded as the city's special protector, and its northern summit (altered by the construction of the Monument of Vittorio Emanuele II) was occupied by the *Arx*, or citadel of Rome. Formerly the hill was accessible only from the Forum but since the 16C the main buildings have been made to face the north, in conformity with the direction of the modern development of the city.

There are three approaches to the hill from Piazza d'Aracoeli. On the left a long flight of steps mounts to the church of Santa Maria in Aracoeli, and on the right, Via delle Tre Pile (a carriage road of 1873), winds up past fragments of temples and a stretch of archaic wall. In the middle the stepped ramp known as the *Cordonata* designed by Michelangelo (and modified c 1578 by Giacomo della Porta) provides the easiest way up the hill. At its foot are two Egyptian lions in black granite (veined with red) of the Ptolemaic period, from the Temple of Isis. In the garden on the left (traversed by another flight of steps, shaded by a pergola) a 19C statue of Cola di Rienzo marks the spot where he was killed in 1354. Higher up is a cage which, until recently, contained a she-wolf, the symbol of Rome.

Piazza del Campidoglio

At the top is **PIAZZA DEL CAMPIDOGLIO** (Pl. 4; 7), beautifully designed by Michelangelo to give grandeur to the historical centre of Rome (it was completed to his design in the 17C). It is surrounded on three sides by stately palaces and a balustrade defines its open end. At the back is Palazzo Senatorio; on the left is Palazzo del Museo Capitolino; facing it, on the right is Palazzo dei Conservatori. The latter has a very unusual design with Ionic columns supporting a flat open loggia below, and handsome windows with coupled columns on the piano nobile, below a prominent entablature with a balcony. The two storeys are united by the use of the giant order, the first time this solution was used in secular architecture. The similar palace opposite, also designed by Michelangelo, was not built until the mid-17C.

The handsome pavement with an oval star design gave prominence to the famous gilded bronze statue of Marcus Aurelius, which, since its restoration, has been displayed in the Capitoline Museum (see below); it was replaced here by a copy in 1538 Michelangelo, having just been made a citizen of Rome, provided its small and elegant base, and its theatrical setting. On the balustrade are colossal figures of the Dioscuri (much restored), late Roman works found in the Ghetto in the 16C, the 'Trophies of Marius', two war memorials of the Flavian period bearing barbarian arms, statues of Constantine and his son Constans (from the Baths of Constantine), and two milestones, the first and seventh of the Via Appia.

The collections housed in the Palazzi del Museo Capitolino, dei Conservatori, and Caffarelli are grouped under the comprehensive title of the **MUSEI CAPITOLINI**. The title is rather confusing, since one of the museums is called the Museo Capitolino (see below). They are famous for their magnificent Roman sculptures, and constitute the oldest public collection in the world, dating from 1471, when Sixtus IV made over to the people of Rome a valuable group of

bronzes (including the 'Spinario' and the she-wolf), which were deposited in Palazzo dei Conservatori. This nucleus was later enriched with finds made in Rome and by various acquisitions, notably the collection of Cardinal Alessandro Albani. A second museum was opened in 1876.

■ **Admission**: 9–19 daily; closed Mon. ☎ 671 02071. Lire 10,000. (C). There is one ticket for all the museums, which can be bought at the entrance to the Museo Capitolino, on the left of the piazza, or at the entrance to Palazzo dei Conservatori, on the right of the piazza.

Museo Capitolino
Palazzo del Museo Capitolino (Pl. 4; 5), built in the reign of Innocent X (1644–55), contains the Museo Capitolino, an extremely interesting collection of ancient sculpture, begun by Clement XII and added to by later popes. It was opened to the public in 1734, during the pontificate of Clement XII. Many of the numbers which distinguish each piece of sculpture are now illegible, and the collection is poorly labelled.

   Ground Floor. Inner Court. The colossal statue of a river-god, known as 'Marforio' (probably 2C AD) was moved from the foot of the Capitoline Hill by Giacomo della Porta in 1596 and incorporated in the fountain here. This was once one of Rome's 'talking' statues (the most famous of which was 'Pasquino', see p 128), used for the display of satirical comments and epigrams. Marforio 'conversed' with another 'talking' statue called Madama Lucrezia, still at the bottom of the hill. In the side niches are two figures of Pan (telamones), from the Theatre of Pompey.

   Portico. The equestrian ***statue of Marcus Aurelius**, formerly in Piazza del Campidoglio, has been displayed here since its restoration. This magnificent colossal gilded bronze is a masterpiece of Roman sculpture. It was beautifully restored in 1981–90 when the gilding was returned to its surface. It is now thought to date from the latter part of the Emperor's reign (AD 161–80), or possibly from the year of his death; it is the only Roman equestrian statue of this

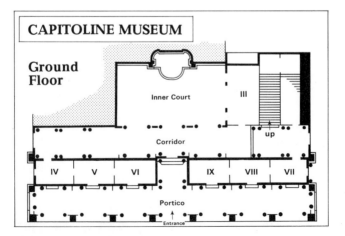

period to survive. This popular statue appears time and again in medieval representations of the city, and it is first documented in the 10C when it was believed to represent the Christian emperor Constantine the Great. It is thought to have been on the Lateran hill as early as 782, and was brought from there by order of Paul III in 1538 to the Capitoline Hill. In 1873 Henry James commented 'I doubt if any statue of King or captain in the public places of the world has more to commend it to the general heart'.

The sculpture in the **atrium** includes a colossal statue of Minerva, from a 5C original, two statues of women after Greek originals, with portrait heads of the 2C–3C AD, and a colossal statue of Mars, dating from the Domitian period. At the left end are three rooms (**IV–VI**; closed indefinitely), containing monuments of Oriental cults (including statues of Mithras).

At the right end of the atrium is the entrance to three more rooms: **Room VII**. Heads, busts and fragments of calendars from the Palatine and Ostia, including a finely preserved Order of Precedence of the citizens of Ostia (from the time of the Emperor Pertinax). **Room VIII**. 1. Roman head from the period of Trajan; *4. Amendola sarcophagus, with a battle between Gauls and Romans; 10. Cippus of a master-mason called Titus Statilius Aper, with his tools. **Room IX**. Colossal double *sarcophagus, a splendid work of the 3C AD, with portraits of the deceased and reliefs representing the story of Achilles; cippus of Vettius Agorius Praetextatus, a proconsul of Achaia in the Peloponnese.

A staircase leads up past fragments of sarcophagi with reliefs of animals to the **First Floor**. Beyond the gallery (described below) is **Room I** which exhibits the ***Dying Gaul**, an exquisitely modelled figure of a Celtic warrior who lies mortally wounded on the ground. It was discovered in 1622 in the gardens of Sallust near the Villa Ludovisi and is a copy from the Roman period of one of the bronze statues dedicated at Pergamon by Attalos I in commemoration of his victories over the Gauls (239 BC). The statue was formerly called the 'Dying Gladiator', 'butcher'd to make a Roman holiday', in Byron's phrase. It was beautifully restored in 1986 when the position of the right arm was changed, having been altered in a 17C restoration.

Nearly all the other statues in this room were found at Hadrian's Villa, near Tivoli: 1. Amazon, a Roman work after an original attributed to Pheidias (wrongly restored); 2. Colossal head of Alexander the Great; 3. Hermes, Hadrianic version of a 4C original; 4. Lycian Apollo, copy of a work by Praxiteles; 6. Head of a youth; *7. Satyr Resting, a good replica of an original by Praxiteles (the 'Marble Faun' of Nathaniel Hawthorne's novel of that title; other replicas in the Vatican); *8. Head of Dionysos; 9. Greek Cynic philosopher, Roman copy in marble of a bronze original; 10. Head of a general, a Pheidian type; 11. Priestess of Isis, period of Hadrian; 12. Eros and Psyche, Hellenistic work.

Room II. In the centre: *1. Laughing Silenus, in red marble, of the Imperial period from a Hellenistic bronze; 2. Alabaster bust of an unknown Roman, period of Gallienus; 5. Sarcophagus depicting the Hunt of the Calydonian Boar; 8. Child with mask, a Hellenistic work; 11. Sarcophagus with figures of Endymion and Selene (early 3C AD); 16. Herm of Hercules (2C AD); 17. Boy with a goose, copy of a bronze by Boethos of Chalcedon (2C BC); 19. Sarcophagus (2C AD) with the life of Dionysos including his birth, a graceful work. On the wall above is a bronze plaque on which is inscribed the *Lex Regia* of Vespasian, the historic decree conferring sovereign power on the emperor; the

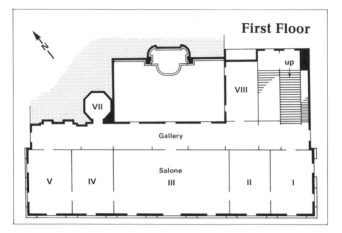

text was used by Cola di Rienzo to demonstrate the greatness and the rights of Rome.

Room III (*Salone*). In the centre are five statues in dark marble or bronze: 1, 5. Statues of Zeus and Asklepios, both from originals of the 4C BC; 2, 4. Young or laughing centaur, Old or weeping centaur, two remarkable works from Hadrian's Villa, signed by his contemporaries Aristeas and Papias of Aphrodisias in Caria; 3. Infant Hercules, a colossal ugly figure in green basalt, of the late Imperial epoch, on a base decorated with scenes from the myth of Zeus.

The marbles exhibited around the walls include: (on the entrance wall) 27. Huntsman, head of the period of Gallienus on a body of the late Archaic type; 28. Statue of Harpocrates, period of Hadrian. On the wall opposite the windows: 13. Hadrian as Mars; 20. Archaic statue of Apollo, copy of the so-called Omphalos Apollo in Athens; 21. Statue of a young Roman of the time of Hadrian as Hermes; *22. Old woman in terror, a striking example of the Hellenistic period; 23. Muse, once probably representing Hera, from a 4C original; 24. Colossal statue of Demeter, restored as Hera, from an Attic original of the 4C BC. On the far wall: 7. Colossal statue of Apollo (the head does not belong); 11. Hera, from an original attributed to Agorakritos (5C BC), badly restored with a portrait head. On the window wall: *30. Apollo, from a work of the first half of the 5C; 31. Pothos, from an original by Skopas; 33. Wounded Amazon, signed by the copyist Sosicles, from a 5C original; 34. Roman couple as Mars and Venus, period of Septimius Severus; 36. Athena Promachos, a 4C type from the Villa d'Este.

Room IV. The identifications of the busts (recently cleaned) of philosophers, poets and others in this room are not all certain. Those whose identity is most probable are Socrates (various types), Theon (17), Sophocles (22–23), Chrysippos (27), Euripides (30–31), Homer (39–41), Demosthenes (43), Aeschines (50), Metrodorus (51), double *portrait of Epicuros and Metrodorus (52), Epicuros (53), Antisthenes (55), and Cicero (56). In the centre, 75. Seated figure ('Marcellus') from an original of the 4C BC (head modern). On the walls are fragments of a frieze, perhaps from the Porticus of Octavia, with sacrificial instruments and parts of ships, and Greek votive reliefs.

Room V contains a rich collection of Roman Imperial busts, interesting as

portraits and also in some cases because of the precious materials used. On columns: *Augustus, wearing a wreath of myrtle; *15. Woman of the late Flavian period; Commodus. Around the walls: 20. Domitia; 21. Plotina, wife of Trajan, considered the best portrait of her; 24. Matidia; 39. Julia Domna; *55. Heliogabalus. Above are reliefs, two of which are works of great delicacy, executed in the first centuries of the Empire and following Hellenistic types: F. Perseus rescuing Andromeda; H. Sleeping Endymion. In the centre: *59. Helena, mother of Constantine, a beautiful seated figure inspired by the Aphrodite of Pheidias.

Gallery. 35. Colossal head of an Emperor, 4C AD; 36. Portrait of Marcus Aurelius as a boy; 53. Colossal head of Aphrodite, perhaps an original of the Hellenistic period; 57. Sarcophagus of the 3C AD with reliefs of the rape of Persephone; 61. Roman matron of the Flavian period in the guise of Venus; 65. Torso of the Discobolos of Myron, badly restored as a fighting gladiator; 67. Cupid as archer, a good copy of a celebrated work by Lysippos; 68. Hercules slaying the Hydra (so restored by Algardi: and the antique model he used can be seen beside it. It was more probably intended to represent Hercules capturing the hind). 4a. Relief of a man and wife, probably reading a will; 7. Leda and the Swan, replica of a work attributed to Timotheos (4C BC); 8. Head of Marsyas, probably a Hellenistic original; 10. Drunken old woman, perhaps after Myron the Younger, a Pergamene sculptor of the end of the 3C BC; 22. Psyche winged, from a Hellenistic original; 24. Head of Dionysos, a good copy from a 4C BC original; 31. Minerva, copy of a bronze of c 400 BC; 34. Decorative vase (krater) of the 1C AD, resting on a *well-head from Hadrian's Villa, with archaistic decoration representing the procession of the 12 gods (Dii Consentes).

Room VII (Cabinet of Venus), contains the celebrated *Capitoline Venus, found in the 17C in a house near San Vitale, a superbly modelled statue of Parian marble. It is a Roman replica of a Hellenistic original, thought to be derived from the Cnidian Aphrodite of Praxiteles, and was beautifully cleaned in 1992.

Room VIII (Hall of the Doves) is named from a delicate *mosaic (9) from Hadrian's Villa, after a work by Sosias of Pergamon; 8. Sarcophagus with the story of Prometheus (3C AD); 23. Herm of Hermes Propylaios; 37. Diana of Ephesus; 52. Front panel of a sarcophagus, with the Triumph of Bacchus. In glass cases: 53. Tabula Iliaca or Trojan Tablet, a plaque with small reliefs representing the Trojan cycle, by Theodorus (1C AD); 76. Piece of a shield of Achilles by the same sculptor. In the centre of the room is a charming little statue of a child protecting a dove, a Roman copy of a Greek work of the 2C BC (wrongly restored with a snake).

Palazzo dei Conservatori

The Palazzo dei Conservatori (Pl. 4; 7) was rebuilt by Nicholas V about 1450 and remodelled after 1564 by Giacomo della Porta and Guidetto Guidetti from a design by Michelangelo. It contains the **Sale dei Conservatori**, the **Museo del Palazzo dei Conservatori** and the **Pinacoteca**. The first two occupy the first floor, and the Pinacoteca is arranged on the second floor. Adjoining the building, and reached from the Museo del Palazzo dei Conservatori, is the **Museo Nuovo**, which is at ground level, but has been closed since 1984.

Ground Floor. Inner Court. On the right are fragments of a colossal statue (c 12m high) of Constantine the Great, including the head, hand and foot, which were brought from the Basilica of Constantine in 1486. The body of the

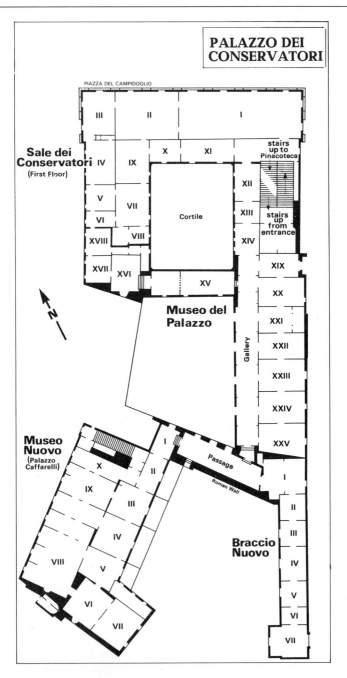

PALAZZO DEI
CONSERVATORI

PIAZZA DEL CAMPIDOGLIO

Sale dei
Conservatori
(First Floor)

III   II   I

X   XI

IV   IX

stairs
up to
Pinacoteca

XII

V   VII

Cortile

XIII

stairs
up
from
entrance

VI

XVIII   VIII

XIV

XVII   XVI

XIX

XV

XX

Museo del
Palazzo

XXI

XXII

Gallery

XXIII

XXIV

Museo
Nuovo
(Palazzo
Caffarelli)

XXV

I

X

Passage

I

II

IX

Roman Wall

III

II

IV

III

Braccio
Nuovo

IV

VIII

V

V

VI

VI

VII

VII

statue was made in wood. Near the head is an inscription from the time of Boniface VIII (1294–1303). On the left are bases and transennae with sculptured representations of provinces and nations subject to Rome, which once decorated the Temple of Hadrian in the Piazza di Pietra. Above is an inscription from the arch erected in AD 51 on Via Lata to celebrate the conquest of Britain by Claudius. Beneath the portico at the further end, a figure of Roma from the time of Trajan or Hadrian, and statues of Barbarians.

Beyond the ticket office a **staircase** leads up to the **First Landing**. Four reliefs from triumphal arches, three of them celebrating Marcus Aurelius and his military victories and triumph in 176, including a scene of the emperor sacrificing before the Temple of Jupiter Capitolinus, have been displayed here since the 16C. The fourth panel comes from an arch in Via di Pietra. **Second Landing**: Hadrian, relief from the demolished Arco di Portogallo. The *statue of Charles of Anjou, by Arnolfo di Cambio or his workshop, was made for Santa Maria in Aracoeli c 1270. From this landing at the top of the stairs open the Sale dei Conservatori.

Sale dei Conservatori

Room I (Sala degli Orazi e Curiazi). Frescoes by Giuseppe Cesari, usually known as the Cavaliere d'Arpino, representing episodes from the reigns of the early kings. *Urban VIII, marble statue, a studio work begun by Bernini; *Innocent X, bronze by Algardi. It was here in 1957 that the Treaty of Rome, the foundation of the European Economic Community, was signed by Italy, Belgium, France, West Germany, Luxembourg and Holland.

Room II (Sala dei Capitani). Handsome doors in carved wood (17C); more frescoes from Roman history by Tommaso Laureti; and 16C–17C statues, including ones of Alessandro Farnese and Marcantonio Colonna.

Room III (Sala dei Trionfi di Mario). Frieze by Michelangelo Alberti and Giacomo Rocchetti representing the triumph of Emilius Paulus over Perseus of Macedon. The most famous of the bronzes presented to the Conservatori by Sixtus IV are exhibited here. In the middle is the celebrated ***Spinario**, or Boy plucking a thorn from his foot. This was formerly known as the 'Fedele Capitolino', because it was thought to be the portrait of Marcius, a Roman messenger who would not delay his mission though tortured by a thorn in his foot. It is a delicate Hellenistic composition in the eclectic style of the 1C BC. Also displayed here: bronze *head, known as L. Junius Brutus, of Etruscan or Italic workmanship of the 3C BC; Camillus, or acolyte (1C AD); bronze krater with an inscription, the gift of King Mithridates to a gymnastic association, part of the booty from a Mithridatic war, found at Anzio; fine sarcophagus front (3C AD).

Room IV (Sala della Lupa), with more frescoes from Roman history. On the wall opposite the windows are fragments of the Fasti Consulares et Triumphales, from the inner walls of the Arch of Augustus in the Forum, in a frame designed by Michelangelo. These are records of Roman magistrates and of triumphs of the great captains of Rome in 13 BC–AD 12. The famous ***She-wolf** of Rome is thought to be an Etruscan bronze of the late 6C or early 5C BC, probably belonging to the school of Vulca, an Etruscan sculptor of Veio. It originally stood on the Capitoline hill and may be the figure of a wolf struck by lightning in 65 BC, when the hind feet are said to have been damaged. It was taken to the

Lateran Palace some time in the Middle Ages. The twins were added by Antonio del Pollaiolo c 1509.

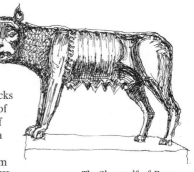

The She-wolf of Rome, *in the Sala dei Conservatori*

Room V (Sala delle Oche), an interesting example of a 17C apartment, contains a figure of Isis and two 'geese', or more probably ducks (antique bronzes); a bronze bust of Michelangelo; and a marble head of Medusa, by Bernini. In the centre is a mastiff in rare green marble.

Room VI (Sala delle Aquile). From here there is access to Rooms XVI–XVIII of the Museo del Palazzo dei Conservatori (see below). **Room VII (Sala degli Arazzi)**. Tapestries showing the goddess Roma, and the Birth of Romulus and Remus (from the painting by Rubens in the Capitoline Gallery).

Room VIII (Cappella Nuova) has an altarpiece by Avanzino Nucci. **Room IX, Sala delle Guerre Puniche**, is decorated with frescoes by Giacomo Ripanda. In the centre, two girls playing, Hellenistic works (removed for restoration). **Room X (Cappella Vecchia)**. On the ceiling, frescoes and stuccoes, by Alberti and Rocchetti; on the walls, Madonna and angels, by Antonio da Viterbo. **Room XI (corridor)**. 16C Flemish tapestry; Roman scenes by Gaspare Vanvitelli. The corridor leads back to the landing, where, to the right, is the entrance to the Museo del Palazzo dei Conservatori.

Museo del Palazzo dei Conservatori

Rooms XII, XIII, XIV (Sale dei Fasti Moderni). These rooms contain lists of the chief magistrates of Rome since 1640, and a collection of busts and herms. **Room XII**. 8. Fragment of a group of a giant fighting two satyrs, derived from the Gigantomachia of Pergamon. **Room XIII**. 2. Cow, Roman copy, thought to be derived from the Cow of Myron; 4. Bust of Faustina, wife of Antoninus Pius; 5. Sarcophagus, depicting a Dionysiac ceremony; 6. Bust of Sabina, wife of Hadrian. **Room XIV**. 4. Panther and wild boar in combat; Roman Imperial busts. From the gallery (see below) is the entrance (right) into Room XV.

Room XV (Sala degli Orti Lamiani), containing sculptures found in the Lamiani Gardens, on the Esquiline. 3. Old fisherman; 5. Old woman with a lamb, two Hellenistic statues of great realism; 4. Seated *girl, a remarkably graceful figure, recently restored, probably a Roman copy of a Greek original of the 3C BC; 7. Centaur's head, probably an original of Pergamene art. (In the second part of the gallery) 12. Bust of Commodus as Hercules, a work of considerable refinement; 13, 14. Tritons, perhaps its supporters; 15. Female statue, after an original of the 4C BC. In the centre, *29. Esquiline Venus, a young girl probably connected with the cult of Isis, an eclectic work dating from the 1C BC. The pavement in marble and alabaster is from the Esquiline.

Room XVI (Sala dei Magistrati, admission from Room VI of the Sale dei Conservatori, see above). 2, 5. Roman umpires starting a race in the time of

Constantine; column of rare green breccia from Egypt; inscriptions recording the conferment of Roman citizenship on Petrarch, Michelangelo, Titian and Bernini; 4. Artemis, from a 4C original, restored to represent Christian Rome; 6. The Emperor Decius as Mars.

The *Sale dei Monumenti Arcaici (Rooms XVII–XVIII). Room XVII. In the centre: *10. Torso of an Amazon (late 6C BC), designed for the angle of the temple pediment of Apollo Daphnephoros at Eretria. 2. Headless female statue from a bronze original c 460 BC; 4. Fragment of a stele (5C or 4C BC); 5. Latona, from a 5C original; 7, 9. Two young initiates of the Eleusinian mysteries. Room XVIII. 6, 7. Korai in the Archaising style of the early Imperial era; 8. Nike, probably from a 5C original; 10. Fragment of a stele of Attic workmanship; 11. Head of a lion (5C); 12. Stele representing a girl with a dove (late 6C).

Gallery. 14. Colossal foot, probably of the Rhodian school; 35. Copy of the 'Grande Ercolanese' (original formerly in Dresden); 41. Relief of a 'Scaenae frons' (1C–2C AD); 44. Shrine dedicated to the Earth Mother; 53, 54. Athletes, from 4C types; 56. Fragment of a relief from the Auditorium of Maecenas; 58. Claudia Justa as Fortune (2C AD); 68. Youth, perhaps from an original of the Polykleitan school. Room XIX has a fine display of *Egyptian works (well labelled), many from the Serapeum in Campo Marzio. They include: statuette of Rameses II; sphinx of Pharaoh Amasis II (568–526 BC); two apes from the tomb of Nectanebes II (359–341 BC); and a Roman crocodile. Room XX. Sarcophagi with the Good Shepherd; inscriptions; 13. Head of a Roman matron (5C–6C AD). Room XXI (Sala del Camino), with remains of a chimneypiece of the Conservatori. The *Capitoline Tensa is the reconstruction of a triumphal chariot overlaid with bronze, which carried the images of the gods at the opening of the Circensian games.

Room XXII (Prima Sala Castellani), contains part of the collection presented by Augusto Castellani, the fruit of excavations between 1860 and 1866 in southern Etruria and Lazio. In glass cases along the walls: Etruscan, Italic and Faliscan vases; Etruscan statuette in terracotta from Cerveteri (end of 7C BC). 1. Sarcophagus, with the Calydonian boar hunt; Greek red- and black-figure vases, and antefixes from Capua (6C–5C); Tragliatella oinochoe (7C BC) with paintings and graffiti, and below, Attic kylix of 470 BC from Cerveteri.

Room XXIII (Seconda Sala Castellani). In glass cases along the walls: Corinthian and Attic vases, with red and black figures (6C BC) including (No. 64) the Amphora of Nikosthenes, and (No. 132) hydria from Ceretani; three sides of an Etruscan funerary bed, with animal reliefs. In the middle of the room: *krater of Aristonothos, with Odysseus and the Cyclops (7C).

Room XXIV (Sala dei Bronzi; closed for restoration). 2, 3, 8. Head, hand, and globe from a colossal statue of Constans II; 5. Rear half of a colossal bull, of very fine workmanship; 6. Globe which originally adorned the Vatican Obelisk, damaged by a musket shot during the Sack of Rome in 1527; *10. Horse, since its restoration thought to be a Greek original dating from the early 4C BC. *11. Bed with exquisite decoration, of the 1C AD; *12. Litter, composed of bronze, found on the Esquiline by Castellani.

Room XXV (Sala degli Orti Mecenaziani), containing sculptures found in the Gardens of Maecenas on the Esquiline. In the centre, *13. So-called 'Auriga', or charioteer mounting (copy of a 5C original). Since its recent restoration this statue is thought to represent a hero, possibly Theseus, driving his chariot (it was

formerly attached to a horse, also displayed here). 2. Statue of Hercules, from an original by Lysippos; 3. Eros or Thanatos, from an early 4C BC original; 6. Punishment of Marsyas, in Phrygian marble, probably of the Rhodian school; 7. Head of Augustus; 8. Hygieia, Roman copy of a Hellenistic original; *9. Dancing Maenad, in relief, from an original by Kallimachos; 10. Headless statue of Aphrodite, a fine copy of an Ionic Greek original; *11. Head of an Amazon, from an original by Polykleitos; in the centre: 18. Rhyton, part of a fountain, by Pontios of Athens, in the neo-Attic style of the 1C AD.

At the end of the gallery is (left) a tufa wall belonging to the Temple of Jupiter Capitolinus (6C BC; see below). The **Braccio Nuovo**, or New Wing, arranged in 1950–52, and **Museo Nuovo** in the **Palazzo Caffarelli**, at the southwest end of Palazzo dei Conservatori, on the other side of the garden (opened as the Museo Mussolini in 1925), have been closed since 1984. They contain more fine Roman sculpture.

Pinacoteca Capitolina

This gallery of paintings, founded in 1749 by Benedict XIV, was based on the Pio and Sacchetti collections, formed respectively by Prince Gilberto Pio of Savoy and Cardinal Sacchetti. In the 19C it lost some of its treasures to the Vatican Picture Gallery and to the Accademia di San Luca. It was later enriched by the Cini bequest, which included some interesting 14C–15C paintings from the Sterbini collection, as well as ceramics. The Pinacoteca is particularly important for its 16C–18C Italian and foreign works.

The gallery is on the second floor of Palazzo dei Conservatori. On the **stair landing**: Apotheosis of Sabina, relief from the Arco di Portogallo (see p 155); head of a priest of Isis(?); bull attacked by a tigress, two examples of marble intarsia work from the basilica of Junius Bassus on the Esquiline (4C AD).

Room I. Scarsellino, *Adoration of the Magi*; Garofalo, *Sacred Conversation*, *Madonna in Glory*, *Annunciation*; Francesco Francia(?), *Presentation in the Temple*; Domenico Panetti, *Portrait of a girl*; Dosso Dossi, *Holy Family*; Mazzolino, *Christ and the Doctors*; Emilian School (1513), *Madonna and Child with Saints*;

Room II. Paolo Veronese, *Strength, Temperance, Rape of Europa*; Girolamo Savoldo, *Portrait of a Lady as St Margaret*; Gentile Bellini (attrib.), *Portrait of a man*; Giovanni Bellini, *Portrait of a young man*; Palma Vecchio, *Woman taken in adultery*; Titian, *Baptism of Christ*; Lorenzo Lotto, *Man with crossbow*; Domenico Tintoretto, *Scourging of Christ, Crown of Thorns, Baptism of Christ, *St Mary Magdalene*.

Room III. Copy of a painting by Jacopino del Conte of Michelangelo; Federico Zuccari, *Self-portrait*; Van Dyck, *The engravers Pieter de Jode, father and son, The painters Luke and Cornelius de Wael*; Guido Reni, *Self-portrait*; Bartolomeo Passarotti, *Double portrait of musicians*; *Portrait of a man, Portrait of a man with a dog*; Rubens, *Romulus and Remus fed by the wolf* (finished by pupils); 17C Roman school, *Portrait of a man*; Salvator Rosa, *Soldier, Witch*; Metsù, *Crucifixion*; Simon Vouet, *Allegory*; Jean Leclerc (attrib.), *Christ with the doctors*; Denis Calvaert, *Marriage of St Catherine*.

Room IV. Mainly 14C and 15C works. Cola dell'Amatrice, *Death and Assumption of the Virgin*; Macrino d'Alba, *Madonna and Saints*; Barnaba da Modena, *Ascension*; Giovanni Antonio Sogliani, *Madonna and Child*; School of central Italy (1376), *Annunciation, Nativity, Presentation in the Temple, Flight into*

Egypt, Massacre of the Innocents; Bartolomeo Bulgarina (attrib.), *St Mary Magdalene and St Bartholomew*; Niccolò di Pietro Gerini, *Trinity*.

To the right is **Room V** (the **Cini Gallery**), which contains part of the bequest of Count Giuseppe Cini (1881), including a fine collection of bronzes and *ceramics from various sources, and excellent Saxon porcelain, clocks and tobacco boxes. At the end, *St John the Baptist* by Caravaggio (there is a replica of this painting in the Galleria Doria). The **Medagliere** (admission by special permission), contains a rich collection of Roman, medieval, and modern coins and medals.

Room VI. Pier Francesco Mola, *Diana and Endymion, Esther and Ahasuerus*; Pietro da Cortona, *Rape of the Sabines, Sacrifice of Polyxena, Triumph of Bacchus*; Raffaellino Bottalla, *Joseph sold into bondage*; Crescenzio Onofri, landscapes. (Above the window), bust of Benedict XIV; inlaid 17C cabinets. The statue of Hercules in gilded bronze was found in the time of Sixtus IV during the demolition of the Ara Maxima, near the Forum Boarium.

Room VII (to right of Room IV). Domenichino, *Sibyl*; Giovanni Lanfranco, *Herminia among the shepherds*; Giovanni Andrea Sirani, *Ulysses and Circe*; Guido Reni, *Cleopatra, Anima Beata*; Guercino, *St Petronilla*, a vast canvas formerly in St Peter's, *Cleopatra before Octavian, St Matthew and the angel, Persian Sibyl*; Francesco Albani, *Nativity of the Virgin*; Caravaggio, *Gipsy fortune-teller*.

Room VIII (left). Pietro da Cortona, *Madonna and Child*; School of Tintoretto, *Pentecost*; Veronese, *Mary Magdalene*; Pietro Paolo Bonzi, two landscapes; Poussin, *Triumph of Flora* (replica of a painting in the Louvre).

Room IX. Garofalo, *Holy Family, Marriage of St Catherine*; Francesco Albani, *Madonna and Child*; Annibale Carracci, *Madonna and Child*; Lodovico Carracci, *Head of a boy*, a very fine early work; Annibale Carracci, *St Francis adoring the Crucifix*.

Palazzo Senatorio

Palazzo Senatorio (Pl. 4; 7), the central palace in Piazza del Campidoglio, is the official seat of the Mayor of Rome, and has recently been beautifully restored. An 11C fortress was built by the Corsi on the remains of the ancient Tabularium (see below), and the Senate was probably installed here c 1150. The medieval castle with four towers was renewed in the 13C and redesigned by Michelangelo in the 16C. The present façade (1592), by Giacomo della Porta and Girolamo Rainaldi, is a modification of Michelangelo's design. In front of the double staircase, with converging flights, is a fountain with two colossal statues (2C AD) of the Tiber (right) and the Nile (left); in the recess is a porphyry statue of Minerva, found at Cori and transformed into the Dea Roma. The palace is crowned by a bell-tower (1582), with a clock, a statue of Minerva, and a gilded cross; two bells (1803–04) replace the famous *Patarina*, which had been installed in 1200 to summon the people to 'Parlamento'.

The **interior** may only be visited by special permission and previous appointment (entrance in Via San Pietro in Carcere). On the first floor in the **Council Chamber** is a colossal marble statue of Julius Caesar (the only statue of him which survives), of the period of Trajan, and in the antechamber, *L'Aurora* by Pietro da Cortona. The **Room of the Flag** contains a fragment of the 14C flag of St George, from the church of San Giorgio in Velabro. In the **Protomoteca** is a large collection of busts of famous people, mostly dating from the 18C and

19C. The **Great Hall** has a Canova monument, and from here there is access to a terrace with a remarkable view of the Forum.

The **Tabularium** (admission only with special permission; apply at Palazzo Caffarelli), or depository of the State archives, survives beneath Palazzo Senatorio, and its great blocks of porous tufa built into the unhewn rock dominate the view of the hill from the Forum. On two storeys, with a rectangular plan and a central court, it was erected in 78 BC by Q. Lutatius Catulus: the inscription stone can still be seen by one entrance on the left flank of Palazzo Senatorio. Beyond this, in Via San Pietro in Carcere, is the arcaded gallery of the Tabularium (no admission) with a splendid view of the Forum. Here, also, is part of the frieze from the Temple of Concord (see p 86), and in the adjoining gallery (seen through a closed iron gate) is a cast of part of the frieze from the Temple of Vespasian, another section of which can be seen through the arch, still in position above three columns at the foot of the Capitoline. It incorporates considerable remains of the **Temple of Veiovis**, erected first in 196 BC, and rebuilt after a fire in the 1C BC. The pronaos is orientated towards Via del Campidoglio, and the podium and cella are well preserved. The external wall of the Tabularium may be seen on two sides; a small gap was left between it and the Temple. Behind the Temple is a colossal marble statue of Veiovis (1C AD, after a 5C BC type), found in the cella. To the right is a perfectly preserved staircase of the Republican period, leading steeply down to the Forum. It was blocked at the bottom by a tufa wall (still in place) when the Temple of Vespasian was built.

From Piazza del Campidoglio the short Via del Campidoglio skirting the right side of Palazzo Senatorio runs downhill, past a stretch of Roman road, to a terrace with an excellent view of the Forum backed by the Colosseum. The rest of the Capitoline Hill can be seen by taking Via di Monte Tarpeo and then Via del Tempio di Giove back uphill from the terrace (or by the staircase which ascends from Piazza del Campidoglio to a portico named after Vignola, the arches of which have been closed in with glass). At the top of Via del Tempio di Giove, enclosed by a modern wall and very much below the level of the road, are the remains of the eastern angle of the façade of the **Temple of Jupiter Optimus Maximus Capitolinus**. The investiture of consuls took place here, and the triumphant procession awarded to victorious generals ended at the temple (see p 82). According to tradition, it was founded by Tarquinius Priscus, completed by Tarquinius Superbus, and dedicated in 509 BC. It is the largest temple known of this period. It was destroyed by fire in 83 BC during the civil wars, rebuilt by Sulla, destroyed again in AD 69, rebuilt by Vespasian and again by Domitian, and was still standing in the 6C. More remains of the temple are incorporated in the Braccio Nuovo of the Musei Capitolini.

From the peaceful gardens on the terrace known as the **Belvedere di Monte Tarpeo**, there is another extensive view of Rome to the south and southeast, taking in the Forum, the Palatine, the Baths of Caracalla, the Aventine and the Tiber. The precipice below is thought to be the notorious Tarpeian Rock of ancient Rome, from which condemned criminals were flung to their death, although some scholars suggest this was on the north side of the hill. The road continues past a little 19C temple to the edge of the hill (where steps lead down to Via di Teatro di Marcello), and then turns right under an arch to skirt the side of the hill above gardens and paths which descend to its foot.

In front of the 16C **Palazzo Caffarelli**, built on the site of the Temple of Jupiter (see above), there is another splendid panorama of Rome, this time towards St Peter's. The palace houses the offices of the Capitoline museums and part of the **Antiquarium Comunale**, an extremely important archaeological collection, with some 60,000 works, most of which has been closed to the public for decades, although a small part of it can now be seen on the Celian Hill (see p 239). It includes material dating from the 9C–6C BC from the Esquiline necropolis, finds from excavations near Sant'Omobono and on the Capitoline, and fragments of the *Forma Urbis* a marble 'map' of ancient Rome in AD 193–211 found in the Forum of Peace in 1562, and one of the most important documents for our knowledge of the topography of the Roman city.

Santa Maria in Aracoeli

Santa Maria in Aracoeli (Pl. 4; 5), an austere brick-built church, dating from before the 7C, when it was already considered ancient, stands on the highest point of the Capitoline Hill (the side door is reached by steps to the east of the Capitoline Museum). The **façade**, never completed, is at the top of a very steep flight of 124 steps from Piazza d'Aracoeli, built in 1348 as a thank-offering for deliverance from a plague.

> The church occupies the site of the Roman citadel. During a siege by the Gauls in 390 BC the Capitol was saved from a night attack by the honking of the sacred geese of Juno kept here, which alerted the Romans to the danger. In 343 BC a temple was erected to Juno Moneta; the name came to be connected with the Mint later established here. The church is on the spot where, according to medieval tradition, the Tiburtine Sibyl foretold to Augustus the imminent coming of Christ in the words, 'Ecce ara primogeniti Dei': hence the name Aracoeli, Church of the Altar of Heaven. In the 10C the church belonged to the Benedictines; in 1250 Innocent IV handed it over to the Franciscans, who rebuilt it in the Romanesque style.
>
> In the Middle Ages the church was the meeting-place of the Roman Council. Here Rienzo addressed the assembly after the events of Whitsun 1347; Charles of Anjou held his parliament of the Romans; and Marcantonio Colonna celebrated his triumph after the battle of Lepanto. 'It was here, as Gibbon himself tells us, that on the 15th of October, 1764, as he sat musing amidst the ruins of the Capitol, while the bare-footed friars were singing vespers, the idea of writing the "Decline and Fall" of the city first started to his mind.' (Augustus Hare). In the tympanum of the south door is a mosaic of the Madonna and two angels by the school of Pietro Cavallini.

The **interior** (open 7–12, 15.30–dusk), hung with chandeliers, although freely restored has retained its grandeur and severity. The ceiling of the **nave**, with naval emblems and much gold ornamentation, dates from 1575 and commemorates the victory of Lepanto (1571). The 22 antique columns in the nave, of varying sizes and styles, were taken from pagan buildings; the third on the left bears the inscription 'a cubiculo Augustorum', and the fourth on the left has a 15C Sienese fresco of the Madonna and Child. Many tombs are set in the Cosmatesque pavement. To the right of the central door is the *tomb of Cardinal

d'Albret, by Andrea Bregno (1465), and the *tomb slab of the archdeacon Giovanni Crivelli (1432; very worn), signed by Donatello; on the left is the tomb of the astronomer Lodovico Grato Margani (1531), by the school of Andrea Sansovino, who himself executed the figure of Christ.

There are coin-operated lights in the apse chapels. **South aisle**. First chapel (Bufalini): *frescoes from the life of St Bernardino, considered among the finest works of Pinturicchio (c 1486; restored by Vincenzo Camuccini); between the second and third chapels, colossal statue of Gregory XIII, by Pier Paolo Olivieri. Fifth chapel (being restored): 16C paintings by Girolamo Muziano; the sixth chapel is a pretty 17C work designed by Giovanni Battista Contini. By the south door (right): monument of Pietro da Vicenza by Andrea Sansovino, and (left) tomb of Cecchino Bracci (d 1545) by Pietro Urbano on a design of Michelangelo. In the last chapel are two Caravaggesque paintings by Daniele Seiter.

In the crossing, on the pilasters facing the high altar, are two *ambones, by Lorenzo and Giacomo di Cosma (c 1200). **South transept**. The Savelli Chapel (or Cappella di San Francesco di Assisi) contains two fine *tombs: on the left is that of Luca Savelli attributed to Arnolfo di Cambio, with a 3C Roman sarcophagus beneath, and on the right, the 14C tomb of Vana Aldobrandeschi, wife of Luca, with a statue of her son Pope Honorius IV. The Cappella di Santa Rosa (seen through the Cappella del Santissimo Sacramento, to the right) has a fine mosaic of the *Madonna enthroned between St John the Baptist and St Francis* dating from the 13C.

Choir. Over the high altar is a small *Madonna, known as the *Madonna d'Aracoeli*, usually attributed to a 10C master. Here from 1512 to 1565 was hung Raphael's *Madonna of Foligno* (now in the Vatican Pinacoteca), commissioned by Sigismondo Conti, whose tomb is in the pavement near the stalls on the south side. In the **apse**, on the left, is the fine monument of Giovanni Battista Savelli (school of Andrea Bregno, 1498).

In the centre of the **north transept** is the little Temple of St Helena, or Santa Cappella, a 17C shrine (reconstructed in the 19C) with eight columns. Beneath it (light) are remains of an altar (12C or 13C) showing the apparition of the Virgin to Augustus. At the end of the transept is the beautiful Cosmati *tomb of Cardinal Matteo di Acquasparta (died 1302), mentioned by Dante (*Paradiso*, xii, 124), with a fresco by Pietro Cavallini. To the right is the entrance to the Cappella del Santissimo Bambino, which contained a figure of the Infant Christ, reputed to have been carved from the wood of an olive tree in the Garden of Gethsemane and an object of immense veneration (see below). This was stolen in 1994, and has been replaced by a copy.

North Aisle, fifth chapel: *St Paul*, by Girolamo Muziano, and the fine tomb of Filippo Della Valle (1494; left), by Michele Marini or the school of Andrea Riccio; third chapel, *St Anthony*, by Benozzo Gozzoli, and the Renaissance tomb of Antonio Albertoni (1509; right); between the third and second chapels: a statue of Paul III. The second chapel (Cappella del Presepio) is open only during the Christmas festival, when the copy of the Christ Child figure is exhibited (from the Cappella del Santissimo Bambino; see above), and children recite little poems and speeches in front of its crib.

The overwhelming **Monument of Vittorio Emanuele II** (Pl. 4; 5) was inaugurated in 1911 to symbolise the achievement of Italian unity. Some 80m high, it changed irrevocably the aspect of the city, throwing out of scale the Capitoline Hill itself, and causing indiscriminate demolition in the area. Familiarly known as 'the wedding cake' or 'Mussolini's typewriter', it can only be described as a colossal monstrosity. It was begun in 1885 by Giuseppe Sacconi, winner of an international competition in which there were 98 entries. He used an incongruous dazzling white 'botticino' marble from Brescia to further alienate the monument from its surroundings. It is occasionally used for exhibitions.

At the sides of the monument are fountains representing the Tyrrhenian Sea, by Pietro Canonica, and the Adriatic, as well as the remains of the tomb of Gaius Publicius Bibulus, dating from the early 1C BC. Above the stylobate are sculptures by Ettore Ximenes, Leonardo Bistolfi, Ludovico Poliaghi, and Augusto Rivalta. The grave of Italy's Unknown Soldier from the First World War, guarded by two sentinels, lies at the foot of the Altare della Patria by Angelo Zanelli. The equestrian statue of Vittorio Emanule II is by Enrico Chiaradia. The two quadrigae are by Paolo Bartolini and Carlo Fontana.

The **Museo Centrale del Risorgimento**, entered from Via di San Pietro in Carcere, has been closed for many years. It contains exhibits illustrating the story of Italy's struggle for independence, important archives, and a section devoted to the First World War.

Museo del Palazzo di Venezia

Across Piazza Venezia (left) is the battlemented **Palazzo di Venezia**, the first great Renaissance palace in Rome. Giuliano da Maiano, Bernardo Rossellino, and Leon Battista Alberti have all been suggested as its architect, but it has recently been attributed to Francesco del Borgo.

It was begun in 1455, enlarged in 1464, and finally finished in the 16C. It was built, partly of stone from the Colosseum, for the Venetian Cardinal Pietro Barbo, afterwards Paul II (1464–71), the first of the great High Renaissance popes. Barbo is said to have built the palace in order to view the horse races in the Corso. It later became a papal residence, and was often occupied as such even after it had been given by Pius IV (1559–65) to the Venetian Republic for its embassy. Charles VIII of France stayed here after entering Rome with 20,000 soldiers in 1494. From the Treaty of Campoformio in 1797 until 1915 it was the seat of the Austrian ambassador to the Vatican. In 1917 Italy resumed possession and the palace was restored. During the Fascist régime it was occupied by Mussolini, who had his office in the Sala del Mappamondo. Some of his most famous speeches were made from the balcony overlooking Piazza di Venezia.

The door in the piazza is finely carved and attributed to Giuliano da Maiano. The picturesque inner court (reached from 49 Piazza di San Marco), with its tall palm trees, has a large unfinished 15C loggia on two sides, of beautiful proportions. In the centre is a fountain by Carlo Monaldi (1730).

Adjoining the palace and facing the Via and Piazza di San Marco, to the south and east, is the **Palazzetto di Venezia**. This was originally (c 1467) in Piazza di Venezia, but was moved to its present position in 1911 because it obstructed the

view of the Vittorio Emanuele Monument. Special permission is needed to visit the beautiful courtyard and garden; apply in advance to the Direttrice del Museo di Palazzo di Venezia, 49 Piazza San Marco, Rome 00100, ☎ 679 8865, fax 699 94221.

The **Museo del Palazzo di Venezia** (open 9–19, Sun 9–13; closed Mon. ☎ 679 8865. Lire 8000) occupies several of the papal apartments and many rooms in the Palazzetto di Venezia. The entrance is in Via del Plebiscito. It is the city's museum of decorative arts (including Romanesque and 14C ivories, majolica, church silver and terracottas), and also has paintings, wood sculptures and bronzes. The collections are displayed in modern showcases designed by Franco Minissi, but some of the 30 rooms are often closed. The State rooms are only open for exhibitions. Rooms 26–30 are closed for restoration for an indefinite period.

From Via del Plebiscito a monumental staircase by Luigi Marangoni (1930) leads up to the first floor and the ticket office. To the left is the Appartamento Cibo, the apartments of the Cardinals of San Marco, with some good ceilings and colourful floors, where the first part of the collection is arranged. The rooms are unnumbered but the works are all labelled. Room 1. Architectural fragments (early 8C–end of 9C) including a well-head; bronzes, ivories, including a 10C *triptych of the 'Deesis' and Saints. Room 2. Sculptural fragments; the marble transenna with donors is attributed to Giovanni di Stefano (fl. 1366–91). Room 3 (to the left). Seated statue of a pope, sometimes identified as Nicholas IV or as Boniface VIII, a Roman work of the late 13C. The *Madonna of Acuto*, an early 13C wood polychrome seated statue, the earliest known work of its kind; *crucifix, probably painted by a follower of Giotto in the last decade of the 13C.

Room 4 (beyond Room 2). *Head of a woman* by Nicola Pisano; 13C relief of an Angel in gilded bronze and cloisonné enamel; 13C Byzantine *crosses, and a *relief of the Crucifixion; Christ Pantocrator, an unusual work in metal and enamel (13C, Byzantine); gilded bronze incised *lunette from the Santuario della Mentorella near Palestrina (thought to be an early 13C German work), possibly the back of an episcopal seat. To the left, **Room 5** has a ceiling with signs of the zodiac. Here are 14C ceramics from Orvieto, and early medieval ceramics from Rome and Lazio, and a valuable series of dower chests.

In **Room 6** (beyond Room 4) is exhibited the Sterbini collection of paintings, mostly Tuscan paintings on gold grounds, all of them in good condition. Three exquisite small works: *triptych by the early 15C Florentine school, *reliquary by the 'Master of Santa Chiara of Montefalco' and *diptych by the early 14C Sienese school. Other works include: Bicci di Lorenzo, *Imprisonment and Martyrdom of St Catherine of Alexandria*; Nanni di Jacopo, triptych with the *Madonna and Child and angel musicians, and four saints*; Cristoforo da Bologna, *Madonna of Humility*; 15C Spanish school, *Madonna enthroned*. In the little chapel: Francesco Zaganelli da Cotignola, *Christ carrying the Cross*; Sassoferrato, *St Francis*; Girolamo da Santacroce, *Rape of Europa, Head of St Michael Archangel*; Bachiacca, *Vision of St Bernardino*.

Room 7 (Salone Altoviti) has *grotteschi* on the ceiling attributed to Vasari. Here are a reliquary by Jacopo Tondi; and a 14C Venetian *triptych in wood, silver and enamel with miniatures of the Madonna and Child, Evangelists, prophets, and stories from the Life of Christ. **Room 8**. Fine wooden statues,

including two of the *Magi (14C works from the Marches). To the left beyond Room 9, **Room 10** displays 12C–13C seals. **Room 11** (beyond Room 8) has a view of the east end of the church of the Gesù.

The long **corridor** (**12**) which connects these apartments to the Palazzetto di Venezia has a splendid view of the delightful courtyard, with palms and a fountain. Here is displayed a representative collection of Italian ceramics with examples from all the main workshops (Faenza, Urbino, Montelupo, Deruta, Pesaro, Casteldurante, etc.). The second half of the corridor displays porcelain (Meissen, Sèvres, Staffordshire, etc). The first rooms (**13–15**) of the Palazzetto contain some furniture. **Room 16** displays a 15C marble bust of the Venetian Cardinal Pietro Barbo (afterwards Paul II) who built Palazzo Venezia.

In **Room 17** begins the splendid display of small *bronzes continued in **Room 18**. Here are works by Il Riccio, Nicolò Roccatagliata, Girolamo Campagna, Giovanni Francesco Susini, Pietro Tacca, Pietro Bracci, Il Moderno, Tiziano Aspetti, Giambologna, François Duquesnoy, Alessandro Algardi, Antonio Susini, and Gian Lorenzo Bernini. **Room 19**. Sculptures by Baccio da Montelupo (*Head of the Redeemer*), and Francesco Segala, and two *reliefs of the *Miracle of St Mark* by Jacopo Sansovino (models for the bronze reliefs in the chancel of the basilica of San Marco in Venice). Beyond Room 20, **Room 21** has small sculptures, including two models for sculptures on the Trevi fountain.

Room 22 displays numerous busts, statuettes, and terracotta *bozzetti* by Bernini (model for an angel on Ponte Sant'Angelo and for details of his Roman fountains), and Alessandro Algardi (bust of Giacinta Sanvitali Conti, and *St Agnes appearing to St Constance*). **Room 23**. Relief of the *Deposition* by Ignazio Marabitti; two 18C portraits by Vincenzo Pacetti. **Room 24** contains a relief by Ercole Ferrata. **Room 25**. Bozzetti attributed to Francesco Mochi and the early 17C Lombard school. Beyond the little room (**26**) with a pretty barrel vault is the last room (**27**) of sculpture, with a head ('Seneca') attributed to Guido Reni, and a bust of Benedict XIII by Pietro Bracci (1724). But note that rooms 26 and 27 are closed at present.

Room 28 has been closed for conservation reasons. It contains paintings: Giorgione(?), double portrait; Lelio Orsi, *Pietà*; Giuseppe Maria Crespi, *Finding of the infant Moses*, *David and Abigail*; Ciro Ferri, *Marriage of St Catherine*; Donato Creti, *Nymphs dancing*; Jacob Cuyp, two portraits; Carlo Maratta, *Cleopatra*; Francesco Solimena, *Marriage at Cana*.

Other paintings not on display include: Giovanni Bellini, *Portrait of a young man*; Nicolò de' Barberi, *Woman taken in adultery*; Giovanni Cariani, *Lovers in a landscape*, *Portrait of a devotee*; Rocco Marconi, *Woman taken in adultery*; Bachiacca, *Lady as St Mary Magdalene*; Federico Zuccari, scenes in the life of Taddeo Zuccari; Benozzo Gozzoli, *The Redeemer* (part of a fresco); Domenico Puligo, *Madonna*; Girolamo da Cremona, *Nativity* and *Annunciation* (triptych); School of Giovanni Bellini, *Moses rescued from the water*, *Meeting of the Madonna and St Anne*; Giovanni da Modena, Crucifixion; Ottaviano Nelli, *Madonna*; Segna di Tura, *Madonna and Child*; Paolo Veneziano, *Angelic choir*; Benedetto Diana, *The Redeemer*; Garofalo, *St Jerome*; Guercino, *St Peter*; Cornelius Johnson, *Child with a puppy*; and Simone Cantarini, Madonna.

The important collection of arms and armour (some of them left to the city by the Odescalchi in 1976) and the 15C–17C tapestries (German, Flemish and Italian) are not yet on display. The deposits also include the Enrichetta Wurts

collection of silver (presented to Mussolini in 1930), mostly German, English and American ware dating from the 17C to the late 19C, and Oriental porcelain and ceramics.

The palace is also the seat of the **Istituto Nazionale di Archeologia e Storia dell'Arte** (entered at 49 Piazza San Marco), founded in 1922. The library, the most important of its kind in Italy, with c 350,000 vols, was partially reopened here in 1993, but is in urgent need of new premises (part of it has been moved to the Collegio Romano).

At the corner of Piazza San Marco is a colossal mutilated bust of Isis, known as '**Madama Lucrezia**'. It has been here since the 15C and was once one of Rome's 'talking statues'. In the garden in front (right) is a fountain (1927) with a pine cone, the emblem of this district, the Rione della Pigna.

In Piazza San Marco is the basilica of **SAN MARCO** (Pl. 3; 6), which forms part of Palazzo di Venezia. It was founded in 336 by St Mark the Pope, restored in 833, rebuilt in the 15C by Paul II, and again restored in the 17C and 1744. The campanile is Romanesque, and the façade an elegant Renaissance work with a portico and a loggia built for the papal benediction ceremony when Palazzo di Venezia was used as a residence by the popes. Under the portico are sculptural fragments and inscriptions, and over the beautiful central door, a relief of St Mark enthroned attributed to Isaia da Pisa (1464).

Steps lead down to the fine **interior** which retains its ancient basilican form with a raised sanctuary. There is a good Renaissance ceiling and remains of a Cosmatesque pavement (east end). The bright columns of Sicilian jasper and the stucco reliefs in the nave (between 17C frescoes) date from the Baroque restoration in the 18C.

South side: first altar: Palma Giovane, *Resurrection*; third chapel, Carlo Maratta, **Adoration of the Magi*. Beyond a niche with a monument to Cardinal Vidman (died 1660) by Cosimo Fancelli, the fourth chapel contains 17C works by Bernardino Gagliardi. By the steps up to the presbytery is the funerary monument of Leonardo Pesaro by Antonio Canova. The chapel to the right of the high altar, by Pietro da Cortona, contains a painting of St Mark the Pope by Melozzo da Forlì and frescoes by Borgognone. In the **apse** (coin-operated light) a **mosaic* (c 829–30) represents Christ with saints and Gregory IV offering a model of the church. Beneath are the Lamb of God with 12 sheep representing the Apostles, and, on the arch, Christ between St Peter and St Paul. In the sacristy (if closed, ring on the left in the church porch), is a recomposed tabernacle by Mino da Fiesole and Giovanni Dalmata, and *St Mark the Evangelist* (much darkened) by Melozzo da Forlì.

The niches on the **north side** contain notable Baroque monuments, and here the fourth chapel has works by Francesco Mola and Borgognone. The second chapel was decorated by Emidio Sintes (1764). Remains of the earlier churches have been found beneath the pavement.

2 · The Roman Forum

■ **Admission**: 9–18, Sun 9–13. ☎ 699 0110. Entrance is free. The main entrance is in Via dei Fori Imperiali, opposite the end of Via Cavour. There is another entrance (more convenient for the Palatine) on Via San Gregorio. There is an exit at the Arch of Titus near the Colosseum, and another exit is usually open on Via del Foro Romano, above the Basilica Julia (closed on Sundays). You need a whole day for a complete visit to the Forum and the Palatine.

In summer the Forum is occasionally lit up and tours are available, ☎ 699 0110.

The Roman Forum (Pl. 4; 7) is the heart of ancient Rome. Here is reflected almost every event of importance in the city's development from the time of the kings through the Republican and Imperial eras to the Middle Ages. The ruins stand in the centre of modern Rome as a romantic testament to her past greatness. The site is planted with trees, flowers and shrubs. The visible remains are difficult to understand in detail without constant reference to the plans provided in the text. Important excavations are being carried out in various parts of the Forum (see below), and some areas are inaccessible because of this. At the foot of the Capitoline Hill, a road which formerly cut off the monuments at the extreme west end of the Forum has been eliminated. There are plans to connect the Forum with the Capitol again via the Clivus Capitolinus.

The best comprehensive view of the Forum is from the Capitoline Hill, from the terrace at the bottom of Via del Campidoglio or from the Belvedere di Monte Tarpeo (see p 71). The Palatine also provides a good view.

The Forum runs west-north-west and east-south-east, following the direction of the Capitoline end of the Sacra Via and that of the Nova Via. In the following description it is taken as running west and east, the left side, looking towards the Colosseum, being north and the right side south. The plans in the text have been given this orientation.

History

The site of the Forum was originally a marshy valley lying between the Capitoline and Palatine Hills. It was bounded on the north and east by the foothills of the Quirinal and Esquiline and by the low ridge of the Velia, which connected the Palatine with the Esquiline. In the Iron Age it was used as a necropolis. Buildings appeared here after the union of the Latin villages of the Palatine with the Sabines of the Quirinal, which is traditionally said to have followed the battle of Romans and Sabines on the Palatine slopes. The first monuments of the Forum, such as the Lapis Niger, the Vulcanal, the Temple of Janus, the Regia, the Temple of Vesta and the Curia date from the period of the kings. Tarquinius the Elder and Servius Tullius (c 616–535 BC) made the area habitable by canalising its stagnant waters into the Cloaca Maxima and it became the market place (Forum) of Rome.

The original Forum was a rectangle bounded on the west by the Lapis Niger and the Rostra, on the east by a line through the site of the Temple of Julius Caesar, and on the north and south by two rows of shops (tabernae)

The Roman Forum from the Capitoline Hill

approximately on the line of the Basilica Emilia (north) and the Basilica Julia (south). This area was about 115m by 57m. Adjacent, on the north-west, was a second rectangle including the Comitium, reserved for political assemblies, or Comitia Curiata, the Curia, or senate-house, and the Rostra, or orators' tribune. Beyond the limits of this second square, to the east, were the Regia, seat of the Pontifex Maximus (head of the college of priests), the Temple of Vesta and the House of the Vestals. In this direction ran the Sacra Via. Other streets were the Argiletum to the north, the Vicus Jugarius and the Vicus Tuscus to the Velabrum, the Clivus Argentarius, which ran between the Capitol and the Quirinal to the Via Flaminia and the Campus Martius, and the Nova Via, on the south side, which ran along the side of the Palatine Hill.

The Forum was therefore divided into three distinct areas: the Comitium, or political centre, the religious centre of the Regia, and the Forum proper. The area of the Forum gradually lost its character as market place and became a centre of civic importance and the scene of public functions and ceremonies. The greengrocers and other shopkeepers were moved to the Velabrum and replaced by money-changers (argentarii).

In the 2C BC a new type of building, the basilica, was introduced. This large covered space was used for judicial hearings and public meetings when these could not be held outside. The new construction involved the demolition of private houses behind the tabernae. The first basilica was the Basilica Porcia, built by the censor Cato in 185 BC and destroyed in 52 BC. Others were the Basilica Emilia (179 BC), and the Basilica Sempronia (170 BC), built by T. Sempronius Gracchus, father of the tribunes, and later replaced by the Basilica Julia. The last to be built was the Basilica of Constantine (4C AD).

In 133 Tiberius Gracchus was killed in the Forum. After Julius Caesar's assassination on the Ides of March, 44 BC, his body was cremated in the Forum. He had begun the enlargement of the Forum which Sulla had planned some years before, and which was completed by Augustus. Between 44 and 27 BC the Basilica Julia, the Curia and the Rostra were

completed, the Temple of Saturn and the Regia restored, the Temple of Julius Caesar dedicated, and the Arch of Augustus erected. According to Suetonius, Augustus found the city brick and left it marble.

By this time the area of the Forum had become inadequate for the growing population and the emperors were obliged to build their own Fora (see Chapter 4). A fire in the old Forum in the 3C AD caused much damage, which was repaired by Diocletian, but the area reflected the general decline of the city. Temples and sanctuaries were neglected under Christian rule and robbed of most of their treasures. The few that remained were finally despoiled in the barbarian invasions and the abandoned buildings were further damaged by earthquakes.

The medieval Roman barons, notably the Frangipani family, used the tallest of the ruined buildings as foundations for their fortress-towers, and a few churches were constructed. But most of the Forum became the Campo Vaccino, or cattle-pasture. Its monuments were used as quarries and its precious marbles were burned in limekilns. In the Renaissance the Forum provided inspiration to numerous artists. Many buildings erected from the 15C to 18C took their plans from monuments here, and often parts of the Roman edifices were reused in these buildings.

At the end of the 18C systematic excavations of the site began, and they continued with little interruption through the 19C, especially after 1870. The distinguished archaeologist, Giacomo Boni, conducted the excavations from 1898 to 1925, and found archaic monuments of great interest; his work was continued by Alfonso Bartoli. Since 1980 excavations have been in progress at the west end of the Forum at the foot of the Capitoline Hill, in the area of Santa Maria Antiqua and the Temple of Castor, behind the Basilica Emilia and the Curia, and on the northern slopes of the Palatine, between the Sacra Via and the House of the Vestals.

Western section of the Forum

From the main entrance on Via dei Fori Imperiali (Pl. 4; 7) a broad path descends between the Temple of Antoninus and Faustina (left; described below) and the Basilica Emilia on the level of the ancient Forum. The **Basilica Emilia** was built by the censors M. Aemilius Lepidus and M. Fulvius Nobilior in 179 BC, restored by members of the Aemilia gens in 78 BC and rebuilt in the time of Julius Caesar. It was rebuilt in AD 22 after a fire and nearly destroyed by another fire during Alaric's sack of Rome in 410. On the side towards the Forum it faces the Sacra Via; on its west side is the Argiletum, once one of the Forum's busiest streets, which led north to the quarter of the Subura through the Forum of Nerva.

Much of this ancient building was demolished during the Renaissance in order to reuse its marble. It comprised a vast rectangular hall 70m by 29m, divided by columns into a central nave and aisles, single on the south side and double on the north. In the fine pavement of the hall, in coloured marble, are embedded some coins that fused with the bronze roof-decorations during the fire of 410. Casts of fragments of a frieze of the Republican era have been assembled below the terrace at the northeastern corner. On the south side, facing the Forum, was a two-storeyed portico covering a row of shops, the **Tabernae Novae**, still well preserved. The portico was restored during the late empire; the three granite columns which have been set up in front of the Basilica date from

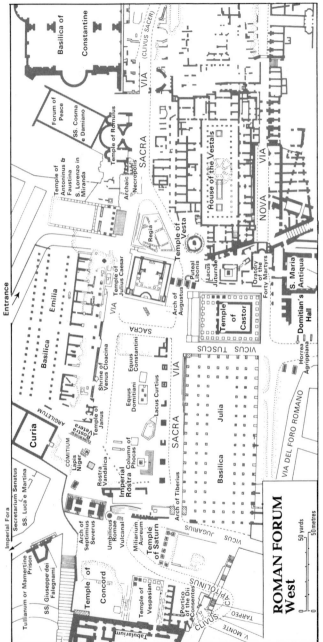

ROMAN FORUM
West

Basilica of Constantine

Forum of Peace

SS. Cosma e Damiano

Temple of Romulus

Temple of Antoninus & Faustina

S. Lorenzo in Miranda

VIA (CLIVUS SACER)

VIA SACRA

Archaic Necropolis

House of the Vestals

VIA NOVA

Regia

Temple of Vesta

Temple of Julius Caesar

Puteal Libonis

Lacus Iuturnae

Oratory of the Forty Martyrs

S. Maria Antiqua

Domitian's Hall

Arch of Augustus

Temple of Castor

Entrance

VIA SACRA

Basilica Emilia

Shrine of Venus Cloacina

Equus Constantini

Equus Domitiani

Lacus Curtius

VICUS TUSCUS

Horrea Agrippiana

VIA DEL FORO ROMANO

Curia

ARGILETUM

Rostra Vetera

Temple of Janus

COMITIUM

Lapis Niger

Rostra Vandalica

Imperial Rostra

Column of Phocas

Arch of Tiberius

VIA SACRA

Basilica Julia

Imperial Fora

Secretarium Senatus

SS. Luca e Martina

Arch of Septimius Severus

Umbilicus Romae

Vulcanal

Miliarium Aureum

Temple of Saturn

Arch of Tiberius

VICUS JUGARIUS

Tullianum or Mamertine Prison

SS. Giuseppe dei Falegnami

Temple of Concord

Temple of Vespasian

Portico of the Dii Consentes

CLIVUS CAPITOLINUS

V. MONTE TARPEO

Tabularium

Capitol

50 yards

50 metres

this time. On the west side are remains (covered) of the earliest basilica. The **Macellum**, a market building paved in peperino and surrounded by columns, built in the late 3C or early 2C BC, has recently been unearthed towards the modern road.

The open space in front of the Basilica Emilia is the original **Forum**; through it runs the Sacra Via (see below). As the meeting-place of the whole population, and a market place, the Forum was kept free of obstructions in Republican days. Here all important ceremonies and public meetings took place. Orators spoke from the Rostra, where magistrates' edicts, legal decisions, and official communications were published. The Forum was where all the main religious festivals were held, and where political offenders were executed, and the funerals of important people took place. The body of Julius Caesar was cremated here. During the Empire the Forum lost its original character, and new buildings encroached on the area. It remained merely an official centre, and was to a great extent replaced by the new Imperial Fora.

The **SACRA VIA**, the oldest street in Rome, traverses the length of the Forum. It was lined with important sanctuaries, and a tradition relates that it was the scene of the peace treaty between Romulus and the Sabine king Titus Tatius. Its oldest section is that between the Temple of Castor and the Velia. The winding road now visible, at a lower level than the later monuments on either side, dates from the late Republican era; the later Imperial road took a slightly different course between the Forum and the Arch of Titus. On the west side it was continued as the Clivus Capitolinus, which climbed round the Portico of the Dei Consentes to the Temple of Jupiter on the Capitol. On the east side, the Republican road left the Forum to the south of the Velia. In late Imperial times it was continued by another road beyond the Arch of Titus to the Arch of Constantine, near the Colosseum.

It was along the Sacra Via that a victorious general awarded a triumph passed in procession to the Capitol to offer sacrifice in the Temple of Jupiter. He rode in a chariot drawn by four horses, preceded by his captives and spoils of war, and followed by his soldiers. In the Sacra Via, by the southeast corner of the Basilica Emilia, is a dedicatory inscription to Lucius Caesar, grandson and adopted son of Augustus, set up in 2 BC; there was probably an arch here dedicated to him and his brother Gaius.

On the south side of the Sacra Via is the **TEMPLE OF JULIUS CAESAR**, the site of which marks the eastern limit of the original Forum. The body of Julius Caesar was brought to the Forum after the Ides of March in 44 BC, and it was probably here that his body was cremated, and his will read by Mark Antony. The temple was dedicated by Augustus in 29 BC in honour of the 'Divine' Julius Caesar ('Divus Julius'). Tiberius gave a funeral oration here over the body of Augustus before it was buried in his mausoleum in AD 14.

This temple (probably Corinthian prostyle hexastyle) was preceded by a terrace which was an extension of the podium. This was called the **Rostra ad Divi Julii**, from the beaks of the Egyptian ships of Antony and Cleopatra captured at Actium with which it was decorated. Nothing remains except for the central block of the podium and the round altar (under cover), probably marking the spot where Caesar was cremated. Fragments, thought to belong to the frieze, are in the Antiquarium of the Forum. Remains of foundations on the

north and south sides of the temple are thought to be those of the arcaded **Porticus Julia**, which surrounded the temple on three sides.

About 50m further west, near the steps of the Basilica Emilia, are the foundations of the circular **Shrine of Venus Cloacina**, which stood on the point where the Cloaca Maxima entered the Forum. This great drain, installed by the Tarquins, crossed the Forum from north to south on its way to the Tiber (see p 257). At the west end of the Basilica Emilia is the presumed site of the Shrine of Janus. Its bronze doors were closed only in peace-time, which is said to have occurred only three times in the history of Rome.

To the west, in front of the Curia building (described below), lies the area of the **Comitium**, the place where the *Comitia Curiata*, representing the 30 *Curiae* into which the city was politically divided, met to record their votes. The earliest political activity of the Republic took place here and this was the original site of the Rostra. During the Empire the Comitium was restricted to the space between the Curia and the Lapis Niger; under the Republic the area was much more extensive.

Here is the **Lapis Niger** with the oldest relics of the Forum. The Lapis Niger was a pavement of black marble laid to indicate a sacred spot. This was traditionally taken to be the site of the tomb of Romulus, or the shepherd Faustulus (finder of the infant Romulus and Remus), or Hostus Hostilius, father of the third king of Rome, but is now identified as the ancient sanctuary of Vulcan, known as the **Volcanal**. The pavement and the monuments below it were discovered in 1899, and are now reached by a flight of iron steps (usually closed). They comprise the base of a truncated column (possibly the base for a statue), an altar, and a square stele with inscriptions on all four sides. These provide the most ancient example of the Latin language (6C or early 5C BC) and seem to refer to a *lex sacra*, i.e. a warning against profaning a holy place. In the space between the pavement and the monuments, bronze and terracotta statuettes and fragments of 6C vases were found, mixed with profuse ashes (indicating a great sacrifice). These are in the Antiquarium of the Forum. Excavations to the east of the Lapis Niger have revealed some remains of the Republican **Rostra**, dating partly from 338 BC, and partly (the curved front and steps) from Sulla's time.

At the north end of the Comitium rises the **CURIA SENATUS**, or **Curia Julia**. Replacing the original *Curia Hostilia* said to have been built by Tullus Hostilius and several times rebuilt, the senate house was begun by Sulla in 80 BC, and rebuilt after a fire by Julius Caesar in 44 BC. Fifteen years after Caesar's death it was completed by Augustus, who dedicated a statue of Victory in the interior. The present building dates from the time of Domitian (restored by Diocletian after a fire in 283). In 630 it was converted into the church of Sant' Adriano. In 1935–39 Alfonso Bartoli restored to it the form it had under Diocletian. The lower part of the brick façade was originally covered with marble; the upper courses were covered with stucco. It was preceded by a portico. The existing doors are copies of the originals, removed by Alexander VII to St John Lateran. A simple pediment with travertine corbels crowns the building.

The remarkable interior, 27m long, 18m wide and 21m high, has a beautiful green and maroon **pavement** in opus sectile, which had been preserved beneath the floor of the church. The three broad marble-faced steps on the two

long sides provided seats for some 300 senators. At the end, by the president's tribune, is a brick base which may have supported the golden statue of Victory presented by Augustus. The side walls, with niches, were partly faced with marble. The porphyry statue of Hadrian or Trajan dating from the 1C–2C AD was found in recent excavations behind the building.

Also exhibited here are the ***Plutei of Trajan**, or Anaglypha Trajani, two finely sculptured balustrades or parapets, found in the Forum in 1872 between the Comitium and the Column of Phocas. Both their date and original location are uncertain. On the inner faces are depicted the animals offered up at public sacrifices (*suovetaurilia*), a boar, a ram and a bull; on the outer faces are famous deeds of the emperor. The first (on the left) represents the emperor burning the registers of outstanding death duties, an event which took place in 118, during Hadrian's reign; in the second (on the right) an emperor standing on a Rostra with a statue of Trajan, is receiving the thanks of a mother for the founding of an orphanage. The architectural backgrounds show the buildings on the west, south and east sides of the Forum systematically depicted. From the right of the first panel to the left of the second are: Temple of Vespasian, an arch without decoration, Temple of Saturn, the Vicus Iugarius, and the arcades of the Basilica Julia. The arches are continued on the second panel, followed by an interval for the Vicus Tuscus(?), Temple of Castor and Rostra of the Temple of Julius Caesar (on which the emperor is standing); his attendants mount the ramp of the Rostra through the Arch of Augustus. On both sides is shown the statue of Marsyas beside the sacred fig tree (see below).

In recent excavations behind the Curia, remains of the Augustan building have come to light. Two doors at the rear end opened into a columned portico of the Forum of Caesar (see p 110), providing an entrance from the old forum to the new. Connected to the Senate House was the *Secretarium Senatus* used by a tribunal set up in the late Empire to judge senators.

Between the Lapis Niger and the Imperial Rostra (see below) is a large marble **column base** (recently restored) bearing an inscription of Diocletian to commemorate the decennial games of AD 303; the reliefs on the other sides depict scenes of sacrifice. Close by is the marble base of an equestrian statue with a dedicatory inscription celebrating the victory of Arcadius and Honorius over the Goths in 403.

The remaining part of the northwestern side of the Forum has been fenced off since 1980 while excavations are in progress and the monuments are being restored. A deposit of ex-votos from the Archaic period has been found, probably connected with an ancient cult of Saturn. The dig has not progressed yet below the medieval level which has revealed an interesting 12C district of the city here. The huge building of the Tabularium, on the edge of the Capitoline Hill which dominates this area, has been restored.

The triple **ARCH OF SEPTIMIUS SEVERUS**, nearly 21m high and over 23m wide, entirely faced with marble, was erected in AD 203 in honour of the tenth anniversary of the emperor's accession, and dedicated by the senate and the people to Severus and his sons Caracalla and Geta in memory of their victories over the Parthians, Arabs, and Adiabenians of Assyria. One half of the monument was restored in 1988, and the other half is now being restored. The name of Geta, elder son of Severus, who was murdered by Caracalla in 212, was

replaced by an inscription in praise of Caracalla and his father, but the holes made for the original letters are still visible. On the well-proportioned arch the four large reliefs depict scenes from the two Parthian campaigns: in the small friezes are symbolic Oriental figures paying homage to Rome, and at the bases of the columns are captive barbarians. There is a small interior staircase (no admission) which leads up to the four chambers of the attic.

To the south of the Arch of Severus (now behind a fence) are the ruins of the **Imperial Rostra**, or orator's tribune, brought from its original site in front of the Curia during Caesar's restoration. It is 3m high, 24m long and 12m deep. The original structure (see above), of very early date, was decorated with the 'rostra' or iron beaks of the ships captured at the battle of Antium (338 BC). On the platform rose columns surmounted by commemorative statues, and its parapet was probably decorated with the sculptured plutei of Trajan (see above). In front, on the right, are the **Rostra Vandalica**, an extension of the 5C AD; the modern name is taken from an inscription commemorating a naval victory over the Vandals in 470.

At the back of the Rostra is a semicircular wall (*Hemicyclium*), formed by alterations during the building of the Arch of Septimius Severus. At its north end, by the Arch, is a cylindrical construction, the **Umbilicus Urbis** (?2C BC), supposed to mark the centre of the city. Opposite the other end of the wall is the site of the Miliarium Aureum, the 'golden milestone', a bronze-covered column set up by Augustus as the symbolic starting-point of all the roads of the Empire, with the distance from Rome to the chief cities engraved in gold letters on its base.

Immediately behind the Umbilicus, protected by a roof, is a quadrangular area once identified as the *Volcanal*, or Altar of Vulcan, but now considered to be an Altar of Saturn, dating from before the 6C BC. Here in Republican times grew two trees, a lotus and a cypress, said to be older than the city itself.

From the southwestern corner of the original Forum, the Vicus Jugarius runs south to the Velabrum between the Basilica Julia on the left (see below) and the Temple of Saturn on the right. The **TEMPLE OF SATURN**, one of the most ancient sanctuaries in the Forum, may have been inaugurated in 498 BC in honour of the mythical god-king of Italy, whose reign was the fabled Golden Age. The temple was rebuilt, after several previous reconstructions, by L. Munatius Plancus in the year of his consulship, 42 BC. It was again restored after fires in 283 and c 400 AD. The high podium and eight columns of the pronaos with part of the entablature survive, all dating from Plancus. The pavement and podium are to be entirely reconstructed after excavations have been completed. The columns are nearly 11m high. Six of them, in grey granite, are in front; the other two, in red granite, are at the sides. The Ionic capitals were added in the 5C restoration. The temple was the State treasury, where gold and silver ingots and coined metal were kept. The room (*Aerarium*) east of the narrow stairway of the temple could be locked (the holes for the lock can still be seen). The 'Saturnalia' was held here every year on 17 December.

Near the Temple of Saturn stood the **Arch of Tiberius**, erected in AD 16 in honour of the emperor and of his nephew Germanicus, who avenged the defeat of Varus in the Teutoburg Forest (AD 9) by his victory over the German tribes at Idisiavisus (on the Weser). Behind the temple, excavations are in progress in an area formerly covered by houses; it is possible another temple may be found beneath the medieval constructions.

The last monuments on the west side of the Forum at the foot of the Capitoline Hill lie beyond the **Clivus Capitolinus**, the whole of which has been uncovered since 1980 beneath the modern Via del Foro Romano (which has been eliminated). This is the ancient road with a flint pavement, built in the 2C BC, which was the western continuation of the Sacra Via (see above) in the Forum, and the only way up to the Capitol in ancient times. It was used for triumphal and other processions to the Temple of Jupiter. There are long-term plans to reopen it to pedestrians when excavations and restorations in this area have been completed.

The **Portico of the Dei Consentes** preserves 12 white columns forming an angle; the original seven columns are in marble, the restorations in limestone. Rebuilt by the prefect Vettius Praetextatus in AD 367, on the pattern of a Flavian structure, and dedicated to 12 Roman deities whose statues were here, it is the last pagan religious monument in the Forum. The portico was reconstructed in 1858 and is being restored.

Beyond are three high columns, all that remains of the hexastyle pronaos of the rich and elegant **Temple of Vespasian** erected in honour of that emperor at the foot of the Tabularium staircase by his sons Titus and Domitian after his death in AD 79. The front part of the basement has recently been excavated. To the north are the remains of the **Temple of Concord**. This was a reconstruction by Tiberius (7 BC–AD 10) of a sanctuary which traditionally was thought to have been built by Camillus in 366 BC to commemorate the concordat between the patricians and the plebeians. Instead it is probable that the temple was built for the first time in 218 BC and then rebuilt in 121 BC with the consent of Opimius after the murder of Gracchus. It became a museum and gallery of paintings and sculptures by famous Greek artists. Only the pavement remains in situ; part of the frieze is in the Tabularium. Excavations are also in progress here.

On the other side of the Temple of Saturn (see above) are the scanty but extensive ruins of the **BASILICA JULIA**, which occupies the area between the Vicus Jugarius and Vicus Tuscus (see below). The basilica, built on the site of the Basilica Sempronia (170 BC), was begun by Julius Caesar in 54 BC, and finished by Augustus. After a fire, it had to be reconstructed and rededicated by Augustus in AD 12. It was again damaged by fire in AD 283 and reconstructed by Diocletian in 305. It was damaged yet again in Alaric's sack of 410 and was restored for the last time by Gabinius Vettius Probianus six years later. The Basilica Julia was the meeting-place of the four tribunals of the *Centumviri*, who dealt with civil cases. In the Middle Ages the church of Santa Maria in Cannapara was built on its west side. The surviving remains mostly date from 305; the brick piers of the central hall are 19C reconstructions.

The basilica was even larger than the Basilica Emilia, and measured 101m by 49m. It had a central hall 82m long and 18m wide, bordered all round by a double row of columns which formed aisles. On the long side, facing west, was a colonnade of arches and piers with engaged columns; this contained a row of shops. On the steps here can be seen graffiti in the marble used as 'gaming boards'.

In front of the Basilica Julia is a row of seven brick bases, dating from the 4C. These mark the southern limit of the original forum which was first paved in the Etruscan period. The surviving pavement was laid by L. Surdinus in the

Augustan era (as the restored inscription records). On the bases stood columns bearing statues of illustrious citizens. Two of the columns have been re-erected. In front, towards the west, rises the **Column of Phocas** (recently restored), not only a conspicuous feature of the Forum but the last of its monuments. It was set up in 608 by Smaragdus, exarch of Italy, in honour of the centurion Phocas who had seized the throne of Byzantium; its erection may have been a mark of gratitude for the emperor's gift of the Pantheon to Boniface IV. The fluted Corinthian column, probably taken from some building of the best Imperial era, is 13.5m high. It stands on a high base, formerly faced with marble and surrounded by steps. On the top was originally a statue of the usurper.

To the north of the column of Phocas is a small square unpaved space, where the statue of Marsyas once stood next to the sacred fig tree, the olive and the vine (all recently replanted here), mentioned by the Elder Pliny. In one of the pavement slabs is incised the name of L. Naevius Surdinus, *praetor peregrinus* in the time of Augustus, who may have had his tribunal here. This legal dignitary had to deal with cases involving *peregrini*, i.e. individuals who were not Roman citizens.

To the east is the paved area of the **Lacus Curtius**, with the substructure of a puteal (covered), surrounded by a 12-sided structure of peperino blocks. The lake must have been a relic of the marsh drained by the Cloaca Maxima. According to one tradition a great chasm opened here in 362 BC which the soothsayers said could be closed only by throwing into it Rome's greatest treasure. Marcus Curtius, announcing that Rome possessed no greater treasure than a brave citizen, rode his horse into the abyss which promptly closed (a relief found here illustrating this legend is now in the Palazzo dei Conservatori; a cast is shown in situ). Livy, instead, suggests the name comes from the consul C. Curtius who fenced off this area in 445 after it had been struck by lightning.

In the southeast corner of the Forum (surrounded by iron railings, and below ground level) three travertine blocks were formerly taken to be the base of the Equus Domitiani (AD 91) but are now considered by some scholars to be the base of the equestrian statue of Constantine (Equus Constantini), probably dedicated in AD 334 (Domitian's statue is now thought to have been in the centre of the Forum).

At the east end of the original Forum is the Temple of Julius Caesar, described above. To the south are the foundations of the **Arch of Augustu**s, which had a central arch flanked by lower and narrower side passages surmounted by pediments. After recent excavations here, this is thought to date from 20 BC, after the standards captured by the Parthians had been returned. The 'Fasti Capitolini' (consular and triumphal registers; see Room IV of the Sale dei Conservatori, p 66) which date from this period, may have belonged to this arch. Another triumphal arch (with a single arch) was erected in another part of the Forum by Augustus in 30 BC to commemorate the victory over Antony and Cleopatra at Actium two years earlier. Next to the south pier foundation of the arch is a rectangular monument in the shape of a well-head, which is a remnant of the Puteal Libonis, a monument which stood beside the tribunal of the Praetor Urbanus, who dealt with cases involving Roman citizens.

The monuments to the south of the Arch of Augustus, including the Temple of Castor and the Lacus Juturnae, have been fenced off since excavations began in

this part of the Forum in 1983. Beyond the Arch and facing the east end of the Basilica Julia across the Vicus Tuscus is the **TEMPLE OF CASTOR**, or Temple of the Dioscuri. It was almost certainly built in 484 BC by the dictator Aulus Postumius in honour of the twin heroes Castor and Pollux, whose miraculous appearance at the battle of Lake Regillus (496 BC) resulted in victory for the Romans over the Tarquins and their Latin allies. This temple, which had three cellae and a deep pronaos, built on a high podium, was restored after 200 BC. It was reconstructed by Metellus Dalmaticus in 117 BC, when a tribune for orators was installed, and it seems to have been used by money changers (as recorded by Cicero).

This temple was destroyed by fire in 14 or 9 BC, and the present building was inaugurated by Tiberius during the reign of Augustus (AD 6). Peripteral in plan, and c 26m x c 40m in area, it had eight Corinthian columns at either end and 11 at the sides. The wide pronaos, excavated in 1982–85, was approached by a flight of steps. Three of the columns, which are 12.5m high, survive from the temple of Tiberius, with their beautifully proportioned entablature. Roman knights regarded the Dioscuri as their patrons; every year, on 15 July, they staged an impressive parade in front of the temple. Fragments of statues of the Dioscuri found here, are now in the Antiquarium. Excavations and restoration work were carried out on the Temple in 1983–87.

On the east side of the temple is the **Lacus Juturnae**, or Basin of Juturna, closely connected to the story of the Dioscuri: a legend related how they were seen watering their horses here immediately after their appearance at the battle of Lake Regillus (see above). Juturna, the nymph of healing waters, was venerated in connection with the springs here. The fountain has a square basin of opus reticulatum lined with marble; a statue probably stood on the rectangular base in the centre. On the parapet is a small marble altar (replaced by a copy; the original is in the Antiquarium), with reliefs of the Dioscuri and their sister Helen on two of its sides, and of their parents Jupiter and Leda, on the other two. In the 4C the Lacus Juturnae was the seat of the city's water administration. In the late Empire a series of rooms was built here presumably for the accommodation of invalids who came to take the waters. These rooms contain fragments of statues of gods and other sculptures. To the south is the shrine itself, an aedicula, restored in 1953–55, with the front built into the brick walls, and with two columns. In front is a marble puteal, with a dedicatory inscription to Juturna by the magistrate M. Barbatius Pollio. The marble altar has a relief of Juturna and her brother Turnus.

Adjoining the shrine, on the south, is an apsidal building of the late Empire, converted into the **Oratory of the Forty Martyrs** and preserving remains of 8C–9C frescoes. The 40 martyrs were soldiers frozen to death in an icy pool at Sebaste, in Armenia. The building closes the west end of the Nova Via.

To the south of the Oratory are the considerable remains of the church of **Santa Maria Antiqua** (closed indefinitely; enquire at the Antiquarium in the Forum), the oldest and most important Christian building in the Forum. The 7C–8C wall-paintings inside are of the first importance in the history of early Christian art. Excavations were carried out here in 1983–87.

On the west side of the church is **Domitian's Hall**, a large rectangular brick building (21m x 28m), originally vaulted. With an entrance on the ancient **Vicus Tuscus**, it was intended as a monumental entrance to Domitian's palace

on the Palatine. The hall was never completed and was transformed into a warehouse. Excavations here in 1983–87 clarified that this was on the site of a large atrium built by Caligula in front of the Temple of Castor which also provided an extension to the Imperial palace on the Palatine. Traces were found of the perimeter wall (26.5m x 22.3m) built of blocks of travertine. On a lower level were Republican buildings facing the Vicus Tuscus, demolished to make way for Caligula's atrium.

Also on the Vicus Tuscus is a vast brick building known as the **Horrea Agrippiana**. This was a grain warehouse built around three courtyards, each provided with three storeys of rooms, built by Agrippa. The church of San Teodoro (see p 257) stands in the second courtyard.

Eastern section of the Forum

The Vicus Tuscus returns north between the Basilica Julia and the Temple of Castor, and then east, past the bases of the Arch of Augustus (see above), to reach the religious centre of the Forum. Here are the Temple of Vesta, the House of the Vestals, and the Regia.

The **TEMPLE OF VESTA**, where the vestals guarded the sacred fire, is a circular edifice of 20 Corinthian columns. It was partially reconstructed in 1930 by Alfonso Bartoli. The circular form recalls the form of the Latin huts, and the first temple on this site was possibly made, like these, of straw and wood. Vesta, goddess of the hearth, protected the fire, which symbolised the perpetuity of the State. The task of the vestals was to keep the fire always alight. Its extinction was the most fearful of all prodigies, as it implied the end of Rome. The origin of the cult is supposed to go back to Numa Pompilius, second king of Rome, or even to Aeneas, who brought the eternal fire of Vesta from Troy, together with the images of the penates.

The temple was burned down several times, notably during Nero's fire of AD 64 and in 191. It was rebuilt as often, the last time by Septimius Severus and his wife Julia Domna. It was closed by Theodosius and was in ruins by the 8C. Up until 1930 all that remained of it was the circular basement surmounted by tufa blocks and a few architectural fragments. In the interior was an *adytum*, or secret place, containing the unknown pledges of the duration of Rome (*pignora imperii*), and the *Palladium*, a statue of Pallas Athena, supposedly taken from Troy by Aeneas. No one was allowed inside the *adytum* except the vestals and the Pontifex Maximus, and its contents were never shown. The Palladium was an object of the highest veneration, as the safety of the city depended on its preservation. When the emperor Heliogabalus tried to steal it, the vestals are supposed to have substituted another statue, keeping the cult statue of Vesta in a small shrine near the entrance to the House of the Vestals.

Immediately east of the Temple of Vesta is the **HOUSE OF THE VESTALS**, a large rectangular atrium arranged round a spacious courtyard. It dates from Republican times, but was rebuilt after the fire of Nero in AD 64, and was last restored by Septimius Severus; remains of both structures can still be seen.

There were six vestals, the virgin priestesses of Vesta, who were chosen by the king, and later, during the Republic and Empire, by the Pontifex Maximus. Candidates, between six and ten years of age, had to be from a Patrician family. After her election a vestal lived in the House of the Vestals

for 30 years; ten learning her duties, ten performing them, and ten teaching novices. During this period she was bound by the vow of chastity. At the end of the 30 years she was free to return to the world and even to marry. The senior vestal was called Vestalis Maxima or Virgo Maxima. If a vestal let out the sacred fire, she was whipped by the Pontifex Maximus, and he then had to rekindle the fire by the friction of two pieces of wood from a felix arbor.

The vestals' other duties included making offerings to Vesta, sprinkling her shrine daily with water from the Egerian fountain, assisting at the consecration of temples and other public ceremonies, and guarding the Palladium. Maintained at the public expense, they had many privileges, such as an exalted order of precedence, and the right of intercession. Wills (including the emperor's) and treaties were entrusted to their keeping. If a vestal broke her vow of chastity she was immured alive in the Campus Sceleratus and the man was publicly flogged to death in the Forum.

The House of the Vestals seems too large for just six vestals, and part of it may have been reserved for the Pontifex Maximus, whose official seat was in the Regia (see below). It has a delightful courtyard, 61m long and 20m wide, in the middle of which are three ponds irregularly spaced and unequal in size. The central pond was formerly partly covered by an octagonal structure of unknown purpose. A charming rose garden has been planted among the ruins. Along the sides of the courtyard are statues and statue-bases of vestals dating from the 3C AD onwards. Near the entrance is a base from which the name of the vestal has been removed, possibly because she became a Christian.

There was a two-storeyed portico surrounding the courtyard. In the middle of the short east side is a large hall paved with coloured marbles and flanked on either side by three small rooms, thought to be the sacristy of the priestesses. Behind this hall, towards the Palatine, are an open courtyard with a fountain, and other rooms. Along the south side, which abuts on the Nova Via, is another series of rooms (no admission) opening out of a corridor. In the first of these are the remains of a mill; the second is probably a bakery. On this side staircases lead to the upper floor and to the Nova Via. Near the last staircase is a small shrine. In the middle of the west side is a large room, perhaps the dining-room, leading to the kitchen and other rooms. The north side of the building is less well preserved; stairways on the second floor show that it had more than two storeys.

The **Nova Via** (not accessible; excavations in progress) runs parallel with the Sacra Via along the southern slope of the Palatine Hill. It provided a means of communication with the buildings on the Palatine. The visible remains of this road probably date from the Flavian period, but recent excavations at the point where it crosses the *Clivo Palatino* have revealed paving which seems to date from the Republican era.

To the north of the Temple of Vesta and east of the Temple of Julius Caesar are the remains of the **REGIA**, traditionally supposed to be the palace of Numa Pompilius, the second king of Rome, and the official headquarters of the Pontifex Maximus. Primitive huts, similar to those on the Palatine (see p 99) were found here, and the earliest permanent construction excavated dates from the 7C BC. The edifice, rebuilt by Domitius Calvinus after a fire in 36 BC, retains its 6C form. The elegance of its architecture can be seen from scattered frag-

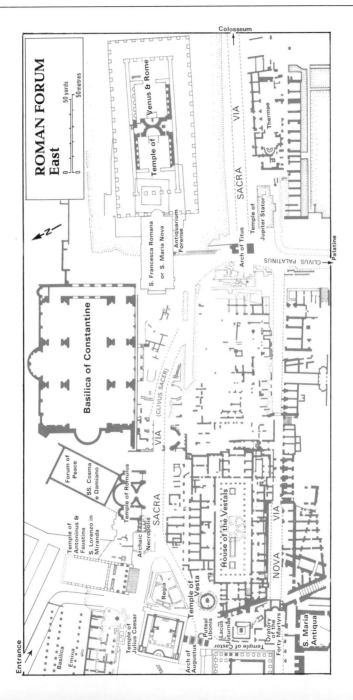

ROMAN FORUM
East

Entrance

Colosseum

Temple of Venus & Rome

S. Francesca Romana
or S. Maria Nova

Antiquarium Forense

VIA SACRA

Thermae

Arch of Titus

Temple of Jupiter Stator

Palatine

CLIVUS PALATINUS

Basilica of Constantine

VIA (CLIVUS SACER)

VIA SACRA

Forum of Peace

SS. Cosma e Damiano

Temple of Romulus

Temple of Antoninus & Faustina

S. Lorenzo in Miranda

Archaic Necropolis

House of the Vestals

VIA NOVA

Regia

Temple of Vesta

Puteal Libonis

Lacus Juturnae

Oratory of the Forty Martyrs

S. Maria Antiqua

Temple of Julius Caesar

Arch of Augustus

Temple of Castor

Basilica Emilia

ments. Other parts of the building date from a reconstruction of the time of Septimius Severus.

The Regia may have been the depository of State archives and of the *Annales Maximi*, written by the Pontifex Maximus. It also included the Sacrarium of Mars, with the *ancilia*, or sacred shields, and the chapel of Ops, goddess of plenty. At the southeast corner of the Regia were discovered the foundations of the arch erected in 121 BC by Q. Fabius Maximus Allobrogicus to span the Sacra Via.

To the north of the Regia rises the **Temple of Antoninus and Faustina** (no adm), near the main entrance to the Forum. One of the most notable buildings of Imperial Rome, it was dedicated by the Senate in AD 141 to the memory of the Empress Faustina and, after his death in 161, also to Antoninus Pius. The temple was converted into the church of **San Lorenzo in Miranda** before the 12C, and given a Baroque façade in 1602. A reconstructed flight of steps leads up to the pronaos, formed from monolithic Corinthian columns (17m high) in cipollino, six in front and two on either side. The architrave and frieze of vases and candelabra between griffins, and the side walls of the cella, of peperino blocks, originally faced with marble, also survive. Sculptures, including a female torso, have been placed in the pronaos. The dedication of the church commemorates the trial of St Laurence, which may have taken place in this temple.

To the east of the temple is an Archaic necropolis, discovered in 1902. This was the cemetery of the ancient inhabitants of the Esquiline or of the original settlement on the Palatine, and dates back to the Early Iron Age, before the date of the traditional foundation of Rome. Tombs were found for both cremations and burials. Cremated ashes were discovered in urns surrounded by tomb furniture, in small circular pits. The burials here were either in tufa sarcophagi, hollowed-out tree trunks, or trenches lined with tufa slabs. The finds are in the Antiquarium.

Here the Sacra Via begins to ascend the Velia to the Arch of Titus. The Velia was a low ridge which connected the Palatine Hill with the Esquiline and which was levelled by Mussolini. On either side of the road are the ruins of private houses and shops (some under cover), including one dating from the Republican era, once wrongly called the Carcer, or prison.

On the left is the so-called **Temple of Romulus** (never open; being restored), a well-preserved 4C structure formerly thought to have been dedicated to Romulus, son of Maxentius who died in AD 309. It has recently been suggested that it could have been the audience hall of the city prefect, or identified with a Temple of Jupiter. It is a circular building built of brick and covered by a cupola flanked by two rectangular rooms with apses, each originally preceded by two cipollino columns (only those on the right survive). The curved pronaos has two porphyry columns and an architrave taken from some other building; the splendid antique bronze **doors** are a remarkable survival.

Behind is a rectangular hall, probably the library of the Forum of Peace built by Vespasian in AD 70 (see p 112). This hall was converted in the 6C into the church of Santi Cosma e Damiano (described on p 112), the temple serving as a vestibule. In the Forum of Peace were probably kept the city plans, cadastral registers, and other documents. The *Forma Urbis*, a famous Roman plan of the ancient city (fragments of which survive in the Antiquarium Comunale) used to decorate the far wall (towards the modern Via dei Fori Imperiali).

Beyond tower the remains of the **BASILICA OF CONSTANTINE**, or **Basilica of Maxentius**, also called the '*Basilica Nova*', the largest monument in the Forum and one of the most impressive examples of Roman architecture in existence. The skill and audacity of its design inspired many Renaissance builders, and it is said that Michelangelo studied it closely when he was planning the dome of St Peter's. The three huge barrel-vaulted niches on the north side still dominate the Forum. It was begun by Maxentius (306–10) and completed by Constantine, who considerably modified the original plan.

The huge building is a rectangle 100m long and 65m wide, divided into a nave and two aisles by massive piers supported by buttresses. As first planned, it had a single apse, on the west side. Against the central piers were eight Corinthian columns 14.5m high; the only survivor was moved by Paul V to Piazza Santa Maria Maggiore. The original entrance was from a side road on the east; Constantine added a portico on the south side which opened onto the Sacra Via. The portico had four porphyry columns, which survive in part. In the middle of the north wall Constantine built a second apse, which was shut off from the rest of the building by a colonnaded balustrade; here the tribunal probably held its sittings. The interior walls, decorated with niches, were faced with marble below and with stucco above.

The three arches of the north aisle are 20.5m wide, 17.5m deep and 24.5m high: the arches of the groin-vaulted nave, whose huge blocks have fallen to the ground, were 35m high and had a radius of nearly 20m. Parts of a spiral staircase leading to the roof can be seen on the ground, having collapsed in an earthquake. A tunnel was built under the northwest corner of the basilica, for a thoroughfare which had been blocked by its construction. The entrance to the tunnel (walled up since 1566) can still be seen. In 1487 a colossal statue of Constantine was found in the west apse, fragments of which are now in the courtyard of the Palazzo dei Conservatori. The bronze plaques from the roof were removed in 626 by Pope Honorius I for the old basilica of St Peter's.

On the opposite side of the Sacra Via is a mass of ruins, among which is a large portico, the vestibule to the Domus Aurea of Nero. Domitian used this to build the Horrea Piperataria, a bazaar for oriental goods, pepper and spices, to the north of the Sacra Via. Later, the area to the south also became commercialised. Domitian's building was finally destroyed in 284. A small circular base with a relief of a Maenad and an inscription recording its restoration by Antoninus Pius (originals in the Antiquarium) in front, on the Sacra Via, may be the remains of a Sanctuary of Bacchus.

On the ascent to the Arch of Titus is the church of Santa Francesca Romana, or Santa Maria Nova (entered from Via dei Fori Imperiali and described on p 106). The former convent of this church is now the seat of the Forum and Palatine excavation offices and contains the **ANTIQUARIUM OF THE FORUM** (or *Antiquarium Forense*). Most of it has been closed for a number of years; it is to be rearranged on two floors of the cloister (admission as for the Forum). In the first room are finds from the Archaic Necropolis, and a model. Rooms II and III contain objects found near the House of the Vestals; yields from wells, Italo-geometric and Etrusco-Campanian vases, votive objects, glassware, and lamps. Room IV (beyond Room II) looks into the impressive *cella of the Temple of Venus and Roma (see p 114), which cannot otherwise be seen. Here are

displayed objects from the area of the Lapis Niger, Comitium, Cloaca Maxima, Regia and Basilica Emilia.

The rest of the collection, not at present on view, includes: a large capital from the Temple of Concord; a marble basin reconstructed from original fragments found near the Lacus Juturnae, and sculptures from the fountain, including a headless statue of Apollo from a Greek original of the 5C BC; fragments of the frieze of the Basilica Emilia, and part of its architectural decoration; and part of a *fresco removed from the chapel of Saints Cyriac and Julitta in Santa Maria Antiqua.

Dominating the summit of the Sacra Via is the **ARCH OF TITUS**, erected by Domitian (AD 81) in honour of the victories of Titus and Vespasian in the Judaean War, which ended with the sack of Jerusalem (AD 70). In the Middle

The Arch of Titus in the Roman Forum

Ages the Frangipani incorporated the arch in one of their castles, but the encroaching buildings were partly removed by Sixtus IV (1471–84) and finally demolished in 1821. Restoration of the arch was then undertaken by Giuseppe Valadier, who used travertine instead of marble to repair the damaged parts.

The beautiful, perfectly proportioned, single archway, with Composite columns, is covered with Pentelic marble. The two splendid reliefs inside the arch are very worn. One of them shows Rome guiding the Imperial quadriga with Titus and Victory; and the other shows the triumphal procession bringing the spoils from Jerusalem, which include the altar of Solomon's temple decorated with trumpets, and the seven-branched golden candlestick. In the centre of the panelled vault is the Apotheosis of Titus, who is mounted on an eagle. On the exterior frieze is another procession in which the symbolic figure of the vanquished Jordan is carried on a stretcher.

The large area on the northern slopes of the Palatine, to the west of the Arch of Titus as far as the House of the Vestals (between the Via Nova and the Sacra Via), has been excavated since 1985 beneath the visible remains of the **Horrea**, large warehouses on several floors. The building nearest the House of the Vestals probably dates in its present form from the time of Hadrian. The larger building to the east may be the **Horreum Vespasiani**, a market which fronted the Horrea Piperataria (see above), destroyed when the Basilica of Constantine was built. A row of shops against the Palatine Hill is prominent: almost in the centre can be seen a well-preserved vaulted edifice, beside which steps led up to the Via Nova and the upper floors.

The most important result so far of the excavations in this area has been the

discovery of **Archaic walls** on three levels: the oldest traces date from 730–675 BC when Romulus is supposed to have founded Rome; above these was a wall in red tufa defended by a ditch (675–600 BC). The latest wall, which seems to be part of the *Roma Quadrata* of Servius Tullius (530–520 BC), was constructed with large blocks of red tufa. Subsequent levels have shown interesting remains of at least four Archaic domus, and at least four Republican houses, one of which, facing the Clivo Palatino, may eventually be opened to the public (see p 97). Evidence was also discovered here of the destruction of numerous buildings by Nero for his huge Domus Aurea which, extending from the Oppian and Celian Hills across the Velia to the Palatine, invaded the centre of the Roman city. The horrea (see above) were part of a general plan of the Flavians to reinstall public edifices in this area after the death of Nero.

The Forum can be left by the gate beyond the Arch of Titus. The path descends along an extension of the Sacra Via, with the Temple of Venus and Roma (see p 114) on the left, to the Colosseum. Otherwise the Palatine is reached directly from the Arch of Titus by the Clivo Palatino.

3 · The Palatine

■ **Admission**: 9–1hr before sunset; Sun & Tues 9–13. ☎ 699 0110. Lire 12,000. The Palatine can be reached from the Roman Forum near the Arch of Titus (see p 94; and see the Plan on p 91), where the Clivo Capitolino begins, or by a separate entrance on Via San Gregorio (through a portal by Vignola and Rainaldi).

The topography of the Palatine is intricate, one level after another of multi-storey buildings having been erected on and through the previous levels. Several of the more interesting sites are apt to be fenced off, because of fresh excavations or damage of some kind. The custodians are informed and helpful. The House of Livia is usually open to the public; other enclosed monuments, including the House of Augustus, the church of Santa Maria Antiqua and the House of Marcus Aemilius Scaurus, can usually only be visited with prior permission from the Sopraintendenza di Archeologia. Contact the Ufficio Permessi, 53 Piazza Santa Maria Nuova, 00186 Rome, fax 678 7689. Requests should give reasons for the visit, names of participants, possible dates and contact information in Rome. Visits for study purposes are given priority. The Palatine Antiquarium has been closed indefinitely for restoration.

The Palatine (Pl. 4; 7) is a four-sided plateau south of the Forum, rising to a height of 40m above it and 51m above sea-level. It is about 1750m in circumference. It was here that the primitive city was founded, and splendid Imperial palaces were later built over its slopes, so that the word Palatine came to be synonymous with the 'palace of the emperor' (hence 'palace'). A park, with a profusion of wild flowers and fine trees, inhabited by birds and beautifully kept, now surrounds the ruins. It is one of the most romantic and charming spots in the centre of the city, remarkably isolated from the traffic-ridden streets at the foot of the hill.

History and topography

The Palatine now has the appearance of a plateau, the intervening hollows having been filled in by the successive constructions in the Imperial era. In ancient times the central summit was called the Palatium. It sloped down towards the Forum Boarium and the Tiber, with a declivity called the Germalus on the west and north (now occupied by the Farnese gardens) looking towards the Capitol. The Velia, a second lower summit, was connected with the Esquiline by a saddle through the Roman Forum. The name Palatium is said to be derived from Pales, the divinity of flocks and shepherds, whose festival was celebrated on 21 April, the day on which (in 754 or 753 BC) the city of Rome is supposed to have been founded. Long before that date, however, the hill was settled, according to legend, from Greece. Sixty years before the Trojan War (traditional date 1184 BC), Evander, son of Hermes and an Arcadian nymph, led a colony from Pallantion in Arcadia, and built a town at the foot of the Palatine Hill near the Tiber, naming it after his native village. Traces of occupation going back to the 9C BC have been discovered during excavations.

When the twins Romulus and Remus decided to found a new city, the honour of naming it was accorded to Romulus by the omen of 12 vultures which he saw on the Palatine. Some time after its foundation on the hill, the city was surrounded by a strong wall forming an approximate rectangle: hence the name Roma Quadrata. Three gates were provided in the walls: the Porta Mugonia on the northeast, the Porta Romanula on the northwest, and the Scalae Caci at the southwest corner overlooking the valley of the Circus Maximus. Excavations begun in 1985 on the lower northern slopes of the hill would appear to have identified a stretch of this wall, as well as traces of even earlier fortifications.

The northern slopes of the Palatine, in the area nearest to the Forum, were for centuries considered one of the most prestigious residential districts. During the Republic many prominent citizens lived here, including Cicero, Q. Lutatius Catulus, the orator Crassus, the demagogue Publius Clodius, the orator Hortensius, and the triumvir Antony. Remains of these residences have recently been unearthed. Augustus who was born on the Palatine, acquired the house of Hortensius and enlarged it. His new buildings included the renowned Temple of Apollo, with Greek and Latin libraries attached. Part of his palace has been excavated. The example of Augustus was followed by later emperors, whose residences became more and more magnificent, and the Palatine tended to become an Imperial reserve.

Recent excavations have revealed that the first palace on the Germalus summit, still called the 'Domus Tiberiana', was in fact part of Nero's huge Domus Aurea. This was reconstructed by Domitian who seems to have called it the 'Domus Tiberiana'. Hadrian added buildings towards the Via Nova and on the northwest side of the hill, but preferred to live on his estate near Tivoli.

The whole of the Palatium was reserved for the constructions of the Palace of the Flavian emperors, which comprised the official palace, the emperor's residence, and the stadium. To provide a water supply, Domitian extended the Acqua Claudia from the Celian hill to the Palatine. Septimius

Severus increased the area of the hill to the south by means of a series of arcades. Other remarkable edifices were the emperor's box overlooking the Circus Maximus and the monumental Septizonium. Heliogabalus built a new temple in the Adonaea, in which he placed the most venerated treasures of Rome.

Odoacer, first king of Italy after the extinction in 476 of the Western Empire, lived on the Palatine; so for a time did Theodoric, king of the Ostrogoths, who ruled Italy from 493 to 526. The hill later became a residence of the representatives of the Eastern Empire. From time to time it was favoured by the popes, and some Christian churches were built here. In the 12C there was an important Greek monastery on the hill.

In the course of time, after a period of devastation, the Frangipani and other noble families erected their castles over the ruins. In the 16C most of the Germalus was laid out as a villa for the Farnese (the Orti Farnesiani). Systematic excavations were begun about 1724 by Francesco Bianchini, shortly after Duke Francis I of Bourbon Parma had inherited the Farnese Gardens. They were mainly concentrated in the area of the Domus Flavia. Little more was done till 1860; in that year the gardens were bought by Napoleon III, who entrusted the direction of the excavations to Pietro Rosa. He continued his work after 1870 when the Palatine was acquired by the Italian Government.

In 1907 D. Vaglieri began to explore the Germalus; he was succeeded by Giacomo Boni, who worked on the buildings below the Domus Flavia. Alfonso Bartoli later carried out research under the Domus Augustana and elsewhere and brought to light much information about the earliest inhabitants. Excavations have been in progress since 1985 on the lower northern slopes of the hill, beneath the Domus Tiberiana, on the southwest corner of the hill in the area of the Temple of Cybele, and near the Vigna Barberini.

The Clivo Palatino ascends from the Forum passing the Nova Via on the right. A Republican house excavated in 1985, facing the Clivo Palatino, has been restored and can be visited by request, see p 95. With some 50 bedrooms, it is thought that it may have been the servants' quarters attached to the residence of Marcus Aemilius Scaurus, in 58 BC before he went into exile in 52 BC.

The Farnese Gardens and the western Palatine

On the right paths and steps lead up to the **Farnese Gardens**, laid out by Vignola in the middle of the 16C for Cardinal Alessandro Farnese, grandson of Paul III. They extended from the level of the Forum, then much higher, to the Germalus; the various terraced levels were united by flights of steps. Vignola's work was completed by Girolamo Rainaldi at the beginning of the 17C. The modern stairs lead up to the first terrace (formerly approached by a monumental ramp from the Nova Via in the Forum) with a nymphaeum. Above another terrace with a fountain stand the twin pavilions of the aviary on the highest level of the gardens, overlooking the Forum. The classical *Viridarium* instituted by Alessandro Farnese was replanted here by the archaeologist Giacomo Boni (1859–1925). The gardens are still very beautiful. Boni's tomb stands beneath a palm tree in the part of the gardens overlooking the Forum. Delightful paths continue through the gardens to the west side of the hill. To the south is an

ancient palm tree beneath which is a box-hedge maze reproducing that in the peristyle of the Domus Flavia.

The gardens cover the site of the so called **Domus Tiberiana**, very little of which is visible. Recent excavations here have revealed that the first palace on this site (formerly occupied by Republican houses) was part of Nero's Domus Aurea. This was reconstructed by Domitian, and extended to the northwest (towards the Clivo della Vittoria) by Hadrian. A cryptoporticus (with entrances, not open to the public, on Via di San Teodoro) dates from the period of Nero. Under Domitian a ramp on four levels was constructed to connect the Domus Tiberiana with the Forum. There is an oval fishpond in the southeast corner near the stairs leading down to the cryptoporticus and a series of rooms with brick vaults on the southern slope overlooking the Temple of Cybele. These rooms (no admission) were built by the Antonines for the accommodation of the Praetorian Guard; graffiti in them indicate their occupation by soldiers.

Excavations have been in progress since 1978 in the southwestern part of the hill around the Temple of Cybele, and the top of the Scalae Caci, so that some of the ruins are sometimes fenced off. From the south side of the gardens a modern flight of steps descends past (left) considerable remains of the Domus Tiberiana (see above). On the right are the ruins of the **TEMPLE OF CYBELE** (or **Magna Mater**) covered by a thicket of ilex. During a critical period of the second Punic War, an oracle had foretold that the battle could only be won if the Romans obtained from Phrygia the black stone which was the attribute of the goddess Cybele. In fact, the Romans—with this sacred cult image—were victorious, and the temple was built in 204 BC, and consecrated in 191 BC.

> Cybele, the Magna Mater, mother of the gods, was the great Asiatic goddess of fertility. She was worshipped in the town of Pessinus in Phrygia (Asia Minor). She, and her young lover Attis, were served by eunuch priests, and the festival of Cybele and Attis was celebrated annually (22–24 March) with primitive orgies.

The temple, raised on a high podium, had six Corinthian columns in antis. Burned down in 111 BC, it was rebuilt by Q. Caecilius Metellus, consul in 109, and restored again in the reign of Augustus (AD 3). It is depicted on a Roman relief set into the garden façade of the Villa Medici. Recent excavations have clarified the various dates of the building. The podium and the walls of the cella date from after the fire of 111 BC. At this time a large platform was built in front of the temple for athletic games and theatrical performances in honour of the goddess, beneath which was a district with an underground road, shops, and a thermal building. Pavements and external architectural decorations survive from the Augustan period. The statue of Cybele and fragments of a marble lion found here have been placed under an arch of the Domus Tiberiana.

To the east of the temple are remains of the **Temple of Victory** built in 294 BC by the consul Lucio Postumio Megello. Between the two temples is a much smaller one, recently identified as the **Temple of Victory Virgo** dedicated by Marco Porcio Cato in 193 BC.

Further east are two **archaic cisterns** (under cover) dating from the 6C BC, one of which is particularly well preserved. It is circular in form, with a beehive

vault of cappellaccio blocks laid in gradually diminishing courses; the top was closed with a single slab. The construction recalls the Mycenean tholos.

The area to the south is the most ancient part of the hill. Here are traces of a wall of tufa and the site of the **Scalae Caci**, one of the three gates of Roma Quadrata. Cacus was the giant who stole the oxen from Hercules, and according to legend had his den in the Forum Boarium, at the foot of the hill, and was killed there by Hercules. Up until the 4C AD it was believed that the house of Romulus, or the hut which belonged to Faustulus where the twins were brought up after they were found by the shepherd, was located in this area. Excavations in 1907–49 revealed the traces of a **hut village** of the Early Iron Age (9C BC). On the rocky level of the hill are numerous holes and channels indicating the plan of three huts. In the holes were placed poles supporting the roofs. The channels were used to carry away the rain-water from the roofs.

Also in this part of the hill was the **Lupercal**, although traces of it have not yet been found. This was the cave sanctuary of the she-wolf, an animal sacred to Rome. It contained an altar and was surrounded by a grove sacred to the god Lupercus. Here the annual festival of the *lupercalia* was held on 15 February, when the priests of the god, the *luperci*, dressed in goatskins, and processed around the hill, whipping whoever they met. It was believed that the castigation of women symbolised fertility. The name February means purification and expiation. These rites were later connected with the mythical legend of Romulus and Remus suckled by the she-wolf.

The part of the hill between the Temple of Cybele and the Temple of Apollo (see below) has been fenced off while excavations (begun in 1961) of the **House of Augustus** (not the Domus Augustana, which is described on p 104) have been carried out. This may be opened to the public; meanwhile admission is only granted by special permission; see p 95.

In the west wing of the house, thought to be the private quarters of the Emperor, have been found rooms with paintings of the highest interest: one has a charming frieze of pine cones, and another architectural and theatrical motifs. A series of larger rooms were probably used for public ceremonies and included two libraries, and a little nymphaeum decorated with shells. The wall-paintings, dating from 25 BC–AD 25, are remarkable for their vivid colour and intricate design (and refined figure studies). Considerable fragments of the stuccoed vaults and pavements of marble inlay have also come to light.

To the southeast of the House of Augustus are some ruins once thought to belong to the Temple of Jupiter Victor, built by Q. Fabius Rullianus in 295 BC after his victory over the Samnites at Sentinum. After a building of the late Republican era was found beneath it, it was identified instead as the famous **Temple of Apollo** vowed by Augustus in 36 BC and dedicated eight years later. A corridor which is thought to have connected the Temple to the House of Augustus has been excavated here, and more wall-paintings have been discovered near the podium of the temple. Fragments of a colossal statue of Apollo were found near the site of the temple, although they do not belong to the famous statue of Apollo by Skopas known to have been placed here. All that survives is the basement of the temple (44m by 24m) reached on the south side by a long flight of steps (no admission; the existing flight is a modern reproduction).

The Temple of Apollo was surrounded by the Portico of the Danaids, on which

THE ROMAN FORUM

Basilica Julia

S. Maria Antiqua
NOVA   VIA
Temple of Augustus
VICUS TUSCUS
Pal. of Caligula
Farnese
CLIVUS VICTORIAE
(Palace of Tiberius)
Cryptoporticus
S. Teodoro
S DI VIA TEODORO
Gardens
Basilica
Aula Regia
Temple of Cybele
House of Livia
Peristyle
Domus Flavia
House of Romulus (Iron age huts)
House of Augustus
Lupercal
Scalae Caci
Temple of Apollo
Triclinium   Anti
Libraries
S. Anastasia
Paedagogium
VIA
Circus   DEI
Maximus

THE PALATINE
0   50   100 yards
0   50   100 metres
N

SACRA VIA
Arch of Titus
Entrance
Thermae
Arch of Constantine

PALATINUS

CLIVUS

S. Sebastiano
Aedes Caesarum

VIA

S. Bonaventura

DI

S.

Entrance

GREGORIO

Lararium

Domus
Augustana
quarium

Aqueduct

Stadium

Baths of
Septimius Severus

CERCHI

were statues of the 50 daughters of Danaus. Some magnificent painted terra-cotta panels (now in the Palatine Antiquarium) were found here. Near by were the renowned Greek and Latin libraries, rebuilt by Domitian.

To the north of the House of Augustus is the so-called **HOUSE OF LIVIA**, famous for its wall-paintings. When it was discovered by Pietro Rosa in 1869, it was identified as the house of the wife of Augustus from some lead pipes bearing the inscription *Iulia Augusta*. It is now considered to be part of the house of Augustus himself (see above). The masonry dates from the 1C BC; the mural paintings are Augustan. The house is usually open to the public.

An original staircase descends into the rectangular **courtyard**, in which there are two pillar bases and architectural paintings. The most important rooms open onto it. In front are the three rooms thought to belong to the Tablinum, or reception suite; on the right is a room which was probably the Triclinium, or dining-room. The decorations of the **tablinum** are in the second Pompeian style (1C BC), which imitates in painting the marble of Greek and Roman domestic architecture, and introduces figures.

The paintings have been detached but are exhibited *in situ*. The paintings in the central room are the best preserved, especially that on the right wall of this room. It has panels separated by columns of fantastic design in a free interpretation of the Corinthian style. In the central panel Hermes is seen coming to the rescue of Io, the lover of Zeus, who is guarded by Argus of the hundred eyes; in the left panel is a street scene; the right panel is lost. In the intercolumniations are small panels with scenes of mysterious rites. The central painting on the rear wall of this room, now almost obliterated, shows Polyphemus pursuing Galatea into the sea; on the left wall, which lost its paintings in ancient times, are exhibited the lead pipes which gave the house its name (see above).

The room on the left has architectural decorations (very ruined), with panels of griffins and other fantastic creatures. The room on the right is also architectural in its decorative scheme. The delicate yellow frieze depicts small landscapes and genre scenes. Below is the representation of a Corinthian portico; between the columns are rich festoons of fruit and foliage. In the **triclinium** (usually closed) the decorations are also mainly architectural. On the wall opposite the entrance is a portico with an exedra; in front is a trophy with spoils of the chase, and below is a pond with ducks. Above are branches of trees.

To the north of the House of Livia is one of the most interesting features of the Palatine. This is the **CRYPTOPORTICUS** (closed for restoration), a vaulted passage 128m long, skirting the Farnese Gardens and the Domus Tiberiana. Decorated in the vault with fine stuccoes (replaced by casts; originals in the Antiquarium) for part of its length, it receives light and air from windows set high on the east side. This was part of the Domus Tiberiana, and a branch corridor was later added to link it with the Domus Flavia. The Cryptoporticus can be reached also by stairs leading down from the Farnese Gardens.

The Palace of Domitian

To the east extends the vast area of the Palace of Domitian, which occupies nearly the whole of the Palatium and the former depression between it and the Germalus. This vast collection of buildings was brilliantly planned for Domitian by the architect C. Rabirius, who levelled the central part of the hill to fill up the depression on the west. In the process he demolished or buried numerous earlier

constructions, from private houses to Imperial palaces; some of these have been revealed by excavations. The complex includes the Domus Flavia, or official palace, the Domus Augustana, or Imperial residence, and the Stadium. Originally it was reached from the north by a monumental staircase of three flights.

The splendour of the **DOMUS FLAVIA**, northwesternmost of the constructions, was praised by numerous Roman poets. On the north side it has a portico of cipollino columns which may have served as a loggia. In the centre of the palace is the spacious **peristyle** with an impluvium in the form of an octagonal maze surrounding a fountain. A box-hedge reproduction of this maze is in the Farnese Gardens. Because of Domitian's constant dread of assassination he is supposed to have had the walls covered with slabs of Cappadocian marble whose mirror-like surface enabled him to see anyone approaching. On the west side is a series of small rooms with apses, statue-bases, and baths; on the east side are traces of three more rooms.

To the north of the peristyle are three large halls (fenced off) facing north onto an open space identified with the Area Palatina. The central hall is the so-called **Aula Regia**, or throne room, originally decorated with 16 columns of pavonazzetto and with 12 black basalt statues: two of the statues were found in 1724 and are now in Parma. In the apse was the Imperial throne where the emperor sat when he presided over meetings of his council and received foreign ambassadors. To the east is the so-called **Lararium** (under cover), in fact thought to be another room used for public ceremonies, or a guardroom protecting the main entrance to the palace. To the west is the **Basilica Jovis**, divided by two rows of columns of giallo antico; it has an apse at the further end, closed by a marble screen. This may have been used as an auditorium. A flight of steps (at present closed) leads down from the Basilica to the Cryptoporticus (see above).

To the south of the peristyle is the **triclinium**, or banqueting hall. It has an apse reached by a high step; in this was placed the table where the emperor dined. The hall was paved with coloured marbles, which are well preserved in the apse. Leading out of the hall on either side was a court with an oval fountain. Around the fountain on the west side, which is well preserved, is a magnificent pavement in opus sectile belonging to the Domus Transitoria of Nero. Here, too, is a pavilion constructed by the Farnese as part of their gardens with a double loggia looking northwest and decorations attributed to the Zuccari.

Behind the triclinium is a row of columns (partly restored) belonging to the Domus Flavia. Further south are two rooms with apses, once thought to be Domitian's reconstruction of the Greek and Latin Libraries of the Temple of Apollo, but now considered to be reception rooms used by Augustus for legates.

The Domus Flavia covers several earlier constructions of considerable interest. These underground areas are sometimes shown by custodians; for permission to visit them, apply at the Forum Antiquarium (9–13).

Beneath the Lararium is the **HOUSE OF THE GRIFFINS**, named after the two griffins in stucco which decorate a lunette in one of the rooms. This is the oldest Republican building preserved on the Palatine (2C or 1C BC). Its wall-paintings, like those in the House of Livia, are in the second Pompeian style. The house is on two levels, the decorations being on the lower level. Of the several rooms reached by the staircase, the large hall is the best preserved. The pavement is in opus sectile. The mural paintings simulate three planes of different depth, while the columns imitate various marbles. Round the top of the room runs a cornice

and the ceiling is stuccoed. Paintings from two of the rooms have been detached and are now in the Palatine Antiquarium. Beneath the Basilica is the **Aula of Isis**, a large rectangular hall, with an apse at one end. The mural paintings have been detached and are now exhibited in a room of the Domus Augustana (see below).

Steps lead down from the triclinium to part of the **Domus Transitoria of Nero** (formerly called the Baths of Tiberius). At the foot of the steps is a court with a partly restored nymphaeum, decorated with rare marbles. Other rooms have traces of pavements with fine marble inlay. Small paintings of Homeric subjects found in a room leading off the court have been removed to the Antiquarium. Beneath the peristyle is the so-called *Palatine Mundus* (no admission; a grate now covers the entrance to the stairs), a pit with a well at one end. This was thought by Boni, when it was discovered, to be the Mundus of Roma Quadrata, but it was more probably a silo. In 1952, on the wall of a building, one of the many destroyed when the Domus Flavia was built, was found a Christian inscription, believed to refer to the celebration of the Eucharist in AD 78 and, if so, the earliest yet discovered.

Overlapping the Domus Flavia on the east are the vast remains of the **DOMUS AUGUSTANA**. This was the private residence of the emperor, 'the Augustus', not that of the Emperor Augustus. It was built on two levels, with two peristyles on the upper and one on the lower level. Only the bases of the columns survive. The first peristyle, towards Via di San Bonaventura, was open. In the middle of the second peristyle is a large basin with a quadrangular shrine, possibly dedicated to Vesta. Around the court are remains of rooms, one of which has been identified as the 4C **Oratory of St Caesarius**. Close by is the Palatine Antiquarium (see below). In another of the rooms is a graceful 16C loggia decorated with grotesques, formerly part of the Villa Mattei. Here are exhibited paintings detached from the Aula of Isis (see above). Dating from the Republican period these were painted before the edict of 21 BC banning the worship of Isis. The fantastic architectural paintings have panels with scenes of the cult of Isis and the fragments of the ceiling decoration are especially interesting. When the hall, with the House of the Griffins, was discovered in 1720–22, the paintings, which were in much better condition than they are now, were copied by Gaetano Piccini and by Francesco Bartoli. Bartoli's watercolours are now in the Topham Collection at Eton.

Another peristyle of the Domus Augustana is on a much lower level (no adm but well seen from above). In the middle is the basin of a fountain. Beyond are rooms with pavements of coloured marbles. A doorway in the bottom wall leads to the exedra of the palace overlooking the Circus Maximus; this was originally decorated with a colonnade.

The **Palatine Antiquarium** occupies the former Convent of the Visitation between the Domus Flavia and the Domus Augustana. It was formed with the material collected in 1860–70 from the excavations begun by Napoleon III in the Farnese Gardens and amplified by Pietro Rosa. It has recently been reopened after years of restoration. The contents include wall decorations and frescoes, stucco, marble intarsia, sculptures, and *painted terracotta panels found near the Temple of Apollo.

To the east of the Domus Augustana lies the **STADIUM**. This is an enclosure

146m long, with a series of rooms at the north end and a curved wall at the south. The interior had a two-storeyed portico with engaged columns covering a wide ambulatory or cloister. The arena has a semicircular construction at either end, presumably once supporting a turning-post (*meta*). In the centre are two rows of piers of a portico of the late Empire. Towards the south end are the remains of an oval enclosure of the early Middle Ages which blocked the curved end of the Stadium. Columns of granite and cipollino, Tuscan, Corinthian and Composite capitals, and fragments of a marble altar with figures of divinities lie on the surface of the arena. In the middle of the east wall is a wide exedra shaped like an apse, of two storeys, and approached from the outside by a curved corridor. This structure is usually identified as an Imperial box, used by the emperor when he commanded the races and athletic contests here. Some scholars, however, suggest the 'stadium' was in fact a garden, used occasionally as a hippodrome.

East of the Stadium was the so-called **Domus Severiana**, which was built over a foundation formed by enlarging the southern corner of the hill by means of enormous substructures that extended almost as far as the Circus Maximus. The scant remains include part of the **baths**. To the north is the **aqueduct** built by Domitian to provide water for his palace; it was an extension of the Acqua Claudia which ran from the Celian to the Palatine. The aqueduct was restored by Septimius Severus.

To the south is the site of the Imperial box built by Septimius Severus, from which he watched the contests in the Circus Maximus. In the southeastern corner of the Palatine is the probable site of the **Septizonium** or **Septizodium**, built by Septimius Severus in AD 203 to impress visitors to Rome arriving by the Via Appia. Here in 1241 Matteo Orsini imprisoned cardinals and forced them to elect Celestine IV; the new pope and three of the cardinals died as a result of the conditions. It was demolished by Sixtus V at the end of the 16C. Renaissance drawings of this building show that it had three floors, each decorated with columns. The façade was divided vertically into seven zones, the number corresponding either to that of the planets or to the days of the week; hence the uncertainty about the name. The columns and blocks of marble and travertine from this ornate structure were reused in various buildings in the city.

Beyond the Severian arches, the south end of the Stadium, and the exedra of the Domus Augustana, lies the **Paedagogium** (1C or 2C AD), halfway down the hill and facing the Circus Maximus, supposed to have been a training school for the court pages. Other rooms (inaccessible), on the edge of the hill above Via dei Cerchi, include the so-called **Schola of the Praecones**.

The Palatine can be left either by descending the hillside to the east of the Domus Augustana to the exit on Via San Gregorio or by returning across the Domus Augustana and descending the Clivo Palatino (see the Plan) to the exit at the Arch of Titus in the Forum.

Outside the arch (and not included in the Palatine enclosure), Via di San Bonaventura ascends to the northeastern summit of the Palatine. Here, approached by a 17C portal in the wall of the Vigna Barberini, the former Barberini vineyard, is the small medieval church of **San Sebastiano al Palatino**, with interesting murals (c 970) in the apse. Excavations in the churchyard have unearthed the probable site of the **Adonaea**, or gardens of

Adonis, where this god was worshipped. Later, Elegabalus built a **Temple of the Sun** in the centre of the gardens. Here he placed numerous treasures from the most ancient cults of the city, including the sacred stone from the Temple of Cybele, and what he took to be the Palladium (see p 89). The district acquired the name Palladii or in Pallara in the Middle Ages, and this was given also to the church of San Sebastiano. Recent excavations here have revealed a semicircular exedra which has the same dimensions as the south exedra of the Domus Augustana (see above) overlooking the Circus Maximus, and is therefore probably part of the same palace. The last section of Via di San Bonaventura (which ends at the church) is flanked by 18C terracotta Stations of the Cross.

4 · The Imperial Fora and the Colosseum

The five Imperial Fora, of Caesar, of Augustus, of Vespasian, of Nerva and of Trajan, occupy the huge area between the Roman Forum and the lower slopes of the Quirinal and Viminal. They are traversed by the wide **Via dei Fori Imperiali** (Pl. 4; 5, 7) opened in 1933 by Mussolini as the Via dell'Impero and lined with gardens. From Piazza Venezia it runs in a straight line to the Colosseum past the Fora of Trajan and Augustus on the left and the Forum of Caesar on the right. It then crosses over the Fora of Nerva and of Vespasian. During the construction of this thoroughfare, built to add dignity to Fascist military parades, numerous 16C buildings were demolished, the Velia Hill levelled, and the Imperial Fora hastily and inconclusively excavated.

Since 1980 projects have been mooted to eliminate the stretch of road between Piazza Venezia and Via Cavour and to carry out systematic excavations of the Fora at a considerably lower level. Meanwhile only one-fifth of the Fora is visible and the traffic along this unfortunate road continues to damage the ancient monuments. The Imperial Fora are all visible from outside (with the exception of the Forum of Vespasian) but for many years only the Markets and Forum of Trajan have been open regularly to the public. Since 1994 the road has been a pedestrian precinct on Sundays. In summer the fora are often floodlit at night.

History

With the ever-increasing population of the city, by the end of the Republican era the Roman Forum had become too small for its purpose. It was congested with buildings and overcrowded by citizens and by visitors from abroad. The only direction in which expansion was possible was to the north, even though numerous buildings had to be demolished here. The purpose of any new forum was to be the same as that of the Roman Forum, namely to serve, with its basilicas, temples, and porticoes, as a judicial, religious, and commercial centre.

The first step was taken by Julius Caesar, who built his Forum during the decade before his death in 44 BC. In it he placed the Temple of Venus Genetrix in commemoration of the victory of Pharsalus (48 BC). His example was followed by his successors, most of whom erected temples in memory of some outstanding event in Roman history for which they took the credit. The Forum of Augustus, with the Temple of Mars Ultor,

commemorated the battle of Philippi (42 BC); the Forum of Vespasian had its Temple of Peace erected with the spoils of the campaign in Judaea (AD 70); and the Forum of Trajan, completed by Hadrian, had a temple to the deified Trajan in honour of his conquest of Dacia (AD 106). The Forum of Nerva had a Temple of Minerva. All the Fora were connected and the whole area was arranged in conformity with a definite plan.

During the Middle Ages and the Renaissance the Fora were pillaged for their building material and robbed of their marbles and bronzes, and the area was later built over. Until the 20C only parts of the Fora of Trajan and Augustus and the so-called 'Colonnacce' were visible; the clearance of the area was begun in 1924 to make way for Via dei Fori Imperiali.

The Imperial Fora

At the west end of Via dei Fori Imperiali, opposite the corner of the Vittorio Emanuele Monument stands Trajan's Column (see below) beside two domed churches of similar design (usually closed). The first, **Santa Maria di Loreto** (usually open in the afternoon), by Antonio da Sangallo the Younger, with a lantern by Giacomo del Duca (1582), is a fine 16C building. It contains an altarpiece attributed to Marco Palmezzano, and a statue of St Susanna by François Duquesnoy (1630). The second church, dedicated to the **Nome di Maria** is by Antonio Dérizet (1738).

In front of the churches extends the **FORUM OF TRAJAN** (entered through the Markets of Trajan; see below), built between 107 and 113 and the last and most splendid of the Imperial fora. It was designed by Apollodorus of Damascus in a site excavated in the saddle between the Capitol and Quirinal Hills. The forum itself is in the form of a rectangle 118m by 89m, with a portico and exedra on each of the long sides. In the centre was an equestrian statue of Trajan. At the west end, occupying the whole of its width, was the Basilica Ulpia. Adjoining on the west, were the Greek and Latin libraries with Trajan's Column between them, and, still further west, beneath the area of the two churches, the Temple of Trajan. The entrance was from the east, adjoining the Forum of Augustus, through a monumental arch. To the north of the forum and virtually adjoining it is the semicircle of the Markets of Trajan. In the opinion of ancient writers these constructions made up a monumental group unequalled in the world. Further excavations are to be carried out here.

TRAJAN'S COLUMN is generally considered to be the masterpiece of Roman sculptural art, still almost intact, and carefully restored in 1980–88. It was dedicated to Trajan by Hadrian in memory of his conquest of the Dacians, the inhabitants of what is now Romania. Around the column shaft winds a spiral frieze 200m long and between 0.89m and 1.25m high, with some 2500 figures in relief illustrating in detail the various phases of Trajan's military achievements in the Dacian campaigns (101–102 and 105–106). The carving was carried out in less than four years by an unknown Roman master and his workshop. It is known that the column could originally be seen from buildings which surrounded it on various levels in the Forum of Trajan: it is now more difficult to appreciate the beautiful details of the carving with the naked eye. Casts (made before restoration) of each panel are kept in the Museo della Civiltà Romana.

The column is 100 Roman feet (29.7m) high, or with the statue, 39.8m; it is

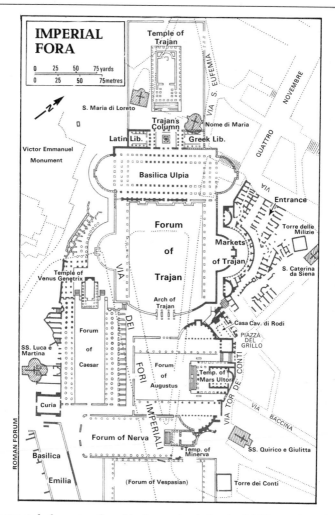

IMPERIAL FORA

0   25   50   75 yards
0   25   50   75 metres

S. Maria di Loreto

Temple of Trajan

VIA S. EUFEMIA

NOVEMBRE

Trajan's Column

Nome di Maria

Latin Lib.

Greek Lib.

QUATTRO

Victor Emmanuel Monument

Basilica Ulpia

VIA

Entrance

Torre delle Milizie

Forum

of

Trajan

Markets

of Trajan

S. Caterina da Siena

Temple of Venus Genetrix

VIA DEI

Arch of Trajan

Casa Cav. di Rodi

PIAZZA DEL GRILLO

SS. Luca e Martina

Forum

of

Caesar

FORI IMPERIALI

Forum of Augustus

Temp. of Mars Ultor

VIA TOR DE' CONTI

VIA BACCINA

Curia

ROMAN FORUM

Forum of Nerva

Temp. of Minerva

SS. Quirico e Giulitta

Basilica

Emilia

(Forum of Vespasian)

Torre dei Conti

constructed of a series of marble drums. A spiral stair of 185 steps (no admission) carved in the marble ascends to the top of the Doric capital on which once stood the statue of Trajan (replaced by the statue of St Peter in 1588). The ashes of the emperor, who died in Cilicia in 117, and of his wife Plotina, were enclosed in a golden urn and placed in a vault below the column. An inscription at the base has been interpreted to indicate that the top of the column reached to the original ground-level, thus giving an idea of the colossal excavations necessary for the construction of the forum.

The entrance to the **MARKETS OF TRAJAN** (open 9–18.30; closed Mon; ☎ 679 0048; Lire 3750) in Via IV Novembre is reached from here by steps (Via Magnanapoli). A second entrance is on the Via dei Fori Imperiali side, just by Trajan's Column, .

The Markets of Trajan were built before the Forum of Trajan, at the beginning of the 2C AD, and consisted of 150 individual shops, used for general trading.

The entrance is through a rectangular **hall** of two storeys, with six shops on each floor; on the upper storey is a large covered hall which may have served as a bazaar. In the shops marble fragments from the forums of Trajan and Augustus are now exhibited, including columns, capitals, reliefs, decorative tondos, and friezes. There are also models of the remains of the Temple of Mars Ultor in the Forum of Augustus. A series of rooms at the end display lions' head waterspouts, a delicately carved *capital from the Temple of Mars Ultor, decorated with winged horses, and two *heads of Jupiter from the Forum of Augustus. Beyond, in a fine domed semicircular hall, are fragments of statues. The shops on the other side have models and plans. The rooms upstairs display more fragments of friezes and colossal seated statues; two colossal heads and fragments of colossal statues, in Greek marble; and statues of Dacian prisoners from the Forum of Trajan in pavonazzetto marble and white marble. Amphorae are kept in the other rooms here.

Beyond the hall is the large semicircle of three superimposed rows of shops with arcaded fronts, built on the slopes of the Quirinal. The semicircle ends on either side in a well-preserved apsidal hall (only the one on the left can be visited). The portico of the fourth shop on the left of the bottom row has been reconstructed. The apsidal buildings on the second floor are particularly well preserved. An ancient paved road, the **Via Biberatica**, passes in front of the markets but is now blocked by Via IV Novembre.

The **Torre delle Milizie** (no admission), behind the markets, is a massive brick-built tower, a conspicuous feature in the skyline of Rome, and one of the most important civic medieval buildings to have survived in the city. It is thought to have been rebuilt in the 13C by the Caetani. In 1312 the emperor Henry VII stayed here. The tower, which acquired its lean after an earthquake in 1348, later belonged to the Conti family, and was restored and isolated from the convent of St Catherine by Antonio Muñoz in 1914. It originally had three storeys: two of these survive.

Steps descend from the markets to the level of the Forum of Trajan. The **North Portico** conforms to the semicircular shape of the markets. In the Middle Ages the portico was stripped of its precious marbles: all that survives are the remains of three steps of giallo antico, a column base, traces of the polychrome marble pavement, and a column of the apse. Behind the apse was the wall of the enclosure; part of this is visible on the left. The site of the South Portico is under Via dei Fori Imperiali.

A passageway leads towards Trajan's Column, in front of which are the extensive remains of the **Basilica Ulpia**, dedicated to the administration of justice, and the largest in Rome. Though not as spacious as the Basilica of Constantine, it was longer (120m; not counting the apses at either end); its width was 60m. It was divided by rows of columns into a nave and four aisles. On each short side was an extensive apse; the north apse was found under Palazzo Roccagiovine beside Via Magnanapoli. The front of the basilica, towards the interior of the forum, had three doors; at the back, towards Trajan's Column, there were two doors. Part of the pavement in coloured marbles has survived; also a fragment of the entablature, with reliefs depicting scenes of sacrifice and candelabra. The roof, covered with bronze tiles, may have been some 50m high.

On the left of the column is the **Latin Library** and on the right the **Greek Library**, both of them rectangular, with wall niches surmounted by marble cornices to hold the manuscripts. Behind the column is a fragment of a colossal granite column (with its marble capital), virtually all that remains of the huge **Temple of Trajan** erected after Trajan's death in 117 by Hadrian. Dedicated to the deified emperor and his wife Plotina c 118 the temple stood between Trajan's column and the Via Lata (now the Corso).

At the beginning of Via dei Fori Imperiali, beyond the Vittorio Emanuele Monument, the steep Via di San Pietro in Carcere (open only to cars with special permits) diverges right to climb above the Mamertine Prison (see below) to the Capitol. Here, well beneath the level of the road, can be seen the remains of the **FORUM OF CAESAR** (no admission), first of the Imperial fora, and said by Dio Cassius to have been more beautiful than the Roman Forum. Recent excavations behind the Curia building in the Roman Forum (see Chapter 2) have shown that Caesar created an entrance to his forum from the Curia. The focal point of this new forum was the **Temple of Venus Genetrix**, from whom Julius Caesar claimed descent. The high base remains, and although it has lost its marble facing, three of its Corinthian columns have been re-erected. In the temple, dedicated in 46 BC, two years after the battle of Pharsalus, were exhibited a statue of the goddess by Arcesilaus, a statue of Julius Caesar, a gilded bronze statue of Cleopatra, and two pictures by Timomachus of Byzantium (1C BC) of Ajax and of Medea. In front of the temple stood an equestrian statue of Caesar. Trajan rebuilt the temple and forum and added the Basilica Argentaria, or exchange building, and five large shops over which was an extensive (heated) public lavatory (*forica*), remains of which survive.

From Via di San Pietro in Carcere (see above) a well-preserved stretch of the *Clivus Argentarium*, the Roman road which ran between the Capitoline and the Quirinal Hills, is open to pedestrians. Lined with remains of shops and a nymphaeum dating from the time of Trajan, it descends to the little church of **San Giuseppe dei Falegnami** (often closed). This was built in 1598 perhaps by Giovanni Battista Montano, above the **Tullianum**, called the **Mamertine Prison** (9–12, 14.30–18) in the Middle Ages, and later consecrated as **San Pietro in Carcere**. This is thought originally to have been a cistern, like those at Tusculum and other Etruscan cities. On the lower level, the form can be seen of a round building which may have had a tholos (which could date it as early as the 6C BC). A spring still exists in the floor. The building was used as a dungeon in Roman times for criminals and captives awaiting execution. Jugurtha, Vercingetorix, the accomplices of Catiline, and—according to Christian tradition—St Peter and St Paul were all imprisoned here.

Beside the church, steps lead up to the Capitol. There is a good view from here of the monuments at the west end of the Roman Forum. Opposite is the handsome church of **SANTI LUCA E MARTINA** (Pl. 8; 2; often closed), probably founded in the 7C by Honorius I on the site of the Secretarium Senatus. It was rebuilt in 1640 by Pietro da Cortona, and is considered one of his masterpieces. The two storeys, the upper dedicated to St Luke and the lower to St Martina, have an original and complex design. The façade, built of travertine, and the dome are particularly fine. The church of St Luke has a centralised Greek-cross plan. The lower church of Santa Martina is reached by a staircase to the left of the high altar.

In a well-designed chapel (left) are the tombs of Saints Martina, Epifanio and Concordio, and a tabernacle by Pietro da Cortona. The side chapel with a pretty scallop motif has a fine terracotta group of the three saints by Alessandro Algardi. In the corridor is the tomb of Pietro da Cortona, and in the vestibule, statuettes by Cosimo Fancelli, and a bas-relief of the *Deposition* by Algardi.

On the other side of Via dei Fori Imperiali, in front of their respective fora, are modern bronze statues of Trajan, Augustus and Nerva. Adjoining the Forum of Trajan is the **FORUM OF AUGUSTUS**, built to commemorate the victory of Philippi (42 BC) and dedicated to Mars Ultor (the Avenger). Closed since 1984, it can be seen from the railings along Via dei Fori Imperiali (which, however, covers half its area).

The forum is dominated by the octastyle **Temple of Mars Ultor**, dedicated in 2 BC, which has columns on three sides. It had a large pronaos and an apsidal cella. A centre of solemn ceremonies and the Imperial sanctuary, it became a museum of art and miscellaneous relics; among these were the sword of Julius Caesar and the Roman standards surrendered by the Parthians in 20 BC. Three columns at the end of the right flank are still standing. Of the eight Corinthian columns in front, four (the two middle and the two end ones) have been partly reconstructed from antique fragments. A broad flight of steps ascends to the capacious pronaos. In the cella, where the effect of undue width is lessened by a colonnade on either side, are the stepped bases of the statues of Mars, Venus and perhaps Divus Julius. Behind is the curve of the large apse. A stairway on the left descends to an underground chamber once thought to be the temple treasury. The huge wall behind was built to isolate the forum from the Subura district.

On either side of the temple, marble steps lead up to the site of twin **basilicas** which were almost completely destroyed during the Renaissance for their marble; each had a great apse, which Augustus decorated with statues of Roman heroes, from Aeneas onwards (some of the niches can still be seen). On the ground between the surviving columns of the temple and the right-hand basilica are architectural fragments of great interest. Behind these is the **Arch of Pantanus**, formerly an entrance to the forum. The left-hand basilica had an extension at the north end known as the **Hall of the Colossus**, a square room which held a colossal statue of Augustus or of Mars, the base of which remains. Two ancient columns have been re-erected at the entrance.

At the east end of the Forum of Augustus is the **FORUM OF NERVA**, or **Forum Transitorium** (excavations in progress), so called because it led into the Forum of Vespasian. Nerva's Forum, which was begun by Domitian and completed in AD 97, was, in effect, a development of the **Argiletum**, the street that led from the Roman Forum to the Subura. In the middle rose the **Temple of Minerva**, the ponderous basement of which remains in place. The temple was still standing at the beginning of the 17C, when it was pulled down by Paul V to provide marble for the Fontana Paolina on the Janiculum. Beyond the temple and close to the enceinte wall are two enormous Corinthian columns (recently restored), the so-called **Colonnacce**. In the attic between the columns is a high-relief of Minerva, after an original of the school of Skopas. In the rich frieze of the entablature Minerva (Athena) is seen teaching the arts of sewing and weaving and punishing Arachne, the Lydian girl who excelled in the art of

weaving and had dared to challenge the goddess. In front of the Colonnacce is a section of the Argiletum.

To the east of the Forum of Nerva extended the **FORUM OF VESPASIAN** or **Forum of Peace**, built in AD 69–79, with the spoils of the Jewish War. Excavations revealed and identified a shrine under the Torre dei Conti, some prone columns, and remains of a pavement in opus sectile; a large hall was converted in the 6C into the church of Santi Cosma e Damiano (see below).

On Piazza del Grillo is the **Casa dei Cavalieri di Rodi**, ancient seat of the Roman priorate of the Order of the Knights of St John of Jerusalem (see p 260). The house was built over a Roman edifice at the end of the 12C, and restored in 1467–70 by Cardinal Marco Balbo, nephew of Paul II. It has a well-preserved colonnaded atrium, dating from the time of Augustus; the roof is a Renaissance addition. It is now used as a chapel by the Knights of St John (open for a service, Sun 10.30).

At the top of a flight of Roman stairs (restored) is a fine Renaissance hall (adm sometimes on request), off which are several contemporary rooms; one of these, the Sala del Balconcino contains part of the attic storey of the portico of the Forum of Augustus, with caryatids. Stairs lead up to a loggia with restored frescoes and fine views over the fora.

Via di Campo Carleo or Via Tor de' Conti lead back to Via dei Fori Imperiali which continues towards the Colosseum, passing the entrance to the Roman Forum. Here a large area of gardens has been fenced off adjoining the Forum of Nerva and excavations have been in progress since 1988. So far only the medieval and 16C levels have been explored.

Excavations begun in 1991 in the area between the present fence of the Roman Forum and the edge of the road have been completed, having revealed excellent evidence of the various uses of this land (remnants of the Forum of Nerva, medieval houses, etc) over the centuries. Also discovered was a Renaissance era sewage conduit, which has been restored and now serves to connect the new excavations with those done in the 1930s on the other side of Via dei Fori Imperiali. At present the area is open for guided tours several nights a week, but there are plans to open the entire area (all the Imperial Fora together) on one ticket.

A stairway on the left of the entrance to the Roman Forum leads to the church of San Lorenzo in Miranda, which encloses the Temple of Antoninus and Faustina (no admission; see p 92). Further on is the church of **SANTI COSMA E DAMIANO**, dedicated to two brothers from Cilicia who were miraculous healers. This church occupies a large rectangular hall (probably a library) of the Forum of Vespasian, which St Felix IV adapted in 527, adding mosaics to the apse. The so-called Temple of Romulus in the Roman Forum served as a vestibule to the church. It was rebuilt in 1632, when the pavement was added to make it a two-storeyed building. The church is reached through the early 17C cloisters of the adjoining convent with contemporary frescoes by Francesco Allegrini.

The **interior** (lights in each chapel) is celebrated for its 6C *mosaics, copied in several Roman churches (especially in the 9C). On the triumphal arch is the Lamb enthroned, surrounded by seven candlesticks, four angels, and the symbols of the Evangelists. In the apse (restored in 1989): Saints Cosmas and Damian presented to Christ at his Second Coming by St Peter and St Paul; on the

right, St Theodore; on the left St Felix IV (restored) presenting a model of the church. There are also palms and the phoenix, symbol of the Resurrection. Below is the Lamb on a mount from which four rivers (the Gospels) flow; 12 other lambs (the Apostles) are shown with Bethlehem and Jerusalem on either side.

The ceiling of 1632 has a fresco by Marco Montagna, who also painted frescoes in the nave. The Baroque altar by Domenico Castelli (1637) is adorned with a 13C *Madonna and Child*. In the first chapel in the right aisle, is a striking fresco of *Christ encrowned on the Cross*, derived from the Volto Santo in Lucca. It dates perhaps from the 13C, but more probably from a repainting in the 17C by an unknown Lucchese artist. In the vault are frescoes by Giovanni Battista Speranza. In the second chapel (being restored) are paintings by Giovanni Baglione. The third chapel has an altarpiece of *St Anthony of Padua* by Spadarino, and frescoes by Allegrini (who also painted the frescoes in the first and second chapels in the left aisle). In a domed Roman vestibule off the cloister is part of an 18C Neapolitan presepio (closed in August). The models and figures in wood, terracotta, and porcelain are of exceptionally fine workmanship.

Via dei Fori Imperiali next passes on the right the colossal ruins of the Basilica of Constantine (described on p 93). The four interesting relief **maps** on a modern brick wall facing the street were set up here in 1932. They show the extent of Roman power at four stages in its history: in the 8C BC; in 146 BC, after the Punic Wars; in AD 14, after the death of Augustus; and in the time of Trajan, AD 98–117.

Adjoining the Basilica of Constantine (and reached by a flight of steps from Via dei Fori Imperiali, or by a short road from Piazzale del Colosseo) is the church of **SANTA MARIA NOVA** or **Santa Francesca Romana** (Pl. 8; 2; open 9.30–12.30, 15.30–19, or 15–17 in winter). It is on the summit of the Velia and encroaches on the Temple of Venus and Rome (see below); a fine stretch of ancient Roman road is conspicuous on the approach to the west door.

The church incorporates an Oratory of St Peter and St Paul built by Paul I (757–67) in the west portico of the Temple of Venus and Rome. In 847, after grave structural damage to the church of Santa Maria Antiqua in the Forum, that church was abandoned and the diaconate was transferred to the oratory, which became *Santa Maria Nova*. The church was enlarged, and the apse mosaic and **campanile** added before it was consecrated anew in 1161. The façade, designed by Carlo Lombardi, was added during his reconstruction in 1615.

Santa Francesca Romana (Francesca Buzzi; 1384–1440), wife of Lorenzo Ponziani, founded the Congregation of Oblates here in 1421, which she herself joined after her husband's death in 1436. Canonised in 1608, she is the patron saint of motorists, and on her festival (9 March) the street between the church and the Colosseum is congested with cars lining up for a blessing. The painter Gentile da Fabriano was buried in the church in 1428. The former conventual buildings now contain the excavation offices and Antiquarium of the Roman Forum (see p 93).

Interior. The Cosmatesque pavement in the raised east end was restored in 1952. In the vestibule of the side entrance (right): tombs of Cardinal Marino Bulcani (died 1394) and of Antonio da Rio (or Rido), castellan of Castel Sant' Angelo (c 1450). South transept: tomb of Gregory XI, by Pietro Paolo Olivieri,

Santa Maria Nova

set up in 1585 by the Roman people in honour of the pope who restored the seat of the papacy from Avignon to Rome (1377). Let into the south wall (behind grilles) are two flagstones from the Sacra Via which are supposed to show the imprint of the knees of St Peter, made as the saint knelt to pray for the punishment of Simon Magus, who was demonstrating his wizardry by flying. The legendary site of Simon's consequent fall is in the neighbourhood. From here stairs lead down to the crypt with the body of St Francesca Romana, and a 17C bas-relief of her with an angel (17C). The confessio, an early work by Bernini, has a marble group of the same subject, by Giosuè Meli (1866).

In the apse are *mosaics of the Madonna and saints (probably completed in 1161), and on either side, statues of angels of the school of Bernini. Above the altar is a 12C *Madonna and Child*, revealed in 1950 and detached from another painting found beneath it. The earlier painting, a colossal *Virgin and Child*, which may have come from Santa Maria Antiqua, is now kept in the **sacristy**. Probably dating from the end of the 6C, it is one of the most ancient Christian paintings in existence. Also in the sacristy: Paul III and Cardinal Reginald Pole (left wall) attributed to Perino del Vaga; fragments of medieval frescoes; *Miracle of St Benedict*, by Subleyras. On the entrance wall, *Madonna enthroned between St Benedict and Santa Francesca Romana*, by Girolamo da Cremona, and *Madonna enthroned with Saints*, by Sinibaldo Ibi of Perugia (1545).

Beyond the church is the summit of the Velia, transformed into a terrace with gardens (no admission), the area of which (145m by 100m) virtually coincides with that of the enormous **TEMPLE OF VENUS AND ROMA**. Built and probably designed by Nero on the site of the vestibule of the Domus Aurea, where Nero had placed a colossal bronze statue of himself as the Sun, it was the largest temple in Rome. The statue had therefore to be moved (see below). The temple was built in honour of Venus, the mother of Aeneas and the ancestor of the gens Julia, and of Roma Aeterna, whose cult appears to have been localised on the Velia. Begun around 125, and dedicated in 135, it dominated this end of the Roman Forum. Its classical proportions show the strong influence Greek architecture had on the emperor. Damaged by fire in 283, it was restored by Maxentius (307). It is said to have been the last pagan temple which remained in use in Rome, as it was not closed until 391 (by Theodosius). It remained virtu-

ally entire until 625, when Honorius I stole the bronze tiles off its roof for the old basilica of St Peter's.

To counteract the unevenness of the ground, it was necessary to build a high platform; this was of rubble, with slabs of peperino and marble-faced travertine. The temple was dipteral, with ten granite Corinthian columns at the front and back and 20 on each of the sides. It had two cellae placed back to back; that facing the Forum was the shrine of Roma and the other that of Venus. The visible remains date from the time of Maxentius. The two cellae (the apses and diamond-shaped coffers were added by Maxentius) are still standing. That facing the Forum has been partly restored, and is visible from a room of the Antiquarium in the Forum (see p 93). The brick walls were formerly faced with marble and provided with niches framed with small porphyry columns. The apse contains the base of the statue of the goddess. The floor is of coloured marbles. The temple was surrounded by a colonnaded courtyard, with propylae on the north and south sides; in 1935 some of the columns and column-fragments on the south were re-erected, and can be seen from the extension of the Via Sacra which leads from the Arch of Titus down to the Colosseum.

The Colosseum

Piazzale del Colosseo (closed to traffic), lies in a valley between the Velia on the west, the Esquiline on the north and the Celian on the south.

The Colosseum (Pl. 5; 7) is the most famous monument of ancient Rome and the emblem of her eternity. Its original name, *Flavian Amphitheatre*, commemorated the family name of Vespasian, who began the building, and of his son Titus, who completed it. The popular name of the amphitheatre first occurs in the writings of the Venerable Bede (c 673–735), who quotes a prophecy of Anglo-Saxon pilgrims: 'While the Coliseum stands, Rome shall stand; when the Coliseum falls, Rome shall fall; when Rome falls, the world shall fall.' This name is thought to be derived from the proximity of Nero's colossal statue (see below), rather than from the size of the building itself.

■ **Admission**: upper level 9–one hour before sunset; Sun and Wed 9–14, ☎ 700 4262. There is free access to the ground floor from the west and north sides. The first floor (admission from the main entrance on the side facing the Roman Forum; Lire 8000) is also open, although the upper storeys have been closed for many years.

History

The amphitheatre, begun by Vespasian between AD 70 and 76 on the site of the lake in the gardens of Nero's Domus Aurea, was completed by Titus in 80. The inaugural festival lasted 100 days, during which many gladiators and 5000 wild beasts were killed. The amphitheatre was restored c 230 under Alexander Severus and in 248 the thousandth anniversary of the foundation of Rome was celebrated here. There is no historical basis for the tradition that Christians were martyred in the arena. Gladiatorial combats were suppressed in 407 and fights with wild beasts in 523. The damage from the earthquake of 422 was probably repaired by Theodosius II and Valentinian III. The building was again shaken by earthquakes in 1231 and 1349. It was later converted into a castle by the Frangipani and the Annibaldi.

In 1312 the Colosseum was presented to the senate and people of Rome by the Emperor Henry VII. By the 15C it had become a recognised quarry for building material. Its travertine was used during the construction of Palazzo di Venezia and Palazzo della Cancelleria. Other parts of the building were reused in St Peter's and Palazzo Barberini. In 1749, however, Benedict XIV dedicated the Colosseum to the Passion of Jesus and pronounced it sanctified by the blood of martyrs. Pius VII, Leo XII, Gregory XVI and Pius IX carried out restorations, erecting buttresses and other supports. In 1893–96 it was freed from obstructive buildings by Guido Baccelli, and the interior structures revealed. Further clearances were carried out after the construction in 1933 of Via dei Fori Imperiali.

The Colosseum was particularly admired by 19C travellers to Rome because of its romantic ruined state. Dickens in 1846 declared: 'It is the most impressive, the most stately, the most solemn, grand, majestic, mournful sight, conceivable. Never, in its bloodiest prime, can the sight of the gigantic Coliseum, full and running over with the lustiest life, have moved one heart, as it must move all who look upon it now, a ruin. God be thanked: a ruin!'

Exterior. The elliptical amphitheatre is built of travertine outside and of brick and tufa in the interior. The travertine blocks were originally fastened together with iron tenons; these were torn out in the Middle Ages and their sockets are conspicuous. Despite being pillaged for centuries, the Colosseum preserves its remarkable grandeur and the northeast side appears almost undamaged. The mighty exterior wall, which supports the complicated interior, has four storeys. The lower three have rows of arches decorated with engaged columns of the three orders superimposed: Doric on the lowest storey, Ionic on the middle, and Corinthian on the top. The fourth storey, dating from the restoration of Alexander Severus, has no arches but is articulated by slender Corinthian pilasters. Statues originally occupied the arches of the second and third storeys. The exterior dimensions are: length 188m, breadth 156m, circumference 527m, height 50m.

There were 80 entrance arches. All were numbered except the four main entrances at the ends of the diameters of the ellipse, situated northeast, southeast, southwest and northwest. That on the northeast (between arches XXXVIII and XXXIX), which was without a cornice and was wider than the others, opened into a hall decorated with stuccoes; it was reserved for the emperor. The numbered arches led to the concentric vaulted corridors giving access to the staircases. Each spectator entered by the arch corresponding to the number of his ticket, ascended the appropriate staircase and found his seat in the cavea by means of one of the numerous passages.

Interior. This was divided into three parts: the arena, the podium and the cavea. Though more than two-thirds of the original building has been removed, and the rows of the seats in the cavea are missing, the magnificence of the amphitheatre, which could probably hold some 50,000 spectators, can still be appreciated (although the best view is from the top storey, at present closed). The effect of the scene is reduced by the fact that the underground passages of the arena are exposed: they were formerly covered by a wooden floor.

The **arena** measures 76m by 46m. Its name comes from the sand which

covered the floor in order to prevent combatants from slipping and to absorb the blood. It was also sometimes flooded for mock sea-battles (*naumachiae*). The subterranean passages which can now be seen were used for the arrangement of the spectacles, and provided space for the mechanism by which scenery and other apparatus were hoisted into the arena. There were also cages for animals here.

The Cross replaces an earlier one which was set up to commemorate the martyrs who were supposed to have died in the Colosseum. The Chapel of Santa Maria della Pietà is open for a service at 10 on Sunday. The arena was surrounded by a wall c 5m high to protect the spectators from the animals. At the top of this wall was the **podium**. This was a broad parapeted terrace in front of

The Colosseum

the tiers of seats, on which was the imperial couch, or pulvinar. The rest of the terrace was reserved for senators, pontiffs, vestals, foreign ambassadors, etc.

The **cavea** was divided into three tiers, or *moeniana*. The lowest tier was reserved for knights, the middle one for wealthier citizens, and the top one for the populace. The tiers were separated by landings (*proecinctiones*), reached by several staircases. Each tier was intersected at intervals by *vomitoria*, 160 in all, passages left between the seats. The section between two passages was called a *cuneus*, or wedge, from its shape. Above the topmost tier was a colonnade, to which women were admitted. At the very top was the narrow platform for the men who were responsible for the *velarium*, or awning, which kept off the sun; the holes for the supporting poles are still visible.

A modern staircase leads up from the second arch on the left of the main entrance to the first storey (for admission, see above). The view of the interior is spectacular. A model of the Colosseum and a few architectural fragments can be seen in a hall (behind glass).

The Antiquarium (closed since 1984), in part of the interesting sub-vaults built by Vespasian and used for all the trappings necessary for the spectacles in the arena above, contains architectural elements (notably capitals) from the highest part of the building, and sculptural fragments from the terminals of the balustrades of the cavea.

Between the Colosseum and the Temple of Venus and Rome is the site (marked by a raised lawn planted with ilexes) of the huge brick base, 7m square, of the **Colossus of Nero**, the remains of which were demolished in 1936. This huge gilt bronze statue of Nero as god of the Sun, by Zenodorus, was nearly 35m high

and the largest bronze statue ever made (it had a concrete core), even larger than its model, the Colossus of Rhodes. The statue was provided with a new base and moved here from the vestibule of the Domus Aurea by Hadrian when he built the Temple of Venus and Rome. Decianus, the architect assigned to the task of removal, used 24 elephants to shift the statue.

Nearby a little garden has been planted with three cypresses. On the other side of a square lawn is an area of recent excavations surrounded by a fence and planted with olive trees. The visible ruins belong to the vestibule of the Domus Aurea. Beneath these were found extremely interesting remains of a temple and a Roman road. A circular fence surrounds the base of the **Meta Sudans**, which was demolished in 1936 by order of Mussolini, and re-excavated in 1982. This marble-faced fountain erected by Domitian marked the boundary of four regions of the Augustan city (II, III, IV and X). It was restored by Constantine, and received its name from its resemblance to the conical turning-post (*meta*) for chariot races in circuses, and from the fact that it 'sweated' water through numerous small orifices. It was surrounded by a circular basin.

The triple **ARCH OF CONSTANTINE** (Pl. 4; 7, 8) was erected in AD 315 in honour of Constantine's victory over Maxentius at Saxa Rubra. This triumphal arch was decorated with sculptural fragments from older Roman monuments, a sad testimony to the decline of the arts in the late Imperial period. However, the proportions of the arch are good, and many of the individual reliefs are of the highest quality. These were severely damaged by the polluted air, but they were beautifully restored in 1989.

The splendid large *reliefs on the inside of the central archway and the two above on the sides of the arch come from the frieze of a monument commemorating Trajan's victories over the Dacians and are probably by the sculptor who carved Trajan's Column. The eight large *medallions on the two façades, with finely carved hunting scenes and pastoral sacrifices, belonged to an unknown monument set up by Hadrian. The eight high-reliefs set into the attic were taken (like the three in Palazzo dei Conservatori) from a monument to Marcus Aurelius, and represent a sacrifice, orations to the army and to the people, and a triumphal entry into Rome. The small bas-reliefs of the frieze, and the victories and captives at the base of the columns, are of the period of Constantine.

5 · The Pantheon and Piazza Navona

The Pantheon

The best-preserved monument of ancient Rome, the Pantheon (Pl. 2; 6) remains the most magnificent symbol of the Empire. Dedicated to all the gods (Pantheon), it was conceived as a secular Imperial monument as much as a shrine. In 609 it was converted into a church, the first temple in Rome to be Christianised. A pedimented pronaos precedes a gigantic domed rotunda, with a rectangular feature as wide as the pronaos and as high as the cylindrical wall inserted between the two. This combination of a pronaos and rotunda gives it a special place in the history of architecture. Originally the pronaos was raised by several steps and preceded by a large rectangular paved forecourt, much larger than the present piazza. Admission: 9–16.30; Sun 9–13. ☎ 683 00230.

The Pantheon

History

The original temple was built apparently of travertine, during the third consulate of Agrippa (27 BC), son-in-law of Augustus, to commemorate the victory of Actium over Antony and Cleopatra. It was damaged by fire in AD 80, restored by Domitian, and struck by lightning and destroyed by another fire in 110. In spite of the dedicatory inscription on the pediment of the pronaos (*M. Agrippa, L.F. Cos. tertium fecit;* Marcus Agrippa, son of Lucius, consul for the third time, made it), it has been conclusively proved (by examination of the brick stamps) that the existing temple, including the pronaos, is not that of Agrippa, but a new one, built and probably also designed by Hadrian, of brick, on a larger scale and on different lines. This second building, begun in AD 118 or 119 and finished between AD 125 and 128, received and retained the name of Pantheon.

It was restored by Septimius Severus and Caracalla. Closed and abandoned under the first Christian emperors and pillaged by the Goths, the Pantheon was given to Boniface IV by the Byzantine emperor Phocas (whose column is in the Forum). Boniface IV consecrated it as a Christian church in 609. It was dedicated to Santa Maria ad Martyres—there was a legend that some 28 wagonloads of martyrs' bones had been transferred here from the catacombs. In 667 Constans II, emperor of Byzantium, on a 12-day visit to Rome, robbed the temple of what the Goths had left, and, in particular, stripped off the gilded roof-tiles (probably of bronze). Benedict II (684) restored it, Gregory III (735) roofed it with lead; in 1153 Anastasius IV built a palace beside it.

When the popes took up residence in Avignon the Pantheon served as a fortress in the struggles between the Colonna and the Orsini. In 1435 Eugenius IV isolated the building, and from then on it was the object of such veneration that the Roman Senator on taking office swore to preserve

'Maria Rotonda' intact for the pontiff, together with the relics and sacred treasures of the City. The monument was greatly admired during the Renaissance; Pius IV repaired the bronze door, and had it practically recast (1563). Urban VIII (Barberini), however, employed Bernini to add two clumsy turrets in front, which became popularly known as the 'ass-ears of Bernini'. Urban VIII also melted down the bronze ceiling of the portico to make the baldacchino at St Peter's and 80 cannon for Castel Sant' Angelo, an act of vandalism that prompted Pasquino's stinging gibe, 'Quod non fecerunt barbari fecerunt Barberini' (what the barbarians did not do, the Barberini did).

Alexander VII had the portico restored by Giuseppe Paglia (1662), and the level of the piazza lowered to provide a better view of the façade; Clement IX surrounded the portico with an iron railing (1668); Benedict XIV employed Paolo Posi (1747) to restore the interior and the atrium. The first two kings and the first queen of Italy are buried here. The incongruous turrets added by Bernini were removed in 1883.

The **portico** is nearly 34m wide and 15.5m deep, and has 16 monolithic Corinthian columns of red or grey granite, without flutings, each 12.5m high and 4.5m in circumference. The superb capitals and the bases are of white marble. The three columns on the east side are replacements, one by Urban VIII (1625), the others by Alexander VII (1655–67); the arms of these popes may be seen in the decoration of the capitals. Eight of the columns stand in front, and the others are disposed in four rows, so as to form three aisles, the central one leading to the bronze door, which dates from the time of Pius IV, and the others to the two great niches which may formerly have contained colossal statues of Augustus and Agrippa.

The visual impact of the domed **interior** is unforgettable. The use of light from the opening in the dome displays the genius of the architect. The height and diameter of the interior are the same—43.3m. The great **dome** has five rows of coffers diminishing in size towards the circular opening in the centre, which measures almost 9m across. The intricate design of the coffers is mainly responsible for the effect of space and light in the interior. They were probably ornamented with gilded bronze rosettes. The diameter of the dome, the largest masonry vault ever built, exceeds by more than 1m that of the dome of St Peter's. Its span, which contains no brick arches or vaults, begins at the level of the highest cornice seen on the outside of the building, rather than, as it appears in the interior, at the top of the attic stage.

The cylindrical wall is 6m thick; it contains seven great niches, or recesses, each, except the central apse, preceded by two Corinthian columns of giallo antico, and flanked by pilasters. The apse instead has two free-standing columns. Between the recesses, which originally contained statues, are eight shrines (aediculae), those flanking the apse and entrance with triangular pediments, and the others with segmented pediments. They are supported by two Corinthian columns in giallo antico, porphyry, or granite. Above the recesses is the entablature with a beautiful cornice, and still higher is an attic, unfortunately restored in 1747, making this stage more pronounced than was intended. Part of the original decoration can be seen over the recess to the right of the apse: between the rectangular openings (fitted with grilles) were shallow

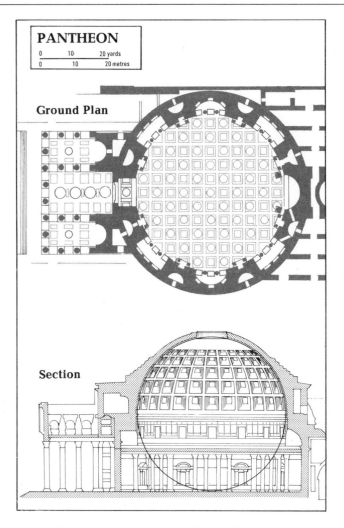

PANTHEON

| 0 | 10 | 20 yards |
| 0 | 10 | 20 metres |

Ground Plan

Section

pilasters of reddish marble alternating with three marble panels. More than half of the original coloured marble sheets on the walls are still in place. The floor, though restored, retains its original design.

Right side. In the first chapel: *Annunciation*, a fresco attributed to Melozzo da Forlì or Antoniazzo Romano, and two 17C marble angels. In the aedicule: 14C fresco of the *Coronation of the Virgin*. Second chapel: tomb of Vittorio Emanuele II, first king of Italy (died 9 January 1878), designed by Manfredo Manfredi; third chapel: 15C *Madonna and Saints*. In the main **apse**, above the high altar is a 7C icon of the *Virgin and Child*.

Left side. In the third chapel: 16C crucifix and (right) a monument by Thorvaldsen to Cardinal Consalvi (died 1824), secretary of Pius VII, who repre-

sented the Holy See at the Congress of Vienna. Third aedicule: **Tomb of Raphael**, inscribed with the famous distich of Bembo, translated by Pope in his Epitaph on Sir Godfrey Kneller ('Living, great Nature feared he might outvie Her works, and dying, fears herself may die'). On the altar is the statue of the *Madonna del Sasso*, by Lorenzetto, probably with the help of Raffaello da Montelupo, from Raphael's original design. The bronze bust is by De Fabris. Below the empty niche on the right is the short epitaph of Maria Bibbiena, niece of Cardinal Dovizi da Bibbiena, who was to have married Raphael but predeceased him.

Second chapel: tomb of Umberto I (who was assassinated at Monza on 29 July 1900), designed by Giuseppe Sacconi. Below Umberto's tomb is that of Margherita di Savoia, first queen of Italy (died 5 January 1926). Among other artists buried in the Pantheon are Giovanni da Udine, Perino del Vaga, Taddeo Zuccari, Annibale Carracci, and Baldassarre Peruzzi.

In Via della Palombella, attached to the back of the back of the Pantheon, can be seen remains of another Roman structure, once called the 'Basilica of Neptune' and attributed to Agrippa. It has similarities to the pronaos and is now known to date from Hadrian's time, but its purpose is unclear.

In **Piazza della Rotonda** is a fountain (1575), on a model of Giacomo della Porta, surmounted by an obelisk of Rameses the Great, formerly belonging to the Isaeum (see below) and erected here in 1711.

Piazza Minerva contains a bizarre but delightful work by Bernini (1667), a marble elephant supporting a small obelisk which belonged to the Isaeum Campense, or Temple of Isis, that formerly stood nearby. Other relics from the temple are in the Museo Capitolino, in Piazza dei Cinquecento, and in the Egyptian Museum in the Vatican. The hieroglyphic inscription on the obelisk relates to Apries, the last of the independent Pharaohs of Egypt (the Hophrah of the Bible), who was the ally of Zedekiah, king of Judah, against Nebuchadnezzar (6C BC).

Santa Maria sopra Minerva

Santa Maria sopra Minerva (Pl. 2; 6; closed 12–16) stands on the site of a small oratory probably built here before AD 800 on the ruins of a Temple of Minerva. It was rebuilt in 1280 by the Dominicans who modelled it on their church (Santa Maria Novella) in Florence (according to Vasari it was by the same architects, Fra Sisto and Ristoro). It was altered and over-restored in the Gothic style in 1848–55. On the right side of the simple façade (1453) small marble plaques register the heights reached by floods on the Tiber before it was canalised.

In the **interior** (coin-operated lights in some chapels) the vault, the rose-windows, and the excessively colourful decorations date from the 19C restoration. On the right of the central door is the tomb of Nerone Diotisalvi, a Florentine exile (died 1482), and, on the right of the south door, that of Virginia Pucci Ridolfi (1567), the latter with a fine bust by an unknown Florentine.

South aisle. By the first chapel, with an altarpiece by Baciccia, tomb of the archivist Castalio, with a fine portrait. The second chapel was decorated by Lazzaro Baldi in the late 17C. The third chapel has vault frescoes by Girolamo Muziano. The fourth chapel was designed by Carlo Maderno. The altarpiece of the *Annunciation* is by Antoniazzo Romano (1500), with Cardinal Juan de

Torquemada (uncle of Tomás de Torquemada, the inquisitor) presenting three poor girls to the Virgin; this commemorates the Confraternity of the Annunziata, founded in 1460 to provide dowries for penniless girls. On the left, tomb of Urban VII, by Ambrogio Buonvicino.

The fifth chapel has a frescoed ceiling by Cherubino Alberti, and an altarpiece of the *Institution of the Eucharist*, by Barocci. At the sides are the tombs of the parents of Clement VIII, by Giacomo della Porta, and (in a niche to the left) a statue of Clement VIII. Some scholars have recently attributed the statue of St Sebastian in a niche on the right wall of the chapel to Michelangelo as a model for his Christ (see below); it seems to have been finished by Nicolas Cordier. Sixth chapel: on the right, tomb of Bishop Juan Diaz de Coca (1477), by Andrea Bregno, with a fresco attributed to Melozzo da Forlì; on the left, tomb of Benedetto Sopranzi, Bishop of Nicosia (died 1495), by the school of Bregno.

South transept. First chapel: wooden crucifix (early 15C). The **Cappella Carafa** is preceded by a fine marble arch (attributed to Giuliano da Maiano), with a beautiful balustrade. It contains celebrated **frescoes* by Filippino Lippi (1489; beautifully restored in 1993). On the right wall, below: *St Thomas confounding the heretics*, the central figures being Arius and Sabellius (the two youths in the right-hand group are probably the future Medici popes, Leo X and Clement VII, both buried in this church). In the lunette above is *St Thomas Aquinas in prayer*, and in the vault, *the Sibyls*. On the altar wall: *Assumption* (with a splendid group of angels) and altarpiece of the *Annunciation, with St Thomas Aquinas presenting Cardinal Olivieri Carafa to the Virgin*, also by Filippino. On the left wall: monument of Paul IV (died 1559) by Giacomo and Tommaso Cassignola, from a design by Pirro Ligorio.

To the left of this chapel: ***tomb of Guillaume Durand** (died 1296), bishop of Mende, by Giovanni di Cosma, with a beautiful 13C mosaic of the Madonna and Child. Third chapel: Carlo Maratta, Madonna and Saints. Fourth chapel: frescoed ceiling by Marcello Venusti; on the right, tomb of Cardinal Capranica (1458).

Choir. At the foot of the steps, on the left, is ***Christ bearing the Cross** by Michelangelo (1514–21), commissioned at a cost of 200 ducats by Metello Vari and Pietro Castellani. The bronze drapery is a later addition. Under the 19C high altar lies the body of St Catherine of Siena (see below). In the apse are the tombs of Leo X (left) and Clement VII, designed by Antonio Sangallo the Younger, with statues by Raffaello da Montelupo and Nanni di Baccio Bigio respectively. In the pavement is the slab-tomb of Cardinal Pietro Bembo (1547), secretary to Pope Leo X from 1512 to 1520, and friend of Michelangelo, Raphael, and Ariosto.

North transept. To the left of the choir, in a passageway which serves as an exit, are several large monuments, including those of Cardinal Michele Bonelli (Alexandrinus), by Giacomo della Porta, and of Cardinal Domenico Pimentel, designed by Bernini. Surrounded by a bronze fence (1975) is the **tomb-slab of Fra Angelico, attributed to Isaia da Pisa. The painter died in the convent here in 1455, and the charming epitaph was composed by Pope Nicholas V. In the second chapel to the left of the choir, is a 15C altarpiece (a standard) of the *Madonna and Child*, attributed to Fra Angelico. The tomb of Giovanni Arberini (died c 1470) is by a Tuscan sculptor (Agostino di Duccio?), who incorporated a splendid *bas-relief of Hercules and the lion, probably a Roman copy of an original Greek work of the 5C BC. To the left is the entrance to the 17C sacristy,

behind which is the room in which St Catherine of Siena died in 1380; it was brought here from Via di Santa Chiara by Cardinal Barberini. The frescoes, poorly preserved, are by Antoniazzo Romano and his school (1482).

At the end of this transept is the Cappella di San Domenico, with the monument of Benedict XIII (died 1730), with sculptures by Pietro Bracci. At the corner of the nave and transept is the charming small tomb of Andrea Bregno (1421–1506). On the second nave pillar is the tomb of Maria Raggi, a colourful early work by Bernini.

North aisle. Between the fourth and third chapels: tomb of Giovanni Vigevano (died 1630) with a bust by Bernini (c 1617). Third chapel: tiny altarpiece (*the Redeemer*), attributed to Perugino or to Pinturicchio; on the right, statue of St Sebastian, attributed to Michele Marini; on the left, St John the Baptist, by Ambrogio Buonvicino; against the side-walls, tombs of Benedetto and Agostino Maffei, attributed to Luigi Capponi (15C). Second chapel: tomb of Gregorio Naro, showing the cardinal kneeling at a prie-dieu, has recently been attributed to Bernini. In the first chapel is a bust of Girolamo Bottigella, perhaps by Iacopo Sansovino. Near the door is the tomb of Francesco Tornabuoni (1480), by Mino da Fiesole, and above is that of Cardinal Tebaldi (1466), by Andrea Bregno and Giovanni Dalmata.

The monastery (no adm.) was once the headquarters of the Dominicans, and where Galileo was tried (1633). In the **cloister** are two funerary monuments attributed to Andrea Bregno and the **Sala dei Papi** with a colossal statue of the Madonna and Child, an unfinished work attributed to Bernini. A small museum has been closed indefinitely.

The Dominicans were left a library by Cardinal Girolamo Casanate which they opened in the convent in 1701. The **Biblioteca Casanatense** (now entered at 52 Via S. Ignazio) specialises in theological texts and works on the history of Rome (350,000 vols).

From the piazza, the narrow Via dei Cestari (with a number of shops selling liturgical articles) runs south towards the busy Corso Vittorio Emanuele. On the right in Via dell'Arco della Ciambella, part of the circular wall of the central hall of the **Baths of Agrippa** is charmingly incorporated into the street architecture. These were the first public baths in the city, begun by Agrippa in 29 BC, and restored by Hadrian. The brick-faced concrete dates from the 3C. Opposite, Via della Pigna leads past the 16C Palazzo Maffei Marescotti to a little piazza in front of the Baroque church of **San Giovanni della Pigna** (usually closed; with interesting tomb slabs inside the entrance wall). At a house here (No. 6) Mussolini met Cardinal Gasparri in 1923 to initiate discussions on the Concordat. Via del Gesù (with a beautiful Renaissance doorway at No. 85) leads down to Palazzo Altieri (1650–60; interesting courtyards) on the traffic-ridden Piazza del Gesù.

The Gesù

The Gesù (Pl. 3; 6; closed 12–16), or the church of the *Santissimo Nome di Gesù*, is the principal Jesuit church in Rome and the prototype of the sumptuous style to which the Order has given its name. It was built between 1568 and 1575 at the expense of Alessandro Farnese. Both the façade (by Giacomo della Porta), cleaned in 1993, and the interior (by Vignola) are important to the subsequent

I SIGNORI VISITATORI SONO TENUTI A
PRENDERE VISIONE DEL REGOLAMENTO
E AD OSSERVARNE LE NORME.

IL PRESENTE BIGLIETTO VA CONSERVATO ED ESIBITO
AGLI ADDETTI CHE NE FACCIANO RICHIESTA

PONTIFICIA COMMISSIONE
DI ARCHEOLOGIA SACRA

BIGLIETTO D'INGRESSO

ALLE CATACOMBE
DI S. PRISCILLA

27699

PONTIFICIA COMMISSIONE
DI ARCHEOLOGIA SACRA

BIGLIETTO D'INGRESSO
ALLE CATACOMBE
DI S. PRISCILLA

№ 27700

I SIGNORI VISITATORI SONO TENUTI A
PRENDERE VISIONE DEL REGOLAMENTO
E AD OSSERVARNE LE NORME.

IL PRESENTE BIGLIETTO VA CONSERVATO ED ESIBITO
AGLI ADDETTI CHE NE FACCIANO RICHIESTA

Torquemada (uncle of Tomás de Torquemada, the inquisitor) presenting three poor girls to the Virgin; this commemorates the Confraternity of the Annunziata, founded in 1460 to provide dowries for penniless girls. On the left, tomb of Urban VII, by Ambrogio Buonvicino.

The fifth chapel has a frescoed ceiling by Cherubino Alberti, and an altarpiece of the *Institution of the Eucharist*, by Barocci. At the sides are the tombs of the parents of Clement VIII, by Giacomo della Porta, and (in a niche to the left) a statue of Clement VIII. Some scholars have recently attributed the statue of St Sebastian in a niche on the right wall of the chapel to Michelangelo as a model for his Christ (see below); it seems to have been finished by Nicolas Cordier. Sixth chapel: on the right, tomb of Bishop Juan Diaz de Coca (1477), by Andrea Bregno, with a fresco attributed to Melozzo da Forlì; on the left, tomb of Benedetto Sopranzi, Bishop of Nicosia (died 1495), by the school of Bregno.

South transept. First chapel: wooden crucifix (early 15C). The **Cappella Carafa** is preceded by a fine marble arch (attributed to Giuliano da Maiano), with a beautiful balustrade. It contains celebrated *****frescoes** by Filippino Lippi (1489; beautifully restored in 1993). On the right wall, below: *St Thomas confounding the heretics*, the central figures being Arius and Sabellius (the two youths in the right-hand group are probably the future Medici popes, Leo X and Clement VII, both buried in this church). In the lunette above is *St Thomas Aquinas in prayer*, and in the vault, *the Sibyls*. On the altar wall: *Assumption* (with a splendid group of angels) and altarpiece of the *Annunciation, with St Thomas Aquinas presenting Cardinal Olivieri Carafa to the Virgin*, also by Filippino. On the left wall: monument of Paul IV (died 1559) by Giacomo and Tommaso Cassignola, from a design by Pirro Ligorio.

To the left of this chapel: *****tomb of Guillaume Durand** (died 1296), bishop of Mende, by Giovanni di Cosma, with a beautiful 13C mosaic of the Madonna and Child. Third chapel: Carlo Maratta, Madonna and Saints. Fourth chapel: frescoed ceiling by Marcello Venusti; on the right, tomb of Cardinal Capranica (1458).

Choir. At the foot of the steps, on the left, is *****Christ bearing the Cross** by Michelangelo (1514–21), commissioned at a cost of 200 ducats by Metello Vari and Pietro Castellani. The bronze drapery is a later addition. Under the 19C high altar lies the body of St Catherine of Siena (see below). In the apse are the tombs of Leo X (left) and Clement VII, designed by Antonio Sangallo the Younger, with statues by Raffaello da Montelupo and Nanni di Baccio Bigio respectively. In the pavement is the slab-tomb of Cardinal Pietro Bembo (1547), secretary to Pope Leo X from 1512 to 1520, and friend of Michelangelo, Raphael, and Ariosto.

North transept. To the left of the choir, in a passageway which serves as an exit, are several large monuments, including those of Cardinal Michele Bonelli (Alexandrinus), by Giacomo della Porta, and of Cardinal Domenico Pimentel, designed by Bernini. Surrounded by a bronze fence (1975) is the *****tomb-slab of Fra Angelico, attributed to Isaia da Pisa. The painter died in the convent here in 1455, and the charming epitaph was composed by Pope Nicholas V. In the second chapel to the left of the choir, is a 15C altarpiece (a standard) of the *Madonna and Child*, attributed to Fra Angelico. The tomb of Giovanni Arberini (died c 1470) is by a Tuscan sculptor (Agostino di Duccio?), who incorporated a splendid *****bas-relief of Hercules and the lion, probably a Roman copy of an original Greek work of the 5C BC. To the left is the entrance to the 17C sacristy,

behind which is the room in which St Catherine of Siena died in 1380; it was brought here from Via di Santa Chiara by Cardinal Barberini. The frescoes, poorly preserved, are by Antoniazzo Romano and his school (1482).

At the end of this transept is the Cappella di San Domenico, with the monument of Benedict XIII (died 1730), with sculptures by Pietro Bracci. At the corner of the nave and transept is the charming small tomb of Andrea Bregno (1421–1506). On the second nave pillar is the tomb of Maria Raggi, a colourful early work by Bernini.

North aisle. Between the fourth and third chapels: tomb of Giovanni Vigevano (died 1630) with a bust by Bernini (c 1617). Third chapel: tiny altarpiece (*the Redeemer*), attributed to Perugino or to Pinturicchio; on the right, statue of St Sebastian, attributed to Michele Marini; on the left, St John the Baptist, by Ambrogio Buonvicino; against the side-walls, tombs of Benedetto and Agostino Maffei, attributed to Luigi Capponi (15C). Second chapel: tomb of Gregorio Naro, showing the cardinal kneeling at a prie-dieu, has recently been attributed to Bernini. In the first chapel is a bust of Girolamo Bottigella, perhaps by Iacopo Sansovino. Near the door is the tomb of Francesco Tornabuoni (1480), by Mino da Fiesole, and above is that of Cardinal Tebaldi (1466), by Andrea Bregno and Giovanni Dalmata.

The monastery (no adm.) was once the headquarters of the Dominicans, and where Galileo was tried (1633). In the **cloister** are two funerary monuments attributed to Andrea Bregno and the **Sala dei Papi** with a colossal statue of the Madonna and Child, an unfinished work attributed to Bernini. A small museum has been closed indefinitely.

The Dominicans were left a library by Cardinal Girolamo Casanate which they opened in the convent in 1701. The **Biblioteca Casanatense** (now entered at 52 Via S. Ignazio) specialises in theological texts and works on the history of Rome (350,000 vols).

From the piazza, the narrow Via dei Cestari (with a number of shops selling liturgical articles) runs south towards the busy Corso Vittorio Emanuele. On the right in Via dell'Arco della Ciambella, part of the circular wall of the central hall of the **Baths of Agrippa** is charmingly incorporated into the street architecture. These were the first public baths in the city, begun by Agrippa in 29 BC, and restored by Hadrian. The brick-faced concrete dates from the 3C. Opposite, Via della Pigna leads past the 16C Palazzo Maffei Marescotti to a little piazza in front of the Baroque church of **San Giovanni della Pigna** (usually closed; with interesting tomb slabs inside the entrance wall). At a house here (No. 6) Mussolini met Cardinal Gasparri in 1923 to initiate discussions on the Concordat. Via del Gesù (with a beautiful Renaissance doorway at No. 85) leads down to Palazzo Altieri (1650–60; interesting courtyards) on the traffic-ridden Piazza del Gesù.

The Gesù

The Gesù (Pl. 3; 6; closed 12–16), or the church of the *Santissimo Nome di Gesù*, is the principal Jesuit church in Rome and the prototype of the sumptuous style to which the Order has given its name. It was built between 1568 and 1575 at the expense of Alessandro Farnese. Both the façade (by Giacomo della Porta), cleaned in 1993, and the interior (by Vignola) are important to the subsequent

development of the design of Baroque churches in Rome. The cupola planned by Vignola was completed by Della Porta.

The Gesù

The heavily decorated **interior** (being restored) has a longitudinal plan, with an aisleless nave and lateral chapels. On the **vault** is a *fresco (recently restored) of the *Triumph of the Name of Jesus*, a remarkably original work, with marvellous effects of foreshortening, by Baciccia. The frescoes of the cupola and the tribune are by the same artist. He also designed the stucco decoration, executed by Antonio Raggi and Leonardo Retti. The marble decoration of the nave dates from 1858–61.

South side. The first chapel has an altarpiece and frescoes by Agostino Ciampelli. In the third chapel, the altarpiece, vault and walls were all painted by Federico Zuccari (the lunettes and pendentives are by Ventura Salimbeni). The four marble festoons incorporated in the decoration are supposed to have come from the Baths of Titus. The elegant **sacristy** is by Girolamo Rainaldi.

South transept. Altarpiece from a sketch by Pietro da Cortona with the *Death of St Francis Xavier*, by Carlo Maratta. The **high altar** and presbytery were redesigned in 1840 by Antonio Sarti. Over the high altar, sumptuously decorated with coloured marbles, is *The Circumcision*, by Alessandro Capalti (1842). On the left, a bust of Cardinal Roberto Bellarmine, by Bernini, was placed in a Neo-classical setting after the tomb was destroyed during the rebuilding in the 19C. The two pretty little circular domed chapels on either side of the main apse were decorated by Giuseppe Valeriani (1584–88).

North transept (light on left). *Altar-tomb of St Ignatius, by Andrea del Pozzo and others (1695–1700), resplendent with marble and bronze; the columns are encrusted with lapis lazuli and their bronze decorations are by Andrea Bertoni. The statue of St Ignatius is a copy by Adamo Tadolini of the original by Legros (melted down during the French Revolution). Above is a group of the Trinity by Leonardo Retti with a terrestrial globe formed from a splendid block of lapis lazuli, the largest known. In front of the altar is a magnificent balustrade, and at the sides are marble groups: *Religion Triumphing over Heresy*, by Legros (right), and *Barbarians Adoring the Faith*, by Jean Baptiste Théodon (left).

North side. Third chapel: altarpiece of the *Holy Trinity* by Francesco Bassano, and *Baptism of Christ* (right wall) by Ventura Salimbeni. The second chapel has vault frescoes by Pomarancio, 17C paintings by Giovanni Francesco Romanelli, and interesting sculptures. The first chapel also has its vault frescoed by Pomarancio and two paintings by Francesco Mola. The singing of a Te Deum in

this church annually on 31 December is a magnificent traditional ceremony.

To the right of the Gesù's façade, at No. 45 Piazza del Gesù is the entrance to the rooms where St Ignatius lived from 1544 to his death in 1556. They have recently been restored, and contain mementoes, paintings and documents, and are open Mon–Sat 16–18; fest. 10–12 (entrance is free). An adjoining corridor was decorated by Andrea Pozzo c 1680.

Via d'Aracoeli leads from Piazza del Gesù towards the Capitol: off it, to the right, is Via delle Botteghe Oscure (with the headquarters of the former Italian Communist Party, now called the Partito Democratico della Sinistra). Nearby are the remains of a **temple** (seen from the railings), probably a Temple of Nymphs, dating from the 1C BC. Palazzo Paganica on the south side of this road was purchased in 1983 by the Italian State and excavations are in progress beneath it and the adjoining site (entrance at 6C Via Caetani). Remains of the small **Theatre of Balbus** inaugurated in 13 BC have been uncovered, adjoined to the west by a cryptoporticus known as the **Crypta Balbi**. Later buildings also excavated here include the medieval church of Santa Maria, and a Renaissance monastery. The interesting remains may one day be opened to the public. In Via Caetani a plaque marks the place where the body of the Prime Minister Aldo Moro was abandoned by his murderers in 1978.

Via delle Botteghe Oscure ends at **Largo Argentina**, a traffic-ridden square with an impressive group of **four Republican temples**, known as the *Area Sacra di Largo Argentina*. The site was demolished in 1926–29 for a new building which, after the temples had been discovered and excavated, was never built. The ruins, now inhabited by cats, are well seen from the railings outside.

All the temples face a courtyard to the east paved with travertine. It is not yet known with certainty to whom they were dedicated, so they are usually identified by letters. The **first temple** ('A') is peripteral and hexastyle; most of the tufa columns and stylobate are preserved. In the Middle Ages the church of St Nicholas was built over it; the apses of the church (otherwise demolished) may still be seen. The **second temple** ('B'), the most recent, is circular, and six columns survive, as well as the original flight of steps and the altar. A podium behind this temple near Via di Torre Argentina, almost certainly belongs to the Curia Pompei where Julius Caesar was murdered. The **third temple** ('C'), oldest of the four, was built at a lower level; it dates from the end of the 4C or the beginning of the 3C BC. In the Imperial era the cella was rebuilt and the columns and podium covered with stucco. In 1935 the altar, with an inscription relating to c 180 BC, was discovered; even this was a replacement of an older altar. The **fourth temple** ('D'), in travertine, is the largest; it has not been completely excavated as part of it is under Via Florida, to the south. During the excavations the medieval **Torre del Papito** here was restored and isolated.

To the north of the square, on Via dei Cestari, is the church of the **Stimmate**, rebuilt at the beginning of the 18C by Giovanni Battista Contini. It contains paintings by Francesco Trevisani, including the high altarpiece of *St Francis Receiving the Stigmata* (1714). On the west side of Largo Argentina is the **Teatro Argentina** dating from 1730, and the most important theatre in Rome during the 18C. The façade is by Pietro Holl (1826). Here in 1816 was held the first performance of Rossini's *Barber of Seville*, and in 1851 that of Verdi's *Rigoletto*. The theatre is now noted for drama productions—'Teatro di Roma' is the resi-

dent company. It has a small museum (admission by appointment, ☎ 6840001).

On the right of the theatre, Via del Sudario leads out of the square past the handsome south façade of Palazzo Caffarelli Vidoni, attributed to Lorenzo Lotti (c 1515). Opposite is the delightful **Casa del Burcardo**, built in 1503 for Bishop Hans Burchard or Burckhardt. He was author of a remarkable account of the papal court under Innocent VIII and Alexander VI, and called the house the 'Torre Argentina', which in turn became the name of the piazza. The back doors of the Teatro Argentina (see above) open on to the courtyard. It now houses a theatrical museum and a library (both closed indefinitely). The **Chiesa del Sudario** (1604) was the court church of the House of Savoy from 1871 to 1946. The façade is by Carlo Rainaldi, and inside (closed) are late 19C works by Cesare Maccari.

Via del Sudario ends in the little Piazza Vidoni where a Roman statue called '*Abate Luigi*' (one of Rome's 'talking' statues) has been placed against the side wall of the church of **SANT'ANDREA DELLA VALLE** (Pl. 3; 6; entrance to right). It was begun in 1591 by Fra Francesco Grimaldi, and continued by Carlo Maderno, who crowned it with a fine dome, the highest in Rome after that of St Peter's. The façade (1665) is by Carlo Rainaldi. The aisleless **interior** (open 7.30–12, 16.30–19.30) has a high barrel-vault and spacious apse. Inspired by the Gesù, it gives the impression of a sumptuous reception hall rather than a house of prayer.

South side. The first chapel, by Carlo Fontana, has green marble columns and fine sculptures by Ercole Antonio Raggi. The design of the second chapel (Cappella Strozzi) shows the influence of Michelangelo and contains reproductions in bronze of his Pietà and of his statues of Leah and Rachel from the projected tomb of Julius II. The third chapel has a Neo-classical monument attributed to Giuseppe de Fabris and Rinaldo Rinaldi. At the east end of the nave, high up, are similar monuments of two popes of the Piccolomini family: on the right, Pius III (died 1503) attributed to Francesco Ferrucci and his son Sebastiano; on the left Pius II (died 1464) attributed to Paolo Taccone and a follower of Andrea Bregno. In the little chapel on the right of the presbytery is a 17C Crucifix.

In the **dome** high up above the crossing is the *Glory of Paradise*, by Lanfranco; in the pendentives, the Evangelists by Domenichino (1623). Domenichino also designed the splendid **presbytery and apse** (restored in 1994) and painted the Six Virtues and the scenes from the life of St Andrew; the gigantic frescoes in the tribune are by Mattia Preti. The sacristy has 17C decorations. In the **north transept** is an altar by Cesare Bazzani (1912) in the Baroque style.

North side. Third chapel: altarpiece of *St Sebastian* by Giovanni de' Vecchi. Second chapel: altarpiece by Francesco Manno (early 19C). The first chapel, frescoed by Passignano, has four good sculptures: on the left, *Mary Magdalene* by Cristoforo Stati, and *St John the Baptist* by Pietro Bernini; and on the right, *St John the Evangelist* by Ambrogio Bonvicino and *Santa Marta* by Francesco Mochi.

Opposite the church façade, at the beginning of Corso del Rinascimento, is a fountain by Carlo Maderno decorated with an eagle and a dragon. Corso Vittorio Emanuele (Pl. 3; 5, 6), now one of the main traffic arteries of Rome running

from Piazza Venezia to the Tiber, dates from 1876. It continues past Palazzo Massimo alle Colonne, skilfully set in a narrow, irregular site, by Baldassarre Peruzzi (1532–36). The convex façade, much blackened by the polluted air, follows the line of the cavea of the Odeon of Domitian which stood here. The beautiful portico is decorated with stuccoes. The palace has two courtyards: one a charming Renaissance work with a frescoed loggia, and a Baroque fountain, and the second (in very poor repair) with 17C decorations. The interior is being slowly restored, and a fresco has been uncovered which may be the work of Giulio Romano. In Piazza dei Massimi, behind the palace (reached from Corso Rinascimento) is the so-called 'Palazzo Istoriato', or Palazzetto Massimi with remains of its painted façade (1523; by the school of Daniele da Volterra). Here Pannartz and Sweynheim transferred their press (from Subiaco) in 1467 and issued the first books printed in Rome. The marble cipollino column set up in the piazza belonged to the Odeon of Domitian (see above).

The Corso widens at a little piazza in front of the church of **San Pantaleo** (open only early in the morning) dating from 1216. It was rebuilt in 1681 by Antonio de Rossi and preserves its 17C interior with a vault fresco by Filippo Gherardi. The façade was added by Giuseppe Valadier in 1806.

The huge **Palazzo Braschi** by Cosimo Morelli (after 1792) houses the **Museo di Roma** (Pl. 2; 8) on four floors. This has been closed for restoration since 1988, although important exhibitions are occasionally held on the ground floor.

The museum was founded in 1930 to illustrate the history and life of Rome from the Middle Ages to the present day. Many of the works of art come from demolished buildings. At the foot of the magnificent staircase attributed to Valadier (1802–04) and decorated by Luigi Acquisti, is a colossal statue of Christ and St John by Francesco Mochi. The collection includes detached frescoes by Cigoli and Lo Spagna, portraits of illustrious members (including Isaac Newton) of the Accademia dell'Arcadia (see p 281), paintings by Pompeo Batoni, Baciccia, Andrea Sacchi, Pietro da Cortona, Guido Reni, Giovanni Paolo Pannini, and Gavin Hamilton. It also has sculptures by Francesco Mochi, Canova and Pietro Tenerani, and mosaics from the old façade of St Peter's. The second floor rooms have ceilings decorated in the early 19C by Liborio Coccetti.

Via di San Pantaleo, which skirts the left side of Palazzo Braschi, ends in Piazza Pasquino. Here is a fragment of a marble group representing Menelaus with the body of Patroclus, a copy of a Hellenistic work of the Pergamene school which may once have decorated the Stadium of Domitian (see below). This famous statue has been known as **Pasquino** since it was placed here in 1501. It became the custom to attach witty or caustic comments on topical subjects to the pedestal of the statue. The credit for originating this method of public satire was ascribed to a certain Pasquino, a tailor in the vicinity, hence the origin of the term 'pasquinade'. There were other 'talking statues' in the city; as Stendhal noted on his visit to Rome in 1816: 'What the people of Rome desire above all else is a chance to show their strong contempt for the powers that control their destiny, and to laugh at their expense: hence the dialogues between "Pasquino" and "Marforio"'. Many printing houses and bookshops were opened in the vicinity of the piazza.

From Piazza Pasquino the narrow Via del Governo Vecchio, an ancient papal thoroughfare with many traces of the early Renaissance, leads west. On the

right (No. 39) is **Palazzo Nardini** (or Palazzo del Governo Vecchio), built in 1473 by Cardinal Stefano Nardini, made Governor of Rome by Paul II. It has a splendid Renaissance portal. Opposite is the remarkable **Palazzo Turci** (1500), once attributed to Bramante.

Piazza Navona

From Piazza Pasquino Via di Pasquino leads into Piazza Navona (Pl. 2; 6) which occupies the site of the Stadium of Domitian.

> Its form, preserving the dimensions of the Roman building which could probably hold some 30,000 spectators, represents a remarkable survival within the modern city. The name, too, is derived from the athletic games, the 'Agoni Capitolini' held here after the stadium was inaugurated in AD 86. In the Middle Ages the piazza was called the 'Campus Agonis'; hence 'agone', 'n'agona', and 'navona'. Historic festivals, jousts, and open-air sports took place here, and it was also used as a market place from 1477 until 1869. From the 17C to the late 19C the piazza was flooded every weekend in August, for the entertainment of the Romans (the nobles enjoyed the spectacle from their carriages).

During the Christmas festival, statuettes for the Christmas crib are sold here, and the fair and toy-market of the Befana, or Epiphany is held. In the total absence of wheeled traffic Piazza Navona remains the most animated square in Rome. It has several well-known cafés.

Three splendid fountains decorate the piazza. At the south end, the **Fontana del Moro** was designed by Giacomo della Porta in 1576, with sculptures by Taddeo Landini, Simone Moschino, Silla Longhi and Egidio della Riviera. In 1874 these were replaced by copies made by Luigi Amici, and in 1909

The Fontana dei Quattro Fiumi in Piazza Navona

the originals were moved to the Giardino del Lago in Villa Borghese (see p 174). The fountain was altered by Bernini in 1653 when he designed the central figure, known as 'Il Moro' (executed by Antonio Mari).

The central **Fontana dei Quattro Fiumi** is one of Bernini's most famous works. In the mass of rocks and grottoes are colossal allegorical figures of the rivers Danube, Ganges, Nile and Plate, representing Europe, Asia, Africa, and America, carved by Bernini's pupils, Antonio Raggi, Giacomo Antonio Fancelli, Claude Poussin, and Francesco Baratta. The tall obelisk was cut in Egypt and

brought to Rome by order of Domitian. It was moved here by Innocent X from the Circus of Maxentius and bears the names of Vespasian, Titus and Domitian in hieroglyphics. The popular story told to illustrate the rivalry between Bernini and Borromini—that the Nile is holding up an arm to block out the sight of Sant'Agnese—is apocryphal, since the fountain was finished in 1651 before Borromini started work on the church.

The fountain at the north end, representing Neptune struggling with a marine monster, Nereids and sea-horses, is by Antonio della Bitta and Gregorio Zappalà (1878). Remains of the north curve of the stadium, with the entrance gate, can be seen beneath the modern buildings north of the piazza, in Piazza di Tor Sanguigna.

On the west side of the piazza is **SANT'AGNESE IN AGONE**, an ancient church built on the ruins of the stadium which Christian tradition marks as the spot where St Agnes was exposed (see p 267). It was reconstructed by Girolamo and Carlo Rainaldi in 1652. The splendid concave **façade** which adds emphasis to the dome was begun by Borromini (1653–57). The lantern of the dome is by Carlo Rainaldi, and the twin bell-towers are by Giovanni Baratta and Antonio del Grande.

The small Baroque **interior** has an intricate Greek-cross plan in which a remarkable effect of spaciousness is provided by the cupola. The fresco on the dome is by Ciro Ferri and Sebastiano Corbellini; the pendentives are by Baciccia. Above the seven altars: 17C bas-reliefs or statues (including an antique statue of St Sebastian altered by Paolo Campi) take the place of paintings. The high altarpiece is a *Holy Family* by Domenico Guidi. Above the entrance is the monument by Giovanni Battista Maini of Innocent X, who is buried here. Beneath the church the Oratory of St Agnes, built before 800, survives (although poorly restored) in a vault of the Stadium of Domitian. It contains badly damaged 13C frescoes, and the last work of Alessandro Algardi, a bas-relief of the miracle of St Agnes.

To the south of the church is **Palazzo Pamphilj** (sometimes called Palazzo Doria) started by Girolamo Rainaldi, and completed by Borromini for Innocent X, in the mid-17C. It was later occupied by the sister-in-law of Innocent, the notorious Olimpia Maidalchini. It is now the Brazilian Embassy (for permission to visit write to Piazza Navona 14, Rome 00100; fax 686 7858).

In the interior the **Sala Palestrina** is a magnificent example of Borromini's secular architecture, using the minimum of surface decoration. The busts are by Alessandro Algardi. It has had an interesting history as a music room, since the first performance of the Concerti Grossi of Corelli took place here in the 17C. The State rooms overlooking Piazza Navona are decorated with delightful friezes, all painted between 1634 and 1671. They contains works by Andrea Camassei, Agostino Tassi, Gaspard Dughet, Giacinto Gemignani, and Giacinto Brandi. The long **Gallery** (designed by Borromini), has a magnificent fresco of the story of Aeneas by Pietro da Cortona. The charming papal bedroom also has a ceiling fresco by Cortona.

On the opposite side of the piazza, is the church of the **Madonna del Sacro Cuore**, formerly San Giacomo degli Spagnoli, which was rebuilt in 1450 and restored in 1879. The entrance from the piazza is by a side door at the east end. On the south side the choir-gallery is almost certainly by Pietro Torrigiani; the **chapel** off the north side is by Antonio da Sangallo the Younger.

Just off the northwest corner of the piazza, in the street of the same name, is the German church of **SANTA MARIA DELL'ANIMA** (Pl. 2; 6), rebuilt in 1500–23. The façade was possibly designed by Giuliano da Sangallo. Above the door is a cast of the Virgin attributed to Andrea Sansovino, a copy of a highly venerated *Madonna Between Two Souls in Purgatory*, which was formerly in the church and was the origin of its name. The original is kept in the sacristy.

The **interior** (entrance through a pretty little courtyard behind the church at 20 Vicolo della Pace, 8–19; fest. 8.30–12.30, 15–19) has an unusual plan, derived from late Gothic German churches. The paintings in the vault and on the walls are by Ludovico Seitz (1875–82), who also designed the window over the central door.

South side. First chapel: *San Benno* by Carlo Saraceni; second chapel: *Holy Family*, by Giacinto Gimignani, and two funerary monuments by Ercole Ferrata; third chapel: *Crucifix* by Giovanni Battista Montano, and 16C frescoes by Girolamo Siciolante da Sermoneta; fourth chapel: *Pietà*, by Lorenzetto and Nanni di Baccio Bigio, in imitation of Michelangelo.

In the **sanctuary**: *Holy Family with saints*, by Giulio Romano, over the high altar; on the right, the magnificent tomb of Adrian VI (died 1523; of Utrecht), designed by Baldassarre Peruzzi, with sculptures by Michelangelo Senese and Niccolò Tribolo; on the left, tomb of Karl Friedrich of Clèves (died 1575), by Gilles de Rivière and Nicolas d'Arras (a bas-relief from this tomb is in the corridor leading to the sacristy).

North side. Fourth chapel: *Descent from the Cross* and frescoes, by Francesco Salviati; third chapel: *Life of St Barbara*, frescoes by Michiel Coxie; first chapel: *Martyrdom of St Lambert*, by Carlo Saraceni.

In the peaceful little piazza here, in a delightful part of the city, is the beautiful church of **SANTA MARIA DELLA PACE** (Pl. 2; 6). It is closed for restoration but the courtyard is open for occasional concerts. The church was rebuilt by Sixtus IV (1480–84) to celebrate the successful outcome of the Pazzi conspiracy and victory over the Turks. There was also a popular legend that a miraculous image of the Virgin in the portico of the old church bled on being struck by a stone. The architect is believed to have been Baccio Pontelli. The church was partly rebuilt in 1611 and again later in the century by Alexander VII, under whose auspices the façade and beautiful semicircular porch with Tuscan columns were erected by Pietro da Cortona; his design

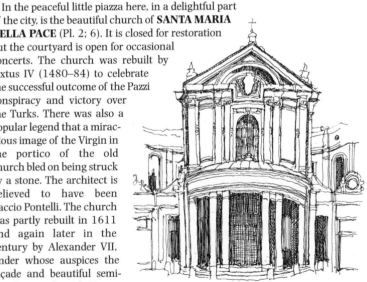

Santa Maria della Pace

of the delightful little piazza and the surrounding area was never completed.

The entrance is beyond the arch to the left of the façade, at 5 Via Arco della Pace. The **cloisters** are among Bramante's finest works in Rome (1504). They have two rows of arcades one above the other—columns of the upper row rise from the centres of the arches in the lower row. The tomb of Bishop Bocciaccio (1497) on the right is by the school of Luigi Capponi.

The **interior** consists of a domed octagon preceded by a simple rectangular nave. Above the arch of the first chapel on the **south side** are frescoes of *Sibyls by Raphael (c 1514), painted for Agostino Chigi, founder of the chapel. They represent (beginning on the left) the Cumaean, Persian, Phrygian, and Tiburtine Sibyls, to whom the future is being revealed by angels; their varying shades of awe and wonder are beautifully conveyed in look and gesture. The paintings were restored in 1816 by Palmaroli. Above them are four Prophets, by Timoteo Viti (Raphael's pupil): on the right, Daniel and David, on the left, Jonah and Hosea. On the altar, Deposition, a fine bronze by Cosimo Fancelli. The second chapel (Cesi) was designed by Antonio da Sangallo the Younger, and has remarkable marble decoration by Simone Mosca (1540–42). The ruined frescoes in the window lunette are by Rosso Fiorentino. The Cesi tombs and sculptures are by Vincenzo de' Rossi.

North side. First chapel: in the niche is a *fresco** of the Virgin, Saints Bridget and Catherine, and the donor Ferdinando Ponzetti, by Baldassarre Peruzzi, who also painted the small frescoes of Old Testament subjects on the vaulting of the niche. At the sides of the chapel are the little *tombs of the Ponzetti family** (1505 and 1509), with delicately carved decoration and four busts. Second chapel: altarpiece (much darkened) with Madonna and saints, by Marcello Venusti, perhaps from a design by Michelangelo.

Octagon. Above the high altar, by Carlo Maderno, is the highly venerated 15C image of the Madonna della Pace. The beautiful marble tabernacle in the chapel of the Crucifix (left) is attributed to Pasquale da Caravaggio. On the octagon, to the right of the high altar is Baldassarre Peruzzi's, *Presentation in the Temple*.

Off the other side of Piazza Navona (see above) Via di Sant'Agostino leads to the church of **SANT'AGOSTINO** (Pl. 2; 6), which was built for Cardinal d'Estouteville by Giacomo da Pietrasanta (1479–83). It is dedicated to St Augustine, author of the *Confessions*. The severely plain façade is one of the earliest of the Renaissance. The **interior** (open 7.45–12, 16.30–19.30), renovated by Luigi Vanvitelli (1750) contains good frescoes on the vault and nave by Pietro Gagliardi (1855), including five prophets on the nave pilasters which accompany the *Prophet Isaiah** (being restored) frescoed on the third pillar on the north side by Raphael. This was commissioned by the Humanist scholar Giovanni Goritz in 1512 for his funerary monument, and shows how much the painter was influenced by Michelangelo's frescoes in the Sistine Chapel. It was restored by Daniele da Volterra. Beneath it is a *Madonna and Child with St Anne*, sculpted from a single block of marble by Andrea Sansovino.

At the west end is the so-called *Madonna del Parto*, by Jacopo Sansovino (1521), a greatly venerated statue and the object of innumerable votive offerings. The two angels holding stoups at the west end are by Antonio Raggi.

South aisle. First chapel: paintings by Marcello Venusti; second chapel:

Madonna della Rosa, a copy by Avanzino Nucci of the original painting by Raphael, which was stolen from Loreto and subsequently disappeared. Third chapel: altarpiece by Giacinto Brandi, and two paintings by Pietro Locatelli. Fourth chapel, *Christ Giving the Keys to St Peter*, sculpted by Giovanni Battista Cotignola. Fifth chapel: 16C Crucifix.

South transept. Chapel of Sant'Agostino: altarpiece by Guercino and side panels by his school; 18C stuccoes, and Baroque tomb of Cardinal Renato Imperiali, by Paolo Posi. On the **high altar** (1628), with two angels designed by Bernini, is a Byzantine Madonna brought from Constantinople. In the chapel to the left of the choir is the tomb of St Monica (mother of St Augustine), by Isaia da Pisa, and vault frescoes attributed to Giovanni Battista Ricci. The next little chapel (seen through a gate) was decorated by Giovanni Lanfranco (1616–19). The chapel in the **north transept** (covered for restoration) has a marble group on the altar finished by Ercole Ferrata.

North aisle. Fifth chapel: altarpiece by Giacinto Brandi; fourth chapel: *St Apollonia*, by Girolamo Muziano; third chapel: altarpiece by Sebastiano Conca; second chapel, designed by Bernini, has a Crucifix by Ventura Salimbeni. In the first chapel: *Madonna di Loreto*, commissioned for this altar by Ermete Cavalletti from Caravaggio (light on right). This is one of the most beautiful paintings by Caravaggio in the city. In the little vestibule at the north door are Four Doctors by Isaia da Pisa, statues belonging to the tomb of St Monica, and a Crucifix by Luigi Capponi (15C).

In Via delle Coppelle, to the right off Via della Scrofa, is (No. 35) **Palazzo Baldassini**, a smaller version of Palazzo Farnese, by Antonio Sangallo the Younger (1514–23), with a handsome courtyard and loggia. Garibaldi lived here in 1875.

Via dei Pianellari skirts the left side of Sant'Agostino as far as Via dei Portoghesi. Here are a delightful 15C doorway and tower and, behind a pretty balustrade, the ornate façade of the 17C church of **Sant'Antonio dei Portoghesi**. The good Baroque interior (usually closed) has a painting (first left altar) of the Madonna and Saints by Antoniazzo Romano. Across Via della Scrofa, Via della Stelletta continues east to the piazza and church of **Santa Maria in Campo Marzio** (Pl. 2; 6). The church, of ancient foundation, was rebuilt in 1685 by Giovanni Antonio de' Rossi on a Greek-cross plan, with a good portico and court. Over the high altar is a Madonna, part of a triptych probably of the 12C–13C. Since 1920 the church has belonged to the Roman Catholic Patriarchate of Antioch of the Syrians (services on fest.).

To the south, reached by a street of the same name is the church of **Santa Maria Maddalena** with a Rococo façade (1735; over-restored in 1991) by Giuseppe Sardi. The pretty **interior** (1695–99), open 7.30–11.45, 17–19.45; fest. 9–11, on an original plan, was designed by Giovanni Antonio de'Rossi and Giulio Carlo Quadrio. The statues of Virtues in the nave are attributed to Paolo Morelli, except for the first and third on the left which are by Carlo Monaldi, and by Giuseppe Raffaelli. The vault is frescoed by Michelangelo Cerruti (1732) and the cupola by Stefano Parrocel (1739). The confessionals are by Giuseppe Palma (1762).

South side. Second chapel: 16C painting of the Madonna and Child; third chapel: elaborate marble altar with a vault fresco by Sebastiano Conca. By the

side door is a fine wooden statue of Mary Magdalene (15C). Over the high altar, *Mary Magdalene in Prayer* by Michele Rocca and, above, a fresco by Aureliano Milani. **North side**. Third chapel: *St Nicholas of Bari* by Baciccio; second chapel: *St Laurence Giustiniani in Adoration of the Child* by Luca Giordano (1704). The elaborate cantoria and organ date from the early 18C. The sacristy (1741) of unique design is entered from the left aisle.

Via delle Colonnelle (which passes the right side of the church dating from the late 17C) leads to Piazza Capranica, which is dominated by **Palazzo Capranica**, partly Gothic and partly Renaissance in style. The tower has a delightful loggia. From the Maddalena, Via del Pantheon (with a hotel at No. 63 on the left where Ariosto stayed in 1513; plaque) returns to the Pantheon (see above).

From Sant'Agostino, Via della Scrofa continues south past the church of **SAN LUIGI DEI FRANCESI** (Pl. 2; 6; closed 12–15.30 and Thur afternoon), the French national church (1518–89). The façade, attributed to Giacomo della Porta, with two superimposed orders of equal height, was over-restored in 1977. The **interior** was heavily encrusted with marble and decorated with white and gilded stucco on a design by Antonio Dérizet (1756–64).

South aisle. Against the first pillar is the monument to the French who fell in the siege of Rome in 1849. Second chapel: ***frescoes** (damaged by restoration) by Domenichino—to the right, *St Cecilia distributing garments to the poor*, and *St Cecilia and her betrothed crowned by angels*; to the left, *St Cecilia refusing to sacrifice to idols*, and *her martyrdom*; on the ceiling, *St Cecilia in Paradise*. The altarpiece is a copy by Guido Reni of Raphael's *St Cecilia* at Bologna. Fourth chapel: altarpiece by Iacopino del Conte, *Oath of Clovis*; to the right, *Army of Clovis*, by Pellegrino Tibaldi; to the left, *Baptism of Clovis*, by Girolamo Sermoneta.

The **high altarpiece** is an *Assumption of the Virgin* by Francesco Bassano. **North aisle**. The fifth chapel (coin-operated light on right) contains three famous and very well preserved ***paintings by Caravaggio** (1597–1602): left, *Calling of St Matthew*; right, *St Matthew's Martyrdom*, and (altarpiece) *St Matthew and the Angel*. On the first pillar is a monument to Claude Lorrain (1600–82) by Lemoyne.

Nearly opposite the church is **Palazzo Giustiniani**, designed by Girolamo Fontana; the main doorway is by Borromini.

The huge **Palazzo Madama** (Pl. 2; 6; occasionally open for guided visits on weekends) has its main façade on the modern Corso del Rinascimento. It has been the seat of the Italian Senate since 1871.

Originally this was a house belonging to the Crescenzi, which passed to the Medici in the 16C as part of the dowry of Alfonsina Orsini. In the 17C the building was enlarged and decorated by Lodovico Cardi and Paolo Marucelli, who are responsible for the interesting Baroque façade. It owes its name to the residence here of 'Madama' Margaret of Parma, illegitimate daughter of Charles V, who married first Alessandro de' Medici and afterwards Ottavio Farnese, and was Regent of the Netherlands from 1559 to 1567. Benedict XIV bought the palace in 1740, and it became successively the residence of the Governor of Rome and the seat of the Ministry of Finance (1852–70), before it became the Palazzo del Senato. The right wing was added in 1931.

Across Via degli Staderari (with a tiny wall fountain) is **Palazzo della Sapienza** (Pl. 2; 6) with a fine Renaissance façade, also on Corso del Rinascimento, by Giacomo della Porta. It was the seat until 1935 of the University of Rome, founded by Boniface VIII in 1303. It now houses the **Archivio di Stato**, and exhibitions are held in a library designed by Borromini. The beautiful **court**, also designed by Borromini, has porticoes on three sides, and the church of **Sant'Ivo** is at the far end (recently cleaned). Begun for the Barberini pope, Urban VIII, both the courtyard and the church incorporate his device (the bee) into their design, as well as Alexander VII's Chigi device of mounds. The church (open on Sunday at 10; or shown by the porter) is a masterpiece of Baroque architecture, with a remarkable light interior. The dome is crowned by an ingenious spiral campanile (copied many times, especially in Germany).

The campanile of Sant' Ivo

In Piazza Sant'Eustachio there is a good view of the campanile of St Ivo, and a charming palace with fine windows, a pretty cornice, and remains of its painted façade. Here also is a house (No. 83) built by Giulio Romano for the Maccarani. The church of **Sant'Eustachio**, of ancient foundation, preserves its campanile of 1196. The pretty interior (usually closed) was designed by Antonio Canevari after 1724 (the two large 18C altarpieces in the transepts are by Giacomo Zoboli). Via della Palombella takes you back to the Pantheon.

6 · Piazza Navona and Campo dei Fiori to the Tiber bend

The area covered in this chapter includes part of the ancient **Campus Martius**, or Plain of Mars, which at first included the whole area between the Capitoline Hill, the Tiber, and the Quirinal and Pincio Hills, but more precisely came to refer to the low-lying ground enclosed in the Tiber bend. It was said originally to have been the property of the Tarquins, and to have become public land after the expulsion of the kings. It took its name from an ancient Altar of Mars here, which gave a predominantly military nature to the area. After the 2C BC many temples and edifices for public entertainments were built, and on other parts of

the land military exercises and athletic competitions were held. The southern part of the Campus Martius was the Prata Flaminia, with the Circus of Flaminius. The area was not included in the walls of Rome until Aurelian built his famous wall round the city (AD 272–79).

Between Piazza Navona (described in Chapter 5) and Campo dei Fiori, opposite Palazzo Braschi (see p 128), on the noisy Corso Vittorio Emanuele, is the elegant little Renaissance palace called the **Piccola Farnesina** (Pl. 2; 8), which now houses the Museo Barracco. It was built in 1523 to the order of the French prelate Thomas Le Roy; the architect was almost certainly Antonio da Sangallo the Younger. The palace is also called the *Farnesina ai Baullari* and *Palazzo Le Roy* or *Regis*.

> Le Roy, who held important posts at the pontifical court, played a significant part in the concordat of 1516 between Leo X and Francis I of France. For his services he was ennobled and permitted to augment his coat of arms with the lilies of France. This heraldic privilege is recorded in the architectural details of the palace: the three floors are divided horizontally by projecting bands displaying the Le Roy ermines and the Farnese lilies, which were substituted for the lilies of France and gave the palace the name of Piccola Farnesina by which it is best known. It has no connection with the Villa Farnesina in Trastevere.

The Piccola Farnesina was built to face Vicolo dell'Aquila, to the south. The construction of the Corso Vittorio Emanuele left exposed the north side of the palace, which backed on houses that had to be pulled down to make room for the new street. A fine new façade on the Corso was therefore built in 1898–1901; the architect was Enrico Guj, who also modified the side of the palace facing Piazza dei Baullari (and added the steps and balustrade).

Museo Barracco

Since 1948 the palace has contained the Museo Barracco, a museum of ancient sculpture, beautifully rearranged and reopened to the public in 1991. The collection, not large but choice, was formed by Senator Giovanni Barracco (1829–1914), and presented by him to the city of Rome in 1902. The entrance to the museum is in Piazza dei Baullari della Farnesina; open: 9–19; Sun 9–13; closed Mon. ☎ 688 06848. Lire 3650.

In the **courtyard** is a bust of Giovanni Barracco by Giuseppe Mangionello (1914) and the foundation inscription of the palace (found during rebuilding). Beneath the portico is a Hellenistic statue (No. 100) of Apollo seated on a rock. The room beyond displays a 4C Christian sarcophagus (245), and a headless funerary statue of a woman (120), a 4C BC Attic work. On the **staircase** are two female statues (175, 166) of young girls.

First Floor. Room I (straight ahead). Egyptian sculpture from the beginning of the 3rd millennium to the end of the Roman era. First case: 1. Fragment of a relief of Nofer, a court official (4th Dynasty). Second case: 2. Bas-relief of a cow being milked and other scenes (5th Dynasty). Third case: 6. Statuette of a woman kneading dough; 7. Wooden statuette of a man; and (17) a polychrome fragment with the head of a pharaoh (perhaps Amenophis IV). Fourth case: 12.

Basalt statuette of a scribe (12th Dynasty). Fifth case: 15. Head of a prince (19th Dynasty); 14. head of a lion in wood (18th Dynasty); 19. head of Rameses II as a young man; amulets, seals and scarabs. In the middle of the room: 13. Sphinx of queen Hatshepsut, with the seal of Thutmosis III (1504–1450 BC), and a basalt lion (20). On the wall: 24. Statue of Osiris; 35, 309. two canopic vases; 23. bust of a warrior; *21. Head of Rameses II, as a young man, with a blue chaplet (1299–1233 BC); *31. Head of a priest wearing a diadem, once thought to be a portrait of Julius Caesar, an interesting example from Roman Egypt.

Room II. Egyptian, Sumerian, and Assyrian works. First case: 30. Ptolomaic male head; second case: 22. Gilded funerary mask; 33. Painted stucco head of a mummy (Roman era). In front of the second case: 26, 246. Sarcophagi; *27. Vase, used as a water-clock, with fine reliefs. The third case displays Sumerian and Assyrian works in bronze, terracotta and alabaster. On the end wall are displayed Assyrian reliefs: 47. Winged deity, from the northwestern palace of Assurbanipal at Nimrud (883–859 BC); 48. Five women prisoners in a palm grove (period of Sennacherib, 705–681, or Assurbanipal, 669–626 BC); 58. Huntsman with a horse.

Room III exhibits Etruscan works. 202, 201. Funerary cippi of the 5C BC from Chianciano and Chiusi; three representations of the Egyptian and Phoenician god Bes, including a statue (60) from a villa in the Alban hills; and three antefixes in the form of female heads, including one (205) from Bolsena, probably dating from the 2C BC.

Room IV contains works dating from the 6C–5C BC from Cyprus. First case: Statuettes (61, 62) of players of musical instruments; 68. Unusual little model of a polychrome quadriga ridden by a woman and child. Second case: 64. Head of a bearded priest wearing a chaplet, showing traces of colour (end of 5C), well preserved.

The **loggia**, with a vault frescoed in the 17C, displays (59) an alabaster lion mask, a Phoenician work found in Sardinia. In the small meeting room at the top of the stairs hang four 4C frescoes detached from the Roman edifice below the building (see below), including one showing a duck with a snake in its mouth, and another with boats.

A pretty staircase continues up to the **Second Floor** with a frescoed vault and tiled floor. In the **loggia** are Roman sculptures, copies of Greek originals.

Room V displays Greek originals of the 5C BC. On the wall opposite the entrance: 73. Fragment of an Attic sepulchral stele with a horseman; 80. Archaic head of a youth; 81. Head of Athena, from Greece or southern Italy; 88. Head of an athlete; *97. Head of Marsyas, replica of the head of the famous statue by Myron; *92. Head of Apollo, after an original by Pheidias, possibly the bronze statue seen by Pausanias near the Parthenon (Athens, before 450 BC); 113. Head of an ephebus (Argive-Sikyonian school).

On the opposite wall are copies of works by Polykleitos: 108. Head of the Doryphoros, good copy of the original bronze; 107. Head of the Diadumenos, after the original bronze; *109. Statuette of Hercules; 110. Head of a young man; 160. Bust of Hermes; *102. Upper part of a statue of an Amazon, after the original in the Temple of Diana at Ephesos, and (103) part of a leg of this statue. In the centre of the room: *99. Replica of the Westmacott athlete in the British Museum, also after an original by Polykleitos, possibly a portrait of Kyniskos, victor at Mantinea.

Room VI continues the display of Greek works. On the right, first case, upper shelf: early works from the Cyclades and Mycenae; lower shelf: ceramics, including (223, 231) two amphorae of the 5C BC, the second attributed to the Berlin Painter. Second case: 101. Head of a girl (5C); statuettes in rosso antico of (115, 116) girls carrying water-vessels, (77) a woman in a peplos (c 470 BC), and (76) a woman wearing a chiton (early 5C). On the left of the entrance are displayed 4C Attic works including: (127, 128) funeral lekythoi, (143) head of an old man, possibly Demosthenes, (135) fragment of a sepulchral relief, (*129) votive relief to Apollo, (132) head of a veiled woman, part of a sepulchral relief; and (*131) head of Apollo Kitharoidos, the best existing replica of the statue by Praxiteles.

Rooms VII and VIII. Hellenistic art. *139. Bitch licking her wounds, perhaps a replica of the masterpiece by Lysippos, formerly in the Temple of Jupiter on the Capitol; 157. Head of Alexander the Great or Mithras (2C BC); portraits, including (140) Demosthenes, from an original attributed to Polieuctes, and (155) Epicurus, after an Ionian original of 270 BC. In two cases are displayed ceramics from Magna Graecia, and sculptures from Taranto. On the wall: 176. Archaistic relief (3C BC), depicting the cave of Pan; 134. Fragment of a relief of a horseman stroking the mane of his horse, from a representation of the Dioscuri (4C, Graeco-Italian). At the end of the loggia, with a frescoed vault (1904) is Room IX which displays Roman and medieval art. On the wall opposite the entrance: 173. Funerary urn in the form of an Ionic temple; *151. Statuette of Neptune, Roman work of the 1C BC from a 4C Greek original; *194. Head of a Roman boy, perhaps Nero; 190. Bust of a young Roman (probably period of Tiberius). By the door: 195. Head of Mars (period of Trajan). On the last wall: 206, 249, 250. Sepulchral reliefs (Palmyra, 3C AD); 208, 207. Two charming marble reliefs from the Duomo of Sorrento (10C–11C); 209. Fragment of a mosaic from old St Peter's with the representation of the *Ecclesia Romana*.

In the basement of the palace are remains of a Roman building of the late Imperial period, discovered in 1899. Here can be seen part of a portico, with fine columns and opus sectile paving.

On the right of the Museo Barracco, opening onto Corso Vittorio Emanuele, is Piazza della Cancelleria, along one whole side of which is the graceful façade of the **PALAZZO DELLA CANCELLERIA** (Pl. 3; 5), a masterpiece of the Renaissance. It was built for Cardinal Raffaello Riario by an unknown architect, probably in 1486, with a double order of pilasters. Showing Florentine influence, it is thought that Bramante may have helped at a late stage, possibly designing the beautiful courtyard; it is also probable that Andrea Bregno was involved in the building. The magnificent **courtyard** has double loggie with antique columns.

Excavations beneath the courtyard in 1988–91 revealed 4C and 5C remains of the huge basilica of San Lorenzo in Damaso, founded by Pope St Damaso I, and one of the most important early Christian churches in Rome (see below). A cemetery in use from the 8C to the 15C was also discovered here, as well as numerous shards of 15C ceramics.

The palace is now the seat of the three Tribunals of the Vatican, including the Sacra Rota, and of the Pontificia Accademia Romana di Archeologia. Special

permission is needed to see the interior, which includes works by Marcantonio Franceschini, Giuseppe Nicola Nasini, Baciccia, Vasari and his pupils (including Raffaellino dal Colle), and Francesco Salviati.

Incorporated into the palace is the basilica of **San Lorenzo in Damaso** (entered by a doorway at the right end of the main façade). The ancient basilica (see above) founded in the 4C was finally demolished in the 15C when the present church (built on part of the site), contemporary with the palace, had been completed. It was entirely restored in 1868–82, and again in this century after fire. It has a double atrium, and over the fine doorway in the right aisle is a lunette fresco of angel musicians by Cavaliere d'Arpino (detached; formerly in the nave). The adjoining chapel has a 14C crucifix in wood. In the main apse, *Coronation of the Virgin, with Saints*, by Federico Zuccari. At the end of the left aisle is the tomb of Cardinal Ludovico Trevisan, called Mezzarota Scarampi (1505), and in the chapel of the Sacrament, a 12C icon of the Virgin brought here from Santa Maria di Grottapinto in 1465.

Campo dei Fiori

At the south end of Piazza della Cancelleria, beyond the interesting old Via del Pellegrino which skirts the side of the Cancelleria, with shops set into the façade on street level, opens CAMPO DEI FIORI (Pl. 3; 5), once a meadow, which became one of the most important piazze in Rome in the 15C. Executions were occasionally held here; the fine monument (by Ettore Ferrari; 1889) to Giordano

Monument to Giordano Bruno in Campo dei Fiori

Bruno, in the centre, stands on the spot where he was burned alive as a heretic by the Inquisition in 1600. Campo dei Fiori has been a market-place since 1869, with attractive old stalls and canvas shades. It is the centre of a distinctive district of the city, with numerous artisans' workshops. The beautiful old Via dei Cappellari which leads out of the northwest side of the piazza, and the parallel Via del Pellegrino are worth exploring.

The huge 15C **Palazzo Pio** (Righetti), at the east end of the piazza, was built over the ruins of Pompey's Theatre (see below), which was surmounted, on the highest part of the cavea, by a Temple of Venus. The late 16C façade of the palace by Camillo Arcucci faces Piazza del Biscione, where at No. 89 is a small house with a painted façade. Impressive remains of the theatre can be seen on request at the restaurant in the piazza. From here a frescoed archway leads into a dark passageway by the old (deconsecrated) chapel of Santa Maria di Grottapinta to Via di Grotta Pinta. If this is closed it is necessary to reach Via di Grotta Pinta via Via del Biscione (where the Albergo Sole is thought to be the oldest hotel in the city), Piazza del Paradiso and Via dei Chiavari (with a good view of the dome of Sant'Andrea della Valle). The semicircular Via di Grotta Pinta follows the line of the auditorium of the **Theatre of Pompey** (55 BC; Rome's first stone-built theatre); to the east of it formerly stood the great rectangular Porticus of Pompey, off which opened the 'Curia' (remains of which have been identified in Largo Argentina, see p 126) where Julius Caesar was murdered (15 March, 44 BC) at the foot of a statue of Pompey (perhaps the one now in Palazzo Spada). The modern Teatro dei Satiri is here.

The animated Via de' Giubbonari, a busy local shopping street (closed to cars), leads out of the Campo dei Fiori, skirting the side of Palazzo Pio. It ends at Piazza Cairoli, with the domed church of **SAN CARLO AI CATINARI** (Pl. 3; 6), by Rosato Rosati (1612–20), many times restored. It takes its name from the basin-makers (*catini*) who used to work in the area. The façade was erected in 1636 by Giovanni Battista Soria.

The spacious **interior** (open 7.30–12, 16.30–19) is interesting for its 17C works. **South side**. The first chapel, decorated in 1698–1702 by Simone Costanzi, has an altarpiece of the Annunciation by Giovanni Lanfranco. Second chapel: *Martyrdom of San Biagio* by Giacinto Brandi. Between the second and third chapels is the Hamerani monument, with exquisite classical carved decoration by Luca Carimini (1830–90). The third chapel, the Cappella di Santa Cecilia, beautifully lit from its little oval dome, was designed by Antonio Gherardi. In the **sanctuary**, the high altarpiece, illustrating *San Carlo carrying the Sacred Nail to the plague-stricken*, is a good late work by Pietro da Cortona. The apse bears a fresco of San Carlo Received in Heaven by Giovanni Lanfranco. In the pendentives of the dome over the crossing are the Cardinal Virtues by Domenichino.

The **sacristy** contains a little bronze crucifix attributed to Alessandro Algardi, and the *Derision of Christ* by Cavaliere d'Arpino, and in an adjoining room (shown by the sacristan) a tondo of *San Carlo in prayer* (a fresco detached from the façade) attributed to Guido Reni, and a painting of San Carlo by Andrea Commodi. **North side**. The third chapel, decorated in the 17C, has frescoed lunettes attributed to Giacinto Gimignani. The altarpiece in the second chapel, of the *Death of St Anne*, is by Andrea Sacchi.

Opposite the church is Palazzo Santacroce, by Carlo Maderno (1602). On the

other side of Via de' Giubbonari several short streets lead into the piazza in front of the **Monte di Pietà** (now a bank), with a long history as a pawnshop. The façade by Ottaviano Nonni (Il Mascherino) was enlarged by Carlo Maderno, with a clock and small marble bell-tower attributed to Borromini. A fine domed chapel (adm on request) by Carlo Maderno (1641; restored 1725) contains high reliefs by Domenico Guidi, Pierre Le Gros, and Giovanni Théodon.

Via dell'Arco del Monte di Pietà skirts the right flank of the building as far as the little piazza in front of the church of **Santissima Trinità dei Pellegrini** (open only for services on Sunday), by Paolo Maggi (1603–16). The façade was added in 1723 by Francesco de Sanctis. The interior contains 17C works by Guido Reni (*The Trinity*), Borgognone, and Cavaliere d'Arpino. In the neighbouring hospice (1625; being restored) the poet Goffredo Mameli, author of the national hymn which bears his name, died in 1849 at the age of 22 from wounds received fighting for the Roman Republic.

From the piazza, Via dei Pettinari leads to the Tiber, here crossed by Ponte Sisto (described on p 277). The little church of **San Salvatore in Onda** (usually closed) was built at the end of the 11C but transformed in the 17C. The interesting crypt was built over a Roman building of the 2C AD.

Via San Paolo alla Regola leads out of Piazza dei Pellegrini beyond the church of San Paolo alla Regola to the Case di San Paolo, a group of over-restored 13C houses now used as offices. Other medieval buildings were demolished to make way for the huge Ministry of Justice built here in 1920 by Pio Piacentini. To the left is the ancient church of **Santa Maria in Monticelli** (closed indefinitely), with a 12C campanile, radically restored in 1860. In the apse is a mosaic head of Christ, and fragments of mosaic decoration dating from the 12C. In the second chapel to the right is a Flagellation (detached fresco) by Antonio Carracci; opposite is a 14C wooden crucifix.

Galleria Spada

The narrow Via Capo di Ferro (where an ancient house has columns set in to the façade) leads out of Piazza dei Pellegrini into Piazza Capodiferro with the huge **PALAZZO SPADA** (Pl. 3; 5), built for Cardinal Girolomo Capodiferro in 1540, probably by Giulio Mazzoni. The palace was acquired in the 17C by Cardinal Bernardino Spada, and is now owned by the State. It has been the seat of the Council of State (or Supreme Court) since 1889. The courtyard and façade are by Giulio Mazzoni or Girolamo da Carpi and are outstanding examples of stucco decoration (beautifully cleaned and restored in 1992).

Borromini restored the palace for his friend Cardinal Spada, and designed a painted niche with a statue on a wall in Piazza Capodiferro to close the view from the garden entrance on Via Giulia. The design of the niche has recently been found beneath the intonaco, and reconstructed here above an ancient sarcophagus which serves as a fountain in the piazza. Borromini also added an ingenious trompe l'oeil perspective on the south side (visible from the courtyard through a large glass window), This makes use of the waste space between the Spada garden and the adjoining Palazzo Massari. The dimension of the tunnel is perspectively multiplied more than four times through the use of light and spacing of the columns. The door into the garden is usually opened on request by the porter.

Reached by a staircase from a corridor at the back of the palace is the **Galleria Spada** (open 9–19; fest. 9–13; closed Mon. ☎ 686 1158. Lire 8000), a collection of paintings formed by Cardinal Spada and augmented by successive generations of his family. Arranged in four rooms which preserve their 17C decoration and furnishings, the important collection of 17C and 18C paintings (and 2C and 3C Roman sculpture) is a fascinating example of a 17C Roman patrician family's private collection, which survives almost intact. It was acquired by the State in 1926. The works are numbered as described below, and handlists are available in each room.

Room I. Two portraits of Cardinal Bernardino Spada by Guido Reni (*32) and Guercino (35). 29. Guido Reni, *St Jerome*. **Room II**. 60. School of Titian, *Musician* (unfinished); *56. Andrea del Sarto, *Visitation*; 94. 15C Umbrian school, *Madonna and Child*; 92. Sigismondo Foschi, *Madonna and St John the Baptist*; 16C tabernacle in carved and gilded walnut, with a bas-relief of the Annunciation; 90. Lavinia Fontana, *Cleopatra*; 89. Parmigianino (attributed), three heads (a fresco); 86. Titian, *Paul III* (a copy); 81. Giovanni Battista Bertucci, *Madonna and Child with St John*; 80. Marco Palmezzano, *Way to Calvary, Eternal Father*; 76. Fiorenzo di Lorenzo, *St Sebastian*; *77. Jan van Scorel, *Young man*; 78. Hans Dürer, *Young man*. On the two long walls, fragments of a larger painted frieze by Perino del Vaga, designs for tapestries originally intended for the wall below Michelangelo's *Last Judgment* in the Sistine Chapel.

Room III. 100. Nicolò dell'Abate, Landscape; 101. Ciro Ferri, *Vestals*; 146. 17C Flemish school, *Winter Scene*; Pietro Testa, 145. *Iphigenia*, 144. *Massacre of the Innocents*; 141. Antonio Carracci, *Young man*; 139. Francesco Trevisani, *Antony and Cleopatra*; 136. Circle of Scipione Pulzone, *Young girl*; 133. Baciccia, *sketch for the vaulting of the Gesù; 132. Guercino, *Death of Dido*; 126. Baciccia, *Christ and the woman of Samaria*; 123. Francesco Furini, *St Lucy*; *120. School of Rubens, *Portrait of a Cardinal*; 117. Circle of Annibale Carracci, *Portrait of a young boy*; J.F. Voet, 119. *Gentlewoman*, 110, 105. *Portrait of Urbano and Pompeo Rocci*; 113. Nicolò Tornioli, *Cain and Abel*; 103. P. Snayers, *Sack of a village*; 106. Giacinto Campana and Guido Reni, *Abduction of Helen*; 102. Jan Breughel the Elder, *Landscape with windmills*. Among the Roman sculpture are a seated philosopher, a bust of a woman of the 2C AD, and two Roman statuettes of boys, one dressed in the lion-skin of Hercules, and another in the philosopher's pallium.

Room IV. 148. School of Gherardo delle Notti, *Betrayal of Christ*; 149. Artemisia Gentileschi, *St Cecilia*; 150. Mattia Preti, *Christ Tempted*; 152. Michelangelo Cerquozzi, *At the water trough*; 155. Orazio Gentileschi, *David* (being restored); 158. Cerquozzi, *Death of the donkey*; 159. Anon 17C, *Boy with a plumed hat*; *161. Cerquozzi, *Masaniello's revolt in Naples*; 165. Willem Reuter (formerly attributed to Sweerts), *Market*; 168. Lubin Baugin, Still life; 171. Bartolomeo Cavarozzi, *Madonna*; 172. Orazio Borgianni, *Pietà* (a replica); 175. 17C Roman school, *Madonna and St Anne*; 176. Nicolò Renieri (also attributed to Bartolomeo Manfredi), *David*; 178. School of Carlo Saraceni (also attributed to Francesco Albani), *Christ Scourged*; 182. Cerquozzi, *Traveller and shepherds*; 184. Le Valentin, *Holy Family*. The Roman bust of a boy dates from the Julio-Claudian period.

The **State Rooms** on the first floor can be seen by appointment (☎ 68271). The **General Council Chamber** has magnificent trompe l'oeil frescoes by the

17C Bolognese artists, Agostino Mitelli and Michelangelo Colonna, with birds and figures peering into the room from around columns and window ledges. The colossal statue of Pompey is traditionally thought to be the one at the foot of which Caesar was murdered. The **Corridor of Stuccoes** is a delightful work by Giulio Mazzoni (1559), complemented by his ornamentation of the façade of the court seen through the windows. Further rooms lead to the **Meridiana**, a corridor decorated by Giovanni Battista Ruggeri, mapping the times at various places in the world. The eight Hellenistic reliefs of mythological subjects of the 2C AD are very fine, and in a good state of preservation.

Vicolo de' Venti continues to PIAZZA FARNESE, created by the Farnese in front of their splendid palace. Here are two huge baths of Egyptian granite brought from the Baths of Caracalla in the 16C and used by the Farnese as a type of 'royal box' for the spectacles which were held in the square. They were adapted as fountains (using the Farnese lilies) in 1626.

PALAZZO FARNESE (Pl. 3; 5), the most magnificent Renaissance palace in Rome, is now the French Embassy; it was first used as such in 1635. It was designed by Antonio da Sangallo the Younger for Cardinal Alessandro Farnese, afterwards Paul III. He began the piazza façade and the two sides, and after his death in 1546 Michelangelo finished the upper storeys and added the superb entablature. The work on the back of the palace was continued by Vignola and Giacomo della Porta. In the 18C the palace became the property of the Bourbons of Naples.

The **interior** is at present closed to the public. Sangallo designed the **vestibule**, with a beautiful colonnade and stuccoed ceiling, and the **courtyard** (the first two storeys). The huge **Salon d'Hercule** is named after the gigantic statue of the Farnese Hercules. On his visit to Rome in 1787 Goethe records the loss of the statue, together with the magnificent Farnese collection of sculpture, to Naples (transferred there by the Bourbons), lamenting: 'If they could detach the Gallery with the Carracci from Palazzo Farnese and transport it, they would.' It has a fine wooden ceiling by Sangallo, and two statues representing Piety and Abundance, by Guglielmo della Porta.

The **Galleria** has *frescoes of mythological scenes, the masterpiece of Annibale Carracci (1597–1603). The ingenious treatment of the angles, and the magnificent overall scheme centring on the Triumph of Bacchus, demonstrate the great imagination of the artist, who here created the model for subsequent Baroque ceiling paintings. Carracci was assisted by his brother Agostino, and (in the frescoes above the doors and niches) by Domenichino.

Just off the square, on Via di Monserrato, is the exterior in Romanesque style (including an elaborate portal by Luigi Poletti) of the church of **St Thomas of Canterbury**, attached to the **Venerable English College** (entrance at No. 45). The ground on which they stand has been the property of English Catholics since 1362, when it was founded as a hospice for pilgrims, and the record of visitors shows the names of Thomas Cromwell (1514), Thomas Hobbes (1635), William Harvey (1636), John Milton (1638), John Evelyn, and Cardinal Manning. The church was rebuilt on a design by Virginio Vespignani in 1866–88, a free adaptation of a Romanesque basilica, with elaborate gilded decorations, and frescoes of English martyrs in the matroneum. It contains the beautiful tomb *effigy of Cardinal Christopher Bainbridge, Bishop of York (died

1514), attributed to Nicola Marini, borne on two Romanesque lions, and a monument to Thomas Dereham (died 1739) by Ferdinando Fuga, with sculptures by Filippo della Valle. The high altarpiece is by Durante Alberti. In the college, of which Cardinal Howard and Cardinal Wiseman were rectors, are portraits of English cardinals.

In Piazza Santa Caterina della Rota is the church of **San Girolamo della Carità** (usually closed; ring at 63 Via San Girolamo), rebuilt in the 17C by Domenico Castelli, with a façade by Carlo Rainaldi. The **funeral chapel of the Spada** (first on the right), formerly attributed to Borromini, is now thought to be the work of Cosimo Fanzago. To the left of the high altar is a decorative chapel (1710) dedicated to San Filippo Neri, by Filippo Juvarra (light to left). The church of **Santa Caterina della Rota** (also usually closed) has a fine ceiling from a demolished church and 18C works.

The Mascherone in Via Giulia

Via dei Farnese (with a charming small palace at No. 83) skirting the right flank of Palazzo Farnese, leads to Via Giulia. Here, through a gate, can be seen the Palace's lovely garden and the rear façade, adapted from Michelangelo's designs by Giacomo della Porta. The design of Michelangelo to connect the palace with the Villa Farnesina by a bridge across the Tiber was never carried out, but a single arch (hung with vines) of the viaduct to the bridge spans Via Giulia at this point. The fountain in the wall on the left, the *Mascherone*, was erected by the Farnese; both the colossal mask and the porphyry basin are Roman.

The straight VIA GIULIA (Pl. 3; 5) runs parallel to the Tiber for over one kilometre. It was laid out by Julius II (1503–13) and was for long the most beautiful of the 16C streets of the city. The church opposite the end of Via dei Farnese, **Santa Maria dell'Orazione e Morte** (open only on Sun and fest. at 18) was rebuilt in 1733–37 by Ferdinando Fuga. **Palazzo Falconieri**, enlarged by Borromini, is distinguished by the giant falcons' heads at either end of its façade (it has been the seat of the Hungarian Academy since 1928). Several rooms inside have fine ceilings decorated in stucco by Borromini.

Further on, the church of Santa Caterina da Siena (closed for restoration), rebuilt by Paolo Posi in 1766, stands opposite Palazzo Varese by Carlo Maderno (c 1617). A street on the left leads to **Sant'Eligio degli Orefici** (open 10–12, except Sat and Wed; ring at 9 Via di Sant'Eligio). This beautiful small 16C church, surmounted by a cupola and Greek-cross in plan, is by Raphael (clearly influenced by Bramante). After his death Baldassarre Peruzzi continued the

building and added the cupola. The façade, following Raphael's designs, was rebuilt by Flaminio Ponzio.

From the Lungotevere here there is a fine view of the Janiculum, the dome of St Peter's, and the Villa Farnesina. Via della Barchetta, on the other side of Via Giulia, leads to Via di Monserrato on which (right) is the church of **SANTA MARIA DI MONSERRATO** (Pl. 2; 7; open only on Sun; for adm apply at 151 Via Giulia), the Spanish national church. It was begun by Antonio da Sangallo the Younger (1518) but altered later, with a façade by Francesco da Volterra.

In the **interior**, the first south chapel contains an altarpiece of *San Diego*, by Annibale Carracci, and the 19C tombs of the two Borgia popes, Calixtus III (died 1458) and Alexander VI (died 1503), and of Alfonso XIII (died 1941). In the third north chapel is a statue of St James, by Iacopo Sansovino, and two fine wall tombs attributed to Andrea Bregno. The first north chapel contains a group of the *Madonna and Child with St Anne*, by Tommaso Boscoli (1544), and a ciborium (behind wooden doors) attributed to Luigi Capponi. In the court, reached through the sacristy at the end of the nave on the right (or at 151 Via Giulia), are several fine tombs, notably that attributed to Andrea Bregno of Cardinal Giovanni de Mella. In a room off the courtyard is the monument to Pedro de Foix Montoya; this incorporates a remarkable portrait bust, an early work (c 1621) by Gian Lorenzo Bernini.

Via Giulia continues past (left) the church of the **Spirito Santo dei Napoletani**, begun by Ottaviano Mascherino in 1619, and restored by Carlo Fontana, and again in the 19C, when the façade was built by Antonio Cipolla. It contains paintings by Pietro Gagliardi and a martyrdom of San Gennaro by Luca Giordano. The street opposite leads to the 16C Palazzo Ricci with a painted façade by Polidoro da Caravaggio, heavily restored, and now badly faded. Via Giulia next traverses an area demolished before 1940 for a new road, never built; the 18C façade by Filippo Raguzzini of San Filippo Neri survives here.

Opposite the church of Santa Lucia del Gonfalone on Via dei Banchi Vecchi, Vicolo Cellini (the sculptor had his workshop in the area) leads to Corso Vittorio Emanuele. Across the Corso is the **CHIESA NUOVA** or Santa Maria in Vallicella (Pl. 3; 5), built under the inspiration of St Philip Neri and with the patronage of Cardinal Angelo Cesi. Among the architects were Matteo Bartolini da Città di Castello and Martino Longhi the Elder (1575–1605), but the façade is by Fausto Rughesi. Born in Florence in 1515 St Philip Neri came to Rome c 1530. He was an outstanding figure of the Counter Reformation and founded an 'Oratorio' here. In recognition of his Order, Gregory XIII gave him Santa Maria in Vallicella in 1575 which he proceeded to rebuild.

In the **interior**, the vault, apse and dome were decorated by Pietro da Cortona (1664), and the whole church is brilliantly gilded. In the **sanctuary** are three *paintings by Rubens* (1608), with splendid colours: over the high altar, *Madonna and Angels*; to the right, *Saints Domitilla, Nereus and Achilleus*; to the left, *Saints Gregory, Maurus and Papias*. On the right of the apse, under the fine 18C cantoria, is the **Cappella Spada**, designed by Carlo Rainaldi, with an altarpiece by Carlo Maratta (*Madonna between St Charles and St Ignatius*). St Philip Neri is buried beneath the altar of the sumptuous **Cappella di San Filippo** (1600–04), on the left of the apse; his portrait in mosaic is copied from a painting by Guido Reni. In the north transept, *Presentation of the Virgin in the Temple*, by Federico Barocci. In the fine 17C sacristy, with a fresco by Pietro da

Cortona, is a statue of St Philip Neri and an angel, by Alessandro Algardi. From here there is access to another chapel and the rooms of St Philip Neri (works by Guercino, Pietro da Cortona, Guido Reni, Garofalo, etc.) with mementoes of the saint.

In the neighbouring **Oratorio dei Filippini**, rebuilt largely by Borromini (1637–52), St Philip instituted the musical gatherings which became known as oratorios, and have given their name to a form of musical composition. The **façade**, between that of a church and a palace, has a remarkably subtle design. The delightful clock-tower can be seen from Via dei Banchi Nuovi, on the right. The extensive convent buildings, also by Borromini, are now occupied by the Vallicelliana Library (history of Rome), the Municipal Archives, and various learned societies. On Corso Vittorio Emanuele at No. 217 (left) is the 16C Palazzo Sora, and (right), in a little piazza, Palazzo Sforza Cesarini (with a 15C court-yard).

Vicolo Cellini (see above) and Via delle Carceri lead back to Via Giulia. The **Carceri Nuove** here, built in 1655 by Antonio del Grande, were long considered a model prison. The **Museo Criminologico** (admission by appointment only, ☎ 683 00234) is arranged in an adjacent prison building designed in 1827 by Giuseppe Valadier (entrance at 29 Via del Gonfalone).

The 16C **Oratorio di Santa Lucia del Gonfalone** (entrance on Vicolo della Scimmia) has a façade by Domenico Castelli. It is usually closed, but concerts are given here. The interior has a fine pavement, and a carved and gilded ceiling by Ambrogio Bonazzini. But it is particularly interesting for its frescoes by painters of the late 16C Tuscan-Emilian school, including Jacopo Bertoia, Raffaellino da Reggio, Federico Zuccari, Livio Agresti, Cesare Nebbia, and Marco Pino.

On Via del Gonfalone and beyond the church of Santa Maria del Suffragio (by Carlo Rainaldi), several large rough blocks of masonry protruding into the street are all that remains of a great court of justice designed for Julius II by Bramante but never finished. Here is yet another church, the small San Biagio della Pagnotta. At No. 66 rises Palazzo Sacchetti, by Antonio Sangallo the Younger (1543).

At the end of Via Giulia is **SAN GIOVANNI BATTISTA DEI FIORENTINI** (Pl. 2; 5), the church of the Florentines. Leo X ordered a competition for its erection. Raphael and Peruzzi were among the contestants; but Iacopo Sansovino was successful and began the work. It was continued by Antonio da Sangallo the Younger and completed by Giacomo della Porta; Carlo Maderno added the transept and cupola. The façade is by Alessandro Galilei (1734).

Interior (open 7–11, 17–19.30). In the **south aisle**, above the door into the sacristy, is a 16C Tuscan statuette of St John the Baptist. On either side of the arch here is a portrait bust; that on the left by Pietro Bernini (1614), and that on the right by his son Gian Lorenzo (1622). Third chapel: Santi di Tito, *St Jerome*; (right wall) Ludovico Cigoli, *St Jerome*, and (left wall) Passignano, Construction of the church. In the **south transept**, *Saints Cosmas and Damian at the stake*, by Salvator Rosa. **North aisle**. First chapel: altarpiece by Giovanni Battista Vanni; fourth chapel: putti on the wall tombs of the Bacelli, carved by François Duquesnoy. Behind the high altar is a crypt sepulchre of the Falconieri family, a fine late work by Borromini (closed for restoration, but normally shown on request by the sacristan).

Return across Corso Vittorio Emanuele and take Via Banco Santo Spirito out of Largo Tassoni. From here Vicolo del Curato leads to the piazza at the beginning of VIA DEI CORONARI (Pl. 2; 5), a beautiful Renaissance street on the line of the Roman Via Recta. It is now famous for its antique shops.

From Piazza dei Coronari Via di Panico leads right into Via di Monte Giordano. Here the 18C Palazzo Taverna (Pl. 2; 5), formerly Gabrielli, has a beautiful fountain by Antonio Casoni (1618) in the court. The palace stands on **Monte Giordano**, a small, apparently artificial, hill already inhabited in the 12C. It takes its name from Giordano Orsini (13C) whose legendary fortress stood here. Dante mentions the 'Monte' (*Inferno*, XXVIII, 12) in the description of the pilgrims crossing the Ponte Sant'Angelo on the occasion of the jubilee of 1300. The Orsini continued to own the castle until 1688, and the buildings, here still crowded together, betray their medieval origins.

At the beginning of Via dei Coronari, on the right (Nos 122–23) stands the so-called House of Raphael. In the piazza on the left is **San Salvatore in Lauro** a church with a Palladian interior by Mascherino (1594). To the left of the church (No. 15) is the entrance to the fine Renaissance cloister (in poor repair). A small courtyard beyond has two Renaissance portals. The refectory contains the *tomb of Eugenius IV (died 1447) by Isaia da Pisa, one of the earliest sepulchral monuments to exhibit the characteristic forms of the Renaissance.

Further on in Via dei Coronari is the Piazzetta di San Simeone with Palazzo Lancellotti (no admission), begun by Francesco da Volterra and finished by Carlo Maderno. From the piazzetta the interesting Via della Maschera d'Oro leads to Palazzo Sacripante Ruiz (a fine building attributed to Bartolomeo Ammannati), while to the south, also parallel to Via dei Coronari, is the medieval Vicolo dei Tre Archi. Via dei Coronari ends in Piazza di Tor Sanguigna at the north end of Piazza Navona (see Chapter 5).

The busy Via Giuseppe Zanardelli leads north from here to Ponte Umberto I past (right) **Palazzo Altemps**, begun c 1480 for Girolamo Riario and completed by Martino Longhi the Elder, with a charming belvedere in the form of a turret. The palace was acquired by the State in 1982 and has been carefully restored. The chapel on the first floor was frescoed by Pomarancio and Ottavio Leoni (1604–17). The Ludovisi collection from the Museo Nazionale Romano (see p 198) may be displayed here. The Teatro Goldoni, which adjoins the palace, preserves its 17C decoration.

In Piazza Ponte Umberto I is **Palazzo Primoli**, seat of the Fondazione Primoli. On the ground floor is the **Napoleonic Museum** (open 9–19; Sun 9–13.30. ☎ 688 06286. Lire 3750. C), presented to the city of Rome in 1927 by Count Joseph Primoli. The collection belonged to Count Joseph and his brother Louis, who were sons of Carlotta Bonaparte. In the 14 period rooms of the museum are paintings, statues and relics of the Bonaparte family, with special reference to the Roman branch. The more important works include paintings by Jacques-Louis David of *Zenaide* and *Carlotta*, daughters of Joseph, King of Naples; by Gérard of *Elisa Baciocchi*; by Jean-Baptiste Wicar of *Louis, King of Holland*; and by Winterhalter of *Napoleon III and the Empress Eugénie*. The collection also includes sculptures by Antonio Canova, Lorenzo Bartolini, J.B. Carpeaux, and Thorvaldsen; miniatures by Jean-Baptiste Isabey; prints illustrating the contest between Napoleon and Pius VII; State robes; and autographs, including the marriage contract of Napoleon and Marie Louise.

On the top floor of Palazzo Primoli is the **Museo Mario Praz** (open 9–13, 14.30–18.30, except Mon morning. ☎ 686 1089. Lire 4000) visitors are accompanied and lent a handsheet), the residence of the art historian and man of letters Mario Praz from 1969 until his death in 1982. The apartment is filled with his remarkable collection of decorative arts, paintings, sculpture, furniture, etc., particularly representative of the Neo-classical period.

Nearby, on the corner of Via di Monte Brianzo, is the **Osteria dell' Orso**. The medieval building was altered c 1460, and it first became a hotel in the 16C. Rabelais, Montaigne and Goethe were among its patrons.

7 · The Corso and Piazza del Popolo

VIA DEL CORSO (Pl. 3; 6, 4, 2), now called simply *Il Corso*, has been one of the most important thoroughfares in the city since Roman times. It is a straight and fairly narrow street, well over a kilometre in length, connecting Piazza Venezia with Piazza del Popolo. It remains one of the busiest streets in Rome, and the pavements are hardly wide enough to accommodate the almost incessant stream of pedestrians in either direction during working hours, and during the evening *passeggiata* (especially crowded on weekends). Many fashionable shops are concentrated in the area between the Corso, Piazza di Spagna and Piazza del Popolo.

> The Corso represents the urban section of the Via Flaminia (221 BC), the main road to northern Italy. In Latin it was called the Via Lata (or 'broad way') because of its width, exceptional in ancient Rome. Its present name is derived from the celebrated races inaugurated here by Paul II in 1466. Many palaces were built along the street from the 16C to the 18C, and the straightness of its line between Piazza Venezia and Piazza Colonna was perfected by Alexander VII, when he demolished two triumphal arches that formerly spanned it. The Carnival celebrations here from the 17C onwards became famous spectacles; John Evelyn, Goethe, Dickens, and Henry James have left vivid descriptions of the festivities. The street has given its name to the principal street in numerous other Italian cities.

The Corso runs north from Piazza Venezia. At its left corner is Palazzo d'Aste Rinuccini Bonaparte by Giovanni Antonio dei Rossi (17C), where Letizia Ramolino, mother of Napoleon I, died in 1836. On the right beyond Vicolo del Piombo, are Palazzo Salviati, by Carlo Rainaldi (1662), and Palazzo Odescalchi, of the 17C–18C, but with a façade (1887–88) in the Florentine 15C style.

Galleria Doria Pamphilj

On the opposite side of the Corso is the huge **Palazzo Doria Pamphilj** (Pl. 3; 6), which dates from 1435, but has suffered many vicissitudes. It has been the residence of this important Roman noble family since the 17C. The façade towards the Corso, by Gabriele Valvassori (1731–34), is perhaps the finest and most balanced Rococo work in Rome. The south façade is by Paolo Ameli (1743); that on the north in Piazza del Collegio Romano is by Antonio del Grande (1659–63), with two very fine wings.

The Palazzo contains the **Galleria Doria Pamphilj** (open 10–15 Mon, Tues, Fri, Sat, Sun; closed Thur. ☎ 679 7323. Lire 12,000. Guided tours of the apartments most mornings. Lire 6000. Private visits can also be arranged), the most important of the Roman patrician art collections to have survived in the city. This is now entered at No. 2 Piazza Collegio Romano, reached off the Corso by Via Lata beyond the church of Santa Maria in Via Lata (described below).

The collection was initiated in 1651 by the Pamphilj Pope Innocent X who decreed that the pictures and furnishings in Palazzo Pamphilj in Piazza Navona should be inherited by his nephew Camillo, son of the Pope's acquisitive sister-in-law Olimpia Maidalchini. Important additions were made to these works of art when Camillo married Olimpia Aldobrandini, widow of Paolo Borghese, and in 1760 with the Doria family bequests. The Doria family still live here, and the collection has been protected by the State since 1816.

The grand staircase leads up to the first floor. The period rooms, richly decorated in white, red and gold, and beautifully maintained, provide a sumptuous setting for the fine paintings. The rooms were restored in 1996, nine more rooms opened for the first time, and the collection rehung as it was arranged after 1760 by the Doria prince Andrea IV (with the Flemish and Italian works side by side). Only a small selection of the works (each identified by its number) has been given below. A handlist is lent to visitors.

The first series of rooms forms part of the Appartamento di Rappresentanza. The walls of the **Sala del Poussin** are covered with 17C landscapes by Gaspard Dughet (known as 'Il Poussin'). The **Sala del Trono** (right) displays more landscapes, this time in tempera, most of them by Crescenzio Onofri, pupil of Dughet. In the **Sala Azzurra** (right) are 19C family portraits. The **Sala dei Velluti**, which retains its late 18C red velvet wall-hangings, contains paintings by Giuliano Bugiardini, and *busts of Innocent X and Benedetto Pamphilj by Alessandro Algardi. The rococo **Saletta Verde** (right), decorated in an elegant 18C Venetian style, has Venetian scenes, including a view of Piazza Venezia by Josef Heintz the Younger and works by the circle of Pietro Longhi.

The **Sala da Ballo** was decorated, together with the adjacent smaller ballroom, at the end of the 19C, with silk hangings. The smaller room has an 18C ceiling fresco of *Venus and Aeneas* by Antonio Nessi, and a Gobelins tapestry woven for Louis XIV from a 16C Flemish design, representing the month of May. The large family **Cappella** was designed by Carlo Fontana (1691; but altered in the 18C–19C). The altar of rare marbles dates from the 17C and the ivory crucifix is by Ercole Ferrata. In the **Saletta Gialla** (right), the 12 tapestries of the signs of the Zodiac by Claude Audran were executed in the Goblins workshops by order of Louis XV. The **Saletta Rossa** has a 17C Gobelins tapestry, four allegorical paintings of the Elements by Jan Brueghel the Elder, and a portrait of James Stuart, the Old Pretender, by Alexis Simon Belle.

In the **Stanza di ingresso alla Galleria** are works derived from David Teniers the younger, and two paintings of the Holy Family by followers of Andrea del Sarto (g12), and Fra' Paolino (g11).

The **Galleria** is arranged around four sides of a courtyard, redesigned by Gabriele Valvassori in 1731–34. The arrangement now follows that of the late

18C. **First Gallery**. Left wall: i1. Annibale Carracci, *Mary Magdalene*; i3. Garofalo, *Madonna in Glory*; i4. Claude Lorrain, *Landscape with dancing figures*; i5. Annibale Carracci, **Flight into Egypt*; i10. Cigoli, *Christ in the house of the Pharisee*; i15. Paris Bordone, *Venus, Mars, and Cupid*; i17. Claude Lorrain, *Meeting with Diana*; i19. Annibale Carracci (attributed), *St Jerome*; i21. Claude Lorrain, *Mercury stealing with the oxen of Apollo*; i22. Garofalo, *Holy Family*; i28. Guercino, *Herminia and Tancred*; i30 Carlo Saraceni, *St Roch and the angel*; i31. David Teniers the Younger (attributed), *Fête Champêtre*; i32. Claude Lorrain, *Sacrifice at Delphi*. Window wall: i42. Andrea del Sarto (copy from), *Madonna and Child*; i47. Quinten Massys, **Userers*; i63. Jan van Scorel, *Portrait of Agatha van Schoonven*; i64. Domenico Beccafumi, *St Jerome*.

The delightful **Galleria degli Specchi (Second Gallery)** was created in the 18C by Valvassori (the vault is decorated by Aureliano Milani). In the **Cabinet** is the **Portrait of Innocent X* commissioned by the Pope in 1650 from Velazquez—the gem of the collection. Also displayed here is a sculpted **bust of the Pope by Gian Lorenzo Bernini. In the gallery are displayed Roman statues and two paintings: a *portrait of Joan of Aragon, princess Colonna* (a copy from Raphael), and *The Crossing of the Red Sea* by Antonio Tempesta.

At the end of the Galleria degli Specchi is a series of four rooms overlooking the Corso with prettily decorated ceilings. Here are exhibited works in the collection grouped according to period. The **Saletta del Settecento** displays Italian views by Hendrick Frans van Lint, Jan Frans van Bloemand, and Gaspar van Wittel. The **Saletta del Seicento** contains two masterpieces by Caravaggio: M5. **Rest on the Flight into Egypt*, and M6. *Penitent Magdalene*. The *San Sebastian* (M8) is by Ludovico Carracci.

Saletta del Cinquecento. N1. Raphael, **Double portrait*; N2. Tintoretto, *Portrait of a young man*; N4. Titian, **Salome with the head of St John the Baptist*; N5. Jacopo and Francesco Bassano, *Return of the Prodigal Son*.

The Saletta del Quattrocento contains 15C works: O/1 Ludovico Mazzolino, *Pietà*; O/2 Antoniazzo Romano, *Madonna and Child*; O/3 Garofalo, *Holy Family*; O/4 Ortolano, *Nativity and saints*; O/5 Ludovico Mazzolino, *Massacre of the Innocents* and *Rest on the Flight*; O/9–O/11. Works by Bernardino Parentino; O/12. Hans Memling, *Deposition*; O/13. Quentin Massys, **The Hypocrites*; and works by Giovanni di Paolo.

At the end is a little **cabinet** with three busts, portraits of Filippo Andrea Doria V, his wife Mary Talbot, and her sister.

Third Gallery. Left wall: q2. Correggio, **Triumph of Virtue* (unfinished sketch for the painting now in the Louvre); q3. Claude Lorrain, *Rest on the Flight into Egypt*; q10. Lorenzo Lotto, *St Jerome*; q13. Guercino, *Return of the prodigal son*; q18. Copy of the portrait of Innocent X by Velazquez, which originally hung here (see above); q19. Guido Reni, *Madonna in adoration of the Child*; q21. Pieter Bruegel the Elder, *Battle in the port of Naples*; q23. Guercino, *St John the Baptist in the desert*; q25. Garofalo, *Marriage of St Catherine of Alexandria*; q31. Alessandro Allori, *Calvary*; q32. Marcello Venusti, *Crucifixion*; Sassoferrato, q34. *Holy Family*, q39. *Madonna in prayer*. Window wall: q46. Giovanni Bellini (and his bottega), *Madonna and Child with St John the Baptist*; q49. Paul Brill, *Landscape with a hunting scene*; q53. Garofalo, *Holy Family with saints*; q56. Leandro Bassano, *Sacrifice of Noah*; q57. Guercino, *St John the Evangelist*; q58. Paul Brill, *Landscape with hunting scene*; q59. Jacopo Bassano, *Adam and Eve in Earthly*

Paradise; q61. Boccaccio Boccaccino, *Holy Conversation*; q65. and q67. Jan Frans van Bloemen, Landscapes; q66. Federico Barocci, Study of a head.

Fourth Gallery. Bust (I) of Olimpia Aldobrandini Pamphilj by Alessandro Algardi. s43. Jan Brueghel the Elder, *Madonna and Child with animals*. Left wall: s60. Jan Brueghel the Elder, Landscape; s57. Caravaggio, *Young St John the Baptist* (a replica of the painting in the Pinacoteca Capitolina); s71. Parmigianino, *Madonna and Child*; s80. Ludovico Mazzolino, *Christ in the temple*; s83. Jan Brueghel the Elder, *Earthly Paradise*; s84. David Ryckaert III, *Rural feast*. The charming little **Saletta degli Specchi** was decorated by Stefano Pozzi in the early 18C. Jan Brueghel the Elder; s90. *Creation of Man*; s92. *Temptations of St Anthony*, s94. *Vision of St John on Patmos*, s.95 *Allegory of Fire*; s96. *Allegory of Water*; s111. *Allegory of Air*; s112. *Allegory of Earth*. s4. Domenichino, *Landscape*. Window wall: s13. Guercino, *St Joseph*; s14. Marco Basaiti, *St Sebastian*; s16. Titian, Angel (fragment); s21. Marcello Venusti, *Christ in the garden*; s22. Ludovico Carracci, *Madonna and Child with saints*; s31. Nicolò Rondinelli, *Madonna and Child*.

Steps lead down from the fourth gallery into the **Salone Aldobrandini** which displays Antique sculptures (not yet fully catalogued) including three large sarcophagi, busts and statues (in the centre, young Bacchus in red basalt and a centaur in red and black marble). The four Brussels tapestries illustrate the battle of Lepanto, and on the far wall are marble reliefs by François Duquesnoy.

In the **Private Apartments** red dominates the decorations. The **Winter Garden** (or conservatory) is decorated with antique busts, a 16C Brussels tapestry, and an 18C sedan chair. The **Fumoir** (or smoking room) was created by Mary Talbot, wife of Filippo Andrea Doria V, in the 19C (her portrait hangs here). In the adjoining room is a large polyptych of the *Madonna and Child with saints and angels*, of the early 15C Tuscan school (attributed to the 'Maestro di Borgo alla Collina') and *St Bernardine* by Sano di Pietro. The 16C Brussels tapestry depicts the month of February. In the **Room of Andrea Doria**, with a 16C ceiling, a glass case contains some of Filippo Andrea Doria's possessions, and there are two more Brussels tapestries with scenes of Lepanto. The portrait of Christopher Columbus is by Mabuse.

The **Small Dining Room** contains a bust of Princess Emily Doria by Canonica, a collection of Trapani corals, ambers and ivories, and a 19C frieze showing the fiefs of the Doria-Pamphilj family. The **Green Salon**, contains a *Madonna* by Beccafumi; a *Deposition* by Hans Memling; a large mid-15C Tournai tapestry with the medieval legend of Alexander the Great; a bronze bust of Innocent X, by Algardi; and a *Portrait of a man*, by Lorenzo Lotto. In the centre is a rare 18C cradle in carved and gilded wood. In the recess to the left is a beautiful *Annunciation*, by Filippo Lippi.

On the north side of Piazza del Collegio Romano (Pl. 3; 6) is the **Collegio Romano**, a large building erected in 1585 by order of Gregory XIII for the Jesuits. The architect was probably the Jesuit Giuseppe Valeriani. It is now partly used by the Ministry of 'Beni Culturali e Ambientali' (Cultural Affairs).

The founder of the Jesuit College was St Francis Borgia, duke of Gandia, third in succession after Ignatius Loyola as General of the Jesuits. Its pupils included eight popes: Urban VIII, Innocent X, Clement IX, Clement X, Innocent XII, Clement XI, Innocent XIII and Clement XII. The Jesuit library founded here

formed the nucleus of the Biblioteca Nazionale Centrale Vittorio Emanuele which was moved to new premises near the Castro Pretorio in 1975. The Salone della Crociera, with its original bookcases, has been used to house part of the library of the Istituto Nazionale di Archeologia e Storia dell'Arte in Palazzo di Venezia (see p 77).

On the south side of the piazza is the former church of **Santa Marta** (restored as an exhibition centre), by Carlo Fontana, with a good doorway. Inside (closed when not in use) is a pretty vault decoration designed by Baciccia, with paintings by him and Paolo Albertoni. Just beyond, on the left of Via del Piè di Marmo, in Via di Santo Stefano del Cacco, is a colossal marble foot (perhaps from an ancient Roman statue of Isis).

On the Corso, next to Palazzo Doria, rises **SANTA MARIA IN VIA LATA**, a small church of ancient foundation, rebuilt in the 15C. The graceful **façade** (recently cleaned) and vestibule are by Pietro da Cortona (1660). The pretty little **interior** is open 16–19. At the end of the left aisle is the tomb (1776) of the poet Antonio Tebaldeo (1463–1537), tutor of Isabella d'Este, secretary of Lucrezia Borgia, courtier of Leo X, and friend of Raphael (who painted his portrait in the Vatican, a copy of which is placed here). The church also contains tombs of the families of Joseph and Lucien Bonaparte. The high altar and apse, decorated with coloured marbles, have been attributed as an early work to Bernini, but they are now thought to be by Santi Ghetti.

The lower level (closed for restoration) has remains of a large Roman building which probably served as a warehouse, converted in the 5C into a Christian chapel and welfare centre, rebuilt and enlarged as a church in the 7C and 11C. Interesting murals (7C–9C) were discovered here (detached). A tradition that St Paul was guarded on this spot during his second visit to Rome, led to excavations as early as the 17C (when a high relief by Cosimo Fancelli was put in place).

Here the Corso was spanned by the *Arcus Novus* erected by Diocletian in 303–04, and demolished in 1491 when the church was rebuilt.

In the Corso, beyond Via Lata, a bank now occupies Palazzo Simonetti (No. 307), once the property of the Boncompagni-Ludovisi and for years the residence of Cardinal de Bernis, ambassador of Louis XV at the papal court. Low down on the corner of the palace, in Via Lata, is the **Fontanella del Facchino** with a sturdy porter holding a barrel; water issues from the bung-hole. Water-sellers are supposed to have resold Tiber or Trevi water from their barrels. *Il Facchino* was one of Rome's 'talking statues'; with his flat beret, he was once thought to be a caricature portrait of Martin Luther, but the figure more probably represents Abbondio Rizio, a heavy drinker. In 1751, Vanvitelli attributed the sculpture to Michelangelo.

Opposite Palazzo Simonetti is **SAN MARCELLO** (Pl. 3; 6), a very old church, rebuilt on a design by Jacopo Sansovino after a fire in 1519, with a **façade** (recently restored) by Carlo Fontana (1683). The **interior** (open 7–12, 16–19) was frescoed in the 17C by Giovanni Battista Ricci da Novara (including the *Crucifixion* on the west wall, the *scenes of the Passion* between the windows, and the apse). On the west wall is the tomb of Cardinal Giovanni Michiel (died 1503) and his nephew Bishop Antonio Orso (died 1511), by Jacopo Sansovino. **South side**. Third chapel: 15C fresco of the *Madonna and Child* in a marble frame, and, on the altar wall, frescoes by Francesco Salviati. On the ceiling of the fourth chapel are frescoes begun by Perino del Vaga (*Creation of Eve, St Mark, and St*

John the Evangelist), completed after the sack of Rome by Daniele da Volterra and Pellegrino Tibaldi. Beneath the altar, which has a fine 14C crucifix, is an interesting Roman cippus. The fifth chapel has paintings by Aureliano Milani (c 1725). The fourth chapel on the **north side** has frescoes by Taddeo Zuccari and busts (on the right wall) of three members of the Frangipane family by Alessandro Algardi. Excavations of the medieval church may one day be opened to the public.

Via del Caravita diverges to the left for the delightful Rococo PIAZZA DI SANT'IGNAZIO, a 'theatrical' masterpiece by Filippo Raguzzini (1728). The Jesuit church of **SANT'IGNAZIO** (Pl. 3; 6) rivals the Gesù in magnificence. It was begun in 1626 by Cardinal Ludovisi as the church of the Collegio Romano (see above), to celebrate the canonisation of St Ignatius de Loyola by the cardinal's uncle Gregory XV. The design by Carlo Maderno and others was carried out by Orazio Grassi, a Jesuit mathematician from the college, who is also responsible for the fine **façade**.

The spacious aisled **interior** (open 7.30–12.30, 16–19.15) is sumptuously decorated. In the vaulting of the nave and apse are remarkable *paintings representing the missionary activity of the Jesuits and the *Triumph of St Ignatius*, the masterpiece of Andrea Pozzo. The amazing trompe l'oeil perspective projects the walls of the church beyond their architectural limits, and Pozzo even provided a cupola, never built because of lack of funds, in a canvas 17m in diameter. The vaulting and 'dome' are best seen from a small yellow disc set in the pavement about the middle of the nave. The second chapel on the south side, lavishly decorated with rare marbles, has an altarpiece of the *Death of St Joseph* by Francesco Trevisani.

In the ornate **chapels of the transepts**, designed by Andrea Pozzo, with marble Solomonic columns, are large marble high reliefs: on the south side, the *Glory of St Louis Gonzaga*, by Pierre Le Gros, with a lapis lazuli urn containing the remains of the saint, and two figures of angels, 18C works by Bernardo Ludovisi; on the north side, the *Annunciation* by Filippo della Valle, and another lapis lazuli urn with the relics of St John Berchmans (died 1621), and two 18C angels by Pietro Bracci. In the chapel to the right of the high altar is the funerary monument to Gregory XV and his nephew Cardinal Ludovico Ludovisi, the founders of the church, by Pierre Le Gros. From the sacristy there is a lift (access by request) to a chapel frescoed by Borgognone.

On the right side of the Corso (No. 239) is Palazzo Sciarra-Colonna, built in the late 16C by Flaminio Ponzio, under which, in 1887, was found part of the Acqua Vergine. Opposite is a bank building by Antonio Cipolla (1874). The street here was once spanned by the triumphal Arch of Claudius (fragments of which are preserved in Palazzo dei Conservatori). Via delle Muratte diverges (right) for the Fontana di Trevi (see p 166).

In Piazza di Pietra, a few metres to the left of the Corso by Via di Pietra, are the remains of the **Temple of Hadrian**, built by Antoninus Pius in 145 and dedicated to his father. The wall of the cella remains, along with the peristyle of the right side with 11 disengaged fluted Corinthian *columns (15m high). They are incorporated in the façade of the stock exchange building.

Piazza Colonna

Via Bergamaschi leads north to PIAZZA COLONNA (Pl. 3; 4), on the Corso, which for centuries was the centre of the city, and is still one of its busiest squares. On the north side rises the great flank of **Palazzo Chigi**, begun in the 16C by Matteo di Castello (and also possibly Giacomo della Porta and Carlo Maderno) and finished in the 17C by Felice della Greca. It is now the official residence of the Prime Minister (no admission; but the interesting 17C courtyard can be seen through the entrance). The famous Chigi library founded by Alexander VII, was presented by the State to the Vatican in 1923. The main façade of the palace faces the Corso and Largo Chigi from which the busy Via del Tritone leads towards Piazza Barberini.

The east side of the piazza is closed across the Corso, by the **Galleria Colonna** (1914), an interior arcade in the form of a Y. On the opposite side of the piazza is the façade of **Palazzo Wedekind** (1838), incorporating on the ground floor a handsome portico, with 12 Ionic marble columns, brought from a Roman building at Veio. The little church on the south side is San Bartolomeo dei Bergamaschi (1561). At the beginning of Via del Tritone (see above) is **Santa Maria in Via** rebuilt in 1594, with a good Baroque front, completed in 1670.

In the centre of the piazza, beside a graceful fountain, designed by Giacomo della Porta (the dolphins, etc., are a 19C addition by Achille Stocchi), rises the monument from which it derives its name, the majestic **COLUMN OF MARCUS AURELIUS** (*Colonna Antonina*; restored in 1984–88). It was erected between AD 180 and 196 in honour of the emperor's victories over the Germans and Sarmatians (169–76), and dedicated to him and his wife, Faustina. The column is made entirely of marble from Luni, and is formed of 27 blocks. The ancient level of the ground was nearly 4m lower than at present. The shaft measures 100 Roman feet (29.6m), and the total height of the column, including the base and the statue, is nearly 42m. In the interior (no admission) are 203 steps lit by 56 tiny windows.

The column was inspired by Trajan's Column, but instead of being the focal point of a forum, it was in the centre of an important group of monuments of the Antonine period. The ancient base was decorated with Victories, festoons and reliefs. The summit was originally crowned with figures of Marcus Aurelius and Faustina, but in 1589 Domenico Fontana replaced the imperial statues with one of St Paul.

Around the shaft a bas-relief ascends in a spiral of 20 turns, interrupted halfway by a Victory; the lower part of the relief commemorates the war against the Germanic tribes (169–73), the upper that against the Sarmatians (174–76). The philosopher-emperor led his troops in all these important battles, which delayed the barbaric invasions for several centuries. On the third spiral (east side) the Roman soldiers are represented as being saved by a rainstorm, which in the 4C was regarded as a miracle brought about by the prayers of the Christians in their ranks. Casts of the reliefs are kept in the Museo della Civiltà Romana (see Chapter 26), but they are not at present on view.

A little further west is Piazza di Montecitorio, with the old façade of **PALAZZO DI MONTECITORIO**, which, since 1871, has been the seat of the Italian Chamber of Deputies. The original palace was begun for the Ludovisi family in 1650 by Bernini, who was responsible for the general plan of the building and for the idea of enhancing the effect of the façade by giving it a convex, slightly

polygonal form. The north façade of the palazzo is in Piazza del Parlamento. In 1918 it was enlarged and given its new façade by Ernesto Basile; the principal entrance is now on this side. The Art Nouveau red-brick front is in contrast to the prevailing style of architecture. In the interior, the Chamber, also of this period, is panelled in oak and brightly illuminated from above by a row of windows pierced in the cornice. Below the cornice is an encaustic frieze by Aristide Sartorio, begun in 1908, representing the development of Italian civilisation. The fine bas-relief in bronze in honour of the House of Savoy is by Davide Calandra.

The **obelisk** (22m high) in the centre of the piazza was originally erected at Heliopolis by Psammetichus II (c 590 BC). It was brought to Rome by Augustus to celebrate his victory over Cleopatra, and set up in the Campus Martius, where it served as the gnomon of an immense sundial. In 1748 it was discovered underground in the Largo dell'Impresa (an open space north of the palace) and in 1792 it was erected on its present site.

In the Corso, beyond Largo Chigi, stands Palazzo Marignoli (1889), and (left) Palazzo Verospi where Shelley lived in 1819 (plaque). Via delle Convertite leads (right) to Piazza San Silvestro, an important bus terminus, with the **Central Post Office** (Pl. 3; 4). The church of **San Silvestro in Capite** (open 7–12.30; fest. 9–12.30, 15.30–19.30; services in English); was originally erected here by Pope Stephen III (752–57) on the site of a Roman building, possibly Aurelian's Temple of the Sun. It was bestowed on the English Roman Catholics by Leo XIII in 1890. The 12C–13C campanile is surmounted by a 12C bronze cock. It contains interesting 17C works, including the organ, and paintings by Giacinto Brandi, Orazio Gentileschi, Francesco Trevisani, Lodovico Gimignani, and Pomarancio.

Further along the Corso (now less busy), beyond Piazza del Parlamento (see above), is Palazzo Fiano (left), built over the remains of the Ara Pacis (see below). This was the site of the Roman Arco di Portogallo, demolished in 1662 by order of Alexander VII. A small square opens out just beyond, opposite the pretty Via Frattina, the first of several long straight pedestrian streets which open off this side of the Corso and end in Piazza di Spagna (see Chapter 8). In the square, on the left, is **SAN LORENZO IN LUCINA** (Pl. 3; 4), a church probably dating from the time of Sixtus III (432–40), or even earlier, rebuilt in the 12C, and again in 1650. Of the 12C church there remain the campanile (restored) which has several rows of small loggie with colonnettes, the **portico** with six Ionic columns, and the doorway.

Interior: **south side**. In the first chapel a reliquary contains part of the gridiron on which St Laurence was supposed to have been martyred. Second chapel: on the left pillar is the tomb of Nicolas Poussin (1594–1665) by Lemoyne, erected by Chateaubriand in 1830. The fourth chapel, designed by Bernini for Innocent X's doctor Gabriele Fonseca, decorated with pretty stuccoes, has a fine portrait bust (left of the altar) by Bernini. The *Crucifixion* on the **high altar** is by Guido Reni.

North side. The decorative fifth chapel was designed by Simon Vouet, and contains two good paintings of *St Francis* by him (on the left and right walls). In the second chapel the altarpiece is by Carlo Saraceni. Pompilia (in Browning's *The Ring and the Book*) was married in this church. Excavations (open at 16.00

on the last Sat of the month) have revealed interesting remains of the early Christian basilica (2C–3C), above Roman edifices, including a private house and a market building.

Beyond is **Palazzo Ruspoli** (No. 418A; left), designed by Ammannati, with a great marble staircase by Martino Longhi the Younger, and frescoes by Jacopo Zucchi. Since 1990 it has been the seat of the Fondazione Roberto Memmo which holds exhibitions here. At Largo Carlo Goldoni three streets converge on the Corso: Via Condotti, with its fine shops, leading past the church of the **Santissima Trinità dei Spagnoli**, with an 18C eliptical interior (open 7–12, 16.30–19.30; closed July & Aug), to Piazza di Spagna (see Chapter 8); Via Fontanella di Borghese, ending in Piazza Borghese (see below); and Via Tomacelli, which leads to Ponte Cavour, an important bridge over the Tiber leading to the Prati district.

Further on, where the street widens, stands **SANTI AMBROGIO E CARLO AL CORSO** (Pl. 3; 4; open 9.30–12, 17–19; winter 8–12, 16–19), built in 1612 by Onorio Longhi, completed by his son Martino. The fine cupola (being restored) is by Pietro da Cortona. The façade (heavily restored) is by Giovanni Battista Menicucci and Fra Mario da Canepina (1690). The altarpiece (poorly lit; *The Madonna presenting San Carlo to Christ*) is one of Carlo Maratta's best works, and on an altar behind it is a rich urn containing the heart of St Charles Borromeo. In the neighbouring Oratory of Sant'Ambrogio (at No. 437, to the left of the church; ring for the porter), on the site of the old church built by the Lombards in 1513 on a piece of land granted them by Sixtus IV, is a marble group of the *Deposition*, by Tommaso della Porta (1618).

Mausoleum of Augustus and Ara Pacis

Behind the apse of San Carlo is the ugly Piazza Augusto Imperatore (Pl. 3; 2; now used by tourist buses) laid out by the Fascist regime in 1936–38 around the **MAUSOLEUM OF AUGUSTUS** (Pl. 3; 2), or *Tumulus Caesarum* (admission by written request only; write to the Ripartizione X del Comune di Roma, 29 Portico d'Ottavia, 00100 Rome, fax 689 2115; part of the interior can be seen through the main south entrance). This was the tomb of Augustus and of the principal members of his family, the gens Julia-Claudia, and was one of the most sacred monuments of ancient Rome. The last Roman emperor to be buried here was Nerva in AD 98. Erected in 28 BC, it is a circular structure 87m in diameter. The smaller cylinder above was originally surmounted by a tumulus of earth some 45m high, planted with cypresses and probably crowned with a statue of the emperor.

The mausoleum was excavated and restored in 1926–30. The circular base, of opus reticulatum, has a series of large niches on the outside. The sepulchral cella in the centre has travertine walls, a central pillar, and three niches which contained the cinerary urns of Augustus and of his wife Livia, his nephews Gaius and Lucius Caesar and his sister Octavia, with an inscription to his beloved nephew Marcellus, who was the first to be interred here in 23 BC. On either side of the entrance were two obelisks, one of which is now in Piazza del Quirinale, and the other in Piazza dell'Esquilino, as well as bronze inscriptions with the official will of Augustus, a copy of which was found at Ankara (it is reproduced on the outside wall of the pavilion protecting the Ara Pacis, see below).

In the Middle Ages the tomb became a fortress of the Colonna. Later it was

pillaged to provide travertine for other buildings, and a wooden amphitheatre was built inside it, where Goethe watched animal-baiting in 1787. Later still it was converted into a concert hall and was used as such until 1936.

To the west of the Mausoleum, between Via di Ripetta and the Tiber, is a platform approached by a flight of steps at either end. Here a building with glass walls was built in 1938 to protect the monumental altar called the **ARA PACIS**, reconstructed in 1937–38 from scattered fragments and from reproductions of other dispersed fragments. The carved decoration is a splendid example of Roman sculpture, influenced by Classical Greek and Hellenistic art. Opening hours: 9–17; Sun 9–13; closed Mon. ☎ 671 1035 69. Lire 3750.

The Ara Pacis Augustae was consecrated in the Campus Martius on 4 July 13 BC, and dedicated four years later, after the victorious return of Augustus from Spain and Gaul, in celebration of the peace that he had established within the Empire. This much is known from the document (Res gestae Divi Augusti) which the emperor had engraved on bronze tablets (see above) in Rome a year before his death in AD 14. This has been copied on the wall of the modern pavilion.

In 1568, during excavations for the foundations of Palazzo Fiano (on the Corso), nine blocks belonging to the frieze of the altar were found and bought by Cardinal Ricci da Montepulciano for the Grand Duke of Tuscany. To facilitate transport, each block was sawn into three. These went to the Uffizi Gallery in Florence. The cardinal overlooked two other blocks unearthed at the same time. One of these eventually passed to the Louvre in Paris; the other to the Vatican Museum.

Three hundred years later (1859), during a reconstruction of Palazzo Fiano, other parts of the altar were found, and they were acquired in 1898 by the Italian Government for the Museo Nazionale Romano. In 1903 and 1937 excavations brought to light the basement of the altar and further fragments. The pieces from the Museo Nazionale Romano and the Uffizi were recovered; those in the Louvre, the Vatican, and the Villa Medici were copied, and the altar was reconstructed, as far as possible, in its original form and appearance.

The monument, built throughout of Luni marble, has a simple base with two horizontal bands. On the base is an almost square-walled enclosure, with two open and two closed sides. The **external decoration** of the enclosure is in two zones divided by a horizontal Greek key-pattern border. The lower zone is covered with an intricate and beautiful composition of acanthus leaves on which are swans with outstretched wings. In the upper zone is the frieze of reliefs, with a decorated cornice above it. Between the jambs of the main or north entrance (approached by a flight of steps) are scenes illustrating the origins of Rome. The left panel (almost entirely lost) represented the *Lupercalia*; the right panel shows *Aeneas sacrificing the white sow*. The panels of the south entrance depict *Tellus*, the earth goddess, possibly an allegory of Peace (left), and Rome (right), much damaged. The side panels represent the ceremony of the consecration of the altar: the procession includes Augustus, members of his family including children, State officials, and priests.

The **interior of the enclosure** is also in two zones; because sacrifices took

place here, the lower part has no decoration other than simple fluting. The upper zone, however, is decorated with beautifully carved bucrania. The **altar** is an exact reconstruction of all recovered fragments. Approached by a flight of steps, it has a back and two side walls; a further flight of narrow steps leads up past the walls to the altar proper. The cornice and the anta of the left side wall are the best preserved; the reliefs indicate the *Suovetaurilia*, or sacrifice of a pig, a sheep and an ox. Little else of the decoration survives.

To the south, on Via di Ripetta, in a district once inhabited by the Serbs (Schiavoni) who came here as refugees after the battle of Kossovo (15 June 1389), are two churches, **San Girolamo degli Schiavoni**, rebuilt in 1587, and **San Rocco** with a Neo-classical façade by Valadier (1834), and an early altarpiece by Baciccia in the sacristy. Further south, Via Borghese diverges left from Via di Ripetta (the name of which is a reminder of the vicinity of the old river bank and port) to **Palazzo Borghese** (Pl. 2; 6, 4; no admission), called from its shape the 'harpsichord of Rome'. It was begun perhaps by Vignola (c 1560) and completed by Flaminio Ponzio, who designed the beautiful terrace on the Tiber front. The palace was acquired by Cardinal Camillo Borghese, who became Pope Paul V in 1605, and was renowned for its splendour. For nearly two centuries it contained the paintings from the Galleria Borghese; they were restored to their former residence in 1891. It is now the seat of the 'Circolo della Caccia', an exclusive club founded in 1869. The pretty courtyard has long lines of twin columns in two storeys, and colossal statues representing Ceres and the empresses Sabina and Julia; a garden beyond contains fountains and Roman sculpture.

In Via Vittoria, across the Corso, is the Accademia Musicale di Santa Cecilia, a renowned musical academy. Further north the Corso passes (left) the church of **San Giacomo in Augusta** (so called from its proximity to the Mausoleum), with a façade by Maderno; it is known also as San Giacomo degli Incurabili from the adjoining hospital. Opposite is the small church of **Gesù e Maria** with a façade by Girolamo Rainaldi who was also responsible for the interior decoration completed c 1675.

At No. 18 (plaque) is the **Goethe Museum** (open 11–18; closed Tues; Lire 5000) in the house where Goethe lived in 1786–88. It has material relating to the poet's travels in Italy; also on display are several views of Rome by Piranesi, many of Tischbein's sketches of Goethe, and an unframed copy of the artist's famous painting, *Goethe in the Roman Countryside*.

Piazza del Popolo

PIAZZA DEL POPOLO (Pl. 3; 2), at the end of the Corso, provides a scenic entrance to the city from Via Flaminia and the north. Numerous famous travellers in the 19C recorded their first arrival in Rome through the Porta del Popolo. The piazza was created by Latino Giovenale Manetti in 1538 for Paul III in strict relationship to the three long straight roads which here penetrate the city as a trident, between the two twin-domed churches added in the 17C. The piazza was given its present symmetry by Giuseppe Valadier after the return of Pius VII from France in 1814. Between four fountains with lions by Valadier (1823; to a 16C design by Domenico Fontana) rises an **obelisk** (24m), the hieroglyphs on which celebrate the glories of the pharaohs Rameses II and

Santa Maria dei Miracoli and Santa Maria de Montesanto, Piazza del Popolo

Merenptah (13C–12C BC); Augustus brought it from Heliopolis, after the conquest of Egypt, and it was dedicated to the sun in the Circus Maximus. Domenico Fontana moved it here in 1589, as part of the urban plan of Sixtus V.

The three streets which converge on the piazza from the south are Via di Ripetta (see above) on the left, the Corso in the middle, and Via del Babuino (from Piazza di Spagna; see Chapter 8) on the right. The ends of the streets are separated by a pair of decorative Baroque churches (not always open), **Santa Maria dei Miracoli** (left) and **Santa Maria in Montesanto** (right); the façades were modified by Bernini and Carlo Fontana (1671–78), after Carlo Rainaldi. In the centre of each hemicycle is a fountain with marble groups (on the left, Neptune with two Tritons, on the right, Rome between the Tiber and the Anio, both by Giovanni Ceccarini; 1824) and at the ends are more Neo-classical statues of the Four Seasons. A winding road designed by Valadier, Viale Gabriele d'Annunzio, descends from the Pincio (see Chapter 8). In the piazza is a fashionable café.

Across the piazza (to the right of the gate) rises the flank of **SANTA MARIA DEL POPOLO** (Pl. 3; 2; open 7–12, 16–19; fest. 8–13.30, 16.30–19), on the site of a chapel erected by Paschal II in 1099 over the tombs of the Domitia family, which were believed to be the haunt of demons, because Nero was buried there. The Pope solemnly cut down a walnut tree that was supposed to shelter them. The church was rebuilt in 1227 and again under Sixtus IV (1472–77). The early Renaissance façade is attributed to Andrea Bregno.

The **interior** (lights in some chapels and the apse) was renovated by Bernini and has many important works of art. **South aisle**. First chapel (della Rovere): ***frescoes** by Pinturicchio (1485–89); over the altar, the *Adoration of the Child*; in the lunettes (very worn and restored), scenes from the life of St Jerome; on the right, tomb of Cardinal de Castro (1506), perhaps by Antonio da Sangallo the Younger; on the left, the tomb of Cardinals Cristoforo and Domenico Della Rovere (1477) by Mino da Fiesole and Andrea Bregno. The second chapel (Cybo) is well designed; the architecture is by Carlo Fontana and its marbles are especially rich and varied. The huge altarpiece (*Assumption* and *Four Doctors of the Church*) is by Carlo Maratta; at the sides are the tombs of the Cybo family, and of Bishop Girolamo Foscari (died 1463).

The third chapel (being restored), with a worn majolica pavement, was fres-

coed by the school of Pinturicchio (1504–07). To the right is the tomb of Giovanni della Rovere (1483; school of Andrea Bregno). Fourth chapel (Costa): altarpiece (1489) by the school of Andrea Bregno. On the right, tomb of Marcantonio Albertoni (1485); on the left, tomb of the founder, Cardinal Giorgio Costa (1508). In the lunettes, frescoes by the school of Pinturicchio (1489). The bronze *effigy of Cardinal Pietro Foscari, formerly attributed to Vecchietta, is now thought to be by Giovanni di Stefano (c 1485).

South transept. The altarpiece of the *Visitation* by Giovan Maria Morandi is in a frame supported by two angels by Ercole Ferrata and Arrigo Giardè. On the right, tomb of Cardinal Lodovico Podocataro of Cyprus (1508). In the dome over the crossing are frescoes by Raffaele Vanni. A corridor, passing an altar from the studio of Andrea Bregno, leads to the **sacristy** which contains a *tabernacle by Bregno, with a painted Madonna of the early Sienese school, and the monuments of Bishop Rocca (died 1482) and Archbishop Ortega Gomiel of Burgos (died 1514).

The triumphal arch is decorated with fine 17C gilded stuccoed reliefs, and over the **high altar** is the venerated *Madonna del Popolo*, a 14C painting. The **apse** of the church, behind the altar, with a shell design, is one of Bramante's earliest works in Rome, commissioned by Julius II (light on left). It is currently being restored. Here are the two splendid *tombs** of Cardinal Girolamo Basso della Rovere (1507) and Cardinal Ascanio Sforza (1505), signed by Andrea Sansovino. The *frescoes** high up in the vault—illustrating the *Coronation of the Virgin, Evangelists, Sibyls*, and *Four Fathers of the Church*—are by Pinturicchio (1508–09). The stained glass, commissioned by Julius II, is by Guillaume de Marcillat.

North transept. In the first chapel to the left of the choir, with a pretty vault, are two dramatic *paintings** by Caravaggio: *Crucifixion of St Peter* (right wall), and *Conversion of St Paul*, (left wall). These famous masterpieces, which have been restored recently, were executed in 1600–01. The altarpiece of the *Assumption of the Virgin* is by Annibale Carracci, who also designed the frescoes in the barrel-vault above, with attractive stuccoes. In the second chapel to the left of the choir, with another pretty vault, is a marble statue of St Catherine of Alexandria by Giulio Mazzoni and two paintings of the *Annunciation* by Giacomo Triga (early 18C). The altarpiece in the north transept of the *Holy Family*, by Bernardino Mei, is in another frame supported by two angels, by Antonio Raggi and Giovanni Antonio Mari; on the left wall is the tomb of Cardinal Bernardo Lonati (late 15C).

North aisle. Fourth chapel: frescoes by Pieter van Lint. The third chapel has fine monuments to the Mellini family: the earliest ones are low down on the right wall, and to the right of the altar (exquisite small tomb of Cardinal Pietro Mellini, 1483). To the left of the altar is a bust of Urbano Mellini by Alessandro Algardi. The *tomb of Giovanni Garzia Mellini (with a half figure of the cardinal) on the left wall, is also by Algardi. The second chapel is the octagonal well-lit *Chigi Chapel**, founded by the great banker Agostino Chigi (1465–1520). It was designed in a fusion of architecture, sculpture and painting by Raphael (1513–16). Work on the chapel was interrupted in 1520 with the death of Agostino and Raphael, and it was only completed after 1652 for Cardinal Fabio Chigi (Alexander VII) by Bernini. Raphael prepared the cartoons for the *mosaics** in the dome, executed by the Venetian artist Luigi de

Pace in 1516. These represent God the Father as Creator of the firmament, surrounded by symbols of the seven planets, each of which is guided by an angel as in Dante's conception. The frescoes depicting the Creation and the Fall, between the windows, and the medallions of the Seasons, are by Francesco Salviati (1552–54). The altarpiece (*Nativity of the Virgin*) is by Sebastiano del Piombo (1530–34); the bronze bas-relief in front, depicting Christ and the woman of Samaria, by Lorenzetto, was intended for the base of the pyramidal tomb of Agostino, but was moved here by Bernini. Statues of Prophets: by the altar, *Jonah (left), designed by Raphael, executed by Lorenzetto, and Habakkuk (right) by Bernini; by the entrance, Daniel and the lion, by Bernini and Elijah, by Lorenzetto.

The remarkable pyramidal form of the tombs of Agostino Chigi and of his brother Sigismondo (died 1526), executed by Lorenzetto, were dictated by Raphael's architectural scheme and derived from ancient Roman models. They were altered by Bernini. The unfinished burial crypt below the chapel, with another pyramid, would in Raphael's original design have been visible and illuminated from the chapel above. The lunettes above the tombs were painted by Raffaele Vanni in 1653. The marble intarsia figure of Death, with the Chigi stemma, in the centre of the pavement was added by Bernini.

On the left of the chapel is a colourful funerary monument, erected in 1771 in memory of Princess Odescalchi. In the **baptistery** are two ciboria by Andrea Bregno, and the tombs of Cardinals Francesco Castiglione (right; 1568) and Antonio Pallavicini (1507). The former Augustinian convent adjoining the church was the residence in Rome of Martin Luther during his mission here in 1511.

At the back of the church, near the steps from the Pincio, the **Sala del Bramante** is used for exhibitions.

Beside the church stands the monumental and historic **Porta del Popolo** (Pl. 3; 2; restored in 1984), which occupies almost the same site as the ancient Porta Flaminia. The inner face of the gate was designed by Bernini in 1655, on the occasion of the entry into Rome of Queen Christina of Sweden; the outer face (1561) is by Nanni di Baccio Bigio, who followed a design by Michelangelo. The two colossal statues of St Peter and St Paul in the outer niches, late works by Francesco Mochi, have been removed since 1979. The two side arches were opened in 1879. Outside the gate, in the busy Piazzale Flaminio, is an entrance to the huge park of the Villa Borghese (see Chapter 9).

8 · Piazza Venezia to Piazza di Spagna and the Pincio

From Piazza Venezia, Via Cesare Battisti leads uphill. On the left opens the long thin Piazza dei Santi Apostoli (Pl. 4; 5), the scene in recent years of political demonstrations. On the west side of the piazza is **Palazzo Odescalchi**, which extends to the Corso; the façade on the piazza is by Bernini, with additions by Niccolò Salvi and Luigi Vanvitelli (1750). At No. 67 is a Museum of Waxworks (open daily 9–20. ☎ 679 6482; Lire 6000), opened in 1953.

Galleria Colonna

The east side of the piazza is occupied by the huge building of **PALAZZO COLONNA** (Pl. 4; 5) which incorporates the church of Santi Apostoli.

The palace was built by Martin V (Oddone Colonna), who lived here as pope from 1424 until his death in 1431. It was rebuilt in 1730, and here, on 4 June 1802, after the cession of Piedmont to France, Carlo Emanuele IV of Savoy, King of Sardinia, became a Jesuit and abdicated in favour of his brother Vittorio Emanuele I. Four arches spanning Via della Pilotta connect the palace with the Villa Colonna (no admission) which has a beautiful garden with tall cypresses (part of which can be seen from the Galleria Colonna; see below). In the garden are the remains of the huge Temple of Serapis, built in the time of Caracalla.

The palace contains the magnificent **Galleria Colonna** (open Sat 9–13; closed Aug. ☎ 679 4362. Lire 4000), begun in 1654 by Cardinal Girolamo I Colonna, who employed the architect Antonio del Grande, but it was not completed until nearly 50 years later. On Del Grande's death in 1671, Girolamo Fontana took over direction. In 1703 the gallery was opened by Filippo II Colonna. One of the most important of the patrician collections in Rome, it is arranged in magnificent Baroque galleries, and is beautifully maintained. The entrance is at 17 Via della Pilotta. The paintings, most of them not labelled, are all numbered according to the description given below.

From the entrance, stairs mount to the **vestibule**, in which is displayed a painting of St Julian, attributed to Perino del Vaga. The **Hall of the Colonna Bellica** is named after a 16C column of rosso antico, surmounted by a statue of Pallas Athena. The ceiling frescoes of the Reception into Heaven of Marcantonio II Colonna, are by Giuseppe Chiari.

The paintings include: 132. Pietro Novelli, *Isabella Colonna with her son Lorenzo Onofrio*; 139. Palma Vecchio, *Madonna and Child, with St Peter and donor*; 66. Van Dyck (attributed), *Lucrezia Tomacelli Colonna*; *25. Bonifacio Veronese, *Holy Family, with Saints Jerome and Lucy*; 28. Hieronymus Bosch (copy from), *Temptation of St Anthony*; *32. Bronzino, *Venus with Cupid and a satyr*; 156. 16C Roman school (formerly attributed to Agostino Carracci), *Cardinal Pompeo Colonna*; 134. Gian Paolo Olmo or Moretto, *Portrait of a man with a dog*; 186. Domenico Tintoretto, *Adoration of the Sacrament*; *147. Scipione Pulzone, *Pius V*; 53. School of Dosso Dossi, *Giacomo Sciarra Colonna* (?); *106. Lorenzo Lotto (attributed), *Cardinal Pompeo Colonna*; 37. Bartolomeo Cancellieri (attributed), so-called *Portrait of Vittoria Colonna*; 189. Jacopo Tintoretto, *Narcissus*; Michele di Ridolfo del Ghirlandaio, 117, 115, 116. *Venus and Cupid, Dawn*, and *Night*.

Sculpture: Hercules, Bacchus, and Head of Antinous. On the steps leading down to the Great Hall is preserved a cannon ball which fell here on 24 June 1849, during the siege of Rome.

The **Great Hall** is superbly decorated. The ceiling paintings, by Giovanni Coli and Filippo Gherardi, depict incidents in the life of Marcantonio II Colonna, who commanded the papal contingent at Lepanto (1571); the central panel illustrates the battle. On the walls are four Venetian mirrors with flower paintings by Mario de' Fiori and Giovanni Stanchi, and putti painted by Carlo Maratta.

The paintings include: Salvator Rosa, *162. St John the Baptist*, once thought to be a self-portrait, 163. *Preaching of St John the Baptist*; 14. Francesco Bassano the Younger, *Christ in the house of the Levite*; 46. Giovanni Domenico Cerrini, *St

Irene taking the arrows from St Sebastian; 192. Follower of Jacopo Tintoretto, *Portrait of a man with his secretary*; Pier Francesco Mola, 123. *Hagar and Ishmael*, 124. *Rebecca at the well*; 104. Lombard school (formerly attributed to Scipione Pulzone), *Family portrait of Alfonso III Gonzaga, Count of Novellara*; 165. Copy from Rubens (formerly attributed to Van Dyck), *Equestrian portrait of Carlo Colonna, duke of Marsi*. Giovanni Lanfranco, 98. *Magdalen in glory*, 99. *St Peter delivered from prison by the angel* (perhaps a copy); 7. Nicolò Alunno, *Madonna del Soccorso* (the Virgin rescuing a child from a demon); 164. Matteo Rosselli (attributed), *Allegory of the Fine Arts*; 151. Guido Reni, *St Francis of Assisi with two angels*; 168. Enea Salmeggia, *Martyrdom of St Catherine*; 82. Guercino, St Paul the Hermit; 6. Alessandro Allori, *Descent into hell*; 180. Sustermans (attributed), *Federico Colonna, viceroy of Valencia*; 40. 17C Roman school (formerly attributed to Ribera), *St Jerome*; 141. Bartolomeo Passarotti, *Family of Lodovico Peracchini*; 167. Rubens (follower of), *Assumption of the Virgin*.

The Roman sculpture includes: Dancing faun; Marcus Aurelius; Gladiator. Fine bas-reliefs and sarcophagi fragments are set into the walls beneath the windows, and into statue pedestals.

The **Room of the Desks** (or 'Room of the Landscapes') derives its name from two valuable *desks displayed here. The first, in ebony, has 28 ivory bas-reliefs by Francis and Dominic Steinhard after drawings by Carlo Fontana; the central relief is a copy of Michelangelo's *Last Judgement*, the other 27 are copies of works by Raphael. The second desk, in sandalwood, is adorned with lapis lazuli, amethysts, and other semi-precious stones; in front are 12 small amethyst columns and at the top gilt bronze statuettes representing the Muses and Apollo seated under a laurel tree. The ceiling frescoes, by Sebastiano Ricci, are of the battle of Lepanto.

In this room is a fine series of *landscapes by Gaspard Dughet (54–65), and a further series by J.F. van Bloemen, with figures probably by Placido Costanzi (21–24). Others include: Borgognone, 49. *Stag hunt*, 50. *Battle scene*; 182. Herman van Swanevelt (formerly attributed to Claude Lorraine), *Landscape with ruins of the Palatine Hill*; 146. Nicolas Poussin (follower of), *Apollo and Daphne*; 126. Jan Brueghel the Elder (and Josse de Momper?), *Landscape with figures*; 31. Paul Brill (attributed), *Antigone recovering the bodies of her brothers*; 121. 16C Flemish school, *Landscape with Noli me tangere*; 89. Jacob de Heusch (formerly attributed to Salvator Rosa), *Seascape*; 181. Herman van Swanevelt, *Landscape with the Good Samaritan*; 113. Circle of Michele Marieschi (formerly attributed to Canaletto), *View of the Campo and Scuola di San Rocco in Venice*.

Sculpture: Susini, copy in bronze of the Farnese bull; two Roman fire irons in polished bronze; bronze group of a centaur and a female figure.

Room of the Apotheosis of Martin V. This room takes its name from the subject of the ceiling painting by Benedetto Luti. Above the windows, Pietro Bianchi, *Fame crowning Victory*. Above the end wall, Pompeo Batoni, *Time discovering Truth*. 159. Roman school(?), *Cain and Abel*; Domenico Tintoretto, 187, 188. Portraits; 152. Workshop of Guido Reni, *St Agnes*; Guercino, 85, 86. *Annunciation*; 183. German School, 1524 (formerly attributed to Mabuse), *Man with clasped hands*; 33. Bronzino, *Madonna and Child with Saints John and Elizabeth*; 190. Jacopo Tintoretto (formerly attributed to Titian), *Onofrio Panvinio, the Augustinian*; Francesco Salviati, *170. Portrait of a Man, 169. Raising of Lazarus*; 1. Francesco Albani, *Rape of Europa*; 83. Guercino, *Guardian angel*; 178.

Giovanni di Pietro Spagna, *St Jerome*; 191. Follower of Jacopo Tintoretto, *Spinet player*; 8. Andrea del Sarto (formerly attributed to Puligo), *Madonna and Child*; 43. Annibale Carracci (also attributed to Bartolomeo Passarotti), *Peasant eating beans*; 26. Paris Bordone, *Holy Family with Saints Jerome, Sebastian, and Mary Magdalene*; *197. Paolo Veronese, *Man in Venetian costume*.

Sculpture: Orfeo Buselli, bust of Cardinal Jerome I Colonna; two Roman marble busts.

The **Throne Room** is reserved, as in other princely houses, for the Pope; the chair is turned to the wall so that no one else can sit in it. 144. Pisanello (copy from), *Portrait of Martin V, Oddone Colonna*; Scipione Pulzone, 149. *Portrait of Marcantonio II Colonna*; 150. (attributed), *Portrait of Felice Colonna Orsini*. In this room are (198) a nautical chart presented by the Roman people to Marcantonio II and a parchment diploma given him by the Roman senate after the battle of Lepanto. French clock by I. Godet of Paris. Statuettes in bronze of a satyr and Aphrodite; and marble busts of Zeus and a woman.

Room of Maria Mancini (or 'Room of the Primitives'). 51. Francesco Cozza, *Birth of the Virgin*; 143. Pietro da Cortona, *Resurrection of Christ, with members of the Colonna family*; 92. Jacob van Amsterdam, *Christ appearing to the Madonna and St John after the Resurrection*; *198. Bartolomeo Vivarini, *Madonna enthroned*; 105. Luca Longhi, *Madonna with the young St John and a monk*; Francesco Albani, 3, 4. *Herminia among the shepherds*; *35. Giuliano Bugiardini, *Madonna*; *154. Rocco Zoppo (attributed; formerly attributed to Melozzo da Forlì), *Portrait of a young man in profile* (traditionally identified as Guidobaldo della Rovere, Duke of Urbino); 10. Iacopo degli Avanzi, *Crucifixion*; 102. Copy from Leonardo da Vinci, *Madonna and Child*; 175. Girolamo Sicciolante da Sermoneta, *Madonna with the infant St John*; *179. Stefano da Zevio, *Madonna and Child enthroned with angels*; 30. School of Botticelli, *Madonna and Child*; 130. Gaspar Netscher (attributed), *Maria Colonna Mancini* (niece of Cardinal Mazarin); 38. Simone Cantarini, *Holy Family*; 166. Rubens (copy from), *Reconciliation of Esau and Jacob*; 29. Workshop of Botticelli (formerly attributed to Jacopo del Sellaio), *Apostle St James*; 137, 138. Bernart van Orley, *The seven joys and seven sorrows of Mary*; 90. Innocenzo da Imola, *Holy Family with St Francis*; 84. Guercino, *Moses with the tables of law*.

Santi Apostoli

The church of Santi Apostoli (Pl. 4; 5) was built by Pelagius I c 560 to commemorate the defeat and expulsion of the Goths by the Byzantine viceroy Narses, and dedicated to the Apostles James and Philip. It was restored and enlarged in the 15C and 16C and almost completely rebuilt by Carlo and Francesco Fontana in 1702–14. The unusual **façade**, which has the appearance of a palace rather than a church, consists of a stately Renaissance double **loggia** of nine arches. This is attributed to Baccio Pontelli, and was built at the cost of Cardinal della Rovere, afterwards Pope Julius II. The upper storey was filled in with Baroque windows by Carlo Rainaldi c 1665 (who also added the balustrade with statues of the Apostles). Behind this and above it can be seen the Neo-classical façade of the church added by Valadier in 1827. In the **portico** (closed by an iron grille), is (left), the tomb of the engraver Giovanni Volpato, by Canova (1807). On the right, *bas-relief of the 2C AD, representing an eagle holding an oak-wreath in his claws; and a lion, signed by Vassalletto. Two 12C red marble lions flank the entrance portal.

The Baroque **interior** (open 7–12, 16–19) is on a vast scale, with a nave 18m broad. The effect of immensity is enhanced by the manner in which the lines of the vaulting continue those of the massive pillars, and the lines of the apse those of the nave. From the end near the entrance can be seen the surprising effect of relief attained by Giovanni Odazzi in his contorted group of Fallen Angels, on the vault above the high altar. On the ceiling are the Triumph of the Order of St Francis, by Baciccia, and the Evangelists, by Luigi Fontana.

South aisle. The first chapel contains a 15C Madonna donated to the church by Cardinal Bessarion (see below). Against the second pillar is a monument to Clementina Sobieska, queen of James III (see below), by Filippo della Valle. The chapel at the end of the aisle has eight columns from the 6C church. In the **sanctuary** the high altarpiece, supposed to be the largest in Rome, of the *Martyrdom of St Philip and St James*, is by Domenico Muratori. On the right are the tombs of Count Giraud de Caprières (1505) and Cardinal Raffaele Riario, perhaps to a design of Michelangelo; on the left, the beautiful monument of Cardinal Pietro Riario, by the school of Andrea Bregno, with a Madonna by Mino da Fiesole. Fragments of the exquisite frescoes by Melozzo da Forlì which formerly covered the 15C apse are preserved in the Quirinal and in the Pinacoteca of the Vatican.

Steps in front of the sanctuary lead down to the **confessio**. Here are preserved the relics of the Apostles Philip and James and, in the chapel to the left, the beautiful *tomb by Andrea Bregno, of Raffaele della Rovere (died 1477), brother of Sixtus IV and father of Julius II. The other chapels were charmingly decorated in 1876–77 in the style of the catacombs, and foundations of the earlier church can be seen here. **North aisle**. At the east end, around the door into the sacristy, is the first important work in Rome by Canova, the *mausoleum of Clement XIV. On the second pillar is an epitaph of 1682 dedicated to Cardinal Bessarion (1389–1472), the illustrious Greek scholar, with a 16C portrait of him (his remains were translated here in 1957). In the second chapel: altarpiece of St Joseph of Copertino (the 'flying monk'), by Giuseppe Cades (1777), between two columns of verde antico, which are the largest known.

The two Renaissance **cloisters** (entered at No. 51) contain a bas-relief of the Nativity by the school of Arnolfo di Cambio, an early Christian sarcophagus and, in the second cloister, a memorial to Michelangelo, whose body was temporarily placed here in 1564 before his burial in Santa Croce in Florence. Also here, is a double inscription in Latin and Greek which was dictated by Cardinal Bessarion for his own tomb.

At the end of Piazza dei Santi Apostoli, is the little Baroque Palazzo Balestra (formerly Muti), which was presented by Clement XI to James Stuart, the Old Pretender, on his marriage in 1719. Here were born his sons Charles, the Young Pretender (1720), and Henry, Cardinal York (1725); and here died James, in 1766, and Charles, in 1788. Via del Vaccaro leads right into Piazza della Pilotta. At the east end of the square is the large Università Gregoriana Pontificia (1930). From here Via dei Lucchesi runs north past (right) Via della Dataria, leading up to Piazza del Quirinale, and (left) Via dell' Umiltà, leading to the Corso.

Fontana di Trevi

Beyond the crossroads the street, now called Via di San Vincenzo, continues to the huge Fontana di Trevi (Pl. 4; 3), one of the most famous sights of Rome, and one of the city's most exuberant and successful 18C monuments. The abundant water, which forms an essential part of the design of the monumental fountain, fills the little piazza with its sound. There is still a rooted tradition that travellers

who throw a coin into the fountain before leaving the city will return to Rome (the money is collected periodically and donated to the Italian Red Cross). It provided the setting for the film *Three Coins in the Fountain*. The fountain was restored for the first time in 1989–91. Its waters are those of the 'Acqua Vergine', which Agrippa brought to Rome for his baths in 19 BC, and which also feed the fountains of Piazza di Spagna, Piazza Navona and Piazza Farnese. The aqueduct, which is nearly 20km long,

The Fontana di Trevi

runs through the Villa Giulia. The name 'Trevi' may come from '*tre vie*', referring to the three roads which converged here.

The original 15C fountain was a simple and beautiful basin by Leon Battista Alberti; it was restored by Urban VIII, who is said to have obtained the necessary funds from a tax on wine. Many famous architects, including Bernini, Ferdinando Fuga, and Gaspare Vanvitelli presented projects for a new fountain. In 1732 Clement XII held a competition and Nicola Salvi was given the commission. His theatrical design incorporates, as a background, the entire façade of Palazzo Poli, which had been completed in 1730. Two giant tritons, one blowing a conch, conduct the winged chariot of Neptune. In the side niches are figures of Health (right) and Abundance (left); the bas-reliefs above represent the virgin of the legend from which the water took its name, pointing out the spring to the Roman soldiers, and Agrippa approving the plans for the aqueduct. The four statues above these represent the Seasons with their gifts. At the summit are the arms of the Corsini family, with two allegorical figures. The fountain was completed in 1762, after Salvi's death.

Opposite is the church of **Santi Vincenzo ed Anastasio**, rebuilt in 1630, with a Baroque façade by Martino Longhi the Younger. In the crypt of this church, the parish church of the neighbouring pontifical palace of the Quirinal, are preserved the hearts and lungs of almost all the popes from Sixtus V (1590) to Leo XIII (1903). Via del Lavatore diverges right to Vicolo di Scanderbeg which

leads to Piazza Scanderbeg in which is the **Museo Nazionale delle Paste Alimentari** (open 9.30–12.30; 16–19; Sun 9.30–12.30. ☎ 699 1120. Lire 12,000) a private museum which illustrates the history of pasta.

Via della Stamperia runs north to the right of the Fontana di Trevi past the garden of the Accademia di San Luca (see below), opposite the **Calcografia Nazionale** or Calcografia di Roma, the most important collection of copper-plate engravings in the world (open 9–13 except Sun). The collection was formed in 1738 by Clement XII and moved in 1837 to its present site; the building is by Luigi Valadier. It contains almost all the engravings of Giovanni Battista Piranesi (1432 plates) and examples of the work of Marcantonio Raimondi, Rossini, Pinelli, and many others. It has a total of more than 19,600 plates. Exhibitions are often held; any items not on display can be seen on request, and copies purchased. The institute was merged with the Gabinetto Nazionale delle Stampe in 1975 as the **Istituto Nazionale per la Grafica**, and there are long-term plans to move it next door to Palazzo Poli.

Galleria dell'Accademia di San Luca

The street opens out into Piazza dell'Accademia di San Luca. Here is Palazzo Carpegna, seat of the Accademia di San Luca, moved from the neighbourhood of the Roman Forum when Via dei Fori Imperiali was built. The academy, founded in 1577 by the painter Girolamo Muziano of Brescia, incorporated the 15C Università dei Pittori whose members used to meet in the little church of San Luca. Muziano's successor, Federico Zuccari, gave the academy its first statutes, and it soon became famous for its teaching and for its prize competitions. The eclectic Galleria dell'Accademia di San Luca contains gifts and bequests from its members, together with donations from other sources. The collection is arranged on the third floor (lift). Open Mon, Wed, Fri and last Sun 10–13. ☎ 679 8850.

Room I (ahead, beyond the gallery). Baciccia, *Portrait of Clement IX*; Girolamo and Giovanni Battista Bassano, *Shepherds and sheep*; Pier Francesco Mola, *Spinster*; Titian (attributed), *St Jerome*; Raphael, *Putto*, fragment of a fresco (1512); Jacopo Bassano, *Annunciation to the shepherds*; Marcello Venusti, *Deposition*; Sassoferrato, *Madonna and Child*; Sebastiano Conca, *Modesty*; Carlo Maratta, *Death of Sisera*; Poussin (copy of Titian), *Triumph of Bacchus*; Francesco Beccaruzzi (formerly attributed to Titian), *Portrait of Marino Cornaro*.

Room II. Donation of Baron Michele Lazzaroni. Paris Bordone, *Seduction*; Titian (attributed), *Portrait of Ippolito Rimanaldo*; Giovanni Battista Piazzetta, *Judith and Holofernes*; School of Moretto, *Portrait of a woman*; Baciccia, *Madonna and Child*; Biagio di Antonio, *Annunciation*; Federico Zuccari, *Self-portrait*; Venetian school, *Madonna and Child*; Alessandro Allori, *Portrait of a woman*; Cavaliere d'Arpino, *Perseus and Andromeda*, *Taking of Christ*. In the centre of the room, Saints Andrew and Bartholomew by Bronzino.

Room III. Works of the 18C and 19C. Domenico Pellegrini, *Augustus Frederick, Duke of Sussex*, *Self-portrait*, *Hebe*; Giuseppe Grassi, portraits of the architect Henry Wood and of Vincenzo Camuccini; Mme Brossard de Beaulieu, *Contemplation*; Angelica Kauffmann, *Hope*; Anton Wiertz, *Portrait of the architect Angelo Uggeri*; Mme Vigée le Brun, *Self-portrait*. Sculpture: Antonio d'Este (attributed), Bust of Canova; Clodion (?; formerly attributed to Bernini), *Bust of a young girl*; and The Three Graces by Bertel Thorvaldsen.

Room IV. Francesco Guarino, *Jacob's Dream*; Nicholas Berchem, *Cattle and shepherds in the Roman Campagna*; P. van Bloemen, *Cattle scene*, *Horses*; Sweerts, Genre scenes; Giovanni van Bloemen, *Pastoral scenes*; Master of the St Lucy Legend, *Virgin*; 16C German school, *Deposition*.

Room V. Cagnacci, *Tarquin and Lucretia*; Canaletto, Architectural perspective; Giovanni Paolo Pannini, Landscapes with Roman ruins; Van Dyck, **Madonna and Child with angels*; Rubens, *Nymphs crowning Abundance*; John Parker, landscape; Jan Asselijn, *Roman Campagna*; Palma Giovane, *Susanna*; Philip Wouwermans, *White horse*; Isaac Mytens, *Admiral Neewszom Kostenaer*; Philip Peter Roos (Rosa da Tivoli), *Shepherd and animals*. A *painting of the *Madonna and Child with angels* (and a drawing) by Van Dyck are not at present on view.

Room VI. (**Gallery**). Francesco Trevisani, *Scourging of Christ*, *St Francis*; Benedetto Luti, *Mary Magdalene at the feet of Christ*, **Self-portrait*; Anton von Maron, portraits of academicians; Raphael Mengs, *Teresa Mengs von Maron*, Vincenzo Pacetti, *Caterina Cherubini Preciado*, Andrea Locatelli, two genre scenes, two landscapes; Guercino, *Venus and Cupid* (detached fresco); Claude Joseph Vernet, **Seascape*; Gaspare Vanvitelli, *View of Tivoli*, *Porto di Ripa Grande*. Sculpture: Giambologna (formerly attributed to Tribolo), Allegorical figure of a river (terracotta).

Room VII. Sebastiano Conca, *Marriage of St Catherine*, *Fame*; Baciccia, study for the *Birth of St John Baptist* in Santa Maria in Campitelli; Placido Costanzi, genre scene; Angelo Massarotti, *Madonna and sleeping Child*; J.F. de Troy, *Faustulus finding Romulus and Remus*; Henrick van Somer, **St Jerome and the Sadducees*; Michele Rocca, *St Cecilia*; Guido Reni, *L'Addolorata*; Ciro Ferri, *Martyrdom of St Luke*.

Room VIII. Alessandro Algardi, *Leo XI and Henry IV*. Terracotta reliefs from prize competitions held in the 18C. Pierre Legros the Younger, *The Arts paying homage to Clement XI*; Michele Slodtz, *St Theresa transfixed by an angel*. **Staircase**. Francesco Hayez, *Il Vincitore*; Aristide Sartorio, *Monte Circeo*; Canova, *Self-portrait* and *Bust of Napoleon*; Guido Reni, *Fortune*, *Bacchus and Ariadne*; Pietro Bracci, terracotta bozzetto.

Not on view are paintings and sculpture by 20C academicians, donated by the artists or their families, including works by Giorgio Morandi, Fausto Pirandello, Felice Casorati, and Emilio Greco. The **Sale Accademiche** have also been closed to the public, except on St Luke's Day (18 October). They contain more important works from the 15C to the present day, including *St Luke painting the Virgin*, begun by Raphael and finished by assistants.

Just north of the Accademia is the busy Via del Tritone. This street ascends gradually from Largo Chigi in the Corso, to Piazza Barberini. Half-way up is Largo del Tritone, entered from the north by Via Francesco Crispi and Via Due Macelli. On the south side, Via del Traforo leads to the *Traforo Umberto I* (Pl. 4; 3), a road tunnel under the Quirinal Gardens, 347m long, built in 1902–05. In Via Crispi, in the former Carmelite convent of San Giuseppe, the **Galleria Comunale d'Arte Moderna** is temporarily arranged, with sculptures on the ground floor and paintings on the upper floors. Italian and foreign 20C artists represented include: Rodin, Guglielmo de Sanctis, Michele Cammarano, Scipione, Vincenzo Cabianca, Norberto Pazzini, Aristide Sartorio, Giacomo Balla, Arturo Noci, Amerigo Bertoli, Antonio Donghi, Fausto Pirandello, Roberto Melli, Renato

Guttuso, Giacomo Manzù, Giorgio Morandi, and Pietro Annigoni.

On the north side of Largo del Tritone, is Via Due Macelli, which runs north-west. In the first street to the left, Via Capo le Case, is the church of **Sant'Andrea delle Fratte**, which belonged to the Scots before the Reformation. Here in 1678 the composer Alessandro Scarlatti was married. The tower (unfinished), and refined fantastical campanile, both by Borromini, were designed to make their greatest impression when seen from Via Capo le Case.

Interior. In the second chapel on the right is the tomb of one Miss Falconet (1856), with a recumbent figure by the American artist Harriet Hossmer. To the left of the side door is the epitaph of Angelica Kauffmann (1741–1807). The cupola and apse were decorated in the 17C by Pasquale Marini, and the three huge paintings depicting the crucifixion, death and burial of St Andrew are by Giovanni Battista Lenardi, Lazzaro Baldi and Francesco Trevisani. By the high altar are two beautiful *angels by Bernini, sculpted for Ponte Sant'Angelo but replaced on the bridge by copies. The cloister has a garden with four cypresses.

Piazza di Spagna

Via Due Macelli leads into the long and irregular Piazza di Spagna (Pl. 4; 1), for centuries the centre of the artistic and literary life of the city. Foreign travellers usually chose their lodgings in the pensiones and hotels in the vicinity of the square, and here the English colony congregated. John Evelyn, on his first visit to Rome in 1644, stayed near the piazza. Keats died in a house on the square, the British Consul formerly had his office here, and there is still a well-known English tea room. In the neighbouring Via del Babuino is the English church. The piazza retains a cosmopolitan atmosphere, always crowded with Romans and visitors. The elegant streets leading out of the west side of the piazza to the Corso are famous for their fashionable shops: Via Condotti, Via Frattina and Via Borgognone are also now pedestrian zones.

At the south end of the piazza, between Via Due Macelli and Via di Propaganda is the **Collegio di Propaganda Fide**, with a façade (on Via di Propaganda) by Borromini (1622). The detailed friezes are particularly fine. The college, which has the privilege of extraterritoriality, was founded for the training of missionaries (including young foreigners) by Urban VIII as an

The Spanish Steps

annexe to the Congregazione di Propaganda Fide established by Gregory XV in 1622. The Column of the Immaculate Conception (1857) commemorates the establishment by Pius IX in 1854 of the dogma of the Immaculate Conception of the Virgin Mary. On the west side, opposite the small Piazza Mignanelli, is **Palazzo di Spagna**, which gave the piazza its name, the residence since 1622 of the Spanish ambassador to the Vatican. It is a good building with a fine courtyard by Antonio del Grande (1647).

In the narrow centre of the piazza is the **Fontana della Barcaccia**, the masterpiece of Pietro Bernini, father of Gian Lorenzo. The design (a leaking boat) is well adapted to the low water pressure of the fountain. The theatrical **Scalinata della Trinità dei Monti** or **SPANISH STEPS** were built in 1723–26 by Francesco de Sanctis to connect the piazza with the church of the Trinità dei Monti and the Pincio. The famous monumental flight of 137 steps (recently restored), which rises between picturesque houses, some with garden terraces, has always been a well loved haunt of Romans and foreigners. It is a masterpiece of 18C town planning. Every day there is a display of flowers for sale at the foot, and the steps are covered with tubs of magnificent azaleas at the beginning of May.

In the elegant pink 18C house, on the right looking up, is the apartment (with a little terrace covered with a vine) where the poet John Keats spent the last three months of his life (plaque), now the **Keats-Shelley Memorial House** (on the second floor, entrance at No. 26 in the Piazza; open 9–13, 15–18; closed Sat & Sun. ☎ 678 4235. Lire 5000). This was a small pensione in 1820, when Keats booked rooms for himself and his friend Joseph Severn, having been advised by his doctor to spend the winter in Rome. Keats led what he described as a 'posthumous life' here until his death from tuberculosis on 23 February 1821, aged 25.

The house was purchased in 1906 by the Keats-Shelley Memorial Association and first opened to the public in 1909 as a delightful little museum and library dedicated to the English writers Keats, Shelley, Byron and Leigh Hunt, all of whom spent much time in Italy. The library contains over 8000 volumes, and numerous autograph letters and manuscripts are preserved here. In the Salone is displayed material relating to Shelley and Byron, including a painting of Shelley at the Baths of Caracalla by Joseph Severn. The kitchen was in the small room opening onto a terrace on the Spanish Steps, and Severn's room now contains mementos of Severn, Leigh Hunt, Coleridge, and Wordsworth. Severn came back to Rome as British Consul in 1860–72. Here is displayed a reliquary of Pius V which was later used as a locket for the hair of Milton and Elizabeth Barrett Browning and was owned by Leigh Hunt (see Keats' poem 'Lines on Seeing a Lock of Milton's Hair'). The death mask of Keats, and a sketch by Severn of the poet on his deathbed, are preserved in the little room where he died. The Landmark Trust has the use of the apartment above the museum, and it is available for short rents (UK ☎ 01628 825925).

In the house opposite (which retains its fine deep russet colour), at the foot of the Spanish Steps, built by De Sanctis to form a pair with the house where Keats lived, 'Babington's English Tea Rooms' survive. The piazza is particularly attractive at its north end with a row of 18C houses and four tall palm trees.

In the fashionable VIA CONDOTTI, named after the conduits of the Acqua Vergine, is the renowned **Caffè Greco** founded in 1760, and a national monument since 1953. Its famous patrons included Goethe, Gogol, Berlioz, Stendhal,

Taine, Baudelaire, Thorvaldsen and Wagner, and it is decorated with personal mementoes, self-portraits, etc. At No. 68 is a 17C palace which is the headquarters of the Sovereign Military Order of Malta (or the order of the Knights of St John of Jerusalem; see p 250, which is accorded extraterritorial rights by the Italian State. At the northwest end of the piazza Via della Croce leads to Via Bocca di Leone in which (right) at the corner of Vicolo del Lupo, was the Brownings' Roman residence.

VIA DEL BABUINO, opened in 1525, connects Piazza di Spagna with Piazza del Popolo. Rubens lived here in 1606–08, and Poussin in 1624. It is now famous for its antique shops. It takes its name from a 16C fountain statue which has been placed beside the church of Sant'Atanasio dei Greci (by Giacomo della Porta). The neo-Gothic English church of All Saints (Pl. 3; 2) was built in 1882 by G.E. Street. On the right, near Vicolo Alibert, was the studio in which the Danish sculptor Thorvaldsen succeeded his English colleague Flaxman as occupant; and parallel on this side is the 16C VIA MARGUTTA, the residence of Dutch and Flemish painters in the 17C. Here at No. 53 Sir Thomas Lawrence founded the British Academy of Arts in 1821. It is still a street of artists with art galleries and studios (with interesting courtyards and gardens towards the Pincio), and in spring and autumn a street fair is held with paintings for sale.

On the terrace at the top of the Spanish Steps is PIAZZA DELLA TRINITÀ DEI MONTI with its church. From the balustrade there is a fine view of Rome, with the dome of St Peter's in the distance (beyond the dome of Santi Ambrogio e Carlo al Corso), and to the left the top of the Column of Marcus Aurelius. On the near right can be seen the Villa Medici (described below). The **obelisk** here, probably brought to Rome in the 2C or 3C AD, when the hieroglyphs were incised (copied from those on the obelisk in Piazza del Popolo), formerly stood in the Gardens of Sallust. It was set up here in 1788 by Pius VI.

The church of the **TRINITÀ DEI MONTI** (Pl. 4; 1), attached to the French Convent of the Minims, was begun in 1493 by Louis XII. It was restored after damage caused by Napoleon's occupation in 1816 at the expense of Louis XVIII. The unusual 16C **façade** has a double staircase (by Domenico Fontana). The **interior** (when closed, ring at the door of the small side staircase on the left, but usually open 9.30–12.30, 16–18) is divided by a grille into two parts, only one of which may ordinarily be visited. **South side**. First chapel: altarpiece and frescoes by Giovanni Battista Naldini. The third chapel is decorated on a plan by Daniele da Volterra (by his pupils) and contains an *Assumption, by him. The painting has a remarkable design, but is in very poor condition (it includes a portait of Michelangelo in the last figure on the right of the picture). In the second north chapel, is a *Descent from the Cross, an especially fine work (although very damaged, since it was transferred to canvas in 1811) by the same painter, possibly executed from a design by his master.

The other part of the church contains *frescoes by Perino del Vaga, Giulio Romano and others, in finely decorated chapels. The fourth chapel on the left (north transept) has the Assumption and Death of the Virgin by Taddeo Zuccari, finished by his brother Federico. The vault is painted by Perino del Vaga. Excavations beneath the convent (no admission) have revealed traces of a Roman villa which seems to have had a terrace on the hillside similar in form to the Spanish Steps.

From the Piazza there is a good view of the long and straight VIA SISTINA, which descends to Piazza Barberini (see Chapter 10) and then ascends the Quirinal Hill as Via delle Quattro Fontane. This handsome thoroughfare was laid out by Sixtus V as the 'Strada Felice' which ran for some 3km via Santa Maria Maggiore all the way to Santa Croce in Gerusalemme. In this street most of the illustrious visitors to Rome between the days of Napoleon and 1870 seem to have lodged. Nikolai Gogol (1809–52), lived at No. 126; No. 48 housed in succession Giovanni Battista Piranesi (1720–78), Bertel Thorvaldsen (1770–1844) and the architect and archaeologist Luigi Canina (1795–1856). At the top end it still has some well-known hotels and elegant shops.

Between Via Sistina and Via Gregoriana is the charming and bizarre **Palazzo Zuccari**, built by the artist Federico Zuccari as his residence and studio. Sir Joshua Reynolds lived here in 1752–53 and the German archaeologist Winckelmann in 1755–68. In 1900 it was bought by Enrichetta Hertz, who left her library, with the palace, to the German government. The Biblioteca Hertziana is now one of the most famous art history libraries in the country.

In the other direction, Viale della Trinità dei Monti leads along the edge of the hill to the **VILLA MEDICI** (Pl. 4; 1), the seat of the French Academy since 1803. Students who win the Prix de Rome at the École des Beaux-Arts in Paris for painting, sculpture, architecture, engraving or music are sent to study here for three years at the expense of the French Government. Admission to the gardens Sun 10–12.30 (guided visits on the half hour). ☎ 676 11. Lire 4000. Important exhibitions are held in the Villa.

The palace built by Annibale Lippi for Cardinal Ricci da Montepulciano, c 1540, was bought by Ferdinando dei Medici, later Grand Duke of Tuscany in 1576. Here also lived Cardinal Alessandro de' Medici (later Leo XI). The villa was modified by Bartolomeo Ammannati for the Medici, who here housed their famous collection of ancient Roman sculpture, the masterpieces of which were later transferred to the Uffizi in Florence. In 1801 it was bought by Napoleon and the French Academy, founded in 1666 by Louis XIV, was transferred here. In the 17C Velazquez was a tenant, and Galileo was confined here by the Inquisition in 1630–33.

The villa is famous for its inner **façade** on the garden front decorated with numerous ancient Roman statues, medallions, columns, and bas-reliefs (including four delicately carved panels dating from AD 43). The beautiful 16C **garden** has long vistas through hedged walks. The formal garden has several fountains and fragments of ancient sculpture, including the head of Meleager which might even be an original by Skopas.

Among the ilexes in front of the Villa Medici the **fountain**, with an ancient Roman red granite vase, was designed in 1589 by Annibale Lippi. The cannon ball is said to have been shot from Castel Sant'Angelo by Queen Christina of Sweden, when late for an appointment with the painter Charles Errard who was staying at the French Academy. The view is familiar from many paintings (including one by Corot dated 1828), although it is now somewhat impaired by trees in the foreground.

The gently sloping Viale della Trinità dei Monti ends at a monument by Ercole Rosa (1883) to the Cairoli brothers, who, as supporters of Garibaldi, died in

1867. From this point Viale D'Annunzio descends to Piazza del Popolo while Viale Mickiewicz ascends to the Pincio.

The Pincio

The Pincio (46m; Pl. 3; 2) was laid out as a Romantic park by Giuseppe Valadier in 1809–14 on the Pincian Hill. Adjoining the Villa Borghese, it forms the largest public garden in the centre of Rome and it is especially crowded on holidays. It was the most fashionable Roman 'passeggiata' in the last century when the aristocracy and foreign visitors came here in their carriages to hear the band play and admire the sunset. Joseph Severn describes his walks here with John Keats in 1820–21 (while staying above the Spanish Steps), during which they frequently met Pauline Borghese, Napoleon's sister. The *view from the terrace of the Piazzale Napoleone is dominated by the dome of St Peter's.

The Pincio was known as the *Collis Hortulorum* of ancient Rome since it used to be covered with the monumental gardens of the Roman aristocracy and Emperors. In the 4C it was owned by the Pinci, from whom the name of the hill is derived. Excavations have found traces of 1C walls here.

On a terrace is the **Casina Valadier** (1813–17), now an open-air café. Among the habitués of its most sumptuous period as a fashionable restaurant were Richard Strauss, Mussolini, King Farouk, Gandhi and Chiang Kai-shek. The view from its terrace is even better than that from Piazzale Napoleone.

The park is intersected by broad avenues passing between magnificent trees, many of them remarkable specimens of their kind. One of these avenues, Viale dell'Obelisco, runs east to join Viale delle Magnolie in the Villa Borghese (see Chapter 9). The obelisk which gives the avenue its name was placed here in 1822 (it was found in the 16C outside the Porta Maggiore where it may have decorated the Circus Varianus). The hieroglyphs suggest that it was originally erected by Hadrian on the tomb of his lover Antinoos who drowned in the Nile in 130. It may have been transported from Egypt by Elegabalus in the 3C. Throughout the park are busts of celebrated Italians from the days of ancient Rome to the present time. Of the fountains, the most notable are the Water Clock, in Viale dell'Orologio, and the Fountain of Moses.

The Pincio is bounded on the north and east by massive walls, part of which is the Muro Torto, or Murus Ruptus, the only stretch of Aurelian's wall that was not fortified by Belisarius against the Goths: he was prevented from doing so by the Romans who told him it would be defended by St Peter. The wall has for centuries seemed on the point of collapsing. Viale del Muro Torto, at the foot of the Pincio, is a busy road running outside the wall from Piazzale Flaminio to Porta Pinciana.

9 · Villa Borghese and Villa Giulia

Villa Borghese

Immediately north of the Aurelian wall is the magnificent Villa Borghese (Pl. 11; 5, 6, 7, 8), Rome's most famous public park, with a circumference of 6km, in which is the suburban villa which houses the celebrated Museo Borghese (see below). The main entrance to the park is, from Piazzale Flaminio, just outside Porta del Popolo. There are four other entrances: from the Porta Pinciana on the

south, from Via Pinciana on the southeast; from Via Mercadante on the north-east; and from Viale delle Belle Arti on the north. Traffic is excluded from the main area of the park.

The Villa owes its origin, in the 17C, to Cardinal Scipione Borghese, Paul V's nephew (see below). In the 18C Prince Marcantonio Borghese (father of Prince Camillo Borghese who married Pauline Bonaparte) employed Jacob More from Edinburgh to design the gardens. Early in the 19C the property was enlarged by the addition of the Giustiniani Gardens. In 1902 it was bought by the State, then handed over to the city of Rome, and opened to the public. The Villa (c 688 hectares) is now connected with the Pincio and the Villa Giulia, so that the three form one great park, intersected in every direction by avenues and paths, with fine oaks, giant ilexes, umbrella pines and other trees, as well as statues, fountains, and terraces.

The Temple of Aesculapius in the Giardino del Lago, Villa Borghese

From the classical main gateway on Piazzale Flaminio (Pl. 11; 7), designed by Luigi Canina (1835), Viale Washington ascends to Canina's Fountain of Aesculapius, 1830–34, with a Roman statue. From here a road leads (right) to the Portico Egiziano, another imposing entrance, in the form of pylons. Ahead on the right is a monument to Victor Hugo (1905), presented by the Franco-Italian League. On the left of the avenue is the **Giardino del Lago**, with hedged walks and arbours, laid out in 1785 by Jacob More and Cristoforo Unterberger, 'all'inglese'. On an island in the little lake is a Temple of Aesculapius by Antonio and Mario Asprucci. Seven statues by Vincenzo Pacetti (partly Roman) have been replaced by copies.

From Piazza delle Canestre the broad Viale delle Magnolie, connecting these gardens with the Pincio, runs southwest, and Viale San Paolo del Brasile runs southeast past a monument to Goethe (by Gustav Eberlein), and the 17C Casina delle Rose, abandoned for years but to be restored. In Piazzale Brasile is a monument, in Carrara marble, to Byron after Thorvaldsen (1959). Beyond is Porta Pinciana, at the top of Via Vittorio Veneto (see Chapter 10).

From Piazza delle Canestre an avenue leads northeast past the so-called **Casina di Raffaello**, reconstructed by Antonio Asprucci in 1792. The interior

(with decorations by Felice Giani) is to be used as a museum of restored sculptures from the garden, including four Tritons (removed here in 1909 from the Fontana del Moro in Piazza Navona where they were replaced by copies in 1874). A huge Neo-classical monument to the Dutch Jurist Jan van der Capellen, made in 1790 by Giuseppe Ceracchi and erected in the gardens in 1845, will also probably be housed here, as well as a Roman sarcophagus with the myth of Phaeton. The Tempietto di Diana is attributed to Mario Asprucci (1789). Beyond is the attractive **Piazza di Siena**, a rustic amphitheatre with tall pine trees, created by Mario and Antonio Asprucci in c 1792, where important equestrian events are held, and opera performances take place in summer. Nearby is a monument to Umberto I, by Davide Calandra. At the end of the avenue is a reproduction of the Temple of Faustina.

On the left 'La Fortezzuola' dates from the 16C; the crenellations were added in the 19C. In 1926 it became the studio of the sculptor and musician Pietro Canonica (born 1869) who lived here until his death in 1959. He left the house and a large collection of his sculpture to the Commune of Rome as the **Museo Canonica** (open 9–19; Sun 9–13; closed Mon. ☎ 884 2279. Lire 3750). The first room contains a portrait sculpture of Donna Franca Florio (1903), a bust of Princess Emily Doria Pamphili (1901), and *Dopo il Voto* (After the Vow), a statue of a young nun exhibited in Paris in 1893. Room II has the model for a monument to Alexander II of Russia (destroyed in the Revolution of 1917). Room III. Plaster casts of equestrian statues of Simon Bolivar (1954), and King Feysal I of Iraq (1933), and several war memorials. The gallery at the right of the entrance contains original models of portraits, notably Lyda Borelli (1920), Alexander II of Russia (1913), Luigi Einaudi (1948), the Duke of Portland (1896), Margaret of Savoy (1903), and casts of portraits of the English royal family made between 1902 and 1922. The house and small studio are also open, with some fine works of art collected by Canonica (some from Palazzo Reale in Turin).

Viale dei Cavalli leads right past the 18C Fontana dei Cavalli Marini, by Christopher Unterberger, a marble basin supported by four seahorses. A road to the left leads to the **Palazzina** or **Casino Borghese** (which can also be approached directly from Porta Pinciana by the Viale del Museo Borghese). The Palazzina was begun for the Borghese in 1608 by Flaminio Ponzio, Paul V's architect, and continued after his death in 1613 by Jan van Santen (Giovanni Vesanzio). It was altered for Marcantonio IV Borghese by Antonio Asprucci and Christopher Unterberger in 1775–90 when the splendid interior decoration was carried out. At the rear of the building is a beautiful formal garden.

Museo Borghese

The villa houses the Museo and Galleria Borghese (Pl. 12; 5, 7), an impressive collection of paintings and sculpture founded by Cardinal Scipione Borghese, which includes classical works as well as some masterpieces by Gian Lorenzo Bernini, Canova, Raphael and Caravaggio.

The Cardinal acquired numerous works of art through the good offices of his uncle Paul V, including Raphael's *Deposition* which he carried off from the church of San Francesco in Perugia. The collection was added to by later members of the family, but much of the sculpture was sold in 1807 to Napoleon I by Camillo Borghese, husband of Pauline Bonaparte, and is now in the Louvre. For nearly two centuries the paintings were housed in Palazzo Borghese; they

were brought here in 1891. The collections were acquired by the State in 1902.

The villa has completely reopened after many years of conservation work, which included major structural improvements and a detailed restoration of the gallery space and reconstruction of the gardens. The works of art have been returned to their original disposition on the two floors of the villa.

■ Open daily 9–19, Sun 9–13.30; ☎ 854 8577; Lire 4000. Entrance is via a central door which leads down to the Lower Ground Level, with tickets and information, bookshop, bar, restaurant and toilets.

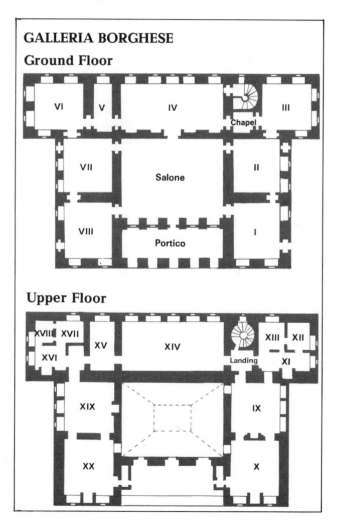

Ground floor. The entrance to the ground floor is through the doors under the central portico, with fragments of a triumphal frieze of Trajan. The **Entrance Hall** has a fine ceiling fresco by Mariano Rossi (1775–78); on the pavement are five fragments of a Roman mosaic (AD 320) with gladiators and wild beasts (found in 1834 at Torrenova, near Rome). The classical sculpture includes the colossal figure of a satyr, colossal heads of Hadrian and Antonius Pius, and statues of Augustus and Bacchus. Most of the other ceilings on this floor were decorated at the time of Marcantonio Borghese (c 1750–60) by Giovanni Battista Marchetti with numerous assistants.

Room I. **Pauline Borghese*, sister of Napoleon, as Venus Victrix, by Canova (1805–08), justly one of his best known works; *Herm of Bacchus* by Luigi Valadier (1773); *Cupid on an Eagle*, attributed to Pietro Bernini (c 1618); Portrait of Pope Clement XII, by Pietro Bracci.

Room II. **David*, a statue carved by G.L. Bernini (1623–24) at the age of 25, the face of which is a self-portrait; sarcophagus with the Labours of Hercules on two sides (AD 160). Paintings here include *Samson in prison* (c 1595) by Annibale Carracci; *Andromeda liberated by Perseus* by Rutilio Manetti; *David with the head of Goliath* (1612) by Battistello Caracciolo; *Still-life with Birds* (1602–07), school of Caravaggio.

Room III. The beautiful **Apollo and Daphne*, by Bernini, was made in 1624; the dramatic moment of capture is well portrayed. Over the doors, two landscapes by Paul Brill (c 1595). In the **Chapel**, frescoed by Claude Deruet (died 1660), is exhibited a fragment found in Rome in 1980 thought to be Michelangelo's first version of the head of Christ for the *Rondanini Pietà* (now in Milan).

Room IV. Busts of Roman emperors, in porphyry and alabaster, carved in the 17C. The decoration of the room is a notable example of 18C skill and taste in the ornamental arrangement of a great variety of precious marbles, and the incorporation of bas-reliefs and paintings into the design. Here are exhibited vases in marble from Luni, with the Seasons, by Maximilian Laboureur. The *Rape of Proserphine* is another early masterpiece by Bernini (formerly in the Villa Ludovisi), and the bozzetto in bronze of Neptune was made by him for a fountain group now in the Victoria and Albert Museum, London. Also here is a bronze replica by Antonio Susini of the Farnese bull (now in the Museo Nazionale in Naples).

Room V. *Hermaphrodite*, a replica of a famous Hellenistic prototype;above, alabaster vase on a red porphyry base; bust of Agrippa the Elder (1C AD); *Head of Aphrodite* (Sappho from Fidia). On the floor is a (3C BC) Roman mosaic of a fishing scene, and above the doors, landscapes by Paul Brill.

Room VI. Bernini's **Aeneas and Anchises* (1613), was carved at the age of 15 jointly with his father, Pietro Bernini; *Truth*, sculpted by Bernini (1645) for the vestibule of his palace on Via del Corso, but left unfinished. Paintings include *Cupid and Psyche* (1589) by J. Zucchi; *Death of the Virgin*, a preliminary sketch for the church of Santa Maria della Pace by G.M. Morandi.

Room VII. Paintings by Tommaso Conca representing the gods and religions of ancient Egypt. Among the sculpture, a *Satyr on a Dolphin* (1C AD), copy of an original from Taranto, head reworked in the 16C.

Room VIII. **Dancing Satyr*, 2C AD copy of an original by Lysippus, discovered in 1824 at Monte Calvo and restored under the direction of Thorwaldsen.

SIMULACRUM VERITAS TEMPORE OLI
RLO LAVERATIS DEANINVS RLMI
OLM COLVMIA AFFFTVIS
IN JALITAAM DOLERIS INVSCLFT
M TRANSMIINI POSTRAIS INLWTIL
TOS BODAN WON FFTEDVSL

Truth, *by Gian Lorenzo Bernini,
in Room VI of the Museo Borghese*

Paintings include masterpieces by **Caravaggio**, *Boy crowned with ivy* (*Il Bacchino malato*; 1592–95), *Boy with a basket of fruit* (1595), **Madonna of the Palafrenieri* (1605), **St Jerome* (1605–06), *St John the Baptist* (1609–10), **David with the head of Goliath* (1609–10); Cavalier d'Arpino's *The Capture of Christ* (1598) and *The Rape of Europa* (1602–03); Cigoli's *Joseph and Potiphar's Wife* (1610); Baglione, *Judith and the head of Holofernes* (1608).

First floor. Visitors must return to the Lower Ground floor, where a staircase leads up to the first floor picture gallery.

Room IX. Beautiful paintings by **Raphael**: **Deposition* (1507), **Portrait of a Lady with a Unicorn* (possibly the portrait of Maddelena Strozzi) (1506), **Portrait of a Man* (1502–04), and 16C copies of his *La Fornarina* (attributed to Raffaellino da Colle) and *Portrait of Pope Julius II*; Perino del Vaga, *The Holy Family with the Infant St John the Baptist* (1511) and *The Holy Family* (1540); Perugino, *St Sebastian* (1490); Botticelli and assistants, *Madonna and Child and the Infant St John the Baptist and angels* (1488); Giulio Romano, *Virgin and Child with Infant St John the Baptist* (1523); Perugino, *Madonna and Child* (16C).

Room X. Andrea del Sarto, **Madonna and Child with the Infant St John the Baptist* (1517); Correggio, **Danaë* (1530–31); Parmigianino, *Portrait of a Man* (1528–30); Bronzino, **St John the Baptist* (c 1525); Lucas Cranach the Elder, *Venus and Cupid with a honeycomb* (c 1531).

Room XI. Garofalo: *Virgin and Child with St Michael and other Saints* (c 1530–32), *The Holy Family* (early 16C), *Madonna and Child with Sts Peter and Paul*; Ortolano, *Deposition* (1520–21).

Room XII. Sodoma: *The Holy Family* (1525–30), *Pietà* (1540); Peruzzi, *Venus* (early 16C); Lorenzo Lotto, *Portrait of Mercurio Bua* (c 1535); copy of Leonardo's *Leda and the Swan* (early 16C).

Room XIII. Franceso Francia: *St Francis* (c 1510), *Madonna and Child* (c 1510), *St Stephen* (1475); Kress Master of Landscapes, *Madonna and Child with St Joseph and the Infant St John the Baptist*; Lorenzo Costa, *The Scourging of Christ* (before 1492).

Room XIV. Sculptures include Bernini's *Goat Almathea* (c 1615), *Bust of Pope Paul V* (1618), two *Portraits of Cardinal Scipione Borghese* (c 1632), and Model for the Equestrian Statue of Louis XIV (1669–70). Paintings include Guido Reni, *Moses with the Tables of the Law*; Bernini, *Self-portrait as a mature man* (c 1630–35), *Self-portrait as a young man* (c 1632), *Portrait of a Boy* (c 1638); Guercino, *The Prodigal Son* (c 1627–28).

Room XV. Jacopo Bassano, *The Last Supper* (1546–47), *Sheep and Lamb* (c 1560); Dosso Dossi, *St Cosmas and St Damian* (1534–42); G. Savoldo, **Tobias and the Angel* (c 1530).

Room XVI. Tibaldi, *Adoration of the Christ Child* (1548); Vasari, *The Nativity* (c 1546); Zucchi, *Allegory of the Creation* (1585).

Room XVII. Sassoferrato, *Madonna and Child* (1650); Pompeo Batoni, *Madonna and Child* (1742).

Room XVIII. Rubens, **The Deposition* (c 1602); Badalocchio, The *Entombment of Christ* (c 1610).

Room XIX. Carracci, *The Laughing Youth* (1583); Domenichino, *Diana* (1616–17), *Sybil* (1616–17).

Room XX. Antonello da Messina, *Portrait of a Young Man* (c 1475); Lorenzo Lotto, *Madonna and Child with Saints* (1508); Titian, *****Sacred and Profane Love**, his early masterpiece (1514), *Venus Blinding Cupid* (c 1565), *St Dominic* (c 1565), *Scourging of Christ* (c 1560).

Viale dell'Uccelliera runs northwest to Viale del Giardino Zoologico, in which is the entrance to the **Zoological Gardens** (Pl. 11; 6; open 8.30–17 or 18. ☎ 321 6564. Lire 10,000), established in 1911 and enlarged in 1935 (it now has an area of about 12 hectares). The collection is strong in bears and large cats. In Via Ulisse Aldovrandi, on the north side of the Zoo and accessible from there also, are the Museo Zoologico (1932) and the Museo Africano with an interesting Shell Collection in an annexe (sometimes open on Saturday).

Galleria Nazionale d'Arte Moderna
Viale del Giardino Zoologico continues to the exit of Villa Borghese on Viale delle Belle Arti. In this avenue, on the right, is the **Palazzo delle Belle Arti** (Pl. 11; 5), built in 1911 by Cesare Bazzani, and enlarged in 1933. It contains the Galleria Nazionale d'Arte Moderna, the most important collection extant of 19C–20C Italian art, founded in 1883. The gallery has been undergoing lengthy structural restoration and rearrangement for many years. It has now been completely reopened. There are long-term plans to arrange all the 20C works in the right wing and all the 19C works in the left wing, with contemporary art in an annexe under construction. Exhibitions are frequently held here.

■ Open 9–19; Sun 10–13; closed Mon. ☎ 322 981. Lire 8000.

The rooms open in the **Right Wing** contain 20C Italian works displayed chronologically. **Room I** has paintings by Giacomo Balla, including: *Portrait in the open*, 1902; *Villa Borghese, Il Parco degli Daini*, 1910; *Line of Velocity + Form + Noise*, 1915; *Bridge of Velocity*, 1913/14; *Stream of Borghetto*, 1938; and *Queue in the street for lamb*, 1942.

Room II exhibits the Futurists: Umberto Boccioni (*Ungracious Portrait, Horse + Rider + house*); Gino Severini, *Girl + Road + Atmosphere*, 1913; Boccioni, *Portrait of Maestro Busoni, Silvia*; Enrico Prampolini, *Figure + Window*, 1914; and works by Alberto Magnelli.

Room III. The Twenties: Piet Mondrian, *Large Composition A*, 1919; Laszlo Moholy-Nagy, *Yellow Cross Q.7*; Marcel Duchamp, *La Boîte-en-valise*; Giorgio de Chirico, *Hector and Andromache*; Roberto Melli, *Study of a head*, 1919; Carlo Carrà, *Oval of the apparitions*, 1918; Giorgio Morandi, *Still life*, 1918 (a good work of the Metaphysical period).

The **Veranda** exhibits sculpture (1920–30). Libero Andreotti, *The Pardon*; Arturo Martini, Relief of Orpheus; Francesco Messina, *Boy at the sea*; Adolfo Wildt, Bust of Arturo Toscanini. Numerous busts by Bruno Innocenti, Francesco Messina, Arturo Martini, and others. Libero Andreotti, *Affrico* and *Mensola*; works by Giacomo Manzù.

The **Salone** is divided into sections. **A.** Ardengo Soffici, *Washing the boy*; Gino Severini, *Group of things*, 1930, *Still life*, 1929; Giorgio de Chirico, Self-portrait, 1925, *Battle of gladiators*, 1933–34, *Horseman with red hat*, *Still Life*, 1929; Alberto Savinio, *Autumn*, 1935. **B.** Carlo Carrà, *Horses*, 1927, *Boy on a horse*, 1936; Mario Sironi, *Solitude*, 1925. **C.** Felice Carena, *Bathers*, 1925; Virgilio Guidi, *Head of a girl*; Ubaldo Oppi, **Fishermen of Santo Spirito*; Virgilio Guidi, **In the tram*; Antonio Donghi, **Hunter*, 1929; Francesco Trombadori, **Still life with basket of fruit*. **D.** Felice Casorati, **Portraits*, **Apples*; Massimo Campigli, **Sailors' wives*, 1934.

E. Works by Giorgio Morandi, and Ottone Rosai, and Arturo Tosi. **F.** Giacomo Balla, *Pessimism* and *Optimism*, 1923; and works by Fortunato Depero, Gerardo Dottori, and Enrico Prampolini. **G.** Works by Mario Mafai (including a self-portrait of 1942); Scipione, *Portrait of his mother*, 1930, *Portrait of the poet Ungaretti*. **H.** Works by Fausto Pirandello; Emanuele Cavalli, **The Bride*, 1934; Giuseppe Capogrossi, *Female portrait*, **The Storm*. The sculpture in the Salone includes *The Sisters* (or *The Stars*) by Arturo Martini.

Room IV. Works by Riccardo Francalancia, Antonio Donghi, Mario Broglio, Roberto Melli (*The checked dress*), Filippo de Pisis (*Still lifes, A road in Paris*, etc.).
Room V, Amerigo Bartoli, *Friends at the café*, 1929; Gregorio Sciltian, *Bacchus at the Hostelry*; Gino Severini, *The married couple*, 1939; Afro, *Self-portrait*, 1935; and works by Alberto Zivieri.

Room VI. The 'Sei' ('Six') of Turin (Enrico Paulucci, Carlo Levi, Gigi Chessa, Francesco Menzio, Nicola Galante, and Jessie Boswell). Walter Richard Sickert, P*ortrait of Baron Aloisi*; Wassily Kandinsky, *Angular Line*, 1930, Joan Miró, *Seated woman*, 1935; Carlo Levi, *Portrait of a friend*, 1930; works by Pio Semeghini; Maurice Utrillo, *Quai d'Anjou*, 1925.

Steps lead up from the Veranda (see above) to a room with paintings by Renato Guttuso. Other rooms in this wing display art from 1945–72 including works by Lucio Fontana, Alberto Burri, Ettore Colla, Umberto Mastroianni, and Alberto Giacometti.

The **Left Wing** displays 19C art. The first two rooms contain European art including works by: De Chirico; Gustav Klimt (*The Three Ages of Man*, 1905); Dante Gabriele Rossetti (*Mrs William Morris*); Rodin (bust of the sculptor Dalou, **Bronze Age*, bozzetto for a ballerina); Amedeo Modigliani; Degas; Vincent Van Gogh (*The Gardener*, and *L'Arlésienne*); and Paul Cézanne. The third room has a display of sculptures by Vincenzo Gemito (1852–1929), including a bust in gilded bronze of Cesare Correnti (1880).

Other artists represented in the collection include: Giovanni Fattori, Aristide Sartorio, Ettore Ximenes, Ercole Rosa, Vincenzo Vela, Adolfo Wildt, Achille d'Orso (*Prosimus Tuus* or 'Weary tiller'), Marco Calderini, Federico Zandomeneghi, Giovanni Boldini (*Portrait of Giuseppe Verdi*), Giuseppe de Nittis (**Bois de Boulogne*), Edoardo Gordigiani, Urbano Nono, Giovanni Battista Amendola, Antonio Mancini, Edoardo dal Bono, Ettore Tito, Gaetano Previati, Leonardo Bistolfi, Teodoro Matteini, Andrea Appiani, Filippo Agricola, Vincenzo

Podesti, Natale Schiavoni, Henry Raeburn, George Romney, Pietro Tenerani, Antonio Canova, Tommaso Minardi, Lorenzo Bartolini, Domenico Induno, Giacinto Gigante, Ippolito Caffi, Massimo d'Azeglio, Francesco Hayez, Il Piccio, Giuseppe Molteni, Filippo Palizzi, Gioacchino Toma, Michele Cammarano, Domenico Morelli, Giovanni Duprè, Giulio Monteverde (*Edward Jenner experimenting on a young boy*), Antonio Fontanesi, Giacomo Favretto, Tranquillo Cremona, Paolo Troubetzkoy, Medardo Rosso, Giuseppe Pellizza, Luigi Galli, Norberto Pazzini, and Luigi Serra.

Prints and drawings from the collection of Luigi Sprovieri, include works by: Hogarth, Gillray, Cruikshank, Rowlandson, Blake, *Goya, Flaxman, Richter and German artists, as well as the Japanese masters Hiroshige, Utamaro and Hokusai. Other 19C European prints and drawings include works by: Prud'hon, Géricault, Delacroix, Ingres, Corot, Millet, Courbet, Fantin-Latour, Rodin, Manet, Degas, Sisley, Renoir, Pissarro, Toulouse-Lautrec, Gauguin, Edvard Münch, Egon Schiele, Whistler, Beardsley, Burne-Jones, William Morris, Fattori and Signorini.

The collection dedicated to the group of Tuscan artists known as the *Macchiaioli* includes works by Antonio Puccinelli, Giovanni Fattori (**Portrait of his first wife*), Giuseppe Abbati, Silvestro Lega (**The visit*), Odoardo Borrani, Vincenzo Cabianca, Cristiano Banti, Adriano Cecioni, Telemaco Signorini, Vito d'Ancona, and Odoardo Borrani.

Outside the gallery, Viale delle Belle Arti widens into Piazza Thorvaldsen, in which, on the right, is a copy of Thorvaldsen's *Jason*, a gift from the city of Copenhagen. Above the steps is a statue of Simon Bolivar (1934). On the hill above, in Via Antonio Gramsci, is the **British School at Rome** (Pl. 11; 5), established in 1901 as a School of Archaeology. After the 1911 International Exhibition of Fine Arts in Rome, the site where the British Pavilion had stood was offered to the School by the Commune of Rome. The pavilion designed by Sir Edwin Lutyens, with a façade based on the west front of St Paul's Cathedral, was reproduced in permanent materials. In 1912, the School widened its scope to the study of the fine arts, literature and history of Italy. Scholarships are awarded, and an annual exhibition is held in June of the artists' work. The researches of the School are published annually in 'The Papers of the British School'.

This district, known as the **Valle Giulia**, was laid out at the beginning of the century after Viale delle Belle Arti had been opened. Numerous foreign academies and cultural institutes have been established here: on the left of the Viale are the Belgian, Dutch, Swedish and Romanian Academies; on the right, in Via Gramsci, beyond the British School, is the Faculty of Architecture of Rome University, and the Austrian Academy.

Museo Nazionale Etrusco di Villa Giulia
Further along Viale delle Belle Arti stands **Villa Giulia**, or correctly *Villa di Papa Giulio* (Pl. 11; 5), built in 1550–55 for Pope Julius III by Vignola, Vasari and Bartolomeo Ammannati, with some help from Michelangelo. In the 17C the villa was used to house guests of the Vatican, including Queen Christina of Sweden in 1665. Since 1889 it has been the home of the Museo Nazionale Etrusco di Villa Giulia, devoted mainly to pre-Roman works found in Lazio,

Umbria and southern Etruria. In 1908 the Barberini collection was donated to the museum, and later acquisitions include the Castellani and Pesciotti collections (in 1919 and 1972). Material from excavations in progress at the Etruscan sites of northern Lazio is also exhibited here. Villa Poniatowsky (1870), in a park to the right of Villa Giulia, has been acquired by the State, and there are long-term plans to use it to enlarge the museum.

■ Open 9–19; closed Mon. ☎ 320 1951. Lire 8000.

This charming suburban villa has lost much of its 16C decoration, including many pieces of ancient sculpture (which were taken to the Vatican). The façade is of two orders: Tuscan on the ground floor and Composite above. The porch, in rusticated masonry, leads to an **atrium**, with Corinthian columns and niches for statues. This opens into a semicircular **portico**, with Ionic columns and arches. The delightful vaulted ceiling is painted with vine trellises, birds and putti, and the wall panels are painted in the Pompeian style (attributed to Paolo Venale). Beyond lies the **courtyard**, enclosed by walls with Ionic columns, niches, and reliefs. Some of the delicate stucco decorations by Ammannati on the **loggia** survive. The **nymphaeum**, which has lost much of its original decoration, was frequently copied in later 16C Italian villas.

Two curved staircases lead down from the loggia to the first level, with fountains adorned with statues symbolising the Tiber and the Arno. On the lower level are a ceiling relief of the miraculous finding of the Acqua Vergine and four marble caryatids. Behind the portico is an aedicula or shrine, with a statue of Hygieia, a Roman copy of a 5C Greek original. The garden extends on either side of the courtyard. On the right is a reconstruction of the Temple of Aletrium (Alatri) by Count Adolfo Cozza (1891), according to the account of Vitruvius and the evidence of the remains (see below).

On the left of the atrium at the entrance is the library, with frescoes attributed to Taddeo Zuccari and Prospero Fontana. A temple relief illustrating the Seven against Thebes from Pyrgi (460 BC), formerly exhibited here, has been temporarily removed. The museum was arranged in galleries flanking the garden in 1960. Many of the rooms and showcases are in need of renovation (and the labelling is erratic and insufficient); part of the museum has been closed for this reason. The entrance is on the left of the semicircular portico.

Rooms 1–5 contain finds from the necropolis of **Vulci** where some 15,000 tombs were found, mostly dating from the 9C–5C BC. **Room 1**. Two stone sculptures, of a man astride a sea-horse and a centaur (showing Greek influence), found at the tomb entrances.

Room 2 contains fine bronze objects, including ossuaries, buckles and razors; a statuette of a warrior in prayer with a pointed helmet, large shield and long plaits (9C from Sardinia); bronze armour dating from the end of the 6C BC; and an *urn in the shape of a hut (mid-7C BC).

Rooms 3 and 4. Attic red and black figure vases imported from Greece, and local Etruscan-Corinthian ware, including a large amphora by the 'Painter of the Bearded Sphinx', and a black-figure hydria showing women at a fountain.

Room 5. Three terracotta models of a temple, a stoa, and a tower, terracotta heads and figurines from Hellenistic Vulci, forming part of a *stipe* (trench for a votive offering). More recent finds include seated figures of children. Stairs lead

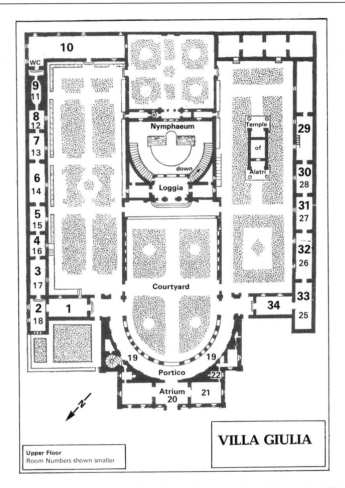

VILLA GIULIA

Upper Floor
Room Numbers shown smaller

down to the reconstruction of a *tomb from the necropolis at Cerveteri, with two chambers, containing beds and the belongings of the dead.

Room 6. Tomb furniture from the Villanovan and archaic necropolis of **Bisenzio-Vesentium**, including 8C geometric pottery, and a small bronze rustic chariot decorated with figurines which was used as an incense burner (late 8C).

Room 7. Finds from the sanctuary of Portonaccio at **Veio** discovered in 1916 and 1939, including the celebrated group of **Apollo and Herakles**. These colossal statues in polychrome terracotta (restored) formed part of a votive group representing the contest between Apollo and Herakles for the Sacred Hind in the presence of Hermes and Artemis, and are a splendid example of Etruscan sculpture of the late 6C or early 5C BC. They were probably the work of Vulca, a celebrated sculptor of Veio, who is said to have been summoned to Rome by Tarquinius Superbus to execute the statue and decorations for the Temple of

Jupiter Capitolinus. Of the other figures in the group there remain only the hind (removed) and the *head of Hermes. From the same temple is the statue of Latoma holding Apollo as a child, and the antefixes with the head of a gorgon and the head of a maenad.

Rooms 8–10 house finds from the necropolis at Cerveteri (the ancient *Caere*; 7C–1C BC). **Room 8**. Terracotta votive heads, sarcophagus 'of the Lions'. Here are displayed copies of the three famous gold-leaf plaques from Pyrgi, the Etruscan port of Cerveteri (the originals belong to the museum but are kept in the vaults), with inscriptions in Etruscan and Phoenician referring to the dedication of the sanctuary to the Phoenician 'Astarte' and the Etruscan 'Uni'. **Room 9**. Terracotta *sarcophagus (6C), representing a husband and wife feasting upon a couch; this remarkable and rare sculpture bears witness to the skill of the Etruscan artists, evident in the expressive rendering of the features, especially the hands and feet.

Room 10. Collection of skyphoi (drinking cups), kylixes (cups on stems), vases for perfume and wine, and amphorae (7C–2C). Case 2: Protocorinthian skyphoi, with geometric decoration, and a Corinthian krater, with warriors on horseback and chariots. Case 3: Bucchero ware. Case 6: collection of small aryballoi (vases for perfume). Cases 7–10: rare Attic kylix, with lively figures of satyrs dancing, story of Polyphemus, vine motif, etc. Cases 14–17: small red-figured kylix, showing two exploits of Theseus and a young cithara player. Case 19: Attic red-figured psykter (global vase with cylindrical support), showing Zeus enthroned on one side, and Theseus fighting the Minotaur on the other. Case 20: Attic red-figured krater, with hoplite running, and, on the neck, athletes, and Herakles struggling with Kyknos. Cases 21–24: Etruscan and Faliscan vases; silver-painted vases from Bolsena.

Upper Floor. Rooms 11–18 contains the Antiquarium; many of the objects here are of unknown provenance. **Room 11**. Bronze plates from a triumphal chariot, with hoplites and horsemen fighting (6C); buckles. **Room 12**. Ploughman at work, found at Arezzo; bronze statuettes, including elongated votive figurines.

Rooms 13 and 14 contain bronze domestic objects including mirrors, candelabra, cistae (see below), horse-bits, strigils and small containers for unguents in leather and metal used by athletes.

Room 15. Statuette of Veiovis, 1C AD, found in 1955 at Monterazzone, near Viterbo. Case 4: *Chigi Vase found at Formello (Veio), of exquisite workmanship and the finest extant example of the Protocorinthian style (first half of the 7C BC); among the subjects depicted are a lion-hunt, a hare-hunt, a troop of soldiers, and the Judgment of Paris.

Room 16. Vases. **Room 17**. Fragment of a krater of Assteas, depicting a comic scene: Ajax, fleeing from Kassandra, clings to the statue of Pallas Athena.

Room 18. Etruscan Biga from Castro. Dating from the 6C BC this two-wheeled chariot was found in 1967 in a tomb beside the skeletons of two horses (also exhibited here). The chariot, with bronze decorations, is very well preserved.

Stairs lead up to the hemicycle (**19**) with the **Castellani Collection of Ceramics** (many of them from Cerveteri). This was amassed in the 19C by Augusto Castellani, a member of a firm of goldsmiths. The rooms have a good view of the courtyard and garden of the villa. Case 1: alabaster vases imported from Greece and Cyprus, Etruscan vases showing Oriental influence. Case 2:

black- and red-figure vases, many decorated with animals. Case 3: two pitchers, one with the rape of Persephone, the other with Herakles and the dog Cerberus before Eurystheus. Case 4: black-figured Attic vases; Laconian krater decorated with lotus-flowers. Case 5: two amphorae signed by Nikosthenes (540–510 BC). Case 6: group of miniature kylixes. Case 7: amphora with large handles, red- and black-figured. Case 8: red-figured Attic vases; pitcher with two young men and leveret. Case 10: red-figured Attic vases including one showing Dionysus, satyrs, and maenads. Case 11: examples of Faliscan, Campanian and Apulian ware. Case 12: ceramics from Egnatia in Apulia, white- and yellow-figured. Part of the hemicycle is also used for exhibitions.

On the right, **Room 20** contains the **Pesciotto collection**, with vases from the Villanovian and Archaic periods (8C–6C BC), including incised bucchero ware and bronzes, and the alto rilievo di Pyrgi. In **Rooms 21 and 22** (closed indefinitely) is the **Castellani jewellery collection**, one of the finest collections of antique jewellery in existence, with Minoan, Hellenistic, Roman and Oriental pieces. There are also copies or reworkings made by the renowned Castellani jewellers in the 19C.

If Rooms 25–28 are closed, you will have to go down the spiral staircase from the hemicycle and cross the courtyard to reach Room 34. **Rooms 25–28,** which have been closed for many years, exhibit material from the Ager Faliscus, the area between Lake Bracciano and the Tiber. The Falisci were an Italic people akin to the Latins but much influenced by their Etruscan neighbours. Finds from Capena include an Etrusco-Campanian *dish with a war elephant and her baby, evidence of the impression made in Italy by the elephants of Pyrrhus. There is a fine collection of vases from the necropolis of Falerii Veteres (Civita Castellana): two bowls with Dionysos and Ariadne and a Faliscan inscription (resembling Latin): 'Today I drink wine, tomorrow I shall have none'; an amphora with volutes, showing Eos and Kephalos and Boreas and Orithyia; interesting stamnoi; *rhytons (drinking horns), masterpieces of Greek ceramic art of the first half of the 5C BC (the one shaped like a knuckle-bone is signed by Syriskos and the one in the form of a dog's head is attributed to Brygos); a large *krater (mid 5C) with girls dancing, and two other red-figured 5C *kraters with Herakles and the Nemean lion, and Herakles being received into Olympos.

In **Room 29** (being rearranged), on two levels, are sculptures and architectonic terracottas from temples (5C–2C BC) near Falerii Veteres, with good antefixes of Persian Artemis and a winged genius. Below are large figured terracottas from the pediments, including *Apollo, a head of Mercury, and a female head, showing the influence of Greek sculpture. In glass cases are excellent examples of temple decoration and cult statues: antefixes with heads of Maenads, of Silenus, and part of an acroterion with two warriors, from Sassi Caduti (early 5C); portraits from the *stipes* of the Temple at Vignale, the acropolis of Falerii Veteres; female head in peperino, crowned in bronze-leaf, from Celle; head of Zeus from Scasato.

Room 30 contains material from the **Temple of Diana at Nemi** (4C–2C BC), the famous sanctuary of the Golden Bough in the sacred wood beside the lake (see p 394): lower portion of a cover-slab in gilded bronze, votive objects, terracotta pediment of the temple. Male head from Antemnae (late 4C).

Room 31. Coffin formed from the trunk of an oak-tree (from Gabii); antefix with maenad's head, from Lanuvium; terracotta model, perhaps of a temple,

from Velletri. **Room 32**. Collection from the Tomba delle Ambre, at Satricum in the territory of the Volsci, including sculptures from the temple of Mater Matuta (6C BC), and a votive *stipe* of the 7C BC.

Room 33. Works from Palestrina, the ancient *Praeneste*, a flourishing centre of Latin and Volscian civilisation. Since the trade and industry of Etruria and Latium were derived from the same sources, the culture here naturally had much in common with the Etruscan culture. The material includes finds from the Barberini and Bernardini Tombs, two important examples of the Oriental period (7C BC). The **Barberini Collection** was formed of objects unearthed between 1855 and 1866 from tombs in the locality of Colombella, just south of the town of Praeneste. It was acquired by the State in 1908, and includes the contents of a large tomb covered with marble slabs of the Oriental period (7C BC), and the contents of deep-laid tombs of the 4C–2C BC. The **Bernardini Tomb**, discovered in 1876, a trench-tomb lined with tufa and covered by a tumulus, exactly corresponds with the style of the Barberini tombs and with that of the Regolini-Galassi tomb in the Vatican.

The tombs of the Oriental period yielded gold and silver articles, bronzes and ivories, in which Egyptian, Assyrian and Greek art are mingled. Notable among the goldsmith's work: two *pectorals, or large buckles, of gold granulated work, decorated with cats' heads, chimaeras, and sphinxes; patera in silver-gilt with Pharaoh in triumph, horses and an Assyrian royal hunt; caldaia, for heating or cooling water, in silver-gilt, with six serpents on the brim, and decorated with horsemen, foot-soldiers, farmers and sheep being attacked by lions. Ivories: cups; lion with dead man on his back; mirror-handles (?) shaped like arms. Bronzes: conical vase-stand with fantastic animals in repoussé; throne in sheet-bronze, with ornamental bands and figures of men and animals.

The contents of the 4C–2C tombs include a full collection of bronze mirrors and **cistae**. The latter contained the mirrors, strigils, spatulae and other implements for the care of the body. The cistae are usually cylindrical, with engraved decoration in repoussé or pierced work, lids adorned with small figures, and feet and handles of cast metal. These toilet boxes were virtually unique to Praeneste. Among them is the **Cista Ficoroni**, the largest and most beautiful yet discovered. It is named after Francesco Ficoroni who bought it and gave it to the Kircher Collection (now incorporated in the Prehistoric and Ethnographic Museum). On the body of the cista is a representation of the boxing match between Pollux and Amykos, king of the Bebryces, an elaborate design pure in its lines and evidently inspired by some large Greek composition, possibly a wall-painting contemporary with those by Mikon in the Stoa Poikile at Athens. The names of both the maker and the buyer of the cista are recorded in an archaic Latin inscription: *Novios Plautios med Romai fecid, Dindia Macolnia fileai dedit*; it was no doubt a wedding present.

Room 34. Goldsmith's work; bronze helmet inlaid with silver, from Todi; Attic *bowl signed by Pampheios, showing Odysseus evading Polyphemos; head from Cagli.

Beyond the Villa Giulia, Viale delle Belle Arti goes on past the red-brick church of Sant'Eugenio (1951), built to celebrate the 25th anniversary of the episcopal consecration of Pius XII in 1942, to the Via Flaminia, on which is the elegant Palazzina of Pius IV, attributed to Pirro Ligorio, who designed the Casina of Pius

IV in the Vatican gardens. The busy Via Flaminia (traversed by buses and trams) leads back to Piazza del Popolo (see Chapter 7).

10 · The Quirinal Hill, Palazzo Barberini and the Museo Nazionale Romano

To the east of the Vittorio Emanuele Monument, beside the two small churches in front of Trajan's Column (see p 107), steps lead up to Via IV Novembre (with the entrance to the Markets of Trajan, described in Chapter 4). Beyond is the Largo Magnanapoli (Pl. 4; 5), at the beginning of the busy Via Nazionale. In the centre of the square is a little group of palm trees, with some remains of the Servian Wall (see also p 51); in the ancient Palazzo Antonelli (No. 158; restored) are other remains in several rooms off the courtyard, including an arch for a catapult. On the right, behind the church of **Santa Caterina da Siena** (being restored), with a good Baroque interior, rises the conspicuous Torre delle Milizie.

At the beginning of Via Panisperna, in a fine position high up on the right, is the tall façade of **Santi Domenico e Sisto** (ring for admission at the college next door; bell by the gate), preceded by a theatrical staircase (1654) by Vincenzo della Greca. Inside is a huge fresco (1674–75) by the Bolognese painter, Domenico Canuti, a sculptured group (*Noli me tangere*) by Antonio Raggi, and a Madonna and Child thought to be an early work by Antoniazzo Romano.

VIA NAZIONALE (Pl. 4; 5, 4) leads from Largo Magnanapoli towards Piazza della Repubblica and the Railway Station. On the right it passes the extensive garden of the **Villa Aldobrandini**, built in the 16C for the Duke of Urbino, acquired by Clement VIII (Ippolito Aldobrandini), and given by him to his nephews. The villa was a famous meeting place for the Roman aristocracy during the Napoleonic era. Now owned by the State, it contains an international law library. A splendid Roman fresco of a marriage scene found on the Esquiline in 1605 was kept in one of the garden pavilions here until 1838, when it was moved to the Vatican museum (where it is still known as the *Aldobrandini Marriage*). Via Nazionale skirts the villa wall as far as Via Mazzarino, in which (right) is an open gate and steps which lead up past impressive 2C ruins to the garden.

Further on in Via Mazzarino, to the left, is the church of **Sant'Agata dei Goti** (if closed, ring at No. 16), built by an Arian community in 462–70, but much restored. The Byzantine plan remains despite the disappointing 20C restorations, with antique columns and decorative capitals with pulvins. In the apse is a well-preserved 12C–13C Cosmatesque tabernacle. The picturesque 17C court is hung with ivy. The original fabric of the building can be seen on leaving the church by the door in the right aisle.

Further along Via Nazionale, on the right, is the huge Neo-classical head office of the Banca d'Italia by Gaetano Koch (1886–1904), behind a row of palm trees and colossal lamp-posts. On the left is the Teatro Eliseo. Just beyond Via Milano (with a road tunnel on the left), rises the monumental **Palazzo delle Esposizioni** (Pl. 4; 5), erected in 1878–82 to a design by Pio Piacentini. As an important exhibition centre, it has been radically restored, and a new system of illumination has been installed.

Beyond the palace, on a much lower level, is the little church of **San Vitale** (usually closed), dedicated in 416 and several times restored. It has a fine portico with old columns and 17C doors. In the interior is a carved wood ceiling, and the walls are decorated with effective 17C trompe l'oeil frescoes with landscapes by Cavaliere d'Arpino, Gaspard Dughet, Andrea Pozzo and others.

The Quirinal Hill

From Largo Magnanapoli, Via XXIV Maggio climbs the Quirinal Hill. This street was named to commemorate the day in 1915 on which Italy declared war on Austria. Near the beginning, on the left, is the entrance to the church of **San Silvestro al Quirinale**, on an upper floor (ring at No. 10 on the right, 9–13), from which the cardinals used to march in procession to shut themselves in the Quirinal when a conclave was held in summer. The **interior** was rebuilt in 1524 on a Latin cross. **North side**. The first chapel, with pretty floor tiles, has two fine landscapes by Maturino and Polidoro da Caravaggio, who also painted the *St Catherine* and *Mary Magdalene* flanking the altar. In the vault are frescoes by Cavaliere d'Arpino. Second chapel: *Nativity* by Marcello Venusti. **South side**. Second chapel: *Pius V* and *Cardinal Alessandrino* by Giacinto Gemignani, with, in the centre, a 13C *Madonna and Child* by a Roman artist. The domed Bandini chapel at the end of the **north transept** contains tondi by Domenichino, and statues of Mary Magdalene and St John the Evangelist by Alessandro Algardi (1628; probably his first Roman commission). The altarpiece of the *Ascension* is by Scipione Pulzone. A door in the north transept admits to a courtyard, off which is an oratory where the poetess Vittoria Colonna used to meet with Michelangelo and others.

The street ascends between two of the most attractive of Rome's princely residences. On the left is the entrance to Villa Colonna, the garden annexe of Palazzo Colonna (see Chapter 8); on the right (behind a high wall), on the site of the Baths of Constantine, is **Palazzo Pallavicini-Rospigliosi** (Pl. 4; 5; admisson only to the garden; see below), built in 1613–16 probably by Carlo Maderno. It later passed to Cardinal Mazarin who enlarged it. In 1704 it was purchased by the Pallavicini-Rospigliosi family who still live here. In the 19C the beautiful gardens were greatly altered and diminished. The **Galleria Pallavicini** (open only with special permission) on the first floor contains some important paintings of Italian and foreign schools (15C–18C). The collection was founded by Nicolò Pallavicini (friend of Rubens) and his son Cardinal Lazzaro, and includes works by Botticelli, Lorenzo Lotto, Annibale and Ludovico Carracci, Guido Reni, Guercino, Federico Barocci, and Rubens (*Christ and the Apostles*).

In the charming little hanging garden is the **Casino Pallavicini** (open first day of month 10–12, 15–17) designed by Giovanni Vesanzio. The fine façade is decorated with numerous good reliefs of mythological subjects from Roman sarcophagi (2C–3C AD). The pavilion contains Guido Reni's celebrated *fresco (1613–14) of *Aurora scattering flowers before the chariot of the Sun*, which is escorted by the Hours. It was greatly admired by travellers to Rome in the 19C. On the walls are four frescoes of the Seasons by Paul Brill, and two 'Triumphs' by Antonio Tempesta. The ceiling frescoes in the two side rooms are by (left) Giovanni Baglione, and (right) Passignano. Here are hung a number of 17C paintings and the sinopia of a fresco of the Allegory of Night by Giovanni da San Giovanni, from the ballroom of the palace.

At the top of Via XXIV Maggio is the spacious and dignified PIAZZA DEL QUIRI-NALE (beware of fast traffic), with its two palaces: the Quirinal in front, and Palazzo della Consulta, to the right. The balustrade on the west side, overlooking Via della Dataria, provides a view across rooftops to the dome of St Peter's in the distance. The piazza occupies the summit of the **Quirinal** (61m), one of the highest of the Seven Hills. It received its name from a Temple of Quirinus, or from *Cures*, an ancient Sabine town northeast of Rome from where, according to legend, the Sabines under their king Tatius came to settle on the hill. The name of Quirinus was a title of Romulus, after he had been deified; the festival in his honour was called *Quirinalia*.

In the middle of the square, on a high pedestal, flanking an obelisk, are two famous colossal groups of the **Dioscuri** (Castor and Pollux), standing by their horses, over 5.5m high. They are Roman copies, dating from the Imperial era, of Greek originals of the 5C BC. The two groups were found nearby in the Baths of Constantine and placed here by Domenico Fontana for Sixtus V (1585–90), who was responsible for the recutting of the false inscriptions on the bases, 'Opus Phidiae' and 'Opus Praxitelis', which probably date from c AD 450. The statues appear in numerous representations of the city from medieval times. They were formerly called the horse-tamers, and the square, known as Monte Cavallo, was named after them. The **obelisk** (shaft 14.5m), originally in front of the Mausoleum of Augustus, was brought here by Pius VI in 1786; Pius VII added the great basin (now a fountain) of dark grey granite, until then used as a cattle-trough in the Roman Forum.

At the corner of Via XXIV Maggio, where Via della Dataria begins, is a part of the Scuderie Pontificie (Papal Stables), built in 1722. The **Palazzo della Consulta**, once the seat of the supreme court of the Papal States ('Santa Consulta') is now the seat of the Corte Costituzionale, a supreme court for matters concerning the constitution. The façade is by Ferdinando Fuga (1739).

PALAZZO DEL QUIRINALE (Pl. 4; 3) has been the official residence of the President of the Republic since 1947. The President's guards, who have to be over six feet tall, have splendid crimson and blue uniforms. The stately front of the palace projects into the piazza, while its flank, known as the 'manica lunga' ('long sleeve'), is in Via del Quirinale. The building was begun in 1574 by Flaminio Ponzio and Ottavio Mascherino for Gregory XIII, on the site of a villa rented by Cardinal d'Este from the Carafa, and was continued by Domenico Fontana, Carlo Maderno, Bernini (who worked on the 'manica lunga'), and Fuga: it was not completed until the time of Clement XII (1730–40). The principal entrance is by Maderno; the tower on the left of it was added in the time of Urban VIII. The palace is open on the first and third Sunday of the month, 8.30–12.30 (the gardens are open on 2 June).

From 1592 the Quirinal was the summer residence of the popes, and some conclaves were held here. Sixtus V died in the palace in 1590. Pius VII left the palace as prisoner of Napoleon, and from its balcony Pius IX blessed Italy at the beginning of his pontificate. From 1870 to 1947 it became the residence of the Kings of Italy. Vittorio Emanuele II died here on 9 January 1878.

In the **interior** most of the furniture, paintings and tapestries belonged to the Italian royal family. The collection of Oriental vases and the Gobelins tapestries were the property of the papacy. On the grand staircase is Melozzo da Forlì's magnificent *fresco of Christ in Glory, with angels,* formerly in the church of the Santi Apostoli. At the top of the stairs is the **Sala dei Corazzieri**, decorated in 1616–17, with a frieze designed by Agostino Tassi and executed by Lanfranco and Saraceni. This and the adjoining **Cappella Paolina** are by Carlo Maderno. The chapel, the same size as the Sistine Chapel in the Vatican, has fine stucco decoration by Martino Ferrabosco. The **Cappella dell' Annunciata** was decorated between 1609 and 1612, under the direction of Guido Reni (who executed the scenes of the life of the Madonna and the prophets, in the pendentives), by Lanfranco, Francesco Albani, and Antonio Carracci. The **Sala del Balcone** contains two paintings by Pietro da Cortona. In the **Salottino di San Giovanni** there is a copy, attributed to Giulio Romano, of the young St John the Baptist by Raphael and his workshop in the Uffizi gallery in Florence. The **Gallery of Alexander VII** has frescoes carried out under the direction of Pietro da Cortona (1656–57) by Grimaldi, Lazzaro Baldi, Ciro Ferri, Mola (*Joseph and his brothers*, which is considered his most successful fresco), Maratta, Gaspard Dughet, Antonio Carracci and others. The extensive **garden** (only open on 2 June) was designed by Ottaviano Mascherino.

Via del Quirinale skirts the 'manica lunga' (see above) of the palace. On the right, beyond a public garden with an equestrian statue of Charles Albert by Romanelli (1900), rises the church of **SANT'ANDREA AL QUIRINALE** (open 8–12, 16–19, except Tues), a masterpiece by Bernini (1658–70), and his pupil Mattia de Rossi. The simple **façade**, of a single order, balances the fine domed elliptical **interior**, with columns, pilasters and frames in pink and grey marble, and gilded and stuccoed decorations. Cherubim look down from the lantern. Each chapel is lit by windows high up behind the altars. The fine 17C altarpieces include (first chapel on the right), *St Francesco Saverio* by Baciccia, and, in the second chapel, *Deposition* by Giacinto Brandi. The high altarpiece, with the *Crucifixion of St Andrew*, by Borgognone, is surmounted by a splendid group of angels and cherubim sculpted by Raggi. On the left of the high altar is an altarpiece by Carlo Maratta. The sacristy has a pretty frescoed ceiling by Giovanni de la Borde (approved by Bernini). The lavabo here is attributed to Bernini.

Beyond a public park, on the right, is another small oval church, **SAN CARLO ALLE QUATTRO FONTANE** (*San Carlino*; open 9.30–12.30, 16–18, closed Sat afternoon and Sun), a masterpiece by Borromini which provides an interesting contrast to the former church by Bernini. The tall curved **façade** (1665–68) is well adapted to the cramped site on the corner of a narrow street. The **interior** (1638) has convex and concave surfaces in a complicated design using triangles in a unifying scheme: the symbolism throughout is of the Holy Trinity. In the chapel to the left of the altar, *Rest on the flight into Egypt*, attributed to Annibale Carracci or Giovanni Francesco Romanelli. The small **cloister**, which can be entered from the church, was also designed by Borromini. From here is the entrance to the **crypt** (not at present open to the public), designed in a fantastical play of curves linked by a heavy continuous cornice. It is thought Borromini intended this as the place of his own burial.

At this point Via del Quirinale ends at the carfax known as the QUATTRO FONTANE (Pl. 4; 4), with its four vistas ending in Porta Pia and the obelisks of the Quirinal, Pincio, and Esquiline, typical of the Rome of Sixtus V. The four small fountains (which give the busy crossroads its name), dating from 1593, personify Fidelity, Strength, the Aniene and the Tiber. Via delle Quattro Fontane leads right to Via Nazionale and left to Piazza Barberini.

Via Venti Settembre leads straight on, beyond the cross-roads, past Palazzo del Drago, by Domenico Fontana (1600), and the large Ministry of Defence, to Piazza San Bernardo (see below). At No. 7 in this street, on the left, is the Scottish Presbyterian church of St Andrew, with a war memorial (1949) to the London Scottish.

To the left Via delle Quattro Fontane descends all the way to Piazza Barberini. Half-way down, on the right, is **PALAZZO BARBERINI** (Pl. 4; 3), one of the grandest palaces in Rome. It was begun by Carlo Maderno for Urban VIII in 1624. The windows of the top storey, the stairs, and some doorways were executed from a design by Borromini. The central block is attributed to Bernini. The garden flanks one side of the street where the huge stone pilasters and iron grille were added in the 19C by Francesco Azzurri.

Galleria Nazionale d'Arte Antica

In 1949 the Barberini palace became the property of the State, and one wing houses part of the Galleria Nazionale d'Arte Antica, a national gallery of paintings; the other section of the gallery is in Palazzo Corsini (see p 278). After the State had purchased Palazzo Corsini with the picture-gallery of Cardinal Neri-Corsini, it was presented with the collections of Prince Tommaso Corsini and later acquired the Torlonia and other collections. The combined collections, opened to the public in 1895, are pre-eminent in Italian Baroque painting; there are also some good examples from the 15C–16C, and a large selection of foreign works. The right wing of the palace was for years occupied by offices and club rooms of the armed forces: these are now being moved and the gallery is in the process of being rearranged. At present only the Salone is open on the first floor, and the rest of the collection is temporarily displayed on the second floor. The rooms are not numbered.

■ Open 9–19; Sun 9–13; closed Mon. ☎ 481 4591. Lire 8000.

Across the garden, planted with palm trees, a door on the left beneath the portico leads into the palace. A monumental flight of stairs probably designed by Bernini leads up to the **First Floor**, with the entrance to the gallery (and the ticket office). Here are displayed three busts by Bernini. On the left is the **Salone**, with a magnificent ceiling fresco of *The Triumph of Divine Providence*, by Pietro da Cortona, his main work, painted between 1633 and 1639 to celebrate the glory of the Papacy of Urban VIII and the Barberini family. It is a *tour de force*, particularly in the organisation of the space, and the reduction of the composition into the angles. On the walls are hung seven cartoons by the school of Pietro da Cortona showing scenes from the life of Urban VIII, executed for tapestries manufactured in the Barberini workshops active in Rome 1627–83 (and now in the Vatican). Also four cartoons for mosaics in the Cappella Colonna in St Peter's by Andrea Sacchi, Bernini and Carlo Pellegrini, and Giovanni Lanfranco.

Many paintings formerly in rooms on the first floor are temporarily displayed here. Simone and Machilone, *Crucifix*; 'Maestro dell'Incoronazione di Urbino', *Birth of St John the Baptist*; Giovanni Baronzio, *Scenes from the life of Christ*; Nicolò di Pietro, *Coronation of Mary*; Filippo Lippi, *Madonna and Child*, *Annunciation with donors*.

Michele Giambono, *Madonna and Child*; Marco Palmezzano, *St Jerome*; Bartolomeo Veneto, *Portrait of a man*; Calisto Piazza da Lodi, *St Catherine of Alexandria*; Andrea Solario, *Lute-player*; Giacomo Francia, *Pietà*; Perugino, *St Nicholas of Tolentino*; Francesco di Giorgio Martini, *Pietà*, a terracotta group restored in 1985 (and formerly attributed to Giacomo Cozzarelli).

Circle of Filippino Lippi, *Madonna enthroned between Saints Peter and Paul*; Piero di Cosimo, *Mary Magdalene*; *Madonnas with Saints* by Lorenzo di Viterbo, Antoniazzo Romano and L'Alunno; 'Maestro di San Sebastiano', *Pilgrims at a sanctuary* (a very unusual work); 15C Provençal school, *Addolorata*.

Francesco Pagano (attributed), *Saints Sebastian and Catherine*; Pietro da Cortona, *Guardian angel*.

Titian, *Venus and Adonis* (replica of a painting in the Prado); El Greco, *Adoration of the Shepherds and Baptism of Christ*; Tintoretto, *Christ and the adulteress*; Giovanni Busi (Il Cariani), *Madonna and Child with St Anne and the young St John the Baptist*; Lorenzo Lotto, *Mystical Marriage of St Catherine*; Niccolò dell'Abate, *Portrait of a young man*; Girolamo Genga, *Marriage of St Catherine*; Sodoma, *Three Fates*, *Rape of the Sabines*, *Marriage of St Catherine*; Siciolante da Sermoneta, *Francesco II Colonna*; Bronzino, *Stefano Colonna*.

The famous portrait of a lady by Raphael is known as *La Fornarina*. The sitter may have been Raphael's mistress, the daughter of a Sienese bakerwoman, although the painting has also been attributed to the master's pupil, Giulio Romano, who also painted the *Madonna and Child*; Beccafumi, *Madonna and Child with the young St John*; Brescianino, *Lady with a turban*; Andrea del Sarto, *Holy Family*.

Guido Reni, *Mary Magdalen*, *Sleeping putto* (a fresco), and *Portrait of a lady* (supposed to be Beatrice Cenci); Guercino, *Et in Arcadia Ego*; Lanfranco, *Transfiguration*; works by Nicolas Poussin; two paintings by Gian Lorenzo Bernini (*David with the head of Goliath* and *Portrait of Urban VIII*); Sassoferrato, *Portrait of Ottaviano Prati*; Pier Francesco Mola, *Portrait of a lady*; Baciccio, *Pietà*, Clement IX, *Portrait of Gian Lorenzo Bernini*.

The other rooms and the chapel (at present closed) on the first floor have vaults painted by Andrea Camassei, Andrea Sacchi (1630–33), Giuseppe Chiari, and Pietro da Cortona and his pupils (including Francesco Romanelli).

Second Floor. In the hallway is a monochrome painting of the Pietà (derived from a work by Michelangelo) by the 'Master of the Manchester Madonna'. Also here: Jacopino dal Conte, *Deposition*; Jacques de Backer, *Dead Christ supported by an angel*; Marcello Venusti, *Prayer in the Garden*, *St Laurence*; Scipione Pulzone, *Cardinal Ricci*; Jacopo Zucchi, *Portrait of a lady*; Federico Zuccari, *Portrait of a man*.

Room I. Bartolomeo Passarotti, genre scenes; Il Scarsellino, *Resurrection of Lazarus*, *Christ in the Garden*, *Pietà*; works by Paul Brill, *Crucifixion of St Peter*, *Martyrdom of St Paul*; Luca Cambiaso, *Venus and Adonis*; Domenico Fetti, *Jacob's Dream*.

Room II. Caravaggio, *Narcissus*, *Judith and Holofernes*, and *St Francis in meditation* (attributed); Orazio Gentileschi, *St Francis supported by an angel*; Giovanni

Baglione, *Sacred and Profane Love*; Carlo Saraceni, *Madonna and Child with St Anne, St Cecilia and an angel*.

Room III. Massimo Stanzione, *Deposition*; Luca Giordano, *Portrait of a capomaestro*; Bartolomeo Manfredi, *Bacchus and a drinker*; Orazio Borgianni, *Portrait of a man*; Mattia Preti, *Resurrection of Lazarus*; Salvator Rosa, Allegories of Poetry and Music. **Room V**. Quentin Metsys, *Portrait of Erasmus*; Hans Holbein, *Portrait of Henry VIII* (possibly a replica); perspectives by Jean François Niceron.

The impressive **18C collection of paintings** is arranged in 12 more rooms. In the entrance corridor are Roman paintings by Placido Costanzi, Sebastiano Conca, Pietro Bianchi, and others. **Room 1** (right), bozzetti by Sebastiano Conca, and small works by Carlo Maratta. **Room 2**. Pierre Subleyras, *Madonna reading, Female nude*; works by Francesco Trevisani; larger works by Marco Benefial (*Pyramus and Thisbe*) and Francesco Mancini. **Room 3** contains bozzetti for frescoes in Roman churches by Baciccio, and Andrea Pozzo (the dome and vault of Sant'Ignazio, see p 153. **Room 4**. Portraits by Ignazio Stern, Pompeo Batoni, and Angelica Kauffmann. **Room 5**. Works by Francesco Solimena, Gaspare Traversi, Giuseppe Bonito (a Neapolitan artist), and Sebastiano Conca (*Adoration of the Magi*). **Room 6** contains works by Giuseppe Maria Crespi, Donato Creti, Alessandro Magnasco, and portraits by Vittore Ghislandi and Pietro Antonio Rotari. **Room 7**. Giovanni Battista Piazzetta, *Judith*; Giovanni Battista Tiepolo, *Old faun and young satyr*.

Room 8, frescoed with chiaroscuri in 1780–90, contains the Cervinara collection of charming small 18C French paintings, including: Nicolas Lancret, *Le Faucon, Family Group*; Jean Baptiste Greuze, *Portrait of a girl*; Jean-Honoré Fragonard, **Annette et Lubin*; Hubert Robert, *Landscapes*; François Boucher, *Le Matin, Le Soir, La petite jardinière*; and Louis-Leopold Boilly, *La Fête du Grand-père*. **Room 9** contains interesting views of Rome by Gaspar van Wittel, and **Room 10** views of ancient ruins by Giovanni Paolo Pannini. In **Room 11** are more works from the Cervinara collection, by Francesco Guardi (*The Giudecca Canal*), and Hubert Robert (*Bridge with washerwomen*). **Room 12**. Views of Venice by Luca Carlevarijs, and Canaletto; Bernardo Bellotto, *The Schlosshof in Vienna*. The last room, with a pretty ceiling, is reserved for recently restored works.

Other rooms contain the exceptionally valuable Numismatic Collection, made by Vittorio Emanuele III.

Also on this floor (but closed) are five rooms containing the **Dusmet Collection** which was left to the State in 1949. **Room I**. 16C majolica from Asia Minor. **Room II**. 17C–18C Chinese porcelain, and a Tien Lungli vase; 16C Flemish tapestries. **Room III**. Neri di Bicci (attributed), *Death of the Virgin, Madonna and Child* (tabernacle); 14C Sienese school, diptych of *San Vescovo* and *San Monaco*; 14C artist from the Marches, *Bishop saint*. **Room IV**. Terracotta works: Leone Leoni, *Deposition*; Francavilla, statuettes of Moses and Aaron; 16C Florentine school, *Pietà*; Susini, *Christ in the Garden*. **Room V**. 16C Flemish tapestries. Guercino (attributed), *Visitation of St Julian*; Annibale Carracci, *Self-portrait*; Lorenzo Costa, *Annunciation*. The delightful 18C **Barberini Apartments** (not open at present), with Rococo decorations, contain furniture, porcelain, costumes, etc.

Opposite the palace was the Scots College from 1604 until 1962, when it moved out of the centre of Rome to Via Cassia. The buildings dating from 1869, and the

church of St Andrew (1645–76), deconsecrated in 1962, are now incorporated in a bank.

Via delle Quattro Fontane ends in PIAZZA BARBERINI, which was transformed between the Wars into one of the busiest traffic hubs in the city. Here converge Via del Tritone (from the Corso), Via Sistina (from the Pincio), Via Vittorio Veneto, via San Nicola da Tolentino, and Via Barberini. Isolated in the centre of the square is this unpleasant setting is Bernini's masterpiece, the **Fontana del Tritone** (1642–43), with four dolphins supporting a scallop shell on which is seated a Triton who blows water through a conch shell held up in his hands. Commissioned by Urban VIII, it is decorated with the beautifully carved Barberini device of the bee. On the north side, at the beginning of Via Veneto, is the small, reconstructed **Fontana delle Api**, designed by Bernini a year later, also decorated with the Barberini bee and with an inscription stating that the water is for the use of the public and their animals.

Here begins the broad and tree-lined VIA VENETO (Pl. 4; 3, 1), which climbs in two sweeping curves to Porta Pinciana. Officially called Via Vittorio Veneto, it was opened in 1886 on part of the site of the beautiful park of the Villa Ludovisi which was obliterated, and which gave its name to this aristocratic district of the city, laid out at the turn of the century. The street with its luxury hotels, great mansions and famous cafés was especially fashionable for its ambience of 'la dolce vita' in the 1960s (after the success of Federico Fellini's film *La Dolce Vita* in 1959).

On the right is the church of the **Cappuccini** or **Santa Maria della Concezione** (Pl. 4; 3), architecturally simple and unpretentious in accordance with Franciscan ideals and in strong contrast to the Baroque works of the time (1626). Its founder was Cardinal Antonio Barberini. In the very dark **interior** all the pictures are labelled. **South side**. First chapel: Guido Reni, *St Michael*; to the left, Honthorst, *Mocking of Christ*; third chapel, Domenichino, *St Francis in Ecstasy*, and *Death of St Francis*; fifth chapel: Andrea Sacchi, *St Anthony raising a dead man*. An inscription on the pavement (*hic jacet pulvis, cinis et nihil*) marks the grave of Cardinal Barberini in front of the high altar.

North side. Fifth chapel: Andrea Sacchi, *The Virgin and St Bonaventura*; first chapel: Pietro da Cortona, *St Paul having his sight restored*. A **cemetery** (entered down the stairs to the right of the church) has five subterranean chapels decorated from the 17C onwards with the bones and skeletons of over 4000 Capuchins, arranged in patterns.

Opposite the church, a street with steps ascends to **Sant'Isidoro** (open Sunday at 10.00) with a pink façade by Carlo Bizzaccheri (1704). The church (1620, by Antonio Casoni) was attached to a college for Irish students, founded by Luke Wadding (1588–1657), the distinguished Irish Franciscan, who instigated the Irish rebellion of 1641 against the confiscation of Ulster. His tomb is in the church, which contains several works by Carlo Maratta, and a chapel designed by Gian Lorenzo Bernini with sculptures attributed to his son Paolo.

Further up Via Veneto, by its second curve (right) is Palazzo Piombino, or Palazzo Margherita, a huge building by Gaetano Koch (1886–90) standing in a garden, now the United States Embassy. Queen Margherita lived here after the death of Umberto I in 1900. Further on, Via Lombardia leads left from Via Veneto to the **Casino dell'Aurora** (No. 46; no admission), a relic of the famous Villa Ludovisi which belonged to Cardinal Ludovisi, nephew of Gregory XV. The

first Roman scene in Henry James's novel *Roderick Hudson* takes place in the gardens here. The garden-house contains a fine ceiling painting of Aurora and Fame by Guercino (1621). Via Veneto ends at **Porta Pinciana**, a handsome fortified gateway erected by Honorius c 403 and since enlarged. Opposite is one of the entrances to the Villa Borghese (Chapter 9).

On the city side of Porta Pinciana, Via di Porta Pinciana branches left from Via Veneto and, passing the grounds of the Villa Medici, runs into Via Francesco Crispi, which ends in Largo del Tritone. Beyond the gate, the broad Corso d'Italia skirts a long stretch of the Aurelian Wall (272–79) with some 18 turrets as far as Piazza Fiume on the site of the demolished Porta Salaria, and continues to Porta Pia (p 275).

VIA BARBERINI, opened in 1926, ascends from Piazza Barberini. On the left, in a side street called after it, is the church of **San Nicola da Tolentino** (closed indefinitely), rebuilt in 1620 by Carlo Buti, and finished by Martino Longhi the Younger and Giovan Maria Baratta, who built the façade in 1670. The high altar was designed by Alessandro Algardi. It contains a chapel thought to be the last work of Pietro da Cortona (1668), with sculptures by Ercole Ferrata, Cosimo Fancelli and Antonio Raggi.

Via Barberini ends at Largo Santa Susanna, another traffic hub, where it is joined on the left by Via Leonida Bissolati, with its numerous travel agencies. The square is dominated by the building of the Ufficio Geologico (1873, by Raffaele Canevari), containing the **Geological Museum** (no admission), with a collection of minerals, marbles (archaeological and modern) and fossils.

Adjoining Largo Santa Susanna on the southeast is the busy Piazza San Bernardo, with its fountain and three churches. It is, in effect, a widening of Via XX Settembre. On its northwest side is the church of **Santa Susanna** (Pl. 4; 4; open 17–19; fest. 10–12.00, 16.30–19), a Paulist church, probably dating from the 4C, restored in 795, and remodelled in the 15C and 16C. It is now the American National church. The façade, by Maderno (1603), is considered by many to be his masterpiece; in the good late Mannerist interior (1595) are large frescoes by Baldassare Croce. Opposite, at the beginning of Via Torino, is the round church of **San Bernardo alle Terme**, built into one of the two circular halls flanking the exedra of the Baths of Diocletian (see below) in the 16C (in an unattractive colour). The domed interior contains eight colossal stucco statues of saints by Camillo Mariani (c 1600–05), and a Neo-classical monument to the sculptor Carlo Finelli (died 1853) by Rinaldo Rinaldi.

The **Fontana dell'Acqua Felice** is fed by an aqueduct (1585–87) from Colonna in the Alban Hills. The fountain dates from the time of Sixtus V and is by Domenico Fontana; the unsuccessful figure of Moses is attributed to Prospero Antichi or Leonardo Sormani. The bas-relief of Aaron is by Giovanni Battista della Porta, and that of Gideon by Flaminio Vacca and Pier Paolo Olivieri; the four lions are copies of Egyptian antiques removed by Gregory XVI to the Egyptian Museum founded by him in the Vatican.

The church of **SANTA MARIA DELLA VITTORIA** (Pl. 4; 4), is a fine edifice by Maderno (1620), with a façade by Giovanni Battista Soria. Originally dedicated to St Paul, it was renamed from an image of the Virgin (burned in 1833) that gave victory to the Catholic army over the Protestants at the battle of the White Mountain, near Prague, on 8 November 1620 (Thirty Years War). The

interior (open 6.30–12; 14.30–19.30) is considered one of the most complete examples of Baroque decoration in Rome, rich in colour and glowing with marbles. It has good stuccowork and a fine organ and cantoria by a pupil of Bernini, Mattia de Rossi. The frescoes are by Giovanni Domenico Cerrini.

The second south chapel has an altarpiece of *The Madonna and St Francis* by Domenichino. The **Cornaro Chapel** (fourth chapel on the north side; recently restored), by Bernini, is a splendid architectural achievement, using the shallow space to great effect. Over the altar is his famous sculptured group, **The Ecstasy of St Theresa* (restored in 1996), and below is a gilt bronze relief of the Last Supper. At the sides are expressive portraits of the Venetian family of Cornaro, by pupils and followers of Bernini. The last half-hidden figure on the left is said to be a portrait of Bernini. The fresco, by Luigi Serra (1885), in the apse of the church, commemorates the triumphal entry into Prague of the Catholic army.

Via XX Settembre continues to Porta Pia (see p 265), passing on the left a building of 1902, built to house the Ministry of Agriculture and Forests, and on the right (no. 97), the colossal Treasury building by Raffaele Canevari (1870), containing a **Numismatic Museum** (open 9–13, except Sat & Sun. ☎ 476 13317. Document required showing proof of identity). Interesting is a collection of wax seals by Benedetto Pistrucci, who designed the St George and dragon on the English sovereign. The short Via Servio Tullio, opposite, leads north to Piazza Sallustio where, behind Villa Maccari (right), is a considerable fragment of a villa which used to stand in the Gardens of Sallust, laid out in 40 BC, on which the historian C. Sallustius Crispus lavished the wealth he had accumulated during his African governorship. Here also are the foundations of the Trinità dei Monti obelisk, showing where it stood in the Middle Ages.

The short Via Orlando runs from Piazza San Bernardo past the Grand Hotel opened in 1894 (when it was the first hotel in Italy with electric light), to the large circular PIAZZA DELLA REPUBBLICA (Pl. 5; 3), formerly *'dell' Esedra'* (from the exedra of the Baths of Diocletian, the buildings of which may be seen on the opposite side). The semicircular porticoed fronts of the palazzi on either side of the entrance to the piazza (by Koch; 1896–1902), follow the line of the exedra. The abundant waters of the **Fountain of the Naiads** (1870) are supplied by the Acqua Marcia. Four groups of reclining nymphs and the central Glaucus were sculpted by Mario Rutelli (1901–11).

Baths of Diocletian

The Baths of Diocletian were built in 298–306 by Diocletian and Maximian. The largest of all the ancient Roman baths, they could accommodate over 3000 people at once. They covered a rectangular area, c 380m by 370m, corresponding to that now bounded on the southeast by Piazza dei Cinquecento, on the southwest by Via Torino, on the northwest by Via XX Settembre, and on the northeast by Via Volturno. The main buildings included a calidarium, tepidarium, and frigidarium. The calidarium, which survived into the late 17C, occupied part of the present piazza. The tepidarium and the huge central hall of the baths are now occupied by the church of Santa Maria degli Angeli (see below). The frigidarium was an open-air bath behind this hall. Numerous large and small halls, nymphaea, and exedrae were located within the precincts.

The only entrance to the baths was on the northeast side, near the present Via Volturno. On the southwest side the closed exedra was flanked by two circular

halls: one of these is now the church of San Bernardo alle Terme (see above; the other is at the corner of Via Viminale and Via delle Terme. A third (octagonal) hall, on the corner of Via Parigi at the northwest angle of the main complex, is open to the public (see below). In the 16C a Carthusian convent was built in the ruins, and the baths were plundered for their building materials in the 16C–19C.

Along the modern Via Parigi stand conspicuous remains of buildings demolished to make way for the Baths. At the beginning of the street is a Roman column, a gift from the city of Paris (1961). On the corner of Via Parigi is the **Octagonal Hall of the Baths of Diocletian**, which provides a splendid setting for some works from the Museo Nazionale Romano (see p 198). The rectangular exterior hides a domed octagonal interior (open 10–19. ☎ 487 0690), a beautiful Roman architectural work. The hall is thought to have connected the open-air gymnasium and gardens of the Baths of Diocletian with the heated calidarium. Roman foundations can be seen through the glass panel in the centre of the hall.

Here are displayed Roman statues and busts (mostly dating from the 2C to 3C AD), many of them found in the Baths of Caracalla, Diocletian, and Trajan, including two famous bronzes: the *Boxer resting*, a magnificent work signed by Apollonius, dating from the 1C BC, and the Hellenistic so-called *Prince* (early 2C BC), a young man leaning on a lance, perhaps Pollus or one of the Seleucids, in the identical pose of the Alexander the Great by Lysippos. Also here is the marble *Aphrodite*, an original Greek work of the 4C BC, possibly by a predecessor of Praxiteles, representing the goddess just risen from the sea; near her right leg is her cloak, supported by a dolphin; the head and arms are missing. The statue was found in the Baths at Cyrene.

SANTA MARIA DEGLI ANGELI (Pl. 5; 3; open 7.30–12.30, 16–18.30) occupies the great central hall of the baths, converted into the church of the Carthusian convent. The work of adaptation was carried out in 1563–66 for Pius IV by Michelangelo, who may also have designed the cloisters and other conventual buildings. Michelangelo placed the entrance of the church at the short southeast side of the rectangle and thus had at his disposal a nave of vast proportions. The effect was spoiled by Vanvitelli who, instructed by the Carthusian fathers in 1749, altered the orientation. He made the entrance in the long southwest side and so converted the nave into a transept. To compensate for the loss of length, he built out on the northeast side an apsidal choir, which broke into the monumental southwest wall of the frigidarium. The façade on Piazza della Repubblica, with Vanvitelli's doorway, incorporates an apsidal wall, all that is left of the calidarium.

In the disappointing **interior**, the circular **vestibule** (being restored) stands on the site of the tepidarium. Here are the tombs of Carlo Maratta (died 1713; right) and Salvator Rosa (died 1673; left). By the entrance into the transept is (right) a fine colossal statue of St Bruno, by Houdon (1766). The vast **transept** is nearly 100m long, 27m wide and 28m high. The eight monolithic columns of red granite, nearly 14m high and 1.5m in diameter, are original; the others, in brick, were added when the building was remodelled. To the right: in the pavement, a meridian dating from 1703; tomb by Antonio Muñoz of Marshal Armando Diaz (died 1928), Italian commander-in-chief in the First World War. The huge paintings include (left): *Mass of St Basil*, by Subleyras; *Fall of Simon Magus*, by Pompeo Batoni. In the **choir**, on the right, Romanelli, *Presentation in*

the Temple; Domenichino, *Martyrdom of St Sebastian*; left, Pomarancio, *Death of Ananias and Sapphira* (painted on slate); Carlo Maratta, *Baptism of Christ*. In the apse, on the left, monument of Pius IV, from Michelangelo's design, which also inspired the monument of Cardinal Serbelloni opposite. The door to the sacristy in the left transept leads to a room with impressive remains of the **frigidarium** of the Baths of Diocletian (see above), and a display explaining the history of the building.

Viale Einaudi leads past a garden with a monument by Azzurri, erected in memory of 548 Italian soldiers ambushed at Dogali, Eritrea, in 1887. It incorporates an Egyptian obelisk found in the Isaeum Campense (its companion is in Florence) inscribed with hieroglyphs recording the glories of Rameses the Great or Sesostris, the Pharaoh of the time of Moses. (The monument, first erected in front of the old railway station was moved here in 1924; in 1936–44 it was decorated with the Lion of Judah plundered from Addis Ababa).

On the right of Santa Maria degli Angeli is the entrance through a garden to splendid vaulted rooms of the **Baths of Diocletian** (open 9–14; Sun 9–13; closed Mon. ☎ 488 0530. Lire 12,000; the same ticket allows entrance to Palazzo Massimo, see below) which, together with the Carthusian convent built inside the ruins in the 16C, provided a superb setting for the collections of the Museo Nazionale Romano, founded here in 1889. Most of the collection has been moved to Palazzo Massimo (see below), but eventually the huge collection of epigraphs and sarcophagi belonging to the museum is to be rearranged here, and a prehistoric section opened on the first floor of the cloister. At present only two rooms and the cloister are open. Temporarily displayed here (before its removal to Palazzo Massimo) is the **Discobolo*, or discus-thrower, from the Lancelotti collection, the finest and best-preserved replica of the famous statue of Myron. It was sold to Hitler in 1938, but recovered ten years later. In the corridor are mosaics, including one of a skeleton with an inscription in Greek ('Know Thyself').

The **Great Cloister** was built in 1565 and is ascribed to Michelangelo, who died the year before. The arcades are supported by 100 travertine columns. The fountain in the garden dates from 1695; it is shaded by four cypresses, one of which is the original. Seven colossal heads of animals (probably from the Forum of Trajan) surround the fountain.

Museo Nazionale Romano

The vast PIAZZA DEI CINQUECENTO (Pl. 5; 4), by far the largest square in Rome, is the terminus or junction of many bus services. **Palazzo Massimo** (Pl. 5; 4), built in 1883–87 by Camillo Pistrucci, which used to house the Jesuit Collegio Massimiliano Massimo, has been restored as the new seat of the Museo Nazionale Romano (Pl. 5; 4), one of the great museums of the world, with numerous masterpieces of classical art. Only seven rooms on the ground floor have so far been opened; some of the most important sculptures are exhibited in the Octagonal Hall of the Baths of Diocletian (see above), and others have been left in the old seat of the Museo Nazionale Romano in the Baths of Diocletian (see above). The Ludovisi collection (except for the Ludovisi throne) is to be exhibited in Palazzo Altemps.

The collection was founded in 1889, and includes archaeological finds made in Rome since 1870, part of the Kircherian collection, and the collection formed

by Cardinal Ludovico Ludovisi, nephew of Gregory XV (Alessandro Ludovisi; pope 1621–23), acquired by the State in 1901.

■ Open 9–14; Sun 9–13; closed Mon. ☎ 488 0530. Lire 12,000. The ticket also admits to the Baths of Diocletian.

On the **Ground Floor** is displayed art from the time of Sulla to Augustus, including portraits, and some Greek originals, in a severe modern arrangement. Near the entrance is a colossal statue of Minerva in pink alabaster, basalt and marble (late 1C BC to early 1C AD), found in Piazza dell'Emporio. In the corridor around the interior courtyard are displayed portrait heads.

Room I. Fragments of a calendar and a list of magistrates, from Anzio (84–55 BC); male portraits from Palestrina and Mentana (1C BC), and a bust (once thought to be a portrait of Caesar) from the von Bergen collection, dated 50–40 BC; statue of a general from Tivoli.

Room II. Stele with a citizen in a toga; funerary relief of the Rabirii (from the Via Appia Antica); and three male portraits from Priverno. In the corridor is a mosaic pavement (1C BC) with the Rape of Hylas (2C BC).

Room III displays portraits of Romans close to Augustus or members of his family, including a supposed portrait of Octavia, two portraits of Livia, portraits of Germanicus (in bronze) and Drusus Minor (from Mentana), and of Tiberius and Drusus Major (from Lanuvio). Also here are a portrait of Octavian, and a bronze head of Cornelius Pusio. The statue of a woman represented as Artemis from Ostia has a fine portrait head. **Room IV** has a very good numismatic display, with *coins arranged chronologically from the 7C BC to AD 68.

Room V, dedicated to Augustus, contains the celebrated ***statue of Augustus as Pontifex Maximus***, one of the finest portraits of the emperor, found in the Via Labicana; *frescoes from the Columbarium on the Esquiline (from the time of Caesar); and an ***altar from Ostia***, with reliefs of the origins of Rome (Mars and Rhea Silvia, Romulus and Remus suckled by the she-wolf, etc.), dated 1 October AD 124.

In the corridor is a mosaic dating from the 1C BC with two ducks and a cat. Beyond Room VI (closed) is **Room VII**. Here is displayed the ***Ludovisi Throne***, found in the Villa Ludovisi; it is thought to have been intended for the statue of a divinity, and is usually considered to be a Greek original of the 5C BC. The back and sides are adorned with reliefs. The central subject is apparently the birth of Aphrodite, who rises from the sea supported by two Seasons; on the right side is the representation of a young woman sitting clothed on a folded cushion; she is taking grains from a box and burning them in a brazier; on the left side is a naked flute girl, also sitting on a folded cushion, playing a double pipe. The ***Daughter of Niobe***, from the Gardens of Sallust, is a Greek original of the 5C BC of the school of Kresilas, and the **Peplophoros** (the headless statue of a girl in a peplos), found in Piazza Barberini, is also probably a Greek original of the first half of the 5C BC.

Room VIII contains neo-Attic works including Athena (found on the Celian hill), Aphrodite (copy of the Cnidian Aphrodite by Praxiteles, signed by the Greek artist Menofantos), and a Muse holding a tragic mask (the replica of a Hellenistic original). Also here are decorative reliefs, including a base with maenads, and a fountain basin with a frieze of marine figures, etc.

The rest of the collection is still being arranged and may be open by the time this book is published. On the **First Floor** will be exhibited sculptures found in Imperial villas (including Hadrian's Villa outside Tivoli, and Nero's Villa outside Subiaco). A room will contain statues of the Muses, the Crouching Venus, and the *'**Maiden of Anzio**', a masterpiece of Greek art dating from the end of the 4C or beginning of the 3C BC by a sculptor of the school of Lysippos who had come under the influence of Praxiteles. It represents a young girl approaching an altar and carrying implements for a sacrifice, and was discovered in the Imperial villa at Anzio in 1878. The ***Ephebus of Subiaco**, a Roman copy of an original of the 4C BC (probably one of the Niobids), and a young girl or nymph sleeping, both come from Nero's villa at Subiaco. A section will be devoted to portraits found in Hadrian's Villa, and another to busts of emperors, including Lucius Verus and Vespasian (one of the best surviving Roman portraits, found at Ostia), and female portraits of the 3C and 4C AD. In another room will be displayed the bronzes from the ships salvaged from Lake Nemi (see p 394).

The **Second Floor** is to be devoted to *wall-paintings* and *mosaics* from the Republican era onwards. The rectangular room from the Imperial Villa at Prima Porta of Livia, wife of Augustus, will be reconstructed; its walls were decorated with splendid *frescoes* of an orchard and flower garden, which constitute the masterpiece of naturalist decoration of the second style of Roman painting. Detached and restored in 1952–53, the frescoes were saved just in time from complete decay. The stuccoed and painted decoration of a building of the Augustan age, discovered in the grounds of the Villa Farnesina near the banks of the Tiber, will also be displayed here. The *ceilings decorated in stucco are masterpieces of their kind, with friezes decorated with festoons and cupids, interspersed with landscapes and mythological scenes. Other decorations come from a villa at Castel di Guido, thought to have belonged to Antoninus Pius. The mosaics include some from the Villa of Septimius Severus at Baccano. The **Basement** will have rooms for the coin collection, medals and jewellery.

Other masterpieces which will probably be exhibited include: an Apollo by the school of Pheidias, or perhaps by Kalamis, found in the Tiber; a dancer wearing a chiton, and Juno, possibly the portrait of an empress as the goddess, both found on the Palatine (5C BC); the 'Torso Valentini', a hero or athlete, a remarkable work of the early 5C BC, formerly in the courtyard of Palazzo Valentini; the head of Hypnos, attributed to Praxiteles, from Hadrian's Villa; the Apollo of Anzio, by an unknown Attic predecessor of Praxiteles; 'Dancer of Tivoli', Roman copy of a Hellenistic original; young satyr turning round to look at his tail, a Hellenistic work; a goddess personifying a seaport, accompanied by a child merman (1C BC; recalling 4C); sepulchral altar, comprising an ossuary and a cippus, with reliefs depicting a nuptial scene, and figures of maenads dancing and of youths carrying implements for a sacrifice; head of a princess of the Julio-Claudian gens wearing a diadem, possibly Agrippina, mother of Nero; Antoninus Pius as a young man; Commodus as a youth; head of Sabina, wife of Hadrian (with traces of colour still visible); the head of Hadrian, found beneath the Stazione Termini; Dionysos, from Hadrian's Villa, Hadrianic copy of a 4C Greek original; and head of a dying Persian, of the school of Pergamon, one of a series of sculptures set up at Pergamon to commemorate the victory of Attalos I over the Gauls; and polychrome marble intarsia panels from the basilica of Giunio Basso on the Esquiline (early 4C AD).

The **Stazione di Termini** (Pl. 5; 4; called after the Baths of Diocletian), on the southeast side of the square, is one of the largest railway stations in Europe. Its reconstruction, begun in 1938, was delayed by the Second World War, and it was not opened until 1950. In front is a gigantic quasi-cantilever construction, sweeping upwards and outwards, serving as a portico. The two metro (underground) lines intersect here.

In front of the station (left), is the best preserved fragment of the **Servian Wall**, formed of massive blocks of tufa. This wall, some 11km long, was traditionally attributed to Servius Tullius, sixth king of Rome; it is now thought that the wall dates from about 378 BC, although sections of an earlier earthen bank (*agger*) have been identified, which may be the work of Servius. There were 12 gates (see the plan on p 51). Further fragments of the wall were unearthed during the reconstruction of the station. Beneath the station have also been found remains of a private house and of baths, with good mosaics, dating from the 2C AD.

11 · The Esquiline Hill and Santa Maria Maggiore

The **Esquiline** (65m), the highest and most extensive of the Seven Hills of Rome, was formerly a region of vineyards and gardens, and had few inhabitants. It has four summits. Most of the *Oppius* or Oppian Hill is covered by a park (the *Parco Oppio*), on the site of the Baths of Titus and of Trajan and Nero's Domus Aurea. The *Cispius*, extending to the northeast, is crowned by the basilica of Santa Maria Maggiore. The other two summits are the *Subura*, above the low-lying district of that name, and the *Fagutalis*, named from a beech grove.

The four summits of the Esquiline, together with the three of the Palatine, formed the early city of the Septimontium. According to the erudite Varro, the name 'Esquiline' was derived from the word excultus, which referred to the ornamental groves planted on the hill by Servius Tullius, including the Querquetulanus (oak grove) and Fagutalis.

Although most of the hill was considered an unhealthy place to live, the region between the modern Via Cavour and the slopes of the Oppian Hill, called the Carinoe, was a fashionable residential district. Pompey lived here, in a small but famous house, occupied after his death by Antony. The site of the villa of Maecenas was afterwards occupied by the Baths of Titus. The villa was eventually acquired by Nero, who incorporated it in his famous Domus Aurea. Virgil had a house near the gardens of Maecenas. Propertius lived in the vicinity and Horace may have done.

VIA CAVOUR (Pl. 8; 2), opened in 1890 and now an important traffic artery of the city, runs from Via dei Fori Imperiali (Chapter 4) to Piazza dei Cinquecento and the railway station. At the beginning on the left is the base of the massive **Torre dei Conti**, all that remains of a great tower erected after 1198 by Riccardo dei Conti, brother of Innocent III. It was damaged by an earthquake in 1348 and reduced to its present state by Urban VIII in the 17C. Via Cavour now

passes through the ancient *Subura*, the scarcely noticeable hill of which was one of the four summits of the Esquiline. The district was connected to the Roman Forum by the Argiletum.

At the first important crossroads, Via degli Annibaldi (right) provides an interesting glimpse of the Colosseum, and Via dei Serpenti (left) leads to the **Madonna dei Monti**, a fine church by Giacomo della Porta (who also designed the fountain nearby). The 17C **interior** contains stuccoes by Ambrogio Buonvicino and frescoes by Cristoforo Casolani. **South side**. first chapel: frescoes by Giovanni da San Giovanni; third chapel (right side): Paris Nogari, *Christ carrying the Cross*. The **dome** (being restored) was decorated in 1599–1600 by Cesare Nebbia, Orazio Gentileschi, and others. In the chapels on the **north side**: *Adoration of the Shepherds* by Girolamo Muziano; two paintings by Cesare Nebbia; and an *Annunciation* by Durante Alberti.

On Via Cavour, at the end of a high wall, a flight of steps, called Via San Francesco di Paola ascends to the right, on the site of the ancient Via Scelerata, so called from the impious act of Tullia, who drove her chariot over the dead body of her royal father Servius Tullius. On the right is the base, with bands of black and white stone, of a medieval tower. To the right is Piazza San Francesco di Paola, with a large 17C palace which houses the administrative offices of the Istituto Centrale del Restauro (a State Restoration Centre), which now has its main laboratories in the former Istituto di San Michele (see p 274). The steps pass beneath an archway above which is an attractive Doric loggia, once part of the house of Vannozza Catanei (1442–1518), mistress of Alexander VI, and mother of four of his children, including Lucrezia and Cesare Borgia.

San Pietro in Vincoli

At the top of the steps is a square in front of the basilica of San Pietro in Vincoli (Pl. 5; 7; open 7–18 or 19), or *Basilica Eudoxiana*, traditionally founded in 442 by the Empress Eudoxia, wife of Valentinian III, as a shrine for the chains of St Peter. The church was restored in 1475 under Sixtus IV by Meo del Caprina, who was responsible for the **façade**, with its beautiful colonnaded portico.

> The two chains with which St Peter was supposed to have been fettered in the Tullianum are said to have been taken to Constantinople. In 439 Juvenal, Bishop of Jerusalem, gave them to the Empress Eudoxia, wife of Theodosius the Younger. She placed one of them in the basilica of the Apostles at Constantinople, and sent the other to Rome for her daughter Eudoxia, wife of Valentinian III. The younger Eudoxia gave the chain to St Leo I (pope 440–61) and built the church of San Pietro in Vincoli for its reception. Later the second chain was sent to Rome. On being brought together, the two chains miraculously united.

The basilican **interior**, much affected by restoration, preserves its 20 ancient columns with Doric capitals (the Ionic bases were added in the 17C). The **nave**, almost four times as wide as the aisles, has a ceiling painting by Giovanni Battista Parodi, representing the cure of a person possessed by an evil spirit through the touch of the holy chains.

South aisle. First altar: Guercino, *St Augustine*; second altar: the tomb on the left was designed by Domenichino, who painted the portraits above both tombs;

the altarpiece is a copy of his *Deliverance of St Peter*, now in the sacristy.

At the end of the aisle is the **Tomb of Julius II**, the famous unfinished masterpiece of Michelangelo, who was so harassed while working on the monument that he called it the 'tragedy of a sepulchre'. Hindered by his quarrels with Julius II and by the jealousy of that pope's successors, Michelangelo finally abandoned work on the tomb, and the great pontiff, who had contemplated for himself the most splendid monument in the world, lies uncommemorated in St Peter's. Some 40 statues were to have decorated the tomb, including the two slaves now in the Louvre, and the four unfinished slaves in the Accademia gallery in Florence. No idea of the original design of the monument (for which many drawings survive) can be gained from this very unsatisfactory grouping of statues and niches. Only a few magnificent fragments remain here, notably the powerful figure of *Moses, Michelangelo's most strongly individualised work, in whose majestic glance is seen the prophet who spoke with God. The satyr-like horns represent the traditional beams of light, an attribute of the prophet in medieval iconography. The beautiful figures of *Leah and *Rachel on either side—symbols of the active and contemplative life (Dante, *Purgatorio*, xxvii, 108)—are also by Michelangelo. The rest is his pupils' work: an ineffectual effigy of the Pope, by Maso del Bosco; a Madonna, by Alessandro Scherano; a Prophet and Sibyl, by Raffaello da Montelupo.

Michelangelo's Moses in San Pietro in Vincoli

The **sacristy** has a pretty 16C frescoed vault by Paris Nogari and a small 15C marble bas-relief of the Madonna and Child. In the vestibule is the original painting of the *Deliverance of St Peter* by Domenichino (removed for restoration). In the last chapel of this aisle is *St Margaret, by Guercino. The bishop's throne in the **apse** is a marble chair brought from a Roman bath. The frescoes by Giacomo Coppi have recently been beautifully restored. The baldacchino (undergoing restoration) over the high altar is by Virginio Vespignani (19C). In the confessio below are the Chains of St Peter, displayed in a tabernacle with beautiful bronze *doors attributed to Caradosso (1477). Stairs lead down to a tiny **crypt** (closed), in which is a fine late 4C Roman sarcophagus with figures representing scenes from the New Testament, supposed to contain the relics of the seven Jewish Maccabee brothers (1C BC).

North aisle. Second altar: 7C mosaic *icon of the bearded St Sebastian, well preserved (coin-operated light, on right); first altar: Pomarancio, *Descent from the Cross*; (near the west wall) tomb of Cardinal de Cusa, with a good coloured relief (1465), attributed to Andrea Bregno. On the end wall (covered with scaffolding) to the right of the entrance door, is the little tomb of the artist brothers Pollaiuolo with two expressive portrait busts attributed to Luigi Capponi. Above

is a very worn fresco of the plague of 1476 by an unknown 15C artist, and to the left, an early fresco of the Head of Christ (behind glass).

The **cloister** (entrance at 16 Via Eudossiana, on the right, now the University Faculty of Engineering), is attributed to Giuliano da Sangallo. The lovely well-head is by Simone Mosca.

The narrow and pretty Via delle Sette Sale leads out of the piazza on the left of San Pietro in Vincoli. This unexpectedly rural street passes between two of the summits of the Esquiline, the Cispius (left) and the Oppius (right). The park which now covers the Oppian Hill contains scattered remains of the huge **Baths of Trajan**, built after a fire in 104 by Apollodorus of Damascus and inaugurated in 109. The conspicuous ruins include an exedra which was decorated as a nymphaeum, and a hall with two apses. Between Via Terme di Traiano and Viale del Colle Oppio is a nymphaeum (well below ground level) on a basilican plan, probably part of Nero's Domus Aurea, restored by Trajan.

At 2 Via Terme di Traiano is the entrance (kept locked; for admission ask at the Auditorium of Maecenas, see below) to the so-called **Sette Sale**, in fact a remarkable large vaulted building with nine sections, the reservoir of the Baths of Trajan. Excavations have shown that a house was built above the reservoir in the 4C. The rest of the park is occupied by Nero's Domus Aurea, see p 223.

At the end of Via delle Sette Sale, by its junction with Viale del Monte Oppio, is the church of **SAN MARTINO AI MONTI** (Pl. 5; 5, 6), the church of the Carmelites, built c 500 by St Symmachus and dedicated to Saints Sylvester and Martin. It replaced an older church founded in the 4C by Pope St Sylvester I, who came from Mount Soracte to cure Constantine of an illness. It was rebuilt in the 9C and given its present appearance c 1650 by Filippo Gagliardi. In this church, the decisions of the Council of Nicaea (325), which recognised that Christ and God were of the same substance, were proclaimed in the presence of Constantine, and the heretical books of Arius, Sabellius and Victorinus were burnt.

In the **interior** the broad nave is divided from the aisles by 24 ancient Corinthian columns which support an architrave, and the presbytery is raised above the crypt. The fine 17C decoration, with statues, stucco medallions, and frescoes, is by Paolo Naldini and Filippo Gagliardi. In the lower side aisles are frescoes of the life of Elijah and landscapes of the Roman Campagna by Gaspard Dughet, and (left aisle) interesting views of the interiors of St John Lateran and St Peter's before reconstruction, by Filippo Gagliardi. *The Council of Pope Sylvester* is by Galeazzo Leoncino.

The tribune, with a double staircase, leading to the high altar, and the tabernacle are by Gagliardi, who also designed the elaborate stucco decoration of the **crypt**. Here, on the left, a door (key in the sacristy) leads to stairs which descend to a private chapel of the 3C, with traces of frescoes and mosaics, incorporated in eight large halls of a Roman building. In the left aisle are (second altar) *St Albert* by Girolamo Muziano, and (first altar), *Vision of St Angelo* by Pietro Testa.

A door on the right of the apse (closed during restoration work) leads out to a busy crossroads with two heavily restored medieval towers, from which the church of Santa Prassede may be reached (see below). Viale del Monte Oppio ends at the Largo Brancaccio, on the busy 19C Via Merulana.

Here (right) is **Palazzo Brancaccio**, built for Mary Elizabeth Bradhurst Field by Gaetano Koch in 1879, and enlarged by Luca Carimini). The interior has decorations in the neo-Baroque style by Francesco Gai. It now houses the Istituto Italiano per il Medio ed Estremo Oriente, and, on the second floor, the **MUSEO NAZIONALE DI ARTE ORIENTALE**, founded in 1957 and the most important collection of Oriental art in Italy. It has recently been reopened after rearrangement. The opening hours are Mon, Wed & Fri 9–14; Tues & Thur 9–19; Sun 9–13. ☎ 487 4218. Lire 8000.

Handsheets are available. **Rooms II and III**. Pre-Islamic Iran. Finds from the urban site of Shahr-i Sokhta, dating from 3200–1800 BC, and from Swat (northeast Pakistan), with finds from a necropolis dated 1500–500 BC. These include accountants' implements, seals, coins, examples of cuneiform writing, terracotta figures and vases and ceramics, bone and metal utensils, fragments of fabric, and jewellery. Also Luristan bronzes, weapons, and horsebits. **Rooms IV and V** contain works from Tibet, Nepal and Gandhara, including architectural fragments in wood, and jewellery. Rooms VI–X are still closed for restoration. Room VI will display Islamic art; Room VII Japanese art (including screen paint-ings, bronzes and ceramics), Room IX finds from southeast Asia, and Room X the Indian collection.

Rooms XI–XIV contain the collection from China: funerary statues, ritual objects and masks, sculptures of Buddha, bronze mirrors, ceramic and porcelain figures, Imperial warming plates, etc.

To the south in Largo Leopardi is the so-called **Auditorium of Maecenas** (open 9–19; Sun 9–13; closed Mon. C). An Augustan apsidal building, this was in the gardens of Maecenas, and may have been a nymphaeum. The unusual apse has tiered seats in a semicircle. It has recently been restored, but the traces of red landscape paintings in the apse and wall niches have all but disappeared. The building is adjoined by a stretch of the Servian Wall.

Via Leopardi leads northeast to the huge 19C PIAZZA VITTORIO EMANUELE II (Pl. 5; 6) surrounded by porticoes and planted with plane trees, cedars of Lebanon, and oleanders. It is the scene of a daily food market (beware of pick-pockets), noted for its abundance of North African and Middle Eastern products. In the pretentiously redesigned garden of the square are the impressive ruins of a fountain, known as the 'Trofei di Mario' (for admission, contact the Ripartizione X del Comune di Rome, ☎ 671 03819, fax 689 2115) built at the time of Alexander Severus. This was formerly the terminal of an aqueduct (either the Acqua Claudia or the Aniene Nuovo), and the marble panoplies known as the 'Trophies of Marius' were removed from here to the balustrade of Piazza del Campidoglio in the 16C. Near the fountain is the curious Porta Magica or Porta Ermetica, with an alchemist's prescription for making gold, dating from 1680. This was removed earlier this century from the villa of Massimiliano Palombara.

In the north corner of the square is the church of **Sant'Eusebio** (only open at 6.30 and 18.30), founded in the 4C and rebuilt in 1711 and 1750. The ceiling painting, the *Triumph of St Eusebius*, is by Raphael Mengs; in the apse are fine, elaborately carved 16C stalls. In the sacristy, in the right aisle, is the carved top of the tomb of St Eusebius (15C) from the earlier church.

Via Carlo Alberto leads northwest from the square to Santa Maria Maggiore,

passing the Arch of Gallienus, the middle arch of a triple gate erected in the time of Augustus and dedicated in AD 262 in honour of Gallienus and his consort Salonina by the city prefect M. Aurelius Victor; it occupies the site of the Porta Esquilina of the Servian Wall. On the left is the church of **Santi Vito e Modesto** (4C; restored in 1900 and again in 1977; only open at 10.00). It contains frescoes by Antoniazzo Romano, and excavations have revealed traces of the Servian Wall and a Roman aqueduct. Further on, on the right, is **Sant'Antonio Abate**, the church of the Russo-Byzantine rite, with a doorway attributed to the Vassalletto family of sculptors (1262–66). The interior (open on Sunday at 10.00) was redesigned c 1730.

At the end of Via Merulana is PIAZZA SANTA MARIA MAGGIORE, occupying the highest point (55m) of the Cispian summit of the Esquiline. In the square rises a fluted cipollino column 14.5m high, from the basilica of Maxentius. It was set up here in 1613 for Paul V by Carlo Maderno (who designed the fountain), and crowned with a statue of the Virgin.

Santa Maria Maggiore

Dominating the square is the ornate porticoed façade of Santa Maria Maggiore (Pl. 5; 6; open 7–18 or 19), once also called the *Basilica Liberiana*. More completely than any other of the four patriarchal basilicas, it retains its original interior magnificence. A basilica was built here by Pope Liberius (352–66) on the site of a Roman edifice. This was reconstructed by Pope Damasus (366–84) and again by Sixtus III (432–40). The present church almost certainly dates from the time of Sixtus III. Nicholas IV (1288–92) added the polygonal apse and transepts, Clement X (1670–76) rebuilt the apse, and Benedict XIV ordered Ferdinando Fuga to carry out further alterations and add the main façade.

According to a 13C legend, the Virgin Mary appeared on the night of 4–5 August c 358, to Pope Liberius and to John, a patrician of Rome, telling them to build a church on the Esquiline on the spot where they would find in the morning a patch of snow covering the exact area to be built over. The prediction fulfilled, Liberius drew up the plans and John built the church at his own expense. The original title was therefore Santa Maria della Neve. The church was afterwards called Santa Maria del Presepe, after a precious relic of the Crib of the Infant Jesus. In 366 supporters of the antipope Ursinus barricaded themselves in the church and surrendered only when the partisans of Pope Damasus I took off the roof and pelted them with tiles. In 1075 Gregory VII (Hildebrand) was carried off from Mass by the rebel Cencio, but was rescued next day by his supporters. In 1347 Rienzo was crowned here as Tribune of Rome.

Excavations (admission only with special permission) carried out in 1967–72 beneath the nave revealed a large Roman building with remains of frescoes including a remarkable rural calendar with illustrations for each month. Two important ceremonies are held in the basilica annually. On 5 August the legend of the miraculous fall of snow is commemorated in a pontifical Mass in the Borghese Chapel (see below). On Christmas morning there is a procession in honour of the Santa Culla, or Holy Crib, which culminates in the exposure of the relic on the high altar. Santa Maria Maggiore has the privilege of extraterritoriality.

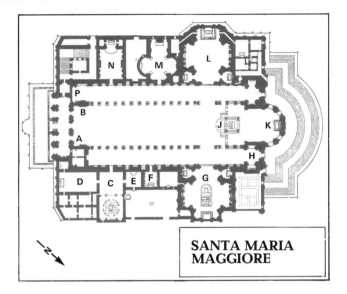

SANTA MARIA
MAGGIORE

Exterior. The fine **campanile**, the highest in Rome, was given its present form in 1377 by Gregory XI, and the polychrome decoration has been restored. The **apsidal façade**, completed c 1673, is approached by an imposing flight of steps from Piazza dell'Esquilino. The right-hand section, with its dome, is by Flaminio Ponzio; the central and left sections by Carlo Rainaldi; the left-hand dome by Domenico Fontana. The **main façade**, masking one of the 12C, was designed by Fuga (1743); it is approached by steps and is flanked by two grandiose wings.

The **portico** is surmounted by a loggia of three arches, above which are statues. In the portico is a bronze statue of Philip IV of Spain, on a model by Bernini. Here tickets may be purchased to visit the **upper loggia** (small groups are usually conducted 9.30–18. Lire 5000). A monumental staircase leads up past a bronze statue of Pope Paul V by Paolo Sanquirico (1605) to the open loggia, from which there is a good view (including the basilica of San Giovanni Laterano at the end of the long straight Via Merulana on the right). From the loggia can be seen the mosaics (recently restored) on the earlier façade, dating from the time of Nicholas IV (1294–1308). The upper part, signed by Filippo Rusuti, depicts Christ Pantocrator with angels and saints. The four scenes below, illustrating the Legend of the Snow (see above), were probably completed by assistants. The four 18C statues of angels by Pietro Bracci were originally over the high altar of the church.

Interior. The vast but well-proportioned interior (86m long), which still preserves its basilican form, is divided into nave and aisles by 36 columns of shining Hymettian marble and four of granite, all with Ionic capitals supporting an architrave, the whole discreetly rearranged and regularised by Ferdinando Fuga. Over the triumphal arch and in the nave are *mosaics, dating from the time of Sixtus III (432–40), the most important mosaic cycle in Rome of this period; of exquisite workmanship, they are in the classical tradition. The small rectangular biblical scenes high up above the architrave in the nave are difficult

to see with the naked eye. On the left, scenes from the life of Abraham, Jacob, and Isaac; right, scenes from the life of Moses and Joshua (restored; in part painted); over the triumphal arch, scenes from the early life of Christ. The coffered **ceiling**, attributed to Giuliano da Sangallo, was traditionally thought to have been gilded with the first gold brought from America by Columbus, presented to Alexander VI by King Ferdinand of Aragon and his wife Isabella, Queen of Castile. The Borgia emblems (rosettes and bulls) are prominent. The fine Cosmatesque pavement dates from c 1150. At the west end (**A**) is the monument of Clement IX (1670), designed by Carlo Rainaldi, with a statue of the pope by Domenico Guidi and statues of Faith and Charity by Cosimo Fancelli and Ercole Ferrata. The tomb (**B**) of Nicholas IV (1574), with sculptures by Leonardo Sormani, was designed by Domenico Fontana.

South aisle. From the baptistery (**C**), with a high relief of the *Assumption* by Pietro Bernini, is the entrance to the sacristy (**D**; no admission), designed, like the baptistery, by Flaminio Ponzio (early 17C). By the entrance, the Santarelli monument has a bust by Alessandro Algardi. In the vault of the Cappella San Michele (**E**), by a side door, are traces of 15C frescoes including two Evangelists by the circle of Piero della Francesca and a Pietà attributed to Benozzo Gozzoli. A column in the adjoining courtyard celebrates the conversion of Henry IV of France. The Cappella delle Reliquie (**F**), designed by Ferdinando Fuga, has ten red porphyry columns, and a 15C wooden crucifix.

The **Sistina Chapel** (**G**), or Chapel of the Holy Sacrament, on a domed Greek-cross plan, is a work of extraordinary magnificence carried out for Sixtus V by Domenico Fontana (1585). It is a veritable church in itself decorated with statues, stuccoes (by Ambrogio Buonvicino), and late 16C Mannerist frescoes by Cesare Nebbia, Giovanni Battista Pozzo, Paris Nogari, Lattanzio Mainardi and Giacomo Stella. The marble decoration was brought from the Septizodium on the Palatine (demolished by Sixtus V) and set up here by Carlo Maderno. The sumptuous tomb of Sixtus V (on the right), has a statue by Valsoldo, and the tomb of Pius V (on the left) a statue by Leonardo Sormani da Sarzana. The temple-like baldacchino, with four gilt bronze angels by Sebastiano Torrigiani, covers the original little Cosmatesque Chapel of the Relics (only open at Christmas), redesigned by Arnolfo di Cambio (late 13C), with figures of the crêche by his assistants. In the chapel (**H**), at the end of the aisle, is the beautiful **tomb of Cardinal Consalvo Rodriguez* (died 1299), a masterpiece by Giovanni Cosmati, showing the influence of Arnolfo di Cambio. The mosaic of the Madonna enthroned, with saints, fits well with the architectonic lines of the tomb, which was completed by the beginning of the 14C.

The **confessio** (**J**), reconstructed in the 19C by Virginio Vespignani, contains a kneeling statue of Pius IX by Ignazio Jacometti. The baldacchino over the high altar, with four porphyry columns, is by Fuga; a porphyry sarcophagus which contains the relics of St Matthew and other martyrs serves as the high altar; the fragment of the Crib of the Infant Jesus is kept below in the Confessio in a reli-quary adorned with reliefs and silver statuettes. At the foot of the sanctuary steps, in the south aisle, is the simple pavement tomb of the Bernini family, including Gian Lorenzo.

The ***mosaic of the apse** (**K**) dating from the time of Nicholas IV (1288–94), is signed by Iacopo Torriti (1290–95), and represents the Coronation of the Virgin, with angels, saints, Nicholas IV, Cardinal Iacopo Colonna, etc. It is the

culminating point of all the mosaics in the church, which commemorate the declaration at the Council of Ephesus (5C) that the Virgin was the Mother of God (Theotókos). The Virgin is seated on the same throne as Christ, a composition probably derived from the 12C mosaic in the apse of Santa Maria in Trastevere. Below, between the windows, are more mosaics by Torriti depicting the life of the Virgin, notably, in the centre, the *Dormition of the Virgin*. The four reliefs, below the windows, are from the old ciborium by Mino del Reame.

North aisle. Balancing the Sistina Chapel is the even more sumptuous **Borghese Chapel** or Cappella Paolina (**L**). This chapel, erected by Paul V, was designed by Flaminio Ponzio (1611). The best known contemporary artists were employed to decorate it, including Cigoli, Cavaliere d'Arpino, Guido Reni, Baglione, and Passignano, and the sculptors Stefano Maderno, Francesco Mochi and Nicolas Cordier. On the altar, surrounded with lapis lazuli and agate, is a *Madonna and Child* with crossed hands, now thought to date from the 12C–13C, although it has also been attributed to a Byzantine artist working before the 10C. The tombs of Clement VIII and Paul V, with statues by Silla Longhi, are on either side. The **Sforza Chapel** (**M**), erected by Giacomo della Porta to a design by Michelangelo, contains an *Assumption*, by Sermoneta. In the **Cesi Chapel** (north, beautifully restored), probably designed by Guidetto Guidetti (c 1550), are two Cesi tombs, by Guglielmo della Porta and an altarpiece of the *Martyrdom of St Catherine*, by Sermoneta. The tomb of Cardinal Philippe de Levis de Quelus and his younger brother Archbishop Eustache (1489), above the Porta Santa (**P**), is in the style of Giovanni Dalmata.

Santa Prassede and Santa Pudenziana

Just off Piazza Santa Maria Maggiore, Via Santa Prassede leads to the inconspicuous side entrance of the church of **SANTA PRASSEDE** (Pl. 5; 6; open 7–12, 16–18.30), built by St Paschal I in 822 and still enveloped on all sides by medieval and later buildings. An oratory is said to have been erected here about AD 150 by St Pius I, and a church is known to have been in existence here at the end of the 5C. Paschal's 9C church was restored in 1450, 1564, 1832 and 1869. The building is dedicated to Praxedes, sister of Pudentiana (see below) and daughter of Pudens, in whose house St Peter is traditionally supposed to have first found hospitality at Rome. Here in 1118 the Frangipani attacked Pope Gelasius II with arrows and stones, driving him to exile in France, where he died.

The main west entrance, on the old Via San Martino ai Monti, is usually kept locked: it is preceded by a medieval porch with two reversed Doric capitals. The only part of the exterior visible is the Zeno Chapel, beside the south entrance. In the **interior**, the **nave** has 16 granite columns and six piers supporting an architrave made up from ancient Roman fragments. The effective trompe l'oeil frescoes date from the late 16C (by Paris Nogari, Baldassarre Croce, Ciampelli, and others). In the well-preserved pavement in the nave a large porphyry disc with an inscription indicates the well where St Praxedes is supposed to have hidden the bones of Christian martyrs.

The **choir** is approached by steps of rosso antico. The fine Baroque baldacchino by Francesco Ferrari (1730) partially hides the splendid 9C *mosaics (coin-operated light on right) showing: on the entrance-arch (outer face) *The New Jerusalem*, whose doors are guarded by angels, (inner face) *Christ and saints*; on the apse-arch, the *Agnus Dei with the seven golden candlesticks*, the

symbols of the Evangelists, and 24 Elders; in the semi-dome, *Christ between* (right) *Saints Peter, Pudentiana, and Zeno*, and (left) *Saints Paul, Praxedes, and Paschal* (the square nimbus indicates that the latter was still alive when the mosaic was executed); below, *the Lamb, the flock of the Faithful* and a dedicatory inscription; above, the monogram of Paschal I. On the left and right of the sanctuary are six Roman *columns of very unusual design incorporating the form of acanthus and laurel leaves. In the crypt (closed for restoration) beneath are four early Christian sarcophagi, including one with the remains of Saints Praxedes and Pudentiana, and a 13C Cosmatesque altar, with a damaged fresco above depicting the Madonna between Saints Praxedes and Pudentiana.

In the **south aisle** is the Byzantine **Chapel of St Zeno** (coin-operated light on left), the most important work of this date in Rome, built in 817–24 by St Paschal as a mausoleum for his mother, Theodora. The entrance is flanked by two ancient porphyry columns with 9C Ionic capitals which support a rich 1C architrave from a pagan temple, elaborately sculptured; on this rests a Roman marble urn (3C). Above is a double row of 9C mosaic busts: in the inner row, the Virgin and Child, Saints Praxedes and Pudentiana, and other saints; in the outer, Christ and the Apostles, and four saints (the lowest two perhaps added in the 13C). The exquisite vaulted interior, the only chapel in Rome entirely covered with **mosaics**, was known as the 'Garden of Paradise'. The pavement is perhaps the oldest known example of opus sectile. Over the door, *Saints Peter and Paul uphold the throne of God*; on the right are *Saints John the Evangelist, Andrew and James*, and *Christ between St Paschal and Valentine*(?); inside the altar-niche, *Madonna and Child between Saints Praxedes and Pudentiana*; on the left, *Saints Praxedes, Pudentiana, and Agnes*, and four female half-lengths including Theodora (with the square nimbus). In the vault, *Christ and four angels*. The bases of the four supporting columns date from the 9C, except for the one on the right of the altar which is a fine 5C Roman work. In a niche on the right are fragments of a column brought from Jerusalem after the 6th Crusade (1228), and said to be that at which Christ was scourged.

In the adjoining funerary chapel is the *tomb of Cardinal Alain Coëtivy (1474) by Andrea Bregno. Outside, on a nave pillar, is the tomb of Giovanni Battista Santoni (died 1592), one of the earliest works of Bernini. At the east end of the aisle, a chapel (being restored) contains the tomb of Cardinal Pantaleon of Troyes (died 1286), with Cosmatesque fragments, attributed to Arnolfo di Cambio, marble architectural fragments, and a 16C crucifix. In the second chapel in the south aisle are two paintings by Ciro Ferri, and ceiling frescoes by Borgognone.

North aisle. First chapel: altarpiece by Giuseppe Severoni; second chapel: *St Charles Borromeo* by Stefano Parrocel, and two paintings on the side walls by Ludovico Stern. Here is preserved the chair used by St Charles Borromeo. Third chapel: *frescoes by Cavaliere d'Arpino, and an altarpiece of *Christ bearing the Cross*, by Federico Zuccari. Against the left wall (in a frame) is the top of the table used by St Charles Borromeo. The fourth chapel was decorated with frescoes and mosaics in 1933. In the **sacristy**, the altarpiece is by Ciampelli. On the right wall is a good painting of the *Flagellation*, attributed to Giulio Romano, and a *Deposition* by Giovanni de Vecchi. To the right, a spiral staircase (admission sometimes on request) leads up to the campanile with 9C wall-paintings.

Behind the apse of Santa Maria Maggiore is Piazza dell'Esquilino with an obelisk, nearly 15m high, set up by Sixtus V in 1587. Like its twin in Piazza del Quirinale it once stood outside the entrance to the Mausoleum of Augustus. Via Cavour (see above) cuts across the piazza. Opposite Santa Maria Maggiore, Via Agostino Depretis runs northwest towards Via Nazionale (see Chapter 10). Via Urbana, on the left, leads in a few metres to **SANTA PUDENZIANA** (Pl. 5; 5), one of the oldest churches in Rome, thought to have been built c 390 above a Roman thermal hall of the 2C. It was rebuilt several times later, notably in 1589. The church is dedicated to Pudentiana, sister of Praxedes (see above), and daughter of the Roman senator Pudens, a legendary figure who is supposed to have given hospitality to St Peter in his house on this site. The church is now well below the level of the modern street.

Exterior. The façade was rebuilt and decorated in the 19C; the fine campanile probably dates from the late 12C. The good doorway preserves a beautiful medieval frieze in relief.

In the disappointing **interior** (open 8–12, 16–18) the nave and aisles are divided by Roman columns built up into piers. The dome was painted by Pomarancio. The precious *mosaic** in the apse, the earliest of its kind in Rome, dates from 390. It was damaged by a 16C restoration, which removed the two outermost Apostles at each end and cut the others in half. It shows Christ enthroned, holding an open book between the Apostles and two female figures, who represent the converted Jews and the converted pagans (or Gentiles), crowning St Peter and St Paul. The Roman character of the figures is marked; the magisterial air of Christ recalls the representations of Jupiter, and the Apostles, in their togas, resemble senators. Above is a jewelled Cross and the symbols of the Evangelists, and buildings (including houses, thermae and a basilica) representing Jerusalem and Golgotha.

In the chapel at the end of the left aisle an altar, presented by Cardinal Wiseman, encloses part of the legendary communion-table of St Peter; the rest of it is in St John Lateran. The marble group of Christ entrusting the Keys to St Peter is by Giovanni Battista della Porta. The Cappella Caetani, opening off the aisle, is a rich Baroque work by Francesco da Volterra, finished by Carlo Maderno. The altar relief is by Pietro Paolo Olivieri. Behind the apse are fragments of frescoes and a statuette of the Good Shepherd.

Through a door in the left aisle (apply to sacristan, but usually closed) is a courtyard, showing part of 2C baths, and, up some stairs, the **Oratorium Marianum** (also kept locked), containing 11C frescoes and brick stamps of Hadrian's time. The building incorporates part of the baths said to have been erected by Novatian and Timotheus, the brothers of Pudentiana and Praxedes, above the so-called house of Pudens. The baths extend on to the pavement in Via Balbo; the frescoes are also visible from here.

Via Urbana continues to the undulating Via Panisperna in which is the church of **San Lorenzo in Panisperna** (Pl. 5; 5), the traditional site of the martyrdom of St Laurence, in a delightful court of old houses, and a villa to the left (part of the Ministry of the Interior, see below). The church contains a vast fresco of the martyrdom by Pasquale Cati. The huge Palazzo del Viminale (1920), now the Ministry of the Interior, fronts Piazza del Viminale on Via Agostino Depretis.

On the parallel Via Napoli, on the corner of Via Nazionale, is the American

Episcopal church of **St Paul's** ('within the Walls'; open for services on Thur at 10.30, and on fest. 8.30, 10.30, and 18 or 19.30), an interesting building by George Edmund Street (1879). The conspicuous red-and-white exterior, in travertine and red brick, is in a Romanesque style (the mosaics are by George Breck, former director of the American Academy in Rome). In the interior the *mosaics in the large apse and choir are by Edward Burne-Jones. The figures in the lower register include portraits of J.P. Morgan, Archbishop Tait, General Grant, Garibaldi and Abraham Lincoln. On both walls of the nave are ceramic tiles designed by William Morris. The stained-glass windows were made by the English firm of Clayton and Bell.

In Via Viminale is the **Teatro dell'Opera**, built in 1880 by Achille Sfondrini for Domenico Costanzi. The Roman première of Verdi's *Falstaff* was performed here in 1893. The theatre was acquired by the Comune of Rome in 1926, and restored and enlarged by Marcello Piacentini in 1959–60. It is the most important lyric theatre in Rome.

12 · St John Lateran and Santa Croce in Gerusalemme

On the edge of the Celian Hill, around the busy PIAZZA DI SAN GIOVANNI IN LATERANO (Pl. 10; 3), are assembled some of the most important monuments in Christian history, including the first church of Rome. Here in 1588, on a line with Via di San Giovanni and Via Merulana, Domenico Fontana set up a red granite obelisk, the oldest in the city. It had been erected by Thothmes IV in front of the Temple of Ammon at Thebes (15C BC), and was brought to Rome by Constantius II (357) to decorate the Circus Maximus, where it was discovered in three pieces in 1587. It is the tallest obelisk in existence (31m high, 47m with the pedestal), though one metre had to be sawn off during its reconstruction. On the west side of the square is the Ospedale di San Giovanni, the main hospital in Rome for emergencies. Excavations in 1959–64 beneath the hospital revealed remains of a villa, thought to be that of Domizia Lucilla, mother of Marcus Aurelius.

St John Lateran

The church of St John Lateran (*San Giovanni in Laterano*; Pl. 10; 3; open 7–18; summer 7–19) is the cathedral of Rome and of the world ('Omnium urbis et orbis Ecclesiarum Mater et Caput'). Founded by Constantine, it was the first Christian basilica to be constructed in Rome. The original five-aisled church with an apse, on a basilican plan, was probably built between 314 and 318, and was dedicated to the Redeemer and later to St John the Baptist and St John the Evangelist. It served as a model for all subsequent Christian churches. Partly ruined by the Vandals, it was restored by St Leo the Great (440–61) and Hadrian I (772–95) and, after the earthquake of 896, by Sergius III (904–11). Nicholas IV (1288–92) enlarged and embellished the building to such an extent that it was considered the wonder of the age; Dante described it with admiration when Boniface VIII proclaimed the first Holy Year in 1300 from the loggia of the east façade.

The church was destroyed by fire in 1308 and rebuilt by Clement V (1305–14) soon afterwards; it was decorated by Giotto. In 1360 it was burnt down again and its ruin was lamented by Petrarch. Under Urban V (1362–70) and Gregory XI (1370–78) it was entirely rebuilt by the Sienese artist Giovanni di Stefano. Martin V (1417–31), Eugenius IV (1431–47) and their successors added to its splendour (Sixtus V employing Domenico Fontana, and Clement VIII, Giacomo della Porta). In 1646–49 Innocent X commissioned Borromini to rebuild the church yet again, and in 1734 Clement XII added the east façade. The ancient apse was entirely reconstructed in 1875–85 and the mosaics reset after the original designs.

The basilica derives its name from the rich patrician family of Plautius Lateranus, who, having been implicated in the conspiracy of the Pisoni, was deprived of his property and put to death by Nero. Recent excavations in the neighbouring Via Aradam have revealed a large Roman building thought to be the house of the Pisoni and Laterani expropriated by Nero. The property afterwards passed to Constantine as the dowry of his wife Fausta. In this 'Domus Faustae' church meetings were probably held as early as 313. The Emperor presented it, together with the land occupied by the barracks (excavated in 1934–38 beneath the nave of the present basilica) built in the 2C for his private horseguards, 'the Equites Singulares', to St Melchiades (pope 311–14), for the purpose of building a church for the see of Rome.

Until 1870 the popes were crowned here, and it has been the seat of five General Councils: in 1123, 1139, 1179, 1215 and 1512. Under the Lateran Treaty of 11 February 1929, this basilica, with those of San Paolo fuori le Mura and Santa Maria Maggiore, was accorded the privilege of extraterritoriality. After the ratification of the treaty the pope, for the first time since 1870, left the seclusion of the Vatican. On 24 June 1929, Pius XI officiated at St John Lateran, and the annual ceremony of blessing the people from the loggia was later resumed. The Pope traditionally attends the Maundy Thursday celebrations in the basilica.

Exterior. The **north front**, on Piazza di San Giovanni in Laterano, built by Domenico Fontana in 1586, has a portico of two tiers. It has been restored after damage from an explosion in 1993 caused by a car bomb placed by the Mafia. Beneath it, on the left, is a statue of Henry IV of France by Nicolas Cordier (c 1610), erected in gratitude for his gifts to the chapter. The two towers behind date from the time of Pius IV (1560). The principal or **east front**, overlooking the vast Piazza di Porta San Giovanni, is a theatrical composition by Alessandro Galilei (1734–36). It consists of a two-storeyed portico surmounted by an attic with 16 colossal statues of Christ with the Apostles and saints. On Maundy Thursday the pope gives his benediction from the central loggia. Beneath the **portico**, the bronze central doors were first used for the Curia, and later the church of Sant' Adriano in the Forum. On the left (**A**) is a statue of Constantine, from his Baths on the Quirinal. On the right is the entrance (only open on the first Saturday of the month) to the Museo Storico Vaticano in the Lateran Palace (see below).

The **interior**, 130m long, with two aisles on either side of the nave, preserves in part its original 4C proportions, although it was entirely remodelled by

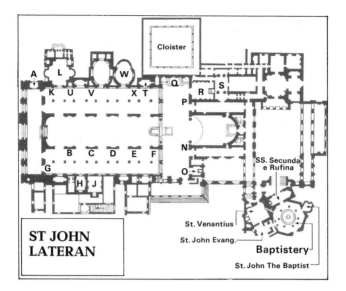

Borromini in 1646–49. In the niches of the massive piers which encase the verde antico pillars are colossal statues of the Apostles made in the early 18C by Lorenzo Ottoni, Camillo Rusconi, Giuseppe Mazzuoli, Pierre Legros, Pierre Monnot, Angelo de Rossi and Francesco Moratti. Above them are stuccoes designed by Algardi with scenes from the Old and New Testaments. Higher still are paintings of prophets (1718) by Domenico Maria Muratori, Marco Benefial, Giuseppe Nicola Nasini, Giovanni Odazzi, Giovanni Paolo Melchiorri, Sebastiano Conca, Benedetto Luti, Francesco Trevisani, Andrea Procaccini, Luigi Garzi, Giuseppe Chiari and Pierleone Ghezzi. The rich ceiling is by Flaminio Boulanger and Vico di Raffaele, and the marble pavement is of Cosmatesque design.

The outer aisles were also decorated by Borromini, and the funerary monuments reconstructed and enclosed in elegant Baroque frames. **South aisles**. In the **inner aisle**, on the nave piers: Boniface VIII proclaiming the Jubilee of 1300 (**B**), a fragment of a fresco from the exterior loggia now considered to be by the hand of Giotto; cenotaph of Sylvester II (died 1003; **C**), by the Hungarian sculptor William Fraknoi (1909); beneath is a medieval memorial slab to the same pope; tomb (**D**) of Alexander III, the pope of the Lombard League; tomb (east) of Sergius IV, with a medieval figure of a pope; tomb (**F**) of Cardinal Ranuccio Farnese, by Vignola. In the **outer aisle**, enclosed in Borromini's Baroque frames: tomb (**J**) of Cardinal Antonio de Chaves (1447) attributed to Isaia da Pisa, and tomb (**H**) of Cardinal Casati (1290), by the Cosmati. Over the window-screen outside the Cappella Massimo (I) is a fragment of the original altar with a statuette of St James, attributed to Andrea Bregno. The **Cappella Torlonia** (**K**), richly decorated by Raimondi (1850), is closed by a fine iron balustrade, and has a sculptured altarpiece (*Descent from the Cross*) by Pietro Tenerani. Beyond is the tomb (**L**) of Giulio Acquaviva (1574), made cardinal at the age of 20 by Pius V. The tomb of Paolo Mellini (1527) is in the embrasure of

the Porta Santa (**M**; opened only in Holy Years), with a damaged fresco.

North aisles. At the beginning of the **outer aisle** (**K**) is a sarcophagus with the cast of a recumbent figure of Cardinal Riccardo degli Annibaldi (1276) by Arnolfo di Cambio (the original is now exhibited in the cloisters, see below). The **Cappella Corsini** (**L**), a graceful early 18C structure by Alessandro Galilei, contains above its altar a mosaic copy of Guido Reni's painting of St Andrea Corsini; on the left, tomb of Clement XII (Lorenzo Corsini; died 1740), a porphyry sarcophagus from the Pantheon, and in the vault below (apply to sacristan), a *Pietà* by Antonio Montauti. In the aisle are tombs of the Archpriest Gerardo da Parma (1061; **U**) and of Cardinal Bernardo Caracciolo (died 1255; **V**); at the end, beyond the pretty Cappella Lancellotti (west), by Francesco da Volterra (1585–90, rebuilt 1675 by Giovanni Antonio de Rossi), is the tomb of Cardinal Casanate (1707; X).

The **transepts** were built under Clement VIII (1592–1605) by Giacomo della Porta, and the large frescoes depicting the conversion of Constantine, his gift to the pope, and the building of the basilica, completed in 1600 under the direction of Cavaliere d'Arpino (by Giovanni Battista Ricci, Paris Nogari, Cristoforo Roncalli, Orazio Gentileschi, Cesare Nebbia, Giovanni Baglione and Bernardo Cesari). In the central space is the **papal altar**, reconstructed by Pius IX, containing many relics, including the heads of Saints Peter and Paul, and part of St Peter's wooden altar-table. Above is the Gothic *baldacchino by Giovanni di Stefano (1367), frescoed by Barna da Siena. In the enclosure in front of the confessio (**M**) is the *tomb-slab of Martin V (died 1431), by Simone Ghini.

In the south transept are the great organ (1598; by Luca Blasi), supported by two columns of giallo antico, and the tomb (north) of Innocent III (died 1216), by Giuseppe Lucchetti (1891), erected when Leo XIII brought the ashes of his great predecessor from Perugia. In the corner in the little Cappella del Crocifisso (**O**), is a kneeling statue of Boniface IX (Cosmatesque; late 14C). In the north transept is the tomb of Leo XIII (**P**), by Giulio Tadolini (1907). At the end is the Altar of the Holy Sacrament (**Q**), by Pier Paolo Olivieri (from the time of Clement VIII), flanked by four antique bronze columns. On the right is the Cappella del Coro (**R**), with fine stalls of c 1625.

The **apse** was reconstructed, at the expense of Leo XIII, by Virginio and Francesco Vespignani in 1885 when the fine apse mosaics were destroyed and replaced by a copy. The original mosaics were designed by Iacopo Torriti and Iacopo da Camerino (1288–94) from an antique model. Beneath the Head of Christ (the copy of a mosaic fabled to have appeared miraculously at the consecration of the church) the Dove descends on the bejewelled Cross. From the hill on which it stands four rivers flow to quench the thirst of the faithful. On either side are (left) the Virgin with Nicholas IV and Saints Peter and Paul, and (right) Saints John the Baptist, John the Evangelist and Andrew; the figures of St Francis of Assisi (left) and St Anthony of Padua (right) were added by Nicholas IV. At their feet flows the Jordan. Kneeling at the feet of the Apostles (in the frieze below) are the tiny figures of Torriti and Camerino.

The doorway beneath Leo XIII's tomb admits to the **sacristy** (**Z**; normally closed to visitors), reached by a corridor (**Y**) containing the tombs of Andrea Sacchi and the Cavaliere d'Arpino, and (behind the apse) two fine statues of St Peter and St Paul by Deodato di Cosma. On the left is the **old sacristy** (**S**), with a beautiful *Annunciation* by Marcello Venusti, after Michelangelo.

Detail of the cloister in St John Lateran

In the north aisle (**T**) is the entrance to the peaceful ***cloister** (open 9–17, 9–18 in summer. Lire 4000), the masterpiece of Iacopo and Pietro Vassalletto (c 1222–32), a magnificent example of Cosmatesque art. The columns, some plain and some twisted, are adorned with mosaics and have fine capitals. The frieze is exquisite. In the centre is a well-head dating from the 9C. Many interesting fragments from the ancient basilica are displayed around the cloister walls.

East side: 27. Large marble inscription (1072) recording the restoration of the basilica by Pope Alexander II; 38. Papal throne, an antique marble chair with Cosmati decorations from the time of Pope Nicholas IV. A door from this walk leads into the little **museum** which contains two Florentine tapestries (1595–1608), an early 16C ex-voto of Tommaso Inghirami, numerous gifts, including a French cope, given to Pius IX, the *cope of Boniface VIII (13C English workmanship), and a model of the Colonna dell'Immacolata (1854) in Piazza di Spagna. At the end of the east side (66) is the tomb effigy of Giovanni Cardelli who died in 1465.

South side: 73. 6C head of a Byzantine empress (on a 2C Roman bust; removed); 84. Inscription recording the papal bull of Sixtus IV (1475); 81. Two half-columns decorated with palm leaves. The *tomb of Cardinal Riccardo Annibaldi was the first important work of Arnolfo di Cambio in Rome (c 1276), and has been reconstructed from fragments, which include reliefs and the recumbent statue. 103. Roman sarcophagus, with four portraits; various pavement tomb-slabs, carved in relief. **West side**: 167–168. Four small columns supporting a marble slab, taken in the Middle Ages to represent the height of Christ; 188. Head from the tomb of Lorenzo Valla (died 1465); bronze door with an inscription of 1196. **North side**: 201. Roman cippus, reused in the 16C; 229. Circular altar dating from the 5C AD. Various pieces of Cosmati work.

Beside the north front of the basilica, in the southwest corner of Piazza di San Giovanni in Laterano, is the **BAPTISTERY OF ST JOHN**, or *San Giovanni in Fonte*, built by Constantine c 315–24, though not, as legend states, the scene of his baptism as the first Christian emperor (337). It is a centrally planned octagonal building, although the original baptistery, designed for total immersion, and derived from classical models, may have been circular. It was remodelled by Sixtus III (432–40), and its design was copied in many subsequent baptisteries. It was restored again by Hadrian III in 884.

In the **interior** (open 9–13, 17–19; winter 9–13, 16–18; the chapels are unlocked by the sacristan) are eight columns of porphyry erected by Sixtus III; they support an architrave which bears eight smaller white marble columns. In the centre is the green basalt font. The 17C decorations were added by Urban VIII, and the harsh frescoes of scenes from the life of St John the Baptist on the

drum of the cupola are modern copies of works by Andrea Sacchi. The **Chapel of St John the Baptist** was founded by the martyred pope, St Hilary (461–68). It preserves its original doors (once thought to come from the Baths of Caracalla), which resound musically when opened. The **Chapel of Saints Cyrian and Justina** (or Saints Secunda and Rufina) occupied the narthex of Sixtus III, altered to its present form in 1154. Over the door is a relief of the Crucifixion after Andrea Bregno (1492). High up on the wall can be seen a fragment of the original marble intarsia decoration of the baptistery. In the north apse is a beautiful 5C *mosaic with vine tendrils on a brilliant blue ground. A door leads out into a courtyard from where can be seen the outer face of the narthex with two beautiful, huge antique columns supporting a fine Roman architrave.

The **Chapel of St Venantius**, added by Pope John IV in 640 contains mosaics commissioned by Pope Theodore I (642–49): in the apse, the head of Christ flanked by angels and the Madonna with Saints and Pope Theodore, and on the triumphal arch, the martyrs whose relics Pope John brought from Dalmatia and (high up) views of Jerusalem and Bethlehem. Remains of 2C Roman baths built above a 1C villa, with a mosaic pavement, may also be seen here. The structure of the original baptistery can be seen in the walls and beneath the apse. The **Chapel of St John the Evangelist**, dedicated by St Hilary, with bronze doors of 1196, is decorated with a vault *mosaic (5C) of the Lamb surrounded by symbolic birds and flowers. The altar has alabaster columns. On the left is Luigi Capponi's, *St Leo praying to St John*.

Adjoining the basilica, and facing Piazza di Porta San Giovanni, is the **LATERAN PALACE** (Pl. 10; 3), used by the popes before the move to Avignon in 1309. The old palace, which dated from the time of Constantine, was almost destroyed in the fire of 1308 which devastated St John Lateran. On the return from Avignon in 1377 the Holy See was transferred to the Vatican. In 1586 Sixtus V demolished or displaced what the fire had left and ordered Domenico Fontana to carry out a complete reconstruction. The new Lateran was intended to be a summer palace for the popes, but they used the Quirinal instead. The exterior is covered for restoration. The interior was restored in 1838. Under the Lateran Treaty of 1929, the palace was recognised as an integral part of the Vatican City. It is now the seat of the Rome Vicariate and offices of the Rome diocese.

Since 1991 the **Museo Storico Vaticano** has been housed here (entrance from the portico at the main (east) façade of the basilica of San Giovanni in Laterano; open first Sat & Sun of month, 8.45–13. Lire 6000). The Papal Apartments, with late Mannerist frescoes (by Giovanni Guerra and others) and some good ceilings, contain interesting 17C and 18C tapestries (Gobelins and Roman works made in San Michele). The historical museum (well labelled) is displayed on three sides of a loggia. It illustrates the history of the papacy from the 16C to the present day, with historical paintings, etc.; papal ceremonies of the past; and the Papal Guards disbanded by Paul VI in 1970.

On the east side of Piazza di Porta San Giovanni are three survivals from the old Lateran Palace: the Scala Santa, the Sancta Sanctorum and the Triclinium. Domenico Fontana, architect of the new Lateran Palace, designed the building in 1589 which houses the **Scala Santa** and **Chapel of the Sancta**

Sanctorum (open 6.15–12.15, 15–18.30; 15–19 in summer). The staircase from the old Lateran Palace was, from the 15C, identified with the staircase of Pilate's house which Christ descended after his condemnation. A legend related how it had been brought from Jerusalem to Rome by St Helena, mother of Constantine. The 28 Tyrian marble steps are protected by boards and only worshippers on their knees are allowed to ascend them. In the vestibule are 19C sculptures by Ignazio Jacometti. The vault and walls of the Scala Santa and the side staircases were decorated at the end of the 16C under the direction of Giovanni Guerra and Cesare Nebbia.

At the top is the **Sancta Sanctorum** (or Chapel of St Laurence), the private chapel of the pope, which preserved the most sacred relics, removed from the old Lateran Palace. Mentioned in the *Liber Pontificalis* in the 8C, it was rebuilt in 1278 and is never open, though partly visible through the grating. It contains frescoes and mosaics carried out for Pope Nicholas III (1277–80), restored for the first time in 1995. Protected by a silver tabernacle presented by Innocent III is the relic which gives the chapel its particular sanctity. This is an ancient painting on wood of Christ which could date from as early as the 5C (many times repainted and restored). It is said to have been begun by St Luke and an angel: hence its name 'Acheiropoeton', or the picture made without hands. The precious relics and their reliquaries are now exhibited in the Vatican Museums. The chapel has a beautiful Cosmatesque pavement. The other rooms in the building have been occupied by a Passionist convent since 1953.

To the east of the Scala Santa is the **Tribune** erected by Fuga for Benedict XIV in 1743 and decorated with good copies of the mosaics from the Triclinium of Leo III, the banqueting hall of the old Lateran Palace. In the centre: Christ sending forth the Apostles to preach the Gospel; on the left: Christ giving the keys to St Sylvester and the labarum, or standard of the Cross, to Constantine; on the right: St Peter giving the papal stole to Leo III and the banner of Christianity to Charlemagne. A fragment of the original mosaic is in the Museum of Christian Art in the Vatican.

The huge PIAZZA DI PORTA SAN GIOVANNI is often used for political demonstrations, or concerts of popular music, and here the festival of San Giovanni is celebrated with a traditional fair on the night of 23–24 June. Porta San Giovanni (Pl. 10; 3), built in 1574 by Giacomo del Duca, superseded the ancient Porta Asinaria, on the site of the Porta Coelimontana of the Servian Wall. The old gate, with its vantage-court, can be seen between two fine towers, to the west of the modern gateway.

Outside the gate the busy Via Appia Nuova leads out of the city through the extensive southern suburbs towards the Alban Hills. About 7.5km from the gate, near the intersection with Via Latina, on Via Arco di Travertino, is the entrance to the **Parco delle Tombe Latine** (open 7–dusk. ☎ 704 74619), which includes a group of tombs dating from the 1C and 2C. Most of them are square and brick built, with recesses on the outside and interior chambers with interesting stucco ornamentation. On the right is the so-called **Tomb of the Valeri** (AD 160), a subterranean chamber decorated with fine reliefs, in stucco on a white ground, of nymphs, sea-monsters, and nereids. On the left is the 2C **Tomb of the Pancrazi,** with landscape paintings, coloured stuccoes, and four bas-reliefs: Judgement of Paris, Admetus and Alcestis, Priam and Achilles, and

Hercules playing a lyre with Bacchus and Minerva. Behind the tomb are the ruins of the 5C Basilica of St Stephen.

A short way outside Porta San Giovanni, Via Tuscolana diverges left and (10km from the gate) it passes **Cinecittà**, the centre of the Italian film industry, opened in 1937. This is probably the only film studio in the world which provides facilities for a complete motion picture production. It covers an area of 600,000 square metres, with 14 theatres. After the war it was used by Visconti, De Sica and Rossellini and soon attracted international film directors and stars from Hollywood. In the 1950s and early sixties 'colossals' such as *Quo Vadis?* and *Cleopatra*, with some of the largest sets ever constructed, were made at Cinecittà. Antonioni and Pasolini worked here, but it is above all associated with the name of Federico Fellini (died 1993), who here created the grandiose sets for many of his films. It is now also often used by television companies.

Santa Croce in Gerusalemme

From Piazza di Porta San Giovanni, Viale Carlo Felice leads east. The first turning on the left is Via Conte Rosso, which runs north to the Villa Wolkonsky, formerly the German Embassy, and now the residence of the British ambassador. Viale Carlo Felice ends in Piazza Santa Croce in Gerusalemme, a busy traffic hub, in an unattractive part of the city. Here is the church of **SANTA CROCE IN GERUSALEMME** (Pl. 10; 2), one of the 'Seven Churches' of Rome, occupied by Cistercians since 1561. According to tradition, this church was founded by Constantine's mother, St Helena. It was in fact probably built some time after 326 within part of the large Imperial palace erected for St Helena in the early 3C on the southwest extremity of the city. The principal edifice was known as the *Sessorium*, and the church took the name of *Basilica Sessoriana*. Here was enshrined a relic of the True Cross saved in Jerusalem by St Helena. It was rebuilt in 1144 by Lucius II, who added the campanile, and completely modernised by Benedict XIV in 1743–44.

The impressive theatrical **façade** and oval **vestibule** were built to a very original design by Domenico Gregorini and Pietro Passalacqua in 1744. The 18C **interior** (open 6–12.30, 13–19) has the nave and aisles separated by granite columns, some of them boxed in pilasters. The Cosmatesque pavement was restored in 1933. The vault paintings of *St Helena in Glory*, and the *Apparition of the Cross* towards the east end are by Corrado Giaquinto (1744). Near the west door (to the right) is the epitaph of Benedict VII (died 983), who is buried here. The second south altarpiece of St Bernard introducing Vittore IV to Innocent II is by Carlo Maratta. Above the high altar, with the basalt tomb which encloses the remains of Saints Caesarius and Anastasius, is a graceful 18C baldacchino. In the apse is a large fresco cycle of the *Invention of the Cross* attributed to Antoniazzo Romano. The tomb on the east wall, of Cardinal Quiñones (died 1540), is by Iacopo Sansovino.

A stairway at the end of the south aisle leads down through the Gregorian Chapel, built by Cardinal Carvajal in 1523, with an early 17C Roman bas-relief of the Pietà, to the **Chapel of St Helena**. It contains a statue of the saint, originally a figure of Juno found at Ostia, copied from the Barberini statue in the Vatican. The altar is reserved for the pope and the titular cardinal of the basilica. The vault *mosaic, the original design of which is probably by Melozzo (c 1480), was restored by Baldassarre Peruzzi and later by Francesco Zucchi. It represents

Christ and the Evangelists, Saints Peter and Paul, St Sylvester (who died here at Mass), St Helena, and Cardinal Carvajal. At the end of the north aisle in the Chapel of the Relics, by Florestano di Fausto (1930), are preserved the pieces of the True Cross, together with other greatly venerated relics. There are long term plans to open a small museum here to exhibit fragments of 12C frescoes detached from the roof of the nave, a 14C fresco of the Crucifixion from the Chapel of the Crucifix, and French 14C statues of Saints Peter and Paul formerly in the Gregorian Chapel.

On the right of the basilica are remains of the **Amphitheatrum Castrense** (no adm), a graceful edifice, built of brick by Heliogabalus or Alexander Severus for amusements of the Imperial court, incorporated with the Aurelian Wall by Honorius. To the left of the basilica, in the gardens of the former Caserma dei Granatieri rises a large ruined apsidal hall known since the Renaissance as the 'Temple of Venus and Cupid'. It was built in the early 4C by Maxentius or Constantine.

In the barracks here are two military museums, and a fine **MUSEUM OF MUSICAL INSTRUMENTS** (open 9–13.30 except Sun. ☎ 701 4796. Lire 4000), with a remarkably representative display dating from Roman times to the 19C, most of it collected by the tenor Evangelista Gorga (1865–1957). The attractive building of c 1903, in the Art Nouveau style, looks north to a section of the Aurelian Wall. On the other side of the building, near the basilica, are more Roman ruins. The collection is beautifully displayed in rooms on the first floor (some of which are sometimes closed because of lack of custodians).

Room 1. Archaeological material, including Roman works in terracotta and bronze. **Room 3**. Exotic instruments from the Far East, America, Africa and Oceania. **Room 4**. Instruments used for folk-dances and folk-songs made in Naples, Russia, Spain, etc. In the centre of **Room 5** is the pianoforte built by Bartolomeo Cristofori in 1722. Also displayed here are other 18C pianos, and a late 17C German clavichord. **Room 6**. Military instruments and instruments used by street musicians: hunting horns; 19C walking sticks which could become violins and flutes; a portable 18C harpsichord; 19C processional organs; hurdy-gurdies; Aeolian harps; and accordions. **Room 7**. Church music (an organ, bells, and a 'marina' trumpet). **Room 9**. A unique organ built by Montesanti, with pipes and reeds of 1777; a glass harmonica; spinets, and lutes. **Rooms 11–15** are arranged in roughly chronological order with instruments from the 11C to 18C. **Room 11** contains the oldest known German harpsichord made in 1537 by Mueller. In **Room 13** is the elaborate Barberini harp. **Rooms 16–18** contains mechanical instruments (musical boxes, etc.).

To the east of the barracks, across Viale Castrense and outside the Aurelian Wall, are the well-preserved remains of the extensive **Circus Varianus**, dating from the reign of Heliogabalus (218–22). From Piazza Santa Croce, Via di Santa Croce leads northwest towards Via Conte Verde and Piazza Vittorio Emanuele. On the left it passes the end of the Villa Wolkonsky (see above). Via Statilia, skirting the north side of the villa, runs parallel to a fine series of arches of the **Aqueduct of Nero**, an extension of the Acqua Claudia (see below), and built by Nero to provide water for his various constructions on the Palatine and Oppian Hills.

Porta Maggiore

The ugly Via Eleniana leads north from Piazza Santa Croce to the large and busy PIAZZA DI PORTA MAGGIORE, in an unattractive part of the city. On the west side of this square is the beginning of Via Statilia, with some arches of the Acqua Claudia(see below), restored to carry the Aqua Marcia (1923). On the east side is the **Porta Maggiore**, or *Porta Prenestina* (Pl. 10; 2), built by Claudius in AD 52, formed by the archways carrying the Acqua Claudia and the Anio Novus over the Via Prenestina and the Via Casilina (see below). The Porta Prenestina was a gate in Aurelian's Wall; it was restored by Honorius in 405. The ancient Via Prenestina and Via Labicana which pass under the arches can still be seen. Also here are foundations of a guardhouse added by Honorius. On the outside of the gate, is the unusual **Tomb of the Baker** (M. Virgilius Eurysaces, a public contractor, and his wife Atistia). This pretentious monument, built entirely of travertine, dates from c 30 BC. The circular openings represent the mouths of a baker's oven; above is a frieze illustrating the stages of bread-making.

> The Acqua Claudia and the Anio Novus, or Acqua Aniene Nuova, were two of the finest Roman aqueducts. Both were begun by Caligula in AD 38; the Acqua Claudia was completed by Claudius in AD 47, and the Anio Novus in 52. They were restored by Vespasian in 71 and by Titus in 81. The water of the Acqua Claudia was derived from two copious springs near Sublaqueum (Subiaco); its length was 74km. The Anio Novus was the longest of all the aqueducts (95km) and the highest; some of its arches were 33m high.

Outside the Porta Maggiore are two main roads, the Via Prenestina on the left, and the Via Casilina on the right. In Via Casilina (in ancient times the Via Labicana), which now traverses ugly suburbs, 5km from the Porta Maggiore are the ruins known as the **Tor Pignattara**. This was the mausoleum of St Helena, the mother of Constantine, who died c 330. It was circular outside, and octagonal within and had terracotta amphorae (*pignatte*) in the vault to diminish the load. It is now in a courtyard near a church built in 1922.

In Via Prenestina, which leads to *Praeneste* (now Palestrina), about 130m from the gate, is the entrance (at No. 17) to the **Basilica di Porta Maggiore** (admission only by special permission; write giving your local telephone number and days of availability to the Ripartizione X del Comune di Rome, 29 Via Portico d'Ottavia, 00100 Rome, ☎ 671 03819, fax 689 2115), unearthed in 1916. It is approached by a modern staircase beneath the railway. This remarkable building of the 1C AD, in near perfect preservation, has the rudimentary form of a cult building, with a central porch, an apse at the east end, a nave and two arched aisles with no clerestory. This became the basic plan of the Christian church. The ceiling and walls are covered with exquisite stuccoes representing landscapes, mythological subjects, scenes of early childhood, etc.; the principal design of the apse is thought to depict the death of Sappho. The purpose for which it was built is still under discussion: it may have been a type of funerary hall, or have been used by a mystical sect, perhaps the Pythagoreans.

Further on is the **Parco dei Giordiani**, a public park surrounding remains of the 3C Villa dei Giordiani, one of the largest suburban Roman villas, including an octagonal hall and a circular mausoleum (known as the Tor de' Schiavi).

Beyond **Ponte di Nona** (at the ninth Roman milestone), a Roman bridge of the Republican era, are the ruins of **Gabii**, an important Latina town in the 7C–6C BC, and half-way between Rome and Palestrina. A legend relates that Romulus and Remus were sent to Gabii to study Greek, and the town was supposed to have been captured by Tarquinius Superbus. Here are remains (with its altar) of a temple known as the Temple of Juno (probably actually dedicated to Fortune), reconstructed in the mid-2C BC. A vast number of bronze statuettes were found in a sanctuary on the site, which is not yet open to the public while excavations continue. In the neighbourhood are the stone quarries from which parts of Rome were built.

From Piazza di Porta Maggiore, the long and straight Via Giovanni Giolitti runs parallel to the railway and Stazione Termini towards Piazza dei Cinquecento (more than 1km from Porta Maggiore). About 300m from Porta Maggiore it passes on the right the so-called **Temple of Minerva Medica** (Pl. 6; 7), now surrounded by ugly buildings. This large ten-sided domed hall is a remarkable survival from the 4C (the ruin is conspicuous on the approach to Rome by train). It was probably the nymphaeum of the Gardens of Licinius, but was given its present name after the discovery inside it of a statue of Minerva with a serpent, which probably occupied one of the nine niches round its walls. The cupola, which collapsed in 1828, served as a model for many classical buildings.

Beyond the temple, Viale Manzoni leads left past the end of Via di Porta Maggiore. Near Via Luzzatti is the **Hypogeum of the Aureli**, a series of tomb-chambers discovered in 1919 (for admission enquire at the Pontificia Commissione di Archeologia Sacra, ☎ 446 5610). On the floor of the first room is a mosaic dedication showing that the vault belonged to freedmen of the Gens Aurelia. The well-preserved wall-paintings (AD 200–250), include the Good Shepherd, the Christian symbol of the peacock, and some landscapes of obscure significance, suggesting a mixture of Christian and gnostic beliefs.

Via Giovanni Giolitti continues to (right) **Santa Bibiana** (Pl. 6; 5), about 600m from Porta Maggiore. This was a 5C church rebuilt by Bernini in 1625, interesting as his first architectural work. It contains eight columns from pagan temples, including (left of entrance) that at which St Bibiana was supposed to have been flogged to death. On the architrave are frescoes by (right) Agostino Ciampelli and (left) Pietro da Cortona. The *statue of the saint, set in an aedicula above the altar, is a fine early work by Bernini.

Just beyond on the left is Piazza Guglielmo Pepe, in which are six arches of an ancient aqueduct. Via Santa Bibiana leads under the railway to Porta San Lorenzo (Pl. 6; 5). Immediately north, in the Aurelian Wall, is Porta Tiburtina, built by Augustus and restored by Honorius in 403. The triple attic carried the waters of the Acquae Marcia, Tepula and Julia. Further north, in Piazzale Sisto V, is an arch formed out of a section of the Aurelian Wall by Pius V and Sixtus V at the end of the 16C to carry the waters of the Acqua Felice.

13 · The Oppian and Celian Hills

The Oppian Hill

The Oppian Hill (Pl. 4; 8), just northeast of the Colosseum, is one of the four summits of the Esquiline and one of the seven hills of the primitive *Septimontium* of Rome. On its slopes is the **Parco Oppio**, with its main entrance in Via Labicana. Near the entrance to the park are traces of the Baths of Titus and the extensive ruins of a wing of the **DOMUS AUREA** of Nero (Pl. 4; 8; Nero's 'Golden House'), overlaid by those of the Baths of Trajan. The site has been closed, partly for conservation reasons, since 1984; for special permission to visit apply to Ripartizione X del Comune di Roma, 29 via Portico d'Ottavia, 00100 rome, fax 689 2115; ☎ 671 03819. Excavations unearthed the vast ramifications of the palace buildings which were buried by the construction of the baths. These subterranean rooms were visited by artists of the Renaissance, who came to see the murals and scratched their names on the walls. The type of decoration known as 'grotesques' takes its name from the Domus Aurea, and clearly inspired Raphael when decorating his Loggia in the Vatican.

Nero already had one palace, the Domus Transitoria on the Palatine, which was destroyed in the fire of AD 64. Even before its destruction he had planned to build another palace (the Domus Aurea) in the heart of the city. With its outbuildings and gardens, it was to extend over part, or all of the Palatine, much of the Celian and part of the Oppian Hills, an area of about 50 hectares. He is reputed to have commented when it was completed that at last he was beginning to be housed like a human being. He employed Severus as architect, and Fabullus as painter, and produced what has been called the first expression of the Roman revolution in architecture. The understanding and use of vaulted spaces in the palace was quite new. It is thought that nearly all the rooms were vaulted, although some of the ceilings in the wing that survives are no longer intact. The atrium or vestibule, with the colossal statue of the emperor (see p 117), was on the summit of the Velia; the main part of the palace was on the site of the so-called Domus Tiberiana on the Palatine (Chapter 3); the gardens, with their lake, were in the valley now occupied by the Colosseum.

This grandiose edifice did not long survive the tyrant's death in 68, and his successors hastily demolished or covered up his buildings, and restored to the city the huge area they had occupied. In 72 Vespasian obliterated the lake to build the Colosseum; Domitian (81–96) buried the constructions on the Palatine (except the cryptoporticus) to make room for the Flavian palaces. Trajan (98–117) destroyed the houses on the Oppian to build his baths; and Hadrian (117–38) built his Temple of Venus and Rome on the site of the atrium, and moved the statue.

Of the Baths of Titus, which occupied the southwest corner of the Oppian Hill, hardly anything remains. The much larger Baths of Trajan are better preserved (and include a reservoir called 'Le Sette Sale', see p 204). The architect of the baths was Apollodorus of Damascus, whose designs were a model for later builders of Imperial baths.

The remains of the Domus Aurea include a **nymphaeum**, with an interesting vault mosaic depicting Ulysses and Polyphemus, and a long **cryptoporticus** decorated with grotesques, on the vault of which artists left their signatures in the 16C. The most important group of rooms are designed around an octagonal **atrium**, which has a particularly original design and structure. It is lit from the side rooms as well as from the wide central opening in the dome. The southern prospect of the rooms would have opened on to an extensive garden, looking across the valley where the Colosseum now stands. A great porphyry vase and the famous *Laocoön* (both now in the Vatican) were found here in the 16C. Numerous rooms have frescoed decorations, painted stucco, and mosaic floors.

At the bottom of the hill, on the east side of the Colosseum and between Via Labicana and Via San Giovanni in Laterano (Pl. 9; 1) are remains of the **Ludus Magnus**, the principal training school for gladiators, constructed by Domitian. Part of the curved wall of a miniature amphitheatre used for training can be seen.

San Clemente

Via San Giovanni in Laterano continues past a new office block (beneath which were found remains of houses built before AD 64 with fine mosaics) to San Clemente (Pl. 9; 2; open 9–12.30, 15.30–18.30; fest. 10–12.30, 15.30–18.30), one of the best preserved of the medieval basilicas in Rome. Dedicated to St Clement, the fourth pope, it consists of two churches superimposed, raised above a large early Imperial building.

The lower church, mentioned by St Jerome in 392, was the scene of papal councils under St Zosimus in 417 and under St Symmachus in 499. Restored in the 8C and 9C, it was destroyed in 1084 during the sack of Rome by the soldiers of Robert Guiscard. Eight centuries later, in 1857, it was rediscovered by Father Mullooly, prior of the adjoining convent of Irish Dominicans, and was excavated in 1861. The upper church was begun in 1108 by Paschal II, who used the decorative marbles from the ruins of the old church. In the 18C it was restored by Carlo Stefano Fontana for Clement XI.

The **upper church** is entered by the side door in Via San Giovanni in Laterano (**B**). The façade (**A**) is turned towards the east and looks onto an atrium with Ionic columns surrounding a courtyard with a little fountain, outside of which is a gabled porch of four 12C columns. The typically basilican **interior** has a nave with a large apse, aisles separated by two rows of seven columns, and a pre-Cosmatesque pavement. The walls of the nave were decorated with a cycle of paintings in 1713–19 under the direction of Giuseppe Chiari, who also executed the *Triumph of St Clement* on the ceiling. The **Schola Cantorum** (**C**), from the lower church, contains two ambones, candelabrum, and a reading-desk, all characteristic elements in the arrangement of a basilican interior. The *screen of the choir and sanctuary, with its transennae, marked with the monogram of John II (533–35), the choir raised above the confessio, the high altar with its tabernacle, the stalls of the clergy, and the bishop's throne, are also well preserved. In the **presbytery** is a delicate baldacchino (**D**) borne by columns of pavonazzetto.

The early 12C *mosaics in the apse** are especially fine; on the triumphal arch: *Christ and the symbols of the Evangelists*, and below (on the south), *Saints*

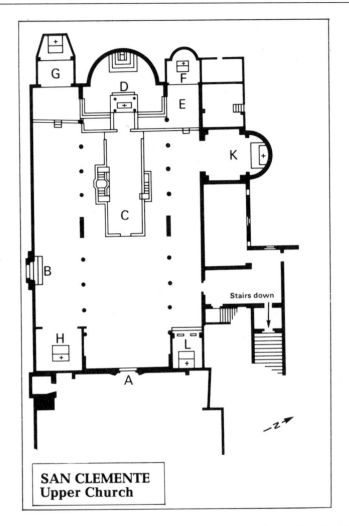

SAN CLEMENTE
Upper Church

Peter and Clement, with boat and oars, *Jeremiah, and Jerusalem*, and on the left, *Saints Paul and Laurence, Isaiah, and Bethlehem*. In the apse-vault: the Dome of Heaven with the Hand of God above the Crucifix. The 12 doves on the Cross represent the Apostles. Beside the Cross are the Madonna and St John. From the foot of the Cross springs a vine with acanthus leaves, encircling figures of St John the Baptist, the Doctors of the Church, and other saints, while the rivers of Paradise flow down from the Cross, quenching the thirst of the faithful (represented by stags) and watering the pastures of the Christian flock. Below are the Lamb of God and 12 companions. On the apse wall below are impressive large 14C frescoed figures of Christ, the Virgin and the Apostles. To the right is a beautiful wall-tabernacle, probably by Arnolfo di Cambio.

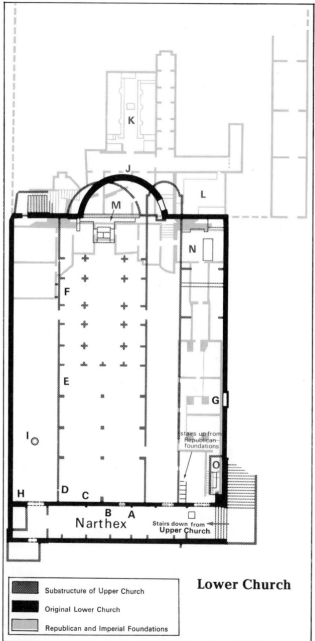

Substructure of Upper Church

Original Lower Church

Republican and Imperial Foundations

Lower Church

In the **south aisle** (**E**): tombs of Archbishop Giovanni Francesco Brusati, by Luigi Capponi (1485), and of *Cardinal Bartolomeo Roverella, by Andrea Bregno and Giovanni Dalmata (1476). In the **Chapel of St John the Baptist** (**F**): late 16C frescoes attributed to Iacopo Zucchi, and a 16C statue of St John the Baptist; in the chapel of St Cyril (**K**), *Madonna*, attributed to Sassoferrato (one of several versions). In the chapel by the west door (**L**) are three paintings of scenes from the life of St Dominic, attributed to Sebastiano Conca.

North aisle. In the chapel to the left of the presbytery (**G**): *Our Lady of the Rosary*, by Sebastiano Conca, and tomb of Cardinal Antonio Venier (died 1479), incorporating columns from a 6C tabernacle. The **Chapel of St Catherine** (**H**) contains *frescoes by Masolino da Panicale, probably executed with the help of his pupil, Masaccio (before 1430): on the left entrance pier, *St Christopher*; on the face of the arch, *Annunciation*; in the archivolt, *the Apostles*; in the vault, the *Evangelists and Fathers of the Church*; behind the altar, *Crucifixion*; south wall, *Life of St Ambrose*; left wall, *Life of St Catherine of Alexandria*. To the right above, outside the chapel, is a sinopia for the beheading of St Catherine (found during restoration) and, on the aisle wall, the sinopia for the Crucifixion.

Off the south aisle is the entrance to the **lower church** (open at the same time as the upper church, see above) the apse of which was built above a mithraeum (3C). This formed part of a late 1C apartment house. Below this again are foundations of the Republican period. The staircase, which has miscellaneous fragments of sculpture, descends to the frescoed **narthex**.

At the foot of the steps a catacomb (see below) can be seen through a grate in the floor. On the right wall is a *fresco (late 11C) of the *Legend of St Clement* (**A**), who was banished to the Crimea and there executed by drowning in the Black Sea. The scenes include the miracle of a child found alive in a church at the bottom of the sea (full of fish). Below are *St Clement and the donor* of the fresco, and further on, to the right, the Translation of St Cyril's body (**B**) from the Vatican to San Clemente (11C). An archway leads into the aisled church which has a wide **nave** obstructed by the foundation piers of the upper church, and is unequally divided by a supporting wall. Immediately to the left is a 9C fresco (**C**) of the *Ascension*, with the Virgin in the centre surrounded by the Apostles, St Vitus, and St Leo IV (with square nimbus). In the corner (**D**), very worn frescoes of the Crucifixion, the *Marys at the Tomb*, the *Descent into Hell*, and the *Marriage at Cana*.

Further along, on the left wall of the nave is the *Story of St Alexis* (east; 11C): the saint returns home unrecognised and lives for 17 years beneath a staircase; before dying he sends the story of his life to the Pope, and is thus recognised by his wife and father. Above, lower part of a fresco of Christ amid angels and saints. Further on, *Story of Sisinius* (**F**): the heathen Sisinius follows his Christian wife in secret, in that way hoping to capture the Pope, but he is inflicted with a sudden blindness; below, Sisinius orders his servants to seize the Pope, but they, also struck blind, carry off a column instead (this fresco more probably depicts the building of the church, as is explained by the painted inscriptions, which are among the oldest examples of Italian writing). Above, *St Clement enthroned by Saints Peter, Linus and Anacletus*, his predecessors on the pontifical throne (only the lower part of the fresco survives).

Right aisle. In a niche: Byzantine Madonna (**G**; 5C or 6C), which may have been originally a portrait of the Empress Theodora; female saints with the crown

of martyrdom; and a beardless Christ. The frescoes, much damaged, probably depict the *Council of Zosimus, the Story of Tobias,* and the *Martyrdom of St Catherine.* At the end, a sarcophagus of the 1C AD with the story of Phaedra and Hippolytus, and a Byzantine figure of Christ (7C or 8C; almost totally obliterated). **Left aisle**. Faded frescoes (**H**) of uncertain subjects. In the floor (**I**) is a circular recess, perhaps an early baptismal piscina. At the end, remains of a tomb perhaps that of St Cyril (869), the apostle of the Slavs.

From the end of the left aisle, a 4C staircase descends to the 1C level with a 'palazzo', and a Mithraic temple of the late 2C or early 3C. Around the corner at the bottom (right) is the pronaos of the **temple** (**J**), with stucco ceiling ornaments (very damaged); opposite is the **triclinium** (**K**) with benches on either side and an altar in the centre showing Mithras, in his Phrygian cap, sacrificing a bull to Apollo, and in the niche behind is a statue of Mithras (temporarily removed); the vault imitates the roof of a cavern. At the far end of the corridor, to the right, is the presumed **Mithraic school** (**L**; closed), where catechumens were instructed, with a mosaic floor and stuccoed vault.

From the pronaos, a door (left) leads to the 1C '**palazzo**', probably belonging to the family of Flavius Clemens, which lies beneath the lower basilica. A long narrow passage (**M**) divides the temple area from the thick tufa wall of the building constructed, after Nero's fire, on Republican foundations. Only two sides of this building have been excavated. Immediately to the right at the bottom of a short flight of steps is a series of rooms; the last two are the best-preserved rooms of the palace, showing the original brickwork. The second side of the building is reached by returning to the opening from the corridor; beyond a room (**N**) with spring water which has been channelled away by tunnels, are seven more vaulted rooms, the last of which (**O**) has a small catacomb (closed), which is probably 5C or 6C, as it is within the city walls. A staircase (right) leads up to the lower church and exit.

•

Opposite San Clemente is Via dei Querceti at the foot of the high wall of the fortified 12C monastery and church of **SANTI QUATTRO CORONATI** (Pl. 9; 2; open 9.30–12.30, 15.30–18; although closed in the afternoons between Christmas and Easter; Sun 9.30–10.45, 16–17.45). The steep Via dei Santi Quattro (left), an unexpectedly rural street, leads up to the entrance to this remarkable castellated building of the Middle Ages. The original 4C or 5C foundation, on a huge scale, was destroyed by Norman soldiers in 1084, and the present church was erected on a smaller scale in 1110 by Paschal II. It was well restored in 1914 by Antonio Muñoz. The church is dedicatd to the four crowned martyrs who were a group of sculptors (Claudius, Nicostratus, Symphorian and Castorius) from the Roman province of Pannonia (near the Danube), who were martyred by Diocletian after they refused to make a statue of Aesculapius. The church is specially venerated by sculptors and marble masons.

The entrance gate passes beneath the unusual **campanile**, dating from the 9C, a squat fortified tower. The small court which succeeds the 5C atrium has a portico with 16C frescoes, and beyond is a second court, once part of the nave, whose columns have survived. On the right of the portico is the **Chapel of St Sylvester** (ring for the key at the monastery of the closed order of Augustinian nuns; first door on the right). It was built in 1246, and contains a delightful *fresco cycle of the same date (particularly well preserved), illustrating the story

of the life of Constantine. It is probably the work of artists from the Veneto, working in the Byzantine style. The first scene in the narrative begins on the left wall: Constantine catches leprosy; the sick Emperor, asleep, dreams of Saints Peter and Paul who suggest he tries to get help from Pope Sylvester; three mounted messengers ride towards Mount Soratte in seach of the pope. The messengers climb the mountain to reach the pope's hermitage; the pope returns to Rome and shows the emperor the effigies of Saints Peter and Paul; Constantine is baptised by total immersion; Contantine, cured of leprosy, presents his Imperial tiara to the pope; the pope rides off wearing it, led by Constantine; the pope brings back to life a wild bull; finding of the True Cross; the Pope liberates the Romans from a dragon. The floor is Cosmatesque, and the 16C frescoes in the presbytery are attributed to Raffaellino da Reggio.

At the back of the second court is the entrance to the church. The aisled **interior** has a disproportionately wide apse, and a 12C matroneum, or women's gallery. The 12C pavement is in opus alexandrinum, and the fine wooden ceiling dates from the 16C. On the west wall and that of the south aisle are remains of 14C frescoes. In the south aisle is an altarpiece of the *Adoration of the Shepherds* by the 16C Flemish school, and in the north aisle an altarpiece of *St Sebastian tended by holy women* by Giovanni Baglione, and (at the west end) an *Annunciation* by Giovanni da San Giovanni. Against the north pillar of the apse is a beautiful 15C tabernacle attributed to Andrea Bregno or Luigi Capponi. The apse is decorated with good frescoes by Giovanni da San Giovanni (1630), depicting the history of the Quattro Coronati and the glory of all saints. The tomb of the four martyrs is in the 9C crypt (usually closed). From the north aisle is the entrance to the delightful tiny **cloister** (ring for admission) of the early 13C, with a 12C fountain and lovely garden. It is one of the most secluded spots in Rome. On the left is the 9C chapel of Santa Barbara interesting for its architecture and fine corbels made from Roman capitals, and with remains of medieval frescoes in the vault.

The Celian Hill

The monastery of the Santi Quattro Coronati is on the edge of the Celian Hill (51m), which extends to the south and west towards the Palatine. Next to the Aventine, it is the southernmost of the Seven Hills of Rome and the most extensive after the Esquiline.

> It is supposed originally to have been called Mons Querquetulanus from the oak forests which covered its slopes. It received its name of Mons Coelius from Caelius (or Coelius) Vibenna, an Etruscan who is said to have helped Romulus in his war against the Sabine king Tatius, and to have settled here afterwards. Tullus Hostilius lived on the hill and transferred to it the Latin population of Alba Longa. It became an aristocratic district in Imperial times. Devastated by Robert Guiscard in 1084, it remained almost uninhabited for centuries. Even today it is sparsely populated, but its ruins and churches are of great interest.

Via dei Querceti leads up to Via Annia and (right) Piazza Celimontana (where traces of *insulae* were excavated in 1991) in front of the huge 19C **Ospedale del Celio**, a military hospital. Excavations in the extensive gardens here in 1991

(during work on new hospital pavilions) revealed remains of an ancient Roman *domus*, thought to be that of the Simmachi. Just south of the military hospital, near a conspicuous survival of the Claudian aqueduct, Via Santo Stefano leads left to **SANTO STEFANO ROTONDO** (Pl. 9; 4; entrance at No. 7), one of the largest and oldest circular churches in existence (open 9–13, 15.30–18; winter 9–13, 13.50–16.20; closed Mon mornings). It dates from the time of Pope St Simplicius (468–83). The original plan included three concentric rings, the largest 65m in diameter, intersected by the four arms of a Greek Cross. This complex design was almost certainly taken from eastern models, perhaps the church of the Holy Sepulchre in Jerusalem, as well as ancient Roman buildings. The outer ring and three of the arms were pulled down by Nicholas V in 1450, so that the diameter was reduced to 40m. The vestibule is formed by the one remaining arm of the Greek Cross.

The circular nave has a double ring of antique granite and marble columns, 34 in the outer and 22 in the inner series, while two Corinthian columns in the centre and two pillars support three arches (recently covered with a bright white plaster). An incongruous wooden floor has been laid following the recent restorations (a mithraeum of the 2C–3C AD, and part of the barracks of the Castra Peregrina were found beneath the floor in 1973). On the left of the entrance is an antique Roman throne, said to be that of St Gregory the Great. In the first chapel on the left is a small 7C mosaic depicting Christ *above* the jewelled cross, with Saints Primus and Felician, showing Greek influence. Outside the second chapel is a fine 16C tomb. The Renaissance altar by Bernardo Rossellino was reconstructed in the centre of the church in 1990. At the height of the Counter-Reformation, the walls were covered with frescoes by order of Gregory XIII by Antonio Tempesta and Pomarancio with vivid scenes of martyrdom in chronological order. Some of them were repainted in the 19C.

On the summit of the hill, across Via della Navicella is the church of **Santa Maria in Domnica** (Pl. 9; 3, 4), or *della Navicella*, of ancient foundation (its title is a corruption of *Dominica*, or Chief). The alternative name is derived from the Roman stone **boat**, which Leo X had made into a fountain in front of the church. The boat was probably a votive offering from the Castra Peregrina, a camp for non-Italian soldiers, situated between Via Santo Stefano and Via Navicella.

The present church, restored by St Paschal I (pope, 817–24), and practically rebuilt by Cardinal Giovanni de' Medici (Leo X) in the 16C from the designs of Andrea Sansovino, has a graceful portico. In the interior (open 9–12, 15.30–18) the nave contains 18 granite columns; over the windows is a frieze by Perino del Vaga from designs by Giulio Romano. On the triumphal arch, flanked by two porphyry columns, is a beautifully coloured 9C *mosaic of Christ with two angels and the Apostles, and Moses and Elijah below; in the semi-dome, St Paschal kisses the foot of the Madonna and Child surrounded by a throng of angels. The confessio contains interesting Roman sarcophagi, fragments of 9C plutei, and a 17C altar.

On the left of the church is the main entrance of the **Villa Celimontana** or Villa Mattei (Pl. 9; 3), built for Ciriaco Mattei in 1582 and celebrated for its splendid gardens (now a public park, open 7–dusk; free jazz concerts are held here at night in summer). It houses the Società Geografica Italiana (with the best library of maps in Italy). In the grounds are ancient marble fragments found on the spot, and a granite Roman obelisk, probably from the Temple of Isis

Capitolina, presented by the Senate to Mattei in 1582. It formed a pair with that in Piazza della Rotonda. The terrace of the casinò and the belvedere at the end of an avenue provide fine views. There is an exit from the park opposite the church of Santi Giovanni e Paolo (see below).

To the north of Santa Maria in Domnica is the entrance to the former Trinitarian hospice of the church of **San Tomaso in Formis**. Here St John of Matha died in 1213: he founded the order of Trinitarians for the redemption of slaves, and above the doorway is a mosaic (c 1218) of Christ between two Christian slaves, one white, the other a Negro. On the left of Via Claudia, which descends from Santa Maria in Domnica to the Colosseum, are remains of the **Temple of Claudius**, built by Nero's mother Agrippina, fourth wife of Claudius, to whom she dedicated the temple (AD 54). Nero converted it into a nymphaeum for his Domus Aurea, and Vespasian rebuilt it in 69.

The **Arch of Dolabella and Silanus** (AD 10), a single archway that Nero afterwards used for his aqueduct to the Palatine, leads into the picturesque Via di San Paolo della Croce, which runs between two garden walls (above which can be seen orange trees) to Piazza dei Santi Giovanni e Paolo. Here is the church of **SANTI GIOVANNI E PAOLO** (Pl. 9; 3; open 8.30–12, 15.30–18; closed Sun morning), beside the 12C convent built above remains of the Temple of Claudius (see above). The travertine blocks of the temple are clearly visible in the base of the beautiful tall **campanile** (45m), the first two storeys of which were begun in 1099–1118, and the five upper storeys completed by the middle of the 12C.

The church occupies a site traditionally connected with the house of John and Paul, two court dignitaries under Constantine II, who were martyred by Julian the Apostate. Two Roman apartment houses (2C–3C AD) were incorporated in the original sanctuary, founded before 410 by the senator Byzantius and his son Pammachius, a friend of St Jerome. This was demolished by Robert Guiscard in 1084, and rebuilding was begun by Paschal II (1099–1118) and continued by Hadrian IV (Nicholas Breakspeare, the only English pope; 1154–59), who was responsible for the apse and the campanile. Excavations carried out in 1949 revealed the early Christian façade and some of the ancient constructions beneath the convent.

The 12C Ionic **portico** has eight antique columns and is closed by an iron grille (1704). Above is a 13C gallery and the early Christian façade with five arches. The 13C Cosmatesque doorway is flanked by two lions. The **interior** (frequently used for weddings), hung with chandeliers, with granite piers and columns, was restored in 1718 by Antonio Canevari. The ceiling dates from 1598 and the floor, in opus alexandrinum, was restored in 1911. A tomb-slab in the nave (protected by a railing) commemorates the burial place of the two martyrs to whom the church is dedicated. Their relics are preserved in a porphyry urn under the high altar. In the third south chapel (by Filippo Martinucci, 1857–80) is the altar-tomb of St Paul of the Cross (1694–1775), founder of the Passionists, whose convent adjoins the church. The apse has frescoes by Pomarancio. In a store-room (unlocked by the sacristan) on the left of the high altar can be seen a remarkable 12C fresco originally over the altar of the church.

From the end of the south aisle (apply to the sacristan) steps lead down to the

Santi Giovanni e Paolo

House of Saints John and Paul (temporarily closed, but restored and normally open at the same time as the church, see above), an interesting two-storeyed construction, with 20 rooms, originally part of three buildings: a Roman palace, a Christian house and an oratory, decorated with frescoes of the 2C or the 3C–4C. Near the foot of the stairs is a well-shaft. Behind it to the right is a **nymphaeum** with a striking fresco of Peleus and Thetis (or Proserpine) and a nereid, and boats manned by cupids. Beyond a foundation wall of the basilica are two rooms. Off the first (left) is the **triclinium** with pagan frescoes of peacocks and other birds and youths bearing garlands. A small adjoining room (reached by a flight of steps) has architectural frescoes.

The series of rooms to the left of the entrance has more frescoes, some with Christian subjects, including a large early Christian figure standing in prayer, with arms extended and eyes raised. The medieval oratory (near the road) has been closed during excavation work (and a fresco of the Passion has been removed for restoration). An iron staircase leads up to the **confessio**, decorated with 4C frescoes the significance of which is not entirely clear: on the end wall is a praying figure, perhaps one of the martyrs, between drawn curtains, at whose feet are two other figures. On the right are Saints Priscus, Priscillian and Benedicta (who tried to find the remains of the martyrs and were themselves killed) awaiting execution with eyes bound; this is probably the oldest existing painting of a martyrdom. Stairs lead down from a room north of the Confessio to another series of rooms which were part of the **baths** in a private house.

Remains of the '**Claudianum**', two storeys of a huge Roman portico, connected with the Temple of Claudius (see above), can be seen beside the convent (for admission, ring at the convent on the right of the portico). On request, the sacristan will open the gate to the pathway between the church and campanile for you to see more Roman remains.

In the piazza outside the church are some arches of Roman shops dating from the 3C. The pretty CLIVO DI SCAURO (the ancient *Clivus Scauri* probably opened in the 1C BC) descends beneath the medieval buttresses of the church spanning the road. Here can be seen the tall façade of a Roman house incorporated in the

left wall of Santi Giovanni e Paolo, and the fine *apse, a rare example of Lombard work in Rome, dating from 1216. Further down on the left are remains of the 6C basilican hall of the library erected by Agapitus I, and, beneath the Chapels of Sant'Andrea and Santa Barbara (see below), a Roman edifice of the 3C AD.

A short road on the left leads up to the church of **SAN GREGORIO MAGNO** (Pl. 9; 3), a medieval church altered and restored in the 17C and 18C. A monastery was founded here by St Gregory the Great (590–604) on the site of his father's house, and dedicated to St Andrew. This was demolished in 1573 except for the two chapels of Santa Barbara and Sant'Andrea (see below).

The *exterior (staircase, façade, and atrium) is by Giovanni Battista Soria (1633) and is considered his masterpiece. In the **atrium** are several fine tombs, including (near the entrance) that of Sir Robert Peckham (died 1569), a self-exiled English Catholic, and a memorial to Sir Edward Carne (died 1561), an envoy of Henry VIII and Mary I; beyond the gate leading to the chapels (see below) are the tombs of Canon Guidiccioni (1643) and (on the right, beside the convent door) the brothers Bonsi (1481), the latter by Luigi Capponi.

The **interior** (only open for services on Sun at 11) has 16 antique columns and a restored mosaic pavement; it was rebuilt in 1725–34 by Francesco Ferrari. At the end of the south aisle is the **Chapel of St Gregory**, with a fine altar-frontal sculptured by Luigi Capponi. The predella is an early 16C painting, depicting St Michael overcoming Lucifer, the Apostles with St Anthony Abbot, and St Sebastian. A small room on the right contains a chair of the 1C BC known as the throne of St Gregory.

Off the north aisle is the **Salviati Chapel**, by Francesco da Volterra and Carlo Maderno; on the right is an ancient fresco of the Madonna (repainted in the 14C or 15C) which is supposed to have spoken to St Gregory; on the left: a fine taber-nacle, of the school of Andrea Bregno (1469). On either side of the apse are 15C–16C statues of Saints Andrew and Gregory.

On the left of the church (reached through a gate in the atrium; open 9–13, 14–18; Sat & Sun 10–13, 16–19) is a pretty group of three chapels surrounded by ancient cypresses. The chapel on the right was built in 1603 and dedicated to **Santa Silvia**, mother of Gregory. It contains her statue by Nicolas Cordier, and a *fresco of an angel choir by Guido Reni. The other two chapels belonged to the medieval monastery and were built above a Roman edifice (visible from the *Clivus Scauri*, see above); they were restored in 1602. In the centre is the chapel of **Sant'Andrea**, preceded by a portico with four antique cipollino columns. Inside is a *Flagellation of St Andrew* (right) by Domenichino, and (left) *St Andrew on the way to his martyrdom*, by Guido Reni. On the entrance wall: Saints Silvia and Gregory by Giovanni Lanfranco. The altarpiece of the *Madonna in glory between Saints Andrew and Gregory* is by Pomarancio; above the altar, in the space between the original roof and the lower Renaissance wooden ceiling, there is an 11C mural.

The third chapel, dedicated to **Santa Barbara**, contains a statue of St Gregory by Nicolas Cordier. The 3C table is supposed to be the one at which he served 12 paupers daily with his own hands, among whom an angel once appeared as a 13th; this legend gave the alternative name to the chapel, the *Triclinium Pauperum*. It was in this convent in 596 that St Augustine received St Gregory's blessing before setting out, with 40 other monks, on his mission to convert the English

to Christianity. A fresco on the left, by Antonio Viviani (1602) commemorates the famous incident of the fair-haired English children, 'non Angli sed Angeli' (not Angles but Angels), which culminated in St Augustine's mission.

On the other side of the Clivo di Scauro (see above), Viale del Parco del Celio (beware of trams) leads up to the Casina dei Salvi, where part of the **Antiquarium Comunale** (or **Antiquarium del Celio**; open 9–19; Sun 9–13.30; closed Mon. ☎ 700 1569. Lire 3750) has recently been reopened. The antiquarium was founded in 1885 for objects found during excavations in Rome, and illustrates the everyday life of the city from earliest times to the end of the Empire. This extremely important collection was first exhibited here in 1894, but much of it, housed in Palazzo Caffarelli on the Capitoline Hill, has remained inaccessible to the public for decades.

The small collection here has finds dating from the Imperial period. In the garden outside are architectural fragments, tombs, reliefs and inscriptions. On the ground floor are frescoes from Roman houses, bronze waterspouts and valves dating from the late Empire (and an interesting model of a water pump), and a mosaic with the scene of a port, found in the gardens of Palazzo Rospigliosi in 1878 during the construction of Via Nazionale. Upstairs are more frescoes. In Room 1 are household items in brass and glass, and jewellery, and in Room 2 are bronze and terracotta cooking and eating utensils. The last room contains bone, ivory, bronze and iron hand tools for working wood and marble, instruments for measuring liquids, solids and distances, and heavy farming tools.

The tree-lined Via di San Gregorio is now a busy road with fast traffic. On the line of the ancient *Via Triumphalis*, it follows the declivity between the Celian and Palatine Hills to the Colosseum. The area to the south, with the Baths of Caracalla, is described in Chapter 14.

14 · The Baths of Caracalla to Porta San Sebastiano

■ Bus No. 118 every 20–40 minutes from the Colosseum via Via delle Terme di Caracalla (for the Baths of Caracalla) and Via di Porta San Sebastiano (with request stops outside the Tomb of the Scipios and at Porta San Sebastiano). On the return, No. 118 can be taken from outside Porta San Sebastiano back to the Baths of Caracalla.

Piazza di Porta Capena (Pl. 9; 3) is a busy road junction at the beginning of Via di San Gregorio (which leads to the Colosseum) and adjoining the rounded end of the Circus Maximus (see Chapter 15). It occupies the site of the Porta Capena, a gate in the Servian Wall, the original starting point of the Via Appia. After Aurelian had built his much more extensive walls, the stretch of the road between Porta Capena and Porta Appia (now Porta San Sebastiano; see below) became known as the 'urban section' of the Via Appia. This part of the Via Appia is now called Via delle Terme di Caracalla as far as Piazzale Numa Pompilio, and,

beyond that square, Via di Porta San Sebastiano. On the northeast side of Piazza di Porta Capena is the **Vignola**, a charming little 16C palace moved here from near Via Santa Balbina in 1911 and reconstructed using the original masonry. The 4C **Stele of Axum** was stolen from the ancient capital of Ethiopia by Mussolini during the Italian occupation in 1935–36 and erected here in 1937. Despite the peace treaty of 1947 and numerous international protests, the monument has never been returned. On the modern Viale Aventino rises the huge building begun in 1938 by Mario Ridolfi and Vittorio Cafiero to house the Ministero per l'Africa Italiano. Since 1951 it has been the seat of the FAO (United Nations Food and Agriculture Organization).

Viale Guido Baccelli leads through the Parco di Porta Capena, opened in 1910. There is an open-air sports stadium here. In Via Santa Balbina is the church of **Santa Balbina** (Pl. 9; 5; open 9–12, 15–17), entered through the former convent on the right of the portico. Founded in the 5C, the church has been rebuilt, and was restored in 1930. The pleasant interior has a wooden ceiling bearing the name of Cardinal Marco Barbo (1489). The transennae in the pretty windows, and the schola cantorum, were installed in 1931. In the floor are set numerous good Roman black-and-white mosaics (1C AD) found in Rome in 1939. The 13C Cosmatesque episcopal chair in the apse is in excellent condition. The apse fresco of the Glory of Christ is by Anastasio Fontebuoni (1523). The fresco fragments include a good Madonna enthroned with four saints and the Redeemer above, attributed to the school of Pietro Cavallini. The bas-relief of the Crucifixion (1460) is attributed to Mino da Fiesole and Giovanni Dalmata, and the *tomb of Stefanus de Surdis (1303) is by Giovanni Cosmati.

Baths of Caracalla

In Via delle Terme di Caracalla is the entrance to the huge **BATHS OF CARA-CALLA** (*Terme di Caracalla*), or *Thermae Antoninianae* (Pl. 9; 5), the best preserved and most splendid of the Imperial Roman baths in the city. The romantic sun-baked ruins, free of modern buildings, are on a vast scale. Opening hours are 9–15; summer 9–18; Mon & Sun 9–13. ☎ 575 8626. Lire 8000.

Begun by Antoninus Caracalla in 212, the baths were opened in 217 and finished under Heliogabalus and Alexander Severus. After a restoration by Aurelian they remained in use until the 6C, when the invading Goths damaged the aqueducts. The baths, built on an artificial platform, have always been above ground, but excavations in this century greatly enlarged the area accessible to the public. In the 16C–17C, the Belvedere Torso (now in the Vatican), the Farnese Hercules, Farnese Bull and Farnese Flora (now in Naples), and many other statues were found among the ruins. The two huge baths (now fountains) in Piazza Farnese, and the mosaic of the athletes, now in the Vatican, also came from here. Shelley composed a large part of his Prometheus Unbound in this romantic setting. From 1937 to 1993 opera performances were given here in summer. After several seasons in other venues, the opera is due to return to the baths in 1998.

The baths were fed by a branch of the Acqua Marcia, an aqueduct built specially for this purpose in 212–17. Roman citizens had free access to the baths, which could accommodate some 1600 bathers at one time (men and women bathed nude, but separately and at different times of the day). The

bathers first went through a series of exercises or sports (including wrestling) in the open or covered gymnasiums, then entered a sequence of baths of varying temperatures. They could then be rubbed down with oil, using a strigil, and massaged. Entertainment was also provided and libraries. The Romans were the first to give importance to the refreshing combination of exercise and cleanliness for the body.

The massive brick-built baths are an architectural masterpiece. Their remarkably complex design (see the plan) included huge vaulted rooms, domed octagons, exedrae, porticoes, etc., as well as an intricate heating system and hydraulic plant beneath ground level (which may be restored and opened to the public). Of the elaborate decoration only a few architectural fragments and some floor mosaics remain, revealing the baroque taste of the 3C in the introduction of divinities on the fine Composite capitals. The walls were formerly lined with marble and stucco.

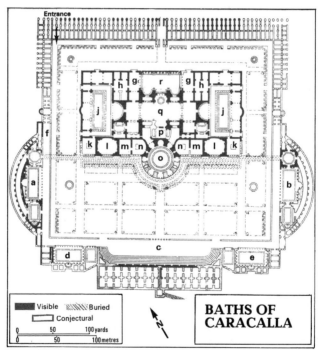

BATHS OF CARACALLA

Visible | Buried | Conjectural

0   50   100 yards
0   50   100 metres

An enclosed garden, now planted with pines, laurel, and cypresses, surrounds the main buildings of the baths (see below), although part of it is closed. Along the boundary wall were two huge exedrae with an apsidal central hall (**a** and **b**), and in the middle of the south side a shallow exedra in the form of a **stadium** (**c**) with tiers of seats concealing the huge water cisterns (which held 80,000 litres each). On either side were two halls (**d** and **e**), probably libraries. The present entrance skirts the boundary wall on the west side past remains of one

of the exedrae (**a**), and older buildings below ground level, including a **mithreum** (**f**), the largest discovered in Rome (admission only with special permission from the excavation offices in the Roman Forum, see p 93). Excavations and restorations (including conspicuous reconstructions) have been carried out in the area of the stadium (**c**) and one of the libraries (**d**), and on the east side of the garden where a house and triclinium of the time of Hadrian have been discovered. This area is fenced off.

The main buildings of the **Baths** (220m x 114m) are symmetrically arranged around the huge central hall (**q**) and the piscina (**r**; see below). The bathers normally entered through a **vestibule** (**g**) to reach the **apodyteria** (**h**) or dressing rooms. The vestibule on the west side has a 15C fresco, from a church on this site. The mosaic, with a pattern representing waves, of the floor of the apodyteria on the eastern side is well seen from the far end of the baths. The two **palestrae** (**j**), for sports and exercises before bathing, consisted of an open courtyard with porticoes on three sides and a huge hemicycle opposite five smaller rooms. The pavement here has remains of fine polychrome geometric mosaics. The series of rooms (**k**, **l**, **m** and **n**) to the south, which may have included a Turkish bath (**laconicum**; **l**) led to the circular **calidarium** (**o**), 34m across, only part of one side of which remains. It had high windows on two levels designed to admit the sun's rays for many hours of the day, and was formerly covered with a dome. From here the bathers passed into the **tepidarium** (**p**) and the large vaulted central hall (**q**). Beyond is the **natatio** (**r**) with an open-air piscina. This has niches on two levels for statues and two hemicycles.

Opposite the Baths, in Piazzale Numa Pompilio, is the church of **Santi Nereo ed Achilleo** (Pl. 9; 5; open 10–12, 16–18 except Tues & Fri; ring for custodian), on the site of the 4C Oratory of the Fasciola, named from the bandage which is supposed to have fallen from the wounds of St Peter after his escape from the Mamertine prison. In 524 the oratory was enlarged into a church by John I, when he brought here the bodies of Nereus and Achilleus, the Christian servants of Flavia Domitilla, who had been martyred at Terracina. The church was enlarged by Leo III c 800, and again by Sixtus IV (pope, 1471–84), and was rebuilt by Cardinal Baronius in 1597.

The aisled **interior** has frescoes by Pomarancio. The ancient ambo and the 15C candelabrum come from other churches; the fine plutei and the high altar, which covers the body of St Domitilla, are of 13C Cosmati work. The mosaic on the choir-arch, of the time of Leo III (815–16), shows the Transfiguration, with a Madonna and an Annunciation at the sides. On the bishop's throne in the apse is carved a fragment of St Gregory's 28th homily, which he delivered from this throne when it stood in the first church dedicated to Saints Nereus and Achilleus in Via Ardeatina.

On the other side of the piazza is the rebuilt church of **San Sisto Vecchio**, with its convent, the residence in Rome of St Dominic (1170–1221). The campanile dates from the 13C. The façade and interior were designed by Filippo Raguzzini in 1725–27. It contains remains of a fresco cycle of the 13C–14C. Remains of the 13C church are visible in the cloister.

Via di Porta San Sebastiano and Via di Porta Latina

From Piazzale Numa Pompilio roads lead to four of the gates in the Aurelian Wall: Via Druso north-northeast to Porta Metronia, Via di Porta Latina southeast to Porta Latina ('one way' from the gate), Via di Porta San Sebastiano south-southeast to Porta San Sebastiano ('one way' to the gate), and the continuation of Via delle Terme di Caracalla south to Porta Ardeatina, adjoining the Bastione del Sangallo.

VIA DI PORTA SAN SEBASTIANO, on the line of the urban section of the Via Appia, is a beautiful road (disturbed by fast traffic) running between high walls behind which are fine trees and gardens. On the right, beyond a walled public garden, is the ancient church of **San Cesareo** (Pl. 9; 6; open Sun 10–13 or by request; for admission ring at No. 4; or ☎ 700 9016) rebuilt at the end of the 16C, with a façade attributed to Giacomo della Porta. Inside is some fine *Cosmati work, including the high altar, the bishop's throne, the transennae, the candelabrum, the ambo, and the fronts of the side-altars. The two angels beneath the high altar are probably from a 15C tomb by Paolo Romano. The beautiful wooden ceiling, gilded on a blue ground, bears the arms of the Aldobrandini pope, Clement VIII (1592–1605). The apse mosaic of the Eternal Father was designed by Cavaliere d'Arpino, who also painted the frescoes. The baldacchino dates from the time of Clement VIII.

Below the church (closed for restoration), is a large black-and-white *mosaic of the 2C AD (suffering from humidity). The fantastic sea-monsters, animals, and figures may have decorated the floor of Roman baths. Two apses and the base of a large column, dividing the excavated area, suggest that the first part was later adapted as a church.

Beyond the church, on the right, at No. 8 is the **House of Cardinal Bessarion** (admission only by appointment and when not in use for receptions held by the Commune of Rome), the famous Humanist scholar (1389–1472), a native of Trebizond, who bequeathed his remarkable collection of Greek and Latin MSS to the Biblioteca Marciana in Venice in 1468. The delightful house and garden are a good example of a 15C summer home. It contains 15C frescoes, and wall-paintings of garlands and ribbons which cast painted shadows, and overall patterns of acanthus leaves and pomegranates.

About 500m further along the road is (left; No. 9) the **Tomb of the Scipios** (closed indefinitely for restoration; for information enquire at the Museo delle Mura, see below). The charming entrance beside two old columns and a little fountain leads into a garden. The tomb, one of the first to be built on the Via Appia, was discovered in 1780. It was built for L. Cornelius Scipio Barbatus, consul in 298 BC, and great-grandfather of Scipio Africanus. Many other members of the gens Cornelia were buried here also, up to the middle of the 2C BC, although Scipio Africanus was buried at Liternum (Patria, near Naples), where he died. The sarcophagus of Scipio Barbatus and the funerary inscriptions found here were replaced by copies when they were removed to the Vatican. The other tombs include those of his son, Lucius Scipio (consul 259 BC), the conqueror of Corsica, of Cornelius Scipio Asiaticus, of Cn. Scipio Hispanus (praetor 139 BC) and Aula Cornelia his wife; also an inscription to Publius, possibly the son of Scipio Africanus. Also here are a three-storeyed house of the 3C which retains traces of paintings and mosaics, and an underground columbarium,

Beside the tomb is an attractive little public park, **Parco degli Scipioni**, with lovely trees and particularly peaceful. Here is the **Columbarium of Pomponius Hylas** (kept locked; for admission enquire at the Museo delle Mura; see below), which is one of the best preserved in existence. The steep original staircase, with a small mosaic inscription giving the name of the founder and his wife Pomponia Vitalis, leads down to the 1C chamber with niches and funerary urns, and decorated with stucco and paintings.

A gate leads out of the park into the pretty rural VIA DI PORTA LATINA, in which to the left is the picturesque church of **San Giovanni a Porta Latina**, in a quiet cul-de-sac, with a large cedar and ancient well. It has a narthex of four Roman columns, and a beautiful 12C campanile. The church, founded in the 5C, was rebuilt by Hadrian I in 772, and several times restored, but the interior retains its beautiful 11C basilican form. It contains 12C frescoes (restored in 1940). The apse has three lovely windows of selenite, and a fine marble pavement in opus sectile.

In the other direction Via di Porta Latina leads to the gate, past the little octagonal chapel of **San Giovanni in Oleo**, traditionally marking the spot where St John the Evangelist stepped out unharmed from a cauldron of boiling oil. It was rebuilt in the early 16C during the reign of Julius II, it has an interesting design, formerly attributed to Bramante, but now usually thought to be by Antonio da Sangallo the Younger or Baldassarre Peruzzi. It was restored in 1658 by Borromini, who added the frieze. The interior (ring at No. 17) contains stuccoes and paintings by Lazzaro Baldi.

Porta Latina is an opening in the Aurelian Wall (see below) with two towers built by Belisarius, the 6C Byzantine general. Outside the gate, Viale delle Mura Latine skirts the wall to Porta San Sebastiano, and Via di Porta Latina runs southeast to Via Appia Nuova.

In Via di Porta San Sebastiano, at No. 13 are other interesting columbaria discovered in the last century in the Vigna Codini, now private property (no adm). The largest had room for some 500 urns, another in the form of a horseshoe has vaulted galleries decorated with stuccoes and paintings. Near the end of the road is the so-called triumphal **Arch of Drusus**, in fact the arch that carried the aqueduct for the Baths of Caracalla over the Via Appia. Only the central of three openings survives; it is decorated with Composite columns of giallo antico.

Porta San Sebastiano (Pl. 9; 8), the *Porta Appia* of ancient Rome, is the largest and best preserved gateway in the Aurelian Wall. It was rebuilt in the 5C by Honorius and restored in the 6C by Belisarius. The two medieval towers at the sides rest on basements of marble blocks. It was at the Porta San Sebastiano that the senate and people of Rome received in state the last triumphal procession to enter the city by the Via Appia, that of Marcantonio Colonna II after the victory of Lepanto in 1571. The interior has been restored as a **Museum of the Walls** (*Museo delle Mura*; open 9–19; winter 9–17.30; Sun 9–13.30; closed Mon. ☎ 704 75284. Lire 3750).

The **Aurelian Wall** was built by Aurelian (emperor 270–75) and Probus (emperor, 276–82), and most of it survives to this day. The enceinte took in all seven hills, the Campus Martius, and the previously fortified area of

Trastevere. It was about 19km round and had 18 main gates and 381 towers (see Plan on p 51). The walls were raised to almost twice their height by Maxentius (306–12), and then restored by Honorius and Arcadius in AD 403. They continued to be the defence of Rome until 1870 when the army of the Kingdom of Italy breached them with modern artillery, northwest of the Porta Pia. Many of the gates are still in use under their modern names.

The museum is arranged in the rooms on two levels above the gate, and in the two towers. It contains prints, models, etc. illustrating the history of the walls. The ramparts along the inner face of the walls, traversing nine defensive towers, are open for some four hundred metres, as far as Via Cristoforo Colombo (see Pl. 9; 8). They provide a very unusual view of rural Rome, bordering overgrown fields and woods, beyond which (towards the end of the walkway) can just be seen, above the trees, the tops of the Vittorio Emanuele Monument, the Baths of Caracalla and the dome of St Peter's. The Bastione del Sangallo, a formidable structure built for Paul III in 1537 by Antonio da Sangallo the Younger, which is beyond Via Cristoforo Colombo, is not yet accessible.

The next stretch of the Via Appia outside the gate is described in Chapter 17.

15 · The Theatre of Marcellus and Piazza Bocca della Verità

The broad and traffic-ridden VIA DEL TEATRO DI MARCELLO (Pl. 3; 8), skirting the western base of the Capitoline Hill, was opened in 1933. It descends past (right) the severe façade of the Monastero di Tor de' Specchi (open to visitors on 9 March every year), founded in 1425 by St Francesca Romana. The Oratory is decorated by Antoniazzo Romano. Beyond rises the Theatre of Marcellus (described below). In Via Montanara is the pretty deconsecrated church of **Santa Rita** by Carlo Fontana, moved here in 1937 from the foot of the Capitoline Hill, below Santa Maria in Aracoeli. It has an interesting oval interior, used for exhibitions. Beyond opens the handsome PIAZZA CAMPITELLI, with a fountain (1589) designed by Giacomo della Porta. Facing the church are three fine palaces: the 16C Palazzo Cavalletti (No. 1), Palazzo Albertoni, and Palazzo Capizucchi (Nos 2 and 3), both dating from the late 16C and attributed to Giacomo della Porta.

The charming façade of **Santa Maria in Campitelli** (Pl. 3; 8) was erected by Carlo Rainaldi when the church was rebuilt (1662–67) in honour of a miraculous image of the Madonna, which was believed to have halted an outbreak of pestilence. The fine **interior** (open 7–12, 16–19) has an intricate perspective effect using numerous arches, columns, and a heavy cornice. In the second chapel on the right is *St Anne, St Joachim and the Virgin* by Luca Giordano (light on the right); the ornate high altar surrounds the miraculous image of the Madonna in pietra dura perhaps dating from the 11C. In the first chapel on the left are two tombs of the Altieri family, inscribed respectively 'Nihil' and 'Umbra'; in the left transept, *Birth of St John the Baptist*, by Baciccia.

Via Cavalletti and Via de' Delfini lead east out of the piazza to the picturesque Piazza Margana, where several houses are hung with old vines. Via de' Funari,

named from the rope-makers who used to live here, leads out of the north side of the piazza, through an area of charming old streets, to **Santa Caterina dei Funari** (Pl. 3; 6), a church with a fine façade by Guidetto Guidetti (1564) and an original campanile. The interior (which has been closed for restoration for many years) contains 16C paintings by Girolamo Muziano, Scipione Pulzone, Livio Agresti, Federico Zuccari and Marcello Venusti, and a fine stuccoed and painted *chapel by Vignola.

Across Via Caetani (described in Chapter 5) is the huge **Palazzo Mattei**, which comprised five palaces of the 16C and 17C. The fine façades in Via dei Funari and Via Michelangelo are by Carlo Maderno. In the little Piazza Mattei, Nos 19 and 17 open onto courts, and a third door gives access to a staircase (left) finely decorated with 17C stuccoes surrounding antique reliefs. Inside are frescoes by Domenichino, Lanfranco, and Albani. Part of the buildings, now owned by the State, are used by the Centro Italiano di Studi Americani.

The charming **Fontana delle Tartarughe** (in Piazza Mattei), by Taddeo Landini (1584), to a design by Giacomo della Porta, was restored in 1658, perhaps by Bernini, when the tortoises (now replaced by copies) were added. At the southwest angle of the piazza is Palazzo Costaguti (no admission), with ceilings on the first floor painted by Albani, Domenichino, Guercino, Lanfranco, and others.

The Ghetto

On the right of the church of Santa Maria in Campitelli the narrow old Via della Tribuna di Campitelli leads past an old house (harshly restored), with Ionic columns set into its façade, to Via Sant'Angelo in Pescheria which continues to the site of the Ghetto (see below) and remains of an entrance to the **Portico of Octavia** (Pl. 3; 8), which is being excavated. It was once a rectangular portico (c 119m x 132m) with about 300 columns, which enclosed two temples, dedicated to Jupiter and Juno. Erected by Quinto Cecilio Metello in 146 BC, it was reconstructed by Augustus in honour of his sister Octavia c 23 BC, and restored by Septimius Severus (AD 203). The southern extremities of the area of the portico have been exposed, and remains of columns to the west, and the stylobate to the east can also be seen.

The entrances consisted of two propylaea with eight columns and four piers; the one on the southwest survives (partly covered for restoration) and serves as a monumental entrance to the church of **Sant'Angelo in Pescheria**, founded inside the portico in 755. The portico was used from the 12C as a fish market (hence the name of the church 'in Pescheria') up until the destruction of the Ghetto in 1888. An arch was added, and the pediment repaired in the Middle Ages. The church (open on Wed at 17.30 and Sat at 17) was rebuilt in the 16C and contains a fresco of the Madonna enthroned with angels, attributed to Benozzo Gozzoli or his school, and an early 12C Madonna and Child. From this church Cola di Rienzo and his followers set out to seize the Capitol on the night of Pentecost, 1347. Here from 1584 until the 19C (Pius IX) the Jews were forced to listen to a Christian sermon every Saturday.

The area roughly occupied by the old Ghetto, between Piazza Cairoli and the Theatre of Marcellus, and Via del Portico d'Ottavio and the Tiber is now recognised as the site of the Circus of Flaminius (221 BC). To the right of the Portico of Octavia are three Corinthian columns of the **Temple of Apollo Medico**,

built in 433 BC and restored by the consul C. Sosius, in 33 BC. Beyond it are the ruins of the **Temple of Bellona**, built in 296 BC.

These two temples are outside the imposing remains of the cavea of the **THEATRE OF MARCELLUS** (Pl. 8; 1). The theatre, together with remains of the temples, are now surrounded by a fence; for admission ask next door at the archaeological offices of the Comune at 29 Via Portico d'Ottavia (open Mon–Sat 9–18). The theatre, planned by Julius Caesar, was dedicated in 13 or 11 BC by Augustus to the memory of his nephew (Octavia's son) and son-in-law, Marcellus, who had died in 23 BC at the age of 19. It was restored by Vespasian and Alexander Severus. The building was pillaged in the 4C for the restoration of Ponte Cestio. It was fortified in the early Middle Ages and made into a stronghold by the Savelli and Orsini family. Renaissance architects frequently studied the theatre. In the 16C it was converted into a palace by Baldassarre Peruzzi for the Savelli; he inserted a façade into the curved exterior of the cavea. The theatre was restored in 1932, when numerous houses and shops on the site were demolished. The cavea originally had at least two tiers of 41 arches, the first with Doric and the second with Ionic engaged columns probably crowned by an attic of the Corinthian order. Only 12 arches in each of the first two tiers survive; the upper stage has disappeared in the course of various alterations. The theatre could probably have held some 15,000 spectators.

The **GHETTO** occupied the district to the west, where from 1556 onwards the Jews were segregated and subject to various restrictions on their personal freedom, although to a lesser degree than in other European countries. The walls were torn down in 1848, and the houses demolished in 1888 before the area south of Via del Portico d'Ottavia was reconstructed around the new synagogue. Many Jewish people still live in the area between Lungotevere Cenci, Via Catalana and Via del Portico d'Ottavia. In Via del Portico d'Ottavia are several medieval houses, and a shop with an ancient Roman architrave framing the door. No. 13 (in very poor repair) has a fine court with loggie. Via della Reginella is a survival from the old Ghetto. At the end of Via del Portico d'Ottavia (No. 1) is the **Casa di Lorenzo Manilio**, with an inscription dating the house in the ancient Roman manner, to 2221 years after the foundation of Rome (i.e. 1468), and decorated with ancient Roman sculptural fragments. The inscription carved in bold stone lettering over the windows on the left side of the building was set up by Manilio, and includes the patriotic invocation 'Have Roma' ('Hail Rome!').

On the left opens Piazza delle Cinque Scole (laid out in the last century when the Ghetto was demolished), with a fountain from Piazza Giudea by Giacomo della Porta. The name of the piazza recalls the five synagogues which once occupied a building here. Here is **Palazzo Cenci**, restored in the 16C, which belonged to the family of Beatrice Cenci who, having killed her father the tyrant Francesco Cenci in 1598, was beheaded for parricide a year later (see Shelley's tragedy *The Cenci*, published in 1819). A short narrow road on the right leads up to **Montecenci**, an artificial mound (probably on Roman remains) with a pretty little piazza between Palazzo Cenci and the church of **San Tommaso dei Cenci** (usually closed). An antique altar is incorporated into its façade. It contains a chapel frescoed by Sermoneta (1575) and two carved Roman brackets supporting a side altar.

Piazza delle Cinque Scole continues to the river; on the left, on Lungotevere

Cenci, rises the monumental **Synagogue** (Pl. 3; 8) built by Vincenzo Costa and Osvaldo Armanni in 1899–1904, with a **Jewish Museum** (open Mon–Thur 9.30–14, 15–17; Fri 9.30–14; Sun 9.30–12.30; closed Sat. ☎ 687 5051. Lire 8000), illustrating the history of the community in the city. A Holy Ark in marble dating from 1523, but incorporating some Roman fragments, which was demolished in 1908–10, has been reconstructed and temporarily exhibited in the vaults of the synagogue.

Isola Tiberina

The debris from the demolitions of the Theatre of Marcellus became known as Monte Savello which gave its name to the traffic-ridden piazza to the south. This faces the Isola Tiberina (Pl. 3; 8), a pretty little island in the Tiber, reached from here by **Ponte Fabricio**, the oldest Roman bridge to have survived in the city, and still in use for pedestrians. The inscription over the fine arches records the name of the builder, L. Fabricius and the date, 62 BC. The bridge is also known as the Ponte 'dei Quattro Capi' from the two herms of the four-headed Janus on the parapet. Remains of the 'Ponte Rotto' (see below) can be seen downstream.

The island, which provides an easy crossing place on the Tiber, is thought to have been settled early in the history of Rome. A temple of Aesculapius was dedicated here in 291 BC (after a plague in 293 BC) and, ever since, the island has been associated with the work of healing. It is now largely occupied by the hospital of the Fatebenefratelli, founded in 1548, and modernised by Cesare Bazzani in 1930–34. On the right is the church of **San Giovanni Calibita** founded in the 11C and reconstructed in 1640. In the 18C interior is a ceiling painting by Corrado Giaquinto. On the left is a tall medieval tower, formerly part of an 11C fortress, and Piazza San Bartolomeo. The island was formerly encircled with a facing of travertine, a portion of which still remains at the extremity, which can sometimes be reached through the archway on the left of San Bartolomeo. It is in the form of a ship with the serpent of Aesculapius carved on it in relief. There are long-term plans to open a museum illustrating the history of the island in the interesting medieval building here, now owned by the Comune.

The church of **San Bartolomeo**, on the site of the temple of Aesculapius, was built in the 10C in honour of St Adalbert, Bishop of Prague, and several times restored, notably by Orazio Torriani in 1624; the tower is Romanesque. The façade has been restored recently. The interior contains 14 antique columns, and an interesting sculptured well-head on the chancel steps, probably from the original church. There is a hall crypt beneath the transept. The south side of the island is joined to Trastevere (Chapter 21) by the **Ponte Cestio**, probably built by L. Cestius in 46 BC, restored in AD 370, and rebuilt in 1892 (the centre arch to its original design and measurements).

Back across Ponte Fabricio, in Piazza di Monte Savello is the apse of the church of **San Nicola in Carcere** (Pl. 8; 1; open 7.30–12, 16.30–19; fest. 10.30–13), the entrance to which is on Via del Teatro di Marcello. This 11C church, probably on the site of an older sanctuary, was reconstructed and consecrated in 1128. It was remodelled in 1599 by Giacomo della Porta, who designed the façade using three columns from a Roman temple (see below), and detached from the surrounding buildings in 1932. The church occupies the site of three

Republican temples in the *Forum Holitorium*, the vegetable and oil market which extended from the Capitoline Hill to the Tiber. The temples are thought to have been dedicated to Janus, Juno Sospita and Spes. The first, to the right of the church, was Ionic hexastyle, with columns on three sides only, the remains of which can be seen incorporated in the south wall of the church; the second, now incorporated in the church, was Ionic hexastyle peripteral; the third, on the left of the church was Doric hexastyle peripteral. The **interior** of the church has fine antique columns from the temples with diverse capitals, and an ancient urn in green porphyry on the high altar. At the end of the left aisle is an altarpiece of the *Ascension*, by Lorenzo Costa. The apse frescoes date from 1865. The Roman remains beneath the church can be visited on Thur (10.30–12), on request to the sacristan.

The main door of the church faces the wide and busy Via del Teatro di Marcello, across which is a medieval fortified mansion (over-restored). A path with steps (called Via di Monte Caprino) leads up from here to the Capitoline Hill. Vico Jugario, a road on the site of the Roman road which connected the Forum Holitorium with the Roman Forum, skirts the foot of the Capitol to Piazza della Consolazione past Sant'Omobono.

At the beginning of Vico Jugario on the left can be seen the arcades of a portico built of peperino in the Rebublican era. On the right is the church of **Sant'Omobono** (open only on the first Sunday of the month at 11.00), with a 16C façade. It contains a 17C lunette showing God as divine tailor putting a fur coat on Adam. Surrounding the church is the **Area Sacra di Sant'Omobono** (Pl. 8; 1; closed, but partly visible through the railings). Excavations begun in 1937 and continued in the 1960s (and still not completed) have revealed interesting remains on seven different levels, the oldest dating from c 1500 BC. Traces of hut dwellings of the 9C–8C BC, similar to those on the Palatine have also been found. The archaeological evidence has provided new light on the origins of Rome and the presence of the Etruscans here in the 7C and 6C BC. Two archaic temples (mid-6C BC), dedicated to Fortuna and Mater Matuta and traditionally founded by Servius Tullius, rest on an artificial mound c 6m high in which were found Bronze Age and Iron Age shards and imported Greek pottery of the 8C BC. In front of the temples are two archaic altars, possibly dedicated to Carmenta. The most conspicuous remains mostly date from after 213 BC when the temples were reconstructed. The material found on the site, including a terracotta group of Hercules and Minerva from one of the temples, is kept in the Antiquarium Comunale.

In Piazza della Consolazione beyond, is the church of **Santa Maria della Consolazione** (open 6–12, 15.30–18). The façade is by Martino Longhi the Elder (1583–1606); the upper part was added in the same style in the 19C. In the first chapel to the right are frescoes by Taddeo Zuccari (1556) of the life of Christ (including the *Flagellation) and the Crucifixion. In the apse, *Birth of Mary* and the *Assumption* by Pomarancio, and over the altar, the *Madonna della Consolazione*, a 14C fresco repainted by Antoniazzo Romano. In the first chapel on the left, is a marble relief of the *Marriage of St Catherine* by Raffaello da Montelupo (1530). The cliff above, on the Capitoline Hill, is thought to be the Tarpeian Rock (see p 71).

Piazza della Bocca della Verità

Via del Teatro di Marcello continues between ugly municipal public offices set up by the Fascist regime in 1936–37 to PIAZZA DELLA BOCCA DELLA VERITÀ (Pl. 8; 3), an open space with a picturesque group of buildings now sadly disturbed on all sides by busy traffic. This occupies part of the site of the *Forum Boarium*, or cattle-market, the oldest market of ancient Rome, and here in a little garden stand two ancient Roman temples and a fine fountain by Carlo Bizzaccheri (1717), opposite the medieval church of Santa Maria in Cosmedin.

On the right of the temples is the eccentric **Casa dei Crescenzi** (no admission), a unique example of a mansion built by a wealthy Roman in the Middle Ages. Formerly a tower guarding the river, it dates from c 1100 and the inscription over the door states that it was erected by one Nicolaus, son or descendant of Crescentius and Theodora, probably members of the Alberic family, the most powerful clan in Rome at the end of the 10C. It is constructed mainly from fragments of classical buildings (or medieval copies of Roman works). The bricks of the lower storey are formed into half-columns, with rudimentary capitals. A fragment of the upper storey and its arcaded loggia survives. It is now used by the Centro Studi per la Storia dell'Architettura, and concerts are occasionally held here.

The **Temple of Portunus** (no admission), dedicated to the god of harbours, was formerly called the *Temple of Fortuna Virilis*. It dates from the end of the 2C BC. In 872 it was consecrated as the church of *Santa Maria Egiziaca*. This pseudoperipteral temple, with four fluted Ionic columns in front of the portico and two at the sides, survives as a precious example of the Graeco-Italian temples of the Republican age.

The little round **Temple of Hercules Victor** (being restored) was for long known as the *Temple of Vesta*. It also dates from the end of the 2C BC (restored under Tiberius) and is the oldest marble edifice to survive in Rome. An inscription from the base of a cult statue found here confirmed its dedication to Hercules Victor. This charming little building consists of a circular cella of solid marble, surrounded by 20 fluted columns. The original ones are those in Greek marble; after severe damage in the 1C AD the temple was restored and some of the columns and capitals replaced, using Luni marble. One of the columns is missing on the north side but its base remains. The exquisite capitals were restored in 1991. In the Middle Ages the temple became the church of *Santo Stefano delle Carrozze* and later *Santa Maria del Sole*. The original roof and ancient entablature have not survived. The entrance to a side conduit of the Cloaca Maxima (see below) can be seen under a travertine lid beside the fountain.

SANTA MARIA IN COSMEDIN (Pl. 8; 3; open 9–12, 15–17) is a fine example of a Roman medieval church, preceded by a little gabled porch and arcaded narthex. The building incorporates two earlier structures, the arcaded colonnade of the Imperial Roman *Statio Annonae*, or market inspector's office, and the side-walls of a porticoed hall, part of an early Christian welfare centre, or *diaconia* (c 600). Nearby was a monumental altar and a temple, both dedicated to Hercules, the latter restored by Pompey. The oratory was enlarged into a basilican church by Hadrian I (772–95); assigned to Greek refugees driven from Constantinople by the iconoclastic persecutions, it became known as the *Schola Graeca*. Its other name, 'in Cosmedin', probably comes from a Greek word meaning decoration, referring to the embellishments of Hadrian. At that period

Santa Maria in Cosmedin and the Piazza Bocca della Verità

it had a matroneum and three apses. Cardinal Alfano, chamberlain of Calixtus II, rebuilt the church c 1123, closed the galleries, and added the schola cantorum.

The fine tall **campanile** of seven storeys also dates from this time. The church was over-restored and the pretty 18C façade torn down in 1894–99; it has again been restored recently.

Beneath the portico, to the left, is the so-called **Bocca della Verità** ('Mouth of Truth'), a large cracked marble disc representing a human face, the open mouth of which was believed to close on the hand of any perjurer who faced the ordeal of placing it there. It is in fact a slab that once closed an ancient drain, and was placed here in 1632. Also here is the tomb of Cardinal Alfano (see above). The principal doorway is the work of Johannes de Venetia (11C).

The fine **interior**, with a nave and two aisles each ending in an apse, closely reproduces the 8C basilica with some 12C additions. The arcades are supported on antique columns with good capitals grouped in threes between piers. In the first part of the nave remains of the arcaded colonnade and side walls of the Statio Annonae and diaconia (see above) can be seen. High up on the walls are the remains of 11C frescoes. The schola cantorum, screen, paschal candelabrum, episcopal throne and pavement (1123) are the *work of the Cosmati family of marble sculptors. The baldacchino over the high altar (an antique porphyry bath) is by Deodatus, third son of the younger Cosma (1294). The paintings in the apses are restored. In the chapel to the left of the sacristy, over the altar, is a *Madonna and Child* attributed to the late 15C Roman school. In the **sacristy**, to the right of the entrance, is a fragment of a mosaic of 706 on a gold ground, representing the *Adoration of the Magi*, formerly in the oratory of John VII at St Peter's. The tiny crypt (no admission) was built into part of the altar dedicated to Hercules, the columns of which remain.

From the Lungotevere Aventino, west of Piazza della Bocca della Verità, the iron *Ponte Palatino* crosses the Tiber to Trastevere (Chapter 21). In the bed of the Tiber, upstream, is a single arch of the *Pons Aemilius*, the first stone bridge over the Tiber (the piers were built in 179 BC, and were connected by arches in 142 BC). From the 13C onwards it was repaired numerous times, and has been known as the 'Ponte Rotto' since its final collapse in 1598. From the parapet of the Ponte Palatino the mouth of the Cloaca Maxima (see below), may be seen under the quay of the left bank, when the river is low.

On the east side of Piazza della Bocca della Verità is Via del Velabro, which perpetuates the name of this ancient district of Rome. The *Velabrum*, once a stagnant marsh left by the inundations of the Tiber, extended between the river and the Palatine, and included the *Forum Boarium* (see above). The derivation of the name is uncertain. The Velabrum is famous in legend as the spot where the shepherd Faustulus found the twins Romulus and Remus. It was drained by the **Cloaca Maxima**, which was an extensive system serving the valleys between the Esquiline, Viminal and Quirinal Hills, as well as the Roman Forum. At first a natural watercourse to the Tiber, it was canalised by Tarquinius the Elder and Servius Tullius (c 616–535 BC), and arched over in c 200 BC; it is still in use.

In the peaceful Via del Velabro (Pl. 8; 3) is the massive four-sided **Arch of Janus** (being restored), which formed a covered passage at a crossroads (*quadrivium*) and provided shelter for the cattle-dealers. Poorly proportioned, it is a work of the decadence, dating perhaps from the reign of Constantine, and is built partly of ancient fragments, with numerous niches for statues. To the left is **SAN GIORGIO IN VELABRO** (Pl. 8; 1) an ancient church probably dating from the 9C or earlier, built over a diaconia established here c 600. The campanile dates from the 12C. The church was restored to its medieval appearance in 1926 by Antonio Muñoz. It was severely damaged in a bomb explosion in 1993 (the work of the Mafia), which destroyed the 9C–12C Ionic portico. This has been carefully reconstructed and the church restored.

The beautiful plain **interior** (open Tue 9.30–12; Fri & Sun 16.30–18.30) is basilican, with nave and aisles separated by 16 ancient columns of granite and pavonazzetto. The pretty windows were restored in this century. The irregularity of the plan which can be seen from the wooden ceiling suggests an earlier construction was incorporated in the 9C building. A room on the right documents the repairs made after 1993. In the apse is a fresco attributed to Pietro Cavallini (c 1296; repainted in the 16C) of Christ with the Madonna and Saints Peter, Sebastian, and George. The altar, with some Cosmatesque decoration, and the canopy, date from the 13C.

To the left of the church is the ornate little **Arcus Argentariorum** (AD 204), which was erected by the money-changers (*argentarii*) and cattle-dealers in honour of the emperor Septimius Severus, his second wife Julia Domna, and their children, Caracalla and Geta. The portrait and name of Geta were effaced as a mark of his disgrace after his assassination by his brother in 212.

To the left of the arch, a street leads to the church of **San Giovanni Decollato** (open on 22 June, or by appointment, ☎ 679 4572). The interior has fine stucco and fresco decoration dating from 1580–90. The altarpiece of the *Decapitation of St John* is by Vasari. In front of the west door is the entrance to the oratory with remarkable *frescoes by the 16C Roman Mannerists, Jacopino del Conte, Francesco Salviati, Pirro Ligorio, and others. There is also a 16C cloister. On the other side of the road, reached by a raised pavement, is **Sant'Eligio dei Ferrari** (open for services on Sun) with an interesting Baroque interior.

Via San Teodoro to the northeast corresponds to the ancient *Vicus Tuscus*, skirting the Palatine on the west. On the right, well below the level of the road, is the small round domed church of **San Teodoro** (Pl. 8; 2; open for services on fest. at 11.30), beside which was found the bronze she-wolf (now in Palazzo dei Conservatori). The first church was built on the site of the great granary warehouse known as the *Horrea Agrippiana*, later turned into an early Christian

diaconia. It is preceded by a delightful courtyard. The present church dates from c 1453 and it contains an early mosaic in the apse of the old oratory (Christ and saints, c 600), much restored. Remains of earlier buildings, including the Roman structures, have been found beneath the foundations (and are sometimes shown on the first and third Sunday of the month after the service).

From Piazza della Bocca della Verità, Via dei Cerchi runs southeast. On the left, in Piazza di Sant'Anastasia (reached also from Via di San Teodoro; see above) is the church of **Sant'Anastasia** (closed for restoration since 1992), dating from 492 and several times restored. The classical façade is by Luigi Arrigucci. Inside, under the high altar, is a recumbent statue of St Anastasia, begun by Francesco Aprile and finished by Ercole Ferrata. Beneath the church are remains of an Imperial building.

Via dei Cerchi skirts the northeast side of the Circus Maximus (with a good view from below of the ancient buildings on the south slopes of the Palatine, see Chapter 3), and Via del Circo Massimo borders its southwest side. In Piazzale Romolo e Remo is a seated bronze statue, by Ettore Ferrari, of Giuseppe Mazzini, unveiled at the centenary (1949) of the Roman Republic.

The **CIRCUS MAXIMUS** (Pl. 8; 4) lies in the Valle Murcia, between the Palatine and the Aventine Hills; now planted with grass, it is used as a public park.

> This was the first and largest circus in Rome. According to Livy, it dates from the time of Tarquinius Priscus (c 600 BC), who is said to have here inaugurated a display of races and boxing matches after a victory over the Latins; but the first factual reference to the circus is in 329 BC. The circus was altered and enlarged on several occasions. In the time of Julius Caesar its length was three stadia (1875 Roman feet) and its width one stadium. The resultant oblong was rounded at one end and straight at the other. Tiers of seats were provided all round except at the straight end; here were the carceres, or stalls for horses and chariots. In the centre, running lengthwise, was the spina, a low wall terminating at either end in a meta, or conical pillar, denoting the turnings of the course. The length of a race was seven circuits of the spina. Though primarily adapted for chariot races, the circus was used also for athletic contests, wild-beast fights, and (by flooding the arena) mock sea battles. It could accommodate from 150,000 to 385,000 spectators; its capacity varied from one reconstruction to the next. The circus was destroyed by fire under Nero (AD 64) and again in the time of Domitian. A new circus was built by Trajan; Caracalla enlarged it and Constantine restored it after a partial collapse. The last games were held under the Ostrogothic king Totila in AD 549.

The extant remains belong to the Imperial period. Some seats and part of the substructure of the stairways can be seen at the curved east end, around the medieval tower near Piazza di Porta Capena, as well as some shops. In the centre of this curve are fragmentary decorative columns of a triumphal arch commemorating Titus's conquest of Jerusalem in AD 80–81, which formed the entrance gate. Excavations have been in progress here since 1984. The obelisks now in Piazza del Popolo and outside the Lateran once stood in the circus. At the west

end of the Circus, on Via dell'Ara Massima, are remains of a large Roman public building (2C AD) with a 3C mithraeum beneath (admission only with special permission from the Comune; write to the Ripartizione X del Comune di Rome, 29 Via Portico d'Ottavia, 00100 Rome, fax 689 2115; ☎ 671 03819).

16 · The Aventine Hill

The Aventine Hill (40m; Pl. 8; 3, 5) rises on the southwest side of the Circus Maximus (see Chapter 15). A secluded residential area with beautiful trees and gardens, it is one of the most peaceful places in the centre of Rome. The Aventine is the southernmost of the Seven Hills of Rome, and was not at first included within the precincts of the city, remaining outside the *pomoerium*, or line of the walls, throughout the Republican era. For centuries it was sparsely populated. It has two summits: the Aventine of ancient Rome, which extends southwest of Via del Circo Massimo in the direction of the Tiber, and the 'Piccolo Aventino', to the south. These are divided by Viale Aventino, which runs southwest from the Porta Capena towards Testaccio. It was to the Temple of Diana on the Aventine that Gaius Gracchus, after failing to obtain his re-election for the third time as tribune in 121 BC, withdrew with his colleague Fulvius Flaccus for their last stand against the Senate. *Aventino* is still a current political term used when the opposition party decide to abstain from participation in the affairs of parliament and abandon the Chamber of Deputies. In the Imperial era the Aventine became an aristocratic district, and in the early Middle Ages it was already covered with elegant mansions.

From Via del Circo Massimo, Clivo dei Publicii and Via di Valle Murcia (bordered by a rose garden) both mount the hill to Via di Santa Sabina. At the top of the rise the road passes (right) the Clivo di Rocca Savelli, a pedestrian lane which leads back down the hill past the wall of the 12C Savelli castle. Beyond is the pretty little walled garden (open to the public) known as the **Parco Savello** (or **Giardino degli Aranci**), planted with orange trees. It has a superb view of Rome to the north and northwest (steps in the far corner lead down to the Clivo di Rocca Savelli, see above). A door in the wall leads into Piazza Pietro d'Illiria, with a splendid wall fountain.

Here is the church of **SANTA SABINA** (Pl. 8; 3; open 6.30–12.30, 16–19), arguably the most beautiful basilica in Rome surviving from the early Christian period. It was built by Peter of Illyria (422–32), a priest from Dalmatia, on the legendary site of the house of the Roman matron Sabina (who was later canonised), near a temple of Juno. It was restored in 824 and in 1216. In 1219 Honorius III gave it to St Dominic for his new Order. It was disfigured in 1587 by Domenico Fontana and skilfully restored by Antonio Muñoz in 1919 and 1937.

The church is preceded by a small 15C portico. The entrance is from the vestibule, to the left, through the far *door, which has 18 remarkable wooden panels carved in the early 5C with scriptural scenes; they include one of the oldest representations of the Crucifixion in existence (the panels are probably not in their original order).

The beautifully proportioned classical **interior** is modelled on the basilicas of Ravenna. Of its mosaic decoration which formerly covered the nave walls and

apse, only one section remains, above the doorway, showing seven hexameters in classical gold lettering on a blue ground, with the founder's name (430), and, at the sides, two female figures which personify the converted Jews (*ex-circumcisione*), and the converted pagans or Gentiles (*ex-gentibus*). The wide and tall nave is divided from the aisles by 24 fluted Corinthian *columns from a neighbouring 2C building. The spandrels of the arcades are decorated with a splendid 5C marble inlay in opus sectile, and the beautiful large windows, 34 in all, have their transennae of varied design based on original fragments.

In the centre of the **nave** is the unusual mosaic tombstone of Fra' Muñoz de Zamora (died 1300), perhaps by Iacopo Torriti. The schola cantorum, ambones, and bishop's throne (in the choir) have been reconstructed from ancient fragments. The unattractive apse fresco by Taddeo Zuccari was repainted by Vincenzo Camuccini in 1836. Below the **right aisle** can be seen an ancient column, older than the church. Adjacent to it, the Chapel of St Hyacinth is frescoed by the Zuccari; and at the end of the aisle is the tomb of Cardinal Auxias de Podio (1485), by the school of Andrea Bregno. Beneath the nave, excavations have revealed remains of a small temple and an edifice of the early Imperial period with a fine marble pavement. The Baroque Elci Chapel, in the **left aisle**, contains, over its altar, the *Madonna of the Rosary with Saints Dominic and Catherine*, by Sassoferrato. In the convent is St Dominic's room, now a chapel, where the saint lived and had a meeting with St Francis. The beautiful *cloister* of 1216–25 (being restored), with 103 columns, is entered from the end of the vestibule (ask the sacristan for admission).

Beyond the convent is another little public park with orange trees, pine trees, a palm tree and bougainvillea. From the parapet, the view (now somewhat hidden by the trees) over Rome includes: in the foreground, the long orange façade of the former Istituto di San Michele, St Peter's with the Janiculum Hill to the left, and to the right the dome of Sant'Andrea della Valle, the little spiral tower of Sant'Ivo, the dome of the Pantheon, the Synagogue, the French Academy (on the skyline surrounded by trees), the Vittorio Emanuele II Monument, the Capitoline Hill, and the Torre Milizie (just behind the tree on the extreme right).

The church of **Sant'Alessio** (Pl. 8; 3; until 1217 *San Bonifacio*), near which the powerful Roman family of Crescentii built a convent in the 10C, is preceded by an attractive courtyard, and retains its fine Romanesque campanile. The interior of the church (open 8.30–12, 15.30–17.30) was modernised by Tommaso de Marchis in 1750, but two tiny mosaic columns remain on either side of the wooden bishop's throne in the apse. At the west end of the left aisle, set in an altar of 1700 by Andrea Bergondi, is a portion of the wooden staircase beneath which St Alexis is supposed to have lived and died in poverty, unrecognised by his wealthy family.

Via di Santa Sabina ends at the delightful PIAZZA DEI CAVALIERI DI MALTA, with elaborate decorations (recently restored) by Giovanni Battista Piranesi, seen against a background of cypresses and palms. He also designed the monumental entrance in the square to the **Priorato di Malta** (Pl. 8; 5), the residence of the Grand Master of the Knights of Malta, and the seat of the Order's embassies to Italy and the Vatican. The Order of the Knights of St John of Jerusalem (or Knights Hospitallers) was founded by a certain Gerard in 1113 to assist pilgrims to the Holy Land. The order was based on the island of Rhodes

from 1310 to 1522, and then on Malta until 1798. Their headquarters are now in Rome (at 68 Via Condotti) and the knights, who take vows of chastity, poverty and obedience, continue to carry out charitable work. The Military Order of Malta is the smallest sovereign state in the world.

There is a remarkable view of the dome of St Peter's at the end of an avenue through the keyhole in the doorway. The villa (admission rarely granted), contains a Chapter Hall with portraits of all the Grand Masters, and an altar-piece from the church by Andrea Sacchi. The beautiful garden, planted with palm trees and bay hedges, has a superb view from a terrace looking over the Tiber towards Monte Mario.

On the left, a drive leads to the back of the villa and the church of **Santa Maria del Priorato**, or *Aventinense* (admission as for the villa), a Benedictine foundation once incorporated in the residence of the patrician senator Alberic, who was the virtual ruler of Rome in 932–54. It passed into the hands of the Templars, and from them to the Knights of Malta. It was rebuilt in 1765 by Piranesi. The fine **façade** of a single order crowned with a tympanum, has rich decorative details. The harmonious **interior** is striking, with fine stucco decoration; the Rococo high altar by Tommaso Righi is cleverly lit. It contains 15C tombs and a statue of Piranesi by Giuseppe Angelini.

On the west side of the Priorato, facing Via della Marmorata, is the ancient brick Arco di San Lazzaro, which may have had some connection with the store-houses (*Emporia*) in this neighbourhood. A large Benedictine seminary (1892–96) stands next to the church of **Sant' Anselmo**, built in 1900 in the Lombard Romanesque style. Mass is held here with Gregorian chant at 9.30 on Sun.

Via Porta Lavernate, Via di Sant'Anselmo and Via Icilio (left) lead towards Santa Prisca on the other side of the hill. The church of **Santa Prisca** (Pl. 8; 5; open only for services), possibly dating from the 4C, is said to occupy the site of the house of Aquila and Prisca, friends of St Peter. In the **interior** the pretty frescoes in the nave are by Fontebuoni. Beneath the church are a **mithraeum** (closed indefinitely), with frescoes and a statue of Mithras slaying the Bull and the recumbent figure of Saturn, and a nymphaeum.

Via di Santa Prisca continues down to the wide and busy Viale Aventino. In Piazza Albania (right) are extensive remains of the Servian Wall (c 87 BC). Across the square, Via San Saba leads up to the 'Piccolo Aventino' and the steps preceding the church of **San Saba** (Pl. 8; 6; open 7–12, 16–18.30), with a little porch and walled forecourt. Beneath the church were found fragments of frescoes (now exhibited in the sacristy corridor), belonging to the first church founded in the 7C by Palestinian monks escaping from the Eastern invasions. The present church may date from c 900, although it has been rebuilt several times and was restored in 1943. In 1463, under Cardinal Piccolomini, the loggia was added above the portico and the four original windows were bricked in.

In the portico are sculptural fragments, some Oriental in character (including a knight and falcon), and a large Roman sarcophagus with figures of a bride-groom and Juno Pronuba. The fine Cosmatesque **doorway** is by Giacomo, the father of Cosma, who also probably designed the floor. In the **interior**, the right aisle has remains of a schola cantorum, a patchwork of Cosmatesque work. On the left-hand side of the church is a short fourth aisle, with remains of 13C

frescoes. High up on the arch over the apse is an Annunciation, another addition for Cardinal Piccolomini. In the apse, above the Bishop's throne is a fine Cosmatesque marble disc and a 14C fresco of the Crucifixion.

Porta San Paolo and the area further south are described in Chapter 25.

17 · The Via Appia Antica and the Catacombs

The Via Appia Antica from Porta San Sebastiano to the church of Domine Quo Vadis is now an unattractive traffic-ridden road, extremely unpleasant to explore on foot except on Sundays, when it is totally closed to traffic from Porta San Sebastiano to beyond the tomb of Cecilia Metella and becomes one of the most interesting and peaceful walks in the city. Beyond the church the road, although very narrow (beware of fast cars), becomes prettier and passes the side entrance to the catacombs of San Callisto and then descends to the basilica and catacombs of San Sebastiano. A short way beyond San Sebastiano are the Circus of Maxentius and the Tomb of Cecilia Metella, the two most interesting monuments on the road. Beyond the tomb the bus (see below) leaves the Via Appia. The remaining 4km as far as the Casal Rotondo are the most beautiful and characteristic section of the road, although in the last few decades some of the monuments have been vandalised, and rubbish of all sorts now abounds. It is not advisable to visit this stretch of the road (one-way for cars leaving Rome) if you are on your own after dark.

■ **Public transport**. On Sundays (9–19) the Via Appia Antica is reached by Bus 760 from Via del Circo Massimo (by the monument to Mazzini) via the Baths of Caracalla and Via di Porta San Sebastiano, terminating at the Catacombs of San Sebastiano.

On weekdays Bus 218 from San Giovanni in Laterano runs via the outside of the Aurelian Walls to Porta San Sebastiano and then follows Via Appia Antica as far as Via Ardeatina (near the Catacombs of San Callisto and San Domitilla).

The Via Appia Antica can also be reached by Underground Line A from Piazza di Spagna and Termini station to 'Colli Albani' where Bus 660 takes Via Appia Pignatelli to the Catacombs of San Sebastiano.

The Via Appia to the catacombs

The Via Appia (Pl. 9; 8) begins outside Porta San Sebastiano, in the Aurelian Wall, continuing the line of its urban section (see Chapter 14). Called by Statius the queen of roads (regina viarum), it was the most important of the consular Roman roads. It was built by the censor Appius Claudius in 312 BC as far as Capua, and later extended to Beneventum (Benevento) and Brundusium (Brindisi). In 37 BC Horace, Virgil, and Maecenas travelled the 375km to Brindisi in 15 days.

The Via Appia served for the first few kilometres as a patrician cemetery, and was lined on either side by a series of family graves. Some of the tombs, usually in the form of a tower or tumulus, can still be seen, although often only their concrete core survives. The solid bases were sometimes used in the Middle Ages as the foundations of watch-towers and small forts. The ancient paving, of massive polygonal blocks of grey basaltic lava from the Alban Hills, with crepidines or sidewalks, has been almost totally covered with asphalt in recent years up to the third milestone. The road was reopened at the end of the 18C and many of the monuments lining the road were erected by Luigi Canina in 1852. The Via Appia was also used by the early Christians for their underground cemeteries, and it is now mostly visited for its famous catacombs. Although the road survives as far as the 12th Roman milestone and its junction with the modern Via Appia Nuova, little or no attempt has been made to preserve it in recent years, and beyond its crossing with the Grande Raccordo Annulare it has been totally abandoned. Despite the institution of a regional archaeological park here in 1988, there are no signs that conservation work is in progress.

The initial section of the Via Appia, the ancient *Clivus Martis*, is now a busy unattractive road, not recommended for walkers. It gently descends from Porta San Sebastiano, and about 120m from the gate is the site of the First Milestone (marked by a column and an inscription; see the Plan on pp 256–257). The road passes under an ugly flyover bearing a new fast road (where excavations have revealed Roman remains), and then under the main Rome-Civitavecchia railway. It crosses the brook Almone (or Marrana della Caffarella), where the priests of Cybele, the Magna Mater, used to perform the annual ceremony of washing the image of the goddess. Tombs appear here and there. On the left, nearly 1km from the gate, is a conical Roman mound with a house on the top, and the little church of **Domine Quo Vadis**. This stands on the spot where— according to tradition—St Peter, fleeing the city, met an apparition of Jesus which shamed him into returning to Rome and martyrdom (the story was the subject of a novel by the Polish writer Henryk Sienkiewicz published in 1896).

By the church, Via Ardeatina branches off to the right to (1km) the Fosse Ardeatine (see below). At this fork is the entrance for cars to the catacombs of San Callisto (see below).

About 100m from the church of Domine Quo Vadis is a turning to the left, called Via della Caffarella. Less than a kilometre along this lane is a path (left), leading to the so-called **Temple of the Deus Rediculus** (now private property), by a mill near the Almone brook. The 'temple' is really a sumptuous tomb of the 2C, once identified as that of Annia Regilla, wife of Herodes Atticus (see below).

After making a short ascent the Via Appia passes a trattoria (No. 87; left) which incorporates remains of the so-called **Columbarium of the Freedmen of Augustus**, where some 3000 inscriptions were found. At No. 101 is the little **Hypogeum of Vibia** (no admission), with pagan paintings of the 3C AD. Beyond (No. 103) is the site of the Second Milestone. At No. 110, on the right, is the entrance to the Catacombs of San Callisto.

The catacombs

The catacombs were used by the early Christians as underground cemeteries outside the walls of Rome, since burial within the walls was forbidden (pagan Romans were cremated). They were often situated on property donated by a wealthy Roman, after whom the cemetery was named (i.e. Domitilla, Agnese, Priscilla and Commodilla). Easily quarried in the soft tufa, the catacombs provided space for the tombs of thousands of Christians. They were in use from the 1C up until the early 5C. Many martyrs were buried here and the early Christians chose to be buried close to them. Later they became places of pilgrimage until the martyrs' relics were transferred to various churches in Rome. They were pillaged by the Goths (537) and the Lombards (755), and by the 9C they were abandoned. They received their name from the stone quarries ('ad catacumbas') on the site of the cemetery of San Sebastiano (see below). In the 16C Antonio Bosio visited the catacombs, but they were not systematically explored until 1850 when the archaeologist Giovanni Battista de Rossi carried out excavations (first at San Callisto), and the Pontificia Commissione di Archeologia Sacra was set up. They were opened to the public and became one of the most famous sights of Rome, when visits by candlelight fired the romantic imagination of 19C travellers. The popular belief that they were used as hiding places by the early Christians has been totally disproved.

The catacombs are a system of galleries of different sizes, often arranged on as many as five levels, and sometimes extending for several kilometres. In the walls simple rectangular niches (*loculi*) were cut in tiers where the bodies were placed wrapped in a sheet. The openings were closed with slabs of marble or terracotta on which the names were inscribed (at first in Greek, later in Latin), sometimes with the date or the words 'in pace' added (almost all of these have now disappeared). Terracotta lamps were hung above the tombs to provide illumination in the galleries. A more elaborate type of tomb was the *arcosolium*, which was a niche surmounted by an arch and often decorated. Small rooms or *cubicula* served as family vaults. The shallowest of the galleries are 7–8m beneath the surface, while the deepest are some 22m below ground level. Openings in the vaults, some of which survive, were used for the removal of earth during the excavations. Most of the tombs were rifled at some time over the centuries in the search for treasure and relics, but the inscriptions and paintings which survive are of the greatest interest.

The **CATACOMBS OF SAN CALLISTO**, the first official cemetery of the early Christian community, are usually considered the most important of the Roman catacombs. They were named after St Calixtus (San Callisto) who was appointed to look after the cemetery by Pope St Zephyrinus (199–217), and who enlarged them when he himself became pope in 217. They were the official burial place of the bishops of Rome. First investigated in 1850 by Giovanni Battista de Rossi (see above), they have not yet been fully explored.

Opening hours are usually 8.30–12 and 14.30 (or 15) to dusk; closed Wed and in Feb. ☎ 513 6725. Lire 8000.

Visitors are conducted by an English-speaking priest to a small basilica with three apses, the **Oratory of Saints Sixtus and Cecilia**, where the dead were brought before burial in the catacombs. Here are inscriptions and sculptural fragments from the tombs, and a bust of De Rossi. Pope St

Zephyrinus is generally supposed to have been buried in the central apse.

The catacombs excavated on five levels are reached by an ancient staircase. The tour usually remains on the second level, from which several staircases can be seen descending to other levels. The *papal crypt* preserves the tombs with original Greek inscriptions of the martyred popes, St Pontianus (230–35), St Anterus (236), St Fabian (236–50), St Lucius (253–54), martyred under Valerian's persecution, St Stephen I (254–57), St Dionysius (259–68), and St Felix I (269–74). In honour of the martyred popes, Pope St Damasus I (366–84) set up the metrical inscription seen at the end of the crypt.

In the adjoining crypt is the **Cubiculum of St Cecilia**, where the body of the saint is supposed to have been buried after her martyrdom at her house in Trastevere in 230. It is thought that it was moved by Paschal I in 820 to the church built on the site of her house. Here has been placed a copy of Maderno's statue of the saint in the church. On the walls are very worn 7C–8C frescoes: Head of Christ, St Urban, and other saints. Beyond the crypt, a 3C passage leads down a short flight of stairs, with Christian symbols carved on stone slabs, to the **Cubicula of the Sacraments**, with symbolic frescoes. In the first cubicle are frescoes of the Raising of Lazarus and, opposite, the Miracle of the Loaves and Fishes. On the end wall is a fine double sarcophagus, with a lid in the form of a roof. The other cubicles have similar frescoes, several depicting the story of Jonah. Further on is the Crypt of St Eusebius, martyred in 310. In the adjoining cubicles are the sepulchral inscriptions of Pope St Gaius (283–96) and two sarcophagi with mummified bodies. Next is the Tomb of Pope St Cornelius (251–53), with a contemporary Latin inscription containing the word 'martyr', and fine 6C Byzantine paintings. Adjoining is the **Crypt of Lucina**, the oldest part of the cemetery.

In 1991 remains of a 4C basilica used as a cemetery were discovered near the Via Ardeatina.

Beyond the via Appia Pignatelli, a road opened by Innocent XII in the late 17C to link the Via Appia Antica with the Via Appia Nuova, is Vicolo Sant'Urbano. It leads left to a villa (now a restaurant) in the park of which is the church of **Sant'Urbano**. This was originally a temple forming part of the villa of the wealthy Herodes Atticus, patron of arts and man of letters of the time of the Antonines, famous above all for his numerous buildings in Greece. The temple was converted into a church in the 9C or 10C and was restored in 1634, when four fluted columns from the pronaos were incorporated into the wall of the church. Inside (ask at the villa for the key) are remains of stucco ornamentation and interesting *frescoes by a certain Bonizzo (1011): over the door, Crucifixion; on the end wall, Christ blessing, with saints and angels; on the other walls, Life of Jesus, and Lives of St Cecilia and her companions, and of St Urban.

Via Appia Antica now descends to a small piazza in which, on the left, is a column set up by Pius IX in 1852 to commemorate his restoration of the Via Appia. On the right are the **BASILICA AND CATACOMBS OF SAN SEBAS-TIANO** (entrance to the left of the church; open usually 8.30–12 and 14.30 (or 15) to dusk; closed Thur and in Nov. Lire 8000). The basilica, one of the seven pilgrimage churches of Rome, was originally dedicated to Saints Peter and Paul and called the *Basilica Apostolorum*. It was built in the first half of the 4C over the

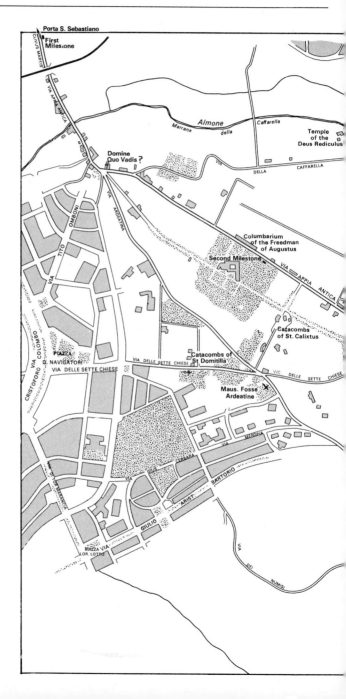

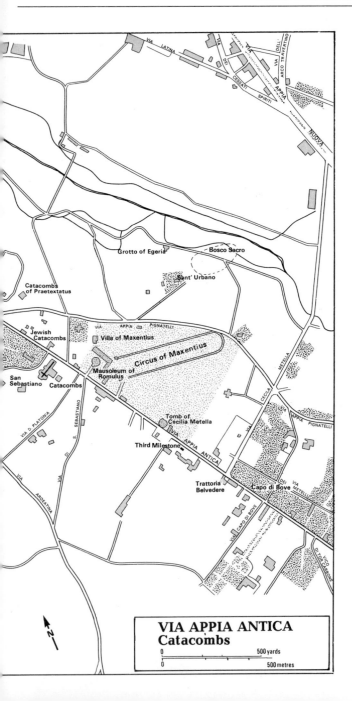

VIA APPIA ANTICA
Catacombs

| 0 | | 500 yards |
| 0 | | 500 metres |

cemetery into which the bodies of the Apostles had been temporarily moved from their tombs in St Peter's and San Paolo fuori le Mura; this is said to have occurred in 258 during the persecution of Valerian. At a later date St Sebastian, who was martyred under Diocletian in 288, was buried here. After the 9C the association with the Apostles was forgotten and the church was named after St Sebastian. From the 3C to the 9C this was the most venerated area of subterranean Rome. The catacombs have two special claims to fame: they are the only ones that have always been known, visited, and therefore damaged, and they were originally the only underground burial place to receive the name of catacombs: *ad catacumbas* (literally, 'by the caves', since they were built in an abandoned stone quarry here).

In the ticket office are fragments of sarcophagi, inscriptions, etc. Visitors are conducted by an English-speaking guide; the order of the tour is sometimes changed. A stairway, with fragments of terracotta lids of sarcophagi bearing Imperial seals, leads down to the **Crypt of St Sebastian** (restored) which contains a copy of a bust of St Sebastian, attributed to Bernini. Beyond are the catacombs excavated on four levels. The **Chapel of Symbols** has carved Christian symbols. An area below the basilica (the walls of which can be seen) known as the '**Piazzuola**' has three elaborate pagan *tombs of the early 2C. They each have a façade with a terracotta tympanum. The first, on the right, has a fresco above the tympanum of a pastoral scene and a banquet. The marble inscription names this as the sepulchre of M. Clodius Hermes. Inside is a vault fresco with a Gorgon's head, and decorative frescoes on the walls, including a beautiful composition with a vase of fruit and flowers flanked by two birds. The floor preserves a mosaic. The centre tomb has a magnificent stucco vault, dating from the early 2C, terminating in a shell design decorated with lotus and acanthus leaves and a peacock. It is believed both pagan and Christian burials took place in this composite tomb on several levels. The tomb to the left has a well-preserved stucco vault which descends to a lunette finely decorated with a grape and vine design. The cubicles here are also decorated with stucco.

A steep staircase ascends to the **Triclia**, a room reserved for the funerary banquets held in honour of the Apostles, Peter and Paul. There is a bench around the wall, and remains of red-painted decorations and fragments of pictures. The walls are inscribed with graffiti invoking the Apostles, including one dating from 260.

The **church** is usually shown at the end of the tour of the catacombs. It originally had a nave and two aisles; the aisles were walled up in the 13C. In 1612 it was rebuilt for Cardinal Scipio Borghese by Flaminio Ponzio; the façade has a portico with six Ionic columns, taken from the preceding 15C portico. The 17C wooden *ceiling is by Vasanzio. Off the south side is the apsidal **Chapel of the Relics** containing a stone which was once believed to bear the imprint of Christ's feet, and other relics, and the **Cappella Albani**, built as a sepulchral chapel for Clement XI by Carlo Fontana. On the high altar are four columns of verde antico. On the third north altar: *St Francis of Assisi*, attributed to Girolamo Muziano. In a chapel off this side: late 14C wooden crucifix (restored). An **Archaeological Museum** (admission only with special permission; write to Pontificia Commissione di Archeologia Sacra, 1 Via Napoleone III, 00185 Rome) is arranged in the ambulatory (where remains of the 4C basilica can be seen). Another chapel on the north side has a recumbent *statue of St Sebastian,

by Antonio Giorgetti, from a design by Bernini. Near the entrance is a stone from the catacombs with an inscription in honour of the martyr Eutychius, by Pope St Damasus.

Other parts of the catacombs not usually shown include the Platonia, the tomb of St Quirinus, and the **Chapel of Honorius III**, with 13C paintings, and an apsidal cubiculum bearing graffiti which indicate that this was the temporary grave of St Peter.

Just short of San Sebastiano, Via delle Sette Chiese, on the right, leads to Via Ardeatina (600m) and (250m further) the Catacombs of St Domitilla (see below). In Via Ardeatina (bus, see above), a little to the left of its junction, is the **Mausoleo delle Fosse Ardeatine**, scene of one of the most horrifying events of the Second World War, during the German occupation of Rome. On 24 March 1944, as a reprisal for the killing on the previous day of 32 German soldiers by the Resistance Movement in Via Rasella, the Germans shot 335 Italians. The victims, who had no connection with the killing of the German soldiers, included priests, officials, professional men, about a hundred Jews, a dozen foreigners, and a boy of 14. The Germans then buried the bodies here under an avalanche of sand artificially caused by exploding mines. Local inhabitants provided a medico-legal commission with the means of exhuming and identifying the bodies after the German retreat. The scene of the massacre, below a huge tufa cliff, now has cave chapels. The victims, reinterred after identification, are commemorated by a huge single concrete slab placed in 1949 over their mass grave, with a group of standing figures, in stone, by Francesco Coccia (1950).

The **CATACOMBS OF ST DOMITILLA** (open usually 8.30–12 and 14.30 (or 15) to dusk; closed Tues, and in Jan. ☎ 511 0342), or Catacombs of Saints Nereus and Achilleus, further along Via delle Sette Chiese, are among the most extensive in Rome and may be the most ancient Christian cemetery in existence. Here were buried St Flavia Domitilla (niece of Flavia Domitilla, sister of Domitian) and her two Christian servants, Nereus and Achilleus, as well as St Petronilla, another Christian patrician, perhaps the adopted daughter of St Peter. The catacombs contain more than 900 inscriptions.

At the foot of the entrance stairway is the aisled Basilica of Saints Nereus and Achilleus, built in 390–95 over the tombs of the martyred saints. There are traces of a schola cantorum, and ancient columns probably from a pagan temple. The area below the floor level has sarcophagi and tombs. By the altar is a rare small column, with the scenes of the martyrdom of St Achilleus carved in relief. The adjoining chapel of St Petronilla (shown during the tour of the catacombs), with a fresco of the saint, contained her sarcophagus until the 8C, when it was removed to St Peter's.

A friar conducts groups from the basilica to the catacombs, excavated on two levels. The **Cemetery of the Flavians** (the family of Domitilla) had a separate entrance on to the old Via Ardeatina. At this entrance is a vaulted vestibule probably designed as a meeting-place for the service of Intercession for the Dead, with a bench along the wall, and a well for water. A long gallery slopes down from here, having niches on either side, with 2C frescoes of flowers and genii. From the original entrance a gallery leads to another **hypogeum**, with four

large niches decorated with 2C paintings (Daniel in the lions' den, etc.). At the foot of a staircase is another ancient section; here is a cubicle with paintings of winged genii and the earliest representation of the Good Shepherd (2C). On the upper level is the **Cubiculum of Ampliatus**, with paintings in classical style. Other sections contain more paintings, including the Madonna and Child with four Magi; Christ and the Apostles; and a Cornmarket.

The Via Appia beyond the catacombs

The Via Appia now leaves behind the area of the catacombs, and becomes more attractive and interesting for its Roman remains. On the left, in a hollow, at No. 153, are the extensive ruins of the **VILLA OF MAXENTIUS** (open in summer, Tues–Sun 9–19; in winter, Tues–Sat 9–17.30; Sun 9–13.30), built in 309 by the Emperor Maxentius. This includes a palace, a circus, and a mausoleum built in honour of his son Romulus (died 307). The **Circus of Maxentius** is the best preserved of the Roman circuses, and one of the most romantic sites of ancient Rome. From it is the best view of the Tomb of Cecilia Metella (see below). The circus was excavated by Antonio Nibby in 1825 for the Torlonia family, and restored in the 1960s and 1970s.

The stadium (c 513m x 91m) was probably capable of holding some 10,000 spectators. The main entrance was on the west side with the 12 *carceres* or stalls for the chariots and quadrigae, and, on either side, two square towers with curved façades. Two arches, one of which has been restored, connected the towers to the long sides of the circus and provided side entrances. In the construction of the tiers of seats, amphorae were used to lighten the vaults (these can still clearly be seen). In the centre of the left side is the conspicuous emperor's box, which was connected by a portico to his palace on the hill behind (see below). At the far end was a triumphal arch where a fragment of a dedicatory inscription to Romulus, son of Maxentius, was found identifying the circus with Maxentius (it was previously attributed to Caracalla). In the centre is the round *meta* and the *spina*, the low wall which divided the area longitudinally (and where the obelisk of Domitian, now in Piazza Navona, originally stood). The course was seven laps around the *spina*. The spina and the carceres were both placed slightly obliquely to equalise, as far as possible, the chances of all competitors, although it is likely that the circus was never actually used since Maxentius fell from power in 312.

On the hillside to the left, towards Via Appia Pignatelli, are the overgrown remains (fenced off) of the **Palace** which include fragments of baths, a basilica, and a cryptoporticus. The conspicuous high wall near the west end of the circus belongs to the quadriporticus around the **Mausoleum of Romulus**, which faces the Via Appia. Some of the pilasters of the quadriporticus survive, as well as much of the outer wall. In the centre is the circular tomb preceded by a rectangular pronaos lying beneath a derelict house. The entrance is in front of a palm tree: beyond the pronaos is the mausoleum with niches in the outside wall for sarcophagi, and a huge pilaster in the centre also decorated with niches. The upper floor, probably covered with a cupola, has been destroyed. Nearby, beside the Via Appia is the so-called **Tomba dei Sempronii**, probably dating from the Augustan era. It is not open to the public while excavations are still in progress.

The road rises to the famous **TOMB OF CECILIA METELLA**, a massive circular tower of the Augustan period, 29.5m (100 Roman ft) in diameter, on a square base, and extremely well preserved (9–18; winter 9–16; Sun & Mon 9–13. ☎ 780 2465; informed custodian). Much of the marble facing is still intact as is also part of the elegant frieze surrounding the upper part, with garlands of fruit and bucrania (hence the name *Capo di Bove* given to the adjacent ground). A relief represents a soldier with Gallic shields and a prisoner from Gaul kneeling at his feet. Also on the side nearest the road is the inscription to Cecilia, daughter of Quintus Metellus Creticus and wife of M. Licinius Crassus (elder son of the triumvir and one of Caesar's generals in Gaul). In the 13C the Caetani transformed the tomb into a crenellated tower to serve as the keep of their castle, which they built across the roadway and included a Gothic church, the ruins of which can be seen on the other side of the road. The interior of the tomb (now inhabited by pigeons), constructed with small flat bricks, is particularly interesting; the roofless room on the right contains a collection of inscriptions and fragments from other tombs. The Third Milestone has recently been set up outside the enceinte of the castle, just to the left of the road, beneath the two-light windows.

A short distance further on is Via Cecilia Metella, where the bus coming from the Colosseum diverges left from the Appia Antica to Via Appia Pignatelli and Via Appia Nuova. The Via Appia Antica, lined by numerous ancient tombs, becomes more and more interesting as the view of the Campagna opens out. To the left can be seen the imposing aqueduct of the Acqua Marcia and the Acqua Claudia.

About 4km from Porta San Sebastiano is the **ancient section of the Via Appia**, excavated in 1850–59 between the 3rd and 11th milestones. This is the best preserved part of the whole road, even though in recent years it has been neglected and partly used as a rubbish dump. For ten Roman miles or more it was bordered with tombs on both sides, and the picturesque remains of some of these were recovered and others reconstructed in the last century by Antonio Canova and Luigi Canina. Some of the original sculptures have been removed to the Museo Nazionale Romano and replaced here by casts (easily identified by their yellow tint); other monuments have been vandalised. In this century, part of the historic area bordering the road has been occupied by luxurious private villas.

On a brick pilaster, on the left, opposite the site of the Fourth Milestone, are fragments of a tomb of a member of the Servilian gens. An inscription records that this was a gift made by Canova in 1808, who, contrary to the general practice of his time, felt that objects found during excavations should be left *in situ*. Beyond is the so-called Tomb of Seneca (left; replaced by casts), immediately followed by the Sepolcro Rotondo, a cella with four loculi, and the Tomb of the Children of Sextus Pompeius Justus (partly replaced by casts). Beyond this, set back from the road, is a so-called **Temple of Jupiter**, square with apsidal niches. On the right, in the Proprietà Lugari (near a clump of huge umbrella pines), is a superb monument in the form of a shrine (supposed to be that of St Urban), surrounded by the ruins of what was probably a villa.

In the next 550m are the scant remains of the Tombs of the Licinii, of Hilarius Fuscus (the five busts replaced by casts), of the Freedmen of the Claudian Gens, and of Q. Apuleius Pamphilius. Beyond a sepulchre in the form of a temple is the

Tomb of the Rabirii (the three busts replaced by casts). Beyond more tombs, one in peperino (decorated with festoons), and another with four busts (casts) the road crosses Via Erode Attico. At a point marked by a group of gigantic pines, near the Fifth Milestone, the road makes a bend, probably to avoid some earlier tumuli, one of which (now surmounted by a tower) passes for the burial place of one of the legendary *Curiatii*, while two others, surrounded by pines, about 350m further on (right), represent those of the *Horatii*. In the field to the right of the first are the remains of an *Ustrinum* (cremation place). A gate on the left opens on a byroad leading to the estate of Santa Maria Nuova, built over ruins (see below); further on, on the same side, is a great pyramidal tomb. Then, opposite the second of the graves of the Horatii, an inscription of the 1C BC marks the tomb of M. Caecilius, in whose family grave (according to Eutropius) was buried Pomponius Atticus, the friend of Cicero.

Just beyond are the magnificent and picturesque ruins of the **VILLA OF THE QUINTILII**, now part of the property of Santa Maria Nuova (see above). The ruins sprawl across fields through which sheep are grazed. These are so extensive as to suggest a town rather than a villa and in fact they used to be called *Roma Vecchia*. The villa, of which the principal mass dates from the time of Hadrian, belonged under Commodus to the wealthy brothers Quintilii, Maximus and Condianus, consuls under Antoninus Pius (AD 151) and writers on agriculture, who were put to death by Commodus for the sake of their possessions, including the villa. This was kept in repair until the 4C. Near the road are the remains of a nymphaeum (converted in the 15C into a castle), a hippodrome and an aqueduct, and, a little in front of them, a cryptoporticus. But the greater portion of these ruins lies nearer the Via Appia Nuova, where there are high walls with windows and impressive arcades, the floor of a small amphitheatre of later date, and traces of baths. Beyond the Via Appia Nuova is a fine monument, converted into a tower by the Saracens.

The road now becomes more deserted, and the monuments more widely scattered. The **Casal Rotondo**, 8km from Porta San Sebastiano, is a large round tomb on a square base, with an incongruous modern house and an olive garden on the summit. This was the largest tomb on the Via Appia, and dates from the Republic; it was enlarged in early Imperial times. It is said to have been erected to the memory of the poet Messala Corvinus by his son Valerius Maximus Cotta. The stylobate is 120 Roman feet (c 36m) in diameter. Attached to a wall close by are fragments of the tomb. Facing this monument is a smaller one attributed to the Aurelian gens. Just beyond the Casal Rotondo are crossroads, on the far side of which was the Sixth Milestone. Here also the Rome–Naples railway passes diagonally below in a short tunnel.

Via di Torricola, on the right leads towards the Via Ardeatina; 4.5km before this intersection is the **Santuario del Divino Amore**, at Castel di Leva. The sanctuary, crowded with pilgrims on Whit Monday, was inaugurated in 1745 to enshrine a picture of the Virgin painted by an unknown 14C artist in the surviving tower of the **Castel di Leva**, a castle of the Orsini which passed to the Savelli before its destruction in the 15C. The painting, credited with miraculous powers of protection, is said to have saved the life of a pilgrim attacked here by mad dogs.

On the left Via di Casal Rotondo, bearing left after a short distance slopes down

to the Via Appia Nuova. This is a convenient point at which to leave the Via Appia Antica; otherwise it can still be followed as far as the Grande Raccordo Anulare.

Beyond the Casal Rotondo is a tomb with reliefs of griffins and a columbarium. Opposite another columbarium, on the right of the road, is a tomb with four busts (casts). Some way further on (about 1km from the Casal Rotondo) is the **Torre in Selce**, a pyramidal tumulus with a medieval tower, 107m above sea-level. The remainder of the road is less interesting, and has been abandoned to rubbish and prostitutes; it soon becomes impracticable for cars.

Beyond inscriptions of M. Julius Pietas Epelides and C. Atilius Eudos, a jeweller, the road swerves a little and begins to descend, and the arches of an aqueduct which formerly brought water from a sulphur spring near Ciampino to the villa of the Quintilii, are prominent. Near this point the Via Appia is cut in two by the Circular Road (Grande Raccordo Anulare), linking all the consular highways that lead out of Rome. The first section was opened in 1951 and completed years later. Its total length is 68km. It is already too narrow to carry the volume of traffic passing round Rome, and is always very busy.

On the other side of the Circular Road the Via Appia is totally abandoned. It passes the Torre Rossa (a 12C–13C structure on a Roman base), and, at about the end of the eighth Roman mile, a sepuchral chamber (or possibly a sanctuary of the mysteries), known as the 'Pillars of Hercules'.

Further along Via Appia, beyond the Torraccio del Palombaro (a monument preserved through having been turned into a church in the 10C), is a path that leads on the right to La Giostra, a little hill upon which are ruins, once identified with the ancient Latin city of *Tellene*, but now thought to be a 4C Roman fortified outpost. Then come other tombs, more or less ruined (including one called the Ruzzica d'Orlando); and at the Ninth Milestone is what is left of the **Villa of Gallienus**, with a fine circular ruin that is regarded as the mausoleum of that emperor. The road is here totally blocked by refuse: it crosses the Rome–Terracina railway and, a little beyond the site of the Twelfth Milestone, joins the busy Via Appia Nuova.

Further along this road are the ruins of tombs and other buildings which lined the Via Appia. There are four imposing stumps of Roman towers, the first of them cylindrical and called the Torraccio (left), the others square. A track to the right leads to the ruins of the small Latin town of *Bovillae*, a colony of Alba Longa. Here can be seen traces of a circus excavated in the 19C, a cistern, and numerous tombs.

18 · San Lorenzo fuori le Mura

■ The basilica of San Lorenzo in Piazzale del Verano is reached by numerous buses and trams from the centre of the city (Bus No. 71 from Piazza San Silvestro, No. 11 from the Colosseum, and trams 19, 19b and 30b).

The basilica of **SAN LORENZO FUORI LE MURA** (Pl. 6; 4) is one of the seven pilgrimage churches of Rome and consists of two churches placed end to end. Though open 8.30–12, 16–18.30, it is often difficult to visit during these hours as it is frequently in use for funerals. Parallel to the 4C covered cemetery basilica

of San Lorenzo, Pelagius II built a new church in 579. In 1216 Honorius III demolished the apse of the 6C church and built onto it another church, with a different orientation (placing the entrance at the opposite end). The churches were skilfully restored in 1864–70 by Virginio Vespignani. San Lorenzo was the only church in Rome to suffer serious damage during the Second World War, when it was partly destroyed in an air raid on 19 July 1943: the façade and the south wall were rebuilt in 1949.

The simple Romanesque **campanile** (being restored) dates from the 12C. The reconstructed 13C **narthex** of six antique Ionic columns has a carved cornice and a mosaic frieze. Inside are two unusual tombs, a tablet (1948) commemorating repairs ordered by Pius XII after war damage, and a monument by Giacomo Manzù to the statesman Alcide De Gasperi, the Christian Democrat who dominated Italian politics between 1943 and 1953; the 13C frescoes depict the lives of Saints Laurence and Stephen.

The basilican 13C **interior** has a chancel and no transept. Twenty-two Ionic columns of granite support an architrave, and the floor is paved with a 12C Cosmatesque mosaic. Near the entrance is the tomb of Cardinal Fieschi, a large Roman sarcophagus converted to its present use in 1256; it was rebuilt from the original fragments after the bombardment. Near the end of the nave on the right is a Cosmatesque ambone and the twisted stem of a paschal candlestick.

The baldacchino in the **choir** is signed by Giovanni, Pietro, Angelo and Sasso, sons of the mastermason Paolo (1147; the upper part was restored in the 19C). The episcopal throne dates from the 13C. Inside the triumphal arch is a 6C mosaic of Christ with saints, and Pelagius offering the church, reset during the Byzantine revival. The raised **chancel** incorporates the 6C church (except for its apse which was demolished), which is on a slightly different axis. The Corinthian columns support an entablature of antique fragments and, above, an arcaded gallery.

The lower level, cloister and catacombs can only be visited by special permission from the monastery. The level of the earliest basilica has some of the original pillars, and in its narthex is the mausoleum of Pius IX (died 1878), rebuilt by Cattaneo in 1881 and decorated by Lodovico Seitz. The **cloister** dates from 1187–91 (a ridiculous fountain has been installed here). Off the cloister are the extensive **Catacombs of St Cyriaca** where the body of St Laurence is said to have been placed after his death in 258.

To the right of the church is the entrance to the huge municipal cemetery called **Campo Verano** (Pl. 6; 4), on the site of the estate of the Emperor Lucius Verus. It was designed by Giuseppe Valadier in 1807–12, with a church and quadriporticus by Virginio Vespignani. The four colossal allegorical figures at the entrance date from 1878. Among the tombs is that of Goffredo Mameli (died 1849), the soldier-poet (first avenue to the left). On the high ground beside Via Tiburtina is a memorial of the battle of Mentana (1867). In the zone of the new plots is a First World War memorial, by Raffaele de Vico.

Piazzale San Lorenzo, a busy traffic hub and bus and tram terminus, is traversed by Via Tiburtina, on the site of the ancient Roman road to *Tibur* (now Tivoli). Viale Regina Elena leads northwest between the Istituto Superiore di Sanità, with a research centre for chemical microbiology, and (left) the **CITTÀ UNIVERSITARIA** (Pl. 6; 3, 4), an interesting example of Fascist architecture. The faculty buildings and chapel were designed on a monumental scale by

Marcello Piacentini and completed in 1935, in which year the seat of the University of Rome was transferred here from Palazzo della Sapienza. Numerous other buildings have been built in this century (some by Giovanni Michelucci) as the university has expanded. The entrance is in Piazzale Aldo Moro, near a bronze statue of Minerva, by Arturo Martini. In the **Rector's Palace** there is a fresco by Mario Sironi. The **University Library** was founded by Alexander VII (with more than a million volumes). In the Faculty of Letters are three study collections (open by appointment, Mon–Fri, 9–13): the Museo delle Origini, which illustrates the prehistory of Italy (founded in 1942); the Museo delle Antichità Etrusche e Italiche, and the Museo dell'Arte Classica (formerly the Museo dei Gessi), with more than 1000 casts of Greek and Hellenistic statuary. The Botanical Institute has an important Herbarium.

The **Policlinico** (Pl. 6; 1, 3) is a large teaching hospital, designed by Giulio Podesti in 1893. To the west are the buildings (entrance on Viale Castro Pretorio), opened in 1975, of the **Biblioteca Nazionale Centrale Vittorio Emanuele II** (Pl. 6; 1). The National Library, the largest in Italy (open weekdays 9–18.30, Saturday 9–13.30) was founded in 1877 with the contents of the library of the Jesuit Collegio Romano (its former seat), and later enriched with the books from 70 monastic libraries. It now has about 4,500,000 volumes (a copy of every book published in Italy has to be sent here), 1935 incunabula, and 6500 manuscripts.

The library is on the site of the **Castra Pretoria**, the huge Roman barracks of the Praetorian Guard. The *Praetoriae Cohortes*, or emperor's bodyguard, originally nine or ten cohorts (9000–10,000 men), were instituted by Augustus and concentrated into a permanent camp here by Sejanus, minister of Tiberius, in AD 23; some portions of his building survive. In later Imperial times the Praetorian Guard acquired undue influence in the conduct of affairs of state. Many an emperor had to bribe them on his accession with a 'donative'; on one occasion, after the death of Pertinax in 193, they put up the Roman Empire for sale by auction; it was bought by Didius Julianus, who enjoyed his purchase for 66 days. Centuries later the Castra Pretoria passed into the hands of the Jesuits, who renamed it *Macao* after their most successful foreign mission. It was again used as barracks in this century.

Via San Martino della Battaglia leads southwest to Piazza dell' Indipendenza (Pl. 5; 4), on the site of the *Campus Sceleratus*, where vestals who had forgotten their vows of chastity were buried alive. Via Solferino continues to Piazza dei Cinquecento in front of the Railway Station (see Chapter 10).

19 · Porta Pia and Via Nomentana (Sant'Agnese fuori le Mura)

■ The important church of Sant'Agnese fuori le Mura, a long way from the centre of the city along a relatively uninteresting road, may be reached from Piazza Venezia by Bus No. 60.

Porta Pia (Pl. 5; 2) was Michelangelo's last architectural work, commissioned by Pius IV in 1561; the exterior face is by Virginio Vespignani (1868). It stands

at the beginning of Via Nomentana. The ancient **Porta Nomentana**, walled up
by Pius IV, is in Piazza della Croce Rossa to the right. The north tower has been
preserved. The Castra Pretoria here and the area to the south are described in
Chapter 18. It was near the Porta Pia that the Italian troops under General
Raffaele Cadorna entered Rome on 20 September 1870 and so brought to an
end the temporal power of the popes. The breach was a few steps to the left of the
gate, in Corso d'Italia (commemorative stones). In the small courtyard of the
gateway is the **Museo Storico dei Bersaglieri** (open 9–13 Tues & Thur),
which documents the wars of independence, the African campaign, and the
First World War. Outside the gate is a monument of 1932.

Inside the gate, on the left, is Villa Paolina, seat of the French Embassy to the
Vatican. It was the home of Pauline Bonaparte from 1816 to 1824, and was
once famous for its garden. On the other side of Via XX Settembre is the **British
Embassy**, a conspicuous building surrounded by water, designed by Sir Basil
Spence and opened in 1971 on the site of the Villa Torlonia, damaged by a
terrorist's bomb in 1946.

The wide VIA NOMENTANA (Pl. 12; 8) runs northeast from Porta Pia,
traversing a residential district of the city, with palaces and villas, many with
beautiful gardens. It follows the line of the ancient Roman consular road to
Nomentum, now Mentana, c 20km northeast of Rome. Any of the buses here
pass the church of Sant'Agnese fuori le Mura (see below).

Beyond Viale Regina Margherita on the left is Villa Paganini (a public
garden), and on the right is the garden of **Villa Torlonia** (Pl. 12; just beyond
8), which became the private residence of Mussolini after 1929. (There is
another Villa Torlonia on the Via Salaria, see Chapter 20.) It is now a municipal park (open 7–dusk) of some 13.5 hectares. By the entrance gate, on Via
Spallanzani, near a grove of palm trees, is a Neo-classical villa built by Giuseppe
Valadier in 1806. The delightful little Art Nouveau **Casina delle Civette** has
been restored and was opened in 1997 as the **Museo della Vetrata** (open
9–17 except Mon; Lire 5000). Designed by Vincenzo Fasolo, it has interesting
stained glass by Cesare Picchiarini (1916–19) and the museum contains other
stained glass by Duilio Cambellotti. There is also a theatre built in 1841–74.
Several neo-Gothic garden buildings, which were built in the grounds in 1840
by Giuseppe Japelli, are due to be restored in the near future.

Sant'Agnese fuori le Mura

About 2km from Porta Pia, opposite a 19C fountain of the Acqua Marcia, stands
the church of Sant'Agnese fuori le Mura, in an important group of early
Christian buildings. These consist of the ruins of a large cemetery basilica built,
probably after Constantine's death, by his elder daughter Constantia in 337–50
on her estate next to the tomb where the martyred St Agnes was buried in 304.
Above the crypt sanctuary and catacombs, Honorius I (625–38) built a second
church, when the Constantinian basilica was already in ruins. Next to the
basilica (and with an entrance from its south aisle), Constantia built the
mausoleum in which she and her sister Helena were buried.

> According to a Christian tradition, St Agnes, having refused the advances of
> a praetor's son, was exposed in the Stadium of Domitian, where her naked-
> ness was covered by the miraculous growth of her hair. She was then

condemned to be burned at the stake, but the flames did not touch her, so that she was finally beheaded by Diocletian. The Pallium (or vestment) worn by the Pope is made of the wool of lambs blessed annually on the day of her festival, 21 January.

The most direct entrance is on Via Sant'Agnese, but you can also enter through the gate of the convent of the Canonici Lateranensi on Via Nomentana, from which the campanile of the basilica of Honorius and the small colonnaded front can be seen. On the right of the court is a hall (originally a cellar) into which Pius IX and his entourage fell unharmed after the collapse of the floor of the room above in 1855.

Beyond a tower is the entrance to the 7C **BASILICA OF SANT'AGNESE FUORI LE MURA** (open 9–12, 16–18; Sunday 16–18; closed Mon afternoon), restored in 1479 by Giuliano della Rovere (Julius II), by Cardinal Varallo after the sack of 1527, and by Pius IX in 1856. It is reached by a staircase of 45 white marble steps (1590), the walls of which are covered with inscriptions from the catacombs, including St Damasus's record of the martyrdom of St Agnes.

In the **interior** of the church (best light in the afternoon), the nave and aisles are separated by 14 ancient Roman columns of breccia and pavonazzetto. There is a narthex for the catechumens, and a matroneum was built over the aisles and the west end in 620. The carved and gilded wood ceiling dates from 1606 (restored in 1855). In the second chapel on the right, over a Cosmati altar, is a fine relief of St Stephen and St Laurence, by Andrea Bregno (1490), and a bust of Christ probably the work of Nicolas Cordier (a copy of a lost work by Michelangelo). There is also a 15C fresco of the Madonna and Child which has recently been restored—for the last centry it had been covered by a painting of the Madonna di Pompeii.

On the high altar, in which are preserved the relics of St Agnes and St Emerentiana, her foster-sister, is an antique torso of Oriental alabaster restored in 1600 as a statue of St Agnes, beneath a baldacchino (1614) supported on four porphyry columns. On the left of the altar is a fine candlestick, thought to be a neo-Attic work of the 2C. In the apse is the original plain marble decoration and an ancient episcopal throne. Above is a *mosaic (625–38), representing St Agnes between Popes Symmachus and Honorius I, two restorers of the basilica, a model of which is held by Honorius. The simplicity of the composition, against a dull gold background is striking. The dedicatory inscription below records how much Honorius spent on the church.

In the left aisle is the entrance to the **Catacombs of St Agnes**. The best preserved and among the most interesting Roman catacombs (open at the same time as the church, see above. Lire 8000), they were discovered in 1865–66. Visitors are conducted. The atmosphere in these catacombs, not normally visited by large groups, offers a striking contrast to that in the more famous catacombs on the Via Appia (see Chapter 17) which are usually crowded with tours. These contain no paintings but there are numerous inscriptions and many of the loculi are intact. They may date from before 258 but not later than 305; the oldest zone extends to the left of the basilica. A chapel was built where the body of St Agnes was found, and a silver coffer provided in 1615 by Pope Paul V.

On the other side of the entrance court a path leads to the round mausoleum of Constantia, known as the church of **SANTA COSTANZA** (open at the same

time as Sant'Agnese, see above; if closed apply at the sacristy in Sant'Agnese; it is often in use for weddings). This was built probably before 354 by Constantia as a mausoleum for herself and her sister Helena. The charming **interior** is annular in plan: 24 granite columns in pairs with beautiful Corinthian capitals and pulvinated imposts support the dome, which is 22.5m in diameter. There are 12 large windows with transennae beneath the dome. On the barrel vaulting of the encircling ambulatory are remarkable early Christian *mosaics (4C), pagan in character. They are designed in pairs on a white ground. Those flanking the entrance have a geometric design, and the next a circular motif with animals and figures. Vintage scenes and vine tendrils with grapes follow, and the fourth pair have roundels with a leaf design, busts and figures. On either side of the sarcophagus are leaves, branches, amphorae and exotic birds. Over the sarcophagus only a fragment remains of a mosaic with a star design. The two side niches also have fine mosaics (5C or 7C). The mosaics in the dome have been lost. Constantia's magnificent porphyry sarcophagus was replaced here by a cast when it was removed to the Vatican.

Two small gates on the right of the mausoleum lead into an overgrown garden and orchard with the remains of the huge **Constantinian basilica** (see above), identified in 1954. They include the outer walls with a round window in the apse, sustained on the outside by huge buttresses. In plan it was typical of the early cemetery basilicas of Rome, such as San Lorenzo fuori le Mura and San Sebastiano.

Beyond the church of Sant'Agnese, Via Nomentana continues northeast towards the river Aniene. On the right, incorporated in the garden wall of the Villa Blanc, is a 2C circular tomb looking like a small copy of the Mausoleum of Cecilia Metella. The gardens of the **Villa Blanc** were designated a public park in 1974, but are still not open to the public and are in a state of abandon. The villa, built in an eclectic style with Art Nouveau elements, is in urgent need of repair.

The road crosses the river Aniene, the ancient *Anio* which rises near Tivoli, by the modern Ponte Tazio. On the right is the Roman **Ponte Nomentano**, rebuilt by Narses in 552 and guarded by a medieval watchtower. Beyond the river is the dismal modern Quartiere di Monte Sacro, named after the *Mons Sacer* (37m), which rises to the right.

20 · Via Salaria (Villa Torlonia and the Catacombs of Priscilla)

■ The Catacombs of Priscilla, a long way from the centre of the city, can be reached from Termini station by bus No. 56 (nearest stop, Via di Priscilla).

Piazza Fiume (Pl. 12; 7) is on the site of the Roman *Porta Salaria*. The gate no longer exists but the bases of two tombs in the square define its width. Here begins the VIA SALARIA (Pl. 12; 7, 5, 4, 2; one-way south), one of the oldest Roman roads. Some 300m outside the gate it passes the large park with umbrella pines (right) of **VILLA TORLONIA** (Pl. 12; 5, 6), formerly *Albani*, built in 1760 by Carlo Marchionni for Cardinal Alessandro Albani, whose valuable

collection of classical sculpture was arranged here in 1765 by Winckelmann, the German archaeologist who had become superintendent of Roman antiquities in 1763. By order of Napoleon 294 pieces of this collection were taken to Paris; after Waterloo nearly all of them were sold at Munich instead of being returned. The rest of the collection continued to increase, and in 1852 it passed into the possession of the Chigi. In 1866 it was bought, with the villa, by Princess Alessandra Torlonia. Visitors are sometimes admitted (except in Aug), but only after previous written application to the Amministrazione Torlonia, 30 Via della Conciliazione. There is another villa of the same name on the Via Nomentana (p 266).

The **Casino**, surrounded by a formal garden, has a hemicycle with 40 Doric columns. In the portico are niches with busts of Roman emperors. Beyond an atrium with caryatids, the first gallery has a collection of herms. The staircase, with Roman reliefs, leads up to the **Oval Hall** with a statue of an athlete, signed by Stephanos (1C BC). In the **Great Hall** the *ceiling painting of Parnassos is by Raphael Mengs. Here is displayed the *Albani Pallas*, a statue of the Attic school. In the **Right Wing** are paintings by Alunno, Perugino, Giovanni Paolo Pannini, Honthorst, Pompeo Batoni, Van Dyck, Taddeo Zuccari, Tintoretto, Ribera and Guercino.

The **Left Wing** has a *relief of Antinous, from Hadrian's villa, the only piece brought back from Paris in 1815; the so-called *Leucothea*, a relief dating from the beginning of the 5C BC; a 5C *relief of a battle scene, showing the influence of Pheidias; the *Apollo Auroktonos*, an ancient copy after Praxiteles; a bust of Quintus Hortensius; and the *Apotheosis of Hercules*, in the style of the Tabula Iliaca in the Capitoline Museum. The so called *Aesop* is a naturalistic nude statue of a hunchback, possibly a portrait of a court dwarf of the time of Hadrian. The paintings include sketches by Giulio Romano of the story of Psyche in Palazzo del Te at Mantua, and works by Borgognone, Luca Giordano and Gaspare Vanvitelli. On the ground floor is the **Stanza della Colonna**, a room with 12 fine columns (one fluted, in alabaster), in which is displayed a *sarcophagus, with a scene of the marriage of Peleus and Thetis, considered by Winckelmann to be one of the finest in existence. The **Kaffehaus** contains Roman mosaics.

Opposite Villa Torlonia is the circular Mausoleum of Lucilius Peto, dating from the time of Augustus. Via Salaria continues to the road junction with Viale Regina Margherita (right) and Viale Liegi (left) which leads to Parioli (see p 297), a fashionable residential district of the city.

Via Salaria continues past St George's English School (left), and now widens with a line of pines down the centre. Via Panama skirts the wall of the vast expanse of VILLA ADA (formerly Savoia; Pl. 12; 1, 2), the garden wall of which extends for a long way along Via Salaria. This was once the private residence of Vittorio Emanuele III, and is now the Egyptian embassy. Part of the grounds are open as a public park.

At 430 Via Salaria is the entrance to the **CATACOMBS OF PRISCILLA** (Pl. 12; 2; usually open 8.30 to 12.30 and 14.30 (or 15) to dusk; closed Mon, and in Jan. ☎ 862 06272), the most important catacombs on Via Salaria, and among the most interesting in Rome. Visitors are taken in groups by an English-speaking nun. The exit is usually on the other side of Via Salaria. A villa of the Roman family of Acilii probably existed above the cemetery, to which the cryp-

toporticus (with cross-vaulting and remains of Pompeian-style frescoes) and a nymphaeum may have belonged. Many popes were buried here between 309 and 555.

The so-called **Greek Chapel** (from the Greek inscriptions found here) is an interesting funerary chapel with frescoes (probably late 3C) of biblical scenes and good stucco decoration. A banquet scene on the apse arch includes the figure of a woman. In the area of the 'arenario' (probably a pozzolana stone quarry) is the Cubiculum of the Velati, with late 3C scenes from the life of a deceased woman, including one of a woman and child.

Via Salaria continues north and a byroad leads left to **Monte Antenne**, the site of the ancient Sabine town of *Antemnae*, said to have been founded by the Siculi. It had probably already disappeared by the time of the kings. At the foot of the hill, with an approach road from the Parioli district, is Rome's first **Mosque**, built in 1984–93, designed by Paolo Portoghesi, Vittorio Gigliotti and Sami Monsawi. The mosque, which can hold up to 3000 people and is the largest in Europe, was financed by some 24 Arab countries. There is also a cultural centre and library here.

Via Salaria crosses the Aniene, near its confluence with the Tiber, by the Roman **Ponte Salario**, rebuilt in 565 by Narses, and then reconstructed after it was blown up by papal troops in 1867. Only two side arches are original.

21 · Trastevere

Trastevere (Pl. 7; 2, 4), the area 'across the Tiber' (*trans Tiberim*), has been, since the Middle Ages, essentially the popular district of Rome, and its inhabitants seem to retain the characteristics of the ancient Romans, who are said to have been proud and independent. This area of the city has been distinguished by its numerous artisans' houses and workshops since Roman times. In the last 20 years or so it has become a fashionable place to live, and it now has a cosmopolitan atmosphere.

In earliest Republican days this bank of the Tiber was occupied by Lars Porsena in his attempt to replace the Tarquins on the Roman throne. Under the Empire it became densely populated by artisans and dock-workers. On the higher ground, and along the waterfront, suburban villas were built by the aristocracy. These included the houses of Agrippa and of Clodia, both of which have been identified with the late Republican villa excavated in 1880 next to the Villa Farnesina (and then destroyed), the magnificent wall-paintings of which are preserved in the Museo Nazionale Romano. Trastevere was home to a great number of Jews before they were confined to the Ghetto. It was the stronghold of independence during the Risorgimento; here Mazzini found support for his Republic of 1849, and here in 1867 Giuditta Tavani Arquati, with her family, made an attempt to incite the city on Garibaldi's behalf. In July, the lively festival of 'Noantri' ('we others') takes place here.

The **Tiber**, or *Tevere* (418km long), is the most famous though not the longest of the rivers of Italy. It is said originally to have been called *Albula* and to have received the name of *Tiberis* from Tiberinus, king of Alba Longa, who was drowned in its waters. It rises in the Tuscan Apennines, northeast of Arezzo and, is fed by numerous mountain streams. The embankments and 'Lungotevere' roads were built in the late 19C to avoid floods. Its swift waters are discoloured with yellow mud, even far from its source: hence the epithet *flavus* ('fair' or 'tawny') given to it by the Roman poets. There are long-term plans to clean its polluted waters.

Ponte Garibaldi (Pl. 7; 2), a modern bridge, with small obelisks, leads to the busy PIAZZA GIOACCHINO BELLI, named after the Roman poet (1791–1863) who wrote popular verses and satirical sonnets in the the Roman dialect. The monument which shows him in a frock coat and top hat, is by Michele Tripisciano (1913). Here begins the wide and traffic-ridden Viale Trastevere. On the left is the over-restored 13C **Palazzetto Anguillara**, with its corner tower, the last of many which once guarded Trastevere. The picturesque courtyard is a modern reconstruction using ancient material. The building is now the Casa di Dante (tablet), where readings from the *Divina Commedia* have been given by leading Italian men of letters since 1914 (now on Sun Nov–mid-Mar, 11–12). The library has the best collection in Italy of works relating to the poet.

On the other side of the Viale is the church of **SAN CRISOGONO** (Pl. 7; 4), founded in the 5C and rebuilt by John of Crema between 1123 and 1130. It was reconstructed by Giovanni Battista Soria in 1623 and restored in 1866. The campanile dates from the 12C. In the **interior** (open 7–11.30, 16–19) are 22 ancient Roman Ionic columns separating the nave from the aisles; the triumphal arch is supported by two huge monolithic porphyry columns. The baldacchino by Giovanni Battista Soria rests on four columns of yellow alabaster. The 13C opus sectile pavement has been restored. A mosaic in a square frame in the apse, attributed to the school of Pietro Cavallini, depicts the Madonna and Child between Saints James and Chrysogonus. Beneath the church (entered through the sacristy in the left aisle, down a steep spiral iron staircase unlocked by the sacristan on request; small donation) is an interesting 5C **early Christian church**, on the site of a late Imperial Roman edifice. The annular crypt was added by Gregory III (731–41); its mural decoration survives, as well as later frescoes and a number of fine sarcophagi.

Behind the church is the huge hospital of San Gallicano, a remarkable utilitarian building by Filippo Raguzzini (1724). The handsome long low façade, with the two floors divided by a balcony, incorporates a church in the centre.

The description below follows a somewhat circuitous route through old Trastevere to the church of Santa Cecilia (Pl. 8; 3); the direct approach to this church is via Via dei Genovesi which runs left from Viale Trastevere.

Across Viale Trastevere the old Via della Lungaretta leads east on the line of the last stretch of the ancient Roman Via Aurelia. The first turning on the right, in Piazza del Drago (Via di Monte Fiore), leads to the **Guardroom of the Seventh Cohort of Vigiles** (Roman firemen). Remains can be seen from the street: the interior (entrance at 9 Via della VII Coorte) can only be seen with special permission (by writing to the Ripartizione X del Comune, 29 Via Portico d'Ottavia, 00100 Rome; fax 689 2115; ☎ 671 03819). It contains interesting

graffiti referring to reigning emperors, from Severus to Giordian III, and a bath or nymphaeum. The barracks were built on the site of a 2C private house.

Via della Lungaretta continues to Piazza in Piscinula (Pl. 8; 3). In the far corner on the right is the small church of **San Benedetto**, with a charming 11C roofed campanile. (If closed, ring at the door to the right of the façade.) On the left of the vestibule, a fine doorway leads into an ancient cross-vaulted cell, in which St Benedict is said to have lived. To the left of the entrance door is a detached 13C fresco of St Benedict (restored). Inside, eight antique columns with diverse capitals divide the nave from the aisles. The fine pavement is Cosmatesque. Above the altar is a 15C painting of St Benedict, and a damaged fresco of the Madonna and Child (15C). Opposite is the medieval **Casa dei Mattei** (restored), with a 15C loggia, and 14C cross-mullioned windows.

Via dell'Arco dei Tolomei leads out of the other side of the piazza through an arch, and Via dei Salumi diverges left. A short way along on the right is Vicolo dell'Atleta (interesting house at No. 14 where the bronze horse now in the Capitoline Museum, and the statue of the Apoxyomenos now in the Vatican, were found), which leads to Via dei Genovesi, and its extension (left), Via Augusto Jandolio. Immediately opposite is a house (Nos 9, 10) with wooden eaves (characteristic of this area). To the left, at the end of the street, can be seen the church of Santa Maria in Cappella (No. 6), dating from 1090, with a contemporary campanile. The lovely old Vicolo di Santa Maria in Cappella leads to Piazza dei Mercanti (with fine 15C houses, including one on the right recently over-restored). The piazza now has several restaurants (not cheap).

Santa Cecilia in Trastevere

In the piazza to the right is the church of Santa Cecilia in Trastevere (Pl. 8; 3; open 10–12, 16–18), on the site of the house of St Cecilia and her husband St Valerian, whom she converted to Christianity. This building was adapted to Christian use probably in the 5C, and the body of St Cecilia was transferred here and a basilica erected by Paschal I (817–24). The church, radically altered from the 16C onwards, was partly restored to its original form in 1899–1901. The slightly leaning campanile dates from 1120.

> St Cecilia, a patrician lady of the gens Cornelia, was martyred in 230, during the reign of Alexander Severus. She was shut up in the calidarium of her own baths (see below), to be scalded to death. Emerging unscathed, she was beheaded in her own house, but the executioner did such a bad job that she lived for three days afterwards. She was buried in the Catacombs of St Calixtus, where her body remained until its reinterment in her church in 820. As the inventor of the organ, she is the patron saint of music. On 22 November churches hold musical services in her honour.

Beyond an elaborate **façade** attributed to Ferdinando Fuga (1725) is the **atrium**, with a fountain made from a large antique marble basin for ceremonial ablutions in a lovely garden. The **portico** with four antique Ionic columns bearing a frieze of 12C mosaic medallions, precedes the Baroque façade of the church. The **interior**, an aisled 18C hall whose piers (1823) enclose the original columns, contains a ceiling fresco of the Coronation of St Cecilia by Sebastiano Conca. **West wall**. On the left of the door: *monument of Cardinal

Niccolò Forteguerri (died 1473), who assisted Pius II and Paul II in their suppression of the great feudal clans—a beautiful work attributed to Mino da Fiesole (restored in 1891). On the other side of the door: tomb of Cardinal Adam Easton (died 1398), a distinguished English churchman who was appointed cardinal in 1381, deposed by Urban VI (c 1386), and reappointed by Boniface IX in 1389. It bears the arms of England and may be the work of Paolo Taccone.

South aisle. In the first chapel (being restored): fresco of the Crucifixion (?14C). A corridor (closed indefinitely), with landscapes by Paul Brill and a marble figure of St Sebastian attributed to Lorenzetto, leads to the ancient **calidarium** (also closed), where St Cecilia was to be scalded to death by steam but was miraculously preserved. The steam conduits are still visible. On the altar is the *Beheading of St Cecilia*, and opposite, *Saints Cecilia and Valerian*, by Guido Reni. Also off the south aisle opens the **Cappella dei Ponziani**, with ceiling frescoes and, on the walls, Saints, all by Pastura, as well as a Cosmatesque altar. The 18C Cappella delle Reliquie is by Luigi Vanvitelli. The last chapel contains the theatrical tomb (1929) of Cardinal Rampolla, who was responsible for the excavations beneath the church. A small room preceding it contained a tondo of the Madonna by Perugino, stolen in 1993. In the chapel at the end of the aisle is a very damaged 12C–13C fresco detached from the portico showing the *Discovery of the body of St Cecilia*.

In the **sanctuary** is a fine *baldacchino (1293), signed by Arnolfo di Cambio. Beneath the altar is a celebrated *statue of St Cecilia, by Stefano Maderno. The body of the saint is represented lying as it was found when her tomb was opened in 1599, on which occasion the sculptor was present. The luminous 9C *mosaic in the **apse** shows Christ blessing by the Greek rite, between (right) Saints Peter, Valerian and Cecilia, and (left) Saints Paul, Agatha and Paschal (the last with the square nimbus); below are the flock of the Faithful and the Holy Cities. In the **north aisle**, the fourth, third and second altarpieces are by Giovanni Baglione, and the first altarpiece is by Giovanni Ghezzi.

The **Roman edifices beneath the church** are entered from the west end of the north aisle (open at the same time as the church. Lire 2000). The excavations have not yet been fully explained, but are generally thought to consist of two Roman houses (possibly including the house of St Cecilia), probably amalgamated in the 4C for Christian use. Some scholars also believe there are remains here of an early Christian basilica. In the various rooms are mosaic pavements and a number of Christian sarcophagi. A 2C room with seven huge basins in the floor was probably used as a tannery. Another room, with Republican columns, contains a niche with a relief of Minerva in front of an altar. A frescoed room (not yet open to the public) was discovered in 1991 with an ancient large font for total immersion. The **crypt** is decorated in the Byzantine style by Giovanni Battista Giovenale (1899–1901), with luminous mosaics by Giuseppe Bravi. Behind a grille are the sarcophagi of St Cecilia, St Valerian and his brother St Tiburtius, St Maximus, and the Popes Lucius I and Urban I. The statue of St Cecilia is by Cesare Aureli.

Inside the **convent** (also entered from the west end of the north aisle; but only open to visitors on Tues and Thur 10–11.30), in the nuns' choir can be seen the splendid *****fresco** of the *Last Judgement* by Pietro Cavallini, a masterpiece of medieval Roman fresco painting (c 1293). This used to be the inside façade of the old church.

From Piazza Santa Cecilia, Via di San Michele leads right. It is fronted by the long bright orange façade of the huge building of the former Istituto San Michele a Ripa (Pl. 8; 3), seat of the Ministero per i Beni Culturali e Ambientali (Cultural Ministry) since 1983, and of the Istituto Centrale del Restauro since 1976. Restoration of this huge complex has almost been completed; it is used for exhibitions and conferences.

The site was purchased in 1686 by Monsignor Tommaso Odescalchi, nephew of Innocent XI, who here founded a hospice and training centre for orphans and vagabond children, built by Carlo Fontana. In 1701 Fontana added a prison building. The façade of the huge building facing the Tiber was completed after Fontana's death by Nicola Michetti. In 1734 Ferdinando Fuga added a women's prison (the prison buildings were in use up to 1870). Numerous artisans' workshops were later installed here, and a renowned tapestry manufactory. The buildings were purchased by the State in 1969 and restoration work was begun in 1973. It is also now the headquarters of the International Center for the Study of the Preservation and Restoration of Cultural Property created by UNESCO in 1956.

The entrance at 22 Via San Michele leads into a large courtyard with a fountain. To the left is a second courtyard, off which is the **Chiesa Grande**, begun in 1713 on a Greek-cross plan by Carlo Fontana, and finished in 1835 by Luigi Poletti, who added the Neo-classical choir. The statue of the Saviour here is by Adamo Tadolini.

At the far end of the building of the former Istituto San Michele, the Tiber is crossed by **Ponte Aventino**. The original bridge at this point, the *Pons Sublicius*, was the first bridge across the Tiber; it is said to have been built by Ancus Marcius, fourth king of Rome, to connect the Janiculum with the city. From the bridge there is a good view of the Roman **port** lining the opposite bank of the Tiber along Lungotevere Testaccio. Here in 193–174 BC a market was constructed, backed by the *Porticus Aemilia*, a wharf with extensive storehouses some 500m in length.

To the right, on this side of the Tiber, the Porta Portese, built by Urban VIII (1623–44) replaces the former *Porta Portuensis*, dating from the time of Honorius. The famous **Porta Portese flea market** (the largest of its kind) is further south, near Stazione Trastevere. Open only on Sunday mornings, 7–13.

From Piazza di Santa Cecilia (see above), Via di Santa Cecilia leads to Via dei Genovesi, which leads left to the church of **San Giovanni Battista dei Genovesi** (1481; restored). The remarkable 15C **cloister** is entered along Via Anicia on the left (ring at No. 12, Tues and Thur, 14–16; summer, except Aug, 15–18). It has an arcaded lower gallery and a trabeated upper storey, and a beautiful garden of orange trees. Via Anicia continues past (right), the church of **Santa Maria dell'Orto**, with an unusual façade attributed to Vignola, crowned with obelisks, and an ornate interior containing 17C and 18C works.

Via Anicia ends in Piazza San Francesco d'Assisi, in which is the church of **San Francesco a Ripa** (Pl. 7; 4; open 7–12, 16–19), built in 1231 to replace the old hospice of San Biagio, where St Francis stayed in 1219. The last chapel on the left has the famous *statue of Beata Lodovica Albertoni, showing her in a

state of mystical ecstasy. It is a late work by Bernini, displayed effectively by concealed lighting. Above is an altarpiece by Baciccia. The Cell of St Francis (apply at the sacristy), contains relics (displayed in an ingenious reliquary), and a 13C painting of the saint.

Via Tavolacci rejoins Viale Trastevere, across which Via Morosini leads past the right side of the Ministero di Pubblica Istruzione (Ministry of Education). Via Roma Libera is the first road to the right, and here, at No. 76 is the **Ospedale Nuovo di Regina Margherita** (formerly the convent of San Cosimato). It has a beautiful 12C cloister with twin columns and, in a garden on the left, the church of **San Cosimato** (open only for services, 7 and 11) dating from the 10C and rebuilt in 1475. It has a good doorway, and contains (on the left of the altar) a 15C fresco of the Virgin with Saints, and the tomb of Cardinal Alderano Cybo (died 1550), ascribed to Iacopo Sansovino (this is now a second altar in a chapel to the left). The second cloister has 15C octagonal columns. From Via Roma Libera the original narthex can be seen, and beyond is Piazza San Cosimato with a food market (Mon–Sat, 8–13).

Via di San Cosimato leads north via Piazza San Calisto to PIAZZA DI SANTA MARIA IN TRASTEVERE (Pl. 7; 4), the characteristic centre of Trastevere. The handsome **fountain**, of Roman origin, was restored by Carlo Fontana (1692). Palazzo di San Calisto on the left of the church, was rebuilt in the 17C by Orazio Torriani.

Santa Maria in Trastevere

The large basilica of Santa Maria in Trastevere (Pl. 7; 4) was constructed by Julius II (337–52), and was probably the first church in Rome dedicated to the Virgin. According to legend a hostel for veteran soldiers existed near the site, and some sort of Christian foundation is known to have existed here under St Calixtus (pope, 217–22). The great basilica of Julius II was rebuilt by Innocent II in 1140, and slightly modified later. The church and its works of art were restored in 1983–96. The campanile is Romanesque.

The **façade** bears a 12C–13C mosaic of the Madonna surrounded by ten female figures with lamps (two of which are extinguished), of uncertain significance. The **portico** added by Carlo Fontana in 1702 (and recently restored) contains an interesting lapidary collection, including Roman and medieval fragments. The worn frescoes of the Annunciation date from the 15C. The three doorways incorporate Roman friezes.

In the splendid 12C **interior** (open 7–12.45, 15–18.45) are 21 vast ancient columns from various Roman buildings, some with fine bases and (damaged) capitals. The opus sectile *pavement is made up from old material; the wooden *ceiling was designed by Domenichino (1617), who painted the central *Assumption*. The decoration on the walls of the nave and triumphal arch was carried out when the church was remodelled by Pius IX in the 19C. The charming tabernacle at the beginning of the south aisle is by Mino del Reame. In the north aisle is the tomb of Innocent II (died 1143), erected by Pius IX in 1869, and the **Avila Chapel**, designed by Antonio Gherardi (1680–86), with a remarkable Baroque dome and very unusual altar.

The **choir** is preceded by a marble screen made up of transennae and plutei, many of them remade in the 19C. Near a Paschal candlestick here is the spot on which a miraculous fountain of oil is supposed to have flowed throughout a

whole day in the year of Christ's Nativity in the Roman building (see above). The baldacchino over the high altar is by Virginio Vespignani. The *mosaics of the triumphal arch and apse (1140) are particularly fine: on the arch, the *Cross with the symbolic Alpha and Omega* between the seven candlesticks and the Evangelical emblems; at the sides, *Isaiah and Jeremiah*, with the rare and touching symbol of the caged bird, representing Christ imprisoned because of the sins of man ('*Christus Dominus captus est in peccatis nostris*'—Lamentations of Jeremiah, Ch IV, v 20). In the semi-dome, *Christ and the Virgin enthroned* beneath the hand of God bearing a wreath and the monogram of Constantine. On the right, *Saints Peter, Cornelius, Julius and Calepodius*; on the left *Saints Calixtus and Laurence, and Pope Innocent II* with a model of the church. Lower are six rectangles with mosaic *scenes from the Life of Mary*, by Pietro Cavallini (c 1291), and, beneath them a mosaic rectangle with *Saints Peter and Paul presenting the donor*, Bertoldo Stefaneschi, to the Madonna (1290). Beneath the mosaics in the apse are late 16C frescoes by Agostino Ciampelli.

To the right of the choir are the Armellini monument (1524), with sculptures by Michelangelo Senese, and the **Chapel of the Winter Choir**, with decorations after Domenichino's designs. The chapel was restored by Henry of York in the 18C. The huge 16C organ is to be restored. To the left of the choir is the **Altemps Chapel**, decorated with frescoes and stuccoes by Pasquale Cati (1588), including an interesting scene of the Council of Trent. On the altar is a photograph of a precious *painting of the *Madonna 'della Clemenza'*, flanked by angels, displayed since its restoration in a little room on the left (seen through a glass door). This remarkable Byzantine work is thought to date from the 8C, or earlier. On the left wall outside the chapel is the tomb of Cardinal Stefaneschi (died 1417) by 'Magister Paulus', beside the monument to Cardinal Filippo d'Alençon (died 1397) which includes his effigy and the relief of the Dormition of the Virgin, also attributed to 'Magister Paulus' or a follower of Orcagna. The **sacristy**, approached by a passage with two exquisite tiny 1C Roman mosaics from Palestrina, one of *marsh birds and the other a port scene, contains a Madonna with Saints Sebastian and Roch of the Umbrian School (very worn).

Via della Paglia skirts the north side of the church. To the right opens Piazza Sant'Egidio, where, at No. 1B there is a **Folklore Museum** (closed for restoration). On the first floor are drawings and engravings of Roman street scenes and views by Bartolomeo Pinelli, and (in the gallery to the right) paintings of 19C Rome, including works by Ippolito Caffi, and Gino Severini (1903). At the end are a series of charming life-size tableaux of Roman scenes by Orazio Amato (1884–1952) based on paintings by Bartolomeo Pinelli. Beyond a room with more engravings, wooden stairs lead up to the reconstructed studio of the poet 'Trilussa' (Carlo Alberto Salustri, 1871–1950). Two more rooms have watercolours of Rome painted in 1878 by Ettore Roesler Franz, and in the last room are some objects from the studio of the musician Maestro Alessandro Vessella (1860–1929). The building is also used as a cultural centre.

Via della Scala leads out of the piazza past the ornate church of **Santa Maria della Scala** (1592), containing (over the first altar on the right), *St John the Baptist* by Honthorst, and a ciborium over the high altar by Carlo Rainaldi (1647). If closed, the church can be entered through the Carmelite Monastery (right) which adjoins the **Pharmacy of Santa Maria della Scala**, adminis-

tered by the monks. Currently being restored, the old 17C pharmacy upstairs may sometimes be seen on request (ring at the door on the left). Via della Scala ends at Porta Settimiana (Pl. 7; 2), incorporated in the Aurelian Wall and rebuilt by Alexander VI (1492–1503).

The street to the right, just before the gate, is Via Santa Dorotea. At No. 20 is the medieval Casa della Fornarina, the supposed house of Raphael's mistress. Other houses of this type may be seen in Vicolo dei Moroni. Via di Ponte Sisto leads to **Ponte Sisto** (pedestrians only), erected for Sixtus IV (1471–84), probably by Baccio Pontelli, to replace the ancient *Pons Janiculensis* (or the *Pons Antoninus*).

The unusual and attractive Via Garibaldi leads uphill from the gate towards the Janiculum (see Chapter 22). At the end of the first straight section of the road (before a sharp turn to the left) is the entrance at No. 27 to the convent of **Santa Maria dei Sette Dolori**. The church was begun by Borromini in 1643, and its unfinished façade (1646) can be seen through the gate. The vestibule and interior of the church are entered through the convent (door to the right of the façade). The church is oblong with rounded ends, with two apses in the middle of the long sides, and a continuous series of pillars connected by a heavy cornice. The disappointing interior decoration was added later in the 17C.

Porta Settimiana marks the beginning of VIA DELLA LUNGARA (Pl. 7; 2, 1), the longest of the long straight streets built by the Renaissance popes. It was laid out c 1507 by Julius II to connect Trastevere with the Borgo. On the left is the building which houses the **Museo Torlonia**, considered to be the most important private collection of ancient sculpture in existence. For years closed 'for restoration', the interior was converted into flats in the 1970s and the works put in store. In 1977 the palace and collection were officially sequestered, and interminable bureaucratic procedures took place in an attempt by the State to acquire the collection. It has never been reopened (for further information apply to the Amministrazione Torlonia, 30 Via della Conciliazione).

The museum was founded by Gian Raimondo Torlonia (1754–1829) with sculptures from Roman collections, to which were added later the yields from excavations on the family estates at Cerveteri, Vulci, Porto, etc. There are over 620 pieces of sculpture, some over-restored, including a few Greek originals. The most important works include the *Giustiniani Hestia*, a splendid statue attributed to Kalamis (5C BC), and a bas-relief of Herakles liberating Theseus and Peirithöos (school of Pheidias; 4C BC). There are numerous Roman copies of works by Greek sculptors, notably Kephisodotos, Polykleitos, Praxiteles and Lysippos. Of the Roman originals perhaps the most striking is a portrait statue of Lucilla, daughter of Marcus Aurelius. The Roman iconographic collection contains over one hundred busts of the Imperial era. The valuable Etruscan paintings (4C BC) are from Vulci. There is also a very fine collection of sarcophagi.

At the end of Via Corsini (No. 24) is the **Orto Botanico** (open 9–18.30; winter 9–17.30; closed Sun. ☎ 686 4193. Lire 4000), founded on the Janiculum in 1660, but on this site only since 1883 when Tommaso Corsini donated the gardens of Palazzo Corsini, on the slopes of the hill, to the State. One of the most important botanical gardens in Italy, it covers some 12 hectares and is beautifully kept. It is famous for its palms and yuccas. A rare collection of orchids is kept in one of the 19C greenhouses.

Galleria Nazionale d'Arte Antica

In Via della Lungara, just beyond Via Corsini, on the left, is **PALAZZO CORSINI** (Pl. 7; 1, 2), built by Cardinal Domenico Riario in the 15C, and rebuilt by Ferdinando Fuga for Cardinal Neri Maria Corsini, nephew of Clement XII, in 1732–36. The palace had been the residence of Queen Christina of Sweden, who died here in 1689. In 1797 General Duphot was killed near here in a skirmish between the French democratic party and the papal dragoons, and in 1800 Madame Letizia, mother of Napoleon, came to live in the palace.

Cardinal Corsini's fine collection of paintings was acquired by the State in 1883 and became part of the Galleria Nazionale d'Arte Antica (which is now divided between this palace and Palazzo Barberini, see Chapter 10). The original Corsini collection (Inventory nos 1–606) has been returned here. The present arrangement is extremely crowded, but more rooms may eventually be opened to the public. The pictures are all labelled.

■ Open 9–14; Sun 9–13; closed Mon. ☎ 688 02323. Lire 8000.

On the **First Floor** is a **vestibule** with Neo-classical sculptures by John Gibson, Antonio Solà, Pietro Tenerani, and others.

Room I. Portraits of the Corsini, and a bust of Clement XII Corsini by Pietro Bracci. Pompeo Batoni, *Nativity*; Sebastiano Conca, *Adoration of the Magi*; Francesco Trevisani, *Nymphs and satyrs*; two 18C bronze statuettes.

Room II. 558. Giovanni da Milano, *Madonna and Child* and scenes from the Life of Christ; *464. Murillo, *Madonna and Child*, one of the finest versions by the painter of this familiar subject; works by David Teniers the Younger, and Marten van Cleve; 111. Van Dyck, *Madonna and Child*, probably painted during his stay in Italy; 388. Rubens, *St Sebastian tended by angels*; 350. Pourbus the Younger, *Portrait of a man*; 347. Joos van Cleve, *Portrait of Bernardo Clesio*; 354. Perino del Vaga, *Portrait of Cardinal Alessandro Farnese*; 318. Federico Barocci, *Self-portrait*; 140. Titian, *Philip II of Spain*; 193. Jacopo Bassano, *Adoration of the shepherds*; Franciabigio, 99. *Madonna and Child*, 488. *Portrait of a man*; 221. 16C Roman school, *La Fornarina*; 116. Fra Bartolomeo, *Holy Family*; 397, 396, 395. Fra Angelico, triptych; 436. Francesco Francia, *St George and the dragon*; 686. Alessandro Algardi, *Baptism of Christ* (small bronze).

Room III (ahead). Works by Michelangelo Cerquozzi and Simon Vouet; 441. Gerard Seghers, *Judith with the head of Holofernes*; *107. Orazio Gentileschi, *Madonna and Child*; *433. Caravaggio, *St John the Baptist*. **Room IV**. Works by Callot, Van Bloemen, Luca Carlevaris, Gaspard Dughet (386. Landscape), and Jan de Momper (73, 75. Landscapes).

Room V survives from the old Palazzo Riario. It is decorated by a follower of the Zuccari brothers. Queen Christina of Sweden is supposed to have died in this room in 1689; her portrait as Diana by Justus van Egmont (c 1656) was placed here in 1991. A terracotta bust of Alessandro VII Chigi attributed to Bernini is also exhibited here, as well as works by Jan Miel and Michael Sweerts. **Room VI**. In the centre is the Corsini throne, dating from the 2C or 1C BC and present in the palace since 1700. 186. Francesco Furini, *Andromeda*; 371. Baciccio, *Portrait of Cardinal Corsini*.

Room VII has a splendid view of the palm trees in the Botanical Gardens (see above), and of the Garibaldi monument on the Janiculum Hill. Here are

displayed: Sassoferrato, *Madonna and Child*; 279, 287. Guercino, *Madonna and Angel*, and *Annunciation*; 79. Donato Creti, *Jacob's Dream*; works by Giovanni Lanfranco; Guido Reni, 222. *St Joseph*, 191. *Salome with the head of the Baptist*; 482. *St Jerome*. **Room VIII**. Works by Salvator Rosa, including (484.) *Prometheus*; Mattia Preti, 1154. *Aeneas and Anchises*, 117. *Tribute Money*; works by Luca Giordano, including (394.) *Jesus in the Temple*.

The palace also houses the **Accademia Nazionale dei Lincei**, founded by Prince Federico Cesi in 1603 for the promotion of learning, and said to be the oldest surviving institution of its kind. Galileo was a Lincean. The administrative offices are in the Villa Farnesina (see below). With it are incorporated the Biblioteca dell'Accademia (1848), with 100,000 volumes and other publications, the Biblioteca Corsiniana, founded in 1754 by Monsignor Lorenzo Corsini, with a valuable collection of incunabula, manuscripts and autographs, and the Fondazione Caetani, whose object is to promote scientific knowledge in the Muslim world.

Opposite Palazzo Corsini is the entrance to the graceful Renaissance **VILLA FARNESINA** (Pl. 7; 2), built by Baldassare Peruzzi (1508–11), as the suburban residence of Agostino Chigi, 'the Magnificent', the Sienese banker who controlled the markets of the East. It is surrounded by a lovely garden, once much larger. Open 9–13, except Sun. ☎ 683 8831. Lire 6000.

Here Agostino Chigi entertained in grandeur Pope Leo X, cardinals, ambassadors, artists and men of letters. He was a patron of Raphael, and died on 10 April 1520, just four days after the artist. At a celebrated banquet in a loggia overlooking the Tiber (demolished in the 19C), as a demonstration of Chigi's extravagance silver plates and dishes were thrown into the river after every course (although it was later learned that a net had been in position to recover them). In 1590 the villa passed to Cardinal Alessandro Farnese, and received its present name, and through the Farnese it was inherited by the Bourbons of Naples in 1731. Since 1927 it has been the property of the State, and houses the administrative offices of the Accademia dei Lincei (see above).

The painted decoration in the villa was carried out between 1510 and 1519. On the ground floor is the festive **Loggia of Cupid and Psyche** (which has been reopened after years of restoration), which formerly opened directly on to the garden. The ceiling has famous frescoes illustrating the legend of Apuleius in a beautiful painted pergola with festoons of fruit and flowers. The decorative programme was provided by Raphael (who probably also made the preparatory cartoons), and the paintings executed by his pupils, Giulio Romano, Francesco Penni, Giovanni da Udine and Raffaellino del Colle. To the right is the **Loggia of the Galatea**. The ceiling is frescoed by Peruzzi with the constellations forming the horoscope of Agostino Chigi. The lunettes, with scenes from Ovid's *Metamorphoses*, are by Sebastiano del Piombo, although the colossal monochrome charcoal head here, a striking work, is now ascribed to Peruzzi. On the walls: the giant *Polyphemus* by Sebastiano del Piombo, and the celebrated *Galatea by Raphael, a superb composition. The latter interrupts the decorative sequence and seems to have been painted just after the works by Sebastiano. The

other scenes were added in the 17C by Gaspard Dughet. A little room off the loggia, known as the Sala del Fregio, contains a beautifully painted frieze with mythological scenes by Peruzzi.

On the upper floor is the **Sala delle Prospettive**, the drawing room, with charming trompe l'oeil views of Rome and mythological subjects by Peruzzi. The bedroom, known as the **Sala delle Nozze di Alessandro e Rossana**, contains *frescoes by Sodoma.

Superb wall-paintings and stuccoes found in a Roman house in the grounds of the villa are kept in the Museo Nazionale Romano. On the second floor of the Villa Farnesina is the **Gabinetto Nazionale delle Stampe** (open 9–13 except Sun and Mon. ☎ 699 801. Free), with an exceptionally fine collection of prints and drawings housed in a series of beautiful rooms. Exhibitions are held here periodically. In 1975 this institute was merged with the Calcografia Nazionale as the Istituto Nazionale per la Grafica, and there are plans to move it to Palazzo Poli, in Piazza di Trevi.

Via della Lungara continues along the right bank of the Tiber past the Regina Coeli prison (1881–1900) and the 16C Palazzo Salviati to Piazza della Rovere (Pl. 2; 5). The Borgo beyond is described in Chapter 23.

22 · The Janiculum Hill

■ The Janiculum is crossed by bus No. 41 from Corso Vittorio Emanuele (Via Paola), near the Tiber (Pl. 2; 5). By foot the prettiest approach is from Trastevere (Via Garibaldi, or Vicolo del Cedro behind Piazza Sant'Egidio; see Chapter 21).

The Janiculum (82m; Pl. 7; 1, and 1; 8; in Italian, *Gianicolo*), not counted as one of the Seven Hills of Rome, is a ridge rising steeply from the Tiber and approximately parallel to its course for the whole of its length. It is now mostly covered with parks and gardens, and has wonderful **views** from the ridge. It has two important churches, San Pietro in Montorio at its southern end and Sant'Onofrio to the north.

The hill's highest point, to the south, is Porta San Pancrazio; to the north it reaches almost as far as Piazza San Pietro. Its ancient name was Mons Aureus which referred to the yellow sand which covers its surface. The name of Mons Janiculus is derived from the old Italian deity Janus, who, according to legend, founded a city on the hill; his temple was in the Roman Forum. Numa Pompilius, the Sabine successor of Romulus, was buried on the Janiculum, and Ancus Marcius, the fourth king, is said to have built the Pons Sublicius over the Tiber to connect the Janiculum with the city of Rome. The hill provided a natural defence against the Etruscans, but it does not appear to have been fortified until after 87 BC, during a period of civil strife between Marius and Sulla, when a wall was built from Pons Aemilius to the Porta Aurelia (Porta San Pancrazio). Part of it was included within the Aurelian Wall, and it was completely surrounded by Urban VIII when he built his wall in 1642. It was the scene of Garibaldi's heroic stand in

defence of the Roman Republic against French troops commanded by Nicolas Oudinot in 1849.

VIA GARIBALDI (Pl. 7; 1, 2) mounts the hill from Trastevere. Above the church of Santa Maria dei Sette Dolori (see p 277), on the right, is the former entrance gate to the Bosco Parrasio, where in 1725 the academy of **Arcadia** was established. It was founded in 1690 to carry on the work of the academy inaugurated by Queen Christina of Sweden ten years before for the discussion of literary and political topics. The object of Arcadia was to eliminate bad literary taste and to purify the Italian language, and it exercised a profound influence on Italian literature during the 18C. In 1786 Goethe was admitted as a 'distinguished shepherd'. Later its importance waned and in 1926 it was absorbed into the Accademia Letteraria Italiana. The paintings which belong to the academy are at present kept at the Museo di Roma. The garden can sometimes be seen on request at 32 Via di Porta San Pancrazio. Beyond a lovely circular dining room with a dome (1725, by Antonio Canevari) is an amphitheatre, from which steps wind down through a small wood, circling a giant Roman pine.

Via Garibaldi continues to mount, in sweeping curves (if you are on foot you can take a short cut via steps to the right of the road), until it reaches a terrace. Here is the church of **SAN PIETRO IN MONTORIO** (Pl. 7; 3, 4), built on a site wrongly presumed to have been the scene of St Peter's crucifixion. Mentioned in the 9C, the church was rebuilt in the late 15C at the expense of King Ferdinand of Aragon and his wife Isabella, Queen of Castile. The apse and campanile, damaged in the siege of 1849, were restored in 1851. Raphael's *Transfiguration* (now in the Vatican) adorned the apse from 1523 to 1809. The church is the burial place of Beatrice Cenci, beheaded as a parricide at Ponte Sant' Angelo in 1599, and Hugh O'Neill of Tyrone and Roderick O'Donnell of Tyrconnel (1608), leaders in the Irish revolt against James I.

In front of the fine simple façade (attributed to the school of Andrea Bregno) is a group of palm trees and a terrace with a view towards the Vittorio Emanuele Monument and, in the distance among the trees of its garden, the Villa Medici.

Interior (open 7.30–12, 16–18.30; lights in some of the chapels), **south side**. First chapel: *Scourging of Christ*, a superb work by Sebastiano del Piombo (1518) from designs by Michelangelo, and frescoes by the same artist; second chapel: *Madonna della Lettera*, a detached fresco fragment attributed to Giovanni Battista Lombardelli, and above, *Coronation of the Virgin*, and four Virtues, attributed to Baldassarre Peruzzi. The fifth chapel has an altarpiece of the *Conversion of St Paul* by Vasari, and a balustrade and two tombs by Bartolomeo Ammannati. The apse is decorated with a copy of Guido Reni's *Crucifixion of St Peter* (now in the Vatican).

North side. The fifth chapel, designed by Daniele da Volterra, contains a *Baptism of Christ* attributed to Giulio Mazzoni. The fourth chapel has stuccowork attributed to Giulio Mazzoni; the *Descent from the Cross* and other frescoes are by Dirk Baburen (1617), a pupil of Caravaggio. Third chapel: altarpiece after Antoniazzo Romano. The second chapel (Raimondi) is an early work by Bernini, with an unusual relief of the *Ecstasy of St Francis*, executed by his pupils Francesco Baratta and Andrea Bolgi. First chapel: *St Francis receiving the stigmata*, by Giovanni de Vecchi. Near the west door, tomb of Giuliano da Volterra (died 1510), by a follower of Andrea Bregno.

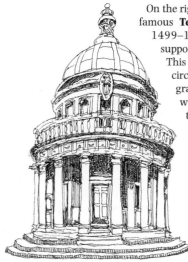

Bramante's Tempietto

On the right of the church is a courtyard with the famous **Tempietto** by Bramante (usually dated 1499–1502, or 1508–12), erected on the supposed exact site of St Peter's martyrdom. This jewel of the Renaissance, a miniature circular building with 16 Doric columns of granite, combines all the grace of the 15C, with the full splendour of the 16C. At the time of writing it was being restored. The interior may sometimes also be seen (ring at the convent, 8–12, 16–19). Stairs designed by Bernini lead down to a crypt with pretty stuccoes by Giovanni Francesco Rossi. To the right of the court is the Spanish Academy.

Via Garibaldi continues to a Neo-classical monument by Giovanni Jacobucci (1941), which commemorates the defenders and deliverers of Rome in 1849–70, and incorporates the tomb of Goffredo Mameli (1827–49), the patriot and poet (author of 'Fratelli d'Italia', the Italian national anthem). Further on is the fountain of the **Acqua Paola**, constructed for Paul V (as the handsome inscription states), by Giovanni Fontana and Flaminio Ponzio (1612), using marble from the Roman Forum. The water, which flows abundantly from the subterranean Aqueduct of Trajan (fed by springs near Lake Bracciano, about 48km northwest of Rome), falls into a large granite basin added by Carlo Fontana in 1690, beneath six columns (four of which are from the façade of Old St Peter's). It now houses a small theatre. On the right of the road is a subsidiary entrance to the Passeggiata del Gianicolo (see below). At the top of the hill is the **Porta San Pancrazio** (Pl. 7; 3), built by Urban VIII, and rebuilt by Virginio Vespignani in 1857 after the decisive battle here between the French forces and Garibaldi in 1849. This gate, once known as the *Porta Aurelia*, was the starting-point of the Via Aurelia.

To the right of the gate is the Villa Aurelia (also rebuilt after 1849), part of the American Academy in Rome since 1911. Viale delle Mura Gianicolensi leads south to the **Villa Sciarra**, a Romantic park laid out in the early 20C, and now a public park (open 7–dusk). It has particularly fine wisteria which flowers in early spring. Beyond is the residential district of **Monteverde**.

In front of Porta San Pancrazio, Via di San Pancrazio leads southwest to the ruins of the Vascello, a Baroque villa where Goffredo Mameli and Luciano Manara were killed in a last sally in 1849. Further on is an entrance to the **VILLA DORIA PAMPHILJ** or *Belrespiro*, by far the largest park in Rome (9km round). It was laid out in 1644–52 for Prince Camillo Pamphilj, nephew of Innocent X. The beautiful park is owned partly by the State and partly by the Commune of Rome and is open to the public (daily, sunrise to sunset). Many of the 19C garden buildings are in need of restoration. Some of the statues have been vandalised (and others removed for safety). The views take in the environs

of Rome (the Campagna) as well as the city, and the splendid umbrella pines are a special feature of the park. The grounds were cut in two in 1960 by the Via Olimpica. The **Casino del Bel Respiro**, built by Alessandro Algardi and Giovanni Francesco Grimaldi in 1644–52, with a formal garden, was used for receptions by the Italian State (but may become a sculpture museum). On Via Aurelia Antica (No. 183) is the **Villa Vecchia** decorated with exquisite stuccoes by Francesco Nicoletti in 1749–51.

Via di San Pancrazio passes the basilica of **San Pancrazio**, on the site of the tomb of St Pancrazio, who—according to Christian tradition—was martyred under Diocletian in 304. A Christian cemetery and 5C oratory existed here, and the present large basilica was built by Honorius I in 630, and remodelled in the 17C. The Baroque interior incorporates the apse, part of the transept and the annular crypt of the 7C church. The 4C **Catacombs of San Pancrazio** (admission from the church, Mon–Sat) contain Oriental inscriptions.

Beyond Porta San Pancrazio is the beginning of the PASSEGGIATA DI GIANI-COLO (Pl. 7; 1), a wide avenue laid out in 1884 (with fine pine trees) across the Villa Corsini above the fortifications of Urban VIII. At Piazzale del Gianicolo the road is joined by that from the Acqua Paola (see above). Here stands the conspicuous equestrian **Statue of Garibaldi**, by Emilio Gallori, erected in 1895 on the site of the hero's exploits of 1849. Around the base are four bronze groups: in front, 'Charge of Manara's Bersaglieri' (Rome, 1849); behind, 'Battle of Calatafimi' (Sicily, 1860); at the sides, 'Europe' and 'America'. The statue itself is 7m high.

The Passeggiata now goes downhill. On the right is the **Villa Lante**, built by Giulio Romano in 1518–27, and owned by Finland since 1950. On the left is the bronze equestrian Statue of Anita Garibaldi, by Mario Rutelli, presented by the Brazilian Government in 1935 to honour her Brazilian origin, and incorporating her tomb. Further on is a memorial tower, by Manfredo Manfredi, presented to Rome in 1911 by Italian residents in Argentina. A cannon shot is fired from here every day at noon.

From this point there is an especially fine **view** of Rome. On the extreme left is the dome of St Peter's, then Castel Sant'Angelo, San Giovanni dei Fiorentini, Palazzo di Giustizia and the modern Prati district, with the green slopes of the Villa Borghese, the Pincio and the gardens of the Villa Medici behind, among which the French Academy and the Trinità dei Monti stand out. To the right is the façade of Montecitorio with its clock. Below the hill is the prison of Regina Coeli, and beyond the river the spiral campanile of the church of Sant'Ivo, the dome of the Pantheon, and the Quirinal. Further to the right is Sant'Andrea and, in the distance, the bell-tower and domes of Santa Maria Maggiore. Then come the Torre delle Milizie, the triple-arched loggia of the Palazzo Farnese, the Vittorio Emanuele Monument, the bell-tower of Palazzo Senatorio on the Capitoline Hill, and the dome of the Synagogue. Behind them are the statues crowning the façade of St John Lateran. Among the trees of the Janiculum, on the extreme right, is the Acqua Paola. The Alban, Tiburtine and Praenestine Hills fall away gradually on the right.

The avenue continues downhill and a short flight of steps leads up to the little Piazzale di Sant'Onofrio, with ilex trees and a fountain. Here is the church of **SANT'ONOFRIO** (Pl. 1; 8; Sun 9–13, or by appointment. ☎ 686 4498),

founded by Blessed Nicolò da Forca Palena in 1419 and restored by Pius IX in 1857. A graceful L-shaped Renaissance portico connects the church and monastery. In the lunettes beneath the portico are three frescoes from the life of St Jerome (*Baptism, Chastisement for reading Cicero, Temptation*), by Domenichino, and over the door, a Madonna by Claudio Ridolfi. By the convent entrance is the tomb of the founder.

The dark **interior** is paved with numerous tombstones. On the left: the first chapel contains a monument to the poet Torquato Tasso, by Giuseppe de Fabris (1857), and the third chapel, the tombstone of Cardinal Mezzofanti (died 1849), who could speak 50 or 60 languages. In the pretty apse over the main altar are repainted frescoes by the school of Pinturicchio. The fresco of St Anne teaching the Virgin to read, on the right, above the monument of Giovanni Sacco (died 1505), is by a pupil of Andrea Bregno. Second chapel on the right: *Madonna di Loreto*, attributed to Annibale Carracci (or his school); in the vault pendentives above the altar in the first chapel, **Annunciation*, by Antoniazzo Romano (light).

The **Monastery**, now occupied by American friars of the Atonement, has a charming 15C cloister (being restored), with frescoes of the life of St Onophrius, by Cavaliere d'Arpino, Sebastiano Strada and Claudio Ridolfi. In the atrium is a monument to the 'Arcadian' poet, Alessandro Guidi (died 1712). In the upper corridor, above a Della Robbia frieze, is a fresco of the Virgin with a donor, much repainted, attributed to Giovanni Antonio Boltraffio. Torquato Tasso (1544–95), the epic poet, spent his last days and died here. The **Museo Tassiano** (admission only by appointment with the Cavalieri del Santo Sepolcro, 33 Via della Conciliazione) contains the poet's death mask, mementoes, MSS, and editions and translations of his works.

The steep Salita di Sant'Onofrio leads down to Piazza della Rovere (Pl. 1; 6), the end also of Via della Lungara. A gentler descent is by the road to the left, which passes the buildings of the pontifical North American College. Ponte Principe Amedeo (1942) crosses the Tiber, and on the left is the road tunnel known as the *Traforo Principe Amedeo*, which leads under the Janiculum to Largo di Porta Cavalleggeri. In front is **Porta Santo Spirito**, an unfinished gateway begun in 1540 by Antonio da Sangallo. It leads by Via dei Penitenzieri into the *Città Leonina*, or Rione of the Borgo (see Chapter 23).

23 · The Borgo and Castel Sant'Angelo

The **BORGO** (Pl. 1; 4, 6 and Pl. 2; 5), the district on the right bank of the Tiber between the Janiculum to the south and Monte Mario to the north, was known in ancient Rome as *Ager Vaticanus*. It was the stronghold of the papacy from 850, when Leo IV surrounded it with a line of walls, until 1586, when it was formally incorporated in the city of Rome.

> The Ager Vaticanus was chosen by Caligula (AD 37–41) for his circus, which was enlarged by Nero (54–68). The site of the Circus of Nero, just south of the basilica of St Peter's, was identified during excavations in this century. In the adjoining gardens many Christians were martyred under Nero in AD 65, including St Peter who was buried in a pagan cemetery nearby. Over his grave the first church of St Peter's was built (c AD 90) to

commemorate his martyrdom. Also within the Ager Vaticanus, Hadrian built his mausoleum (now Castel Sant'Angelo) in 135.

Inscriptions found on the temples of Cybele and Mithras suggest that paganism retained its hold with great tenacity here up until the late 4C. Despite this tendency, churches, chapels and convents were built round the first church of St Peter, and the district, attracting Saxon, Frank and Lombard pilgrims, came to be called the Borgo (borough), a name of Germanic origin from 'borgus' meaning small fortified settlement. In 850 Leo IV (847–55) surrounded the Borgo with walls 12m high, fortified with circular towers, to protect it from the incursions of the Saracens: hence the name Civitas Leonina or Città Leonina. Remnants of Leo IV's wall survive to the west of St Peter's. The Leonine City became the papal citadel: within its walls John VIII was besieged in 878 by the Duke of Spoleto; in 896 Arnulph of Carinthia attacked it and Formosus crowned him emperor. Gregory VII took refuge in the Castel Sant'Angelo from the Emperor Henry IV, and was rescued by Robert Guiscard in 1084. After the coronation in 1167 of Barbarossa in St Peter's, the Romans beseiged the Leonine City (and it was attacked again 12 years later).

During the 'Babylonian captivity' (1309–78) the Borgo fell into ruin, but when the popes returned from Avignon to Rome they chose the Vatican as their residence in place of the Lateran. In the 15C Eugenius IV and Sixtus IV, and early in the 16C Julius II and Leo X were active in developing and embellishing the Borgo as well as the Vatican. The original area of the Borgo was enlarged to the north of Borgo Angelico. However, after the sack of Rome in 1527 the Borgo became one of the poorest and least populated districts of Rome, and in 1586 Sixtus V relinquished the papal claim to this area, so that it was united to the city of Rome.

Five (originally seven) streets in the Leonine City have the prefix Borgo. Borgo Sant'Angelo and Borgo Santo Spirito run respectively north and south of Via della Conciliazione. In the construction of that street, the central Borgo Nuovo and Borgo Vecchio were destroyed. The remaining streets, the Borghi Angelico, Vittorio and Pio survive between the Castel Sant'Angelo and the Vatican.

The celebrated **Ponte Sant'Angelo** (Pl. 2; 5; pedestrians only), the ancient *Pons Aelius* or *Pons Adrianus*, was built by Hadrian (Aelius Hadrianus) in 134 as a fitting approach from the Campus Martius to his mausoleum, known since the Middle Ages as the Castel Sant'Angelo. Although the Roman bridge was decorated with statues, it was transformed by Gian Lorenzo Bernini when he designed the ten **statues on the balustrade** of angels holding the symbols of the Passion. These were executed in 1688 by his pupils, including Ercole Ferrata, Pietro Paolo Naldini, Cosimo Fancelli, and Antonio Raggi; two of the angels are copies of the originals which were removed to the church of Sant'Andrea delle Fratte. At the end towards the castle, the statues of St Peter and Paul, by the school of Lorenzetto and Paolo Taccone (1464), were set up by Clement VII in 1534. The three central arches are part of the original structure; the end arches were restored and enlarged in 1892–94 during the construction of the Lungotevere embankments. Upstream is **Ponte Vittorio Emanuele** (1911), decorated with monumental sculptures in travertine, and bronze victories.

Castel Sant' Angelo

Castel Sant'Angelo

Facing the bridge is Castel Sant'Angelo (Pl. 2; 5), an enormous circular structure begun by Hadrian c 128 as a mausoleum for himself and his family. It was completed in 139, a year after his death, by his successor Antoninus Pius. In the early Middle Ages the tomb was surrounded with ramparts and became the citadel of Rome. In its general plan, the castle follows the design of Hadrian's mausoleum, the exact design of which is unknown. Rising to a height of nearly 50m, it had a square base and a circular structure above supporting a central tower. The curtain walls of the inner ward, between the medieval bastions, are original; so is the entrance (no longer in use), except that the Roman threshold was lower. The round tower is Hadrian's, without its marble facing and its statues. Above it are additions of the Renaissance and later, such as the arcaded galleries. The central tower was the base of Hadrian's quadriga (see below), now replaced by a bronze angel. The pentagonal outer ward, added in the 16C, used to have five bastions (two of them were demolished during the construction of Piazza Pia and of the Lungotevere). The ditch between the two fortifications, planted with trees and covered with lawns, is a public park.

History

The mausoleum consisted of a base 89m square, supporting a round tower 64m in diameter, of peperino and travertine overlaid with marble. Above this was an earthen tumulus planted with cypress trees. At the top was an altar bearing a bronze quadriga driven by a charioteer representing Hadrian, as the Sun, ruler of the world. Inside the building was a spiral ramp (still in existence), which led to a straight passageway ending in the cella, in which was the Imperial tomb. Hadrian and Sabina (his wife), and his adopted son Aelius Caesar, were buried in the mausoleum, as were succeeding emperors until Septimius Severus. When Aurelian built his wall round Rome, he carried it on the left bank of the Tiber above the Porta Settimiana. He built the Porta Aurelia Nova on the city side of the Pons Aelius and made Hadrian's mausoleum into a bridgehead on the other side of the river. He surrounded his bridgehead with a wall strengthened with towers.

The mausoleum was gradually transformed into a castle. Theodoric

(474–526) used it as a prison and for a time it became known as the Carceri Theodorici. According to legend, St Gregory the Great, while crossing the Pons Aelius at the head of a procession to pray for the cessation of the plague of 590, saw on the top of the fortress an angel sheathing his sword. The vision accurately announced the end of the plague and from then onwards the castle has born its present name.

In the following centuries the possession of Castel Sant'Angelo was contested between popes and antipopes, the imperial forces and the Roman barons (Alberic, Crescentii, etc.). In 1084 Gregory VII was rescued from Henry IV's siege by Robert Guiscard. By the late 12C the castle was established as papal property. It was from here that Cola di Rienzo, at the end of his first period of dictatorship, fled to Bohemia on 15 December 1347. In 1378 the castle was severely damaged by the citizens of Rome, resentful of foreign domination. In the reign of Boniface IX rebuilding began. Alexander VI had Antonio da Sangallo the Elder complete the four bastions of the square inner ward (see below) which had been begun by Nicholas V. Julius II built the south loggia, facing the river. When Clement VII and some 1000 followers (including 13 cardinals and 18 bishops) took refuge here in 1527 from the troops of Charles V, Benvenuto Cellini took part in its defence (in his Autobiography he gives a colourful description of his gifts of valour and marksmanship on this occasion). Paul III built the north loggia and decorated the interior with frescoes. The outer ward, with its defensive ditch, was added by Pius IV. Urban VIII provided the castle with cannon made of bronze taken from the ceiling of the Pantheon portico, and he employed Bernini to remodel the outer defences.

From 1849 to 1870 the castle was occupied by French troops. Under the Italian Government it was used as barracks and as a prison until 1901, when the work of restoration was begun. In 1933–34 the castle was adapted for use as a museum and the surrounding area was cleared.

The castle, particularly interesting for its architecture, now contains the **MUSEO NAZIONALE DI CASTEL SANT'ANGELO**, inaugurated in 1925. The 58 rooms, some of which have fine 16C stuccoes and frescoes, contain a collection of paintings, furniture, tapestries, etc., and a military museum (partially closed). The views of Rome and the Tiber are superb. The interior is a labyrinth of rooms, staircases, courtyards and terraces, making it easy to get lost. The various features are numbered with arabic numerals, which correspond to the numbers given in the description below, and to the four plans within the text. Some rooms are often closed, and sometimes certain areas of the castle are temporarily inaccessible; the works of art are frequently rearranged. There is a café (**60**) on the Gallery of Pius IV. The lift is reserved for the staff and the disabled.

■ Open in the summer 9–19; closed second and fourth Tues of the month. ☎ 687 5036. Lire 8000.

The castle is entered from the gardens on the east side. A ramp leads down to the **Portone Peruzzi** (see the plan), an entrance gate to the castle built in 1556 by Giovanni Sallustio Peruzzi for Paul VI. It was adapted in 1628 for the use of

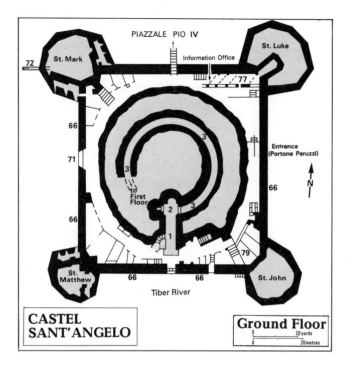

PIAZZALE PIO **IV**

Information Office

St. Luke

72   St. Mark

77

66

71

3

3
to
First
Floor

2

1

3

Entrance
(Portone Peruzzi)

N

66

66

66

79

St.
Matthew

66   66

St. John

Tiber River

**CASTEL
SANT'ANGELO**

Ground Floor

0   20 yards

0   20 metres

barracks built by Urban VIII, and was demolished in 1892 when the Lungotevere was built and moved to this side of the castle. Inside the gate a cobbled street leads left between the foot of Hadrian's splendid round tower and the medieval castle walls past two vaulted oil stores (**79**), where architectural and sculptural fragments found in the castle have been arranged, including Roman and Byzantine pieces. Also displayed here is a model of Hadrian's tomb. At the entrance to the interior is a spacious **vestibule** (**1**), with a model of the castle. On the left is the shaft (**2**) of a lift built for the infirm Leo X and, in front, a niche for a statue of Hadrian. On the right is a **spiral ramp** (**3**), 125.5m long, which rises gently to the sepulchral cella (see below). The ramp is in a remarkable state of preservation; the floor has remains of mosaic decoration. Along it are four vents, one of which was converted into a prison, mentioned by Benvenuto Cellini.

The **Staircase of Alexander VI** (**5**) cuts diametrically across the circular Roman building. By means of a bridge (**6**) built in 1822 by Valadier in place of a drawbridge the staircase passes above the Roman **sepulchral cella** (**7**), of which only the travertine wall blocks survive, with some fragments of marble decoration. Here were kept the urns containing the Imperial ashes. Hadrian's porphyry sarcophagus was taken by Innocent II (1130–43) for use as his own tomb in St John Lateran, where it was destroyed by fire in 1360.

At a landing lit by a round window (**9**), the staircase of Alexander VI originally turned to the right. Paul III closed this section and opened one to the left

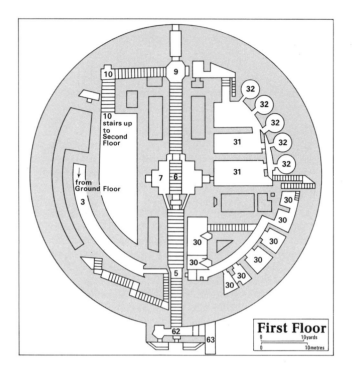

First Floor

0   10 yards
0   10 metres

(**10**; by Antonio da Sangallo the Younger), to give access to the **Courtyard of the Angel** (**11**), named from the marble statue of an angel (**13**) by Raffaello da Montelupo, removed here from the terrace at the top of the castle.

At the end of the court are the Staircase of Urban VIII and the façade by Michelangelo of the **Medici Chapel**, built c 1514 for Leo X (**12**). On the right is a series of rooms (**14**, **15**, **II–VII**, on two levels) which house a **Museum of Arms and Armour** (partly closed). The collection has material from the Stone Age to the 20C, and includes 15C–18C arms found during excavations within the castle precincts. There is a display of prehistoric weapons, 14C–17C defensive arms, swords, pikes and firearms. The 19C–20C material includes exotic arms from Africa and China, and 19C uniforms. Also off the Court of the Angel are the Rooms of Clement VIII (**16**, **17**) and the Hall of Justice (**18**) which are usually open only for exhibitions. The **Hall of Justice** is so called because it was the seat of the tribunal of the 16C–17C. It was built in Roman times above the sepulchral cella, and has a fresco of Justice attributed to Domenico Zaga.

Another door in the courtyard leads into the **Hall of Apollo** (**19**), named after the 16C mythological grotesques on the ceiling attributed to Luzio Luzi. On the right is a trapdoor covering a cellar 9m deep; adjacent is the top of the lift-shaft seen from the spiral ramp (see above). On the right is the **Chapel Of Leo X** (**20**), with a relief of the Madonna and Child attributed to Raffaello da Montelupo.

Opposite are the **Rooms of Clement VII** (**21**, **22**). The first room (**21**) is

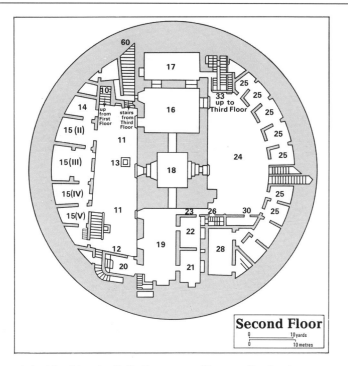

Second Floor

0   10 yards
0   10 metres

decorated with a frieze by Giulio Romano, and has a coffered ceiling. Here are displayed detached frescoes by Niccolò l'Alunno, Lorenzo Lotto, *St Jerome*; the Zavattari brothers, Polyptych; 15C Tuscan school, *Madonna enthroned*; *St Sebastian and St John the Baptist*; Carlo Crivelli, *Christ blessing, St John the Baptist*. In the second room (**22**): Martino Spanzotti, *Pietà*; Bartolomeo Montagna, *Madonna and Child*; Luca Signorelli, *Madonna and Saints*; Giampietrino, *Mocking of Christ*.

A passage (**23**) leads right out of the Hall of Apollo into the large **Courtyard of Alexander VI** (**24**), with a fine marble well, stone cannon balls, and cata-pults. Theatrical performances were given here in the time of Leo X and Pius IV. A small staircase (**26**) leads up to the charming **Bathroom of Clement VII** (**27**) decorated with stuccoes and frescoes attributed to Giovanni da Udine. This room communicates with a small dressing room on the next floor (closed). The Courtyard of Leo X (**28**) with a loggia is also usually closed; below it is a 15C casemate. Adjacent is a small triangular courtyard from which stairs lead to a chamber which had a stove for heating the bath water and the air which circu-lated between the hollow walls.

On the right side of the Courtyard of Alexander VI is a semicircular two-storeyed building, the rooms of which (**25**) were formerly used as prison cells. In the second room from the right, Benvenuto Cellini was imprisoned during the first period of his captivity. A staircase leads down from the courtyard to the **historical prisons** (**30**; closed). Two large underground oil stores (**31**) contain 84 jars, with a capacity of c 22,000 litres. The oil not only served to feed the

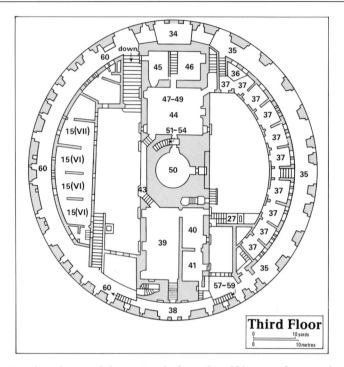

Third Floor

0   10 yards

0   10 metres

garrison, but also as a defence, since boiling oil could be poured on attackers. The five grain silos (**32**) were later used as prison cells. Other macabre prison cells open off a corridor; numerous bones found under the floors indicate that the prisoners were buried where they died. Benvenuto Cellini is said to have passed the second period of his captivity in the last cell.

Stairs lead back up to the Courtyard of Alexander VI, and from there a staircase (**33**) continues up to the semicircular **Gallery of Pius IV** (**35**), a terrace with a splendid *view. A series of small rooms here were used originally as quarters for the household of the papal court and later as political and military prison cells. Rooms 36–37, with the reconstruction of a political prison in the first half of the 19C, and an interesting muster of uniforms, decorations and medals of the various Italian states before the Unification, have been closed indefinitely. To the left is the **Loggia of Paul III** (**34**), with another fine view, built by Antonio Sangallo the Younger and decorated with stuccoes and Mannerist grotesques in 1543–48. The Loggia Of Julius II (**38**), on a design by Giuliano da Sangallo, faces south towards the Ponte Sant'Angelo.

A staircase leads from here to the **Papal Apartments** (**39–49**), decorated for Paul III in 1542–49 and appropriately furnished. The **Sala Paolina** or **del Consiglio** (**39**) has *stuccoes by Girolamo da Sermoneta and Baccio da Montelupo. The walls are decorated by Pellegrino Tibaldi, Domenico Zaga, Perino del Vaga, Polidoro da Caravaggio, Giovanni da Udine, and others. On the right is an amusing trompe-l'oeil fresco of a courtier entering the room through a painted door. In the floor is the coat of arms of Innocent XIII who restored the

room. The **Camera del Perseo** (**40**) takes its name from the beautiful frieze by Perino del Vaga and his bottega. The carved wooden ceiling dates from the 16C. The tapestries come from State collections and include one showing an episode in the life of Julius Caesar. The painting of *Christ carrying the Cross* is by Paris Bordone.

The **Camera di Amore e Psiche** (**41**; seen beyond a railing) has another frieze (recently restored) by Perino del Vaga and his bottega, illustrating the story of Cupid and Psyche in 17 episodes. It has a fine carved gilt 15C ceiling, a large 16C canopied bed, a clavichord, and other furniture. The paintings include: *Christ carrying the Cross* by Sebastiano del Piombo, and a *Girl with a unicorn* by a 16C artist. The statuette is attributed to Jacopo della Quercia.

From the Sala Paolina a corridor (**43**) frescoed in the Pompeian style by Perino del Vaga and his bottega leads to the **Hall of the Library** (**44**), with ceiling frescoes by Luzio Luzi and stuccoes by Sicciolante da Sermoneta (16C). The marble chimneypiece is by Raffaello da Montelupo. The furniture includes four dower chests and a 15C wardrobe. The **Room of the Mausoleum of Hadrian** (**45**) is named after a frieze by Luzi and his school. Here are hung two paintings depicting Bacchanals, one a copy by Poussin of an original by Bellini, and the other by Jordaens. The fine painting of the *Madonna between saints Roch and Sebastian* is a copy from Lorenzo Lotto. A case contains 15C–17C ceramics. Beyond **Room 46** a short flight of stairs (closed) leads to the **Appartamento Cagliostra** (**47–49**; now offices), three 16C rooms decorated with *grotteschi* by Luzi and containing a collection of majolica (15C 'albarelli' (cylindrical pots), floor tiles, Deruta and Faenza ware).

A small vestibule leads out of the Hall of the Library into the central **Room of the Secret Archives**, or **of the Treasury** (**50**). The walnut cupboards in this room were used for the archives inaugurated by Paul III. In the middle are some large chests in which Julius II, Leo X and Sixtus V kept the Vatican treasury. A Roman staircase ascends to the **Round Hall** (**51**), situated beneath the statue of the angel and above the last room. Formerly used as a political prison, it now contains the iron core of Verschaffelt's angel (see below), a cast of the head, and the original sword. A short staircase leads to the **Hall of the Columns** (usually closed) which contains a charming 15C polychrome wood group of the Deposition, and a wooden model of the Archangel Michael attributed to Pietro Bracci. The two adjoining rooms (**52–53**) are only open for exhibitions.

The staircase continues up to the **terrace** (**54**) at the top of the castle, scene of the last act of Puccini's opera *Tosca*. Above, on a small higher terrace, can be seen the huge bronze *angel in the act of sheathing his sword (4m high) by Peter Anton Verschaffelt (1752). This commemorates the vision of Gregory the Great in 590 (see above) after which the castle is named. The bell known as the *Campana della Misericordia* used to announce the execution of capital sentences.

The *view from the terrace is superb. On the left, in front, is the Palace of Justice, with the Villa Medici just visible behind. Further to the left, the Prati district; in the distance, the green park of the Villa Borghese and of the Pincio. Across the Tiber, the Ministry of Finance, with the orange Quirinal building in front; then Palazzo della Consulta, with Santa Maria Maggiore behind it. To the right, on the skyline, the Torre delle Milizie, with the cupola of the Pantheon in front. Next comes the Vittorio Emanuele Monument, with St John Lateran behind it. In the background, the Alban hills. Continuing to the right, the bell-

tower of Palazzo Senatorio on the Capitoline Hill; in front, the two cupolas of Sant'Andrea della Valle and San Carlo ai Catinari. Then can be seen the Aventine, with San Paolo fuori le Mura in the background. Further right, beyond Ponte Sant'Angelo, is Trastevere and the Janiculum; St Peter's and the Vatican; Monte Mario. Immediately below, Ponte Sant'Angelo and Ponte Vittorio Emanuele, with the Lungotevere.

From the terrace the descent is sometimes signposted by a modern staircase which passes three rooms of the Appartamento del Castellano, beyond which stairs continue down to the Gallery of Pius IV and the Courtyard of the Angel. Otherwise you are obliged to return from the terrace down the same staircase to the Hall of the Library (**44**), which you cross diagonally to the door on the left of the fireplace. Stairs lead from here to the loggia of Paul III, from which another flight of stairs continues down to the Courtyard of Alexander VI. After this the route follows Paul III's staircase (**10**), and Alexander VI's staircase (**5**) to the exit.

The **ramparts** are traversed by open walkways (**66**) which encircle the Roman structure and connect the four **bastions** of the square inner ward (signposted to the right from the drawbridge near the entrance; **63**). The first part of the walkway passes above a terrace with four 15C cannon and piles of marble and stone cannon balls, once part of the castle's ammunition store. Beyond the Bastion of St Matthew are the mills (**71**) used from the time of Pius IV to grind flour for the castle. The Bastion of St Mark is closed for restoration. Here can be seen the beginning of the **covered way** (*Corridoio* or *Passetto*; **72**) which connects the castle with the Vatican. This was built in 1277–80 by Nicholas III above Leo IV's 9C defensive wall of the Borgo. It was reconstructed by Alexander VI, who used it as an escape route from the Vatican in 1494. It was again used in 1527 when Clement VII took refuge in the castle from the troops of Charles V.

Between the bastions of St Mark and St Luke is a passageway (closed) leading into the public gardens (Piazzale Pio IV). Just before the Bastion of St Luke is the Chapel of the Crucifix, or of Clement XII (**77**), in which condemned criminals had to attend mass before execution. The circuit continues above the reconstructed gate of 1556 (the present entrance to the castle) to the Bastion of St John, beyond which steps lead down to ground level.

Beside Castel Sant'Angelo, on the river front, is the huge **Palazzo di Giustizia** (Pl. 2; 3), the Palace of Justice, known as the 'Palazzaccio'. A colossal ornate building in solid travertine, decorated with sculptures by Enrico Quattrini and Ettore Ximenes, it was built between 1889 and 1910. It was evacuated in 1970 because it was in danger of collapse; although it is still under restoration, it has been partially reopened. New judiciary offices and law courts have been built by Giuseppe Perugini, and others in the Città Giudiziaria (Pl. 15; 7), in Piazzale Clodio.

To the north, beyond Piazza Cavour, an important traffic centre and terminus for buses, are the Prati and **Trionfale** districts. In Via Pompeo Magno is the church of **San Gioacchino** (Pl. 2; 3), erected by Raffaele Inganni in 1890, with bronze capitals and an aluminium cupola painted inside to represent a star-strewn sky.

About 500m north is Piazza Mazzini. In Viale Mazzini to the right is the church of **Cristo Re** built in 1930 by Marcello Piacentini, with a sculpture by Arturo Martini over the central door. It contains frescoes by Achille Funi and sculptures by Corrado Vigni and Alfredo Biagini. Next to it is the headquarters

of the R.A.I. (the Italian State-owned radio and television network). About 700m further north, at 31 Lungotevere della Vittoria, is the **Museo dell'Arma del Genio** (Pl. 15; 6; open Tues, Thur, Sat 9–12. ☎ 372 5446), illustrating Italian military transport, bridge building and communications. It includes a military aircraft of 1909, and models of historical fortifications and armoury from Roman times to the present day. **Monte Mario** which rises to the north-west is described in Chapter 24.

From Castel Sant'Angelo the unattractive, cold VIA DELLA CONCILIAZIONE (Pl. 1; 6) leads towards St Peter's. The approach to the great basilica was trans-formed by this broad straight thoroughfare, typical of Fascist urban planning, which was completed in 1937. In its construction two characteristic streets of the Città Leonina, the Borgo Nuovo (opened in 1499) and Borgo Vecchio (known as the Spina di Borgo), and the buildings between them were destroyed, except for one palace which was moved (see below). The colonnaded piazza in front of St Peter's was not originally designed to be seen from a distance; its impact is therefore lessened by this monumental approach.

Via della Conciliazione first passes (right) the Carmelite church of Santa Maria in Traspontina (1566–87). Beyond is **Palazzo Torlonia** (formerly Giraud), a delightful reproduction of the Palazzo della Cancelleria, built by Andrea Bregno in 1495–1504 for Cardinal Adriano da Corneto. Then comes **Palazzo dei Convertendi**, built in the second half of the 17C, and re-erected in its present position in 1937. It originally occupied the site of a house built by Bramante for Raphael, who died in it in 1520. On the south side of the street is **Palazzo dei Penitenzieri** built (probably) by Baccio Pontelli for Cardinal Domenico della Rovere in 1480. It is now occupied by the Penitentiaries, who hear confessions in St Peter's. Via della Conciliazione ends in Piazza Pio XII, in front of Piazza San Pietro (described in Chapter 27).

Parallel to Via della Conciliazione to the north is Borgo Sant'Angelo which is skirted by the wall (in urgent need of restoration) which supports the covered way which connects Castel Sant'Angelo with the Vatican (see above). Borgo Pio, one street further north is the prettiest street to have survived in the Borgo. Partly closed to traffic, it is a local shopping street and has several pizzerie.

On the other side of Via della Conciliazione is Borgo Santo Spirito. Here a flight of steps leads up to the little church of **San Michele e Magno** (open on Sun morning), founded in the 8C and retaining a 13C campanile. Inside is the tomb of the painter Raphael Mengs (died 1779).

On the corner of Via dei Penitenzieri is **SANTO SPIRITO IN SASSIA** (Pl. 1; 6), a church founded in 726 for Saxon pilgrims by Ine, king of Wessex, who died in Rome in the same year. The church was rebuilt in 1540 by Antonio da Sangallo the Younger: the design of the **façade** was probably his, but the work itself was done in 1585 by Ottavio Mascherino. The **campanile**, entirely Tuscan in char-acter, and attributed to Baccio Pontelli, is one of the most graceful in Rome.

In the **interior** the wooden ceiling dates from 1534–49. On the west wall are two interesting paintings in elaborate frames: *Visitation* by Francesco Salviati, and *The Conversion of Saul*, attributed to Marco da Siena. **South side**. First chapel: *Pentecost* by Jacopo Zucchi; second chapel: *Assumption* by Livio Agresti. The interesting little porch in front of a side door with two columns has 16C fres-coes and a pretty ceiling. It supports the organ of 1546–52. The huge apse was

covered with frescoes by Jacopo and Francesco Zucchi in 1583. **North side**. The third chapel has a 16C crucifix and frescoed decorations in Roman style imitating precious marbles with figures in grisaille. On the second altar, *Coronation of the Virgin* by Cesare Nebbia.

It was from the ramparts of the Leonine City near here that Benvenuto Cellini, according to his own statement, shot the Constable de Bourbon in 1527; a plaque on the outer wall of the church, however, attributes the deed to Bernardo Passeri, another goldsmith. Adjoining the church are the buildings of the huge **Ospedale di Santo Spirito**, founded by Innocent III c 1198 as a hospital and hostel, and rebuilt for Sixtus IV by various architects (c 1473–78). The first building, the Palazzo del Commendatore (i.e. the house of the director of the hospital), with a spacious courtyard, dates from c 1567. The harmony of the proportions of the main building was spoilt by Alexander VIII, who added a storey, and by Benedict XIV, who blocked up the arches of the portico. The portal is an effective example of the early Renaissance style. The chapel (admission by special permission only) contains an altar with a baldacchino of the time of Clement VIII (1592–1605) and an altarpiece (*Job*) by Carlo Maratta. The river-front, the Lungotevere in Sassia, was rebuilt and extended in 1926 in harmony with the old style.

The hospital contains institutions devoted to the history of medicine: the Lancisiana Library (founded 1711; in the Palazzo del Commendatore) and the Historical Medical Academy. The National Museum of the History of Medicine, unique in Italy at 3 Lungotevere in Sassia (open Mon, Wed & Fri 10–13. ☎ 683 52353). It includes anatomical drawings by Paolo Mascagni (1752–1815), the collection of the surgeon Giuseppe Flajani (1741–1808), surgical instruments, and the reconstruction of a 17C pharmacy, and of an alchemist's laboratory.

24 · Monte Mario and Ponte Milvio

■ The foot of Monte Mario (Piazza Maresciallo Giardino) is reached by bus No. 90 from the Corso. Bus 186 (weekdays) from Piazza Venezia for the Foro Italico.

Monte Mario (139m; Pl. 15; 5) is the ancient *Clivus Cinnae* and the medieval *Monte Malo*. Its present name is taken from the Villa Mario Mellini built on the summit (see below). Via di Villa Madama climbs the east slope of the hill to **Villa Madama** (Pl. 15; 3). This suburban villa, begun for Cardinal Giulio de' Medici (Clement VII) by Giulio Romano was designed by Raphael. It was altered by Antonio da Sangallo the Younger. Later it came into the possession of 'Madama' Margaret of Parma and was afterwards owned by the kings of Naples. Today it is used by the Italian Government as accommodation for prominent visitors.

The beautiful **loggia**, decorated with stucco reliefs by Giovanni da Udine and paintings by Giulio Romano (1520–25) after Raphael's designs, rivals and even excels the famous loggia of the Vatican. In one of the rooms is a frieze of Cupids by Giulio Romano. There is a lovely *view of Rome from the balcony of the main façade. The attractive hanging garden served as a model for many Italian gardens.

On the south slope of the hill is the round church of Santa Maria del Rosario, built in 1650 by Camillo Arcucci (Pl. 15; 7, 5 *view). Beyond the ditches of the

Fort of Monte Mario, a road leads right to the summit at the Villa Mario Mellini, now incorporated in the **Astronomical and Meteorological Observatory** (Pl. 15; 5), with the **Copernican Museum** (open Wed & Sat 9–13. ☎ 353 47056), founded in 1873. It contains mementoes of Copernicus, astrolabes, sextants, quadrants, telescopes, etc. and a large collection of globes.

At the foot of Monte Mario, extending along the riverfront is the **FORO ITALICO** (Pl. 15; 4, 2), an ambitious sports centre built in 1928–31 by the former Accademia Fascista della Farnesina, one of the most impressive building projects carried out by Mussolini in imitation of ancient Roman Imperial architecture. It was altered during work on preparations for the World Cup in Italy in 1990. It was designed by Enrico Del Debbio, and finished by Luigi Moretti in 1936. Facing the entrance is Ponte Duca d'Aosta (1939).

A marble monolith, 17m high, inscribed 'Mussolini Dux', rises at the entrance in front of an imposing avenue paved with marble inlaid with mosaics designed by Gino Severini, Angelo Canevari, and others. It ends in a piazza decorated with a fountain and with a huge marble sphere. On either side of the avenue are marble blocks, with inscriptions recording events in the history of Italy. At the end, beyond the piazza, is the **Stadio Olimpico**, finished for the Olympic Games in 1960, with accommodation for 100,000. It was reconstructed for the World Cup in 1990, with little respect for the setting. To the right is the **Stadio dei Marmi**, capable of seating 20,000 spectators, with 60 colossal statues of athletes. There are open-air and enclosed swimming-pools, the latter with mosaics by Giulio Rossi and Angelo Canevari. Another building has mosaics by Gino Severini. There are also lawn-tennis and basketball courts, running tracks, gymnasium and fencing halls, etc.

Lungotevere Maresciallo Diaz continues along the Tiber passing the Casa Internazionale dello Studente, and, behind it, the Italian Foreign Office (1956), known as the 'Farnesina' from the name of the road here. The sculpture is by Arnaldo Pomodoro (1968). In this district, also is the French Military Cemetery, with the graves of 1500 French who died in the Second World War. The Lungotevere ends at Piazzale Milvio (Pl. 15, just beyond 2), where several roads converge.

The church of the Gran Madre di Dio was designed by Cesare Bazzani in 1933. Ahead, Viale di Tor di Quinto continues along the river to Ponte Flaminio, opened in 1951, a seven-arched entrance to the city from the north. Along it runs Corso di Francia, which passes above the **Villaggio Olimpico**, built to accommodate athletes in 1960, and now a residential district.

Ponte Milvio or Ponte Molle (Pons Milvius), which carried the Via Flaminia over the Tiber (now only used by pedestrians), was built by the censor Marcus Aemilius Scaurus in 109 BC. It was here that Cicero captured the emissaries of the Allobroges in 63 BC during the Catiline conspiracy; and it was from this bridge that the Emperor Maxentius was thrown into the Tiber and drowned after his defeat by his co-emperor Constantine on 28 October 312 (see below). Remodelled in the 15C, by Nicholas V, who added the watchtowers, it was restored in 1805 by Pius VII, who commissioned Giuseppe Valadier to erect the triumphal arch at the entrance. Blown up in 1849 by Garibaldi to arrest the advance of the French, it was again restored in 1850 by Pius IX.

On the south side of Ponte Milvio is Piazza Cardinal Consalvi, with a shrine

containing a statue by Paolo Taccone, erected by Pius II in 1462 on the spot where he had met Cardinal Bessarion returning from the Morea (Peloponnese) with the head of St Andrew. The straight Via Flaminia returns from here to Piazza del Popolo and the centre of the city.

A short way along Via Flaminia which runs parallel with Viale Tiziano ('one-way' going out of the city) is Piazza Apollodoro. To the left is the **Palazzetto dello Sport**, an adventurous and striking construction by Pier Luigi Nervi and Annibale Vitellozzi, designed for the Olympic Games in 1960. Beyond is the Villaggio Olimpico (see above). A little to the south is the **Stadio Flaminio**, designed in reinforced concrete by Pier Luigi and Antonio Nervi in 1959. In addition to the football ground, which can accommodate 45,000 spectators, there are gymnasiums, a fencing school and a swimming-pool. On the right of Piazza Apollodoro, in Via Guido Reni, is the church of Santa Croce, built by Pius X in 1913.

Further south, on the left, Viale Tiziano widens to form Piazzale Manila, from which Viale Maresciallo Pilsudski leads northeast and then east towards the exclusive **PARIOLI** residential district (Pl. 11; 2, 3), the centre of which is at Piazza Euclide, with the huge church of the Sacro Cuore Immacolato di Maria by Armando Brasini (1923).

The Parco di Villa Glori (Pl. 11; 1) was converted in 1923–24 by Raffaello de Vico into the **Parco della Rimembranza**, to commemorate the heroism of the brothers Enrico and Giovanni Cairoli, who were killed in 1867 during Garibaldi's attempt to liberate Rome from papal rule. The park is planted with cypresses, oaks, elms, maples, horse chestnuts, etc. A clump of oak trees commemorates heroes of the First World War. There is a fine *view of the Tiber valley. Beyond is the mineral spring called Acqua Acetosa; the well-head (1661) is probably by Andrea Sacchi.

Via Flaminia continues to the graceful little circular church of **Sant'Andrea in Via Flaminia** by Vignola (1550–55), erected by Julius III to commemorate his deliverance from Charles V's soldiers while he was a cardinal. It is now between Via Flaminia and Viale Tiziano. Further south, on the left, is the beginning of Viale delle Belle Arti, which passes Villa Giulia (see Chapter 9). On the right, beyond Piazzale delle Belle Arti, is **Ponte del Risorgimento** (1909–11), the first bridge to be built in the city in reinforced concrete, with a single span of 100m.

At the corner of Viale delle Belle Arti is the Palazzina of Pius IV (see p 186), and where Via di Villa Giulia leads left, is a fountain erected by Julius III, beneath an imposing façade, originally of only one storey, by Bartolommeo Ammannati (1553); the second part was added by Pirro Ligorio in 1562. In Piazza della Marina is the vast Marine Ministry, by Giulio Magni (1928), which has another façade on the Tiber. Via Domenico Alberto Azuni leads to Ponte Matteotti. Beyond the wooded grounds on the left of Villa Strohl Fern is Piazzale Flaminio (Pl. 2; 2), the starting-point of the Via Flaminia. On the east side are the main entrance to the Villa Borghese (see Chapter 9), and the beginning of Viale del Muro Torto, which runs outside the Aurelian Wall to Porta Pinciana.

Porta del Popolo opens into Piazza del Popolo (see Chapter 7).

25 · Porta San Paolo and San Paolo fuori le Mura

■ The Underground (line B) from the Station and Colosseum runs to Porta San Paolo ('Piramide') and the basilica of San Paolo fuori le Mura ('San Paolo'). Bus No. 673 from the Colosseum via Porta San Paolo, or No. 170 from the Station, Piazza Venezia and Largo Argentina, both terminate at San Paolo fuori le Mura.

The well preserved **Porta San Paolo** (Pl. 8; 7), the *Porta Ostiensis* of ancient Rome, preserves its inner side, with two arches from the time of Aurelian. The outer face, rebuilt by Honorius in 402, has been restored. The gate houses the **Museo della Via Ostiense** (open 9–14; Tues & Thur also open 14.30–16.30; closed Mon. and 2nd & 4th Sun of month ☎ 698 83333), which illustrates the history of the road to Ostia. It includes milestones and reliefs (some only casts), together with models of Ostia and its port in Imperial times. Among the tomb paintings are three frescoed lunettes from a tomb of the Servian period. On the south side of the gate the square is called Piazzale Ostiense, an important traffic hub, with a station of the Underground, and the railway station for the branch line to Ostia and Lido di Ostia (and on the branch line from Tiburtina station to Fiumicino).

On the west side of the square, across the line of the city wall, is the **Pyramid of Gaius Cestius** (died 12 BC), praetor, tribune of the plebs, and member of the college of the Septemviri Epulones (Roman priests), who organised public banquets at important festivals. This is a tomb in the form of a tall pyramid of brick faced with marble, 27m high with a base 22m square. An inscription records that it was built in less than 330 days. It was included in the Aurelian walls in the 3C, and remains one of the most idiosyncratic and best preserved monuments of ancient Rome. Admission only by special permission; write to Ripartizione X del Comune di Rome, 29 Via Portico d'Ottavia, 00100 Rome; fax 689 2115, ☎ 671 03819.

Beyond the pyramid, to the left, extends the so-called **PROTESTANT CEME-TERY** (Pl. 8; 7; open 7–dusk; ring at 6 Via Caio Cestio), in a romantic setting with tall cypresses. The earliest recorded grave dates from 1738.

It was of the **Old Cemetery** (left of the entrance), that Shelley wrote: 'It might make one in love with death to think that one should be buried in so sweet a place.' The tomb in the far corner is that of John Keats (1796–1821; 'Here lies one whose name was writ in water'); close by lies his friend Joseph Severn (1793–1879); behind, John Bell (1763–1820), the Scottish anatomist and surgeon. In the **New Cemetery** lies the heart of Percy Bysshe Shelley (1792–1822; '*cor cordium*', 'the heart of all hearts'), brought here after his cremation by his friend the writer Edward Trelawny (1792–1881), who is buried nearby. Shelley's monument is by Onslow Ford (1891). Here are buried also J. Addington Symonds (1840–93), the historian of the Renaissance; the sculptor John Gibson (1790–1886); the writers William Howitt (1792–1879) and his wife Mary (1799–1888); Robert Michael Ballantyne (1825–94), author of children's books; and Julius Goethe (died 1830), the only son of the poet.

Just beyond the Protestant Cemetery, at the end of Via Caio Cestio, and across

Via Nicola Zabaglia is the **Rome British Military Cemetery**, where 429 members of the three Services are buried. The cemetery is beautifully sited along the line of the city wall. If the gates are locked, telephone the Area Office (address and telephone number are given on a notice).

To the north of the British Military Cemetery and west of Via Nicola Zabaglia rises **Monte Testaccio** (Pl. 8; 7), an isolated mound 54m high and some 1000m round, entirely composed of potsherds (*testae*) dumped here from the Augustan period up to the middle of the 3C AD, from the neighbouring store-houses of the Republican port which lined the Tiber between Ponte Testaccio and Ponte Sublicio (now Ponte Aventino; see Chapter 21). Among the finds here was a hoard of amphorae, used to import oil from Spain, with official marks scratched on them, which are of fundamental importance to our knowledge of the economic history of the late Republic and early Empire. From the top of Monte Testaccio (entered from the corner facing Via Galvani and Via Zabaglia) there is a fine view. Jousts and tournaments were held in this part of the city during the Middle Ages. The district of **Testaccio**, near the 'ex-Mattatoio', a huge building of 1888–89, which used to be used as a slaughterhouse, has recently become a centre of cultural activities with several small theatres and a cinema complex. It is now also renowed for its restaurants (of all categories).

From Piazzale Ostiense the broad uninteresting VIA OSTIENSE leads almost due south through a depressing part of the town. It is not recommended on foot; bus No. 23 follows it to (2km) the basilica of San Paolo. Some distance along it, on the left, is the site of an oratory marking the spot where, according to tradition, St Peter and St Paul greeted each other on their way to martyrdom. In the middle of the road just before San Paolo is a small necropolis known as the **Sepolcreto Ostiense**, which contained pagan and perhaps Christian tombs. The site, seen through railings (admission only by special permission; write to the Ripartizione X del Comune di Roma, 29 Via Portico d'Ottavia, Rome; fax 689 2115, ☎ 671 03819) extended over a wide area; another part is visible left of the road.

San Paolo fuori le Mura

San Paolo fuori le Mura (2km from Porta San Paolo; Pl. 8; 7; open 7–18.30) is the largest church in Rome after St Peter's. The ancient basilica was virtually destroyed by fire in 1823 and the present building is a frigid 19C reconstruction 'which looks outside like a very ugly railway station' (Augustus Hare, *Walks in Rome*). In plan and dimensions, if not in spirit, the new basilica follows the old one almost exactly. One of the four great patriarchal basilicas, it commemorates the martyrdom of St Paul and is believed to contain the Apostle's tomb.

According to Christian tradition, the Roman matron Lucina buried the body of Paul in a vineyard on this spot. A small shrine existed here when, in 384, a large basilica was begun by Valentinian II and Theodosius the Great at the request of Pope Damasus. It was enlarged by Theodosius's son Honorius and decorated with mosaics by Galla Placidia, sister of Honorius. After the additions made by Leo III (Pope, 795–816), it became the largest and most beautiful church in Rome. In the 9C it was pillaged by the Saracens and John VIII (872–82) enclosed it in a fortified village known as Giovannipolis. It was restored c 1070 by Abbot Hildebrand, later Gregory

VII. The façade, overlooking the Tiber, was preceded by a colonnaded quadriporticus. Before the Reformation, the king of England was ex officio a canon of San Paolo and the abbot, in return, was decorated with the Order of the Garter. This great basilica was almost entirely destroyed by fire on the night of 15–16 July 1823.

Leo XII ordered the reconstruction, which was directed by Pasquale Belli, Pietro Bosio and Pietro Camporese, and afterwards by Luigi Poletti. In the rebuilding it was decided to use new materials instead of repairing the damaged stucture. The transept was consecrated by Gregory XVI in 1840 and the complete church by Pius IX in 1854. In 1891 an explosion in a neighbouring fort broke most of the stained glass which was replaced by slabs of alabaster. A service took place here in March 1966 performed by Pope Paul VI and the Archbishop of Canterbury, when they issued a joint declaration of amity. It is one of the three basilicas of Rome which has the privilege of extraterritoriality.

Exterior. The Romanesque campanile was pulled down to make way for the unattractive campanile by Luigi Poletti on Via Ostiense. Poletti was also responsible for the **north portico** which incorporates 12 Hymettan marble columns from the old basilica. On one of the nearest columns, beneath the frieze, is a 4C inscription of Pope Siricius (384–99). The façade (right) is preceded by a great **quadriporticus** with 146 enormous monolithic granite columns, added by Guglielmo Calderini (1892–1928). The elaborate frescoes on the façade date from 1885. The central bronze doors (**1**) are by Antonio Maraini (1928–30). The **Porta Santa** (**2**) has the bronze *doors (seen from the inside of the basilica) which belonged to the old basilica. They were made at Constantinople by Staurakios in 1070, and inlaid with silver in 54 panels of scenes from the Old and New Testament.

Interior. The nave and transept form in plan a tau, or Egyptian cross, 132m by 65m; the height is 30m. The highly polished marble, alabaster, malachite, lapis and porphyry give an impression of Neo-classical splendour. The **nave**, with double aisles separated from one another by 80 columns of Montórfano granite, is the new part of the basilica. In the centre of the ceiling, which is richly decorated with stuccoes in white and gold, are the arms of Pius IX. The paintings between the windows, executed in the mid-19C, depict scenes in the life of St Paul (by Pietro Gagliardi, Francesco Podesti, Guglielmo de Sanctis, Francesco Coghetti and Cesare Mariani); under these (and in the aisles), forming a frieze, are the portraits in mosaic of all the popes from St Peter to John Paul II. In the outermost aisles are niches with statues of the Apostles. The six huge alabaster columns beside the doors were presented by Mohammed Ali of Egypt. The statue of St Peter (**3**) is by Alberto Giacometti and of St Paul (**4**) by Salvatore Revelli.

The **triumphal arch**, a relic of the old basilica, is supported by two colossal granite columns. Its mosaics (much restored) are due to Galla Placidia. They represent Christ blessing in the Greek manner, with angels; symbols of the Evangelists; the Elders of the Apocalypse; Saints Peter and Paul. On the other face of the arch are the remains of mosaics by Pietro Cavallini. Over the **high altar**, supported by four porphyry columns, is a splendid *tabernacle (**5**), by Arnolfo di Cambio and his companion Pietro (Oderisi?, 1285). The tomb of St

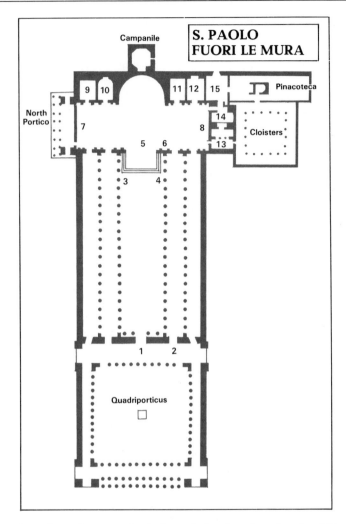

Paul is traditionally supposed to be beneath the altar where there is a 1C tomb, surrounded by Christian and pagan burials. The inscription 'Paolo Apostolo Mart', dates from the time of Constantine. The huge 12C paschal *candlestick (**6**) is by Nicolò di Angelo and Pietro Vassalletto.

The magnificent ceiling of the **transept** is decorated with the arms of Pius VII, Leo XII, Pius VIII and Gregory XVI, as well as with those of the basilica (an arm holding a sword). The walls are covered with rare marbles. The Corinthian pilasters are made up of fragments of the old columns. The great *mosaic of the **apse** was executed c 1220 by Venetian craftsmen sent by Doge Pietro Ziani at the request of Pope Honorius III. It was heavily restored in the 19C after damage in the fire of 1823. The subjects are: Christ blessing in the Greek manner, with

Saints Peter, Andrew, Paul and Luke; at the feet of Christ, Pope Honorius III; below this, a gem-studded cross on the altar, angels and apostles. On the inner face of the arch are the Virgin and Child with St John blessing Pope John XXII.

At either end of the transept is an altar of malachite and lapis lazuli, presented by Nicholas I of Russia: the *Conversion of St Paul* (**7**) is by Vincenzo Camuccini, and the mosaic (**8**), a copy from the *Coronation of the Virgin*, by Giulio Romano. The **Chapel of St Stephen** (**9**) has a statue of St Stephen by Rinaldo Rinaldi, and paintings of his expulsion from the Sanhedrin, by Francesco Coghetti, and of his stoning, by Francesco Podesti. The **Chapel of the Crucifix** (**10**), by Carlo Maderno was the only chapel saved in the fire. On the altar: crucifix attributed to Tino da Camaino; in a niche to the right of the door, statue of St Bridget by Stefano Maderno; to the left, statue of a saint in wood. In this chapel, in 1541, St Ignatius de Loyola and the first Jesuits took the corporate oaths formally establishing their society as a religious order. The **Chapel of the Choir**, or of St Laurence (**11**), is by Guglielmo Calderini. It contains a 15C marble triptych. The **Chapel of St Benedict** (**12**) is a sumptuous work by Luigi Poletti, with a reproduction of the cella of an ancient temple; the 12 fluted columns are from Veio.

The **Sala del Martirologio** (**13**), has badly damaged 13C frescoes, and a bust of Luigi Poletti. The **baptistery** (**14**; designed by Arnaldo Foschini on a Greek-cross plan in 1930) leads into the **vestibule** (**15**) preceding the south door of the church, which contains a colossal statue of Gregory XVI by Rinaldo Rinaldi, and 13C mosaics from the old basilica.

A door to the right off the vestibule leads to the **Cloisters** (open daily 9–13, 15–18) belonging to the old Benedictine convent. They have coupled colonnettes of different forms decorated with mosaics and with tiny couchant animals (most of which have now disappeared) between the columns. In the centre is a rose garden. The cloisters were begun under Abbot Pietro da Capua (1193–1208) and finished after 1228, and are the work, at least in part, of the Vassalletti family of scuptors. Along the walls are placed inscriptions and sculptured fragments: XIV. Statue of Boniface IX; XVII. Sarcophagus with the story of Apollo and Marsyas; XIX. An inscription recording the suicide of Nero (probably a 17C forgery); XX. Statue of a prophet. Off the cloister is the **Chapel of Reliquaries**, with a gilded silver cross, and the **Pinacoteca**, with works by Antoniazzo Romano (*Madonna and four saints*) and Bramantino (*Flagellation*), as well as old prints showing the damage caused by the fire.

From San Paolo the road continues south. After a short distance, a road to the right leads via Viale Marconi to Via del Mare (for Ostia, see Chapter 28). For EUR and the Monastery of Tre Fontane (see Chapter 26), Via Laurentina forks left from Via Ostiense under the railway, and soon joins Via Cristoforo Colombo.

26 · The district of EUR (Esposizione Universale di Roma)

■ EUR is easily reached in 12 minutes from the Station and Colosseum by the underground railway (line B), on which it is the penultimate station. It is also reached by numerous buses, including No. 714 from Stazione Termini and No. 761 from San Paolo fuori le Mura.

From the Porta Ardeatina (Pl. 9; 8) it is approached by Via Cristoforo Colombo (c 6km) which, as a ten-lane highway, passes straight through the middle of EUR.

Esposizione Universale di Roma (now always abbreviated to EUR, prounced 'ay-oor'; Plans 13, 14) was begun in 1938 to the designs of Marcello Piacentini. An ambitious project to symbolise the achievements of Fascism, it was to have been opened for the 1942 World Expo, which was cancelled because of the war. Its buildings were only partly completed, however, and the site suffered some war damage. After 1952 the original structures were restored, new ones were added, and Government offices and public institutions were moved to the site, which has also developed as an exclusive residential district. The monumental white marble buildings are spaciously set out between wide avenues and empty roads, in a setting which recalls the metaphysical paintings of Giorgio De Chirico. Many are now in need of restoration. Some of the huge buildings house museums, arranged for educational purposes and mostly visited by school parties.

Piazza delle Nazioni (Pl. 14; 1) has twin palaces whose façades form two hemicycles. Viale della Civiltà del Lavoro leads right to the Palazzo EUR and, at the end, the Palazzo della Civiltà Italiana built in 1938–43 by Giovanni Guerrini, Ernesto Bruno La Padula, and Mario Romano, now called **Palazzo della Civiltà del Lavoro** (Pl. 13; 2). Known as the 'square Colosseum', it has statues symbolising the arts beneath the lowest arches. At the opposite end of Viale della Civiltà is Palazzo dei Congressi, by Adalberto Libera (1938–54), with paintings by Gino Severini in the atrium.

Beyond is the vast PIAZZA MARCONI (Pl. 14; 3), in the centre of which is a stele of Carrara marble (45m) by Arturo Dazzi (1938–59), dedicated to the inventor Guglielmo Marconi. On the right are two edifices with symmetrical fronts (Palazzi dell'Esposizioni), while between them, further back, is the Grattacielo (skyscraper) Italia (1959–60).

On the left, joined by a huge colonnade, are two palaces of similar design. The one to the left facing the colonnade contains the **Museo Nazionale delle Arti e delle Tradizioni Popolari** (Pl. 14; 3; open 9–14; Sun 9–13. ☎ 592 6148. Lire 4000). The museum contains material collected by Lamberto Loria (1855–1913) for the Museo di Etnografia Italiana, founded in Florence in 1906, and illustrates with models, reconstructions, etc., the various aspects of Italian life. On the ground floor are exhibits relating to transport. The sections on the upper floor include furniture from rural houses, toys, crib figures, carnival and theatrical costumes, musical instruments used during local festivals, and puppets. There is a large collection of 19C and early 20C jewellery. A section on

religious festivals includes ex-votos. On the stair landing is a gondola of 1882. The great hall, with frescoes of 1941, exhibits arts and crafts, with reconstructions of artisans' workshops. The next section illustrates agricultural life. The sections on seafaring and pastoral life are closed for rearrangement.

To the right of the colonnade is the Palazzo delle Scienze which contains the **MUSEO PREISTORICO ED ETNOGRAFICO LUIGI PIGORINI** (Pl. 14; 3). The museum, one of the most important of its kind in the world, is derived from the collection formed in the late 17C by Father Anastasius Kircher in the Collegio dei Gesuiti. From 1871 onwards it was greatly enlarged by Luigi Pigorini, and in 1876 it became the Museo Preistorico del Nuovo Regno d'Italia. After 1913 the protohistoric objects went to Villa Giulia, classical and Christian antiquities to the Museo Nazionale Romano, and medieval exhibits to Palazzo di Venezia.

Opening hours are 9–14; Sun 9–13; closed Mon. ☎ 549 521. Lire 8000.

The **Museo Preistorico** is arranged geographically to indicate the way civilisation developed regionally through the Stone, Bronze and Iron Ages. Most of the exhibits are Italian, of the prehistoric period. They include material from all parts of the peninsula, so that a complete idea may be obtained of the growth of its civilisation and of the commercial and artistic influences of the East and of the countries bordering on the Aegean. The descriptive labels, maps and diagrams are very informative. The most interesting exhibits include: material from cemeteries in the Lazio area; finds of the Italian School in Crete; curious Sardinian statuettes of priests and warriors in bronze; a tomb from Golasecca, representative of the western civilisation of Northern Italy. The objects found in the cemeteries of western and southern Etruria (Vetulonia, Tarquinia, Vulci, Veio, etc.) are particularly interesting; among them are well-tombs (10C–8C BC), with ossuaries resembling those of Villanova, closed with a flat lid or shaped like a house, and trench-tombs (8C–7C BC) showing the influence of Greek commerce, especially on pottery.

The **Ethnographical Collection** includes material from the Americas, Africa, and Oceania collected by Lamberto Loria, Vittorio Bottego, Guido Boggiani, and Enrico Hillyer Giglioli. There is a pre-Columbian archaeological collection from Mexico and the Andes, and artefacts made by the Invits of the Arctic Circle. The collections from Oceania and Africa are at present closed: the African collection includes material from Angola and Zaire. Much of the material which belonged to Loria was collected by him in New Guinea.

Further along the colonnade, on the right, at Viale Lincoln, is the entrance to the **Museo dell'Alto Medioevo** (open 9–14; fest. 9–13. ☎ 592 5806. Lire 4000), which is on the first floor of the Palazzo delle Scienze. A disappointing and small collection made in 1967, it contains Italian material from the fall of the Roman Empire to the 10C AD.

Room I. Heads of a Byzantine Emperor and Empress, gold fibula, all of the late 5C found on the Palatine. **Room II**. Pottery, glass and gold work (including beautiful jewellery) found in a 7C tomb at Nocera Umbra. **Room III**. Contents of a 7C tomb at Castel Trosino, including more very fine jewellery (B, 115, 16), a blue glass rhyton (119), a gold dagger case (F), glass containers (37–45), and fragments of a shield (T).

Rooms IV–V. Collection of 7C–10C church reliefs and friezes. **Room VI**. Finds from the site of Santa Cornelia, near Formello, excavated by the British

School in 1963–65. Remains from three distinct phases were found: early Roman agricultural trenches, a farm and church built by Pope Hadrian I c 780, and a monastic complex (c 1035–41). Also in this room, 8C–9C pottery from the Roman Forum. **Room VII**. Finds from San Rufina, on the Via Cornelia, including mosaics. **Room VIII**. Coptic materials and fabrics of the 5C–8C.

Beyond the colonnade, Viale della Civiltà Romana, leads to the piazza flanked by two symmetrical buildings, again joined by a colonnade, the building of which was financed by the Fiat organisation. Here the **MUSEO DELLA CIVILTÀ ROMANA** (Pl. 14; 4) was inaugurated in 1955. The entrance is in the right wing (open 9–19; Sun 9–13.30; closed Mon. ☎ 592 6041. Lire 5000). The museum, created to house the material from exhibitions held in Rome in 1911 and 1937, consists entirely of plaster casts of famous statues and monuments, and reconstructions of buildings which illustrate the history of ancient Rome and the influence of Roman civilisation throughout the world. They are displayed in 59 rooms of monumental proportions, which have been undergoing lengthy structural repairs for many years.

Each room illustrates a period of the history of Rome, in chronological sequence. **Room VI**: origins of the city; **Room VII**: the conquest of the Mediterranean; **Room VIII**: Julius Caesar; **Room IX**: Augustus (including a reproduction of the pronaos of the temple of Augustus at Ancyra); **Rooms X–XIV**: the Roman emperors; **Room XV**: Christianity; **Rooms XVI–XIX**: the Roman army. **Room XXXVII** in the opposite wing of the museum (reached by returning to the entrance and crossing the piazza) contains a celebrated *model of Rome (on a scale of 1:250) as it was in the 4C.

The other rooms are closed at present. They include displays devoted to the navy; ports; central administration; the Imperial court; the 'triumphs' celebrated in Rome for victorious generals; the provinces of the Roman empire; the 11 'regions' of Italy; methods of construction (quarries and mines); baths and aqueducts; theatres, amphitheatres and circuses; fora, temples and basilicas; military architecture; Roman roads; education; funerary monuments; domestic architecture; the family; religion; portraits; law; libraries; music; science and letters; medicine; artisans; agriculture; hunting and fishing; commerce; and art. In **Room LI** is a complete collection of *casts made in 1860 from Trajan's Column, and in **Room LIX** the reconstruction of part of the Column of Marcus Aurelius.

Viale dell'Arte leads left; the second turning to the right is Viale Europa. Here are the ministries of Foreign Trade and Finance, built after the war. On the corner of Via Cristoforo Colombo is the Ministry of Postal Services and Communications, with the well-arranged **Museo Storico delle Poste e delle Telecommunicazioni** (Pl. 13; 4; open 9–13; closed Sun. Lire 1000). The postal display begins with a casket of 1300 used by the Pontifical Post Office of Urbino and 17C letter boxes, including a 'bocca di leone', and there is a fine copy on tile of the Peutinger Table (an ancient map of the military roads of the western Roman Empire). Later postal history (pioneer air-mail flights; Ethiopian military cancellers, etc.) is well chosen. Here also is displayed the electronic calculator invented by Enrico Fermi, and made in 1956. The history of telegraph and telephone is copiously illustrated by original appliances, including apparatus used by Marconi in his 1901 experiments between Cornwall and Newfoundland.

Viale Europa ends in steps which lead up to the massive church of **Santi Pietro e Paolo** (Pl. 13; 3), with a cupola almost as large as that of St Peter's. Dating from 1938–55, it was designed by Arnaldo Foschini. The first turning right at the foot of the steps leads to the Piscina delle Rose in Viale America and a large open-air theatre. Parallel to this road is a lake about 1km long, divided into three basins, the sides of which are planted with a thousand cherry trees from Japan. This area is perhaps the most successfully planned within the EUR complex. Bridges lead to the **Palazzo dello Sport** (Pl. 13; 6), designed by Pier Luigi Nervi and Marcello Piacentini for the Olympic Games of 1960, and an outstanding work of modern architecture. Constructed of prefabricated concrete, it is covered by a fine rib-vaulted dome 100m in diameter, and seats 15,000 spectators. The well designed Velodromo Olimpico, for cycling events, is about 500m east.

About 1km east of the point where Via Cristoforo Colombo crosses Via delle Tre Fontane, and reached by the latter and Via Laurentina, is the **Abbazia delle Tre Fontane** (Pl. 14; 2). This was built on the traditional site of the martyrdom of St Paul, whose severed head, rebounding three times, is supposed to have caused three fountains to spring up. A monastic community from Asia Minor was established here by 641. St Bernard is believed to have stayed here on his visit to Rome in 1138–40. Three churches were built, but the locality was afterwards abandoned as malarial. In 1868 it was acquired by the Trappists, who drained the ground and planted large groves of eucalyptus. A eucalyptus liqueur is distilled in the community. This and chocolate made by the monks are on sale.

An ilex avenue leads to a medieval fortified gate, with a frescoed vault. A small garden contains classical fragments, and is filled with the sound of doves and a fountain. Ahead is the porch of **Santi Vincenzo ed Anastasio**. It was founded by Honorius I (625), rebuilt by Honorius III (1221), and restored by the Trappists. The spacious plain interior preserves its marble windows. In the nave are poorly restored frescoes of the Apostles (16C).

On the right, on high ground, is **Santa Maria Scala Coeli**, an old church with an octagonal interior, rebuilt by Giacomo della Porta (1582). The design can best be appreciated from the outside. It owes its name to the legend that St Bernard, while celebrating mass, saw in a vision the soul for which he was praying ascend by a ladder from purgatory to heaven. The Cosmatesque altar which was the scene of this miracle is still preserved in the crypt. The mosaics in the left-hand apse (Saints with Clement VIII and his nephew Aldobrandini) are by Francesco Zucchi from designs by Giovanni de' Vecchi.

From the left of this church an avenue leads to **San Paolo alle Tre Fontane**, a 5C church, rebuilt by Della Porta in 1599, with a good façade. Inside to the right is the pillar to which St Paul is supposed to have been bound; on the floor are two Roman mosaic pavements from Ostia.

27 · The Vatican City. St Peter's and the Vatican Museums

Vatican City

The Vatican City (*Città del Vaticano*; Pl. 1; 5, 6) lies on the right bank of the Tiber. Through the Lateran Treaty (or Concordat) signed at the Lateran Palace on 11 February 1929, the Vatican City has the status of an independent sovereign state. With an area of 43 hectares (less than half a square kilometre) and a population of about 550, it is, in size, the smallest independent state in existence. The States of the Church before the unification of Italy in 1870 extended for 44,547 square kilometres. As the residence of the Pope and the site of St Peter's, the most important Roman Catholic church, it attracts hundreds of thousands of visitors from all over the world. The decorations in the Vatican Palace include the famous frescoes in the Sistine Chapel and the 'Stanze' which, respectively, are the masterpieces of Michelangelo and Raphael. The Vatican museums are unique in their scope, quality, and abundance.

■ An **Information Office** is open 8.30–19 (except Wednesday when papal audiences are being held in the Piazza) in Piazza San Pietro to the left of the façade of the basilica (☎ 698 84466 for general information and 698 83333 for museum information).

■ **Dress**. You are not allowed inside St Peter's or the Vatican City wearing shorts or mini-skirts, or with bare shoulders.

The Concordat defined the limits of the Vatican City (see Plan on p 310) which is surrounded by a high wall, skirted by Viale Vaticano for the whole of its length. There are three **entrances to the Vatican City**, protected by members of the Swiss Guard, and not open to the general public. The Portone di Bronzo, in the colonnade to the right of St Peter's, is the official entrance to the Holy See. The Arco delle Campane, to the left of St Peter's is the entrance for cars (and the bus which runs from Piazza San Pietro to the Vatican Museums); it is also used for access to the Audience Hall, and for the organised tours of the gardens and City, and of the necropolis below St Peter's. The Cancello di Sant'Anna, in Via di Porta Angelica, is used for the Polyglot Printing Press, the offices of the *Osservatore Romano*, etc. The **entrance to the Vatican Museums and the Sistine Chapel** (see p 325) is in Viale Vaticano. **For admission to St Peter's**, see p 313.

The Pope and the Vatican State

The Hierarchy. The Pope is **Sovereign Pontiff**, the Bishop of Rome, successor to St Peter, and, as such, the head of the Roman Catholic Church and the Vicar of Christ. He enjoys the *primatus jurisdictionis*, that is, the supreme jurisdictional power over the whole Church. By the Vatican City law of Pius XI (1921), the Pope is head of the legislature, executive and judiciary, and he nominates the General Council and the Governor of the Vatican. He is assisted by the Sacred College of Cardinals and by the Roman Curia. The **Sacred College of**

Cardinals was limited by Sixtus V to 70, but after the consistory of March 1962 the number was increased to 87. John XXIII created 46 new cardinals, and gave them all episcopal dignity. At present there is no limit to the number of cardinals who can be appointed. The College consists of six Cardinal Bishops (whose dioceses are the suburbicarian sees of Ostia, Velletri, Porto and Santa Rufina, Albano, Frascati and Palestrina), nearly 70 Cardinal Priests, and 14 Cardinal Deacons. The **Roman Curia** comprises the 12 **Sacred Congregations**, which deal with the central administration of the Church, the three *Tribunals*, and the six *Offices* (which includes the *Cardinal Secretary of State*, who represents the Vatican in international relations).

The Vatican State has its own postal service, and its own currency. Its newspaper, the *Osservatore Romano*, has a world-wide circulation. It owns a radio transmitting station (prominent in the Second World War). Policing is carried out by the **Swiss Guard**, a corps founded in 1506, which retains the picturesque uniform said to have been designed by Michelangelo. The Noble Guards and Palatine Guards established in the 19C were disbanded by Pope Paul VI in 1970, and the Pontifical Gendarmes transformed into a private corps.

The *Lateran Treaty* (or Concordat) also granted the privilege of extraterritoriality to the basilicas of St John Lateran (with the Lateran Palace), Santa Maria Maggiore and San Paolo fuori le Mura, and to certain other buildings, including the Palazzo della Cancelleria, and to the Pope's villa at Castel Gandolfo. Special clauses in the treaty provided for access to St Peter's and the Vatican Museums. Under the treaty, Italy accepted canon law on marriage and divorce and made religious teaching compulsory in secondary as well as primary schools. Italy also agreed to make a payment in final settlement of the claims by the Holy See for the loss of papal property taken over by the Italian Government. After the signing of the Lateran Treaty the Pope, for the first time since 1870, came out of the Vatican. A new Concordat was signed between the Italian Government and the Vatican in 1984 in Villa Madama (this made religious instruction in schools optional, and contained modifications regarding marriage, etc.)

Conclave (from the Latin, a room that can be locked). On the death of a pope, cardinals under the age of 80 are confined in a chosen locality, usually the Sistine Chapel, to elect a new pope. The place chosen is locked both inside and outside and it includes rooms for the cardinals and their attendants. The internal guardian is the Camerlengo; the external guardian the Commander of the Swiss Guard. The cardinals meet twice daily before the voting procedure takes place. The result of the vote is indicated by the colour of the smoke which issues from a vent above the Sistine Chapel. If the smoke is black the election is still in doubt; if white, the new pope has been elected. The old practice of burning the voting papers (mixed with damp straw for the black) to produce the smoke, was discontinued after the conclave of 1958. The new pope is proclaimed by the senior cardinal-deacon from the central balcony on the façade of St Peter's, from where also he gives his blessing. Since the proceedings take some time, there is always an interregnum between the death of a pope and the election of his successor; John Paul I died on 29 September and John Paul II was elected on 16 October 1978.

Holy Year. The Roman Catholic Church adapted the secular Jewish idea of the jubilee, giving it an exclusively religious meaning; the remission of the temporal punishment of sins substituted for the remission of debts. The first Holy Year was proclaimed from the balcony of St John Lateran on 22 February 1300, by Boniface VIII. The pope gave a plenary indulgence to those confessed communicants who, on the occasion of every centenary of the birth of Christ, visited the four major basilicas—St Peter's, San Paolo fuori le Mura, St John Lateran and Santa Maria Maggiore—within a specified time. In 1343 Clement VI reduced the interval from 100 to 33 years and Paul II (1464–71) to 25 years. This quarter-century interval has been maintained, with few exceptions, ever since: i.e. in 1900, 1925, 1950 and 1975. In addition to the regular celebrations, a Jubilee has occasionally been proclaimed for a special reason, as in 1933, when Pius XI commemorated the 19th centenary of the Crucifixion, or in 1983/4 when John Paul II commemorated the 1950 years since the Death and Resurrection of Christ. The next Holy Year will be in the year 2000.

A Holy Year is usually inaugurated on the preceding Christmas Eve with the opening of the Holy Doors (*Porte Sante*) of the four major basilicas. The Holy Door of St Peter's is opened by the Pope; the other three are opened by their archpriests. The Pope used to wield a silver hammer and a temporary wall in front of the door would fall inwards. In 1983 the Pope used a bronze hammer and the Porta Santa was unlocked for him. In the ceremony the Pope crosses the threshold bareheaded and carrying a torch, followed by cardinals and attendants. At the end of the Holy Year the Holy Doors are reclosed by the Pope.

Papal Audiences. General Audiences usually take place at 10.00 or 11.00 on Wed mornings (9.00 in September) in the New Audience Hall or on the Piazza. The New Audience Hall is reached under the colonnade to the left of the façade of St Peter's. A special section is set aside for newly married couples. Audiences are now also sometimes held in St Peter's, or in the Piazza (when the Pope is transported by jeep). Application to attend an audience can be made in writing to the Prefetto della Casa Pontificia, Città del Vaticano, 00120 Rome (☎ 698 83017; fax 698 85863). Otherwise you can apply in person at the Portone di Bronzo (open 9–13) in the colonnade to the right of St Peter's. At the far end of the Corridore del Bernini is the Scala Regia, the staircase leading to the Sala Regia. At a table at the entrance you are asked to fill in a form and take it to the office of the Prefettura, on the first floor reached by the Scala Pia.

Piazza San Pietro

Piazza San Pietro (Pl. 1; 6), the masterpiece of Gian Lorenzo Bernini (1656–67), is one of the most superb conceptions of its kind in civic architecture, and is a fitting approach to the world's greatest basilica. Partly enclosed by two semicircular colonnades, it has the form of an ellipse adjoining an almost rectangular quadrilateral. At the end, above a triple flight of steps, rises St Peter's basilica, with the buildings of the Vatican towering on the right. Each of the two colonnades has a quadruple row of Doric columns, forming three parallel covered walks. There are in all 284 columns and 88 pilasters. On the Ionic entablature are 96 statues of saints and martyrs.

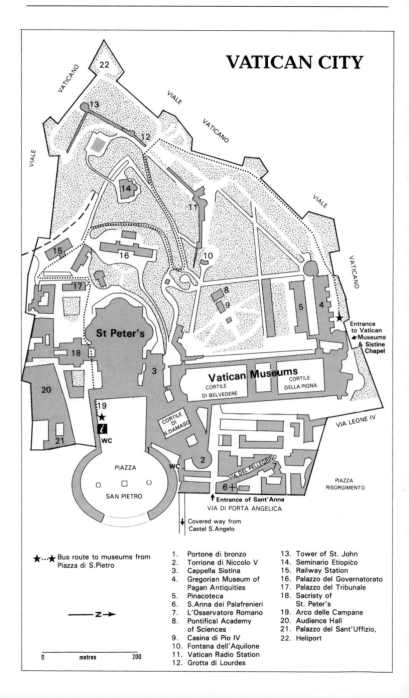

VATICAN CITY

VATICANO

VIALE

VATICANO

VIALE

VIALE

VATICANO

St Peter's

Vatican Museums

CORTILE
DI BELVEDERE

CORTILE
DELLA PIGNA

Entrance
to Vatican
Museums
& Sistine
Chapel

VIA LEONE IV

CORTILE
DI
S.DAMASO

WC

PIAZZA

SAN PIETRO

WC

VIA DEL PELLEGRINO

PIAZZA
RISORGIMENTO

Entrance of Sant'Anna
VIA DI PORTA ANGELICA

Covered way from
Castel S.Angelo

★···★ Bus route to museums from
Piazza di S.Pietro

→—Z→

0   metres   200

1. Portone di bronzo
2. Torrione di Niccolo V
3. Cappella Sistina
4. Gregorian Museum of
   Pagan Antiquities
5. Pinacoteca
6. S.Anna dei Palafrenieri
7. L'Osservatore Romano
8. Pontifical Academy
   of Sciences
9. Casina di Pio IV
10. Fontana dell'Aquilone
11. Vatican Radio Station
12. Grotta di Lourdes

13. Tower of St. John
14. Seminario Etiopico
15. Railway Station
16. Palazzo del Governatorato
17. Palazzo del Tribunale
18. Sacristy of
    St. Peter's
19. Arco delle Campane
20. Audience Hall
21. Palazzo del Sant'Uffizio,
22. Heliport

In the middle of the piazza, on a tall plinth, is an **Obelisk**, devoid of hiero-glyphics, 25.5m high. It was brought from Alexandria (where it had been set up by Augustus) in AD 37, and it is thought that Caligula placed it in his circus, later called the Circus of Nero. In 1586 Sixtus V ordered its removal from the south of the basilica to its present site and put Domenico Fontana in charge of operations. No fewer than 900 men, 150 horses and 47 cranes were required. In the 18C the delightful story was invented that the Pope forbade the spectators, under pain of death, to speak while the obelisk was being raised into position. A sailor called Bresca, seeing that the tension on the ropes had not been correctly assessed and that they were giving way under the strain, transgressed the order, and shouted 'Acqua alle funi!' ('wet the ropes!'). It is said that the Pope rewarded him by granting his family the privilege of supplying St Peter's with palms for Palm Sunday. Round the foot of the obelisk is a plan of the mariner's compass, giving the names of the winds. The globe which surmounted the obelisk until 1586, when it was replaced by a cross, is now in Palazzo dei Conservatori.

The two abundant **fountains** are supplied by the Acqua Paola. The one on the right was designed by Carlo Maderno (1614; a similar fountain had existed in the piazza since 1490). It was moved to its present site and slightly modified by Bernini in 1667, when the second fountain was begun. Between the obelisk and each fountain is a round porphyry slab from which you have the illusion that each of the colonnades has only a single row of columns. In this piazza on 13 May 1981 a Turk, Mehmet Ali Agca, made an attempt on the life of John Paul II.

Covered galleries, also decorated with statues, unite the colonnades with the portico of St Peter's. The gallery on the right, known as the *Corridore del Bernini* and leading to the Scala Regia, is closed by the Portone di Bronzo. A great stair-case, of three flights, leads up to the portico of the basilica. At the foot are colossal statues of St Peter (by Giuseppe de Fabris) and St Paul (by Adamo Tadolini), set up here by Pius IX.

St Peter's

St Peter's, or the *Basilica di San Pietro in Vaticano* (Pl. 1; 5, 6), is perhaps the most imposing church in Christendom. Though neither a cathedral nor the mother church of the Catholic faith (that position is held by S. Giovanni in Laterano), it is the composite work of some of the greatest artists of the 16C, and a master-piece of the Italian High Renaissance. Orientated towards the west and approached through its monumental piazza, the church has its fitting culmina-tion in Michelangelo's dome.

History
According to the Liber Pontificalis, Pope St Anacletus built an oratory (c AD 90) over the tomb of St Peter, close to the Circus of Nero, near which he had been martyred. It is now thought that there may have been a confusion of names, and that Pope St Anicetus (155–66) was probably responsible for the oratory. On the site of this oratory the Emperor Constantine, at the request of Pope St Sylvester I, began a basilica c 319–22, which was conse-crated on 18 November 326. The basilica was 120m long and 65m wide, about half the size of the present edifice. It was preceded by a great quad-

rangular colonnaded portico. The nave and double aisles were divided by 86 marble columns, some of which were said to have been taken from the Septizonium on the Palatine (if so, this was long before the demolition of that building by Sixtus V). It contained numerous monuments of popes and emperors, was decorated with frescoes and mosaics, and was visited by pilgrims from all over Europe. Charlemagne was crowned here by Leo III in 800. Some of its relics are preserved (see below). Its façade is shown in Raphael's fresco the Incendio di Borgo in the 'Stanze' in the Vatican.

In the middle of the 15C the old basilica showed signs of collapse, and Nicholas V, recognising its importance to the prestige of the Roman Catholic faith, decided to rebuild it. He entrusted the work to Bernardo Rossellino, Leon Battista Alberti, and Giuliano da Sangallo, but on the Pope's death in 1455, building work was virtually suspended for half a century. Julius II decided on a complete reconstruction, and he employed Bramante, who started work in 1506. Most of the old church was dismantled, and much was destroyed which could have been preserved: Bramante was nicknamed 'Bramante Ruinante'. The new basilica was on a Greek-cross plan surmounted by a gigantic central dome and flanked by four smaller cupolas. By the time of Bramante's death in 1514, the four central piers and the arches of the dome had been completed.

Leo X employed Raphael to continue the building (on a Latin-cross plan) in collaboration with Fra Giocondo (died 1515) and Giuliano da Sangallo (died 1516). On Raphael's death in 1520 Baldassarre Peruzzi reverted to Bramante's design. Neither Adrian VI, the austere theologian who regarded art as hostile to the Church, nor Clement VII (1523–34) overwhelmed by political disturbances brought about by the Reformation and culminating in the sack of Rome (1527), were interested in the completion of the basilica. However, under Paul III the work received fresh impetus from Antonio da Sangallo the Younger. In 1539 he made a huge wooden model of the basilica readopting the Latin-cross plan (this remarkable work, 736cm x 602cm, and 468cm high, survives and was restored in 1994, although it is not at present on display). At Sangallo's death in 1546, Michelangelo, then 72 years old, was summoned by Paul III. Michelanglo decided on the original Greek-cross plan, and developed Bramante's idea with even greater audacity. He took Brunelleschi's Florentine cupola for his model, and replaced Bramante's piers with new, stronger, ones. His plan for the façade was derived from the Pantheon. Confirmed in his appointment by Paul III's successors, he continued to direct the work until his death in 1564. Vignola and Pirro Ligorio then took over the work, and were followed by Giacomo della Porta (assisted by Carlo Fontana), who completed the dome in 1590, and added the two smaller domes.

In 1605 Paul V demolished what had been left of the old basilica, pulled down the incomplete façade, and directed Carlo Maderno to lengthen the nave towards the old Piazza San Pietro. The present façade and portico are Maderno's work. Thus, after many vicissitudes, the basilica was completed on a Latin-cross plan. On 18 November 1626, the 1300th anniversary of the original consecration, Urban VIII consecrated the new church. Bernini, who succeeded Maderno in 1629, and was commissioned to decorate the interior, wanted to erect two campanili by the façade, but the one that he

completed began to crack on its sinking foundations and was pulled down. Alexander VII kept Bernini as architect of St Peter's, and under him the piazza was begun in 1656. The sacristy was built in the 18C.

In 1940 the ancient cemetery in which St Peter was buried after his crucifixion was discovered beneath the Vatican Grottoes, and on 23 December 1950, the Pope announced that the tomb of St Peter had been identified (see below).

Dimensions. The exterior length of the church, including the portico is 211.5m; the cross on the dome is 136.5m above the ground. The façade is 115m long and 45.5m high. Inside, the church is 186m long and 137m wide across the transepts. The nave is 60m across (including the aisles) and 44m high; the diameter of the dome is 42m, or 1.5m less than that of the Pantheon. The total area is 49,737 sq m (St Paul's in London is 26,639 sq m).

■ **Admission**. The basilica is open daily from 7–19 (7–18 in Oct–Mar). You are not allowed to enter the church wearing shorts or mini-skirts, or with bare shoulders. Mass is held on Sunday at 7, 8, 9, and 10 (Sung Mass at 10.30), and frequently during the week. Holy Communion can be taken in the Cappella del Santissimo Sacramento throughout the day on Sunday. For information on services, ☎ 698 85318.

Exterior

At the top of the triple flight of steps rises the long **façade**. Its great size impairs the view of the dome from the piazza. Eight columns and four pilasters support the entablature. A dedicatory inscription on the frieze records its erection in 1612, during the pontificate of Paul V. The attic, almost without ornament, is surmounted by a balustrade on which are statues of Christ, St John the Baptist and 11 of the Apostles (St Peter's statue is inside), and two clocks, by Giuseppe Valadier (near the ends). Under the left-hand clock are the six bells of the basilica, electrically operated since 1931. The oldest bell dates from 1288; the largest (1786) is 7.5m round and weighs 9.75 tonnes. Above the doors and extending beyond them on either side is a row of nine large windows with balconies. The central balcony is that from which the senior cardinal-deacon proclaims the newly elected pope and from which the new Pope gives his blessing. Below the balcony is a relief, by Ambrogio Bonvicino, of Christ handing the keys to St Peter.

The **portico** is prolonged by vestibules at both ends connecting with the covered galleries of the piazza. The pavement was designed by Bernini. The vault is magnificently decorated in stucco, by Martino Ferrabosco; in the lunettes below it are 32 statues of canonised popes. Of the five entrances to the church, that on the extreme right is the **Porta Santa**, which is sealed from the inside and opened only in Holy Years (it will next be open from Christmas 1999 to Christmas 2000). The panels on the door are by Vico Consorti (1950). The door on the right of the main door is by Venanzio Crocetti (1968). The bronze **central door**, from Old St Peter's, was decorated by Filarete in 1439–45 with reliefs of Christ, the Virgin, Saints Peter and Paul and their martyrdom, and events in the life of Pope Eugenius IV. Around them is a frieze of classical and mythological subjects, animals, fruits, and portraits of emperors. The door to the

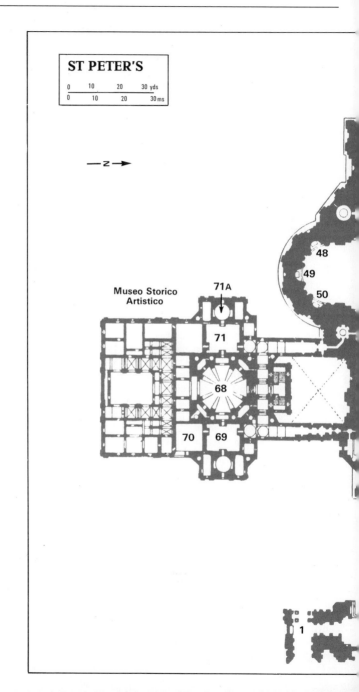

ST PETER'S

0   10   20   30 yds
0   10   20   30 ms

—z→

48
49
50

Museo Storico
Artistico

71A

71

68

70   69

1

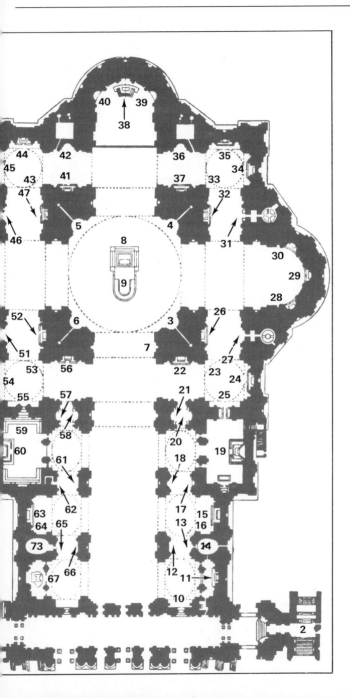

left is by Giacomo Manzù, (1963), with sculptures depicting the death of religious figures and abstract themes of death; the door on the extreme left is by Luciano Minguzzi (1977).

High up on the wall between the doors are three framed inscriptions: the one on the left commemorating the donation by Gregory II of certain olive trees to provide oil for the lamps over the tomb of St Peter; the Latin epitaph of Hadrian I (772–95), attributed to Charlemagne; and the bull of Boniface VIII proclaiming the first jubilee or Holy Year (1300). In the tympanum, above the central entrance (that is, looking backwards, against the light) is the **navicella**, a mosaic representing Christ walking on the waters, executed by Giotto for the old basilica. It has frequently been moved, and has suffered from resetting and restoration; it is now virtually a copy of the original. The equestrian statue of Charlemagne (**1**), at the left end of the portico, is by Agostino Cornacchini; that on the right, of **Constantine** (**2**), is by Bernini.

Interior

The immensity of the interior is disguised by the symmetry of its proportions. The work of Bernini for this majestic church, which had begun with the approach to it and his decorations on Ponte Sant'Angelo, and was continued in the piazza, culminates in the magnificent baldacchino and exedra in the tribune. As the shrine of St Peter, the church has a ceremonial air, with temporary pews beneath the gilded coffered ceiling designed by Bramante. The coloured marble of the walls and pavement is the work of Giacomo della Porta and Bernini.

Nave. The first part of the nave, with its aisles and three side chapels, is Maderno's extension, which transformed the plan of the church from a Greek to a Latin cross. The round slab of porphyry let into the pavement in front of the central door is that on which the emperors used to kneel for their coronation in front of the altar of the old basilica. Further on are metal lines indicating the lengths of the principal churches of Europe. The nave is separated from the aisles by colossal piers, each decorated with two fluted Corinthian pilasters, supporting great arches. In the niches between the pilasters of the nave and transepts are statues of the founders of the religious orders. The aisles have sumptuous decorations by Bernini. Over the spaces between the piers are elliptical cupolas, three on either side, decorated with elaborate mosaics. In addition to these six minor cupolas there are four circular domes over the corner chapels in the main body of the church.

Michelangelo's **dome** is an architectural masterpiece. Simple and dignified, and flooded with light, it rises immediately above the site of St Peter's tomb. Four pentagonal piers support the arches on which rests the drum of the cupola. The **piers** are decorated with balconies and niches designed by Bernini. Each balcony has two spiral columns taken from the saint's shrine in the old basilica (another of these columns is the Colonna Santa; see below). The niches are filled with colossal statues, which give each of the piers its name: St Longinus (**3**), by Bernini; St Helena (**4**), by Andrea Bolgi; St Veronica (**5**), by Francesco Mochi; and St Andrew (**6**), by François Duquesnoy. On the balconies are reliefs referring to the 'Reliquie Maggiori'; these precious relics, which are displayed in Holy Week, are preserved in the podium of the pier of St Veronica. They are the lance of St Longinus, the soldier who pierced the side of Christ on the Cross, presented to Innocent VIII; a piece of the True Cross, collected by St Helena; and the cloth

of St Veronica, with the miraculous image of Christ. The head of St Andrew, presented to Pius II in 1462 by Thomas Paleologos, despot of the Morea, was recently returned to the Greek Orthodox Church at Patras.

The Latin inscription on the frieze of the dome is a continuation of the Greek inscription in the tribune. In the pendentives of the dome are huge mosaics of the Evangelists (the pen held by St Mark is 1.5m long). On the frieze below the drum is inscribed in letters nearly 2m high: 'Tu es Petrus et super hanc petram aedificabo ecclesiam meam et tibi dabo claves regni caelorum.' ('You are Peter, and upon this rock I will build my church; and I will give you the keys of the kingdom of heaven'). The dome is divided into 16 compartments, corresponding to the windows of the drum, by ribs ornamented with stucco; in these compartments are six bands of mosaic by Cavaliere d'Arpino, representing saints, angels, and the company of Heaven; in the lantern above is the Redeemer.

Under a canopy against the pier of St Longinus is the famous bronze **statue of St Peter (7)**, seated on a marble throne. It was once believed to date from the 5C or 6C, but, since its restoration in 1990, is considered to be the work of Arnolfo di Cambio (c 1296). The extended foot of the statue has been worn away by the kisses of the faithful. The statue is robed on high festivals. Above is a portrait in mosaic of Pius IX (1871).

Over the high altar rises the great **baldacchino (8)**, designed by Bernini and unveiled on 28 June 1633 by Urban VIII. This colossal Baroque structure, a combination of architecture and decorative sculpture, is cast from bronze taken from the Pantheon. Four gilt bronze Solomonic columns rise from their marble plinths, which are decorated with the Barberini bees. The columns resemble in design the Colonna Santa (see below) but are decorated with figures of genii and laurel branches. They support a canopy from which hang festoons and tassels and on which angels (by Duquesnoy) alternate with children. From the four corners of the canopy ascend ornamental scrolls, which support the globe and cross. Inside the top of the canopy is the Dove in an aureole.

The **High Altar**, at which only the Pope may celebrate, is formed of a block of Greek marble found in the Forum of Nerva and consecrated by Clement VIII on 26 June 1594. It covers the altar of Calixtus II (died 1123) which in turn encloses an altar of Gregory the Great (died 604). It stands over the space which is recognised as the tomb of St Peter.

In front (**9**) is the **confessione**, built by Maderno and encircled by perpetually burning lamps. It is directly above the ancient Roman necropolis, where the Tropaion of Gaius (see below) was found, below the Vatican Grottoes.

South aisle. Above the Porta Santa is a mosaic of St Peter (**10**), designed by Ciro Ferri (1675). The Cappella della Pietà (**11**) is named after **Michelangelo's Pietà** (1499; restored and protected by glass since its damage in 1972). This exquisite work was made at the age of 25 for the French ambassador, Cardinal Jean de Bilhères de Lagraulas. It is perhaps the most moving of all Michelangelo's sculptures and is the only one inscribed with his name (on the ribbon falling from the left shoulder of the Virgin). The mosaic decorations of the cupola, by Pietro da Cortona and Ciro Ferri, depict the Passion. The *Triumph of the Cross* is by Lanfranco.

The monument to Queen Christina of Sweden (**12**) is by Carlo Fontana (1689), and the statue of Leo XII (**13**), by Giuseppe de Fabris (1836). Beneath it

is the entrance to the small Cappella del Crocifisso (**14**; usually closed), with a *Crucifixion* ascribed to Pietro Cavallini.

The Cappella di San Sebastiano (**15**) has an altar mosaic of the saint's martyrdom, after Domenichino. The monument (**16**) to Pius XI (died 1939) is by Francesco Nagni. Opposite is a monument to Pius XII (died 1958) by Francesco Messina. Under the next arch (**17**) are a fine Baroque monument to Innocent XII (died 1700), by Filippo Valle, and one by Bernini (**18**) of the Countess Matilda of Tuscany (died 1115), whose remains were moved from Mantua in 1635.

The iron grille of the **Cappella del Santissimo Sacramento** (**19**) was designed by Borromini. Over the altar is a gilt bronze ciborium by Bernini, modelled on Bramante's 'tempietto' at San Pietro in Montorio. The two angels also form part of this unfinished composition. Behind is the Trinity, by Pietro da Cortona. Over the altar on the right is a mosaic of the Ecstasy of St Francis, after Domenichino.

Under the next arch are the interesting monument (**20**) to Gregory XIII (died 1585), the reformer of the calendar (by Camillo Rusconi; 1723), and the unfinished tomb (**21**) of Gregory XIV (died 1591). Opposite (**22**), is a *mosaic of the Communion of St Jerome, after Domenichino.

The **Cappella Gregoriana** (**23**) was built by Gregory XIII from designs by Michelangelo, with a cupola 42m above the floor. The chapel is dedicated to the *Madonna del Soccorso*, an ancient painting (**24**) on part of a marble column from the old basilica, placed here in 1578. Beneath the altar is the tomb of St Gregory Nazianzen, and on the right is that of Gregory XVI (died 1846), by Luigi Amici (1855; **25**). Under the next arch is a mosaic (**26**) of the Mass of St Basil, after Subleyras. Opposite is the tomb of Benedict XIV (**27**), by Pietro Bracci; the statue of the Pope (died 1758) shows him proclaiming the Holy Year of 1750.

The **south transept** has three altars decorated with mosaics, depicting St Wenceslas (**28**), after Angelo Caroselli; the Martyrdom of Saints Processus and Martinian, St Peter's gaolers (**29**), after Valentin; and the Martyrdom of St Erasmus (**30**), after Nicolas Poussin (1629). The splendid *monument of Clement XIII (**31**) is by Canova, and the Altar of the Navicella (**32**) has a mosaic of Christ walking on the waters, after Lanfranco; the subject is the same as that of Giotto's mosaics in the portico.

The **Cappella di San Michele** (**33**) contains mosaics of St Michael (**34**), after Guido Reni, and of *St Petronilla (**35**), after Guercino. To the left (**36**) is the monument of Clement X (died 1676), by Mattia de Rossi; opposite (**37**) is a mosaic of St Peter raising Tabitha, after Placido Costanzi.

Two porphyry steps from the old basilica lead to the **tribune**, the most conspicuous object in which is the **Chair of St Peter** (**38**), an ambitious and theatrical composition by Bernini (1665). This enormous gilt bronze throne is supported by statues of four Fathers of the Church: Saints Augustine and Ambrose, of the Latin Church (in mitres), and Saints Athanasius and John Chrysostom, of the Greek Church (bareheaded). It encloses an ancient wooden chair inlaid with ivory, said to have been the episcopal chair of St Peter. A circle of flying angels surrounds a great halo of gilt stucco in the centre of which, providing the focal point of the whole church, is the **Dove** set in the window above the throne.

On the right of St Peter's Chair (**39**) is the fine **monument to Urban VIII** (died 1644), also by Bernini, with statues of the pope and allegorical figures of

Charity and Justice. The design of the tomb is clearly influenced by the Medici tombs in Florence by Michelangelo. The use of different materials in the sculpture give an effective colour to the monument. On the left (**40**) is the monument to Paul III (died 1549), by Guglielmo della Porta, a less successful attempt at the same type of tomb sculpture and design. Beyond the tribune (**41**) is a mosaic of St Peter healing the paralytic, after Francesco Mancini; opposite (**42**) is the monument to Alexander VIII (died 1691), by Arrigo di San Martino; the bronze statue of the pope is by Giuseppe Bertosi, and the other sculptures are by Angelo de Rossi.

North aisle. The **Cappella della Colonna** (**43**), one of the corner chapels with round cupolas, was decorated in 1757 with figures of angels carrying garlands and with symbols of the Virgin. The lunettes have mosaics after Francesco Romanelli. In this chapel is the tomb of St Leo the Great (died 461; **44**); above is a *relief by Alessandro Algardi (1650), representing St Leo arresting the progress of Attila with the help of Saints Peter and Paul. On the altar (left, **45**) is an ancient and greatly venerated representation of the Virgin painted on a column from the old basilica. In the middle of the chapel is the tombstone of Leo XII (died 1829). The monument (**46**) of Alexander VII (died 1667), is Bernini's last work in St Peter's. Opposite is a mosaic (**47**), Apparition of the Sacred Heart, after Carlo Muccioli, set here in 1922 by Benedict XV in place of an oil-painting on slate (*Punishment of Simon Magus*, by Francesco Vanni).

The **north transept** contains confessionals for foreigners, served by the Penitentiaries, who hear confessions in ten languages. The three altars are decorated with mosaics: St Thomas (**48**), after Vincenzo Camuccini; Crucifixion of St Peter (**49**), after Guido Reni; and St Joseph (**50**). In front of the central altar is the tomb of the composer Palestrina (1594) by Achille Funi.

Over the door to the sacristy (**51**) is the Neo-classical monument to Pius VIII (died 1830), by Pietro Tenerani; opposite (**52**), a mosaic of Ananias and Sapphira, after Pomarancio. The **Cappella Clementina** (**53**) is the fourth of the corner chapels with round cupolas; the cupola is decorated with mosaics after Pomarancio. The chapel is named after Clement VIII (died 1605), who ordered Giacomo della Porta to decorate it for the jubilee of 1600. It contains the tomb of St Gregory the Great (died 604; **54**), beneath the altar. Above it is a mosaic of a miracle of St Gregory, after Andrea Sacchi. To the left of the altar (**55**) is a monument to Pius VII (died 1823), by Thorvaldsen, a classical work showing the influence of Canova.

On the pier of St Andrew is a mosaic of the Transfiguration (**56**), a copy (enlarged four times) of Raphael's painting in the Vatican Pinacoteca. Opposite, beneath the aisle arch (**57**), is the *monument of Leo XI, who reigned for only 27 days (died 1605), by Alessandro Algardi, and that of Innocent XI (died 1689; **58**), by Pierre Monnot (the urn decorated with a relief of the liberation of Vienna by John Sobieski).

The **Cappella del Coro** (**59**; closed) is richly decorated in stucco by Giovanni Battista Ricci after designs by Giacomo della Porta. It has a fine gate with the arms of Clement XIII, elegant classical stalls by Bernini, and two large organs. The altarpiece (**60**), after a painting by Pietro Bianchi, represents the Immaculate Conception. In the pavement is the simple tombstone of Clement XI (died 1721).

The bronze **monument to Innocent VIII (61)**, by Antonio Pollaiuolo, is the only monument from the old basilica to be re-created in the new. The pope, who died in 1492, is represented by two bronze statues, one recumbent on the urn, the other seated and holding the spearhead which was supposed to have pierced the side of Christ (given to the Pope by the Sultan Bajazet II). Opposite (**62**) is the monument to St Pius X (died 1914, and canonised in 1954), by Pier Enrico Astorri.

The **Cappella della Presentazione (63)** is named after its altar mosaic of the Presentation of the Virgin, after Francesco Romanelli; beneath the altar is the tomb of St Pius X. The cupola is decorated with a mosaic, after Carlo Maratta, exalting the glory of the Virgin. On the right is a monument to Pope John XXIII, by Emilio Greco. On the left is a monument to Benedict XV (died 1922; **64**), by Pietro Canonica. Under the next arch are the **Stuart monuments**: above the door on the right (now used as an exit from the cupola, see below) is the monument (**65**) to Clementina Sobieska (died 1735), wife of James Stuart, the Old Pretender (she is here called Queen of Great Britain, France and Ireland), by Filippo Barigioni; on the left is the *monument to the last Stuarts (**66**), by Canova, with busts of the Old and Young Pretenders (died 1766 and 1788) and of Henry, Cardinal York (died 1807). George IV contributed to the expense of this monument.

In the **baptistery (67)** the cover of a porphyry sarcophagus, placed upside-down, is used as the font. It formerly covered the tomb of the Emperor Otho II (973–83; in the Grottoes). The present metal cover is by Carlo Fontana. The mosaics reproduce paintings of the Baptism of Christ, by Carlo Maratta; of St Peter baptising the centurion Cornelius, by Andrea Procaccini; and of St Peter baptising his gaolers Saints Processus and Martinian, by Giuseppe Passeri. At the end of the nave can be seen the back of the doors by Giacomo Manzù, with a dedicatory inscription.

The **Treasury** (open 9–18.30; Oct–Mar 9–17.30. Lire 8000), or **Museo Storico Artistico**, is entered by the door under the monument to Pius VIII (**51**). In the vestibule is a large stone slab with the names of the popes buried in the basilica, from St Peter to John Paul I. A corridor leads to the entrance to the treasury, rearranged in 1975 in dark modern exhibition rooms (the harsh illumination has been justly criticised). The treasury was plundered in 846 by the Saracens, and again during the sack of Rome in 1527 by Imperial troops, and was impoverished by the provisions of the Treaty of Tolentino (1797), which Pius VI was forced to conclude with Napoleon. It still, however, contains objects of great value and interest. The exhibits include vestments, missals, reliquaries, pyxes, patens, chalices, monstrances, crucifixes, and other sacred relics, as well as candelabra and ornaments.

Room I. The *Colonna Santa, a 4C Byzantine spiral column, one of 12 from the old basilica (eight decorate the balconies of the great piers of the dome in St Peter's; the remaining three are lost). The column was once thought to be that against which Christ leaned when speaking with the doctors in the Temple. The gilt bronze cock (9C) used to decorate the top of the campanile of the old basilica.

Room II (Sagrestia dei Beneficiati; **71**). Here is displayed the *Crux Vaticana, the most ancient possession of the treasury, dating from the 6C, the gift of the

emperor Justinian II. It is made of bronze and set with jewels. Also here are the so-called *dalmatic of Charlemagne, now usually considered to date from the 11C or the early 15C; a Byzantine case with an enamelled cross; fragment of a Byzantine diptych in ivory; copy (1974) of the ancient Chair of St Peter, now incorporated in Bernini's decoration in the tribune of St Peter's.

In the **Cappella della Sagrestia dei Beneficiati (71A)** is displayed a beautiful *ciborium by Donatello (c 1432), from the old basilica. It encloses a painting of the *Madonna 'della Febbre'* (the protectress of malaria) attributed to Lippo Memmi. Over the chapel altar is *St Peter receiving the keys*, by Girolamo Muziano. A plaster cast of Michelangelo's Pietà in St Peter's is also displayed here. **Room IV**. *Monument of Sixtus IV**, a masterpiece in bronze by Antonio Pollaiuolo (1493). It can be seen to advantage from the raised platform. **Room V**. Ceremonial ring of Sixtus IV (1471–84); reliquary bust of St Luke the Evangelist (13C–14C), and a wooden crucifix probably dating from the 14C.

A passage containing illuminated manuscripts, including one from the Giulia choir (1543) and a 17C ivory crucifix leads to **Room VI**. Here are displayed a cross and candelabra by Sebastiano Torrigiani; a crucifix and six candelabra (1581) made by Antonio Gentili for Cardinal Alessandro Farnese and presented by him to the basilica in 1582; and two huge *candelabra of the 16C, traditionally attributed to Benvenuto Cellini.

Room VII. 13C Slavonic icon in a jewelled silver frame, and reliquaries; model of an angel in clay by Bernini (1673), used for one of the angels flanking the ciborium in the Cappella del Sacramento. **Room VIII**. Gold chalice set with diamonds (18C), bequeathed to the Vatican by Henry Stuart, Cardinal York; platinum chalice, presented by Charles III of Spain to Pius VI, interesting as the first recorded use of platinum for such a purpose; gilt bronze tiara (17C) for the statue of St Peter; on high festivals this statue is attired in full pontificals. **Room IX**. *Sarcophagus of Junius Bassus, prefect of Rome in 359. This was found near St Peter's in 1505, and is superbly carved.

From the entrance to the museum, a second corridor leads right, off which is the **sacristy** (**68**; open 7–19; until 18 in Oct–Mar), built for Pius VI by Carlo Marchionni (1776–84). It is an octagonal hall with a cupola supported by pilasters of yellow Siena marble and grey marble columns from Hadrian's Villa near Tivoli. To the left, the Sagrestia dei Canonici (**69**; open 7–19; until 18 in Oct–Mar) has paintings by Francesco Penni, and Giulio Romano. The adjoining Chapter House (70) contains paintings by Andrea Sacchi.

The Dome

■ Open daily 8.00–one hour before the basilica closes, except Christmas Day and Easter Day, and when the Pope is in the basilica (often on Wednesday morning). The entrance is from outside the basilica at the right end of the portico.

The dome was completed as far as the drum by Michelangelo; the vault and the lantern were added by Giacomo della Porta in 1588–90. Clement VII covered the vault with strips of lead reinforced with bronze ribs.

A lift (or staircase) ascends to the **roof** from which there is a close view of the spring of the dome, with the Cross 92m above. The two side cupolas by Giacomo della Porta are purely decorative and have no opening into the interior of the

church. On the roof are buildings used by the *sampietrini* (workmen permanently employed on the fabric of St Peter's). Two stairways lead to a curving corridor from which is the entrance into the first circular gallery around the interior of the drum of the dome (53m above the ground and 67m below the top of the dome). From here there is an impressive view of the pavement far below and of the interior of the dome; the decorative details and mosaics are on a vast scale. The higher circular gallery is closed to the public.

Signs indicate the way on up via a spiral staircase with lancet windows, and a curving narrow stair between the two shells of the dome. The first big window has a view south, with the roof of the huge Audience Hall (1971) directly below. Iron stairs continue up to the tiny marble stairs which emerge on the loggia around the pretty **lantern**, 537 steps above the pavement of the basilica. There is a *view of the Vatican City and gardens, and beyond, on a clear day, of the whole of Rome and of the Campagna from the Apennines and the Alban hills to the sea. The Cross surmounting the copper ball (2.5m in diameter, just large enough to hold 16 people) is 132.5m above the ground. Another staircase leads down and out onto the roof with a view from the parapet, beside the huge statues on the façade, of Piazza San Pietro. The exit is at present inside St Peter's, under the Sobieska monument, next to the baptistery (**65**).

The Vatican Grottoes

The Vatican Grottoes are open on weekdays 7–one hour before the basilica closes, except when the Pope is in the basilica. The entrance is at present by the pier of St Longinus (**3**) although one of the other three entrances at the piers is sometimes used (see the Plan). The exit is on the outside of the church, to the right of the portico. In the space between the level of the existing basilica (30m above sea-level) and that of the old one (27m), the Renaissance architects built the so-called **Sacred Grottoes** and placed in them various monuments and architectural fragments from the former church. They were used for the burial of numerous popes. Excavations were carried out below the level of the old basilica from 1940 to 1957.

The grottoes, which follow the outline of the basilica above them (except for their annexes), are in two adjoining sections. The **Old Grottoes** have the form of a nave with aisles (corresponding to Maderno's nave but extending beyond it); on either side are the annexes discovered during the excavations. The **New Grottoes** are in the form of a horseshoe, with extensions. The centre is immediately below the high altar of St Peter's. Four of the extensions reach to points below the four piers of St Longinus, St Helena, St Veronica and St Andrew.

Stairs lead down from the church to the **New Grottoes** and a horseshoe corridor, lined with fine reliefs attributed to Matteo del Pollaiuolo of the life of St Peter which decorated the tabernacle over the high altar of the old basilica.

Beyond a modern chapel is the 14C chapel of the Madonna della Bocciata (**2**) and the 15C chapel of the Madonna delle Febbri (**3**). The Clementine Chapel (**4**) is immediately beneath the centre of the church above. Here the rear wall was breached during the excavations for St Peter's tomb. Behind is the foundation of the altar of Calixtus II enclosing that of Gregory I. The Tropaion of Gaius (see below) is therefore beneath (**5**). Openings to the left and right show the structure of the foundations more clearly (visible only when the grille is opened on a guided tour of the necropolis, see below). Opposite the chapel is (**6**) the tomb of

VATICAN GROTTOES

```
0     10     20     30 yards
0     10     20     30 metres
```

Pius XII (died 1958). Another chapel (**7**) has the unfinished tomb of Paul II (died 1471) by Mino da Fiesole, Giovanni Dalmata, and others.

The area of the Old Grottoes lies at the west end of the right aisle. Immediately to the right is a chapel (**8**) with a 15C altar of the Virgin, and the tomb (**9**) of Pius VI (died 1799) in an early Christian sarcophagus. At the west end of the nave, flanked by two lions and two angels, can be seen the **Tomb of St Peter** (**10**). Continuing down the aisle, the route passes the tomb of Pope John XXIII (died 1963; **11**). Beyond on the left (**12**) is the tomb of Queen Christina of Sweden (died 1689), and opposite (**13**), the tomb of Queen Charlotte of Cyprus (died 1487). After a short flight of steps are more tombs: on the left (**14**) Innocent IX (died 1591), and right (**15**) Benedict XV (died 1922), followed by (**16**) Marcellus II (died 1555), and (**28**) John Paul I (died 1978). The chapel (**17**) beyond has a relief of the Madonna attributed to Isaia da Pisa. Here is the plain tomb slab of Paul VI (died 1978).

A turning left leads away from the Old Grottoes, passing some mosaics, and (left) (**18**) the tomb of Julius III (died 1555) into the **North Annexe**, a series of rooms (**19–22**; usually closed) containing interesting inscriptions and fragments from the old basilica. In the two rooms to the left (**19** and **20**; sometimes unlit) is the sarcophagus of Anicius Probus, Prefect of Rome in 395. At the west end of the grottoes (**23**) is a kneeling *statue of Pius VI by Canova. The present

exit is through a corridor where some column bases from Constantine's basilica can be seen, and the cenotaph of Calixtus III with good reliefs. The corridor leads out to the portico of the church beside the equestrian statue of Constantine I by Bernini (keyed 2 on the plan of St Peter's).

The Necropolis and St Peter's Tomb

■ Apply in writing or in person to the Ufficio Scavi (beneath the Arco della Campana, left of St Peter's; open 9–17; ☎ 698 85318) for permission to join the groups of 15 which are conducted on most days (9–12, 14–17; the visit takes c 1hr 30 mins).

A double row of mausoleums, dating from the 1C AD, running from east to west, were discovered below the level of the old basilica. The extreme west series of these is on higher ground and adjoins a graveyard which is immediately beneath the high altar of the present church. Constantine significantly chose to erect his basilica above this necropolis, presumably knowing that it contained the tomb of St Peter. This was a most difficult undertaking because of the slope of the hill; he had to level the terrain and make use of supporting foundation walls.

A baldacchino in the presbytery covered the **Tropaion of Gaius**, a funerary monument in the form of a small aedicule or niche, referred to c 200, and probably built by Pope Anicetus. This monument was discovered during excavations. It backs on to a supporting wall plastered with red, dating from the same period. An empty space beneath it is believed to be St Peter's tomb. This was probably a mound of earth covered by brick slabs, and it shows signs of the interference which history records. That this was a most revered grave is evident from the number of other graves which crowd in on it, without cutting across the tomb. In front of the red wall, on which a Greek inscription is taken to name the saint, is a later wall, scratched with the names of pilgrims invoking the aid of Peter. Bones, obviously displaced, of an elderly and powerfully built man, were found beneath this second graffiti wall and declared by Paul VI to be those of St Peter. The site of the Circus of Nero, the most likely place of St Peter's martyrdom, lay along the south flank of the basilica, and extended as far as Via Sant'Uffizio.

You are usually asked to enter the Vatican City through the Arco delle Campane, and meet in Piazza dei Protomartiri Romani. The visit normally starts at the **South Annexe (24)** of the Old Grottoes, through two rooms (**25** and **26**) with 14C–15C tomb slabs and sarcophagi. A third room (**27**) has transennae and architectural fragments of the 4C–9C, and part of the nave foundation wall of the old basilica; from here stairs lead down to the necropolis. (If, however, work on the excavations prevents this route being used, the group is taken into St Peter's and through the New Grottoes (**5**), from which these stairs can also be reached.)

The **necropolis** is well preserved and was in use until Constantine's reign. Among the 18 loculi cleared, the one purely Christian mausoleum provides the most ancient mosaics yet discovered on a Christian subject. Here, on the vault richly decorated with a vine pattern, Christ is depicted as Helios, the sun-god. On the walls the sinopie remain of mosaics which have become detached from the surface (on the left, Jonah, and ahead, fishermen). In the other mausoleums Oriental cults and those of Greece and Rome are combined. Christians were also

buried in the mausoleum of the Caetenii, with the grave of Aemilia Gorgonia; in the magnificent stuccoed mausoleum of the Valerii, with reliefs in niches, where, despite the pagan sarcophagus (3C), the inscription of Valerinus Vastulus specifies his Christian burial; and in the so-called Egyptian chamber. The paintings of peacocks in the mausoleum of the family of P. Aelius Tyrannus, the marble bust of the woman in that of the Valerii, and the remarkable sarcophagus of Q. Marcius Hermes and his wife, mirror the tastes and wealth of the families of freedmen to whom the loculi belonged. Among the many sarcophagi is one for a child, with figures of the mourning parents.

The Vatican Museums

■ **Admission**. The opening times often vary, but at present the museums and galleries are open Mon–Sat 8.45–13; usually from Easter to mid-June, Sep, and Oct they are open 8.45–16 (the ticket office closes one hour before closing time). They are closed on Sun except for the last Sun of the month when they are open free, unless it is a holiday (see below). The admission fee in 1997 was Lire 15,000, and Lire 10,000 for students in possession of a Student Card. The museums and areas of the palace coverered with this ticket, for one single visit, are the Gregorian Museum of Pagan Antiquities (sculpture) and the Pio Christian Museum (sculpture), the Picture Gallery, the Pio-Clementino Museum (sculpture), the Chiaramonti Museum (sculpture), the Egyptian Museum, the Etruscan Museum, the exhibition rooms of the Library, the Museum of Christian Art, the Borgia Rooms and the Gallery of Modern Religious Art, the Raphael Rooms, the Sistine Chapel, the Chapel of Nicholas V, the Gallery of Maps, the Gallery of Tapestries, and the Ethnological Missionary Museum (open only Wed & Sat). The Etruscan Museum is closed Wed and Sat (and closes early at 13.30 on other days), and the Ethnological Museum is only open on Wed and Sat (until 13.30). For information, ☎ 698 83333.

The Vatican collections are closed on Sun (except the last in the month) and on: New Year's Day, 6 Jan, 11 Feb (anniversary of the founding of the Vatican City State), Easter Mon, 1 May, Ascension Day, Corpus Christi, 29 Jun, 14 & 15 Aug, 1 Nov, 8 Dec, Christmas Day and Boxing Day, and whenever special reasons make it necessary.

The **main entrance** is on Viale Vaticano (see the plan on pp 328–9). There is another entrance from the Vatican gardens which you can use only if you take the bus from St Peter's (see below). It should be noted that on most days (except Wed) it is usually possible to leave the museums by the Scala Regia from the Sistine Chapel which descends to the portico in front of St Peter's.

A **bus service** runs daily, except Sun and Wed (if a Papal audience is being held on the Piazza), every half hour (between 8.45 and 12.45, and between 8.45 and 13.45 when the museums are open until 16) at a quarter past and a quarter to the hour. It leaves from beside the information office and goes under the Arco delle Campane (left of the façade of St Peter's) through the Vatican gardens (described on p 365) to a side entrance to the Museums, at

the ambulatory (5 mins; Lire 2000). This is recommended not only as the most convenient way of reaching the museums from St Peter's (and a way to avoid the queues and tour groups at the main entrance), but also it provides the opportunity of seeing part of the Vatican City and gardens, which can otherwise be seen only on an organised tour (see below). The bus can also be taken back from the Museums to St Peter's (last bus at 14).

Facilities are provided for the **disabled** in the Vatican Museums.

There is a self-service **restaurant** and **café** below the courtyard outside the *Quattro Cancelli*. There are some benches on the terraces and courtyard outside the *Quattro Cancelli* where it is possible to eat a snack. A small café near the Sistine Chapel is open in summer.

The Vatican Palace

The Vatican Palace contains some of the world's greatest art treasures. The extensive buildings and interior courts cover an area of 5.5 hectares. Most of the palace is open to the public, as the apartments reserved for the Pope and the papal court are contained in a relatively small area. The gardens and city can only been seen on an organised tour (see below). As well as the remarkable Greek and Roman sculpture museums, the gallery of paintings, the library, the Egyptian and Etruscan collections, ethnological material, etc. the palace contains the famous Sistine Chapel frescoed by Michelangelo and the 'Stanze' decorated by Raphael. Because of the number of different museums it contains and the vast extent of the halls and galleries on two floors, it is not practicable to see them all in a single visit. You are strongly recommended not to attempt to see too much, and to plan to return at least two or three times. Over two million people a year visit the Sistine Chapel, which is the exclusive goal of almost all the tour groups which enter the palace. Some of the other areas of the palace remain comparatively peaceful, and a number of the galleries with exceptional masterpieces receive many fewer visitors simply because they are not 'on the way' to the Sistine (see 'Plan of Visit', below).

History

In the days of Pope St Symmachus (498–514), a house was built beside the first basilica of St Peter. This house was not the residence of the popes as, until the migration to Avignon in 1309, they lived in the Lateran Palace; but it was used for state occasions and for the accommodation of foreign sovereigns. In it Charlemagne stayed in 800 and Otho II in 980. By the 12C it had fallen into disrepair. Eugenius III (1145–53) was the first of numerous popes to restore and enlarge it. In 1208 Innocent III built a fortified residence here which was added to by his successors. When Gregory XI returned from Avignon in 1378 he found the Lateran uninhabitable and so took up residence in the Vatican. On his death in the same year, the first conclave was held in the Vatican. A covered way which connected the Vatican Palace to Castel Sant'Angelo was used in emergencies (see p 293).

Nicholas V transformed the house into a palace which he built round the Cortile dei Pappagalli. In 1473 Sixtus IV added the Sistine Chapel. Innocent VIII had Giacomo da Pietrasanta build the Belvedere Pavilion on the north

summit of the Vatican hill. Alexander VI decorated a suite of rooms on the first floor of the palace of Nicholas V and they became known, after his family name, as the Appartamento Borgia; he also added the Borgia Tower. Julius II began to form the famous collection of classical sculpture, which he installed in the courtyard of the Belvedere Pavilion. He also commissioned Bramante to unite this pavilion with the palace of Nicholas V by means of long corridors, thus creating the great Courtyard of the Belvedere.

Leo X decorated the east side of the palace with open galleries looking on to the Courtyard of St Damasus, one of which became known as the Loggia of Raphael. Paul III employed Antonio da Sangallo the Younger to build the Cappella Paolina and the Sala Regia. Under Pius IV and Gregory XIII various additions were made by Pirro Ligorio. Sixtus V assigned to Domenico Fontana the construction of the block overlooking Piazza San Pietro and of the great Library, which was built at right angles to the long corridors and thus divided the Courtyard of the Belvedere in two. The Scala Regia of Bernini was begun under Urban VIII and completed under Alexander VII. The Museum of Pagan Antiquities was founded by Clement XIII.

Clement XIV converted the Belvedere Pavilion into a museum which his successor Pius VI enlarged; hence its name 'Pio-Clementino'. The architect was Michelangelo Simonetti, who altered the courtyard and added several rooms. Pius VI was also the founder of the Picture Gallery. Pius VII (Chiaramonti) founded the Sculpture Gallery which bears his name and added the New Wing (by Raffaele Stern), which paralleled the Library. Its construction divided the Courtyard of the Belvedere into three. From now on the sections became known as the Courtyard of the Belvedere (retaining the old name; nearest the pontifical palace), the relatively small Courtyard of the Library, and (nearest to the Belvedere Pavilion) the Courtyard of the Fir Cone (Pigna; after a bronze fir cone placed in it by Paul V). Gregory XVI was responsible for the Etruscan and Egyptian Museums. Pius IX closed the fourth side of the Courtyard of St Damasus and built the Scala Pia. Leo XIII restored the Borgia Rooms and reopened them to the public.

Under Pius XI were built the new Picture Gallery and the new entrance to the Vatican Museums in the Viale Vaticano, both of them dating from 1932. A new building was opened in 1970 by Paul VI to house the former Lateran museums (the Gregorian Museum of Pagan Antiquities and the Pio Christian Museum); in 1973 the Ethnological Missionary Museum was opened beneath, and a Historical Museum was built under the gardens (this has since been transferred to the Lateran Palace). An extensive series of galleries in and around the Borgia apartments were opened in 1973 as a Museum of Modern Religious Art.

The most convenient way of reaching the Vatican Museums from St Peter's is by the Vatican bus service (see above). Otherwise, from St Peter's it is a long and rather unpleasant walk along Via di Porta Angelica (Pl. 1; 4) to the right (north) of Bernini's colonnade in Piazza San Pietro. At the beginning of the street is the battlemented covered way to Castel Sant'Angelo (see p 293). The site of Porta Angelica was the modern Piazza del Risorgimento. On the left is the Cancello di Sant'Anna, one of the entrances to the Vatican City. The road skirts the city wall, and turns left out of Piazza del Risorgimento.

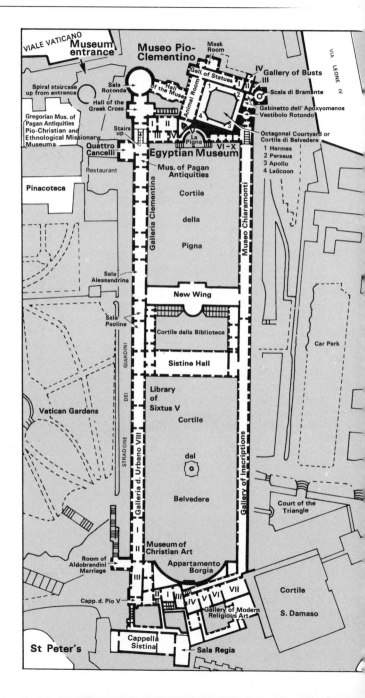

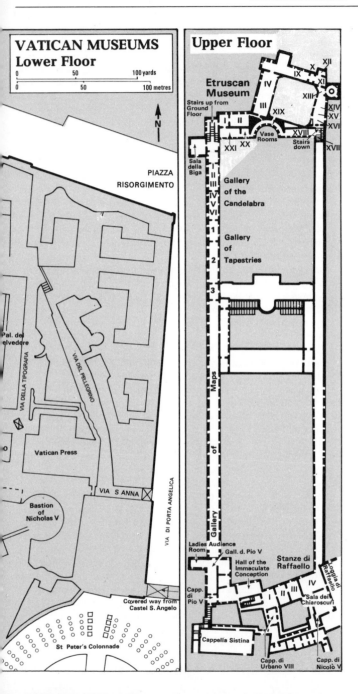

Continuing along the wall, Viale Vaticano leads left to the **entrance to the Vatican Museums** (see the plan on pp 328–9; also atlas plan 1; 3, 4). The **entrance hall** has a ticket office for tour groups (for individual visitors see below), an information office, and lifts for the museums. The monumental **double staircase**, built in 1932 by Giuseppe Momo, has independent ascending and descending spirals, carved out of the hill, to connect the street level with that of the museums. The bronze balustrade is by Antonio Maraini.

The **ambulatory** at the top of the staircase, with mosaics and busts, has the **ticket office for individual visitors** (separate office for students), the bus terminus from St Peter's, a bank, a post office, telephones, bookstalls, cloakrooms, etc.

Beyond the ticket gates, a short flight of steps mounts to the **vestibule** decorated with three mosaics from Hadrian's Villa. In summer (and on fine days) visitors are directed instead outside to the **Cortile delle Carozze** where the *base of the Column of Antoninus Pius has been placed since its restoration. A monolithic block of Greek marble, it has high reliefs on three sides showing the apotheosis of Antoninus and his wife Faustina, who are being conducted to heaven by a winged genius personifying Rome, and delightful scenes of cavalcades (AD 138–61). It was found in 1703 in Via della Missone, near Montecitorio. On the right is the entrance to the new building which houses the Gregorian Museum of Pagan Antiquities and the Pio Christian Museum. Beyond is an open court (below which is a self-service restaurant and café). On the left is a vestibule known as the **Quattro Cancelli**, from which the various museums and galleries are signposted.

■ **Plan of visit**. The collections are so extensive and their layout is so complicated that it is not practicable to see them all in a single visit. To add to the complication four one-way itineraries have been imposed by the Vatican authorities and you are expected to chose one of the four 'tours' depending on the time at your disposal. This is primarily to regulate the flow of people to the Sistine Chapel, and tour groups have to take the signposted routes. If you are not in a tour these can be disregarded to some extent, but if you want to see one particular collection only, the one-way systems are usually a hindrance, and in some cases access from one part of the museums to another is no longer possible.

The number of guided tours in the Vatican can seriously impede the other visitors' enjoyment of the museum. If you have time, it can be a good idea to go straight to the Sistine Chapel at opening time in order to enjoy it in comparative peace, and then return to the Quattro Cancelli to begin the detailed tours described below. However, you are now often able to leave the museums through the Sistine Chapel by the Scala Regia (usually closed on Wed) which descends directly to the portico of St Peter's. The museums which are not 'on the way' to the Sistine Chapel are usually comparatively deserted (anyway before 11): these include the Picture Gallery, the Gregorian Museum of Pagan Antiquities, the Etruscan Museum, the Chiaramonti Museum, and the New Wing.

The four separate tours suggested below can at present be made taking into account the one-way systems.

I. Quattro Cancelli, Simonetti staircase, Egyptian Museum, Chiaramonti

Museum, New Wing, Pio-Clementino Museum, upstairs to the Room of the Biga, Etruscan Museum, and return to the Quattro Cancelli.

II. A very long and tiring route which should, if time permits, be taken in two stages. Quattro Cancelli, upstairs to the Gallery of the Candelabra, Gallery of Tapestries and Gallery of Maps, Hall of the Immaculate Conception, Raphael Rooms, Room of the Chiaroscuri, Chapel of Nicholas V, Chapel of Urban VIII, Borgia Rooms and Gallery of Modern Religious Art, Sistine Chapel, Museum of Christian Art, Sistine Hall and Library, returning to Quattro Cancelli.

III. Quattro Cancelli, Vatican Picture Gallery, and back to Quattro Cancelli.

IV. Vestibule, Gregorian Museum of Pagan Antiquities, Pio Christian Museum, Ethnological Missionary Museum, and back to the Vestibule.

The itineraries described below follow the above scheme.

I. The Egyptian Museum, Chiaramonti Museum, New Wing, Pio-Clementino Museum and Etruscan Museum

The Vatican Palace houses the largest collections of ancient sculpture in the world. These collections owe their origin to the Renaissance popes, and in particular to Julius II. However, many of the pieces were later dispersed, in particular by Pius V who made numerous gifts to the city of Rome and to private individuals. The popes of the late 18C and early 19C tried to reassemble the old collections and formed new ones.

The contents of the sculpture galleries are mainly Greek originals, Roman originals, or Roman copies of Greek originals executed in the 1C and 2C AD. In some cases the Roman sculptor, when copying a Greek model, placed a contemporary portrait head on his copy; later restorers often made additions in marble, stone or plaster and also, in some cases, put heads on statues to which they do not belong. In addition, all the male sculpture was ludicrously disfigured by prudish plaster additions, and there are few undraped female statues (this does not apply to the Gregorian Museum of Pagan Antiquities).

The **numbers of each work** given in the description below are those attached below each work on prominent numbered labels, usually in red. Some of these, however, are missing or difficult to decipher. The Vatican Inventory Numbers are inconspicuously marked in black on the right side or back of the works themselves, and have been ignored, although in some rooms the keyed plans to the most important works also carry the Vatican Inventory Numbers.

The one-way systems (see above) make it, at present, obligatory to approach the sculpture galleries through the Egyptian Museum.

Egyptian Museum

The Egyptian Museum occupies rooms in the lower floor of the Belvedere Pavilion adjoining the Pio-Clementino Museum. The entrance is at the top of the first flight of the Simonetti Staircase outside the Hall of the Greek Cross (described below). The museum was founded by Gregory XVI in 1839 and was arranged by Father Luigi Maria Ungarelli, one of the first Italian Egyptologists to continue the scientific research of Jean-François Champollion, (1790–1832), the French archaeologist and founder of modern Egyptology. The rooms were decorated in the Egyptian style in the 19C by Giuseppe de Fabris. The collection was beautifully rearranged in 1989 (and it is well labelled).

Room I. Funerary stelae and tomb reliefs arranged in chronological order from c 2600 BC–AD 600. **Room II**. Wooden painted mummy cases (1000 BC); two marble sarcophagi (6C BC); jewellery, ornaments, figurines, etc. found in tombs (1500–525 BC); canopic jars (1500–500 BC); model of a boat (2000 BC); and funerary masks and a painted fabric from the Roman period. **Room III**. *Sculptures from the Serapeum of the Canopus of the Egyptian Delta, built by Hadrian in his villa at Tivoli after his journey to Egypt in 130/31 (see Chapter 30), including Serapis, a colossal bust of Isis, and statues of Antinous. **Room IV**. Colossal grey marble statue personifying the Nile (1C AD); two statues of Hapy, the god representing the Nile in flood; and works from the Serapeum in the Campus Martius.

Room V, the Hemicycle, conforms in shape to the Niche of the Bronze Fir Cone (described below). *Head in sandstone of Mentuhotep II (c 2060–2040 BC), the oldest portrait in the museum; statues in black granite of the lion-headed goddess Sekhmet (1390–1352 BC); colossal *statue of Queen Tuaa, mother of Rameses II, brought to Rome by Caligula; colossal granite statue of Ptolemy Philadelphos (284–246 BC) and his wife Arsinoë; black bust of Serapis (2C AD). **Rooms VI and VII** contain the Grassi collection of small bronzes of sacred animals and gods, terracotta statuettes from Alexandria, lamps, utensils, Islamic ceramics, Syrian glass from Palestine (1C–5C AD), etc. **Room VIII**. Material from Mesopotamia and Persia (3000–1000 BC). **Room IX**. Exquisite *bas-reliefs from Mesopotamia (884–626 BC).

The **Niche of the Bronze Fir Cone,** reached from the Hemicycle, is the apse at the north end of the extensive courtyard of the Fir Cone (*Cortile della Pigna*; open in fine weather), one of the three sections into which Bramante's Courtyard of the Belvedere was eventually divided. Here Paul V (1605–21) placed the colossal bronze **fir cone**, over 4m high, found near the Thermae of Agrippa. It formed the centrepiece of a fountain (there are holes in the top of the scales) beside the Temple of Isis, and was made by a certain Cincius Salvius, in the 1C AD. In the Middle Ages it was in the portico of Old St Peter's, together with the two bronze gilt peacocks (here replaced by copies; originals in the New Wing), on either side of it. The fir cone was seen by Dante (*Inferno*, XXXI, 53) and gave its name to a district of the city, the *Quartiere della Pigna*. Also here are seated black granite statues of the goddess Sekhmet, and, in the courtyard below, two lions once part of a monument to Nectanebo I (XXXth Dynasty), removed by Gregory XVI from the Fontana dell'Acqua Felice. An incongruous sculpture, donated by Arnaldo Pomodoro, was installed in the centre of the courtyard in 1990.

From the landing outside Room IX of the Egyptian Museum, stairs lead down to the Chiaramonti Sculpture Gallery, and a door into the Courtyard of the Fir Cone.

The Chiaramonti Museum

The Chiaramonti Museum is reached by stairs leading down from the landing outside the Egyptian Museum and near the Round Vestibule (see below). This gallery is named after its founder Pius VII (Chiaramonti) and it was arranged by Canova who designed the lunette frescoes with scenes from the life of Pius VII as patron of the arts (by Francesco Hayez, Philippe Veit, etc.). The New Wing and the Gallery of Inscriptions are extensions of this museum. The Chiaramonti

gallery, in Bramante's east corridor, is 300m long. The exhibits are divided into 59 sections, numbered on the wall above with roman numerals (odd numbers on left, even numbers on right). Here are displayed Roman works, many of them copies of Greek originals made in the 5C or 4C BC (indicated as 'copy of a 5C original', etc.).

Section I. 3. Sarcophagus of C. Junius Euhodus and his wife Metilia Acte, a priestess of the Magna Mater at Ostia, with a relief of the story of Alcestis; the faces of Alcestis and her husband Admetus are portraits of the Roman couple (2C AD). **Section II.** 15. Herm of Hephaistos (Vulcan), copy of a 5C original, with a head which may be derived from a statue by Alkamenes; **Section IV.** 3. Statue of Hygieia, part of a group of Hygieia and Asklepios, copy of a 4C original attributed to the sons of Praxiteles in the Asklepieion on the island of Kos. **Section V.** 3. Antoninus Pius, wearing armour. **Section IX.** 3. Herakles with his son Telephos, a Roman synthesis of a 4C and 3C original.

Section X. 26. Sepulchral monument of Nonnius Zethus and his family (1C AD), a square marble block with eight conical cavities for the various members of the family. The reliefs of a mill being turned by a donkey and of baking implements probably indicated the man's trade. **Section XI.** 12. Portrait bust of Cicero. **Section XII.** 4. Relief from a 3C sarcophagus, with a mule in blinkers turning a winepress. **Section XIII.** 1. Hermes, from a 5C original; 4. Ganymede and the eagle, copy of a 3C Hellenistic original. **Section XV.** 14. Portrait bust of Pompey.

Section XVI. *4. Head of Athena, copy of a 5C original; the eyes are restorations but they indicate the skill with which Greek artists caught the expression of the human eye. The whites of the eyes were probably of ivory, the pupils of semi-precious stone, and the lashes and brows of bronze. **Section XVII.** 3. Silenus with a panther, copy of a 3C Hellenistic original. **Section XIX.** Portrait-head of a priest of Isis (1C BC); 13. Head of a Roman of the late Republican period. **Section XX.** 5. Athena, from a 5C original. **Section XXI.** 1. Eros bending his bow, probably a copy of a bronze original by Lysippos; *statue of a boy. **Section XXIII.** *3. Fragment of a relief of Penelope in her characteristic attitude: sitting on a chair and resting her head on her right hand; from a 5C original. **Section XXVI.** 15. Head of the Discobolos of Myron, copy of the 5C original; limestone *head from a sepulchral relief from Palmyra, in a fusion of Syrian and Hellenistic-Roman styles (2C AD).

Section XXIX. 2. Colossal head of Augustus; statue (4.) and head (5.) of Tiberius. **Section XXXI.** 2. Archaic relief of the Three Graces. **Section XXXII.** 3. Dacian prisoner of high rank (2C AD). **Section XXXVI.** 3. Resting athlete, copy of a 4C original. **Section XXXVII.** 3. Statue of Herakles, from a 4C original. **Section XL.** 1. Statue of the Muse Polyhymnia, copy of a Hellenistic original of the 3C or 2C BC; 3. Statue of Artemis (Diana), copy of a 4C original. **Section XLIII.** *18. Statuette of Ulysses, part of a group of Ulysses offering wine to Polyphemus, copy of a 3C original. **Section XLV.** 3. Colossal head of Trajan.

Section XLVII. 14. Portrait bust of a lady of the Julio-Claudian gens; the hair is typical of the fashion of the age of Augustus (1C AD). **Section LVIII.** 8 Personification of Winter; the female figure is wrapped in a cloak and holds pine branch in her left hand; she is reclining near a stream where cupids catching waterfowl and fishes; a Hellenistic-Roman work of the 2C AL Sepulchral relief of a Roman family (1C BC). **Section LIX.** 7. Personificati

Autumn, a companion piece to Winter (above); the female figure is surrounded by cupids gathering grapes.

At the end of the Chiaramonti Museum is a gate (closed), beyond which is the **Gallery of Inscriptions** (*Galleria Lapidaria*), open only to scholars. It occupies the remaining part of Bramante's east corridor. The gallery was founded by Clement XIV and reorganised and classified by the epigraphist Monsignor Gaetano Marini (1742–1817). It contains over 5000 pagan and Christian inscriptions from cemeteries and catacombs.

On the right a door leads into the **New Wing**, or *Braccio Nuovo*, an extension of the Chiaramonti sculpture gallery constructed by Raffaele Stern (1817–22) for Pius VII. It contains some of the most valuable sculptures in the Vatican. The impressive hall, 70m long and 8m wide, has a vaulted coffered ceiling and an apse in the middle of the south side, facing the Courtyard of the Library. The floor is inlaid with mosaics of the 2C AD from a Roman villa at Tor Marancia.

5. Caryatid, copy of one of the caryatids of the Erechtheion on the Acropolis of Athens (5C BC); 9. Head of a Dacian, from the Forum of Trajan (2C AD); 11. Silenus carrying the infant Dionysos, copy of an original ascribed to Lysippos. *14. The **Augustus of Prima Porta** is one of the most famous portraits of the emperor, found in 1863 in his wife Livia's villa at Prima Porta, 12km north of the centre of Rome above the Via Flaminia. The emperor, who appears to be about 40 years old, is wearing a cuirass over his toga; he held a sceptre in his left hand; his raised right hand shows that he is about to make a speech. The head is full of character and the majestic pose suggests the influence of Polykleitos. The cuirass, a remarkably delicate piece of work, is decorated with scenes that date the statue. The central scene depicts the restoration by the Parthians in 20 BC of the eagles lost by Crassus at Carrhae (northern Mesopotamia) in 53 BC. The small cupid riding a dolphin, placed as a support for the right leg, may be a portrait of Gaius Caesar, grandson of Augustus. *26. 'Modesty', probably Mnemosyne, copy of an original of the 3C; 23. Statue of Titus.

In the recess: 32. Priestess of Isis; 30. *Bust of Julius Caesar; 30a. alabaster cinerary urn said to be that of Livilla, daughter of Germanicus. The two bronze gilt peacocks (30c,d; recently restored), probably stood at one of the entrance gates to Hadrian's Mausoleum. The six tombstones (30a,b,e–h) were found near the Mausoleum of Augustus; five of them belong to the Julian family and the sixth to Vespasian's. 37. Wounded Amazon (see below); 47. Bust of Trajan; 43. Selene (the Moon) approaching the sleeping Endymion, copy of a Hellenistic original of the 4C–3C; 46. Statue of a tragic poet (the head of Euripides does not belong), copy of a 4C original (?Aeschylus); *53. Portrait bust of a Roman (1C ᵔ).

ᵔ the opposite wall: *64. **Demosthenes**. This is a replica of the original ᵇy Polyeuctos of Athens, set up in Athens in 280 BC to the memory of ᵉnes, the orator and statesman. The hands were originally joined, with ᶜrossed. The mouth plainly suggests the stutter from which the great ᶠᶠered. 65. Portrait bust of Ptolemy of Numidia (1C AD); *67. ᵒn, a replica of one of the statues from the Temple of Diana at ᵉitos. According to the Elder Pliny, this statue won the prize in ᵘch Polykleitos, Pheidias, Kresilas and Phradmon all entered. ᵉt were restored by Thorvaldsen in the early 19C; 74. Bust of

Hadrian wearing armour; 76. Statue of Hera, copy of a 5C original (attributed to Alkamenes); 79. Fortune, copy of a 4C statue (the head, though Roman, is from another figure; the oar and globe are Roman additions); 80. Portrait bust of an unknown Roman of the 2C AD; 82. statue of a man, a Greek portrait of the 4C BC; *85. Statue of Artemis, from a 4C original.

In the apse. *Bust of a man of the late Republican era, possibly Mark Antony; bust of Marcus Aurelius as a young man; statuettes of athletes; Statue of Diana; in the floor, mosaic of Diana of the Ephesians. *106. **The Nile**, a fine Hellenistic work, found in 1513, with a statue of the Tiber (now in the Louvre), near the Temple of Isis. The river-god, who reclines near a sphinx and holds a horn of plenty, has the calm benevolent expression of a benefactor who enjoys his munificence. The 16 children who frolic over him are supposed to symbolise the 16 cubits which the Nile rises when in flood. The plinth is decorated with characteristic scenes of life on the banks of the Nile.

108. Statue of Julia, daughter of Titus; *111. The **Giustiniani Athena**, after a Greek original of the 4C BC; this is the best existing copy of an original in bronze attributed to Kephisodotus or to Euphranor; it portrays the goddess's twofold function as the divinity of the intellect and of arms. 112. Portrait bust of an unknown Roman of the 1C AD, possibly Cn. Domitius Ahenobarbus; 114. Statue of a man wearing a toga, with the head of Claudius; *117. **Resting Satyr**, copy of the famous statue by Praxiteles (replica in the Gallery of Statues; others in the Gregorian Museum of Pagan Antiquities and in the Capitoline Museum); 118. Bust of Commodus (180–92); 120. Statue of an athlete with the head of Lucius Verus; the body is a copy of a 5C original; 121. Bust of the emperor Philip the Arabian (244–49); ***Doryphoros of Polykleitos**, one of numerous copies of the famous bronze statue of a young spear-bearer by Polykleitos, the greatest sculptor of the school of Argos and Sikyon, who made a careful study of the proportions of the human body. 124. Head of a Dacian, from Trajan's Forum; 126. *statue of Domitian, wearing a cuirass.

It is now necessary to return through the Chiaramonti Sculpture Museum to the landing outside the exit from the Egyptian Museum.

The Pio-Clementino Museum

This sculpture gallery occupies the Belvedere Pavilion, which was adapted as a museum by Michelangelo Simonetti. The present entrance is from the landing outside the exit from the Egyptian Museum.

In the first vestibule is the *sarcophagus, in peperino, of Lucius Cornelius Scipio Barbatus, from the Tomb of the Scipios; the sarcophagus is in the form of a Doric altar but the general character is Etruscan. The archaic inscription, in Saturnine verse, is said to be by Quintus Ennius, the great Roman poet. Above are two inscriptions, also from the Tomb of the Scipios, to the son of Scipio Barbatus, who conquered Corsica in 259 BC.

Ahead is the **Round Vestibule** (*Vestibolo Rotondo*). Here are a large bowl made of pavonazzetto and sculptural fragments. Beyond is the **Gabinetto dell'Apoxyomenos**, with the ***Apoxyomenos**, a finely built athlete scraping the oil from his body with a strigil, from a bronze original by Lysippos; this w the masterpiece of the sculptor's maturity (c 330 BC) and illustrated his car of proportions. The statue was found in Trastevere (Vicolo dell'Atleta) in 1 Above, Archaic Latin inscriptions from the Tomb of the Scipios; to the

inscriptions, among them that of Lucius Mummius Achaicus, the conqueror of Greece (146 BC). In the atrium beyond are three circus scenes (3C AD) and a funerary niche (957.) from near Todi (late 1C AD). Through a glass door here can be seen the spiral **Staircase of Bramante**, which ascends to the floor above. The design is masterly; at each turn the order changes, starting with Tuscan at the bottom and ending with Corinthian at the top.

From the Round Vestibule is the entrance to the **Octagonal Courtyard of the Belvedere** (there is another, larger, courtyard of the Belvedere, to the south), where Julius II placed the first classical sculptures which formed the nucleus of the great Vatican collections. When Pius VI had the museum enlarged in 1775, Michelangelo Simonetti made the courtyard into an octagon by forming the recesses (*gabinetti*) in the four corners.

To the left is the **Gabinetto dell'Apollo**. Here is the famous **Apollo Belvedere*, a 2C Roman copy of a bronze original probably by Leochares (4C BC). The slender elegant figure of the young god is stepping forward to see the effect of the arrow that he has just shot. The statue has been greatly admired as one of the masterpieces of classical sculpture since it was brought to the Vatican in 1503. It was beautifully restored in 1982. Under the adjoining colonnade: *relief of a procession, from the Ara Pacis (nearly all the heads are restorations).

The **Gabinetto del Laocoonte** contains the famous group of **Laocoön* and his two sons in the coils of the serpents, a vivid and striking illustration of the story related by Virgil in the *Aeneid*. Laocoön, priest of Apollo, warned his fellow Trojans against the trickery of the Greeks and entreated them not to admit the wooden horse into the city. In punishment Apollo or Athene sent serpents to crush him and his young sons to death in their coils. This group, of Greek marble, was found on the Esquiline Hill, in 1506, and was at once recognised as that described by Pliny, though it is not carved from a single block, as he states, but from at least three pieces. It was purchased by Julius II after its discovery and brought to the Vatican. It is ascribed to the Rhodian sculptors Agesander, Polydoros and Athenodoros (c 50 BC). The violent realism of the conception as well as the ˙xtreme skill and accurate detail with which the agonised contortions of the ¹ies are rendered are typical of late Hellenistic sculpture. One of the best ·n classical sculptures, it influenced Renaissance and Baroque artists, and ·rticularly admired in the 19C (Byron, in *Childe Harold*, describes ·s torture dignifying pain'). The group was restored in 1957: its more ·earance as restored by Giovanni Montorsoli (on the advice of ·is preserved in a plaster cast which can be seen from a window of ·useum of Pagan Antiquities (see below).

·orway beyond are two *Molossian dogs of the school of ·tto dell'Hermes**. *Hermes (formerly thought to be ·ps Hermes Psychopompos, the conductor of souls to the under-

The Apollo Belvedere in the Pio-Clementino Museum

world, copy of an original by Praxiteles at Olympia. In the portico beyond (niche), Venus Felix and Cupid: the body is copied from the Venus of Knidos in the Mask Room; the inscription on the plinth states that the group was dedicated to Venus Felix by Sallustia and Helpis. It has stood in the courtyard since Julius II began the collection here. Also here is a small marble funerary urn in the shape of a house or shrine, and beyond, a sarcophagus with a battle of the Amazons, with Achilles and Penthesileia, grouped in the centre (3C AD).

The **Gabinetto del Canova** contains three Neo-classical statues of Perseus (inspired by the Apollo Belvedere) and the boxers Creugas and Damoxenes, by Antonio Canova, placed here when most of the classical masterpieces were taken to Paris by Napoleon in 1800, after the Treaty of Tolentino.

Beneath the following portico: sarcophagus of Sextus Varius Marcellus, father of Heliogabalus; sarcophagus with curved ends and a relief of a Bacchic procession. Beneath the porticos are six granite basins, the four smaller ones from the Baths of Caracalla.

The door flanked by the two hounds leads out of the courtyard and into the **Animal Room** (*Sala degli Animali*). Most of the animal statues are by Francesco Antonio Franzoni (1734–1818), who made them for this room for Pius VI. Some are entirely Franzoni's work; others were made up by him from ancient fragments. The Roman pieces include: (in the room on the left) sow with a litter of 12, perhaps of the Augustan period; (under the far window) colossal head of a camel (fountain head), copy of a Hellenistic original of the 2C BC; *Meleager with his dog and the head of a boar, copy of a 4C original by Skopas; 464. Triton and nereid, with cupids, perhaps a Hellenistic original of the 2C BC; head of a minotaur, copy of a 5C original. In the room on the right: Mithras slaying the bull (2C AD); (on the wall behind) *mosaics with animals, from Hadrian's Villa at Tivoli (2C AD). In the pavement of each room, mosaics with animals and plants (2C AD).

The **Gallery of Statues** (right) is part of the original Belvedere Pavilion built by Innocent VIII. Remains of paintings by Pinturicchio may still be seen on the walls. To the right: *769. **Eros of Centocelle**, replica of an original of the early 4C. Also called the 'Genius of the Vatican', it is probably a statue of Thanatos, the god of death, from an original attributed to Kephisodotos. It was found at Centocelle by Gavin Hamilton. 767. Discobolos of Polycletus, replica of the second half of the 5C; 762. Seated statue of Paris, possibly a copy of an original by Euphranor (4C); 756. Apollo Kitharoidos, restored as Minerva, late 5C; 754. Seated statue of Penelope (so called; with a head from another antique statue); *750. **Apollo Sauroctonos**, representing the god watching a lizard that he is about to kill, copy of the famous bronze original by Praxiteles; 748. So-called Mattei Amazon, from an original attributed to Kresilas (head from another statue); 747. Satyr; 745. Muse, restored as Urania, belonging to the series of sculptures found at Tivoli (see above). On either side of the door (735, 588.) a pair of seated statues of Poseidippos and Menander(?), the comic poets, copies of Hellenistic originals; 573. Roman, traditionally identified as the Emperor Macrinus (AD 217–18); 571. Asklepios and Hygieia, of Alexandrian type; 567. Two children of Niobe, fragment of the Florentine group; 563. Danaid, or nymph, holding a cup.

*561. **Resting Satyr**, one of several known replicas of the famous statue of Praxiteles. At the end of the room: *551, 547. The **Barberini Candelabra**,

with representations of divinities, from Hadrian's Villa at Tivoli, Roman works in neo-Attic style (2C AD); *548 Sleeping Ariadne, copy of a Hellenistic original of the 3C or 2C; below, 549. Sarcophagus with a gigantomachia, 2C AD after a Hellenistic original of the 2C BC; 540. Relief of Bacchus and Ariadne, from Hadrian's Villa; 544. Hermes, copy of a 5C Greek original (school of Myron); 541. Statue of Augustus of the 1C AD with the head of Lucius Verus (AD 161–69). On the bases of several of the statues are inscriptions relating to the gens Julia-Claudia found near the Mausoleum of Augustus.

At the end is the **Gallery of Busts** divided by arches into four little rooms. **Room I**. To the right (above) 711. Caracalla; 704. Marcus Aurelius; 703. Antoninus Pius; (below) 723. Trajan; 718. Nero idealised as Apollo; 716. Old man wearing a crown of vine-leaves, possibly a priest of Dionysos, Hellenistic, 2C BC; 715. Head of Augustus as one of the Fratres Arvales, and as a boy (714); Julius Caesar; column with three dancing Hours, found near the Ara Pacis; 598. Porphyry bust of a youth, perhaps Philip the Arabian, emperor in 244–49; *592. Portrait group, Cato and Porcia, probably from a Roman tomb, 1C BC. **Room II**. 702. Apollo; 698. Saturn, after an original of the 5C or 4C BC; (above) 689. Colossal bust of Serapis; 697. Isis; 694. Head of Menelaus, from a group of Menelaus with the body of Patroclus (see Pasquino, p 128). In the middle of the room, base in the form of a rectangular chest standing on legs of winged lions, the lid decorated with flowers and foliage.

Room IV (the recess to the left). 641. Mask of Jupiter Ammon, copy of a 4C original; 637. Woman in the attitude of prayer, Augustan after a 5C original *636. Bust of Antinous, an exquisite portrait; 626. Head of Juno, after an original of the 5C. **Room III**. *671. Seated statue of Zeus (Jupiter Verospi), copy of a Hellenistic original (the lower part is a restoration); 784. Celestial globe; 654. Head of one of the Diadochoi wearing a regal headband. 53. Augur; 651. Mithras in the Phrygian cap; 675. Pan.

The so-called **Open Loggia** (*Loggia Scoperta*), usually closed to the public, skirts the north side of the Belvedere Pavilion as far as the Mask Room. 858. Fragment of relief depicting a youth taking part in a Bacchic procession, 3C AD; 862. Frieze, in two sections, with scenes of farm activities and of the sale of bread in a baker's shop, 3C AD; over the door to the Mask Room, sepulchral relief of Galatea, a priestess of Isis, with her husband, 2C AD.

The **Mask Room** (*Gabinetto delle Maschere*; usually locked, but visible through a glass door), with an entrance also from the Gallery of Statues, derives its name from four *mosaics of theatrical masks in the pavement. They came from Hadrian's Villa and date from the 2C AD. The border is of the time of Pius VI and bears his coat of arms. Opposite the entrance, *812. **Venus of Knidos**, a fine copy of the famous statue of Praxiteles. The head belongs to another copy of the statue; the limbs are mainly restorations. The goddess is about to bathe; she has a towel and, near by, a pitcher (hydria). On the left, 810. The Graces, from an original perhaps of the 2C BC. In the niche opposite, 801. Satyr, in rosso antico, from a bronze original (Hellenistic, 2C BC). On the wall between the doors, 815. Venus at her bath, copy of a larger original by Doidalsas, a Bithynian sculptor of the 3C BC.

From the Animal Room (see above) is the entrance to the **Hall of the Muses** (*Sala delle Muse*), an octagon with a vestibule at either end, built in 1782 by Michelangelo Simonetti (the paintings are by Tommaso Conca). **First**

Vestibule: herms (including, 322. Sophocles), and reliefs (321. Pyrrhic dance, a 4C Attic work; Birth of Bacchus). **Octagon**, a magnificent hall with 16 columns of Carrara marble: seven of the statues of the Nine Muses in this room were found, together with that of Apollo, in a villa near Tivoli, and are thought to be copies of originals, apparently of bronze, by Praxiteles or his school, but possibly they do not all belong to the same group. 317. Erato; 312. Calliope; 310. Apollo Kitharoidos; 308. Terpsichore. Nos. 303 and 293 (Euterpe and Urania) were not found with the rest and were not, in fact, originally intended as muses. 299. Melpomene; 295. Thalia; 291. Clio; 287. Polyhymnia. The statues alternate with herms: Metrodorus; so-called Alcibiades; 315. Homer; 314. Socrates; Strategos (Alcibiades?); 305. Plato (not Zeno); 302. Euripides; 301. Epicurus; 289. Demosthenes. In the centre, *1192. **Belvedere Torso**, found in the Campo dei Fiori at the time of Julius II, and bearing the signature of Apollonios, an Athenian sculptor of the 1C BC. The figure is sitting on a hide laid over the ground. Greatly admired by Michelangelo, Raphael, and other Renaissance artists, it may represent Hercules, Polyphemus, Prometheus, Sciron, Marsyas or Philoctetes. **Second Vestibule**: Herm of Pericles, copy of a 5C original by Kresilas; herms of Bias and Periander.

The domed **Circular Hall** (*Sala Rotonda*) was also designed by Simonetti (c 1782), modelled on the Pantheon. In the pavement is a mosaic from Otricoli, representing a battle between Greeks and centaurs, tritons, and nereids; in the centre of the room, a huge monolithic porphyry vase found in the Domus Aurea; *257. Jupiter of Otricoli, a colossal head of majestic beauty, attributed to Bryaxis (4C BC); 256. Antinous (died AD 130) as Bacchus, from a Greek prototype of the 4C (the drapery, which was originally of bronze, was restored in the early 19C by Thorvaldsen); 255. Faustina the Elder (died 141), wife of Antoninus Pius; *254. Female divinity, perhaps Demeter, wearing the peplos, after a Greek original of the late 5C BC. 253. Head of Hadrian, from his mausoleum; 252. Hercules, colossal statue in gilded bronze, an early Imperial copy of a work of the school of Skopas; 251. Bust of Antinous; 249. Juno (the Barberini Hera), a Roman copy of a cult-image in the manner of the late 5C; 248. Marine divinity (from Pozzuoli), believed to personify the Gulf of Baiae, an interesting example of the fusion of marine elements and human features; *246. Nerva (or Galba), after a statue representing Jupiter; 245. Bust of Serapis, after a work by Bryaxis; 243. Claudius as Jupiter; 242. Head of Claudius; 241. Juno Sospita from Lanuvium, dating from the Antonine period; 240. Head of Plotina (died 129), wife of Trajan; 258. Head of Pertinax(?); 259. Genius of Augustus; 260. Head of Julia Domna (died 217), wife of Septimius Severus.

Hall of the Greek Cross (*Sala a Croce Greca*), another Neo-classical room by Simonetti. To the left of the doorway, 199. Caesar, nephew of Augustus, sacrificing. *238. Sarcophagus in porphyry of St Helena, mother of Constantine, decorated with Roman horsemen, barbarian prisoners and fallen soldiers; *237, Sarcophagus of Constantia, daughter of Constantine, in porphyry, decorated with vine-branches and children bearing grapes, peacocks and a ram (Christian symbols), from Santa Costanza (see p 267). 236, 239. Two granite sphinxes; and, in the pavement, mosaics: *basket of flowers, shield with the head of Minerva and the phases of the moon.

Ahead is the landing of the Simonetti Staircase. It ascends to a second landing outside the Gallery of the Candelabra (see below) and the Room of the Biga (right).

The **Room of the Biga** (with glass doors, usually locked) is a circular domed hall by Giuseppe Camporese. *2368. **Biga**, or two-horsed chariot, a reconstruction in 1788 by Francesco Antonio Franzoni from ancient fragments; only the body of the chariot and part of the offside horse are original. The chair was used as an episcopal throne in the church of San Marco during the Middle Ages. The bas-reliefs suggest that the biga was a votive chariot dedicated to Ceres and that it dates from the 1C AD. Along the wall, from the left, 2344. Charioteer; with the head from another statue; *2346. Discobolos, a copy of Myron's work with the head wrongly restored; 2347. Hermes (so-called Phokion), from a 5C original (head a copy of a head of a 4C *strategos*); *2349. Discobolos, from a bronze original by Naucides, nephew and pupil of Polykleitos, a fine example of Peloponnesian sculpture of the 5C BC; *2355. Roman in the act of sacrifice (early Empire), with voluminous draperies; *2363. Bearded Dionysos, called Sardanapalus, a work of the early 4C BC, attributed to Kephisodotos. 2364, 2356, 2348, 2341. Sarcophagi of children (3C AD); the first three have circus scenes, with cupids as competitors; the fourth represents the chariot race between Oinomaos and Pelops.

The Simonetti Staircase continues up to the Etruscan Museum.

Etruscan Museum

The Etruscan Museum (closes at 13.30, and not open Wed & Sat), reached by a staircase from the landing outside the Room of the Biga, was founded in 1837 by Gregory XVI and its official name is the *Museo Gregoriano Etrusco*. One of the most important collections of its kind in existence, many of the objects come from Southern Etruria, but there are also outstanding examples of Greek and Roman art, and a notable collection of Greek vases. In 1989 the Giacinto Guglielmi collection of finds from Vulci was acquired (including Attic vases and Etruscan material). The collection has been beautifully rearranged and well labelled (also in English) and all the rooms were reopened in 1996. Apart from the first two rooms, the exhibits are subdivided according to material (i.e. bronze, stone, terracotta, precious objects, and ceramics). At the top of the stairs, outside the entrance, is a beautiful krater in grey stone.

Room I displays Early Iron Age material (9C–8C BC). In the case on the left are finds from Etruria including Villanovan cinerary urns, and in the case on the right objects from Latium Vetus (south of the Tiber), including a reconstructed chariot and weapons of the late 8C BC.

Room II has interesting frescoes by Federico Barocci and Taddeo Zuccari, with good stuccoes. The room contains objects found in 1836 in an Etruscan necropolis south of Cerveteri where a small group of tumulus chamber-tombs were unearthed; the most important is the ***Regolini-Galassi tomb**, named after its discoverers. Three important people were buried here in 650 BC, including a princess (called Larthia), a warrior of high rank, and a priest-king who was cremated. Their funeral equipment includes: gold jewellery (a gold *clasp, with decorations in relief, necklaces, and bracelets); ivories; cups; plates; and silver ornaments (of Graeco-Oriental provenance); a bronze libation bowl, with six handles in the shape of animals; and a reconstructed throne. Also here were found a *cremation urn; a series of pottery statuettes; a bronze incense-burner in the shape of a wagon; a bronze stand with figures in relief; two five-handled jars; silverware including a drinking cup and jug; and small dishes of

Eastern origin. The biga has been reconstructed, as well as a funeral carriage with a bronze bed and funeral couch. The two cases on the window wall contain finds from tombs in the immediate vicinity of the Regolini-Galassi Tomb, including Bucchero vases in relief, and ceramics from another tomb in the necropolis.

Room III. The frescoes were painted for Pius IV by Niccolò Pomarancio and Santi di Tito. It contains a rich collection of bronze objects in common use, including an incense-burner, tripod, buckles, jars, small throne, candelabra, etc., and two statuettes of children. In the centre, *__Mars of Todi__, wearing armour, a bronze statue dating from the beginning of the 4C BC, but inspired by Greek art of the 5C BC. The collection of **mirrors** includes a particularly fine one engraved with Herakles and Atlas, and another with Chalchas, the sooth-sayer, both designs derived from Greek models of 5C–4C BC. The **cistae** (caskets used by women for their jewellery or as toilet-cases) come mostly from Palestrina, and include a fine oval *cista, found at Vulci, decorated with a battle between Greeks and Amazons, with a handle formed by a satyr and a nymph riding on swans. Among the **paterae** (round flat dishes used for libations) is one with the figure of Eos (Aurora) carrying away Kephalos.

Two steps lead up to **Room IV**, which exhibits works in stone. The two lions (late 6C BC) used to guard a tomb at Vulci. The sarcophagus of Circeo has a poly-chrome relief of a procession from a tomb at Cerveteri (late 5C or early 4C BC) with the deceased lying on the roof. Beyond some small inscribed funerary cippi of the Volsinii type (4C–3C BC), is a cippus from Todi with a bilingual inscription in Latin and Celtic on both sides. A sarcophagus from Tuscania has a relief of the Battle of the Centaurs. Beyond is a female sandstone seated statue from Chiusi (3C–2C BC), and cippi in the form of pine cones from Palestrina. The sculpted heads include some from Vulci. A sarcophagus from Tarquinia (2C BC) shows the Thebans. The works from Vulci (4C BC) include two horses' heads and a funerary cippus in the form of a capital.

Steps lead up to Room IX (described below), and on the left a modern flight of stairs continues up to Rooms V–VIII. **Rooms V–VI** display works in **terracotta**. In Room V are three antefixes. Room VI, on two levels, displays a group of votive statues, and a high relief from the pediment of a temple in Tivoli. The poly-chrome ornament in the form of a winged horse comes from the corner or top of a pediment. In cases are numerous portrait *heads of both sexes and all ages, models of legs, feet, etc., all of them ex-votos. The *bust of an elderly woman, dating from the 3C BC, is particularly remarkable. **Rooms VII** and **VIII** have a magnificent display of gold *__jewellery__, displayed chronologically from the 7C BC. Most of it is from Vulci and includes a necklace with pomegranate drops, coronets and diadems used as funerary wreaths, beautiful earrings, etc.

At the bottom of the stairs is **Room IX** which displays the **Guglielmi Collection from Vulci** (half of it was donated to the Vatican in 1937, and the other half was purchased from the Guglielmi in 1988). It is especially important for its **Attic black- and red-figure vases**, a number of them attributed pieces (displayed in the central cases). It also has Villanovan objects, bronzes (including fine stamnoi), bucchero vases, and Corinthian ware. From the windows the view over the northern districts of the city extends to Monte Mario.

Room X displays alabaster cinerary urns from the Hellenistic period from Volterra and Chiusi. **Room XI**. Funerary *monument with the figure of the

dying Adonis from Tuscania (second half of the 3C BC); cinerary urns in travertine from Perugia, and two urns from Bomarzo. The little **Room XII**, with a view of the Borghese gardens and Villa Medici, and (to the right), Castel Sant'Angelo, and the Vittorio Emanuele monument, displays the **Falcioni collection** acquired in 1898, and typical of a 19C private collection, with a variety of objects including small bronzes, terracottas, and jewellery, some from the neighbourhood of Viterbo, and others of unknown provenance. **Room XIII** has three terracotta sarcophagi from Tuscania. The spiral **staircase of Bramante** which descends to the Pio-Clementino Museum (see above) is at present closed.

The **Antiquarium Romanum** is displayed in Rooms XIV–XVI. **Room XIV** contains fragments of large bronze statues, including the portrait head of the Emperor Treboniano Gallo (251–53 AD); part of a bronze folding table; silver vases with a dedication to Apollo from Vicarello on the Lago di Bracciano, dating from the 1C AD; Roman scales; bronze weight in the shape of a crouching pig, marked C (i.e. 100 Roman pounds); armour in bronze and iron; rings, pins, keys, etc. The view from the window takes in Castel Sant'Angelo, the dome of the Pantheon, the Vittorio Emanuele monument, the tower of Palazzo Senatorio on the Campidoglio, all of them backed by the Alban Hills.

Room XV displays architectural terracottas, lamps, glass, and three fine terracotta panels with reliefs of the Labours of Hercules from the Augustan age. Finds from the 'Ager Vaticanus', the area on the right bank of the Tiber near the Vatican, are displayed in **Room XVI**.

A short flight of stairs leads down to Rooms **XVII–XXI** which have a valuable *****Collection of Greek, Italic and Etruscan vases**. Most of them come from the Etruscan tombs of Southern Etruria, discovered during excavations in the first half of the 19C. At the time of their discovery the vases were all indiscriminately called Etruscan. In fact many of them are Greek in origin and illustrate the importance of the commercial relations between Greece and Etruria; from the end of the 7C to the late 5C BC many Greek vases were imported. By the middle of the 4C BC the Greek imports were largely replaced by the products of Magna Graecia, Lucania and Campania.

The **Hemicycle (Room XIX)** has charming 18C frescoes with views of Rome and the Vatican, and scenes of the Papal States. The building which houses the sacristy of St Peter's can also be seen, built at about this time. (In the Cortile della Pigna, a building 12m below ground level was opened in 1981 to house the Secret Archives of the Vatican Library.)

The hemicycle has a splendid display of **Attic vases**. At the right end: case of black-figure oinochoë; the black-figure amphorae (500–490 BC) include one with a battle scene and chariot by the 'Edinburgh Painter'. Displayed in a case on its own is a *hydria of the Leagros group (c 500 BC). Another case has four black-figure amphorae showing athletes in the presence of Athena by the 'Berlin Painter' (500–480 BC). Beyond the door are kylixes of the 6C BC, including one with red-figure and black-figure decorations. In another case, black-figure *amphora signed by Exekias, who worked in 530–520 BC. One side shows Achilles and Ajax playing with dice; on the other side Castor and Pollux are being welcomed on their return home by their parents, Tyndareus and Leda. The red-figure amphorae (being restored) is attributed to the 'Kleophrades Painter' (510–500 BC). The wall case has red-figure vases including three signed hydria. In a case on its own is a red-figure amphora attributed to the

'Hector Painter', showing Hector carrying out libations before a battle, and taking leave of his parents Priam and Hecuba. In the last case are red-figure amphorae, and a *kylix by the famous 5C vase painter Duris, with Oedipus trying to solve the riddle of the Sphinx.

Room XX frescoed by Pomarancio, contains the private collection left to the museum in 1967 by Astarita of Naples. Exhibited on its own is a large krater of the late Corinthian period showing Ulysses and Menelaus asking for the return of Helen. **Room XXI**. Black-figure vases from Vulci and Cerveteri (6C BC), attributed to the 'Madrid Painter' and the 'Vatican Painter', and works in the Corinthian style (650–615 BC). The upper hemicycle (**Room XXII**), at present closed, will exhibit vases from Magna Graecia.

The Simonetti Staircase leads back down to the Quattro Cancelli.

II. Gallery of Tapestries, Raphael Rooms, Borgia Rooms and Gallery of Modern Religious Art, Sistine Chapel, Museum of Christian Art, Sistine Hall and Library

From the Quattro Cancelli the Scala Simonetti leads up two flights of stairs to the landing outside the Room of the Biga. Here is the beginning of Bramante's long West Gallery with the Gallery of the Candelabra, the Gallery of Tapestries, and the Gallery of Maps.

The Gallery of the Candelabra

The gallery of the Candelabra (80m long) is named after the pairs of marble candelabra, of the Roman Imperial period, placed on either side of the arches which divide it into six sections. The ceiling has frescoes by Domenico Torti and Ludovico Seitz illustrating events in the 16C pontificate of Leo XIII. In the pavement are marbles from the warehouses of ancient Rome.

Section I. 20. Sarcophagus of a child, Roman, 3C AD; pair of candelabra from Otricoli, with reliefs of Bacchic rites and of Apollo and Marsyas, Roman, 2C BC. **Section II**. 10. Pan extracting a thorn from a satyr's foot, copy of a 2C Hellenistic original; 22. Diana of the Ephesians, 3C AD; candelabra of the 2C AD from a Roman villa; 83. Ganymede carried off by the eagle, after a bronze original by Leochares.

Section III. On the walls, fragments of frescoes from a Roman villa at Tor Marancia (near the Catacombs of Domitilla), with flying figures, 2C AD; 12. Mosaic of fish, fruit, etc.; 13. Apollo from an archaic Greek type; 40. Satyr with young Dionysos on his shoulders (1C AD).

Section IV. *30. Sarcophagus with Dionysos and Ariadne and Dionysiac scenes, 2C AD; *38. Fisherman, a realistic work of the school of Pergamon (3C BC); *66. Boy with goose, from a bronze by Boethus of Chalcedon, 3C BC; *85. Sarcophagus with the slaughter of the Niobids, a fine work of the 2C AD; 93. Boy of the Julio-Claudian family, 1C AD.

Section V. *Girl running in a race during a Peloponnesian religious festival, Roman copy of a Greek bronze original of the 5C BC; 25. Young satyr playing the flute. **Section VI**. Artemis, from a Praxitelean original; the head (which does not belong) is a copy of a 5C bronze; 5. Statuette of a woman wearing a cloak, copy of a Hellenistic original of the 4C or 3C BC; 8. sarcophagus with Diana and Endymion; 20. Youth wearing the Phrygian cap, in the manner of Praxiteles; 24. Niobid, copy of a Hellenistic original of the 4C or 3C BC; *32. Fighting

Persian, statuette after an original bronze belonging to the series of statues given by Attalos I of Pergamon to the Athenians which were placed on the Acropolis in Athens; 35. Sarcophagus with the rape of the daughters of Leukippos.

The Gallery of Tapestries

The gallery of Tapestries (*Galleria degli Arazzi*) is divided into three rooms, and contains the so-called 'New School' series of tapestries executed after Raphael's death from cartoons by his pupils, some of which were copied from drawings he had left. Also displayed here are Roman and Flemish tapestries. **Room 1**. Raphael 'New School' tapestries, woven in Brussels in the 16C: *Adoration of the Shepherds and *Adoration of the Magi. Opposite are tapestries illustrating the life of Urban VIII, the most important product of the Barberini workshop active in Rome, 1627–83. **Room 2**. Raphael 'New School' tapestries: Massacre of the Innocents (from a cartoon attributed to Tomaso Vincidor), in three parts; Christ appearing to Mary Magdalene; *Resurrection of Christ; Supper at Emmaus. Opposite are more 17C Roman tapestries illustrating the life of Urban VIII. **Room 3.** Death of Julius Caesar, Flemish (1594).

The Gallery of Maps

The Gallery of Maps (*Galleria delle Carte Geografiche*) was decorated at the time of Gregory XIII, the reformer of the calendar, with numerous *maps and plans painted in 1580–82 by Egnazio Danti, the celebrated Dominican cosmographer, architect and painter. They are extremely important to our knowledge of 16C Italy and represent the Italian peninsula, the Italian regions and the neighbouring islands, as well as some of its most important ports, and the papal territory of Avignon. It is the largest decorative scheme of its kind: it was intended to be seen from the far door, since the regions of northern Italy are at the southern entrance.

Taking the central axis of the gallery as the Apennine range, the west wall (overlooking the Vatican gardens) represents the Adriatic and Alpine regions, and the opposite wall the Ligurian and Tyrrhenian side of Italy. Each map is labelled in Latin at the top. By the far door is *Venice, and two general maps showing the country under the Roman Empire ('Italia antiqua') and in the 16C ('Italia nova'). The paintings were restored several times up until the 17C. The ceiling was decorated at the same time with stuccoes and frescoes illustrating the importance of history and geography to the Church, by a group of painters (including Cesare Nebbia) under the direction of Girolamo Muziano.

Beyond the Gallery of Maps is the **Gallery of Pius V** in which are more tapestries of the late 15C: Scenes of the Passion; *The Creed. On the right, Religion, Grace and Charity, woven in 1525 in Brussels; Coronation of the Virgin, also made in Brussels in the 16C from a cartoon of the 'New School' of Raphael.

To the right is the **Ladies' Audience Room** (closed indefinitely), added by Paul V (1605–21), frescoed by Guido Reni.

At the end of the gallery is the **Chapel of St Pius V**; to the left is the **Sobieski Room**. The floor is inlaid with mosaics from Ostia, and there is a painting by Jan Alois Mateiko (1883) depicting the Liberation of Vienna by John Sobieski on 12 September 1683.

Beyond is the **Hall of the Immaculate Conception**, a room decorated with

frescoes by Francesco Podesti (1858) which illustrate the definition and procla-
mation of the dogma of the Immaculate Conception pronounced by Pius IX on
8 December 1854. The floor has 2C mosaics from Ostia. Beyond are the Stanze
di Raffaello (Raphael Rooms).

Stanze di Raffaello

This series of rooms was built by Nicholas V, and the walls were originally
painted by Andrea del Castagno, Piero della Francesca, and Benedetto Bonfigli.
Julius II employed a group of great artists to continue the decoration, including
Luca Signorelli, Perugino, Sodoma, Bramantino, Baldassarre Peruzzi, Lorenzo
Lotto, and the Flemish painter Jan Ruysch. Bramante recommended his fellow
citizen, Raffaello Sanzio, and the Pope sent for him, and set him to work immediately on his arrival in Rome in 1508. The result proved so satisfactory that
Julius dismissed all the other painters, ordered their works to be destroyed, and
commissioned Raphael to decorate the whole of this part of the Vatican.

The Stanze are the painter's masterpiece; they show the extraordinary development which took place in his art during the years between his coming to
Rome and his death at the age of 37 in 1520. When Raphael arrived, the court
of Julius II was an intellectual centre of the first rank; the College of Cardinals
and the Curia included among their members many celebrated savants, human-
ists and men of letters; and a crowd of artists, led by Bramante and
Michelangelo, were at work in the city. In this highly cultured environment
Raphael, who had great powers of assimilation, acquired an entirely new
manner of painting. He began work in the Stanza della Segnatura (II), with the
frescoes of Astronomy, Apollo, Adam and Eve, and Judgement of Solomon,
which were probably his trial works; he then carried out the other frescoes in
this room. After this he decorated, successively, the Stanza d'Eliodoro (III), the
Stanza dell'Incendio (I), and the Stanza di Costantino (IV). A careful restoration
programme is under way of the frescoes.

The entrance to the Stanze has been altered. A covered balcony (overlooking
the Cortile del Belvedere) from the Hall of the Immaculate Conception leads
direct to the furthest room, the Sala di Costantino (IV), so that the rooms now
have to be visited in reversed chronological order, as described below.

Room IV: Sala di Costantino, painted almost entirely in the time of Clement
VII (1523–34), after Raphael's death, by Giulio Romano with the assistance of
Francesco Penni and Raffaellino del Colle. On the wall facing the window is the
Victory of Constantine over Maxentius near the Pons Milvius, for which Raphael
had made some sketches. The reddish tint which suffuses the picture is charac-
teristic of Giulio Romano. To the right are figures of St Urban, Justice, and
Charity; to the left, St Sylvester, Faith, and Religion.

On the entrance wall: *Constantine Addressing his Soldiers and the Vision of the
Cross*, by Giulio Romano, perhaps from Raphael's design; to the right of this, St
Clement, Temperance, and Meekness; to the left, St Peter, the Church, and
Eternity. On the wall opposite the entrance: The *Baptism of Constantine by St
Sylvester* (a portrait of Clement VII), by Francesco Penni, and at the sides (right)
St Leo, Innocence, and Truth, and (left) St Damasus, Prudence, and Peace. On
the window wall: *Constantine's Donation of Rome to Sylvester*, by Raffaellino del
Colle. At the sides: (right) Gregory VII(?) and Fortitude; (left) St Sylvester and
Courage. Below are other scenes from the life of Constantine. On the ceiling, *The*

Triumph of Christianity, interesting for its unusual iconography, by Tomaso Laureti. In the floor is a 2C Roman mosaic with the Seasons.

It is now necessary to interrupt the visit to the Stanze in order to see the Room of the Chiaroscuri and the Chapel of Nicholas V. From the Sala di Costantino a door leads into the **Room of the Chiaroscuri**, or the *Room of the Grooms* (*Sala dei Palafrenieri*), with a magnificent carved and gilded *ceiling, with the Medici arms. The monochrome frescoes were restored in 1560 by Taddeo and Federico Zuccari and additions were made to them in 1582 by Giovanni Alberti. The little adjoining **Chapel of Nicholas V** is entirely decorated with *frescoes by Fra Angelico, painted between 1448 and 1450. These represent scenes from the lives of the deacon saints Stephen (upper section) and Laurence (lower section); especially fine is the painting of St Stephen preaching. On the ceiling are the four Evangelists and on the pilasters the Doctors of the Church.

The **Loggia of Raphael** (formerly reached from the Sala di Costantino) has been closed to the public for many years. The long gallery of 13 bays overlooks the Courtyard of St Damasus with a fine view of Rome beyond. It was begun by Bramante about 1513 and completed after Bramante's death by Raphael and his pupils. The vault of each bay has four little paintings of Old Testament scenes. The *grotteschi* of the borders are thought to have been inspired by those in the Domus Aurea of Nero, which were discovered in 15C and known to Raphael. The designs were carried out by Giulio Romano, Giovanni da Udine, Franceso Penni, Perino del Vaga, Polidoro da Caravaggio, and others. Controversial restoration work was carried out on the paintings in 1978.

A door leads back into the Raphael Rooms from the Room of the Chiaroscuri. **Room III**: **Stanza d'Eliodoro**, painted by **Raphael** in 1512–14; the subjects were nearly all chosen by Julius II. On the principal wall (right) is the **Expulsion of Heliodorus from the temple at Jerusalem**, alluding to Julius II's success in freeing the States of the Church from foreign powers. The picture illustrates a story in the Apocrypha (Maccabei II, 3): King Seleucus sends his treasurer Heliodorus to Jerusalem to steal the Temple treasure, but the crime is avenged by a horseman assisted by two angels with whips. In the middle of the crowd on the left is Julius II, carried on the sedia gestatoria (the front bearer is a portrait of the engraver Marcantonio Raimondi). In the centre of the composition, under the vault of the temple, the high priest Onias renders thanks to God before the Ark of the Covenant.

On the left is the **Mass of Bolsena**, representing the famous miracle which took place at Bolsena in 1263. A Bohemian priest, who had doubts about the doctrine of Transubstantiation, was convinced when he saw blood drop from the Host on to the altar cloth (the stained corporal is preserved in the cathedral at Orvieto.) This alludes to the vow made by Julius II when, on his first expedition against Bologna in 1506, he stopped at Orvieto to pay homage to the relic. He is shown kneeling opposite the priest, in place of Urban IV, the contemporary pope. The warm colours and, especially, the harmony of reds in the composition show how much Raphael was influenced by Venetian painters (Sebastiano del Piombo and Lorenzo Lotto arrived in Rome at this time).

On the long wall is *Leo I repulsing Attila*, a subject originally selected by Julius II and taken up again at the suggestion of Leo X, when considerable changes

were made in the design. It was executed partly by Raphael's school. The scene representing the banks of the Mincio, where the historic event took place, was replaced by the environs of Rome, and the figure of the Pope, on a white mule, was brought from the back of the picture into the foreground in order to accentuate the allusion to the battle of Ravenna (11 April 1512), at which Leo X, then a cardinal, was present, and which resulted in the expulsion of the French from Italy. Attila, mounted on a white horse, and the Huns behind him, are struck with terror by a vision of St Peter and St Paul.

On the fourth wall is the *Liberation of St Peter*, alluding to the captivity of Leo X after the battle of Ravenna. Three night scenes, with remarkable light effects, illustrate three different episodes: in the middle, the interior of the prison is seen through a high barred window, with St Peter waking up as the angel frees him from his chains; on the left are the guards outside the prison; and on the right St Peter escaping with the angel.

The decoration of the lower part of the walls, with caryatids and four herms, is attributed to Perino del Vaga. The ceiling paintings of God appearing to Noah, Jacob's dream, the Burning Bush, and Abraham's Sacrifice are generally attributed to Peruzzi.

Room II. The **Stanza della Segnatura**, where the pope signed bulls and briefs, has the most beautiful and harmonious frescoes in the series. It was painted entirely by Raphael in 1508–11. On the long wall opposite the entrance is the famous **Disputa** or *Disputation on the Holy Sacrament*, representing a discussion on the Eucharist but essentially intended as a glorification of Catholicism. Given an extremely difficult subject, Raphael succeeded in making the relatively limited space occupied by the composition, which is divided into two zones, appear far larger than it is. In the celestial zone Christ appears between the Virgin and St John the Baptist; above is God the Father surrounded by angels; beneath, the Holy Dove between the four angels holding the book of the Gospels; on the left are St Peter, Adam, St John the Evangelist, David, St Laurence, and Jeremiah(?); on the right, St Paul, Abraham, St James, Moses, St Stephen, and Judas Maccabaeus. In the middle of the terrestrial zone is a monstrance with the Host on an altar. On the right are Saints Augustine and Ambrose, and on the left Saints Gregory and Jerome; they are surrounded by an assembly of Doctors of the Church, popes, cardinals, dignitaries, and the faithful. Certain figures are thought to be portraits of Duns Scotus (the British medieval theologian), and Saints Dominic, Francis, Thomas Aquinas and Nicholas of Bari. On the right is the profile of Dante crowned with laurel, and, beyond him (just visible at the back of the figures in a black hat), is Savonarola. On the extreme left is Fra Angelico in the black Dominican habit and, in the foreground, Bramante.

Beneath the picture are three monochrome paintings by Perino del Vaga: *a pagan sacrifice, St Augustine and the child on the seashore*, and the *Cumaean Sibyl showing the Virgin to Augustus*.

On the wall nearest the Courtyard of the Belvedere is the **Parnassus** (recently restored). Apollo is playing the violin in the shade of laurels, surrounded by the nine Muses and the great poets. Calliope is seated on the left, and behind her are Melpomene, Terpsichore and Polyhymnia; on the right, also seated, is Erato, and behind her are Clio, Thalia, Euterpe and Urania. In the group of poets on the left is the figure of the blind Homer, between Dante and Virgil; lower are Alcaeus,

Corinna, Petrarch and Anacreon, with the voluptuous form of Sappho seated beside them. In the group on the right are Ariosto(?), Ovid, Tibullus and Propertius, and, lower, Sannazaro, Horace and Pindar, seated.

Below the picture are two monochrome scenes: that on the left is thought to show *Alexander placing Homer's poems in the tomb of Achilles* (or, possibly, the discovery of a sarcophagus containing Greek and Latin MSS on the Janiculum in 181 BC). The subject of the scene on the right is either Augustus preventing Virgil's friends from burning the *Aeneid*, or Roman consuls ordering the burning of Greek works considered harmful to the Roman religion. Below these again is some very fine painted intarsia-work by Fra Giovanni da Verona.

On the wall facing the *Disputa* (being restored) is the splendid **School of Athens** (restored), symbolising the triumph of Philosophy, and forming a pendant to the triumph of Theology opposite. The setting is a portico, representing the palace of Science, a magnificent example of Renaissance architecture, inspired by Bramante. The remarkable vaulting, well depicted in light and shade, recalls the Baths of Caracalla. At the sides are statues of Apollo and Minerva. On the steps are the greatest philosophers and scholars of all ages gathered round the two supreme masters, Plato and Aristotle. Plato (probably intended as a portrait of Leonardo da Vinci) points towards heaven, symbolising his system of speculative philosophy, while Aristotle's calm gesture indicates the vast field of nature as the realm of scientific research.

At the top of the steps, on Plato's side, is the bald head and characteristic profile of Socrates; near him, in conversation, are Aeschines, Alcibiades (represented as a young warrior), Xenophon, and others. The beckoning figure next to Xenophon is presumably Chrysippus. At the foot of the steps on the left is Zeno, an old man with a beard, seen in profile; near him Epicurus, crowned with vine-leaves, is reading a book; in the foreground Pythagoras is writing out his harmonic tables, with Averroës, in a turban, and Empedocles looking over his shoulder. The young man sitting down is Federico Gonzaga, who was included by order of Julius II; the handsome youth standing up is Francesco Maria della Rovere; beside him, his foot resting on a block of marble, is a figure which may represent Anaxagoras, Xenocrates, or possibly, Aristoxenus. The seated figure of Heracleitus, isolated in the centre foreground, was not part of the original composition; obviously inspired by Michelangelo's work in the Sistine Chapel (the first section of the vault was uncovered in 1510), it may, according to a recent suggestion, have been intended as a portrait of him.

On the right, around Aristotle, are the students of the exact sciences; standing at the foot of the steps is Ptolemy, with his back to the spectator, and, because of a confusion with the Egyptian kings of the same name, wearing a crown. Opposite him is Zoroaster, holding a sphere. On the extreme right of the composition, Raphael has introduced portraits of himself and Sodoma. To the left is Archimedes or Euclid (with the features of Bramante), surrounded by his disciples and bending over a blackboard on which he is tracing figures with a compass. The solitary figure on the steps is Diogenes, also thought to be a portrait of Michelangelo.

The monochromes beneath the picture are by Perino del Vaga, and represent *Philosophy, astrologers in conference*, and the *Siege of Syracuse* with the death of Archimedes.

On the fourth wall, above the window, are the three Cardinal Virtues—

Fortitude, Temperance, and Prudence. On the left of the window, *Justinian publishing the Pandects*, representing Civil Law, and beneath, *Solon haranguing the Athenians*, by Perino del Vaga. On the right, Gregory IX (in the likeness of Julius II) is shown handing the Decretals to a jurist (1227), to represent Canon Law. The prelates around the Pope are portraits of Raphael's contemporaries; on the left, in front, is Giovanni de' Medici, afterwards Leo X, then Cardinal Antonio del Monte, Alessandro Farnese (Paul III), and others.

Beneath is *Moses bringing the Israelites the Tablets of Stone*, by Perino del Vaga. The ceiling was also painted by Raphael: above the *Disputa*, Theology; above the *Parnassus*, Poetry; above the *School of Athens*, Philosophy; and above the window wall, Justice. In the pendentives, Adam and Eve, Apollo and Marsyas, Astronomy, and the Judgement of Solomon. The small central octagon is attributed to Bramantino. The floor, in opus alexandrinum, shows the arms of Nicholas V and Leo X, and the name of Julius II.

Room I: Stanza dell'Incendio. On the ceiling is the *Glorification of the Holy Trinity* by Perugino, Raphael's master (the only work not destroyed when Raphael took over the decoration of the Stanze). The walls were painted in 1517 by Raphael's pupils (Giulio Romano, Francesco Penni, and perhaps Perino del Vaga) from his own designs. The subjects chosen were events of the times of Leo III (795–816) and Leo IV (847–55), most of which, however, allude to episodes in the history of Leo X.

Facing the window is the **Incendio di Borgo**, illustrating the fire that broke out in Rome in 847, and was miraculously extinguished when Leo IV made the sign of the Cross from the loggia of St Peter's. This was probably intended as an allusion to the achievement of Leo X in restoring peace to Italy. In the background, flames threaten the old church of St Peter's (the façade of which is shown); on the right, the Pope leaves the Vatican. On the left is a scene of the Burning of Troy, with naked figures scaling the walls and Aeneas carrying his father Anchises on his back, followed by his wife Creusa and their son Ascanius.

Opposite the entrance wall is the *Coronation of Charlemagne by Leo III* in 800, an obvious reference to the meeting of Leo X and Francis I at Bologna in 1516, since Leo and Charlemagne have the features of the later pope and king. On the opposite wall the subject is the *Victory of Leo IV over the Saracens at Ostia* (849), in allusion to the Crusade against the Turks proclaimed by Leo X, who is again represented in the figure of Leo IV. The two cardinals behind him are portraits of Cardinal Bibbiena and Giulio de' Medici. On the window wall is the *Oath of Leo III*, made in St Peter's on 23 December 800. On this occasion the Pope cleared himself of charges that had been brought against him. This alludes to the Lateran Council held by Leo X.

The monochrome figures below the paintings represent Godfrey de Bouillon, Ethelwulf of England (Astolfo), Charlemagne, Lothair I and Ferdinand of Castile.

From the Stanza dell'Incendio a door leads into the **Chapel of Urban VIII**, richly decorated with frescoes and stuccoes by Pietro da Cortona.

Outside the chapel, a stairway leads down (right) to the Borgia Rooms and the Museum of Modern Religious Art. It is possible at this point to proceed direct (left) to the Sistine Chapel instead of approaching it through the Borgia Rooms and the Museum of Modern Religious Art. However, it is well worth visiting the first six Borgia Rooms to see Pinturicchio's frescoes, even if you do not intend to continue through the 50 subsequent galleries of modern religious art.

The Borgia Rooms and Gallery of Modern Religious Art

The six Borgia Rooms (*Appartamento Borgia*) are named after Alexander VI (Borgia), who adapted this suite in the palace of Nicholas V for his personal use, and had it decorated with **frescoes by Pinturicchio** and his school (1492–95). After the death of Alexander VI, the Borgia apartment was abandoned since the Borgia family were in disgrace, and it was not until 1889 that Leo XIII had the rooms restored by Lodovico Seitz and opened them to the public. Incongruous modern paintings were hung here in 1973.

Room I, of the Sibyls, is square and has 12 lunettes each with a sibyl accompanied by a prophet. The juxtaposition of sibyls and prophets illustrates an ancient belief that the sibyls foretold the coming of the Messiah. Here Cesare Borgia was imprisoned by Julius II in 1503, in the very room where he had had his cousin Alfonso of Aragon murdered in 1500. **Room II** (left) contains copes designed by Matisse.

Room III, of the Creed, is named after the scrolls on which are written the sentences of the Creed, held by the 12 Apostles depicted in the lunettes. Each Apostle is accompanied by a prophet holding an appropriate inscription. These frescoes are attributed to Pier Matteo d'Amelia, a successor of Pinturicchio.

Room IV, of the Liberal Arts, symbolises the seven liberal arts: the *Trivium* (grammar, dialectic, rhetoric) and the *Quadrivium* (geometry, arithmetic, astronomy, music) which were the basis of medieval learning. The paintings are attributed to Antonio da Viterbo, a pupil of Pinturicchio. The Arch of Justice, in the middle, was painted in the 16C. The ceiling is decorated with squares and grotesques alternating with the Borgia bull. The fine chimneypiece is by or after Sansovino. The hidden treasure of Alexander VI was found in this room.

Room V, of the Saints. The walls and the vault are covered with more splendid *frescoes by Pinturicchio, his masterpiece. The room is divided by an arch into two cross-vaulted areas forming six lunettes. On the ceiling, *Legend of Isis*; *Osiris and the bull Apis* (in reference to the Borgia arms; see above), with reliefs in gilded stucco. Above the door, *Madonna and Child with saints* (medallion). Entrance wall, *The Visitation*; *Saints Paul the Hermit and Anthony Abbot in the desert* (right); End wall, *Disputation between St Catherine of Alexandria and the emperor Maximian*; the saint was once thought to be a portrait of Lucrezia Borgia or Giulia Farnese. The figure behind the throne is a self-portrait by Pinturicchio, and in the background is the Arch of Constantine. Window wall, Martyrdom of St Sebastian, with a view of the Colosseum. On the exit wall, *Susanna and the Elders*; *Legend of St Barbara*.

Room VI, of the Mysteries of the Faith. The frescoes, partly by Pinturicchio, represent the *Annunciation, Nativity, Adoration of the Magi*, *Resurrection (the kneeling pontiff is Alexander VI), Ascension, Pentecost*, and *Assumption of the Virgin*. The last fresco includes a portrait of the donor, perhaps Francesco Borgia. In the ceiling are stuccoes and paintings of prophets.

Room VII, of the Popes, formerly decorated with portraits of popes. The frescoes and stucco decoration of the splendid vaulted ceiling were commissioned by Leo X from Perino del Vaga and Giovanni da Udine.

The **Gallery of Modern Religious Art** was arranged in 1973 in the Borgia Apartments, and in 50 or so rooms, lavishly renovated. The works were presented to the Pope by invited artists from all over the world. They include: Pietro Annigoni, Francis Bacon, Giacomo Balla, Bernard Buffet, Carlo Carrà,

Marc Chagall, Salvador Dalí, Giorgio de Chirico, Filippo de Pisis, Max Ernst, Paul Gauguin, Renato Guttuso, Wassily Kandinsky, Paul Klee, Oskar Kokoschka, Fernand Léger, Carlo Levi, Giacomo Manzù, Marino Marini, Arturo Martini, Henri Matisse, Henry Moore, Giorgio Morandi, Edvard Munch, Ben Nicholson, José Clemente Orozco, Pablo Picasso, Auguste Rodin, Georges Rouault, David Alfaro Siqueiros, Mario Sironi, Ardengo Soffici, Graham Sutherland, Maurice Utrillo, Maurice de Vlaminck, and numerous others. They are arranged in no particular order, but they are fully labelled.

Stairs lead up from the last gallery to the Sistine Chapel.

The Sistine Chapel

The present entrance to the Sistine Chapel is in the west wall, to the right of the altar.

The chapel takes its name from Sixtus IV, who had it rebuilt by Giovanni de' Dolci in 1473–81 as the official private chapel of the popes, and for the conclaves for the election of the popes which are still held here. It is famous for its superb frescoes by Michelangelo, perhaps the greatest pictorial decoration in Western art. The hall is a rectangle 40m long, 13m wide, and nearly 21m high, lit on either side by six windows, placed rather high up.

The barrel-vaulted ceiling is entirely covered by the celebrated **frescoes of Michelangelo**. He is known to have been reluctant to take up this commission from Julius II, but having accepted, he completed the vault between 1508 and 1512. The complex design, which has received various theological interpretations, combines Old and New Testament figures, as well as themes from pagan prophecy and Church history. The powerful sculpturesque figures are set in an architectural design with an effect of high relief and rich colour on a huge scale. Work on the ceiling was begun at the main entrance, in the area furthest from the altar: the development in the artist's skill and his facility in the technique of fresco painting can be seen in the later figures at the altar end. The scaffolding was taken down and the first half of the ceiling revealed in 1510 to the wonder of all who came to see it.

The frescoes were restored in 1980–94. They had been discoloured by dirt and candle smoke, and damaged by poor restorations in the past. Important details about the way in which Michelangelo worked on this great commission were discovered. The holes for the scaffolding were found beneath the windows which would seem to confirm that the scaffolding bridge from which the whole ceiling was painted was without support on the ground. The lunettes were painted in three days directly onto the fresh plaster, without the help of a preliminary cartoon or the transfer of a preparatory sketch. There is now considerable concern about the conservation of the frescoes, since up to 20,000 people a day enter the chapel.

Looking towards the high altar, on the lower curved part of the vault are the *Hebrew prophets* and *pagan sibyls* sitting on architectonic thrones with mouldings in warm grisaille. Above the Last Judgement is the splendid figure of *Jonah issuing from the whale*. Nearest the altar, on the left side: the *Libyan Sibyl; Daniel writing; the Cumaean Sibyl; Isaiah*, in deep meditation; and the *Delphic Sibyl*. At the far end above the entrance is *Zachariah*. On the right side, from the altar end: *Jeremiah; the Persian Sibyl; Ezekiel*, with a scroll; the *Erythrean Sibyl*; and *Joel*.

Along the centre of the vault itself are nine scenes from Genesis, from the

Creation to events in the life of Noah. Again beginning from the altar, these are: *Separation of Light from Darkness*; *Creation of the Sun, Moon, and Planets*; *Separation of Land and Sea and the Creation of the fishes and birds*; *Creation of Adam*, perhaps the most beautiful work on the ceiling; *Creation of Eve*; *Temptation and Expulsion from Paradise*; *Sacrifice of Noah*; *The Flood*; and the *Drunkenness of Noah*. These are framed by decorative pairs of nudes, Michelangelo's famous *'ignudi'*, the most idiosyncratic elements in the ceiling and a remarkable celebration of the nude figure. In the lunettes over the windows are figures representing the forerunners of Christ. In the spandrels on either side of the prophet-sibyl sequence are scenes of Salvation from the Old Testament; over the altar, *Moses and the Brazen Serpent* (right) and the *Death of Haman* (left); at the other end, *Judith and Holofernes* (right) and D*avid and Goliath* (left).

More than 20 years later, in 1535–41, Michelangelo was commissioned by Paul III to paint his huge fresco (20m by 10m) of the **Last Judgement** on the altar wall. This involved the walling-up of two windows and the destruction of two frescoes (both by Perugino) on the side walls. The crowded composition, with innumerable nude figures, contains a remarkable sense of movement and high relief. The strong colour of the background was produced by Michelangelo's liberal use of lapis lazuli. In the upper centre is the enigmatic figure of Christ, beardless, and probably derived from classical models. Near him are the Madonna and (probably) Adam, and on the right St Peter with the keys. At Christ's feet are seated St Laurence and St Bartholomew with his flayed skin (the caricature of a face seen in the folds of the skin is a self-portrait of Michelangelo). In the lunettes high up above the figure of Christ are two groups of angels with the instruments of the Passion.

Beneath, in the central zone, on the left, are the elect ascending to heaven with the help of angels; in the centre is a group of angels with trumpets; on the right the damned are being hauled down into hell. In this group is the famous figure of a soul in despair (known as the *Disperato*) looking down into the abyss. In the lowest zone, on the left, there is a scene representing the Resurrection of the Body; in the centre is a cave full of devils; on the right is the entrance to hell, with the boat of Charon (as in Dante's description) and Minos, the guide to the infernal regions. According to Vasari, Minos has the features of Biagio Martinelli (with ass's ears) who was master of ceremonies to Paul III and had objected to the nudity of Michelangelo's figures. Pius IV also protested about this and at one time intended to destroy the fresco, but in the end he commissioned Daniele da Volterra to paint clothes on some of the figures. An extremely complex restoration operation was carried out on the fresco in 1990–94, since it had deteriorated and been blackened by candle smoke and incense, as well as by the glues used as varnishes in restorations from the late 16C up to the 18C.

A graceful marble screen by Mino da Fiesole, Giovanni Dalmata, and Andrea Bregno divides the chapel into two unequal parts, a larger choir and a small nave. The same artists were responsible for the cantoria. The 15C mosaic pavement is a fine example of opus alexandrinum.

The **frescoes on the long walls** were painted in 1481–83 by some of the greatest artists of the time (some of them are being restored). They depict parallel events in the lives of Moses (left) and of Christ (right). There are six (originally seven) on either side; the two nearest the altar were eliminated to make

room for Michelangelo's *Last Judgement.* On the left (south) wall, beginning from the altar: Pinturicchio, *Moses and Zipporah* (his wife in Egypt) *and the Circumcision of their son*; Botticelli, **Burning Bush*, with Moses slaying the Egyptian and driving the Midianites from the well; school of Ghirlandaio, *Passage of the Red Sea*; Cosimo Rosselli, *Moses on Mount Sinai* and the *Worship of the Golden Calf*; Botticelli, **Punishment of Korah, Dathan and Abiram* (in the background are the Arch of Constantine and the Septizonium); Luca Signorelli and Bartolomeo della Gatta, *Moses giving his rod to Joshua*, and *Mourning for the death of Moses*.

Right (north) wall, beginning from the altar: Perugino(?) and Pinturicchio, *Baptism of Christ*; Botticelli, *Cleansing of the Leper* and the *Temptation in the Wilderness* (in the background, the hospital of Santo Spirito); Domenico Ghirlandaio, **Calling of Peter and Andrew*; Cosimo Rosselli and Piero di Cosimo, *Sermon on the Mount* and *Healing the Leper*; Perugino, **Christ giving the keys to St Peter*; Cosimo Rosselli, *Last Supper*. On the east wall are two frescoes, *The Resurrection* by Domenico Ghirlandaio, and *St Michael defending the body of Moses* by Salviati, overpainted at the end of the 16C by Arrigo Fiammingo and Matteo da Lecce. In the niches between the windows are 28 portraits of the first popes, by Fra Diamante, Domenico Ghirlandaio, Botticelli and Cosimo Rosselli. The celebrated tapestries designed by Raphael, now in the Vatican Pinacoteca, were first exhibited in the Sistine Chapel in 1519.

Through the main door of the Sistine Chapel the sumptuous **Sala Regia** (no admission) can sometimes be seen. It was begun by Antonio da Sangallo the Younger in 1540. It contains stucco decoration by Perino del Vaga and Daniele da Volterra, and frescoes by Vasari, Salviati and the Zuccari. Here the first official meeting since the Reformation took place between the Pope and the Archbishop of Canterbury in 1966. The **Cappella Paolina** (also closed to the public), by Antonio da Sangallo the Younger, has two remarkable **frescoes by Michelangelo (*Conversion of St Paul* and *Crucifixion of St Peter*), painted in 1542–45 and 1546–50.

If you do not wish to

The Scala Regia

continue the tour of the museums, you are often able to leave the chapel by the **Scala Regia** (usually open every day except Wed), an imposing staircase built by Bernini which descends past a statue of Constantine to the portico of St Peter's. The other exit from the Chapel is by a small door in the north wall of the nave, which leads to the Museum of Christian Art.

Museum of Christian Art

The Museum of Christian Art (*Museo Sacro*) was founded by Benedict XIV in 1756, and enlarged in the 19C, partly by the acquisitions of Pius IX but mainly by finds made during excavations in the catacombs by Giovanni Battista de Rossi and his successors.

Beyond a room with vestments, is the **Chapel of St Pius V**, decorated by Giacomo Zucchi to designs by Vasari. In the wall case is part of the **treasury of the Sancta Sanctorum**, the pope's private chapel. The relics were preserved in precious reliquaries inside a case made of cypress wood for Leo III (795–816). The 9C–12C works include: an enamelled *cross presented by St Paschal I (817–24), containing five pieces of the True Cross; a 9C case in the form of a cross; and the Reliquary of Santa Prassede.

The **Room of the Addresses** (*degli Indirizzi*), was so called because in the time of Pius XI, the address or congratulatory documents sent to Leo XIII and Pius X were kept here. Here is displayed a splendid collection of liturgical objects in ivory, enamel, majolica, silver, metal, etc. In the cases opposite the window: *ivories, including diptychs and triptychs (9C–15C). The *Ramboyna diptych (c 900) has Christian scenes with the representation of the Roman wolf in the bottom of the left-hand panel. A five-panelled *tablet with Christ blessing was part of the cover of a New Testament (the other half is in the Victoria and Albert Museum, London). Another *book cover from the Convent of St Gall, Switzerland, is illustrated with the Nativity. The collection of enamels includes Limoges enamels (12C–16C). Other cases display 14C–16C silver crosses and 18C–19C missals. On the window wall: Church silver; crosses and amulets; 16C German, French and Roman silver; hammers used to open the Porta Santa in Holy Years; Roman silver made by Santi Lotti (1629–59); glass; seals and cameos.

The **Room of the Aldobrandini Marriage** (left) was built by Paul V in 1611 and restored by Pius VII in 1817. The ceiling frescoes are by Guido Reni. In the pavement is a 2C geometric mosaic; in the octagon in the centre is Achilles with the body of Hector. On the upper part of the walls are *frescoes of the 1C BC, with scenes from the *Odyssey*, found on the Esquiline in 1848. Lower down are paintings of famous women of antiquity, five of them from Tor Marancia, and paintings of children, from Ostia (1C AD). On the end wall is the *Aldobrandini Marriage* (*Nozze Aldobrandine*), a masterpiece of Augustan art inspired by a Greek model of the 4C or 3C BC, found on the Esquiline in 1605 and kept in one of the garden pavilions of the Villa Aldobrandini until its removal to this room in 1838 by Gregory XVI. The painting of a marriage scene combines realism and symbolism. Two cases contain 3C–5C gilt-engraved glass found in the catacombs.

The **Room of the Papyri** dates from 1774 when 6C–9C papyri from Ravenna were displayed here (now replaced by facsimiles). The frescoes are by Raffaello Mengs and his assistant Christopher Unterberger.

The last room displays **early Christian Antiquities** from the Catacombs of St Calixtus, St Domitilla and St Sebastian, and other cemeteries. These include a collection of glass, some of the finer specimens gilded, engraved 4C glass from Ostia, and 2C–3C multicoloured glass. Christian and pagan lamps (1C–4C), some with symbols of the Good Shepherd, the fish, the peacock, and the monogram of Christ; terracottas; bronze lamps (3C–5C); fabrics including 11C–13C Church embroideries; objects in gold.

Beyond is the first of the exhibition rooms of the Vatican Library.

The Vatican Library

The Vatican Library (*Biblioteca Apostolica Vaticana*) was founded by Nicholas V with a nucleus of some 350 volumes, which he increased to 1200. Sixtus IV brought the total to 3650. The library was pillaged in the sack of 1527. Before the end of the 16C Sixtus V commissioned Domenico Fontana to build the great Sistine Hall. Later popes adapted numerous rooms in Bramante's west corridor to house the steadily increasing collection of gifts, bequests and purchases. Among the most important acquisitions were the Biblioteca Palatina of Heidelberg (1623), the Biblioteca Urbinas (1657, founded by Federico, Duke of Urbino), Queen Christina of Sweden's library (1690), the Biblioteca Ottoboniana, bought in 1748 (formerly the property of Alexander VIII Ottoboni), the Jesuit Library (1922), the Biblioteca Chigiana (1923), and the Biblioteca Ferraioli (1929). There are now about 60,000 MSS, 7000 incunabula, and 1,000,000 other printed books. Leo XIII added a reference library; Pius X reorganised the manuscripts and provided a study-room; and Pius XI carried out further reorganisation. A disastrous collapse in December 1931 of part of the ceiling of the Sistine Hall was repaired two years later. The library and archives are open in the mornings to scholars (with a letter of introduction).

The exhibition rooms of the Library are the Gallery of Urban VIII, the Sistine Rooms, the Sistine Hall, the Pauline Rooms, the Alexandrine Room, the Clementine Gallery, and the Museum of Pagan Antiquities. All the rooms, except the Sistine Hall, are in Bramante's west corridor.

The first room is the **Gallery of Urban VIII**. By the entrance wall are two statues: on the left Aelius Aristides (AD 129–89), dating from the 3C, and on the right the Greek orator Lysias, dating from the 2C. Here are shown astronomical instruments, sailing directions dating from the early 16C, and the Farnese Planisphere (1725), given to Leo XIII by the Count of Caserta.

Beyond are the two **Sistine Rooms**, part of the Library of Sixtus V (see below). In the first, paintings of St Peter's as planned by Michelangelo, and of the erection of the obelisk in Piazza San Pietro. Here is kept a press designed by Bramante for sealing papal bulls. Over the doors of the second room: *Sixtus V proclaiming St Bonaventura Doctor of the Church in the church of the Santi Apostoli* (Melozzo's frescoes are seen in their original place on the wall of the apse); *Canonisation of San Diego in Old St Peter's.*

The **Sistine Hall**, named after its founder Sixtus V, was built in 1587–89 by Domenico Fontana across the great Courtyard of the Belvedere, cutting it into two. It was later paralleled by the New Wing, the construction of which created a small central courtyard, known as the Courtyard of the Library. Beneath this an underground depository was constructed in 1983 to house the precious

collection of Vatican manuscripts, and incunabula. The hall is divided into two vaulted aisles by seven columns, and is decorated with themes glorifying literature and the pontificate of Sixtus V, with interesting views of Rome. **Exhibitions** here of the precious possessions of the library are changed annually.

In the vestibule is a pair of colossal enamel and gilt candelabra used at Napoleon I's coronation and presented by him to Pius VII. Above the doors are paintings of the Lateran Palace, before and after its reconstruction, by Domenico Fontana.

The two **Pauline Rooms** were added by Paul V, and decorated in the Mannerist style of 1610–11. Here are displayed the largest and smallest MSS in the Vatican Library, namely the Hebrew Bible of Urbino (1295) and the Masses of SS Francis and Anne, decorated with 16C miniatures. The **Alexandrine Room** was adapted in 1690 by Alexander VIII, and decorated with scenes in the life of Pius VII by Domenico de Angelis. It contains an early embroidered cope and altar cloth (11C–12C).

The **Clementine Gallery**, in five sections, was added to the Library by Clement XII in 1732; in 1818, under Pius VII, it was decorated by De Angelis with paintings of scenes in the life of that pope. The first two rooms contain a collection of plans of Rome, including one by Antonio Tempesta (1606), and valuable 16C–17C Italian and German bookbindings, and bozzetti by Bernini. The last room has a bronze head of a Muse (Roman copy of a Hellenistic original), and two bronze griffins of the Imperial period. On either side of the entrance are two Mithraic divinities.

Beyond is the main hall of the **Museum of Pagan Antiquities of the Library** (*Museo Profano della Biblioteca*), a museum and coin collection begun by Clement XIII in 1767, with additions from excavations in 1809–15. It was completed in the time of Pius VI, when it was decorated by Valadier. The ceiling paintings symbolise Time. In the cupboards in the right wall: carved Roman ivory, busts in semi-precious stones, a miniature torso, and a mosaic from Hadrian's Villa at Tivoli. Beyond, Roman bronze statuettes (1C–3C AD) and plaques with inscriptions. In the cupboards on the left wall: head and arm of a gold and ivory statue of Minerva, claimed to be a 5C BC Greek original; Etruscan bronzes and carved Roman ivory. Beyond, Etruscan and Roman objects found in Rome and the Pontine Marshes. On the end wall in a niche to the left, *bronze head of Augustus; on right, bronze head of Nero.

Beyond the Museum of Pagan Antiquities of the Library is (left) the Quattro Cancelli.

III. The Vatican Picture Gallery

The Vatican Picture Gallery (*Pinacoteca Vaticana*) is reached by the passageway from the open court beyond the Quattro Cancelli.

The Vatican Picture Gallery

The gallery owes its origin to Pius VI, but under the Treaty of Tolentino (1797), he was forced to surrender the best works to Napoleon. Of these, 77 were recovered in 1815. The present building in the Lombardic Renaissance style, by Luca Beltrami, was opened in 1932.

Room I: Byzantine School and Italian Primitives. Antonio Veneziano, 16. *St James*, 19. *Mary Magdalene*; 18. Jacopo da Bologna, *Death of St Francis*; 17. Vitale da Bologna, *Madonna and Child*; 20. 12C Roman school, *Christ in Judgement*; 23. Giunta Pisano, *St Francis*, and panels illustrating his life; *526. Giovanni and Niccolò (Rome; late 11C), *Last Judgement*, the oldest picture in the gallery; 2. Margaritone d'Arezzo, *St Francis of Assisi*; (window wall) 14. Giovanni del Biondo, *Madonna and Child with saints*; 169. Taddeo di Bartolo, *Death of the Virgin*; 9. Giovanni Bonsi, *Madonna and saints*, signed and dated 1371; *146–150, 158–161. Bernardo Daddi, *Legend of St Stephen*. Also works by Niccolò di Pietro Gerini, and the Florentine school.

Room II. In the centre, *120. The **Stefaneschi Triptych**, by Giotto and assistants. This altarpiece for the Confessio of Old St Peter's painted on both sides, represents Christ enthroned, the martyrdom of Saints Peter and Paul (at the foot of the throne is the donor, Cardinal Stefaneschi); on the back, St Peter accepting the triptych from the Pope; at the sides, four Apostles; on the predella, other Apostles. Around the walls is an exquisite series of small paintings: 168, 166, 163, 170. Pietro Lorenzetti, *Christ before Pilate, St John the Baptist, St Peter, The Virgin*; 165. Simone Martini, *The Redeemer*; *174. Bernardo Daddi, *Madonna of the Magnificat*; 102, 97, 101. Mariotto di Nardo, *Nativity, St Nicholas freeing three knights, Annunciation*; works (136, 138) by Sano di Pietro; 132. Giovanni di Paolo, *Nativity*; 234. Sassetta, *Vision of St Thomas Aquinas*; 193. Lorenzo Monaco, Stories from the life of St Benedict; 247–50. Gentile da Fabriano, Stories from the life of St Nicholas of Bari; 2139. Sassetta, *Madonna and Child*; (window wall) 263. Francesco di Gentile, *Madonna and Child*.

Room III: Fra Angelico and others. Masolino da Panicale, 260. *Crucifixion*, 245. *Transition of the Virgin*; Fra Angelico, *251, 252. Scenes from the life of St Nicholas of Bari, 253. *Madonna and Child with saints*; 243. Filippo Lippi, *Coronation of the Virgin*, a triptych; 262. Benozzo Gozzoli, *St Thomas receiving the Virgin's girdle*.

Room IV: Melozzo and Palmezzano. 269. Remaining fragments of a *fresco of the Ascension, with eight angel musicians, by Melozzo da Forlì, formerly in the church of the Santi Apostoli; another part is in the Quirinal. *270. Melozzo, Sixtus IV conferring on the humanist Platina the librarianship of the Vatican in the presence of Giuliano della Rovere (afterwards Julius II), his brother Giovanni, and Girolamo and Raffaele Riario, a fine fresco transferred to canvas. On the right wall, Marco Palmezzano, *619, 273. *Madonna and saints*.

Room V: 15C Artists. 286. Francesco del Cossa, predella with *Miracles of St Vincent Ferrer*; 275. Lucas Cranach, *Pietà*; 294. Giovanni Battista Utili, *Madonna and Child*.

Room VI: Polyptychs. Carlo Crivelli, 297. *Madonna* (dated 1482), 300. *Pietà*. Vittorio Crivelli, *Madonna with saints* (dated 1481); Niccolò l'Alunno, 299. *Crucifixion*, 307. *Polyptych of Montelparo*; Antonio Viviani, *St Anthony Abbot* (in relief) and other saints (signed and dated 1469).

Room VII: Umbrian School. 312. Pinturicchio, *Coronation of the Virgin*;

313. Umbrian 15C school, *Madonna with St John*; 316. Lo Spagna, *Adoration of the Magi* ('*Madonna della Spineta*'); Perugino, *317. *Madonna enthroned with saints* (318. *Resurrection*), 319–321. Part of predella with saints Benedict, Flavia and Placidus; 326. Giovanni Santi (father of Raphael), *St Jerome.*

Room VIII, the largest room in the gallery, is devoted to the **works of Raphael**. It contains three of his most famous paintings, two predellas, and ten tapestries made from his original cartoons. *334. *The Coronation of the Virgin*, belongs to his early Perugian period and was his first large composition, painted in 1503, when he was 20 years old. In a table case: 335. Predella to the above, with the *Annunciation, Adoration of the Magi*, and *Presentation in the Temple*. *329. The *Madonna of Foligno*, is a mature work painted about 1511. It was a votive offering by Sigismondo Conti in gratitude for his escape when a cannon ball fell on his house during the siege of Foligno. He is shown with St Jerome, and in the background is Foligno during the battle. The painting was kept in the Convent of Sant'Anna in Foligno from 1565 until it was stolen by Napoleon in 1797.

*333. The *Transfiguration*, Raphael's last work, was commissioned in 1517 by Cardinal Giuliano de' Medici for the cathedral of Narbonne. From 1523 to 1809 it was in the church of San Pietro in Montorio. It was restored in 1972–77. The superb scene of the transfiguration of Christ is shown above the dramatic episode of the healing of the young man possessed of a devil. It is not known how much of the painting had been finished by the time of Raphael's death in 1520, and, although the composition is Raphael's, it seems likely that the lower part was completed by his pupils Giulio Romano and Francesco Penni.

The ten celebrated **tapestries** represent scenes from the Acts of the Apostles. Intended for the Sistine Chapel, they were commissioned by Leo X and woven in Brussels by Pieter van Aelst from cartoons drawn by Raphael in 1515–16. They are being restored, one by one. Seven of the cartoons (the other three have been lost) are in the Victoria and Albert Museum, London, though some scholars believe that these seven, which were bought in 1630 by Charles I of England, are 17C copies and that all the originals have been lost. Other tapestries from the same cartoons, but of inferior quality, are in Hampton Court Palace near London, in the Palazzo Ducale at Mantua, and in the Palazzo Apostolico at Loreto.

The tapestries were first exhibited in 1519 in the Sistine Chapel. They have borders of grotesques and broad bases decorated with bronze-coloured designs; most of this work is by Giovanni da Udine. The subjects are: A. *Blinding of Elymas* (this tapestry was cut in halves during the sack of Rome in 1527), B. *Conversion of St Paul*, C. *Stoning of St Stephen*, D. *St Peter healing the paralytic*, E. *Death of Ananias*, F. *St Peter receiving the keys*, G. *The miraculous draught of fishes*, H. *St Paul preaching in Athens*, I. *Inhabitants of Lystra sacrificing to Saints Paul and Barnabas*, L. *St Paul in prison at Philippi*. These tapestries belong to the so-called 'Old School' series. Ten of the 'New School' series are in the Gallery of Tapestries (see above). Also displayed here is (80.) a 16C Flemish tapestry of the Last Supper (after Leonardo's fresco in Milan).

Room IX: Leonardo da Vinci and other 15C–16C Masters. *337. Leonardo da Vinci, *St Jerome*; 340. Lorenzo di Credi, *Madonna*; 339. 16C Lombard school, *Christ at the Column*, portrait of Bramante(?); *290. Giovanni Bellini, *Pietà*.

Room X: Titian, Veronese, Fra Bartolomeo. 347. Girolamo Genga, *Madonna and saints*; 346. Veronese, *Allegory*; 349. Moretto, *Madonna and Child enthroned with saints*; 351. Titian, *Madonna of San Niccolò de' Frari*; *445. *Doge Niccolò Marcello*; 352. Veronese, *St Helena*; 354. Paris Bordone, *St George and the Dragon*; 355. Garofalo, *Apparition of the Virgin to Augustus and the Sibyl*; *359. Giulio Romano and Francesco Penni, '*Madonna of Monteluce*'; 336. Lombard 16C school '*Madonna della Cintura*'.

Room XI: Barocci and others. 363. Vasari, *Stoning of St Stephen*; 365. Cavaliere d'Arpino, *Annunciation*; 368. Muziano, *Raising of Lazarus*; 372. Cola dell'Amatrice, *Assumption of the Virgin*; Barocci, 375. *Head of the Virgin*; 376. *Annunciation*, *377. *Rest on the Flight into Egypt*, 378. *The Blessed Michaelina*, 380. *St Francis receiving the stigmata*. In the centre, 742. Marble bas-relief of Cosimo I by Pierino del Vaga.

Room XII: 17C Masters. There is a fine view of the cupola of St Peter's from the window. 381. Valentin, *Martyrdom of Saints Processus and Martinian* (mosaic in St Peter's); *382. Sacchi, *Vision of St Romauld*; 383. Guercino, *Incredulity of St Thomas*; *384. Domenichino, *Communion of St Jerome* (signed and dated 1614, his first important work; mosaic in St Peter's), 385. Caravaggio (copy), *Denial of St Peter*; *386. Caravaggio, *Descent from the Cross*, 1602 (copy in St Peter's Sacristy); Guido Reni, 387. *Crucifixion of St Peter* (mosaic in St Peter's). *389. *Virgin in glory with saints*; 388. Giuseppe Maria Crespi, *Holy Family*; Guercino, 391. *Mary Magdalene*, 392. *St Margaret of Cortona*; 394. Nicolas Poussin, *Martyrdom of St Erasmus* (signed); 381. Valentin de Boulogne, *Martyrdom of Saints Processo and Martiniano*; *395. Guido Reni, *St Matthew*.

Room XIII: Maratta, Ribera, Van Dyck, and others. *396. Sassoferrato, *Madonna and Child*; 1059. Orazio Gentileschi, *Judith*; *775. Van Dyck, *St Francis Xavier*; 1931. Pier Francesco Mola, *Vision of St Bruno*; 405. Pietro da Cortona, *Appearance of the Virgin to St Francis*; 408. Ribera (or his pupil Henry Somer), *Martyrdom of St Laurence*; 410. Pietro da Cortona, *David and a lion*; 415. Pompeo Batoni, *Appearance of the Virgin to St John Nepomuc*. In the centre, wooden model of Michelangelo's dome of St Peter's, by Giacomo della Porta and Vanvitelli.

Room XIV: Flemish, Dutch, German, French, and Italian Painters (17C–18C). Daniel Seghers, 416, 418. Small religious pictures with flower borders; 421. Rosa da Tivoli, *Hunter*; 419. Matthias Stomer, *Orpheus, Pluto, and Proserpina*; 784. Rubens, *Triumph of Mars*, mainly executed by his pupils; 432–439. Donato Creti, *Astronomical Observations*; 815. Nicolas Poussin, *Gideon*; 423. Van Bloeman, *Horses*; 460. Carlo Maratta, *Clement IX*.

Room XV. 446. Bernardino Conti, *Francesco Sforza*, 447. Pieter Meert, *Philosopher*; 448. Sir Thomas Lawrence, *George IV of England;* 451. David Teniers the Younger, *Old man*; 1210. Muziano, idealised portrait of *Gregory XII*, who abdicated in 1415; 455. Pompeo Batoni, *Pius VI*; 457. Scipione Pulzone, *Cardinal Guglielmo Sirleto*; 458. Giuseppe Maria Crespi, *Benedict XIV*, painted while still a cardinal (the papal robes were added afterwards); *460. Carlo Maratta, *Clement IX*.

Room XVI. Works by Wenceslao Peter (1742–1829), including Paradise and a self-portrait.

IV. The Gregorian Museum of Pagan Antiquities, Pio Christian Museum and Ethnological Missionary Museum

The striking building housing these museums was designed by a group of Italian architects headed by Fausto and Lucio Passarelli, and opened in 1970. The well displayed collections were formerly in the Lateran.

Gregorian Museum of Pagan Antiquities

The Gregorian Museum of Pagan Antiquities (*Museo Gregoriano Profano*) is reached from the vestibule by the entrance to the museums. The Museo Profano was founded by Gregory XVI (1831–46) to house the overflow of the Vatican Museums and the yields of excavations during his pontificate at Rome, Ostia, Veio and Cerveteri. It was enriched by further excavations up to 1870, and at the end of the 19C by a collection of pagan inscriptions.

The numbers used in the description below refer to the plan on p 361.

Near the entrance (left) are Roman copies of original Greek sculpture (torsos, statuettes and heads), and (ahead) Marsyas (**1**), a marble copy of a bronze by Myron which formed part of a group placed at the entrance to the Acropolis in Athens in the mid-5C BC. **Marsyas** is attracted by the sound of the double flute, which Athena had invented and just thrown away. He is foiled in his attempt to pick up the instrument by Athena's commanding gesture (the statue of Athena is a cast).

To the right (**2**) are displayed some ***Greek originals**, including a superb sepulchral stele, showing a young man with his young slave handing him a strigil and a flask of oil (5C BC); two heads (fragments from one of the metopes and from the north frieze of the Parthenon), and the fragment of a horse's head from the west pediment of the Parthenon, probably one of Athena's horses. The head of Athena is also a 5C BC original; it was made to wear a helmet, probably of bronze. The eyes are of polished grey stone in which were set glass pupils; the eyebrows and eyelashes were made of thin strips of bronze, and the ears had gold earrings. Two relief fragments of horsemen, perhaps part of a frieze, resemble in style the Parthenon frieze. The relief of dancing nymphs is an Attic work of the 4C BC. Stairs (**3**) lead up to an area which contains the **Lateran collection of pagan inscriptions** (open only to scholars with special permission).

There follow a series of herms (**4**), and, on the floor, the ***Heraclitus Mosaic** (**5**) of an unswept floor from the triclinium of a house on the Aventine, showing the remains of a banquet. It is signed 'Heraclitus', and may be a copy of a celebrated work by Sosus of Pergamon. Other works in this section include: round altar, with a faun playing for two dancing women; triangular tripod base, with reliefs of dancing figures taking part in Dionysiac rites, a neo-Attic work in Pentelic marble of the 1C BC, after a 4C BC original; copy of the Resting Satyr of Praxiteles (others in the Museo Pio-Clementino and the Capitoline Museum); colossal statue of Poseidon (Neptune), after a bronze original by Lysippos (with several restorations); colossal statue of Zeus.

In the next section, by the windows, is a relief of Medea and the daughters of Pelias whom she is inducing to kill their father, neo-Attic copy of a late 5C BC original. It is one of a series of four relating to the dramatic competitions in Athens.

Beyond a marble statue of Sophocles from Terracina, with fine drapery (a copy

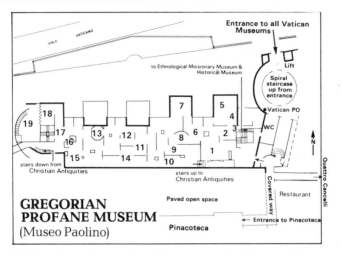

Entrance to all Vatican Museums

to Ethnological Missionary Museum & Historical Museum

Lift

Spiral staircase up from entrance

Vatican PO

WC

N

stairs down from Christian Antiquities

stairs up to Christian Antiquities

Quattro Cancelli

Covered way

Restaurant

GREGORIAN PROFANE MUSEUM (Museo Paolino)

Paved open space

← Entrance to Pinacoteca

Pinacoteca

of a 4C BC work) are the remains of the large circular **Vicovaro Monument** (**6**), dating from the early 1C AD. In the next recess is the **Chiaramonti Niobid** (**7**), a fine Roman copy of an original by Leochares of the 4C BC. The head of a Muse, crowned with ivy, is in the manner of Praxiteles (good copy of a 4C BC original). The torso of a statue of Diana is a Roman copy of a Greek original of the 4C BC; the motion expressed in the drapery is particularly fine. Also here are two Roman orators in togas (1C AD), and fine Roman portrait heads (the last two perhaps portraits of Virgil).

The following sections contain Roman sculpture in chronological order, beginning with the late Republican era. Opposite two statues of the sleeping Silenus (copies of Hellenistic works), found in the Roman theatre at Caere (see below), are a series of funerary reliefs: the first with portraits of parents and a young son, and the second with five busts of members of the Furia family. The circular altar dedicated to Piety comes from Veio; it is decorated with garlands, lyres, and the attributes of Vulcan (1C AD).

Around to the left are a group of **statues from the Roman theatre at Caere** (**8**), mainly of the Julio-Claudian family: Agrippina, mother of Nero and wife of Claudius, as a goddess; colossal seated statue of Claudius as Jupiter; relief with figures symbolising the three Etruscan cities of Vetulonia, Vulci and Tarquinia, found with the statue and believed to have been part of the throne; colossal head, probably of Augustus; colossal seated statue of Tiberius idealised as Jupiter; series of inscriptions found with the statues, explaining their identity; Drusus and elder, with a cuirass decorated with bas-reliefs of two griffins and above, a gorgon; altar dedicated to Manlius, a censor of Caere, by his clients (1C AD); statue of an emperor in a cuirass, decorated with reliefs.

Next comes the so-called **Altar of Vicomagistri** (**9**), 1C AD, found near the Cancelleria. The relief is of a sacrificial procession, followed by four figures carrying statuettes of household deities and by priestly officials known as *vico-magistri*. Two statues of young boys wearing togas, belonging to the Julio-Claudian family (one with a 3C head); more Roman portrait busts and heads.

To the left is an area with **cinerary urns** (**10**), among them one with finely

carved reliefs: the head of Medusa in the centre, below a cock-fight, and festoons with eagles and genii at the sides. A covered urn has good reliefs and an inscription relating to Quinto Volusio Antigono. The next section has architectural fragments, and some exquisite decorative reliefs with small Bacchic scenes and vine-leaves (1C AD). The area is dominated by two large **Cancelleria reliefs** (**11**), dating from the Flavian period (AD 70–96). The frieze on the left (damaged) represents the return to Rome of Vespasian (who appears on the extreme right of the third panel). Surrounding the Emperor are vestals, the Roman Senate and people, and the seated figure of Rome. The frieze on the right represents the departure from Rome of Domitian who appears (restored as Nerva) in the second panel from the left, surrounded by (left) Minerva, Mars and Victory, and (right) Rome with soldiers.

Beyond more portrait busts is sculpture from the **Tomb of the Haterii** (**12**), near Centocelle. Two similar niches have well-modelled portrait busts of a man and woman. Three reliefs illustrate a woman's funeral: the body lying in state, surrounded by relatives and mourners in the atrium of a house; the funeral procession, passing buildings on the Via Sacra; and the sepulchral monument of the Haterii, with a view of the inside and the apparatus used in its construction. Above, high relief with three busts of gods of the underworld; triangular pillar, beautifully carved, with candelabrum, rose branches, and birds. Relief of a procession of Roman magistrates in front of a temple (1C AD); one of the heads was restored (erroneously) in the early 19C by Thorvaldsen to represent Trajan.

Towards the windows, large funerary relief of a woman (the head is a portrait) lying on a bed with a small dog. A sepulchral relief of a chariot race (with a side view of the circus seen from above) shows the organisers of the games, in whose memory the relief was made, on the left (early 2C AD). Two columns are carved with a papyrus motif and lotus leaves around the base.

To the right, colossal **statue of a Dacian** (**13**), dating from the time of Trajan, found in 1841 in Via dei Coronari, on the site of a sculptor's studio of the Imperial era.

A series of capitals and antifixes follow, with two fragments of an architectural frieze from the forum of Trajan, with cupids and griffins and a neo-Attic amphora.

The next sections contain ***pagan sarcophagi** (**14**), with mythological scenes. Among them, several depicting the story of Adonis, of Hippolytus and Phaedra (with scenes of the wild boar hunt), of Orestes, and of the slaughter of the family of Niobe. Further on, is a fine sarcophagus dating from the 3C AD, with a scene of the triumph of Dionysos (Bacchus): he is represented as a victor on his return from India in a triumphal carriage drawn by two elephants, being crowned by Nike (Victory).

Beyond is a colossal statue of Antinous as the god Vertumnus (with finely modelled drapery; the head is modern); fragment of a relief with two boxers, presumably part of a large monument (2C AD).

Fragment of the large oval **Plotinus Sarcophagus** (**15**), with figures in relief in philosophical discussion(?), and part of a lion hunt; on the wall behind, sepulchral relief with the deceased man reading from a large scroll, surrounded by his family and pupils (3C AD); on the right, funerary monument in high relief of a warrior saluting his wife who is seated; a horse stands ready, and a snake is depicted in the tree above. Fragments of draped **Imperial porphyry statues**

(**16**). Towards the windows, relief of a nymph feeding an infant satyr from a large horn-shaped vessel, while in a grotto nearby a young Pan plays the syrinx. Known as the Amaltheia relief, this was originally part of a fountain. To the right is a **statue of Dogmazio** (**17**). Another area (**18**) contains Roman religious sculpture, including statues of Mithras and the bull (3C AD), Diana of the Ephesians, and Asklepios.

To the right of the stairs are fragments of a group with a boy riding a horse, and a river nymph on a sea centaur. Upstairs a walkway passes above a **mosaic of athletes from the Baths of Caracalla** (**19**) and a black marble statue of a stag (Roman copy of a 4C BC Greek original). A corridor has Hebrew inscriptions. Beyond, a balcony overlooks a second fine mosaic from the Baths of Caracalla (and there is a view of the dome of St Peter's from here).

Pio Christian Museum and Ethnological Missionary Museum

The rest of the upper floor is occupied by the **Pio Christian Museum**, founded by Pius IX in 1854 with objects found mainly in the catacombs, and displayed by subject matter. The display begins at the other end of the mezzanine floor, at the entrance to the building. The first section is devoted to the valuable collection of Christian sarcophagi of the 2C–5C, of the highest importance for the study of early Christian iconography; some famous sarcophagi owned by the Vatican but not on view here are represented by casts (numbered with Roman numerals). At the beginning on the left wall, are fragments of sarcophagi representing the Nativity and Epiphany (124, 190) of the 4C AD. Further on (right) is a sarcophagus showing the Crossing of the Red Sea.

Three steps lead up to the next section. In the middle: cast of the sarcophagus of Junius Bassus (the original is in the Treasury of St Peter's). Round the corner to the left is a sarcophagus (164) with five niches showing Christ triumphant over death, Cain and Abel, Peter taken prisoner, the Martyrdom of Paul, and Job. Another short flight of steps ascends past (right) 152. Sarcophagus of the husband and wife Crescentianus and Agapene, found in the Vatican necropolis. At the top of the stairs (left) is a large sarcophagus (104) with episodes from the Bible. To the right: panels (184, 189, 178, 175, 183A) with scenes from the Old and New Testaments; cast of the sarcophagus from Sant'Ambrogio in Milan. The next part of the gallery contains more sarcophagi (including one from St Calixtus) and some mosaic fragments. Three steps lead up to the last section of the museum. On the left is a well-preserved sarcophagus (150.) with traces of the original polychrome decoration. At the end, 191A. Sarcophagus illustrating the Good Shepherd.

On the right wall begins the collection of epigraphs from the **Museum of Christian Inscriptions**, the largest and most important collection of Christian inscriptions in existence. The whole collection was arranged and classified by Giovanni Battista de Rossi (1822–94) in four series. **First series**: inscriptions from public monuments connected with Christian worship. Fragment of the sepulchral inscription of Publius Sulpicius Quirinus (Cyrenius), Governor of Syria, who took the census at the time of the birth of Christ; inscriptions of Pope St Damasus (366–84). **Second series**: dated sepulchral inscriptions. Dogmatic inscriptions, including the (fish) acrostic. Inscriptions relating to the ecclesiastical hierarchy, virgins, catechumens, senators, soldiers, officials, workers, etc. **Third series**: symbols and representations of Christian dogma. The **fourth**

series is arranged topographically (2C–6C) from cemeteries in Rome and Ostia.

The statue of the Good Shepherd is a fine work dating from the late 3C. A passage continues past (177) a sarcophagus from San Lorenzo fuori le Mura, and the cast of a seated statue of the martyred doctor St Hippolytus. On the left of his chair is a list in Greek of the saint's works, and on the right a paschal calendar for the years 222–334. The original is now at the entrance of the Biblioteca Vaticana, in the Belvedere Court (see below). On the balcony overlooking a mosaic from the Baths of Caracalla (see above) is a fragment of the tombstone of Abercius, bishop of Hierapolis (Phrygia), who lived in the reign of Marcus Aurelius (161–80), discovered by Sir William Ramsay and presented to Leo XIII. The Greek text is in three parts: in the first part Abercius says that he is a disciple of Christ the Good Shepherd, in the second he mentions his journey to Rome and the East, in the third he asks the faithful to pray for him and threatens defilers of his grave.

The **Ethnological Missionary Museum** (only open on Wed and Sat) occupies the whole of the area below ground level. It was established by Pius XI in 1927 as a development of the Vatican Missionary Exhibition of 1924–26. The primitive and more recent cultures of each country have been arranged according to subject matter; labelling is kept to a minimum. The countries are indicated by a letter (see the plan). The exhibits illustrate the ways of life and religious customs in: China (**A**), with fine Buddhist sculpture and religious figures of the Ming and T'ang dynasties; Japan (**B**), with ceremonial masks and paintings of martyrs; Korea (**C**); Tibet, Mongolia (**D**); Indochina (**E**), where examples of local art and manufacture show the adaptation of European sacred art to the local genius; *Indian sub-continent (**F**), illustrating Shivaism and Vishnuism; Indonesia, Philippines (**G**); Polynesia (**H**); *Melanesia (**I**), with protective spirits, ceremonial masks and costumes, and the reconstruction of a hut of the spirits from New Guinea; Australia (**J**); North Africa (**K**); Ethiopia (**L**); Madagascar (**M**); West Africa (north), with statuettes of tribal gods; Central Africa (**O**); East Africa (**P**); Southern Africa (**Q**); Christian Africa (**R**); South America (south), including ancient wood sculpture from Colombia; Central America (**T**); North America (**U**); Persia (**V**); Middle East (west); and Christian art from countries penetrated by the missions. A mezzanine floor contains study collections open to scholars.

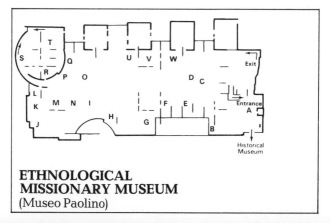

**ETHNOLOGICAL
MISSIONARY MUSEUM**
(Museo Paolino)

The **Padiglione delle Carrozze**, built by Paul VI in 1973 houses carriages and the first automobiles used by the popes. The **Historical Museum** has been transferred to the Lateran Palace.

The Vatican City and Gardens

■ Tours of part of the Vatican City and gardens are organised at the Information Office to the left of St Peter's façade (☎ 698 84466 or 698 84866). Tickets (Lire 18,000) should be booked at least one day in advance. The tours, partly by bus and partly on foot (c 2 hrs) usually depart at 10 every day except Wed and Sun. Individual visitors are not admitted to the city or gardens.

The **Vatican Gardens**, laid out in the 16C, cover the north and west slopes of the Vatican Hill. The Arco delle Campane is protected by a sentry of the Swiss Guard, armed with a rifle instead of the halberd carried by the guard at the Bronze Door. The square beyond is Piazza dei Protomartiri Romani, the site of the martyrdom of the early Christians near the Circus of Nero. On the left is the Camposanto Teutonico, dating from the 8C, and probably the oldest medieval cemetery; it is still reserved for the Germans and Dutch. Adjacent is the Collegio Teutonico. Beyond, against the wall of the city, is the **Audience Hall** (1971), by Pier Luigi Nervi. Designed in the shape of a shell, it has seating for 8000 people.

In the pavement in front of the first arch of the passage beneath the sacristy of St Peter's, a slab marks the former site of the obelisk in Piazza San Pietro. A road leads beneath the sacristy to Piazza Santa Marta. Here, on the right, is a fine view of the left transept of St Peter's; on the left is the Palazzo dell'Arciprete di San Pietro. At the west end of the square is the Palazzo del Tribunale.

Opposite the majestic west end of St Peter's is the little church of **Santo Stefano degli Abissini**, built by Leo III as Santo Stefano Maggiore. In 1479 Sixtus IV conceded it to Coptic monks; it was rebuilt by Clement XI.

A road ascends past the Studio del Mosaico, with an exhibition room, and (right) the Governor's Palace (Palazzo del Governatorato), built in 1931 as the seat of the civic administration of the Vatican City. To the south is the little-used Vatican Railway Station. On the first floor a **Philatelic and Numismatic Museum** was opened in 1990. It preserves all the postage stamps and coins issued by the Vatican since 1929. It is open for group visits by request, ☎ 698 84081.

Viale dell'Osservatorio continues up through the gardens past the Seminario Etiopico. At the western extremity of the city is a stretch of the wall built by Nicholas V on the site of the ancient walls put up by Leo IV. Here the Tower of St John, once an observatory, is now used as a guest house. On the westernmost bastion of the city walls is the Heliport. The road passes a reproduction of the Grotto of Lourdes, presented by the French Catholics to Leo XIII.

A road leads down through exotic vegetation past the old Vatican Radio Station, designed by Marconi, and inaugurated in 1931. Since 1957 Vatican Radio has transmitted from a station at Santa Maria di Galeria, 25km outside Rome. The Fontana dell'Aquilone, by Giovanni Vesanzio, has a triton by Stefano Maderno. Nearer the huge Museum buildings is the **Casina of Pius IV**, two small buildings by Pirro Ligorio (1558–62), which are a masterpiece of Mannerist architecture. In the villa, now the seat of the Pontifical Academy of Sciences, Pius IV held the meetings which received the name of *Notti Vaticane*; at

them were held learned discussions on poetry, philosophy, and sacred subjects. Pius VIII and Gregory XVI used to give their audiences here.

Towards St Peter's a group of buildings include the Floreria, formerly the Mint (Zecca), founded by Eugenius IV, and the Fontana del Sacramento. The Stradone dei Giardini is an avenue which skirts Bramante's west corridor of the Vatican Museums. The exit is usually through Piazza del Forno (overlooked by the Sistine Chapel), around St Peter's, and through the Arco delle Campane.

The northern part of the city, normally closed to visitors, is entered through the Arco della Sentinella, beyond which is the Borgia Tower and a series of small courtyards, in the heart of the Vatican Palace, including the Cortile dei Pappagalli (so called from its frieze of parrots, now almost obliterated). The larger Cortile di San Damaso is overlooked by the Loggia of Raphael. On the other side of the huge museum buildings (and entered from the Cancello di Sant'Anna on Via di Porta Angelica) are various offices of the Vatican State, including the Polyglot Printing Press, the Post Office, the Casa Parrochiale, and the *Osservatore Romano* newspaper. Also here are the barracks of the Swiss Guard, a restoration centre for tapestries, and the restored church of San Pellegrino. In 1956 a Pagan necropolis (tombs of 1C–4C) was discovered beneath the car park. The cemetery was alongside Via Triumphalis, the line of which is now followed by Via del Pellegrino. Beside the Cancello di Sant'Anna is **Sant' Anna dei Palafrenieri**, the parish church of the Vatican City, built in 1573 by the Papal Grooms (Palafrenieri della Corte Papale) to the designs of Vignola.

To the south of St Peter's Colonnade, outside the Vatican City but granted the privilege of extraterritoriality, is **Palazzo del Sant'Uffizio**. The Holy Office, or tribunal, commonly known as the Inquisition, was established here in 1542 by Paul III to investigate charges of heresy, unbelief, and other offences against the Catholic religion. The preparation of the Index of Prohibited Books was originally entrusted to the Congregation of the Holy Office. In 1571 Pius V established a special Congregation of the Index, which survived until its suppression by Benedict XV in 1917, when these duties were resumed by the Holy Office. The tribunal was formally abolished by the Roman Assembly in February 1849, but it was re-established by Pius IX a few months later.

Days Out of Rome

The chapters in this section cover the immediate environs of Rome which are easily accessible in a day by public transport from the centre of the city. These include two extremely important Roman sites, both of them still in beautiful settings: the ancient city of Ostia and Hadrian's famous villa at Tivoli (one of the most interesting classical sites known).

■ Details of public transport are provided at the beginning of Chapters 28–30; for information about the bus services run by 'COTRAL', ☎ 591 5551/2/3/4.

The Roman Campagna

The Roman Campagna, the country surrounding Rome, is an undulating plain, with indeterminate limits, extending from the Tyrrhenian sea to a semicircle of hills (Monti della Tolfa, Sabatini, Tiburtini, Prenestini, Lepini and Ausoni), some distance inland. The area is traversed by the Tiber, into which flow the Aniene and other tributaries. In the Tertiary Age the plain was occupied by a gulf of the sea in which volcanic eruptions formed numerous islands. In the centre, the islands became the Alban Hills. In the northwest, they formed a series of ranges, one behind the other, with craters which are now filled up by lakes: the Monti Sabatini, with the Lago di Bracciano, the Monti Cimini, with the Lago di Vico, and the Monti Volsini, with the Lago di Bolsena. The lava from the eruptions spread as far as the hills where Rome was later built.

The name of *Campania Romana*, dating from the time of Constantine and replacing that of *Latium*, was used to distinguish the area from that of the *Campania Felix*, which surrounds Naples. In the widest sense of the term, the Roman Campagna includes the *Agro Pontino*, formerly the Pontine Marshes. In a more restricted sense it is taken to comprise the area between the sea, the Monti Sabatini and the Alban Hills, corresponding roughly to that of the *Agro Romano*, or administrative division of the Commune of Rome, with an area of 2074sq km.

The Campagna was the focus of almost all the people who were to form the Italic race. In the early days of Rome the growing of grain was the main activity of the Campagna, but after their Mediterranean conquests the Romans were able to import cereals, and gardens and orchards were planted here, sustained by irrigation. The ruins of villas, aqueducts, and cisterns found in every part of the Agro Romano testify to the productivity of the farms that once surrounded the city. In the early days of the Empire the farms began to be displaced by large landed estates (*latifundia*), fertility declined, and malaria increased, so that the population dwindled. During later centuries some of the popes tried without success to help the area with schemes of repopulation and agricultural centres to provide food for the city.

By the time of the Unification of Italy the Agro Romano was a vast malarial swamp. In 1878 the Government began to drain the marshes and stagnant waters and reclaim a belt extending to 10km from the centre of the city. The estates of the suppressed religious organisations were divided up, and in 1883 a principle of compulsory cultivation was established, and a law to this effect

regarding the whole of the Agro Romano was passed in 1921. In the years following the First World War, and under the Fascist regime, land reclamation took place on a large scale.

Ancient Roman roads

The ancient Roman roads leading out of Rome in all directions are still partly in use, and still carry their Roman names. The **Via Aurelia Antica** (which leaves Rome at the Porta San Pancrazio) follows the line of an even older road which linked Rome with the Etruscan towns on the Tyrrhenian coast. It reached the shore at *Alsium* (Palo Laziale), a port of the Etruscan city of *Caere* (Cerveteri) and then followed the coastline to Pisa and Genoa. It ended in Gaul at *Forum Julii* (Fréjus) on the French Riviera. One of the most important ancient Roman roads, named after the Aurelia gens, it was built before 109 BC.

The **Via Cassia** (which leaves Rome north of Ponte Milvio) was originally a rough road which ran north out of Rome to Etruria. It was paved by Cassius Longinus, consul in 107 BC, and named after him. It runs through Viterbo to Siena and Florence. The **Via Flaminia**, which also leaves Rome north of Ponte Milvio, was begun in 220 BC and was named after Gaius Flaminius, censor and afterwards consul, who was killed at the battle of Lake Trasimene in 217 BC. It leads north out of Rome across Umbria to Fano and Rimini on the Adriatic. It leaves the Tiber at Prima Porta (12km from the centre of Rome) near the site of the battle of *Sax Rubra* where Constantine defeated Maxentius in 312, after being converted to Christianity by a vision of the flaming Cross with the words 'conquer by this'.

Via Salaria (see Chapter 20) takes its name from its association with the salt trade between the Romans and the Sabines. It runs (now the modern N4) via Rieti and Antrodoco to Ascoli Piceno and the Adriatic near San Benedetto del Tronto.

Via Latina, probably in use as early as the 7C or 6C BC, ran south from Rome down the valley of the river Sacco in Latin territory and continued to the Campania around Naples. It was used by the armies of Pyrrhus and Hannibal, and in Roman times joined the Via Appia at *Casilinum* near Capua. The **Via Appia Antica** is described in Chapter 17.

Via Ostiense was one of the earliest consular roads, and dates from the victorious campaign of the Romans against the inhabitants of Veio to secure their salt supply (5C BC). It ran to Ostia, and from there, under the name of **Via Severiana**, it followed the coast to *Laurentum* (near Castel Fusano), *Antium* (Anzio), and Terracina, where it joined the Via Appia.

28 · Ostia Antica

■ **Public transport from Rome**. The fastest way of reaching Ostia is by metro-train. Services run by the *Ferrovia Roma-Lido* (for information, ☎ 591 5551) from Porta San Paolo (on Line B of the underground railway from Stazione Termini) has services about every half hour for Ostia Antica (in 35 minutes) going on to Ostia Lido. From the station of Ostia Antica, Via Ostiense and Via del Mare are crossed by a footbridge which leads straight to the entrance to the excavations.

There is a train service from Stazione Termini (in 30 minutes) and Stazione Tiburtina (via Ostiense and Trasevere) in 40 minutes for the airport of Fiumicino which is next to the Museo delle Navi Romane.

■ **By road**. The **Via del Mare** (N8) from Viale Marconi (beyond San Paolo fuori le Mura) is a fast 'superstrada' reaching the coast (28km) at the west end of the Lido di Ostia. It was opened in 1928, when the Lido became Rome's seaside resort. You should take care not to miss the turning right (23km from Rome) signposted for 'Scavi di Ostia Antica', as otherwise the fast main road continues (with no more exits) straight on to Lido di Ostia (now usually called just 'Ostia'), an ugly modern suburb of Rome on the coast, with a complicated system of one-way roads.

The old **Via Ostiense** (see above) runs parallel to the Via del Mare for the whole of its length.

The Roman city of Ostia Antica

The extensive excavations of the Roman city of Ostia Antica (open every day from 9 to one hour before sunset), in a beautiful park of umbrella pines and cypresses, are one of the most interesting and beautiful sights near Rome. The excavations give a remarkable idea of the domestic and commercial architecture prevalent in the Empire in the late 1C and 2C AD (hardly any of which has survived in Rome itself). The remains are as important for the study of Roman urban life as those of the older cities of Pompeii and Herculaneum. At least half a day is needed for the visit, and it is a splendid place to picnic (refreshments can be bought in the village of Ostia Antica, close to the entrance to the excavations). Some of the *mosaics discovered in the ruins are occasionally covered with wind-blown sand. In the description below only the most important monuments are mentioned as the ruins are well labelled (also in English).

History

Ostia, now called Ostia Antica, is named after the ostium, or mouth of the Tiber. The river formerly flowed past the city in a channel to the north, the Fiume Morto, dry since a great flood in 1557. According to legend, Ostia was founded by Ancus Marcius, fourth king of Rome, to guard the mouth of the river Tiber. The surviving remains are not, however, older than the 4C BC, and the city, which was probably the first colony of Rome, may have been founded about 335 BC. It was originally a fortified city (castrum), whose walls survive in part; later it became a much larger commercial city (urbs), also surrounded with walls. Its first industry was the extraction of salt from the surrounding marshes, but it soon developed into the commercial port of Rome and, shortly before the outbreak of the First Punic War (264 BC), it also became a naval base. The link between the port and the capital was the Via Ostiense, which, carrying as it did all Rome's overseas imports and exports until the construction of the Via Portuensis, must have been one of the busiest roads in the ancient world.

The commerce passing through Ostia was vital to the prosperity and even the existence of Rome. One of its most important functions was the organisation of the annona, the supply of produce, mainly grain, to the capital. At the head of the Annona was the Quoestor Ostiensis, who had to live at

Ostia. He was appointed by lot and his office, according to Cicero, was burdensome and unpopular. By 44 BC the Quoestor was replaced by the Procuratores Annonoe, answerable to the Praefectus Annonae in Rome. The organisation involved the creation of a large number of commercial associations or guilds covering every aspect of trade and industry. There are numerous inscriptions referring to these associations in the Piazzale delle Corporazioni. Ostia suffered a temporary setback in 87 BC, when it was sacked by Marius, but Sulla rebuilt it soon afterwards and gave it new walls.

As the city continued to thrive, it outgrew its harbour and by the 1C AD, the construction of another port became an imperative necessity. Planned by Augustus, this was built by Claudius, to the northwest of Ostia, and later enlarged by Trajan (Porto; see below). For a time Ostia remained the centre of the vast organisation for the supply of food to the capital. It added to its temples, public buildings, shops and houses, and it received special marks of favour from the emperors.

The decline of Ostia began in the time of Constantine, who favoured Porto. The titles conferred by the emperor on the newer seaport must have been particularly galling to the inhabitants of Ostia. But even in the 4C, though it had become a residential town instead of a commercial port, it was still used by notable people travelling abroad. In 387 St Augustine was about to embark for Africa with his mother, St Monica, when she was taken ill and died in a hotel in the city. In the following centuries, Ostia's decline was accelerated by loss of trade and by the increase of malaria. Its monuments were looted: columns, sarcophagi and statues stolen from the ruins have been found as far afield as Pisa, Amalfi, Orvieto and Salerno. An attempt to revive the city was made by Gregory IV, when he founded the borgo of Ostia Antica. In 1756 the city, which at the height of its prosperity had had a population of some 80,000, had 156 inhabitants; half a century later only a few convicts of the papal Government lived here; Augustus Hare, writing in 1878, speaks of one human habitation breaking the utter solitude.

Excavations of the site began on a small scale at the beginning of the 19C, under Pius VII. Further work was instituted in 1854 under Pius IX, but systematic excavations did not begin until 1907. They have been continued with few interruptions, until the present day. The work carried out in 1938–42 by Guido Calza and others brought to light many monuments of great interest. The excavated area is now c 34 hectares, or two-thirds of the area of the city at its greatest extent.

Domestic architecture. One result of research has been the great increase in knowledge of the various types of house occupied by Romans of the middle and lower classes. Since it is not likely that the domestic architecture of Ostia differed radically from that of the capital, the examples that have been unearthed of the lower-grade house at Ostia may be taken as typical of such buildings in Rome itself. The middle- and lower-class house at Ostia (insula) was in sharp contrast to the typical Pompeian residence (domus), with its atrium and peristyle, its few windows and its low elevation (and houses of this type are rare at Ostia).

The ordinary Ostia house (insula) usually had four storeys and reached a height of 15m, the maximum permitted by Roman law. It was built of brick,

probably not covered with stucco, and had little ornamentation, although sometimes bricks of contrasting colours were used. The entrance doors had pilasters or engaged columns supporting a simple pediment. There were numerous rooms, each with its own window. The arches over the windows were often painted in vermilion. Mica or selenite was used instead of glass for the windows. The façades were of three types: living-rooms with windows on all floors; arcaded ground floor with shops and living-rooms above; and ground floor with shops opening on the street, and living-rooms above. Many of the houses had balconies of various designs. The apartment houses contained numerous flats or sets of rooms designated by numbers on the stairs leading to them. They too, were of different types; some were of simple design and others were built round a courtyard. The rare domus, built for the richer inhabitants, were usually on one floor only and date mostly from the 3C and 4C. They were decorated with apses, nymphaea and mosaic floors, and the rooms often had columns and loggias.

Religion. In Ostia, as elsewhere in the Roman world, different religious cults flourished without disharmony. As well as temples dedicated to the traditional deities such as Vulcan, Venus, Ceres, and Fortuna, there was a popular cult of the emperors and a surprisingly large number of eastern cults, such as the Magna Mater, Egyptian and Syrian deities, and especially Mithras. Singularly few Christian places of worship have been found.

The city of Ostia seems to have been divided into at least five *Regiones*. The various monuments have been classified according to the region to which they are believed to have belonged: the streets and buildings are marked with signs indicating (**a**) the number of the region, (**b**) the number of the block (**c**) the type of construction, such as temple, warehouse, dwelling-house (insula), residence (domus), etc., (**d**) the traditional name of the street or building.

Beyond the **entrance to the excavations** is a stretch of the Via Ostiense, outside the walls. Parallel on the south is Via delle Tombe, also outside the walls, since Roman law forbade burials within the city limits: here can be seen a few terracotta sarcophagi and sealed graves, as well as columbaria for the urns holding the ashes from cremations.

The entrance to the city is by the **Porta Romana,** with remains of the gate in the walls of the Republican period; some fragments of a marble facing of the Imperial era have been found and placed on the inner walls of the gate. The PIAZZALE DELLA VITTORIA is dominated by a colossal statue of Minerva Victoria, dating from the reign of Domitian and inspired by a Hellenistic original, which may once have decorated the gate. On the right of the square are the remains of *horrea* (warehouses), later converted into baths. In the **Thermae of the Cisiarii** on the far side of the warehouses are several mosaics, one with scenes of life in Ostia.

Here begins the **DECUMANUS MAXIMUS**, the main street of Ostia. It runs right through the city and is c 1200m long. A little way along this street, on the right, is a flight of steps leading to a platform, on the second storey of the **Baths of Neptune**. From the platform can be seen the tepidarium and calidarium, remains of columns, and the floor of the large entrance hall with a *mosaic of Neptune driving four sea-horses and surrounded by tritons, nereids, dolphins,

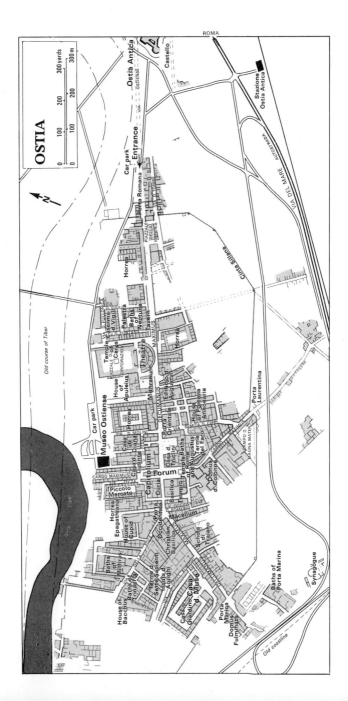

OSTIA

0   100   200   300 yards
0   100   200   300 m

N

ROMA

Ostia Antica

VIA OSTIENSE

Castello

Car park

Entrance

Stazione Ostia Antica

Porta Romana

VIA DEL MARE

VIA DEL MARE AUTOSTRADA

Old course of Tiber

Car park

Museo Ostiense

CARDO MAXIMUS

Fiume Tevere

Piccolo Mercato

Horrea Epagathiana

House of Cupid

Baths of Mithras

House of Bacchus

Baths of Buticosus

Terme d. Sette Sapienti

Casa d. Ariani

Casa delle Ierodule

Casa d. Muse

Porta Marina

Domus Fulminata

Baths of Porta Marina

Synagogue

Old coastline

Horrea

Temple of Ceres

Palestra

Baths of Neptune

Taverna

Theatre

PIAZZALE DELLE CORPORAZIONI

House of Apuleius

Mithraeum

Horrea

CARDO MAXIMUS

Casa di Diana

Casa P. Molin

Capitolium

Curia

Basilica

Tempio Rotondo

Forum

Macellum

Basilica Cristiana

Schola di Traiano

Casa d. Triclini

Horrea d. Oriente

Casa d. Giove e Ganimede

House of Fortuna Annonaria

Termi del Faro

Domus d. Colonne

Temple of Augustus and Roma

Porta Occidentale

CAMPO D. MAGNA MATER

Porta Laurentina

Canale Stagno

etc. In an adjoining room is a mosaic of Amphitrite escorted by Hymen. The platform provides a fine view of the excavations (in the distance straight ahead can be seen the buildings of Fiumicino airport). Nearby is the *palaestra* (gymnasium) a large colonnaded courtyard surrounded by rooms.

Just before the Baths of Neptune is VIA DEI VIGILI (street of the firemen), the construction of which involved the demolition of some earlier buildings, to which belonged a mosaic (displayed nearby) representing the Four Winds and Four Provinces (Sicily, Egypt, Africa Spain). The street leads to the **Caserma dei Vigili** (firemen's barracks), built in the 2C AD. It has an arcaded courtyard, a shrine dedicated to Fortuna Santa, and an *Augusteum*, or shrine for the cult of the emperors.

An archway leads into VIA DELLA FONTANA, one of the best-preserved streets in Ostia. Here is a typical apartment house, with shops and living-rooms over them. To the right the street joins Via della Fullonica, named from its well-equipped **fuller's workshop**, for cleansing cloth, complete with a courtyard for drying.

The street rejoins the Decumanus Maximus at the **Tavern of Fortunatus** in which is a mosaic pavement with the broken inscription: 'Dicit Fortunatus: vinum cratera quod sitis bibe' ('Fortunatus says: drink wine from the bowl to quench your thirst'). The next street to the right (west) is VIA DELLE CORPO-RAZIONI; in it is a well-preserved apartment house, with paintings on the walls and ceilings. On the other side of the street is the **Theatre**, built by Agrippa and enlarged by Septimius Severus in the 2C. It has two tiers of seats (originally three), divided by stairways into five sections or *cunei*. It could accommodate 2700 people. A tufa wall with some marble fragments and three marble masks survive from the stage, behind which some cipollino columns have been set up, which once decorated the third tier of the auditorium. In the main façade, towards the Decumanus Maximus, is a series of covered arcades, formerly shops. Between the arcades and the street are areas paved with travertine and, at either end, a fountain. A Christian oratory in honour of St Cyriacus and his fellow-martyrs of Ostia, was later built over the fountain on the east side.

Behind the theatre extends the spacious PIAZZALE DELLE CORPORAZIONI (Square of the Guilds). In this square were 70 offices of commercial associations ranging from workers' guilds to corporations of foreign representatives from all over the ancient world. Their trademarks are preserved in the mosaic floors of the brick-built arcade running round the square. The trademarks of the foreign representatives tell where the merchants came from (e.g. Carthage, Alexandria, Narbonne, etc.) and what their trade was, and those of the citizens indicate their trade, such as ship repair and construction, maintenance of the docks, ware-houses and embankments, dockers, salvage crews, and customs and excise offi-cials. In the middle of the square are the stylobate and two columns of a small temple *in antis* known as the Temple of Ceres, and the bases of statues erected to the leading citizens of Ostia.

Beyond the square is the handsome **House of Apuleius**, of the Pompeian type, rare at Ostia, with an atrium and rooms decorated with mosaics. Beside it is a **mithraeum**, one of the best preserved of the many temples dedicated to Mithras in the city. It has two galleries for the initiated, on the walls of which are mosaics illustrating the cult of the god. There are also casts of the marble relief of Mithras which was found here, with several inscriptions. In front are four

small tetrastyle temples, erected in the 2C BC on a single foundation of tufa. They are supposed to have been dedicated to Venus, Fortuna, Ceres and Hope. In the square in front of the temples are the remains of a nymphaeum and of a sanctuary of Jupiter.

From the Decumanus Maximus can be seen, on the right, **horrea**, large warehouses for the storage of corn. They have over 60 small rooms, some of them arranged round a central colonnaded courtyard. At the corner of the next street on the right, VIA DEI MOLINI, with a building containing millstones, are the remains of a Republican temple. Here is the **Porta Orientale,** the East Gate of the original fortified city, or Castrum; to the left are the original tufa walls. At this point the Decumanus Maximus has been excavated down to the level of the ancient city and is liable to flooding in bad weather.

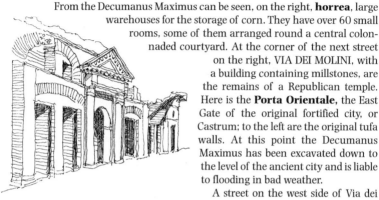

One of the horrea in Ostic Antica

A street on the west side of Via dei Molini, VIA DI DIANA, takes its name from a house called the **Casa di Diana**. It has a characteristic façade with shops on the ground floor, rooms with windows on the first floor, and a projecting balcony on the second floor. The house is entered through a vaulted corridor. On the ground floor is a room (left) whose ceiling and walls have been restored with fragments of frescoes. The small interior courtyard has a fountain and a relief of Diana. At the back of the premises are two rooms converted into a Mithraeum. Opposite the entrance to the Casa di Diana, Via dei Lari opens into PIAZZETTA DE LARI, with a round marble altar dedicated to the lares (or household gods) of the district.

In Via di Diana beyond the Casa di Diana, is (left) the **Thermopolium**, which bears a striking resemblance to a modern Italian bar. Just outside the entrance, under the balcony, are two small seats. On the threshold is a marble counter, on which is a small stone basin. Inside the shop is another counter for the display of food dishes; above are wall paintings of fruit and vegetables. On the rear wall is a marble slab with hooks for hats and coats. Beyond is a delightful court and fountain.

At the end of Via di Diana (right) is an apartment house, originally of four storeys, called the Casa dei Dipinti. A staircase leads up to the top floor from which there is a fine view of the excavations. The ground floor (entered around the corner from Via dei Dipinti) has been closed for many years: the corner room has a mosaic floor and 'architectural' wall-paintings; beyond is a fine *hall painted with mythological scenes, human figures, and landscapes. In the garden of the house are numerous *dolii*, large terracotta jars for the storage of corn and oil. At the end of the street is the Museum, which contains the principal finds from the excavations.

Museo Ostiense

The Museo Ostiense is housed in a building dating from 1500 and originally used by the authorities concerned with the extraction of salt; it was given its Neo-classical façade in 1864.

Room I (left). *Bas-reliefs showing scenes of everyday life (including various arts and crafts, the scene of a birth, a surgical operation, etc.); by the window, two bas-reliefs with the plan of a temple and the topographical plan of a city.

Room II. Architectural and decorative terracotta fragments; statue of Fortune (2C AD). Off the Atrium (with a statue of Apollo Kitharoidos of 2C AD) are (left) Rooms III and IV with works relating to Eastern cults.

Room III. In the niche at the end, *Mithras slaying the bull, from the Baths of Mithras, signed by Kritios of Athens (first half of the 2C BC); in the niche to the right, group of 18 cult statues found in the Sanctuary of Attis (AD 140–70); circular *altar with reliefs of the Twelve Gods, a neo-Attic work of the 1C BC.

Room IV. Recumbent figure of a priest of Cybele (second half of 3C AD); Egyptian-Roman relief in black basalt of Asklepios; stele with a boy initiated in the cult of Isis (early 4C AD).

Steps descend from the Atrium into Room VI. To the left is **Room V** with sculpture inspired by Greek art of the 5C BC: inscribed bases testifying to the presence of Greek artists; head of Hermes; votive relief (an original Greek-Italiot work of the first half of 5C BC); three heads of Athena, from originals of the Phidias type, the Kressilas type, and the Kephisodotos type (first half of 4C BC); upper part of a herm of Themistocles, copy of an original of the 5C; Omphalos Apollo, from the 5C original; head of an unknown man.

Room VI contains sculpture inspired by Greek art of the 4C and 3C BC: two copies of Eros drawing his bow (one a replica of an original by Lysippos); cult statue of Asklepios(?); two herms of Hermes (of the Alcamene type); Dionysos (with elements inspired by Praxiteles). In the centre, fragment of a group of Wrestlers dating from the Trajan era on a Hellenistic model.

Room VII. Sculpture inspired by Hellenistic works. Head of a satyr and of a barbarian of the Pergamene type (2C BC); two heads of Korai; head of Victory (Giulio-Claudian era); Perseus with the head of Medusa; Cupid and Psyche from the House of Cupid and Psyche; replica of the crouching Venus of Doidalsas (3C BC); statue of the Three Graces.

The glass cases between Room VI and Room VIII contain Attic pottery (including a fragment of a red-figure cup showing Orpheus dating from the second half of 5C BC) and Aretine vases with a shiny red glaze. **Room VIII (Sala Guido Calza)**. Roman sculpture from the 1C BC to the mid-2C AD. Headless male *statue, nude except for the drapery over the left arm, signed with the name of the donor Cartilius Poplicola, whose sarcophagus is near Porta Marina. This statue is regarded as the best extant copy of the type known as the 'Hero in Repose'; portraits of Augustus, Trajan (including a statue of him wearing a cuirass), Hadrian, Sabina, wife of Hadrian, and a group of portraits of members of the family of Marcus Aurelius. Herm of Hippocrates (from an original of the 3C BC); funerary statue of Giulia Procula; relief (fragment of an architectural frieze) showing the sacred geese in front of the Temple of Juno Moneta on the Capitoline. The small cases between Room VIII and Room X contain kitchen pottery, terracotta statuettes, and oil lamps.

Room IX (left of Room X). Roman sarcophagi of the 2C–3C AD. The

*sarcophagus of a boy, from the Isola Sacra Necropolis, is a magnificent example of the Attic type, dating from the 2C AD; on the lid is the figure of a boy lying on a couch decorated with bas-reliefs; and the three sides have reliefs of Dionysiac rites with a charming frieze of putti (illustrating the direct influence sarcophagi of this type had on artists of the Renaissance). On the back is the scene of a wrestling match which was left in a rough, unfinished state. The *sarcophagus from Pianabella (c 160 AD) has scenes from the *Iliad*, and another sarcophagus has a scene of Lapiths and Centaurs.

Room X. Roman sculpture (end of 2C to 4C AD). Maxentius(?) as Pontifex Maximus, found in the Edificio degli Augustali; statue of Fausta, sister of Maxentius (AD 310–12); Giulia Domna, in the semblance of Ceres, bust of Septimius Severus, her husband; statue in grey marble of Isis Pelagia, with two fragments of a serpent, also in grey marble, at her feet.

Room XI. Roman art of the 4C–5C AD. Magnificent opus sectile *panels found in an edifice near Porta Marina. The design includes various portraits, and a head thought to be that of Christ (with a halo), and two scenes of a lion attacking a horse. Relief showing scribes recording an orator's speech (thought to have a Christian significance), and two portrait busts in marble tondos. Between Room IX and Room XII cases display Roman glass (including a cup engraved with the figure of Christ, the Cross, and the Monogram, 4C–5C), and objects in bone, ivory, bronze, and lead. **Room XII** (partly under restoration) displays Imperial wall paintings and mosaic fragments.

Parallel with Via dei Dipinti, on the west is the wide CARDO MAXIMUS with arcaded shops, which runs from the Tiber to the Forum and from there to the Porta Laurentina. To the west of this street and also parallel is the narrow VIA TECTA, on the brick walls of which are displayed many of the best preserved inscriptions found in the ruins. Via Tecta runs beside a grain warehouse called the **Piccolo Mercato**. In the south wall have been incorporated several layers of the tufa blocks of the primitive city walls. The Cardo Maximus runs south to the **FORUM**, which is traversed from east to west by the Decumanus Maximus. At the north end of the Forum is the **Capitolium**, the city's most important temple, dedicated to Jupiter, Juno and Minerva. This prostyle hexastyle building, dating from the first half of the 2C, had six fluted white marble columns. The pronaos is reached by a wide flight of steps, in front of which is an altar (reconstituted). In the cella are niches and a plinth for statues of the deities. During the Barbarian invasions the temple was stripped of nearly all its marble facing, but a magnificent slab of African marble is still in place on the threshold and a few surviving marble fragments have been placed to the east of the building under a colonnade, which defined the sacred area.

Opposite the Capitolium, on the south side of the Forum, are the remains of the 1C **Temple of Rome and Augustus**. Like the Capitolium it had six fluted marble columns across the front, but with two side staircases. Fragments of the pediment have been placed on a modern wall to the east; the cult statue of Rome as Victory, dressed as an Amazon, has been placed inside the temple on a plinth, and a headless statue of Victory near the rearranged pediment fragments.

On the east side of the Forum are the **Baths of the Forum**, built in the 2C and restored in the 4C. When restored the baths were decorated with mosaics and cipollino columns; some of the columns have been re-erected. The frigi-

darium survives, together with a series of rooms warmed by hot air. Off the north side is the town **forica** (public lavatory), with its 20 seats almost perfectly preserved. Also on the east side, at the corner where the Decumanus Maximus enters the Forum, is the **Casa dei Triclini**, so called from the couches in each of the three rooms on the right wing of the central courtyard. Behind the courtyard is a room with a high podium decorated with coloured marbles.

Opposite, on the west side of the Forum, is the **Basilica**, or law courts and place of assembly. The façade towards the Forum had a portico of marble arches with a decorated frieze. Fragments of this decoration and of the columns have been preserved. To the south of the Basilica is the **Tempio Rotondo**, dating from the 3C and probably an Augusteum, or temple erected to the worship of the emperors. The peristyle was paved with mosaics and surrounded by marble-faced niches. It was reached by a flight of steps (preserved), which led to the pronaos; this comprised a portico with brick piers faced with marble and with cipollino columns. In the cella are seven niches, three rectangular and four circular. Between the niches are column bases; to the right are the remains of a spiral staircase that led to the dome.

Also on the west side, north of the Decumanus Maximus, is the **Curia**, or senate house. The inscriptions on the walls are lists of *Augustales*, citizens of Ostia belonging to the cult of the emperors. Beside the Curia is the **Casa del Larario**, or House of the Shrine of the Lares, a combination of a house and shopping centre.

Leaving the Forum the Decumanus Maximus continues to the **Porta Occidentale**, the West Gate of the original Castrum; the ancient walls are well seen in Via degli Horrea Epagathiana, a turning on the right. In this street are the **Horrea Epagathiana et Epaphroditiana**, warehouses in a remarkable state of preservation, and used as a shard store (no admission). They were built by two Eastern freedmen, Epagathus and Epaphroditus, whose names are preserved on a marble plaque above the entrance; this is a brick portal with two engaged columns supporting a pediment. The inner courtyard was surrounded by an arcade of brick piers, repeated on the upper floor. On the walls of the vestibule and courtyard are four intact aediculae. In a large vaulted room at the rear of the Horrea are further remains of the primitive town wall.

The region to the west of the Decumanus Maximus was excavated in 1938–42. The Decumanus Maximus now forks. The right fork is VIA DELLA FOCE (Street of the River Mouth); it has been excavated for c 270m. The left fork is the continuation of the Decumanus Maximus (see above) and runs southwest to the Porta Marina, or Sea Gate.

In Via della Foce, on the left, a long passageway leads to the **Mitreo delle Pareti Dipinte**, built in the 2C into a house of the Republican period. The mithraeum is divided into two sections by partly projecting walls with ritual niches. The two stucco-faced galleries of the inner section also have niches. In the rear wall is the brick-built altar, with a marble cippus on which is a bust of Mithras. On the north wall are paintings of initiation rites.

A short street to the right leads to the sacred area of three Republican temples. The central and largest is the prostyle hexastyle **Temple of Hercules Invictus**. The pronaos, paved with mosaics, is reached by a flight of nine steps as wide as the façade. Inside the cella was a small marble column carved to represent the club of Hercules with the lion skin thrown over it. The temple, which may date

from the time of Sulla, was given an altar in the 4C AD by Hostilius Antipater, Praefectus Annonae. On the north side of the Sacred Area is a **tetrastyle temple** (dedication unknown) of the same date as the first. Between the Temple of Hercules and Via della Foce is the **Temple of the Amorini**, named after a round marble altar with winged cupids found there. It was built in the early Republican and rebuilt in the Imperial period. Its final form was *in antis* with just two columns in the portico.

Behind the temple is a street leading to the **House of Cupid and Psyche**, a domus dating from the end of the 3C. It is named after a marble group found in it and now in the Museum. On the west side of the central atrium are four rooms, one with a pavement of coloured marbles (and a copy of the statue); on the east is an attractive nymphaeum in a courtyard with columns and brick arches. At the north end of the atrium is a large room paved with opus sectile, and preserving some marble mural facing. Further along Via della Foce is VIA DELLE TERME DI MITRA (right). The **Baths of Mithras** date from the time of Trajan and were rebuilt in the 2C. They had elaborate systems for heating and for pumping water. In the basement is a mithraeum, in which was found the group of Mithras and the Bull, now in the Museum.

On the left side of the main street are three blocks of small apartment houses; then follows a complex of two apartment blocks with baths between them. The Insula di Serapide is named after a figure of Serapis in an aedicula in the courtyard. The **Terme dei Sette Sapienti** were so called from a satirical painting of the Seven Sages found in one of the rooms. The Sages are distinguished by name (in Greek); to each of them is attached a crude inscription on the subject of health. The baths have a round central hall (once domed), paved with a beautiful *mosaic with five concentric rows of hunting scenes, including what appears to be a tiger. In a room next to a marble plunge pool is a painting of Venus Anadyomene. A passage leads to the extensive **Insula degli Aurighi**, an apartment block with a large central courtyard. Two small paintings of charioteers belonging to opposing factions in the east wall of the arcade give the house its name. Off the north walk is a flat of six rooms with interesting paintings. Beyond the east side of the courtyard is a shrine presumably of Mithras.

Further along Via della Foce, on the left, is a group of buildings of Hadrian's time. The **Baths of Trinacria** preserve good mosaics, and interesting installations for heating and conducting the water. On the other side of Via Serapeo is the House of Bacchus and Ariadne, with rich floral mosaics. The Serapeum, behind, was dedicated in AD 127, and included a temple, with courtyard flanked by porticoes and cult rooms. To the west, originally connected with the Serapeum, is a fine domus, with more mosaics.

Beyond the Insula degli Aurighi is VIA DEGLI AURIGHI, which runs east to join the extension of the Decumanus Maximus. In this street are the Insula delle Celle (left), a type of warehouse with small rooms, and, opposite, a modest hotel with a stable called Albergo con Stalla. This inn also faces a street named after the Insula delle Volte Dipinte (no admission), with painted ceilings. Across the street is the **Casa delle Muse** (closed for many years), dating from the time of Hadrian. This house has a central courtyard with a covered arcade. The restored wooden roof of the arcade rests on the ancient brick cornice. Several rooms contain paintings, and on a wall of the arcade are some graffiti, one of them representing the lighthouse of Ostia.

To the right is the Casa a Pareti Gialle (House with the Yellow Walls). This looks on to a vast square of four large apartment houses built round a garden and known as the Case a Giardino. The scale of construction, the provision of a private garden, and the absence of shops all indicate that the flats in these buildings were intended for the wealthier inhabitants of Ostia.

The Decumanus Maximus, and its extension from the fork outside the West Gate, continues southwest and runs for 350m to the Porta Marina and, beyond it, to the sea-coast. The **Porta Marina** was an opening in the walls built by Sulla, remains of which may be seen. Just inside the gate is a wine-shop, the Caupona di Alexander, and, outside, a large square. The extension of the Decumanus Maximus beyond the gate, built in the time of Augustus, ran through an earlier cemetery (see below). On this section is the **Santuario della Bona Dea,** a small prostyle tetrastyle temple dedicated to a goddess worshipped exclusively by women, whose four column bases survive. Further towards the sea is the Domus Fulminata, with a small monument recording the fact that the house had been struck by lightning. Opposite, Via di Cartilio Poplicola leads to the Baths of Porta Marina past the **Tomb of L. Cartilius Poplicola**, a prominent citizen. The surviving fragment of its decorative frieze shows a trireme with the helmeted head of a goddess. This and another tomb close by attest to the existence of a cemetery in the Republican era.

On the outskirts of the town towards the shore, and between the sea and the ancient Via Severiana (on the southwest side of this street), is the most ancient **Jewish Synagogue** known from monumental remains. It was in continuous use from the 1C to the 5C AD. Ritual carvings and poorly preserved mosaics have been found; several Ionic columns have been re-erected. It was discovered in 1961–63 when the new road to Fiumicino airport was constructed.

The Decumanus Maximus returns past the charming Fontana a Lucerna. In a street to the south beyond the junction with Via degli Aurighi is a block of shops with windows beside their doors. Close by is the **Schola di Traiano**, seat of an Ostian corporation named after a statue of Trajan found in it. In the courtyard, which has stuccoed brick columns, is a long basin provided with niches. The central room has a headless statue of Fortuna and a mosaic pavement. The school overlays earlier constructions, among them a 1C domus; its nymphaeum has been partly restored.

On the opposite side of the main street is the **School of the Naval Smiths**, with a temple. The arcade of the courtyard in front of the temple was evidently a marble store: unused and partly finished columns, bases and capitals have been found in it. The store appears to have belonged to Volusianus, a senator of the 4C, as his name is carved on some of the column shafts. Adjoining is the **Christian Basilica,** an unpretentious structure with two aisles divided by columns and ending in apses. Vico del Dionisio leads south to the Cortile di Dionisio, surrounded by several houses, and to the Mitreo delle Sette Porte, a mithraeum which displays in seven arches the seven grades of the Mithraic cult.

The Decumanus Maximus continues to (right) the **Macellum**, or market, which occupies the area between the Decumanus and a street running south, VIA OCCIDENTALE DEL POMERIO. The market has numerous shops; two fish shops open on to the Decumanus. Behind them is the market-place. Via Occidentale del Pomerio and Via del Tempio Rotondo, behind the Tempio Rotondo at the south end of the Forum, lead to the south continuation of the

Cardo Maximus. On the right here is the **Domus di Giove Fulminatore**, a house of the Republican period remodelled in the 4C, with a striking phallic 'doormat' mosaic. Beside it is the **Domus della Nicchia a Mosaico**, another Republican house, twice rebuilt. It is named after a semicircular niche faced with polychrome mosaic in the room (tablinum) beyond the atrium. Adjoining is the **Ninfeo degli Eroti**, with well-preserved marble floor and walls and niches in which were found two copies of the Eros of Lysippos. The next building is the **Domus delle Colonne**, a large corner house, with façades on the Cardo Maximus and on Via della Caupona del Pavone (right). In the centre of the courtyard is a stone basin with a double apse and short white marble columns; beyond is the large tablinum with its entrance between two columns.

In the side street is a wine-shop, the 3C **Caupone del Pavone**. One of its rooms is decorated with paintings of flying bacchanals and muses; beyond is the bar, with a counter and small basins. On the opposite side of the street is the **Domus dei Pesci**, evidently a Christian house. A vestibule has a mosaic with a chalice and fish. A large room on the south side, with two marble columns, has a fine *mosaic floor.

The Cardo Maximus passes on the right the Portico dell'Ercole; opposite is a fulling mill. Adjoining are the **Terme del Faro**. In a floor of the frigidarium of the baths is a mosaic with fish, sea monsters, and a lighthouse (pharos), after which the baths were named. One of the rooms has a white marble pool and frescoed walls in the 3C style. A ramp leads from the Cardo to the triangular **Campo della Magna Mater**, one of the best preserved sacred areas of the Roman world. At the west corner is the prostyle hexastyle Temple of Cybele. At the east corner the Sanctuary of Attis has an apse flanked by telamones in the shape of fauns. On the same side is the Temple of Bellona, dating from the time of Marcus Aurelius, and, opposite, the Schola degli Hastiferes, seat of an association connected with the cult of Bellona, the goddess of war. The sanctuary is close to the **Porta Laurentina**, which retains the tufa blocks of Sulla's circumvallation (c 80 BC).

Some way south of Porta Laurentina, along the line of the ancient Via Laurentina, is the **Cemetery of the Porta Laurentina**, first excavated in 1865 and systematically explored in 1934–35. Many of the inscriptions relate to freedmen. Beyond the motorway, in the locality called **Pianabella**, excavations, begun in 1976, revealed a necropolis and Christian basilica.

A short distance back along the Cardo Maximus, the SEMITA DEI CIPPI leads to the right (north). This street is flanked by two cippi and contains a 3C domus (Casa del Protiro), its reconstituted portal prettily flanked by cypresses. To the north a right turn leads into a street named after the **House of Fortuna Annonaria**, which has a garden in its peristyle. On the west side of the peristyle is a large room with three arches, columns, and a nymphaeum. At the end of the street, on the right, is another temple of Bona Dea, with a mithraeum next door, notable for its mosaic pavement. Also in the street is the Domus Republicana, with four Doric columns; it is adjoined by the Edificio degli Augustali, the headquarters of the *Augustales* (those in charge of the imperial cult). This building has another entrance in Via degli Augustali, which leads to the Decumanus Maximus, and the main entrance.

The village of Ostia Antica

Across the road from the entrance to the excavations is the borgo of Ostia Antica, a fortified village whose walls are still standing, founded by Gregory IV in 830 and given the name of *Gregoriopolis*. There are now some modern houses outside the walls which enclose a tiny picturesque hamlet beside the castle and church. The **Castle** (closed many years ago for restoration), is a splendid building erected in 1483–86 by Baccio Pontelli for Julius II while still a cardinal. It houses archaeological collections from the excavations, medieval material, and frescoes by Baldassarre Peruzzi. The church of **Santa Aurea**, by Baccio Pontelli or Meo del Caprina, contains the body of the martyred St Aurea (died 268) and, in a side chapel, a fragment of the gravestone of St Monica (who died at Ostia in 387; see above), mother of St Augustine. The Episcopal Palace, with fine frescoes by Baldassarre Peruzzi (1508–13), is the residence of the Bishop of Ostia.

Lido di Ostia

Via del Mare continues to Lido di Ostia (61,600 inhabitants), now usually called just **Ostia**, on the coast. The lido became Rome's seaside resort after the First World War, and under the Fascist regime was planned as a district of the capital (and connected, in 1936, to EUR by a fast road, Via Cristoforo Colombo). Ostia is now an ugly suburb of Rome with numerous high-rise blocks of flats, and is still used as a resort by thousands of Romans in summer. It has some monumental edifices erected in 1916–40, but has been ruined by indiscriminate new building. On the seafront, in Piazza Anco Marzio, a monument by Pietro Consagra was set up in 1993 to the writer and film director Pier Paolo Pasolini found murdered on 2 November 1975 at the Idroscalo, a former seaplane station near the mouth of the Tiber, west of the esplanade (where another neglected monument stands). Nearby survives the Tor San Michele, built in 1568 by Nanni di Baccio Bigio in 1568 to a design by Michelangelo.

To the east is the **Lido di Castel Fusano** in a beautiful pine forest. The first pines were planted here c 1710, and in 1755 the property was acquired by the Chigi family and was afterwards let as a royal hunting reserve. It has belonged to the Commune of Rome since 1932 and part of it is open as a public park. There are long-term plans to connect it, as one huge nature reserve of some 6000 hectares, to the forests of Castel Porziano and Capocotta to the south. This is the largest coastal forest left in the country.

Necropoli di Porto (Isola Sacra)

From Ostia Antica (see above) a branch road (signposted for Fiumicino) skirts the fence protecting the excavations, curving right on a spur from Via del Mare. It passes close to the remains of the synagogue (described above). Beyond the Tiber and a set of traffic lights, the road passes a huge old industrial building, and at a pedestrian crossing (traffic lights) a narrow road (inconspicuous sign for 'necropoli di Porto') leads right. The first byroad left ends at the entrance to the Necropoli di Porto or Isola Sacra (open Tues–Sun 9–sunset; free), in a pretty group of trees. This was the necropolis of the port of Claudius and the later port of Trajan (which came to be known as Porto, see below), particularly important for its 2C–3C tombs. It is situated on the Isola Sacra, a tract of land made into an island by the cutting of the Fossa Traiana from Porto to the sea. Only part of the

site has been excavated as much of it is under cultivation (and some of the tombs are at present being restored).

Since the necropolis was the burial place of the middle- and lower-class inhabitants of Porto such as merchants, artisans, craftsmen and sailors, there are no elaborate mausolea. The tombs, which have been preserved by the sand that covered them for centuries, are arranged in groups. They have or had barrel vaults of brick and masonry faced with stucco; some of them had gable roofs. Internally they are decorated with stuccoes, paintings and mosaics. Sarcophagi and urns in columbaria have been found, often in the same tomb, evidence of the simultaneous practice of burial and cremation. Many of the sarcophagi are adorned with mythological reliefs; terracotta reliefs have representations of arts and crafts, indicating the trade of the deceased. Nearly every tomb has a name inscribed over the door. The tombs of the wealthier citizens have sepulchral chambers, with fanlights. Outside, by the door, are couches for funeral feasts.

Some of the tombs are like old-fashioned round-topped travelling trunks, and recall similar examples in North Africa. The poorest citizens, who could not afford the cost of a monument, buried their dead in the ground and marked the place with amphorae through which they poured libations; or they set up large tiles to form a peaked roof over the remains. The Isola Sacra, once a flourishing horticultural centre, was abandoned after the fall of the Western Empire, and became an uninhabited malarial marsh. It was reclaimed in 1920 when the swamps were drained, roads ballasted, and canals dug.

The road through the cemetery, the Via Flavia, is a section of the ancient road from Ostia to Porto. The tombs are numbered with small marble plaques. Of particular interest are: a **chamber tomb (11)**, with a marble sarcophagus with a scene of a funeral feast, and two other sarcophagi; the **Tomb of the Children (16)**, with an entrance mosaic of the Nile; the **Tomb of the Smith (29)**, with a façade divided by three pilasters and terracotta reliefs indicating the man's trade; the **Tomb of Telesphorus and Julia Eunia (39)**, with the Christian symbols of the lamb, dove and anchor, apparently unique in this cemetery; a two-storeyed tomb **(41)**; a tomb with a mosaic of a ship and the lighthouse of Porto **(43)**. In the row behind are two tombs **(55** and **56)**, the first pedimental, the second with a square-corniced façade, both preserving their inscriptions. Close by is a series of **four chamber tombs (77–80)**, with pedimental façades bearing reliefs.

Near the necropolis is the church of **Sant'Ippolito** where excavations, still in progress, have revealed interesting early Christian remains and a large medieval basilica (not yet open to the public).

Museo delle Navi Romane at Fiumicino, and the ports of Claudius and Trajan

The main road continues towards the airport of Fiumicino (leaving on the right a road signposted 'Fiumicino' and 'Isola Sacra'). Beyond a viaduct, and a road left for Fiumicino and Fregene, the road crosses a railway and a canal before entering the **Airport of Fiumicino** (sign across the road). The airport, officially

called 'Leonardo da Vinci', takes its other name from the nearby ugly seaside town, which was heavily bombed in the Second World War. With graceful cantilevered buildings, it was opened in 1961. At the roundabout this road keeps right, and on the left of the road, just before a war memorial and the main airport buildings, is the **Museo delle Navi Romane** (open Tues–Sun 9–13.30; Tues, Thur also 14.30–16.30. Lire 4000), at 35 Via Alessandro Guidoni. This fine purpose-built museum, opened in 1979, houses remains of five Roman boats found here at the entrance to the Port of Claudius. They include four flat-bottomed cargo ships or barges used to carry goods upstream to Rome, dating from AD 300–400, and a fishing boat (1C AD). Various objects found in the excavations, including lead seals and anchors, are also displayed here, and explanatory diagrams illustrate the history of the ports. There is a good view of the boats from the balcony.

The museum stands in the area once occupied by the **Port of Claudius**. When the harbour of Ostia, already inadequate for its trade, began to silt up with the action of the Tiber, Augustus planned this larger seaport. In AD 42 Claudius began operations. It was connected to the Tiber by a canal. The work was completed in 54 by Nero, who issued commemorative coins stamped Portus Augusti. With an area of some 80 hectares, and a wharf frontage of 800m, it was the most important commercial port in the Mediterranean. Part of the site is now covered by the airport buildings, and by the grassy fields near the museum, in which fragments of the quays and buildings can be seen. Still extant is part of the quay incorporating the form of Caligula's ship (104m x 20m) which brought from Egypt the obelisk now in Piazza San Pietro. The ship was sunk and used as the base of a huge four-storeyed lighthouse.

However, even this harbour soon silted up, and in 103 Trajan constructed a hexagonal artificial basin, the **Port of Trajan** further inland to the south, and better protected. It was connected to the Port of Claudius by a series of docks. This is reached from the airport by Via Portuense, an ancient road which followed the right bank of the Tiber from Rome to the Port. The remains of the port include the **hexagonal basin** (650m across), perfectly preserved, constructed with travertine blocks. More than one hundred ships could be moored here at any one time, and it was surrounded by warehouses. It shows up excellently from the air when landing at Fiumicino, but it is fenced off and can only be visited with special permission or on guided tours organised by the Soprintendenza Archeologica di Ostia (information at the Museo delle Navi).

This area, still private property owned by the Sforza Cesarini family, is occu-pied by a safari park. Attempts have been made to expropriate it and save it from further destruction, and there are long-term plans to create a coastal archaeo-logical park and nature reserve here. Excavations have unearthed the remains of granaries, a wall, a high arch in red brick, an underground passageway, etc. To the west are more ruins, including a monumental portico, at present still over-grown and abandoned. Trajan as well as Claudius dug canals in connection with the seaport. The Fossa Traiana (now the Canale di Fiumicino) survives as a navi-gable canal between the Tiber and the sea. Numerous marble columns and coloured marbles, imported from all over the Empire destined for ancient Rome, have been found in the area.

The village of **Porto**, 2km from the airport, on the Via Portuensis, takes its name from the ancient city of *Portus*, which grew up around the ports of Claudius and Trajan. It was favoured as a seaport by Constantine at the expense of Ostia; in 314 it had its own bishop and became known as *Civitas Constantina*. In the village are the church of Santa Rufina (10C, rebuilt), an old episcopal palace, and the Villa Torlonia. The suburbicarian see of Porto and Santa Rufina is one of the six held by the cardinal bishops.

A motorway (26km) leads directly back to Rome from the airport, which is also connected by a railway line opened in 1990 with Stazione Termini (in 30 minutes) and (via Ostiense and Trastevere) with Stazione Tiburtina (in 40 minutes).

29 · The Alban Hills

The Alban Hills (*Colli Albani*) are an isolated volcanic group rising from the Roman Campagna, with foothills reaching to within 12km of Rome. They enclose the two attractive crater lakes of Nemi and Albano, and 13 picturesque towns known as the **Castelli Romani** (Frascati, Monte Porzio Catone, Montecompatri, Rocca Priora, Colonna, Rocca di Papa, Grottaferrata, Marino, Castel Gandolfo, Albano Laziale, Ariccia, Genzano and Nemi), most of them founded by popes or patrician Roman families. Castel Gandolfo is famous as the Pope's summer residence. Crossed by a confusing number of roads, the hills are now an elegant residential area with numerous villas amid chestnut woods. Vineyards on the outer slopes produce the once famous 'Vini dei Castelli'. Some of the towns are visited as summer resorts.

■ **Information Offices**. Azienda Autonoma dei Laghi e Castelli Romani, 1 Viale Risorgimento, Albano (☎ 932 4081). Azienda Autonoma del Tuscolo, 1 Piazza Marconi, Frascati (☎ 942 0331). Azienda Autonoma di Velletri, ☎ 963 0896.

■ **Public transport from Rome**. Train services from Termini station to Frascati, Velletri, Marino Laziale and Albano. Buses from the Anagnina station of the underground (line A) run by COTRAL (☎ 591 5551) to Frascati, Rocca di Papa, Grottaferrata, Marino, Castel Gandolfo, Albano, Ariccia, Genzano, Nemi and Velletri.

■ **By road from Rome**. The ancient **Via Tuscolana** ran to *Tusculum*, to the east of present-day Frascati. It was a short branch of the **Via Latina**, which left Rome by the Porta Capena (see p 234) passed through *Ferentinum* (Ferentino), *Frusino* (Frosinone), *Aquinum* (Aquino), *Casinum* (Cassino), and *Venafrum* (Venafro) to *Beneventum* (Benevento) where it joined the Via Appia. The main approach from Rome to the other localities in the Alban Hills is by the **Via Appia Nuova** and the modern **Via dei Laghi**.

■ **Hotels** (mostly 3-star and 2-star) at Albano, Rocca di Papa, Nemi, Castel Gandolfo, Genzano, Ariccia, Frascati (3-star *Villa Tuscolana*) and Grottaferrata (2-star *Villa Fiorio*).

■ **Restaurants** of all categories in all the towns, especially good in and near Grottaferrata.

■ **Annual Festivals. Marino**: Sagra dell'uva (a wine festival) on the first Sun in Oct; **Nemi**: festival of wild strawberries (June); **Genzano**: Infiorata, when the main street is carpeted with flowers on the first Sunday after Corpus Domini; **Frascati**: summer drama festival in the theatre of Villa Torlonia.

Frascati

Frascati (18,000 inhabitants) in a beautiful position on the northwest slopes of the Alban Hills, is perhaps the most elegant of the Castelli Romani, famous for its villas and parks. Over 80 per cent of its buildings were destroyed or damaged in 1943–44 when it was the army headquarters of Field-Marshal Kesselring. The white wine of Frascati was once renowned.

> Frascati was overshadowed by Tusculum in Roman days. A small village in the Middle Ages, it expanded in 1191, when the inhabitants of Tusculum, after the destruction of their city, moved to the area around the ancient churches of Santa Maria and San Sebastiano in Frascata. Later it was a feudal holding, and at the beginning of the 16C it was taken by the Holy See. Henry, Cardinal York, was Bishop of Frascati and died here in 1807; the body of his brother, the Young Pretender (died 1788) was buried in the Duomo of Frascati, before being moved to the Vatican Grottoes.

The huge PIAZZA MARCONI is dominated by the Villa Aldobrandini (see below) splendidly sited on a hill above the square. Below its terraced gardens a magnificent clipped hedge descends to the entrance gate. Opposite the villa is a balustrade with a wide view of the plain (and the railway station below, reached by a long flight of steps through gardens). In the centre of the square, with a few palm trees, is a First World War memorial by Cesare Bazzani. Opposite the yellow Municipio (admission 9–12), which escaped serious war damage (and which contains a statue of Giovanni Ceccarini by Antonio Canova), is the entrance to the disappointing public park of **Villa Torlonia** (the lower part used as a car park). The villa where Annibal Caro, the writer and secretary to a number of cardinals, lived from 1563 until his death in 1566 was destroyed in the war. The gardens, above monumental terraces on the hillside, contain a fountain terrace by Carlo Maderno.

Villa Aldobrandini is the finest of the Frascati villas. It was designed by Giacomo della Porta and built by Carlo Maderno in 1598–1603 for Cardinal Pietro Aldobrandini. The superb **GARDEN** (entrance in Via Cardinal Massaia; open 9–13, 15.30–18 except Sat and Sun, with permission from the Azienda Autonoma del Tuscolo in Piazza Marconi), laid out at the same time, and was much admired by diarist John Evelyn who was here in the 17C. It was carefully repaired after war damage. There is a magnificent view extending to Rome. Paths lead up to the gardens behind the villa. Facing the fine rear façade is the

Teatro dell'Acqua, a large semicircular nymphaeum with statuary and fountains designed by Giacomo della Porta and completed by Giovanni Fontana and
Carlo Maderno. In the central niche the figure of Atlas is supposed to represent
Pope Clement VIII, Pietro Aldobrandini's uncle. On the wooded hillside above, a
water-staircase bordered by tall hedges descends from two 'Columns of
Hercules' decorated with mosaic. From the columns there is a view of the large
park with magnificent ilexes and chestnut trees. A small formal garden survives
to the right of the Teatro dell'Acqua. The villa, still owned by the Aldobrandini,
is not open to the public: the rooms are decorated with paintings by the Zuccari,
Cavaliere d'Arpino, and the school of Domenichino.

To the left of the entrance gate of Villa Aldobrandini, Viale Catone leads uphill
between the 16C Villa Lancellotti, (no adm; still owned by the Lancellotti), with
a graceful nymphaeum in its beautiful gardens, just above the road on the right,
and the public Parco dell'Ombrellino on the left. Adjoining Piazza Marconi is
Piazza Roma. From here Via Battisti leads to Piazza San Pietro, rebuilt after its
devastation in the war, with a restored fountain by Girolamo Fontana. The
Duomo, on the right, has preserved most of its façade, also by Girolamo
Fontana, as well as the unattractive bell-towers of later date. The interior has an
interesting plan by Mascherino (1598). It contains a *Madonna of the Rosary* after
Domenichino (third chapel on right) and a relief by Pompeo Ferrucci over the
high altar. To the left of the main door is the cenotaph of Prince Charles Edward
(see above).

In Piazza del Gesù, beyond the fountain, is the church of the **Gesù**, attributed
to Pietro da Cortona, also restored after war damage. It contains remarkable
perspective paintings by Andrea dal Pozzo. Via Cairoli, to the left of the church,
leads to Piazza Paolo III, in which is the **castle**, built with three towers; it is now
the bishop's palace. Beyond it is the rebuilt church of Santa Maria del Vicario, or
San Rocco, with a fine Romanesque campanile.

The road for Tusculum passes a byroad (signposted) for the Villa Falconieri ('La
Rufina'; no admission) built in 1545–48 for Bishop Alessandro Ruffini and
enlarged for the Falconieri by Borromini. Before reaching the entrance the road
passes a splendid gateway by Borromini (with a tree growing through it). The
villa was occupied before 1914 by Wilhelm II of Germany, and presented by the
State to the patriot and poet Gabriele d'Annunzio in 1925. It is now a European
Centre for Education. The once-famous garden has been altered.

About 1.5km east of Frascati is **Villa Mondragone**, built in 1573–75 for
Cardinal Altemps mainly by Martino Longhi the Elder. In 1613 it was bought by
Cardinal Scipione Borghese, who enlarged it. The so-called *portico of Vignola is
by Vasanzio. The terrace commands a good view of Rome. On 24 February 1582
Gregory XIII here issued his famous bull for the reform of the calendar. The villa,
now owned by the University of Torvergata, is being restored.

On the Grottaferrata road is the 17C **Villa Muti** with a splendid formal green
*garden, probably laid out by Cardinal Pompeo Arrigoni in 1595 with box
parterres, surrounded by a large park. The villa and its grounds were
sequestered in 1987 to prevent their alteration. The once beautiful Villa Grazioli
(privately owned), also on this road, is being restored as a hotel and conference
centre.

Tusculum

From Frascati the road for Tusculum climbs uphill past the church of the **Cappuccini** which contains a replica of an altarpiece by Giulio Romano, and paintings by Girolamo Muziano, and Paul Brill. Here also is the tomb of Cardinal Guglielmo Massaia (died 1889), with a statue by Cesare Aureli. Massaia spent 35 years as a missionary in Ethiopia and an interesting museum contains the material he collected there. Beyond is the entrance gate of the **Villa Tuscolana** (now a hotel), surrounded by gardens, fountains and woods. The 16C villa, damaged by bombing, had several owners, including Lucien Bonaparte, Queen Maria Cristina of Sardinia, and Vittorio Emanuele II, passing c 1874 to the princely family of Lancellotti.

Further uphill the road joins a road from Grottaferrata and follows a fence (right), beyond which can be seen a fine stretch of ancient paved Roman road, to end at a car park by the ruins of **TUSCULUM** (610m), 4km outside Frascati, an Etruscan centre said to have been founded by Telegonus, son of Ulysses and Circe. It was the birthplace of Cato the Censor (234–149 BC). The vicinity became famous in the Imperial period as a resort for wealthy Romans who built numerous suburban villas here, no fewer than 43 of which are mentioned in classical literature. The most famous of these was Cicero's villa, the 'Tusculanum', where the Tuscan Disputations were supposed to have been held. The exact site of the villa has been disputed for centuries. In 1191 the Romans destroyed Tusculum in revenge for their defeat at Monte Porzio Catone in 1167 (see below), and the inhabitants escaped to Frascati. Excavations of the ancient city were begun by Lucien Bonaparte in 1804–20, and continued by Maria Cristina of Sardinia.

The site has been acquired by the XI Comunità Montana del Lazio but it is closed to the public while excavations are in progress. From the car park it is a few minutes' walk to the summit of the lower hill with a few overgrown ruins from which the splendid site can be appreciated. There is a fine view of the Alban Hills and of the sea. The so-called **Forum** may have been a quadrilateral annexe to the elegant little **Theatre** (probably dating from the 1C BC) which is beyond to the left. It is the best preserved of the ruins, although the cavea, hewn out of the hillside, was heavily restored and bears a large inscription commemorating pope Gregory XVI's visit here in 1839. On the hill above is the site of the acropolis and nearby are fine stretches of Roman road, and traces of walls. In the other direction, beyond the car park, are traces of a sanctuary called, since the 16C, the 'Villa of Cicero' and, at the westernmost point of the city, beneath the hillside, the **Amphitheatre**, almost totally overgrown. It measured 80m by 53m, with an arena of 48m by 29m and had room for 3000 spectactors, and probably dates from the 2C AD.

On a hill nearby is the **Convent of Camaldoli,** dating from 1611, often visited by James Stuart, the Old Pretender.

The small towns of Monte Porzio Catone, Montecompatri and Rocca Priora, on low hills, form part of the 13 Castelli Romani. At **Monte Porzio Catone**, the inhabitants of Tusculum, helped by Frederick Barbarossa, won a victory over the Romans in 1167. **Montecompatri** is the successor to the ancient *Labicum*, and it was later owned by the Annibaldi and the Colonna. **Rocca Priora** (768m) is on the north side of the great crater of the Alban Hills, overlooking

the classical Valle Latina. It was probably the first town built in the neighbour-hood after the destruction of Tusculum in the 12C. In the 14C it belonged to the Savelli, after which it was taken by the Holy See.

Grottaferrata

Grottaferrata (11,300 inhabitants) is known for its important monastery. Some of the finest Castelli wines were once produced in the area. At the lower end of the Corso del Popolo is the entrance (poorly signposted) to the **ABBAZIA DI GROTTAFERRATA**, enclosed by massive walls and bastions erected by order of Cardinal della Rovere (later Pope Julius II), in 1483–91, probably by Baccio Pontelli or Antonio da Sangallo. Cars can be parked in the castle courtyard, which has a statue of St Nilus by Raffaele Zaccagnini (1904). On the left is the entrance gate to the abbey founded by St Nilus, a Greek abbot who came from Rossano Calabro, and died here in 1004. The monastery was built by his disciple St Bartholomew (also from Rossano; died c 1065), who was a composer of Greek hymns and wrote a biography of St Nilus. Some 26 Basilian monks still live here; they are Roman Catholics who celebrate according to the Byzantine Greek rite.

The interesting **Museum**, founded in 1875, is shown by a monk (ring at the gate; 8.30–12, 16.30–18; Sun 8.30–10, 16.30–18; closed Mon). The entrance is from the second courtyard beneath a beautiful portico with Corinthian columns attributed to Giuliano da Sangallo, beneath which are archaeological fragments.

Room I contains a beautiful classical Greek *stele dating from 430–420 BC, showing a seated male figure reading from a scroll. The relief of the burial of a warrior dates from the time of Hadrian. **Room II** has busts of Euripides and Homer, and Roman statues. Sarcophagi of the 2C–4C AD are displayed in **Room III**.

Room IV. 13C detached frescoes from the nave of the church (see below) with Old Testament scenes (and copies of them made at the end of the 19C). The 15C chalice and paten were presented to the monastery by Cardinal Bessarion. A good painting of Saints Benedict and Nicola is attributed to Stefano d'Antonio or Neri di Bicci. Church silver and crosses as well as 12C–13C Sicilian ceramics are also displayed here.

A few steps lead up to **Room V** which contains finds from excavations in the area, including an Iron Age tomb of a woman discovered in 1960 at Rocca di Papa. On the other side of Room IV is **Room VI** with a 15C French statue of the Madonna and Child, and a bowl made in Orvieto in the 16C. The vault of this room was frescoed with grotesques illustrating the life of Fabio Massimo by Francesco di Siena in 1547. In the last room are 16C and 17C paintings and 18C copes. The monastery has an important **Library** with precious MSS, and there is also a book restoration laboratory.

From the first courtyard (see above) there is access to the church of **Santa Maria**, consecrated by John XIX in 1025, redesigned internally in 1754 and restored in 1902–30. The pronaos was beautifully reconstructed in 1930, and the campanile well restored in 1912. A finely carved Romanesque portal surrounds the 11C wooden door. Above is a *mosaic of Christ between the Virgin and St John the Baptist. The font is an antique marble urn, decorated with unusual fishing scenes. In the **interior**, the roof of the nave dates from 1595; the Byzantine mosaic of the Apostles on the triumphal arch and the damaged fresco above date from the 13C. Frescoes from the clerestory walls have been

detached and are now in the museum. At the beginning of the south aisle is the 'crypta ferrata' (always open), two small vaulted Roman rooms (probably once a tomb) with, as the name suggests, iron grilles in the windows, transformed in medieval times into a Christian chapel. It is thought that the name of the monastery, and later the town, originated here.

Also off the south aisle opens the **Cappella Farnesiana**, with *frescoes (1609–10) of the lives of St Nilus and St Bartholomew, by Domenichino, considered by many to be his finest works. They were commissioned by Odoardo Farnese and greatly admired by artists and travellers over the centuries. They were restored in 1819 by Vincenzo Camuccini, and again in 1990. To the right of the entrance, St Nilus before the Crucifix, and averting a tempest by his prayers. Inside the chapel, to the left: St Nilus and the Emperor Otho III (the page holding the emperor's horse is Domenichino, and the figures on the right of the horse are Guido Reni and Guercino). On the right: St Bartholomew averting the fall of a pillar during the building of the convent; on the end wall (left of the altar): exorcism of a devil and (right) the Virgin presenting a golden apple to Saints Nilus and Bartholomew; in the lunette: death of St Nilus; in the triumphal arch: the Annunciation. The altarpiece of the Madonna and Child with the two founders is by Annibale Carracci. The monastery was built on the site of a large Roman villa, and near the church, is a splendid Roman cryptoporticus.

On the Via Anagnina (towards Rome) outside Grottaferrata is the **Borghetto**, or Castello Savelli, a ruined 13C castle with 13 towers, built on Roman foundations, which passed from the counts of Tusculum to the Savelli, and later to Julius II, who converted it into an outwork of the Abbey of Grottaferrata. Also on this road near Villa Senni is the entrance gate to the **Catacombs of ad Decimum** (open on Sun & fest. 10–12.30, 15 or 16–17 or 19), probably in use from the 3C to the 5C, and so called because they are at the tenth Roman mile from Rome on the Via Latina. They have been owned by the monastery of Grottaferrata since 1910. The well preserved tombs have traces of frescoes and numerous inscriptions. Nearby is a stretch of the ancient Roman paving of Via Latina.

The Lago di Albano

The Lago di Albano is a small crater lake, 10km round and 170m deep. It is fed by underground sources and by the drainage of the surrounding crater, and its waters are full of fish. The *Lacus Albanus* was surrounded by villas in the Imperial Roman era and naumachiae were held here. In 1985 Middle Bronze Age finds were made in the lake. It is surrounded by the scenic Via dei Laghi, and it is possible to walk round the lake in 2 hrs by a track.

Marino

Marino, at the north end of the lake, with 23,800 inhab., is less of a tourist centre than some of the other Castelli, and is celebrated for its wines. It suffered much damage during the Second World War. A colourful market is held here on Sunday mornings.

The town was built near the ancient *Castrimoenium*, colonised under Sulla, of which no traces remain. The modern name first appears in the 11C. In the 13C

Marino was a stronghold of the Orsini; in 1347 Giordano Orsini, who had been driven out of Rome by the tribune Cola di Rienzo, was here besieged unsuccessfully by him. In 1419 the town passed to the Colonna. Many of its inhabitants took part in the battle of Lepanto (1571). Vittoria Colonna (1490–1548) and the musician Giacomo Carissimi (1604–74) were born in Marino.

In Piazza San Barnaba is the restored 17C church of **San Barnaba**. It contains a *Martyrdom of St Barnabas* by Benedetto Gennari, and a Turkish shield taken at the battle of Lepanto. In the neighbouring Piazza Lepanto is the bomb-damaged **Fountain of the Four Moors**, by the local sculptor Pompeo Castiglia (1642), commemorating the battle of Lepanto. The 16C **Palazzo Colonna** is now the Town Hall, and contains an antiquarium. In the church of the **Trinità** is a painting attributed to Guido Reni, and in the church of **Santa Maria delle Grazie** a *St Roch*, of the Emilian school. Attached to the Dominican convent is the church of **Madonna del Rosario**, with an elegant Rococo interior. Near the station is a mithraeum, with interesting frescoes.

Rocca di Papa

A byroad leads uphill off Via dei Laghi for Rocca di Papa (7800 inhab.), built up in picturesque terraces on the side of Monte Cavo, the highest of the Castelli Romani (681m). Surrounded by chestnut woods, it is a summer resort. The lower part of the town is modern, the upper part medieval. Originally called 'Rocca di Monte Cavo' it had adopted its present name, derived from a papal castle here, by the 12C. It was later owned by the Annibaldi and the Colonna. From Piazza della Repubblica there is an excellent view of the medieval town, with the observatory at its top, and of Monte Cavo. Relics of the **castle** can still be seen at the highest point of the town, from which there are views of the Campagna and of the lakes of Albano and Nemi.

A private road winds up to the summit of Monte Cavo. A short way up, a sign indicates the ancient **Via Sacra**, called *Via Triumphalis*, which climbs up the hillside to the left. Perfectly preserved, it can be followed on foot for a considerable way, through beautiful woods. It was built to reach the Temple of Jupiter Latiaris on the summit of Monte Cavo (see below), and for the triumphal processions of generals whose feats of arms were not considered important enough for a triumphal procession along the Via Sacra in Rome.

Another path ascends to the edge of the crater of Monte Cavo from the castle of Rocca di Papa. In the crater a flat floor known as the Campi d'Annibale, is traditionally thought to be the site of the halting-place of Hannibal in his march on Tusculum and Rome in 211 BC. In fact this was probably a Roman military station protecting the Via Appia and Via Latina. The path, with splendid views, follows for some time the Via Triumphalis (see above).

Monte Cavo (949m), the second highest summit of the Alban Hills, is the sacred *Mons Albanus* of the Latins. On its summit stood the Temple of Jupiter Latiaris, the sanctuary of the Latin League, whose religious festivals, the *Feriae Latinae*, were celebrated in spring and autumn by the 47 towns of the confederation. Excavations have failed to find any trace of the temple. On the presumed site of the temple Henry, Cardinal York, built a Passionist Convent in 1783; this later became an observatory, founded by Father Angelo Secchi in 1876. The walls of the convent garden are built partly with blocks from ancient buildings. There is also a television station here. The splendid *view extends along the coast

from Monte Circeo to Civitavecchia, and takes in the Tolfa and Cimini ranges, the Sabine, Tiburtine and Praenestine Hills, and the Monte Lepini. A path descends from here through woods to Nemi.

Castel Gandolfo

Castel Gandolfo, often called just 'Castello' is a lively little town built on the western lip of the Lake Albano crater. It is famous as the summer residence of the Pope. It occupies the site of the citadel of *Alba Longa*, founded, according to legend, by Ascanius, son of Aeneas. It was so called because it extended in a long line up the slopes of Mons Albanus. Head of the Latin League, Alba was the mother city of many of the Latin towns, and of Rome itself. Its war with Rome at the time of Tullus Hostilius, decided by the single combats of the three Roman Horatii and the three Latin Curiatii, the treachery of its dictator Mettius Fufetius, and its destruction around the middle of the 7C BC, are famous episodes in the legendary history of Rome. The town was never rebuilt though its temples were respected and were still standing in the days of Augustus. Domitian built a villa here, ruins of which are visible (see below). There is no trace of the ancient town, but to the west of Castel Gandolfo there is an extensive necropolis of the early Iron Age (9C–7C BC), discoveries from which are in the Museo Preistorico in Rome.

Castel Gandolfo derives its name from a castle of the Gandolfi, a Genoese family of the 12C. The castle passed to the Savelli and, in 1596, to the Camera Apostolica (a department of the Papal Curia). In 1604 it was declared an inalienable domain of the Holy See. After the papal palace was built (see below), it became the summer residence of the popes and it has been used as such ever since, except for the period from 1870 to 1929. Many distinguished people have lived at Castel Gandolfo, among them Goethe, Winckelmann, Angelica Kauffmann and Massimo d'Azeglio.

At the north entrance of the town extends the vast **Papal Palace** (not open to the public), built on the ruins of the castle and retaining some of its towers and walls. It was erected in 1624 by Carlo Maderno for Urban VIII and enlarged by Alexander VII, Clement XIII and Pius IX. The palace, with its gardens and the former Villa Barberini (see below), enjoys the privilege of extraterritoriality.

Since 1936 the palace has housed the **Vatican Observatory**, founded by Gregory XIII, and one of the most important in Europe. It specialises in the study of variable stars, and contains a laboratory of astrophysics.

A short alley to the right of the palace leads to a terrace with a fine view. In the piazza are an elegant fountain and the church of **San Tomaso da Villanova** (1661, with a good cupola), both by Bernini. Inside are a painting of *St Thomas of Villanova*, by Pietro da Cortona, and an *Assumption* by Maratta.

At the south end of the town is the **Villa Barberini** (now Vatican property; no admission). The splendid gardens were laid out in the 1930s by Emilio Bonomelli. This site was once occupied by the Villa of Domitian. Traces of nymphaea, cisterns and a small theatre, are still visible. The sculpture and architectural fragments found during excavations in 1841 and the 1930s are kept here in an Antiquarium (admission only with special permission, ☎ 9320001, Ville Pontificie). At the beginning of the road to Ercolano is the **Villa Torlonia** (no admission), with sculptures by Thorvaldsen and a fine park.

Below Castel Gandolfo, on the west shores of Lake Albano, are two nymphaea,

the so-called **Ninfeo Dorico**, dating from the 1C BC, and possibly part of the Villa of Claudius, and the **Ninfeo Bergantino**, which was part of the Villa of Domitian. Nearby is the **Emissarium**, or outlet of Lake Albano, which maintains the water of the lake at a constant level. It is a tunnel (similar to the outlet of Lake Nemi) cut through the solid rock, 1425m long, 1m wide and 1.5m high; it pierces the rim of the crater and emerges at Le Mole, to the southwest. This is a very early Roman work, traditionally dated before 396 BC and said to have been constructed after the oracle at Delphi had declared that Veio would not fall until the lake was drained.

Castel Gandolfo is connected to Albano Laziale by two scenic roads, built by order of Urban VIII. They are known as 'tunnels' (the 'Galleria di Sopra' and the 'Galleria di Sotto') as they are bordered with ilexes, the interlacing branches of which form arbours over the roads. The upper road has magnificent views of the lake and the Roman Campagna. The lower road passes on the right (near the junction with the Via Appia) a Republican **tower sepulchre**, once some 45m high. This is thought to have been the Tomb of Pompey.

Albano

Albano (378m; 24,400 inhabitants), officially Albano Laziale, is an important town of the Castelli. It rises in the form of a triangle from the Via Appia towards the top of the crater of Lake Albano; the crater cuts off the view of the lake from the town. Albano was badly damaged in the Second World War, when nearly two-thirds of its buildings were destroyed or damaged.

The name of Albano is derived from Alba Longa, but the town owes its origin to Septimius Severus, who established here (c AD 195) the *Castra Albana* for the 2nd Legion (Parthica), to protect (among other duties) the Via Appia. The camp occupied virtually the whole of what is now the town of Albano. Adjoining the camp was a small settlement which gradually developed and eventually overran the military area. Albano became a bishopric in 460; the see was held by Nicholas Breakspeare before he became the only English pope as Hadrian IV (1154–59). Devastated by the Barbarian invasions and in the struggles between the papacy and empire, the town passed in the 13C to the Savelli, whose castle survives to the west of the town. In 1697 it was acquired by the Camera Apostolica. The eccentric Earl of Bristol, bishop of Derry, died here in 1803.

The town centre is the spacious Piazza Mazzini, a widening of the Via Appia. Here is the **Villa Comunale**, a public park shaded by tall pines and occupying the site of a Roman villa formerly identified with a villa of Pompey, traces of which remain. There is a good view from the Belvedere, extending to Rome. From Piazza Mazzini, Via Cairoli leads to Piazza Sabatini, in which is the **Duomo** (San Pancrazio), built and rebuilt on a temple dating from the time of Constantine. The temple columns can be seen incorporated in the walls.

Corso Matteotti leads out of Piazza Mazzini, past the town hall in Palazzo Savelli. In the square opposite is the church of **San Pietro,** built in the 6C over the remains of the thermae of the Roman camp. The right flank of the church incorporates masonry blocks from the baths; the jambs of a door on the left side are made up of fragments of an ancient architrave. There is an attractive Romanesque campanile. In the spacious interior an acanthus cornice supports the modern altar rails.

Via Aurelio Saffi climbs to the upper part of the town. A turning to the left, Via

Don Minzoni, leads to the ruins of the **Porta Praetoria**, revealed by bombing in February 1944. This front gate of the camp of Castra Albana, opening from its short south side and facing the Via Appia, had three openings and was flanked by two towers. It was constructed of blocks of peperino. Its frontage was 36m and its height 13m. Only the east opening survived the bombing; of the main central entrance only the lower part is extant.

Via della Rotonda leads left out of Via Saffi to **Santa Maria della Rotonda** (for admission ask at the Museo Civico. Lire 4000), restored in 1937. This medieval circular domed church, once a nymphaeum belonging to the Villa of Domitian, has a Cosmatesque pulpit supported on a Roman capital. In the sacristy is a small Antiquarium with fragments of sarcophagi, inscriptions, brick stamps and a funerary stele of the 3C AD. Nearby are remains of the walls of the Roman camp. Continuing its ascent, Via Aurelio Saffi leads into the charming Piazza San Paolo, in which is the church of **San Paolo**, built in 1282 and remodelled in 1769. It stands at the apex of the triangle formed by the town. In the wall of the neighbouring seminary are incorporated further remains of the camp walls. At the top of the hill, beyond the cemetery, Lake Albano can be seen far below on the other side.

At 100 Via Aurelio Saffi is the entrance to the **Cisternone** (for admission ask at the Museo Civico. Lire 4000), a reservoir hewn out of rock for the use (probably) of the legionaries of the camp. It is a quadrangular underground construction 46m by 30m, reached by 31 steps and divided into five compartments, each furnished with rows of columns. The ceilings, 12m high, are perfectly preserved. The floor slopes gently towards the west corner, where there is an underground outlet. Near the civil hospital, off Via San Francesco, are a rectangular tower and remains of what was probably the *Porta Principalis Sinistra*, or east gate of the camp, now walled up.

Via San Francesco leads to the ruins of the **Amphitheatre** (closed for restoration; visible from the outside) between the church of San Paolo and the Capuchin Convent; it dates from the second half of the 3C and could accommodate 15,000 spectators. On the hill above is the Capuchin Convent (1619), surrounded by a turreted wall. On the hillside extends the **Bosco dei Cappuccini**, a public park with fine views. The parallel street to the southeast, in which are long tracts of wall, returns to the centre of the town.

The continuation of Corso Matteotti, Borgo Garibaldi, continues past the gardens of the Villa Comunale. To the left, at 3 Viale Risorgimento, is the entrance to the **Museo Civico Albano** (open 9–12.30; Wed & Thur also 16–19.30. Lire 4000; a ticket for this and two other sites costs Lire 10,000), arranged in 15 rooms and containing material from the palaeolithic era up to early Christian times.

To the west of the town is the **Castel Savelli**, a 13C stronghold, last restored in 1660.

Just outside Albano, on the right of the road to Ariccia, is a majestic tomb in the Etruscan style, known as the **Tomb of the Horatii and Curiatii**, perhaps modelled on the Tomb of Aruns, son of Porsenna. It has a base, 15m square, made of peperino blocks, surmounted by two (originally five) truncated cones. The tomb in fact dates from the late Republican era.

Between Albano and Ariccia is a road constructed during the pontificates of Gregory XVI (1831–46) and Pius IX (1846–78), with four viaducts over the

Valle Ariccia, one of the smaller craters of the Alban Hills. One of the viaducts, known as the **Ponte di Ariccia**, was built 59m above the valley floor by Ireneo Aleandri in 1847–54 (rebuilt in 1947), partly blown up by the Germans in 1944, and rebuilt in 1947.

Ariccia

Ariccia (412m; 10,700 inhab.) is in a charming position in wooded country, with numerous villas. It too suffered damage in 1943–44.

> The ancient Latin city of Ariccia, mentioned in the legends of the kings, took a leading part in the wars with Rome until the dissolution of the Latin League in 338 BC. With three other Latin towns it then lost its independence and received full Roman citizenship. In Cicero's time it was a flourishing municipium. It was the first stage in Horace's journey along the Via Appia to Brundusium. In the Middle Ages the town was owned by the counts of Tusculum and later passed to the Savelli; in 1661 it was sold to the Chigi. Henrik Ibsen, 'disillusioned with the theatre', settled at Ariccia with wife and child in 1864 and wrote *Brand* here. In the town in 1826 Massimo d'Azeglio, statesman and artist, entertained Joseph Severn, the artist and friend of Keats.

In Piazza della Repubblica, with two fountains, is **Palazzo Chigi,** in the form of a medieval castle with four towers, restored by Bernini and later enlarged. It has a delightful and extensive *park. Recently acquired by the Comune, it is partially open on request. On the right is the round church of **Santa Maria dell'Assunzione**, built by Bernini in 1664; it has a large dome and two campanili; inside is a fresco of the Assumption, by Borgognone. In the centre of the town are remains of a small Republican temple.

Outside the town, on the northeast edge of the Valle Ariccia, is the **Sanctuary of Santa Maria di Galloro** (429m) by Bernini, with a venerated painting of the Madonna.

The Lago di Nemi

The beautiful and unspoiled Lago di Nemi (316m) is another of the crater lakes in the Alban Hills. Almost circular in shape, it is 5.5km round, with a maximum depth of 34m. It is surrounded by hills with woods of ilex and manna-ash, and no ugly buildings. There is a well-known painting by Turner of the lake (c 1828–9; in London's Tate Gallery).

> This is the ancient Lacus Nemorensis, also called the 'Mirror of Diana'. The Temple of Diana Nemorensis, and a grove on the northeast side of the lake, became one of the most celebrated sanctuaries in central Italy. Only very scanty ruins survive on the hillside outside Nemi of the temple, first excavated in the 17C, and a theatre (some of the finds are in the Museo di Villa Giulia in Rome). Diana was worshipped here with savage rites: only a runaway slave who succeeded in breaking off a branch ('the golden bough') from a certain tree in the grove could become her priest, called Rex Nemorensis. He had to fight the reigning priest in single combat; if he killed him he became the next Rex Nemorensis. The new priest-king, in his turn,

was liable at any time to be challenged by a further aspirant. This sinister rule of succession to the priesthood of Diana was described by Sir James Frazer in *The Golden Bough*, first published in 1890. The first temple was probably built in the late 4C BC.

Nemi

The attractive and quiet little resort of Nemi lies in a picturesque position above the northeast side of the lake. The impressive **Palazzo Baroniale** belonged in the 9C to the counts of Tusculum, then to Cistercian monks, and in 1428 to the Colonna. It was subsequently owned by the Orsini, and the Ruspoli. A very narrow old cobbled road (signposted) for the lakeside passes under its entrance bridge.

On the lakeside is the **Museo delle Navi Romane** (open 9–14 except Mon; May–Sep 9–18). The vast double pavilion erected in 1936 is an interesting building of its period. From 1936 to 1944 it housed two ancient ships built by Caligula (AD 37–41) to convey visitors across the lake for the festival of Diana. The ships were sunk at the time of Claudius, and they were located at the bottom of the lake in 1446 by Leon Battista Alberti, but only when the lake was partly drained in 1927–32 were the huge ships salvaged. The smaller was 71m long and had a beam of 20m; the other was 73m by 24m. On 1 June 1944 they were burned in the museum by German soldiers. The huge building is now almost empty: it contains models of the ships, on a scale of one-fifth, and beneath the floor are stretches of Roman road which led to the Sanctuary of Diana. Fragments of small mosaics, bronze and iron nails, ceramics, anchors and other fittings from the boats are preserved here, but the splendid *bronzes which survived the fire are still in Rome. On the upper floor are diagrams, etc. illustrating how the boats were salvaged, and explanations of the Roman edifices excavated in the vicinity, including the Sanctuary of Diana.

The *emissarium* of the lake, comprising two superimposed tunnels 1650m long, is used when necessary to drain it.

Genzano

Genzano, officially Genzano di Roma, is built in terraces on the outer slope of the crater of Lake Nemi. The town grew up round a castle built in 1235 facing the lake, rebuilt in 1621 by Prince Giuliano Cesarini to face the Via Appia.

The town centre is Piazza Tommaso Frasconi, with a terrace on the right. On the left, beyond an interesting fountain, are three streets, Via Garibaldi, Via Bruno Buozzi and Via Italo Belardi, all going uphill fanwise from the square. The last-named street, scene of the *Infiorata* (flower festival), climbs past the Municipio to the church of Santa Maria della Cima. Via Bruno Buozzi leads to the modern Palazzo Cesarini, which overlooks the lake, 90m below. Via Garibaldi leads to Piazza Dante, where there is a road down to the lake (see above).

Three kilometres south of Genzano is the site of the ancient city of *Lanuvio*, famous for its sanctuary of Juno Sospita, parts of which are incorporated in the seminary and the Villa Sforza. The emperors Antoninus Pius and Commodus were born at Lanuvio.

Velletri

Velletri (37,900 inhabitants) is a busy town with a largely modern appearance on a spur of the Artemisio range. It was reconstructed after serious war damage.

Velletri is the Volscian *Velester*, subjugated by Rome in 338 BC and called *Velitrae*. It was the home of the gens Octavia, of which Augustus was a member. It was an independent commune from c 1000 to 1549, when it was absorbed in the States of the Church. From a window in the Palazzo Ginnetti, Charles of Bourbon escaped in August 1744 from the Irish General U.M. Brown's Austrian troops, later decisively defeating the Austrians in the same battle.

Via Vittorio Emanuele runs through the town from north to south following the contour of the hill from Piazza Garibaldi, site of the Porta Romana, to Porta Napoli. About one-third of the way along opens Piazza Cairoli, the town centre, almost completely rebuilt except for the **Torre del Trivio** (c 50m), a striking Romanesque campanile, dating from 1353, of alternate black-and-white courses, with single and double window-arches; it was cleverly restored after bomb damage.

To the right Via del Comune leads up to the piazza of the same name, the highest part of the town. Here is Palazzo di Giustizia (1835); in front are the little church of San Michele (1837) and the octagonal oratory of Santa Maria del Sangue, by Alessandro da Parma (1523–79). To the left is the 16C **Palazzo Comunale**, with porticoes by Giacomo della Porta (on a design by Vignola), reconstructed since 1945 almost from the foundations.

At the back is the entrance to the **Museo Civico Archeologico** (closed indefinitely), founded in 1893. Beyond the first room with inscriptions, the second room displays a *marble tomb relief with Old and New Testament scenes dating from the second decade of the 4C, one of the most important Christian carvings known of this period. Room III is filled with a splendid Roman *sarcophagus of Parian marble found in 1955 6km outside Velletri. Dating from AD 190–93, and complete with its lid, it is decorated all over with mythological scenes, including the Labours of Hercules. The last two rooms on this floor contain sarcophagi, funerary cippi, and a circular relief showing a Deposition scene. On the floor above are interesting terracotta panels delicately carved in bas-relief in the 6C BC (found in 1910 in Velletri).

Via Collicello leads down from the piazza to the 18C church of **San Martino**, with a Neo-classical façade. Over the second north altar is a detached fresco of the Madonna and Child of 1308. From Piazza Mazzini a road continues south to Piazza Umberto I. In a small square to the left is the entrance to the **Cathedral** (San Clemente), a 13C church built on the remains of a Roman basilica many times altered, rebuilt in 1660, and patched up after the war. The basilican **interior** has a rebuilt 13C apse and a restored ceiling, with a huge painting (1954) by Angelo Canevari. The organ dates from the 16C. The baldacchino over the 17C high altar is surmounted by a Cosmatesque tabernacle (difficult to see). The carved marble candelabrum is attributed to Jacopo Sansovino. On the lower walls of the apse are 14C frescoes. Beside the Renaissance sacristy doorway is a 15C fresco of the Madonna enthroned with four saints. In the second south chapel is a detached fresco of the Crucifixion with a donor.

The **Museo Capitolare**, with a particularly fine collection of works of art, is only partially open (ask for a permit to the Cathedral of San Clemente). It contains paintings of the Madonna by Gentile da Fabriano (restored) and Antoniazzo Romano; fragments of an *Exultet* (school of Montecassino; 12C); *Story of the Passion* (late 13C; French or English); jewelled 12C Byzantine reliquary *cross; and *ornaments from the chasuble of Benedict XI (1303–04).

30 · Tivoli and Hadrian's Villa

■ **Public transport from Rome**. Tivoli can now be reached by the underground line 'B' from the Colosseum or Termini railway station to its terminus at Rebibbia which is connected by a COTRAL bus service (every 20 minutes) to Tivoli (20km, in 45 minutes). There is also a bus (c every hour) from Rebibbia (along the Via Prenestina) which has a stop outside the entrance of Hadrian's Villa. There is a local bus service (No. 4) from Tivoli (with a stop outside the entrance to the Villa d'Este) to the entrance of Hadrian's Villa. By rail, there is a somewhat roundabout route (infrequent service) from Rome (Termini) to Tivoli via Guidonia, on the Rome–Pescara line (40km in 40mins–1 hr).

■ **By road from Rome**. Tivoli is reached by the Via Tiburtina, on the line of the old Roman road to *Tibur* (Tivoli). It passes Bagni di Tivoli and a branch road (right), at 'Bivio Villa Adriano', for Hadrian's Villa.

Tivoli

Tivoli, the classical *Tibur*, is now a busy noisy town (52,000 inhabitants), surrounded by ugly high-rise buildings. In the centre of the town are the famous gardens of the Villa d'Este, and below the hill, protected by a beautiful park, are the magnificent ruins of Hadrian's Villa. Tivoli was built in a delightful position on the lower slopes (230m) of the Sabine Hills at the end of the valley of the Aniene, the classical *Anio* which here narrows into a gorge and forms spectacular cascades. The river makes a wide loop round the town and borders it on three sides. It joins the Tiber north of Rome, near the Ponte Salario, and in Roman times its waters were carried to Rome by two aqueducts, the *Anio Vetus* (70km), begun in 273 BC, and the *Anio Novus* (95km) begun in AD 36.

■ **Information Office**, Azienda Autonoma, Largo Garibaldi, ☎ 0774 334522.

■ **Hotels** of all categories in Via di Villa Adriana (below the town, near Hadrian's Villa).

■ Numerous **restaurants** all over the town. Hadrian's Villa is a superb place to **picnic**.

■ **Transport** from Rome (see above). Railway station, Viale Mazzini (a few hundred metres from the Villa Gregoriana). Bus station in Piazza Garibaldi (local bus No. 4 from here, via the Villa d'Este, to the entrance of Hadrian's Villa).

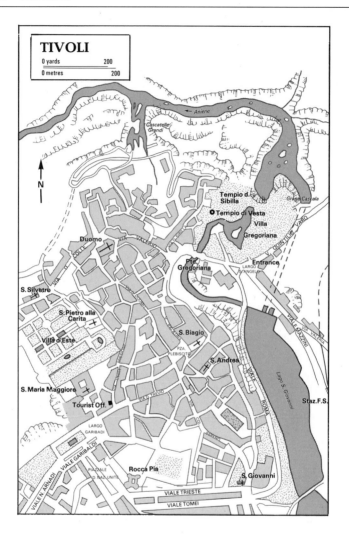

TIVOLI

0 yards   200

0 metres   200

History

Tibur is supposed to have been founded four centuries before the birth of Rome, by the Siculi, who were later expelled by Tiburtus and his brothers, grandsons of Amphiaraus. It was captured by Camillus in 380 BC. By the end of the 1C BC numerous wealthy Romans came to live here or pass the summer here: the area was noted for its abundance of water and its cool climate. Temples were erected to Vesta, Hercules and other deities. Marius, Cassius, Sallust, Maecenas and Quintilius Varus all had sumptuous villas in the town or nearby. Augustus and the poets Catullus, Propertius and Horace frequently visited the town. Trajan also favoured Tibur, but it reached its

greatest fame when Hadrian chose it as his residence and built his remarkable villa on the outskirts of the town. Tibur was sacred to the cult of the Sybil Albunea. Later it was used for the confinement of state prisoners.

In the 6C Totila, the Ostrogoth, sacked the town, but then rebuilt it as his capital. By the 10C it had recovered its prosperity, and withstood a siege by Otho III. It became independent as an Imperial free city, and was occupied by the Caraffa in the 16C. It did not lose its autonomous character until 1816. Among its natives were Munatius Plancus (consul 42 BC), the founder of Lyons, Pope Simplicius (468–83) and Pope John IX (898–900).

The road from Rome, Via Tiburtina, enters the town from the southwest as Via Nazionale and ends at Largo Garibaldi, a busy traffic hub. On the left is the Giardino Garibaldi, with a splendid *view of the open country below: almost due west is Rome, and to the southwest the Roman Campagna extends to the sea.

Viale Nazioni Uniti leads out of the right side of the square up past the bus station to the imposing **Rocca Pia** (no admission), a castle built by Pius II (1458–64) to dominate the inhabitants of Tivoli. It is rectangular in shape and has four crenellated cylindrical towers, two large and two smaller. The castle was built over the ruins of a Roman amphitheatre, best seen from Vicolo Barchetto to the north. Viale Trieste continues to Porta San Giovanni, now the entrance to a hospital. Here is the little church of San Giovanni Evangelista, containing good frescoes by Antoniazzo Romano.

From the other side of Largo Garibaldi (see above) Via Boselli leads to Piazza Trento outside the Romanesque church of **Santa Maria Maggiore**, with a fine rose-window attributed to Angelo da Tivoli above a later Gothic narthex (which contains a 13C fresco of the Madonna and Child, in a fine tabernacle). The **interior** contains remains of the original floor at the east end. In the presbytery are two triptychs, the one on the right dates from the 16C, and the one on the left is signed by Bartolomeo Bulgarini of Siena (14C). Above the latter, *Madonna and Child*, by Iacopo Torriti. Over the high altar is a Byzantine Madonna (12C?), in the right aisle, a crucifix attributed to Baccio da Montelupo.

The Villa d'Este

Adjoining the church, on the right, is the present entrance to the Villa d'Este (open 9 to dusk except Monday), celebrated for its remarkable gardens decorated with spectacular fountains. These were created by Pirro Ligorio for Cardinal Ippolito II d'Este (1509–72), a rich Renaissance prince and collector and patron of the arts, who was a friend of Ariosto, Tasso, Benvenuto Cellini, and the musician Pierluigi da Palestrina.

Originally a Benedictine convent, the property was confiscated as a residence for the governor of Tivoli. When Cardinal Ippolito II d'Este became governor in 1550 he commissioned Pirro Ligorio to transform the convent into a sumptuous villa. The district of the town below the convent was destroyed and the hillside was levelled to provide space for the gardens. An underground conduit was constructed from the Aniene, to increase the water supply. The use of water as the main theme of the gardens may have been inspired by Hadrian's Villa and the plan, based on a series of terraces,

is similar to that of the Temple of Fortune at Palestrina. The work had not been completed by the time of the Cardinal's death in 1572, and it was continued by his successor Cardinal Luigi d'Este who employed Flaminio Ponzio after 1585.

In the 17C numerous additions and restorations were carried out for Cardinal Alessandro d'Este, and (by Gian Lorenzo Bernini) for Cardinal Rinaldo d'Este. In the 19C the villa and gardens were neglected, and all the Roman statues were sold. It passed by bequest to Austria, but after 1918 the Italian Government resumed possession and undertook a general restoration. The top floor was the Italian home of Franz Liszt (1811–86) from 1865 to the year of his death; from this base he travelled to many parts of Europe and, while here, he composed the third book of his *Années de Pèlerinage*, in which one of the most popular pieces is *Les Jeux d'Eau à la Villa d'Este*. A fine Roman mosaic pavement was found beneath the villa in 1983. There is a café in the villa.

The entrance (formerly the back entrance) leads into a courtyard designed in 1567 on the site of the cloister of the convent. The Fountain Of Venus here incorporates a Roman statue. Off the courtyard is the Appartamento Vecchio (closed indefinitely), with frescoes by Livio Agresti.

A staircase descends to the **Appartamento Nobile** on the ground floor, a series of rooms off a long corridor, overlooking the gardens. The largest room is the **Salone** with the **Fontana di Tivoli**, a wall fountain in mosaic, begun by Curzio Maccarone and completed in 1568 by Paolo Calandrino. The frescoes are by the school of Gerolamo Muziano and Federico Zuccari. On the walls are views of the garden painted by Matteo Neroni in 1568. From the loggia stairs lead down to the gardens. The two rooms behind the fountain were decorated by Cesare Nebbia and assistants, and the rooms on the other side of the Salone have frescoes by Federico Zuccari and assistants. Beyond the Sala della Caccia, with 17C frescoes, a spiral staircase descends to the gardens (which can also be reached from the loggia off the Salone).

The main façade of the villa overlooking the gardens has an elegant **loggia** (1567) in the centre on two storeys, connected to the gardens by a double flight of steps. The **GARDENS** are laid out on terraces which descend from the villa and are connected by steps and paths. The original vegetation (which included many plane trees and elms) was altered when evergreen trees (ilexes, pines and cypresses) were introduced in the 17C, and sequoia and cedars were planted in the 19C. The terrace along the front of the palace is called the Passeggiata del Cardinale with a balcony on which is a pretty fountain basin. Beneath it is a loggia with a mosaic vault, and on a lower level the **Fontana del Bicchierone**, added in 1661 by Gian Lorenzo Bernini.

A path descends to a lower walk, at the far left end of which is the Grotto of Diana, with Mannerist decorations (in stucco, mosaic, coloured glass, and shells) by Lola and Paolo Calandrino. Steps descend from here to the elaborate **Fontana di Roma**, or **Rometta**, designed by Pirro Ligorio and executed by Curzio Maccarone. This has a model of the Tiber with an islet (representing the Isola Tiberina) in the form of a boat, on which is an obelisk. Behind are a seated statue of Rome, with the wolf suckling Romulus and Remus, and miniature reproductions of the principal buildings of ancient Rome.

From the Rometta the **Viale delle Cento Fontane** leads right across the garden, parallel to the villa. It is skirted by a long narrow basin lined with hundreds of jets of water, surmounted by a frieze of obelisks, models of boats, Estense eagles, and lilies of France, and below, overgrown with maidenhair fern and moss, are waterspouts in the form of animal heads. At the far end is the grandiose **Fontana di Tivoli** or *dell'Ovato*, by Pirro Ligorio, with the end of the conduit from the Aniene, one of the water supplies for the fountains, which descends in an abundant casade. In the hemicycle of the fountain are statues of nymphs, by Giovanni Battista della Porta. Above, in a laurel grove on the steep hillside, is the Fontana di Pegaso. On the right of the hemicycle is the Grotta di Venere and the rustic Fontana di Bacco (very ruined).

On a lower level, still against the perimeter wall of the gardens, is the monumental **Fontana dell'Organo**, built around a water-operated organ (1568) in the centre of the niche (later protected by a little temple). This was one of the most original and famous features of the garden. The mechanism of the organ was destroyed in the 18C; only the outer structure survives. This fountain faces another scenic terrace which runs parallel to the façade of the villa. Below the organ fountain is the **Fontana di Nettuno**, with high jets of water (reached by Viale del Drago and the first ramp on the right), created in 1927. In front extend the three Peschiere or fish ponds.

In the centre of the lowest terrace is the **Rotonda dei Cipressi**, surrounded by some of the mightiest cypresses in Italy (three of them survive from the 17C). New trees have replaced some that were struck by disease and had to be felled. At the end of the gardens (left) a box and laurel hedge leads to the **Fontana della Madre Natura**, with a statue of Diana of the Ephesians. From the Rotonda dei Cipressi a central path leads back up towards the villa across the terrace with the fish ponds and up to a terrace with the **Fontana del Drago** by Pirro Ligorio. This was probably intended as a homage to Gregory XIII (it reproduces the dragons in his coat of arms), who was a guest of the Cardinal in 1572.

The Viale del Drago leads right past the **Scala dei Bollori** an ingenious water staircase designed in 1567, to the bizarre **Fontana della Civetta,** which once used water power to produce birdsong interrupted by the screech of an owl. It was begun in 1565 by Giovanni del Duca, and finished by Raffaello Sangallo in 1569. Nearby is the Fontana di Proserpina (1570) used as an outside dining room. There is a splendid view of unspoilt countryside from this side of the gardens. Above are the Fontana di Roma and Grotta di Diana, described above.

The church of **San Pietro alla Carità**, outside the garden to the northeast, contains ten cipollino columns, probably from a Roman villa, and an interesting crypt (open Sun mornings; otherwise ring at the base of the campanile). From Largo Garibaldi, Via Pacifici and Via Trevio lead towards Piazza del Plebiscito (see the plan), the town centre. Here is the church of **San Biagio**, founded in the 14C. Rebuilt in 1887, it is a remarkable example of the neo-Gothic style, with three impressive stained-glass windows. On the second south altar is a good painting of San Vincenzo by an artist of the 15C Tuscan school. Behind the altar is a 15C detached fresco of the Crucifixion. Off the north side are interesting 15C fresco fragments of the Madonna enthroned and the Glory of St Thomas.

To the south, in Via Sant'Andrea, is the church of **Sant'Andrea**, with a

Romanesque campanile. From the square, Via Palatina and Via Ponte Gregoriano, with interesting medieval houses, lead to Piazza Rivarola, an important traffic centre. From here Via San Valerio leads left to the **Duomo** (San Lorenzo), rebuilt in 1650 but retaining a Romanesque campanile of the 12C. In the **interior**, the fourth chapel in the south aisle (light on right), contains a 13C *group of five carved wooden figures representing the Descent from the Cross. The third chapel in the north aisle contains the so-called 'Macchina del Salvatore', which encloses a precious 11C or 12C triptych, painted in tempera, with silver and gilt decoration of the 15C and 16C. It is shown only on high religious festivals (copy in the adjoining chapel). Also in this aisle are two episcopal tombs (late 15C and early 16C).

From Piazza Duomo, the medieval Via del Duomo (partly stepped) leads past (No. 78) the entrance to the *Ponderarium*, containing two tables with measures of capacity, used by Roman inspectors of weights and measures. In Piazza Tani, outside the side entrance to the Cathedral, is a pretty fountain made up from a medieval sarcophagus. From here the narrow Via del Colle (impracticable for cars) descends steeply past medieval houses and remains of ancient buildings through one of the most picturesque parts of the town. It passes the Romanesque church of **San Silvestro** (if closed ring to the right of façade at No. 2), recently restored. Inside are interesting 12C or 13C frescoes and a wooden figure of St Valerian of 1138 (right wall).

At the end of the street, outside Porta del Colle, is the **Sanctuary of Hercules Victor**, in a large area until recently occupied by a paper mill. It is now being excavated and studied and there are long-term plans to open it to the public. This huge Hellenistic sanctuary was mentioned by numerous classical authors as being the most important in the city. There was an oracle here similar to the one in Palestrina. The buildings are thought to date from the end of the 2C BC. The most conspicuous remains are the Cyclopean substructures to the northwest where the hill descends to the Aniene valley. Above the mighty foundations are arches and vaults which supported a huge piazzale, with a portico on three sides, a temple, and a theatre. A market was connected to the sanctuary.

From Piazza Rivarola (see above), Via della Sibilla leads northeast to the edge of the cliff which dominates the valley, the site of the Roman acropolis. Here is the so-called **Temple of Vesta**, a circular Roman temple famous for its picturesque position. It is not known to whom the temple was actually dedicated; it is circular peripteral and dates from the last years of the Republic. It was converted in the Middle Ages into the church of Santa Maria della Rotonda. Ten of its 18 fluted Corinthian columns survive, and there is a frieze of bucrania, garlands, rosettes and paterae. The doors and windows of the well-preserved cella are trapezoidal. Close by is an earlier temple, known as the **Temple of the Sibyl**, also of uncertain attribution. It is rectangular with a tetrastyle Ionic façade. Until 1884 it was the church of San Giorgio.

From Piazza Rivarola, Ponte Gregoriano leads over the Aniene to an open space by the Porta Sant'Angelo, a busy traffic centre. Here is the entrance to the **VILLA GREGORIANA**, a park on a very steep hillside with the cascades of the river Aniene (admission daily 9–dusk). The park commemorates Gregory XVI, who took decisive steps to put an end to the periodic local floods, which in 1826 had seriously damaged the town. On his accession to the papacy in 1831, he instructed the engineer Folchi to build a double tunnel under Monte Catillo, to

ease the flow of the river. From this tunnel (300m and 270m), known as the Traforo Gregoriano, the water plunges down in another waterfall, known as the Great Cascade. The park is not very well maintained, and the climb down to the floor of the valley is extremely strenuous.

From the ticket office a path bears a little right, following the signpost ('Grande Cascata') to a terrace, with a view through an arch of the temples of Vesta and of the Sibyl across the valley. The path continues along the side of the hill to a parapet overlooking the crest of the **Great Cascade**. Steps lead down to another terrace from which you can see the mouth of the tunnel. Here the Aniene makes a leap of 108m as it emerges from the Traforo Gregoriano. The tunnel (no admission) bears inscriptions recording the visits of popes and kings. From the first terrace, a path marked 'Ruderi della Villa-Grotte della Sirena, di Nettuno, e Cascata Bernini' descends to another terrace planted with ilexes, at the end of which is a tunnel which passes through impressive remains of a Roman villa.

At the exit a path continues to descend with a good view of the **Little Cascades** and of the **Bernini Cascade**. Further down, a little square is reached marked with two signposts, to the right of which there is a viewpoint about half the height of the Great Cascade, which gives you an idea of its volume, its noise and the rainbow colours of its spray. From the little square a path follows the signpost marked 'Grotte Nettuno e Sirena, Cascata Bernini', descending for some distance and bearing sharp left at a signpost marked 'Ingresso Grotta della Sirena' to reach the fantastic **Grotto of the Siren**, a limestone cavern in which the water tumbles down a narrow ravine. A path climbs the other side of the valley. From a fork marked 'Grotta di Nettuno e Tempio di Vesta', a path turns left, passing through two tunnels lit from the side. At another fork a path descends (left) to the **Grotto of Neptune**, through which the Aniene originally flowed, and another one on the right leads to an exit gate (closed Monday) through a restaurant beside the Temple of Vesta.

From Porta Sant'Angelo, Viale Mazzini leads south to the station. Here, in a park, the tomb of the Vestal Virgin Cossinia has been set up. Also from Porta Sant'Angelo, Via Quintilio Varo leads to VIA DELLA CASCATELLE (3km long) which winds above olive plantations, and passes several times beneath the viaducts of the Rome–Tivoli railway. From the **belvedere** there is a fine view of the Great Cascade, and, after crossing beneath the railway for the last time, there is an excellent *view of the Great Cascade, the Cascatelle, the town of Tivoli, and the Campagna. The road passes the church of Sant'Antonio (left) and the ruined arches of the **Acqua Marcia**. This aqueduct, 58km long and dating from 144 BC, ran from Via Valeria to Rome. Five hundred metres further on, a byroad (left; unsignposted) diverges from the main road and leads down past a group of houses to the conspicuous **Santuario di Santa Maria di Quintiliolo**, near the ruins of a Roman villa, said to have been that of Quintilius Varus.

The road soon deteriorates and becomes less interesting. Further on it crosses the Ponte dell'Acquoria over the Aniene, and, going straight on, begins to climb the *Clivus Tiburtinus*, partly levelled by Constantine. On the right, is the so-called **Tempio del Mondo**, with a large interior chamber and further on, also on the right, is a Roman building known as the **Tempio della Tosse**. Probably dating from the 4C, this is an octagonal building with a circular exterior. Traces of

Byzantine decoration suggest it may have been adapted for Christian worship. The road passes round the ruins of the Temple of Hercules Victor (see above), and re-enters Tivoli by Porta del Colle.

Hadrian's Villa

About 5km below the town of Tivoli, beyond a beautiful olive grove on the hillside, and reached off the Via Tiburtina, the main road to Rome, is Hadrian's Villa, the largest and richest Imperial villa in the Roman Empire. Hadrian became emperor on the death of Trajan in 117, and began the villa the following year, completing it ten years later. It is known that Hadrian prided himself on his abilities as an architect, and it is therefore presumed that the remarkably original buildings, many of them inspired by famous buildings in Greece and Egypt, were directly designed by him. They were spaciously laid out between numerous gardens. It seems to have been used as a residence for the Emperor and his court, particularly in the summer months. Of all the splendid buildings left which were erected by Hadrian throughout the Empire this is probably the most interesting. It is now one of the most evocative classical sites to survive in Italy, protected by a beautiful park.

■ **Open** every day from 9 to dusk. The road for the Villa leaves the Via Tiburtina (the main road from Rome to Tivoli) at the *Bivio Villa Adriana*, 28km from Rome, and 4km from Tivoli. From the turn an ugly byroad (1.5km) continues to the entrance. For transport from Rome and from Tivoli, see p 397. The Villa is a splendid place to picnic, and there is a café near the entrance.

History

It is difficult to understand why Hadrian, with all the resources of the Empire at his disposal, should have chosen such an unprepossessing site for his magnificent estate. Though little over 5km from the scenic Roman health resort of Tivoli, the low-lying surroundings of the villa have no particular attraction. In the emperor's day the flat plain was not even healthy. One reason for the choice of this site is probably the fact that its owner was the Empress Sabina; another reason may have been the emperor's desire to keep himself apart from his courtiers, many of whom owned villas on the hills around Tivoli. Parts of a smaller country house of the 1C BC, overlooking the 'Vale of Tempe', were incorporated into the emperor's villa.

Many of the buildings of the villa are derived from famous classical monuments, some of which Hadrian saw during his prolonged travels in the Empire. These were the Lyceum, the Academy, the Prytaneum and the Stoa Poikile in Athens; the Canopus of the Egyptian Delta; and the Vale of Tempe in Thessaly. He also included a representation of Hades, as conceived by the Greek poets. An extensive system of underground passages (no admission), some mere corridors and others wide enough for a horse and carriage, exist beneath the villa; these were presumably service areas. Hadrian's successors enlarged the villa, but Constantine is supposed to have stolen some elements to decorate Byzantium. Barbarian invaders plundered the site, and it later became a quarry for builders and lime-burners. Until the Renaissance the ruins continued to be neglected or abused.

The first excavations were ordered by Alexander VI and Cardinal Alessandro Farnese. Soon after he took up residence at the Villa d'Este in 1550, Cardinal Ippolito II d'Este employed Pirro Ligorio to continue excavations, but he took many of the finds to decorate his villa. Further excavations were carried out in the 17C–19C. Giovanni Battista Piranesi drew a plan of the site, and made engravings of the buildings and sculptures (now in the Calcografia Nazionale in Rome). In 1730 Count Fede planted cypresses and pines among the ruins. In 1870 the Italian Government acquired most of the site, and systematic excavations were begun (still far from complete). The works of art discovered in the villa (more than 260) are scattered in museums all over Europe, as well as in Rome (the Museo Nazionale Romano, the Capitoline Museum, and the Vatican Museums).

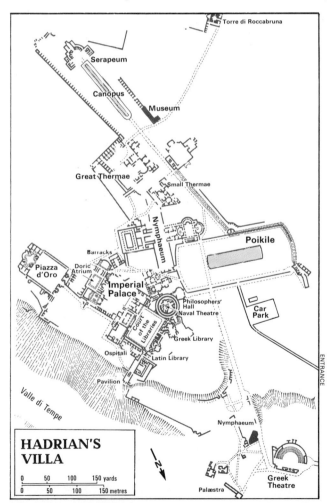

The general plan of the villa, which covers some 120 hectares, is capricious, although the buildings are grouped round four principal structures: the Poikile, the Canopus, the Academy, and the Imperial Palace. Excavations and restorations are in progress on the hillside overlooking the Canopus. Recent studies and excavations suggest that the traditional interpretation of many of the buildings is probably wrong (see the description below), and some of them were used for different purposes than those formerly ascribed to them. Numerous areas between the buildings were reserved for gardens and open courtyards. All the ruins are labelled with explanatory diagrams (also in English). It is not easy to understand the connection between all the buildings since the order of the visit does not begin at the main entrance to the villa (only recently identified). A whole day is needed for a detailed visit to the vast site.

From the **ticket entrance** (with a car park), a short drive leads on to a second car park. There is a café here, and a building which houses a model of the villa. On the far right (not well signposted) an 18C villa is used as a **museum** with an excellent didactic display on three floors, providing a useful introduction to the ruins. On the ground floor are models of various parts of the villa. The first floor illustrates its architecture, with fragments of friezes, capitals, and a Roman marble model of a stadium. The building techniques are illustrated, and the various brick stamps shown. The finds from the villa now in museums are recorded by photographs. On the second floor are engravings of the site (including copies of Piranesi's works) and examples of the various marbles used in the buildings. Fragments of floors, mosaics and painted plaster are displayed.

The **entrance to the ruins** is now through the massive north wall of the **Pecile**, which seems to have been inspired by the *Stoa Poikile* (painted porch) in Athens, famous for its paintings by Polygnotos and Panainos, and for its association with the Stoic philosophers. Hadrian's version is a rectangular peristyle (232m x 97m) with the ends slightly curved, similar to a Greek gymnasium. The huge north wall (9m high), running almost due east and west, still exists. On the south side the wall is no longer standing, but there are remains of a pavilion with three exedrae and a fountain. This was probably a monumental atrium. On both sides of the Pecile ran roofed colonnades; here the sun or shade could be enjoyed at any hour of the day, and either warmth or coolness, depending on the season. In the middle of the rectangle the fish pond has been restored. The free area round it was probably used for exercise. On the southwest the Pecile had as a substructure a wall with three rows of small chambers, now called the Cento Camerelle, which are thought to have been used as accommodation for the Praetorians.

At the northeast angle of the Pecile, a few steps lead up to the so-called **Sala dei Filosofi** (17m x 9m), with an apse, seven niches and four side-doors. This is now thought to have been a large throne room, or *Auditorium*, where the emperor held audiences, and met in council with court dignitaries. It was probably part of the complex which includes the Pecile and the so-called 'Terme con Eliocamino'. Beyond is a charming circular building, with an Ionic marble peristyle, known as the **Teatro Marittimo, almost certainly a private retreat for the emperor, where he could be totally isolated. A circular moat (3.5m broad), lined with Luni (Carrara) marble, encloses an island on which stand an atrium with fluted Ionic columns in an intricate design, and a series of living-rooms,

and baths. It could be reached only by two small wooden (removable) bridges. A reconstruction of one part of the building is displayed on the south side.

On the east side, stairs lead up to the first nucleus of buildings belonging to the **IMPERIAL PALACE**, which is disposed parallel to the Vale of Tempe (see below); its elements are grouped round four peristyles. The so-called **Cortile delle Biblioteche** is now a secluded olive plantation. The 'Greek and Latin Libraries' on the northwest side have recently been identified as the monumental **entrance to the villa**, with towers, on three floors. The third floor had a heating system and may have been used by the emperor before the villa had been completed. Behind, excavations have revealed part of a delightful garden.

To the north of the Cortile delle Biblioteche are the **ospitali**, rooms used by the high-ranking staff of the villa who were particularly close to the emperor. Here are ten well-preserved small rooms leading off either side of a wide corridor. Rectangular alcoves indicate space for the beds (three in each room). Lighting was provided by the high openings. The rooms are decorated with well-preserved mosaics. Steps lead down to a **triclinium**, a dining room with (left) some capitals with a lotus motif, and a mosaic floor. To the right is a long corridor with oblique openings in the vault, to allow the light of midday to enter. This leads to the **Padiglione** (Pavilion) which overlooks a valley with a stream which is thought to have been landscaped by Hadrian to recreate the **Vale of Tempe** in Thessaly, famed for its beauty. The stream, now called the Pussiano, represented the ancient Peneios.

From here steps lead up to a path (south) which leads to the **Great Peristyle** of the palace, with a private library and other small rooms overlooking the Cortile delle Biblioteche. Here also is the **Room of Three Naves**, a delightfully proportioned room with two rows of small columns. Nearby, stairs lead underground to a cryptoporticus, with well-lit corridors. At the other end of this nucleus of the palace is the **Room of the Doric Pilasters**, with a fine entablature, which connected the east and west parts of the villa. The so-called **Caserma dei Vigili**, beyond the apse of the basilican hall (right), was more probably a storehouse near the kitchens. Beyond it is a **quadriporticus**, with a pool and a portico of fluted composite columns. Formerly known as the 'Palazzo d'Inverno', this is now considered to be at the centre of the most important part of the Imperial palace and the residence of Hadrian. The upper floors were supplied with heating systems. Beneath it is a well-preserved extensive cryptoporticus. Beyond it, on a lower level, is the large nymphaeum, described below.

On the left is another nymphaeum, which had two round fountain basins, and from here a path leads to the **Piazza d'Oro**, a rectangular area at the southeast end of the palace. It was so named because excavations here yielded such rich finds. It is entered through the fine octagonal **vestibule**. The peristyle was formed of alternate columns of cipollino and granite in two rows. On the far side (southeast) is an intricate series of exedrae and nymphaea; the central one seems to have been a summer **triclinium**. This was an open courtyard with a remarkable Greek-cross plan, with alternate convex and concave sides. The plan of the portico recalls Greek gymnasiums. It was formerly thought that this was used for banquets, but a recent interpretation is that it was in fact a stoa with libraries, similar to that which Hadrian had built in Athens in this period.

A path continues west past the back of the Caserma dei Vigili and of the main

nucleus of the palace, and descends to a clump of mighty cypresses and the **Small Thermae** and the **Great Thermae**. The small baths are well preserved, with a large rectangular hall, perhaps the frigidarium, and an octagonal hall with a domed vault. They were particularly elegant and refined and may have been reserved for the use of the emperor alone. The large baths, on a simpler design, were probably used by court dignitaries, visitors, etc. They include a circular hall, with cupola and skylight. The huge **Sala Absidata** had an apse and a superb cross-vault, now mostly collapsed. Opposite is another cross-vaulted room (closed; but well seen from the southeast) decorated with exquisite stucco reliefs. On the east is a swimming-pool, bounded on the northwest by a cryptoporticus with, on its ruined walls, numerous graffiti of the 16C and 17C. This gives access to the so-called **Praetorium**, a tall edifice which was divided into three storeys by wooden floors. It may have been used as a warehouse, or as a service wing.

Beyond a row of six huge ilexes is the celebrated **CANOPUS**, designed to imitate the famous sanctuary of Serapis, that stood at the 15th milestone from Alexandria. Hadrian dug a hollow (185m by 75m), in which he constructed a basin, bordered on the east by a block of 20 rooms and a portico, and on the west by a heavy buttressed wall (238m long), against which were more rooms (some of them now used for the Museum; see below).

Around the curved north end of the canal, reproductions of statues found on the site have been set up between marble columns surmounted by an epistyle arched over alternate pillars. Along the west side are reproductions of colossal caryatids and telamons (the originals were found in the basin in the 1950s). At the south end is the so-called **Serapeum**, a monumental triclinium, in the form of a temple of Isis, with a half-

The Canopus at Hadrian's Villa

dome formerly covered with mosaics, above a semicircular banqueting table (reconstructed) from which the diners had a scenic view of the canopus. Some scholars think this may have been intended as a symbolic representation of the Nile: a series of fountains represent its source (in the niche behind), the cataracts, and its delta (in the piscina in front). The basin would then have represented the Mediterranean, with Athens to the west (represented by the caryatids), and Ephesus to the east (represented by statues of Amazons). The canopus may have been built by Hadrian in honour of his lover Antinoos, who was represented as an Egyptian divinity in numerous statues found here. Most of the Egyptian sculptures now in the Capitoline and Vatican museums come from here (those in the Museo Gregoriano Egiziano have recently been rearranged, according to the above interpretation).

There is a fine view of most of the villa from the hill behind. On the northwest

side of the hollow is the **Museum**, housing finds from excavations since 1950. The statues include: a bust of Caracalla; Venus, copy of a work by Praxiteles; Wounded Amazons, one a mutilated copy of a Polykleitan original, the other a fine replica of the famous original by Pheidias; portrait of Verres; Athena and Mars, both from mid-5C originals; two athletes; a crocodile; tondo with the bas-relief of a satyr; four marble caryatids, copies of the 5C originals on the Erechtheion at Athens; and two sileni.

A path leads from here west to the **Torre di Roccabruna**, a belvedere or pharos, which has square outer walls and is circular inside. This is possibly an imitation of the Tower of Timon of Athens, which stood near the Academy. It stands in the Oliveto Roccabruna, which is famous for the size of its olive trees, one of them (the 'Albero Bello') claimed to be the largest in the Tivoli district.

To the southeast, in another olive grove, is the so-called **Accademia**, a complex of buildings which some scholars identify as a secondary palace. The group includes a round hall, known as the **Temple of Apollo**, a peristyle, and the remains of three rooms with delicate stucco ornamentation. About 300m southeast are the remains of an **Odeion**, or **theatre** (45m in diameter), with the Imperial box in the centre of the cavea. To the east of the Odeion a path descends to a hollow (150m long), hewn in the tufa and overshadowed by thick vegetation, which leads to a semicircular vestibule (once perhaps guarded by an image of Cerberus). This was the entrance to **Hades** or the **Inferi**, represented by a quadrangle of four subterranean corridors, 5.5m wide and 91m in total length, with 79 apertures for light. Smaller tunnels connected Hades with various parts of the Villa.

A broad main path returns towards the entrance. To the right, just before the Poikile, is the large **Nymphaeum**, formerly called the 'Stadio' from its elongated form. It was a decorative garden surrounded by porticoes, with three exedrae. Between it and the 'Teatro Marittimo' are remains of the first **baths** constructed in the Villa, formerly known as the 'Terme Con Heliocaminus', which had a large circular room with a heating system used for 'Turkish baths'. On the other side of the Nymphaeum, reached by steps which lead up past a well-preserved cryptoporticus, is the main part of the Imperial palace (see above). A path leads back across the Poikile to the entrance.

From here a fine avenue of cypresses leads north to the Greek Theatre, passing the Casino Fede (now the excavation office), built on part of the ruins of the so-called 'Nymphaeum', a semicircular portico. This frames a small **Temple of Venus**, a goddess particularly venerated by Hadrian. The temple was modelled on the Temple at Cnidos; a statue of Aphrodite of Cnidos discovered here, a copy of the famous statue by Praxiteles, has been replaced by a cast (original in the Museum, see above). Beyond, to the right, a walk leads to the modernised Fontana di Palazzo, near which are a few traces of the **Palaestra**. Beyond this extends the 'Vale of Tempe' (see above). Descending (left) through olives and cypresses, the path passes the **Greek Theatre**, c 36m in diameter; its cavea, or auditorium, is carved out of the hillside.

A few kilometres west of Hadrian's Villa, on Via Tiburtina, is **Bagni di Tivoli**, a spa (hotels of all categories) which uses the water from two nearby lakes. These are fed by hot springs (24°C), the Roman Aquae Albulae, charged with sulphuretted hydrogen which gives a strong smell to the locality. There are

remains of the Roman baths. Nearby are travertine quarries which provided stone for the Colosseum, St Peter's, and many other buildings in ancient and modern Rome. The stone is the lapis tiburtinus, which hardens after cutting. The five-arched **Ponte Lucano**, a Roman bridge over the Aniene, was named after Lucanus Plautius and rebuilt at various times from the 15C to the 19C. Next to the bridge is the tower-like **Tomb of the Plautii**, dating from AD 10–14, and resembling the Tomb of Cecilia Metella on the Via Appia. Aulus Plautius commanded the army which invaded Britain in AD 43.

Glossary

Aedicule, small opening framed by two columns and a pediment originally used in classical architecture

Ambo (pl. ambones), pulpit in a Christian basilica; two pulpits on opposite sides of a church from which the gospel and epistle were read

Amphora, antique vase, usually of large dimensions, for oil and other liquids

Antefix, ornament placed at the lower corners of the tiled roof of a temple to conceal the space between the tiles and the cornice

Antiphonal, choir-book containing a collection of antiphonae—verses sung in response by two choirs

Antis, in antis describes the portico of a temple when the side-walls are prolonged to end in a pilaster flush with the columns of the portico

Apodyterium, dressing-room in a Roman bath

Arca, wooden chest with a lid, for sacred or secular use. Also, monumental sarcophagus in stone, used by Christians and pagans

Architrave, the lowest part of an entablature, the horizontal frame above a door

Archivolt, moulded architrave carried round an arch

Atlantes (or Telamones), male figures used as supporting columns

Atrium, forecourt, usually of a Byzantine church or a classical Roman house

Attic, topmost storey of a classical building, hiding the spring of the roof

Badia, abbazia; abbey

Baldacchino, canopy supported by columns, usually over an altar

Basilica, originally a Roman hall used for public administration; in Christian architecture, an aisled church with a clerestory and apse, and no transepts

Borgo, a suburb; a street leading away from the centre of a town

Bottega, the studio of an artist: the pupils who worked under his direction

Bozzetto, sketch, often used to describe a small model for a piece of sculpture

Bucchero, Etruscan black terracotta ware

Bucrania, a form of classical decoration—heads of oxen garlanded with flowers

Caldarium or **Calidarium**, room for hot or vapour baths in a Roman bath

Campanile, bell-tower, often detached from the building to which it belongs

Camposanto, cemetery

Canephora, figure bearing a basket, often used as a caryatid

Canopic vase, Egyptian or Etruscan vase enclosing the entrails of the dead

Carceres, openings in the barriers through which the competing chariots entered the circus

Cardo, the main street of a Roman town, at right angles to the Decumanus

Cartoon, from cartone, meaning large sheet of paper. A full-size preparatory drawing for a painting or fresco

Caryatid, female figure used as a supporting column

Cavea, the part of a theatre or amphitheatre occupied by the row of seats

Cella, sanctuary of a temple, usually in the centre of the building

Chiaroscuro, distribution of light and shade, apart from colour in a painting

Ciborium, casket or tabernacle containing the Host

Cipollino, a greyish marble with streaks of white or green

Cippus, sepulchral monument in the form of an altar

Cista, casket, usually of bronze and cylindrical in shape, to hold jewels, toilet articles, etc., and decorated with mythological subjects

Columbarium, a building (usually subterranean) with niches to hold urns containing the ashes of the dead

Confessio, crypt beneath the high altar and raised choir of a church, usually containing the relics of a saint

Corbel, a projecting block, usually of stone

Cryptoporticus, vaulted subterranean corridor

Cuneus, wedge-shaped block of seats in an antique theatre

Cyclopean, the term applied to walls of unmortared masonry, older than the Etruscan civilisation, and attributed by the ancients to the giant Cyclopes

Decumanus, the main street of a Roman town running parallel to its longer axis

Diaconia, early Christian welfare centre

Dipteral, temple surrounded by a double peristyle

Diptych, painting or ivory tablet in two sections

Exedra, semicircular recess

Ex-voto, tablet or small painting expressing gratitude to a saint

Forum, open space in a town serving as a market or meeting-place

Fresco, (in Italian, affresco), painting executed on wet plaster. On the wall beneath is sketched the sinopia, and the cartone is transferred onto the fresh plaster (intonaco) before the fresco is begun either by pricking the outline with small holes over which a powder is dusted, or by means of a stylus which leaves an incised line on the wet plaster. In recent years many frescoes have been detached from the walls on which they were executed

Frigidarium, room for cold baths in a Roman bath

Giallo antico, red-veined yellow marble from Numidia

Gonfalone, banner of a medieval guild or commune

Graffiti, design on a wall made with an iron tool on a prepared surface, the design showing in white. Also used loosely to describe scratched designs or words on walls

Greek cross, cross with the arms of equal length

Grisaille, painting in various tones of grey

Grotesque, painting or stucco decoration in the style of the ancient Romans (found during the Renaissance in the Domus Aurea in Rome, then underground, hence the name, from 'grotto'). The delicate ornamental decoration usually includes patterns of flowers, sphinxes, birds, human figures, etc. against a light ground

Herm (pl. hermae), quadrangular pillar decreasing in girth towards the ground, surmounted by a bust

Hexastyle, temple with a portico of six columns at the end

Hypogeum, subterranean excavation for the interment of the dead (usually Etruscan)

Impasto, early Etruscan ware made of inferior clay

Insula (pl. insulae), tenement house

Intarsia (or Tarsia), inlay of wood, marble or metal

Krater, antique mixing-bowl, conical in shape with rounded base

Kylix, wide shallow vase with two handles and short stem

Laconicum, room for vapour baths in a Roman bath

Latin cross, cross with a long vertical arm

Loggia, covered gallery or balcony, usually preceding a larger building

Lunette, semicircular space in a vault or ceiling often decorated with a painting or relief

Matroneum, gallery reserved for women in early Christian churches

Metope, panel between two triglyphs on the frieze of a Doric temple

Mithraeum, temple of the god Mithras

Monolith, single stone (usually a column)

Narthex, vestibule of a Christian basilica

Naumachia, mock naval combat for which the arena of an amphitheatre was flooded

Niello, black substance used in an engraved design

Nimbus, luminous ring surrounding the heads of saints in paintings; a square nimbus denoted that the person was living at that time

Nymphaeum, a sort of summer-house in the gardens of baths, palaces, etc., originally a temple of the Nymphs, and decorated with statues of those goddesses

Octastyle, a portico with eight columns

Oinochoe, wine-jug usually of elongated shape for dipping wine out of a krater

Opus Alexandrinum, mosaic design of black and red geometric figures on a white ground

Opus incertum, masonry of small irregular stones set in mortar (a type of concrete)

Opus quadratum, masonry of large rectangular blocks without mortar; in Opus Etruscum the blocks are placed alternately lengthwise and endwise

Opus reticulatum, masonry arranged in squares or diamonds so that the mortar joints make a network pattern

Opus sectile, mosaic or paving of thin slabs of coloured marble cut in geometrical shapes

Opus spicatum, masonry or paving of small bricks arranged in a herring-bone pattern

Opus tessellatum, mosaic formed entirely of square tesserae

Opus vermiculatum, mosaic with tesserae arranged in lines following the design contours

Palazzo, any dignified and important building

Palombino, fine-grained white marble

Pavonazzetto, yellow marble blotched with blue

Pax, sacred object used by a priest for the blessing of peace, and offered for the kiss of the faithful, usually circular, engraved, enamelled or painted in a rich gold or silver frame

Pendentive, concave spandrel beneath a dome

Peperino, earthy granulated tufa, much used in Rome

Peripteral, temple surrounded by a colonnade

Peristyle, court or garden surrounded by a columned portico

Pietà, group of the Virgin mourning the dead Christ

Piscina, Roman tank; a basin for an officiating priest to wash his hands before mass

Pluteus, (pl. plutei), marble panel, usually decorated; a series of them used to form a parapet to precede the altar of a church

Podium, a continuous base or plinth supporting columns, and the lowest row of seats in the cavea of a theatre or amphitheatre

Polyptych, painting or tablet in more than three sections

Pozzolana, reddish volcanic earth (mostly from Pozzuoli, near Naples) largely used for cement

Predella, small painting or panel, usually in sections, attached below a large altar-piece

Presepio, literally, crib or manger. A group of statuary of which the central subject is the Infant Jesus in the manger

Pronaos, porch in front of the cella of a temple

Propulaea, columned vestibule approaching a temple

Prostyle, temple with columns on the front only

Pulvin, cushion stone between the capital and the impost block

Pulvinar, Imperial couch and balcony on the podium of a theatre

Pulvinated, convex in profile; a term usually applied to a freize

Putto, (pl. putti) figure sculpted or painted usually nude, of a child

Rosso antico, red marble from the Peloponnese

Rhyton, drinking-horn usually ending in an animal's head

Schola Cantorum, enclosure for the choristers in the nave of an early Christian church, adjoining the sanctuary

Sinopia, large sketch for a fresco made on the rough wall in a red earth pigment called *sinopia* (because it originally came from Sinope, a town on the Black Sea). When a fresco is detached for restoration, it is possible to see the sinopia beneath, which can also be separated from the wall

Situla, water-bucket

Solomonic column, barley-sugar or twisted column, so called from its supposed use in the Temple of Solomon

Spandrel, surface between two arches in an arcade or the triangular space on either side of an arch

Spina, low stone wall connecting the turning-posts (metoe) at either end of a circus

Stamnos, big-bellied vase with two small handles at the sides, closed by a lid

Stele, upright stone bearing a monumental inscription

Stereobate, basement of a temple or other building

Stoa, a porch or portico not attached to a larger building

Strigil, bronze scraper used by the Romans to remove the oil with which they had anointed themselves

Stylobate, basement of a columned temple or other building

Telamones, see Atlantes

Temenos, a sacred enclosure

Tepidarium, room for warm baths in a Roman bath

Tessera, a small cube of marble, glass, etc., used in mosaic work

Tetrastyle, having four columns at the end

Thermae, originally simply baths, later elaborate buildings fitted with libraries, assembly rooms, gymnasia, circuses, etc.

Tholos, a circular building (Greek)

Tondo, round painting or bas-relief

Transenna, open grille or screen, usually of marble, in an early Christian church

Travertine, tufa quarried near Tivoli; the commonest of Roman building materials

Triclinium, dining-room and reception-room of a Roman house

Triglyph, small panel of a Doric frieze raised slightly and carved with three vertical channels

Triptych, painting or tablet in three sections

Trompe l'oeil, literally a deception of the eye. Used to describe illusionist decoration, painted architectural perspectives, etc.

Tropaeium, (or Trophy), victory monument

Tumulus, a burial mound

Velarium, canvas sheet supported by masts to protect the spectators in an open theatre from the sun

Verde antico, green marble from Tessaglia

Zoöphorus, frieze of a Doric temple, so-called because the metopes were often decorated with figures of animals

List of Popes

Various points in early papal history are still uncertain: the evidence for Dioscuros as legitimate pope is perhaps stronger than the evidence for Boniface II (No. 55); Leo VIII (No. 132) is an antipope if the deposition of John XII (No. 131) was illegal, and if Leo VIII was a legitimate pope, Benedict V (No. 133) is an antipope; and if the triple deposition of Benedict IX (No. 146) was illegal, Sylvester III, Gregory VI, and Clement II (Nos. 147, 149, 150) must rank as antipopes. Among the popes named John there was never a John XX. The title 'pope' was first assumed by John VIII (d. 882); the triple tiara first appears on the sepulchral effigy of Benedict XII (d. 1342). Adrian IV (d. 1159) was the only English pope, Gregory XI (d. 1378) the last French pope and Adrian VI (d. 1523) the last non-Italian pope, before John Paul II. Anacletus II (d. 1138) was a converted Jew. 'Pope Joan' is placed between John V (d. 686) and Conon.

The names of antipopes and of illegal occupants of the papal chair and particulars as to papal tombs imperfectly identified or no longer in existence are enclosed in square brackets[]. Conjectural dates are followed by a query (?). The title of each pope is given, together with the date of his consecration (for the early popes) or of his election (from Gelasius II onward; No. 162), the date of his death, the duration of his pontificate, and, as far as possible, his birthplace, family name, and place of interment. Martyred popes are indicated by the letter M. Most of the early tombs in the old basilica of St Peter were scattered or lost on the demolition of the church by Julius II; but some of the remains of the popes were collected in two ossuaries in the Grotte Vaticane.

St Peter's remains are preserved beneath the altar of the Confession in St Peter's and the thirteen following popes are believed to be interred close by. Churches mentioned below are in Rome, unless otherwise indicated.

1. **St Peter**; M.; 42–67
2. **St Linus** of Tuscia (Volterra?); M.; 67–78
3. **St Anacletus I**, of Rome; M.; 78–90 (?)
4. **St Clement I**, of the Roman Flavian gens; M.; 90–99 (?).
5. **St Evaristus**, of Greece (or of Bethlehem); M.; 99–105 (?)
6. **St Alexander I**, of Rome; M.; 105–115 (?)
7. **St Sixtus I**, of Rome, M.; 115–125 (?)
8. **St Telesphorus**, of Greece; M.; 125–136 (?)
9. **St Iginus**, of Greece; M.; 136–140(?)
10. **St Pius I**, of Italy; M.; 140–155 (?)
11. **St Anicetus**, of Syria; M.; 155–166 (?)
12. **St Soter**, of Campania (Fundi?); M.; 166–175 (?)
13. **St Eleutherus**, of Epirus (Nicopolis?); M.; 175–189

14. **St Victor I**, of Africa; M.; 189–199
15. **St Zephyrinus**, of Rome; M.; 199–217.
16. **St Calixtus**, of Rome; M.; 217–222. [**Hippolytus**, 217–235]
17. **St Urban I**, of Rome; M.; 222–230.
18. **St Pontianus**, of Rome; M.; 21 July 230–28 Sept. 235
19. **St Anterus**, of Greece; M.; 21 Nov. 235–3 Jan. 236.
20. **St Fabian**, of Rome; M.; 10 Jan. 236–20 Jan. 250.
21. **St Cornelius**, of Rome; M.; March 251–June 253.
[**Novatian**, 251–258]
22. **St Lucius I**, of Rome; M.; 25 June 253–5 March 254.
23. **St Stephen I**, of Rome; M.; 12 May 254–2 Aug. 257.
24. **St Sixtus II**, of Greece (?); M.; 30 Aug. 257–6 Aug. 258.
25. **St Dionysius**, of Magna Graecia (?);

M.; 22 July 259–26 Dec. 268.

26. **St Felix I**, of Rome; M.; 5 Jan. 269–30 Dec. 274.

27. **St Eutychianus**, of Luni; M.; 4 Jan. 275–7 Dec. 283.

28. **St Caius**, of Dalmatia (Salona?); M.; 17 Dec. 283–22 April 296.

29. **St Marcellinus**, of Rome; M.; 30 June 296–25 Oct. 304.

30. **St Marcellus I**, of Rome; M.; 27 May 308–16 Jan. 309.

31. **St Eusebius,** of Greece; M.; 18 April 309–17 Aug. 309 or 310.

32. **St Melchiades** or *Miltiades*, of Africa; M.; 2 July 311–11 Jan. 314.

33. **St Sylvester I**, of Rome; 31 Jan. 314–31 Dec. 335.

34. **St Mark**, of Rome; 18 Jan. 336–7 Oct. 336.

35. **St Julius I**, of Rome; 6 Feb. 337–12 April 352.

36. **Liberius**, of Rome; 17 May 352–22 Sept. 366.

[**St Felix II**, 355–22 Nov. 365.] Tomb on the Via Aurelia Vetus

37. **St Damasus I**, of Spain; 1 Oct. 366–11 Dec. 384.

[**Ursinus**, 366–367]

38. **St Siricius**, of Rome; 15 Dec. 384–26 Nov. 399.

39. **St Anastasius I**, of Rome; 27 Nov. 399–19 Dec. 401.

40. **St Innocent I**, of Albano; 22 Dec. 401–12 March 417.

41. **St Zosimus**, of Greece; 18 March 417–26 Dec. 418.

42. **St Boniface I**, of Rome; 29 Dec. 418–4 Sept. 422.

[**Eulalius**, 27 Dec. 418–3 April 419]

43. **St Calelestinus I**, of Campania; 10 Sept. 422–27 July 432. I

44. **St Sixtus III**, of Rome; 3 July (?) 432–19 Aug. 440. I

45. **St Leo I** the Great, of Tusculum; 29 Sept. 440–10 Nov. 461.

46. **St Hilarius**, of Sardinia; 19 Nov. 461–29 Feb. 468. I

47. **St Simplicius**, of Tivoli; 3 March 468–10 March 483.

48. **St Felix III** (II), of Rome, of the Gens Anicia; 13 March 483–1 March 492.

49. **St Gelasius I**, of Africa; 1 March 492–21 Nov. 496.

50. **St Anastasius II**, of Rome; 24 Nov. 496–19 Nov. 498.

51. **St Symmachus**, of Sardinia; 22 Nov. 498–19 July 514.

[**Laurentius**, Nov. 498–505]

52. **St Hormisdas**, of Frosinone; 20 July 514–6 Aug. 523.

53. **St John I**, of Tusculum; M.; 13 Aug. 523–18 May 526. Died at Ravenna.

54. **St Felix IV** (III), of Samnium (Benevento?); 12 July 526–22 Sept. 530.

55. **Boniface II**, of Rome; 22 Sept. 530–7 Oct. 532.

[**Dioscurus**, 22 Sept. 530–14 Oct. 530]

56. **John II**, of Rome; 2 Jan. 533–8 May 535.

57. **St Agapitus I**, of Rome; 13 May 535–22 April 536. Died at Constantinople.

58. **St Silverius**, of Frosinone; M.; 8 June 536–deposed 11 March 537. Died in exile on the island of Ponza 538 (?).

59. **Vigilius**, of Rome; June 538 (?)–7 June 555 (but elected 29 March 537). Died at Syracuse.

60. **Pelagius I**, of Rome; 16 April 556–4 March 561.

61. **John III**, of Rome; 17 July 561–13 July 574.

62. **Benedict I**, of Rome; 2 June 575–30 July 579.

63. **Pelagius II**, of Rome; 26 Nov. 579–7 Feb. 590.

64. **St Gregory I** the Great, of Rome, of the Gens Anicia; 3 Sept. 590–13 March 604.

65. **Sabinianus**, of Tusculum; 13 Sept. 604–22 Feb. 606.

66. **Boniface III**, of Rome; 19 Feb. 607–12 Nov. 607.

67. **St Bonifaee IV**, of Valeria de' Marsi; 25 Aug. 608–8 May 615.

68. St Deusdedit I, of Rome; 19 Oct. 615–8 Nov. 618.

69. **Boniface V**, of Naples; 23 Dec. 619–25 Oct. 625.

70. **Honorius I**, of Campania; 27 Oct. 625–12 Oct. 638.

71. **Severinus**, of Rome; 28 May 640–2 Aug. 640.

72. **John IV**, of Dalmatia; 24 Dec. 640–12 Oct. 642.

73. **Theodore I**, of Jerusalem (? or Greece); 24 Nov. 642–14 May 649.

74. **St Martin I**, of Todi; M.; 21 July 649–exiled 18 June 653–16 Sept. 655. Died at Sebastopol

75. **St Eugenius I**, of Rome, 16 Sept. 655–2 June 657.

76. **St Vitalian**, of Segni; 30 July 657–27 Jan. 672.

77. **Deusdedit II**, of Rome; 11 April 672–17 June 676.

78. **Donus**, of Rome; 2 Nov. 676–11 April 678.

79. **St Agatho**, of Sicily; 27 June 678–10 Jan. 681.

80. **St Leo II**, of Sicily; 17 Aug. 682–3 July 683.

81. **St Benedict II**, of Rome; 26 June 684–8 May 685.

82. **John V**, of Antioch; 23 July 685–2 Aug. 686.

83. **Conon**, of Thrace; 21 Oct. 686–21 Sept. 687.

[**Theodore**, 22 Sept. 687–Oct. 687]
[**Paschal**, 687]

84. **St Sergius I**, of Palermo; 15 Dec. 687–8 Sept. 701.

85. **John VI**, of Greece; 30 Oct. 701–11 Jan. 705.

86. **John VII**, of Greece; 1 March 705–18 Oct. 707.

87. **Sisinnius**, of Syria; 15 Jan. 708–4 Feb. 708 708

88. **Constantine**, of Syria; 25 March 708–9 April 715.

89. **St Gregory II**, of Rome 19 May 715–11 Feb. 731.

90. **St Gregory III**, of Syria; 18 March 731–10 Dec. 741.

91. **St Zacharias**, of Greece; 10 Dec. 741–22 March 752.

92. **Stephen II**, of Rome; 23 March 752–25 March 752

93. **St Stephen III**, of Rome; 26 March 752–26 April 757.

94. **St Paul I**, of Rome; 29 May 757–28 June 767.

[**Constantine II**, 5 July 767–murdered 769]

[**Philip**, elected 31 July 768–abdicated 768]

95. **Stephen IV**, of Sicily; 7 Aug. 768–3 Feb. 772.

96. **Hadrian I**, of Rome; 9 Feb. 772–26 Dec. 795

97. **St Leo III**, of Rome; 27 Dec. 795–12 June 816.

98. **St Stephen V**, of Rome; 22 June 816–14 Jan. 817.

99. **St Paschal I**, of Rome; 25 Jan. 817–11 Feb. 824.

100. **Eugenius II**, of Rome; 21 Feb. 824–27 Aug. 827. 824

101. **Valentine**, of Rome; Aug. (?) 827–Sept. (?) 827.

102 **Gregory IV**, of Rome; Oct. 827–25

Jan. 844.

103. **Sergius II**, of Rome; Jan. 844–27 Jan. 847.

[**John**, 844]

104. **St Leo IV**, of Rome; 10 April 847–17 July 855.

105. **St Benedict III**, of Rome; 6 Oct. 855–17 April 858.

[**Anastasius**, 29 Sept. 855–20 Oct. 855] 855

106. **St Nicholas I**, the Great, of Rome; 24 April 858–13 Nov. 867.

107. **Hadrian II**, of Rome; 14 Dec. 867–14 Dec. 872.

108. **John VIII**, of Rome, 14 Dec. 872–16 Dec. 882.

109. **Marinus I** (Martin II) of Gallesium; 16 Dec. 882–15 May 884.

110. **St Hadrian III**, of Rome; 17 May 884–17 Sept. 885.

111. **Stephen VI**, of Rome; Sept. 885–Sept. 891.

112. **Formosus**, bishop of Porto; 6 Oct. 891–4 April 896.

113. **Boniface VI**, of Gallesium; April 896 896

114. **Stephen VII**, of Rome; May 896–Aug. 897.

115. **Romanus**, of Gallesium; Aug. 897–end of Nov. 897 897

116. **Theodore II**, of Rome; Dec. 897–Dec. 897 897

117. **John IX**, of Tivoli; Jan. 898–Jan. 900.

118. **Benedict IV**, of Rome; Jan. 900–end July 903.

119. **Leo V**, of Ardea; end of July 903–Sept. 903. Deposed and imprisoned.

[**Christopher**, of Rome; 903, deposed in Jan. 904]

120. **Sergius III**, of Rome; 29 Jan. 904–14 April 911.

121. **Anastasius III**, of Rome; April 911–June 913.

122. **Lando**, of Sabina; end of July 913–Feb. 914 913

123. **John X**, of Ravenna; March 914–May 928. Strangled in prison.

124. **Leo VI**, of Rome; May 928–Dec. 928.

125. **Stephen VIII**, of Rome; Jan. 929–Feb. 931 929

126. **John XI**, of Rome; Son of Pope Sergius III and Marozia; March 931–Dec. 935.

127. **Leo VII**; 3 (?) Jan. 936–13 (?) July 939 936

128. **Stephen IX**, of Germany (?); 14 (?)

July 939–end of Oct. 942 939
129. **Marinus II** (Martin III), of Rome; 30 (?) Oct. 942–May 946 942
130. **Agapitus II**, of Rome; 10 May 946–Dec. 955.
131. **John XII**, Ottaviano, of the family of the Counts of Tusculum, aged 19 yr; 16 (?) Dec. 955–deposed 14th May 964.
132. **Leo VIII**, of Rome, 4 Nov. 963–1 March 965 963
133. **Benedict V**, Grammatico, of Rome; 22 (?) May 964 expelled from the pontical see 23 June 964; died at Bremen 4 July 966.
134. **John XIII**, of Rome; 1 Oct. 965–5 Sept. 972.
135. **Benedict VI**, of Rome; 19 Jan. 973–June 974. Strangled in prison 973
[**Boniface VII**, Francone, of Rome; June–July 974 for the first time]
136. **Benedict VII**, of the family of the Counts of Tusculum, of Rome; Oct. 974–10 July 983.
137. **John XIV**, of Pavia; Dec. 983–20 Aug. 984; killed by Francone (Boniface VII).
[**Boniface VII**, Francone; for the second time, Aug. 984–murdered July 985]
138. **John XV**, of Rome; Aug. 985–March 996 985
139. **Gregory V**, Bruno, of the family of the Counts of Carinthia; 3 May 996–18 Feb. 999.
[**John XVI**, John Philagathus, of Greece; March 997–Feb. 998]
140. **Sylvester II**, Gerbert of Aurillc, Auvergne; 2 April 999–12 May 1003.
141. **John XVII**, Sicco, of Rome; June (?) 1003–6 Nov. 1003.
142. **John XVIII**, of Rapagnano; Jan. (?) 1004–July (?) 1009.
143. **Sergius IV**, of Rome; 31 July 1009–12 May 1012.
144. **Benedict VIII**, John, of the family of the Counts of Tusculum, of Rome; 18 May 1012–9 April 1024 1012
[**Gregory**, 1012]
145. **John XIX**, of Rome, brother of Benedict VIII; April 1024–1032 1024
146. **Benedict IX**, Theophylact, of the family of the Counts of Tusculum; elected (at 15 yr of age) for the 1st time in 1032–deposed in Dec. 1044; elected for the 2nd time 10 March 1045–deposed 1 May 1045; elected for the 3rd time 8 Nov. 1047–deposed 17 July 1048.
147. **Sylvester III**, John, bishop of

Sabina; 20 Jan. 1045–deposed 10 March 1045 1045
148. **Gregory VI**, Gratian, of Rome; 5 May 1045–banished 20 Dec. 1046; died 1047 1045
149. **Clement II**, Suidger, bishop of Bamberg; 25 Dec. 1046–died at Pesaro 9 Oct. 1047.
150. **Damasus II**, Poppo, bishop of Bressanone, of Bavaria; 17 July 1048–9 Aug. 1048. Died at Palestrina.
151. **St Leo IX**, Bruno, of Germany, bishop of Toul; 12 Feb. 1049–19 April 1054.
152. **Victor II**, Gebhard, of Germany, bishop of Eichstätt; 16 April 1055–28 July 1057. Died at Arezzo.
153. **Stephen X**, Frédéric, of the family of the Dukes of Lorraine; 3 Aug. 1057–29 March 1058.
[**Benedict X**, of Rome; 5 April 1058–deposed 24 Jan. 1059.
154. **Nicholas II**, Gérard de Bourgogne; 24 Jan. 1059–27 (?) July 1061 1059
155. **Alexander II**, Anselmo of Milan; 30 Sept. 1061–21 April 1073.
[**Honorius II**, appointed by Imperial Diet of Basle 1061–1072]
156. **St Gregory VII**, Hildebrand, di Bonizio Aldobrandeschi, of Sovana; 22 April 1073–25 May 1085.
[**Clement III**, Ghiberto; 25 Jan. 1080–Sept. 1100]
157. **B. Victor III**, Desiderio Epifani, of Benevento; elected 24 May 1086, consecrated 9 May 1087–16 Sept. 1087.
158. **B. Urban II**, of Reims; 12 March 1088–29 July 1099.
159. **Paschal II**, Rainiero, of Breda; 14 Aug. 1099–21 Jan. 1118.
[**Theodoric**, Sept.–Dec. 1100; epigraph in the cemetery of La Cava]
[**Albert**, Feb.–March 1102]
[**Sylvester IV**, 18 Nov. 1105–12 April 1111]
160. **Gelasius II**, Giov. Caetani, of Gaeta; 24 Jan. 1118–28 Jan. 1119
[**Gregory VIII**, Maurice Bourdain, of Limoges, 8 March 1118–deposed April 1121]
161. **Calixtus II**, Gui de Bourgogne, of Quingey; 2 Feb. 1119–13 Dec. 1124.
162. **Honorius II** Lamberto Scannabecchi, of Fanano (Modena); 15 Dec. 1124–13 Feb. 1130.
163. **Innocent II**, Gregorio Papareschi, of Trastevere; 14 Feb. 1130–24 Sept. 1143.

[**Anacletus II**, Pierleone, a converted Jew; 14 Feb. 1130–25 Jan. 1138]

[**Victor IV**, Gregorio da Monticelli, elected 15 March 1138, abdicated 29 May 1138]

164. **Celestine II**, Guido, of Città di Castello; 26 Sept. 1143–8 March 1144.

165. **Lucius II**, Gerardo Caccianemici dell'Orso, of Bologna; 12 March 1144–15 Feb. 1145.

166. **B. Eugenius III**, Bernardo Paganelli, of Montemagno (Pisa); 15 Feb. 1145–8 July 1153.

167. **Anastasius IV**, Corrado, of the Suburra, Rome; 12 July 1153–3 Dec. 1154.

168. **Hadrian IV**, Nicholas Breakspeare, of Bedmond (Hertfordshire, England); 4 Dec. 1154–1 Sept. 1159. Died at Anagni.

169. **Alexander III**, Rolando Bandinelli, of Siena; 7 Sept. 1159–30 Aug. 1181. Died at Civita Castellana.

[**Victor IV** (V), Ottaviano; 7 Oct. 1159–20 April 1164]

[**Paschal III**, Guido da Crema; 22 April 1164–20 Sept. 1168]

[**Calixtus III**, John of Strumio, a Hungarian, Sept. 1168, abdicated 29 Aug. 1178]

[**Innocent III**, Lando Frangipane of Sezze, elected 29 Sept. 1179, deposed in Jan. 1180]

170. **Lucius III**, Ubaldo Allucingoli, of Lucca; 1 Sept. 1181–25 Nov. 1185. Died in exile at Verona.

171. **Urban III**, Uberto Crivelli, of Milan; 25 Nov. 1185–20 Oct. 1187. Died at Ferrara.

172. **Gregory VIII**, Alberto di Morra, of Benevento; 21 Oct. 1187–17 Dec. 1187.

173. **Clement III**, Paolino Scolare, of Rome; 19 Dec. 1187–Mar 1191.

174. **Celestine III**, Giacinto Bobone Orsini, of Rome; 30 March 1191–8 Jan. 1198.

175. **Innocent III**, Lotario dei Conti di Segni, of Anagni; 8 Jan. 1198–16 July 1216. Died at Perugia.

176. **Honorius III**, Cencio Savelli, of Rome; elected in Perugia, 18 July 1216–died at Rome, 18 March 1227.

177. **Gregory IX**, Ugolino dei Conti di Segni, of Anagni; elected at the age of 86; 19 March 1227–22 Aug. 1241.

178. **Celestine IV**, Castiglione, of Milan; 25 Oct. 1241–10 Nov. 1241.

179. **Innocent IV**, Sinibaldo Fieschi, of Genoa; 25 June 1243–7 Dec. 1254. Died at Naples

180. **Alexander IV**, Orlando dei Conti di Segni, of Anagni; 12 Dec. 1254–25 May 1261. Died at Viterbo .

181. **Urban IV**, Hyacinthe Pantaléon, of Troyes; elected at Viterbo 29 Aug. 1261; died at Perugia 2 Oct. 1264.

182. **Clement IV**, Gui Foulques Le Gros, of St-Gilles; elected at Viterbo 5 Feb. 1265–died at Viterbo 29 Nov. 1268.

183. **Gregory X**, Teobaldo Visconti of Piacenza; elected at Viterbo 1 Sept. 1271–died at Arezzo 10 Jan. 1276.

184. **Innocent V**, Pierre de Champagny, of the Tarentaise; 21 Jan. 1276–22 June 1276.

185. **Hadrian V**, Ottobono de' Fieschi, of Genoa; elected at Rome 11 July 1276–18 Aug. 1276.

186. **John XXI**, Pedro Juliao, of Lisbon; elected at Viterbo 8 Sept. 1276–20 May 1277.

187. **Nicholas III**, Giov. Gaetano Orsini, of Rome; elected at Viterbo 25 Nov. 1277–died at Soriano nel Cimino 22 Aug. 1280.

188. **Martin IV**, Simon de Brion, of Montpincé in Brie; elected at Viterbo 22 Feb. 1281–died at Perugia 28 March 1285.

189. **Honorius IV**, Iacopo Savelli, of Rome; elected at Perugia 2 April 1285–3 April 1287.

190. **Nicholas IV**, Girolamo Masci, of Lisciano di Ascoli; 15 Feb. 1288–4 April 1292.

191. **St Celestine V**, Pietro Angeleri da Morrone; of Isérnia, 5 July 1294–abdicated 13 Dec. 1294. Died in the Castello di Fumone near Alatri 19 May 1296. I

192. **Boniface VIII**, Benedetto Gaetani, of Anagni; 24 Dec. 1294–11 or 12 Oct. 1303.

193. **B. Benedict XI**, Niccolò Boccasini, of Treviso; 22 Oct. 1303–died at Perugia 7 July 1304.

194. **Clement V**, Bertrand de Got, of Villandraut, near Bordeaux; elected at Perugia 5 June 1305, died at Roquemaure 14 April 1314.

195. **John XXII**, Jacques d'Euse, of Cahors; elected at Avignon 7 Aug. 1316–died at Avignon 4 Dec. 1334.

[**Nicholas V**, Pietro da Corvara, 12 May 1328–30 Aug. 1330]

196. **Benedict XII**, Jacques Fournier, of Saverdun, near Toulouse; 20 Dec.

1334–25 April 1342.

197. **Clement VI**, Pierre Roger de Beaufort, of Château Maumont, near Limoges; 7 May 1342–6 Dec. 1352.

198. **Innocent VI**, Etienne d'Aubert, of Mont, near Limoges; 18 Dec. 1352–12 Sept. 1362.

199. **Urban V**, Guillaume de Grimoard, of Grisac, near Mende in Languedoc; 16 Oct. 1362–19 Dec. 1370.

200. **Gregory XI**, Pierre Roger de Beaufort, nephew of Clement VI, of Château Maumont, near Limoges; elected at Avignon 30 Dec. 1370–died at Rome 27 March 1378.

201. **Urban** VI, Bart. Prigano, of Naples; 9 April 1378–15 Oct. 1389.

202. **Boniface IX**, Pietro Tomacelli, of Naples; 2 Nov. 1389–1 Oct. 1404.

203. **Innocent VII**, Cosimo de' Migliorati, of Sulmona; 17 Oct. 1404–6 Nov. 1406.

204. **Gregory XII**, Angelo Correr, of Venice; 30 Nov. 1406–abdicated 4 June 1415–died at Recanati 17 Oct. 1417.

Popes at Avignon:

[**Clement VII**, Robert of Savoy, of Geneva; elected at Fondi 20 Sept. 1378–16 Sept. 1394]

[**Benedict XIII**, Pedro de Luna, of Aragon; 28 Sept. 1394–23 May 1423]

Antipopes at Avignon:

[**Clement VIII**, Gil Sanchez Muñoz, of Barcelona; 10 June 1423–16 July 1429]

[**Benedict XIV**, Bernard Garnier; 12 Nov. 1425–1430 (?)]

Popes at Pisa:

[**Alexander V**, Pietro Filargis, of Candia; 26 June 1409–3 May 1410.

[**John XXIII**, Baldassarre Cossa, of Naples; 17 May 1410, deposed 29 May 1415–died at Florence 23 Dec. 1419.

205. **Martin V**, Oddone Colonna, of Genazzano; elected (aged 50) at Constance, 11 Nov. 1417–20 Feb. 1431.

206. **Eugenius IV**, Gabriele Condulmero of Venice; elected (aged 48) 3 March 1431–23 Feb. 1447.

[**Felix V**, Amadeus, duke of Savoy; 5 Nov. 1439–7 April 1449; died 1451 at the Château de Ripaille on the Lake of Geneva] 1447

207. **Nicholas V**, Tommaso Parentucelli, of Sarzana; elected (aged 49) 6 March 1447–24 March 1455.

208. **Calixtus III**, Alfonso Borgia, of Xativa, in Spain; elected (aged 78) 8 April 1455–6 Aug. 1458.

209. **Pius II**, Aeneas Silvius Piccolomini,

of Corsignano (Pienza); elected (aged 53) 19 Aug. 1458–15 Aug. 1464.

210. **Paul II**, Pietro Barbo, of Venice; elected (aged 48) 30 Aug 1464–26 July 1471.

211. **Sixtus IV**, Fr. della Rovere, of Savona; elected (aged 57) 9 Aug 1471–12 Aug 1484.

212. **Innocent VIII**, G. B. Cibo, of Genoa; elected (aged 52) 29 Aug 1484–25 July 1492.

213. **Alexander VI**, Roderigo Lenzuoli-Borgia, Valencia, Spain; elected (aged 62) 11 Aug 1492–18 Aug 1503.

214. **Pius III**, Fr. Todeschini-Piccolomini, of Siena; elected (aged 64) 22 Sept. 1503–18 Oct 1503.

215. **Julius** II, Giuliano della Rovere, of Savona; elected (aged 60) 31 Oct 1503–21 Feb 1513.

216. **Leo X**, Giov. de' Medici, of Florence; elected (aged 38) 9 March 1513–1 Dec 1521.

217. **Adrian VI**, Adrian Florisz Dedel, of Utrecht; elected (aged 63) 9 Jan 1522–14 Sept 1523.

218. **Clement VII**. Giulio de' Medici, of Florence; elected (aged 45) 19 Nov 1523–25 Sept 1534.

219. **Paul III**, Aless. Farnese, of Camino (Rome) or of Viterbo (?), elected (aged 66) 13 Oct 1534–10 Nov 1549.

220. **Julius III**, Giov. Maria Ciocchi del Monte, of Monte San Savino, near Arezzo; elected (aged 63) 7 Feb 1550–23 March 1555.

221. **Marcellus II**, Marcello Cervini, of Montefano (Macerata); elected (aged 54) 9 April 1555–30 April 1555.

222. **Paul IV**, Giov. Pietro Caraffa, of Capriglio, Avellino; elected (aged 79) 23 May 1555–18 Aug 1559.

223. **Pius IV**, Giov. Angelo de' Medici, of Milan; elected (aged 60) 26 Dec 1559–9 Dec 1565.

224. **St Pius V,** Ant. Ghislieri, of Bosco Marengo, near Tortona; elected (aged 62) 7 Jan 1566–1 May 1572.

225. **Gregory XIII**, Ugo Boncompagni, of Bologna; elected (aged 70) 13 May 1572–10 April 1585.

226. **Sixtus V**, Felice Peretti, of Grottammare; elected (aged 64) 24 April 1585–27 Aug 1590.

227. **Urban VII**, G. B. Castagna, of Rome; elected (aged 69) 15 Sept 1590–27 Sept 1590.

228. GREGORY XIV, Niccolò Sfondrati, of

Cremona; elected (aged 55) 5 Dec 1590–15 Oct 1591.

229. **Innocent IX**, Giov. Ant. Facchinetti, of Bologna; elected (aged 72) 29 Oct 1591–30 Dec 1591.

230. **Clement VIII**, Ippolito Aldobrandini, of Fano; elected (aged 56) 30 Jan 1592–3 March 1605.

231. **Leo XI**, Aless. de' Medici, of Florence; elected (aged 70) 1 April 1605–27 April 1605.

232. **Paul V**, Camillo Borghese, of Rome; elected (aged 53) 16 May 1605–28 Jan 1621.

233. **Gregory XV**, Aless. Ludovisi, of Bologna; elected (aged 67) 9 Feb 1621–8 July 1623.

234. **Urban VIII**, Maffeo Barberini, of Florence; elected (aged 55) 6 Aug 1623–29 July 1644.

235. **Innocent X**, G. B. Pamphilj, of Rome; elected (aged 72) 15 Sept 1644–7 Jan 1655.

236. **Alexander VII**, Fabio Chigi, of Siena; elected (aged 56) 7 April 1655–22 May 1667.

237. **Clement IX**, Giulio Rospigliosi, of Pistoia; elected (aged 67) 20 June 1667–9 Dec 1669.

238. **Clement X**, Emilio Altieri, of Rome; elected (aged 80) 29 April 1670–22 July 1676.

239. **Innocent XI**, Bened. Odescalchi, of Como; elected (aged 65) 21 Sept. 1676–11 Aug 1689.

240. **Alexander VIII**, Pietro Ottoboni, of Venice; elected (aged 79) 6 Oct 1689–1 Feb 1691.

241. **Innocent XII**, Ant. Pignatelli, of Spinazzola (Bari); elected (aged 76) 12 July 1691–27 Sept 1700.

242. **Clement XI**, Giov. Fr. Albani, of Urbino; elected (aged 51) 23 Nov 1700–19 March 1721.

243. **Innocent XIII**, Michelangelo Conti, of Rome; elected (aged 66) 8 May 1721–7 March 1724.

244. **Benedict XIII**, Vinc. Maria Orsini, of Gravina (Bari); elected (aged 75) 29 May 1724–21 Feb 1730.

245. **Clement XII**, Lor. Corsini, of Florence; elected (aged 79) 12 July 1730–6 Feb 1740.

246. **Benedict XIV**, Prospero Lambertini, of Bologna; elected (aged 65) 17 Aug 1740–3 May 1758.

247. **Clement XIII**, Carlo Rezzonico, of Venice; elected (aged 65) 6 July 1758–2 Feb 1769.

248. **Clement XIV**, Giov. Vincenzo Ganganelli, of Sant'Arcangelo di Romagna (Forlì); elected (aged 64) 19 May 1769–22 Sept 1774.

249. **Pius VI**, Angelo Braschi, of Cesena; elected (aged 58) 15 Feb 1775–29 Aug 1799. Died at Valence, France; int. in the Grotte Vaticane.

250. **Pius VII**, Giorgio Barnaba Chiaramonti, of Cesena; elected (aged 58) at Venice; 14 March 1800–died at Rome, 20 Aug 1823.

251. **Leo XII**, Annibale della Genga, born at La Genga, near Foligno; elected (aged 63) 28 Sept 1823–10 Feb 1829.

252. **Pius VIII**, Francesco Saverio Castiglioni, of Cingoli; elected (aged 69) 31 March 1829–30 Nov 1830.

253. **Gregory XVI**, Bart. Cappellari, of Belluno, elected (aged 66) 2 Feb 1831–1 June 1846.

254. **Pius IX**, Giov. Maria Mastai Ferretti, of Senigallia; elected (aged 54) 16 June 1846–7 Feb 1878.

255. **Leo XIII**, Gioacchino Pecci, of Carpineto Romano, elected (aged 68) 20 Feb 1878–20 July 1903.

256. **St Pius X**, Giuseppe Sarto, of Riese (Treviso); elected (aged 68) 4 Aug 1903–20 Aug 1914.

257. **Benedict XV**, Giacomo della Chiesa, of Genoa; elected (aged 60) 3 Sept 1914–22 Jan 1922.

258. **Pius XI**, Achille Ratti, of Desio (Milan); elected (aged 65) 6 Feb 1922–10 Feb 1939.

259. **Pius XII**, Eugenio Pacelli, of Rome; elected (aged 63) 2 March 1939–9 Oct 1958.

260. **John XXIII**, Angelo Roncalli, of Sotto il Monte, Bergamo; elected (aged 77) 28 Oct 1958–3 June 1963.

261. **Paul VI**, Giov. Battista Montini, of Brescia; elected (aged 65) 21 June 1963–6 August 1978.

262. **John Paul I**, Albino Luciani, of Forno di Canale, Belluno; elected (aged 65) 26 August 1978–29 September 1978.

263. **John Paul II**, Karol Wojtyla, of Wadowice (Krakow), Poland; elected (aged 58) 16 October 1978

Index to Artists and Architects

This index lists the Italian artists and architects mentioned in the guide. Only a few foreign artists are featured, namely those whose works are particularly well represented in Italy, such as Poussin and Rubens. In many cases the first names have been abbreviated to Ant. (Antonio or Antonello), Fr. (Francesco), Giac. (Giacomo), Giov. (Giovanni), Gius. (Giuseppe), Mich. (Michele). Artists' dates have been included where they are known.

297, 307, 312, 327, 365, 399, 400,
401, 405
Lippi, Ann. (1563–81) 172
Lippi, Filippino (son of Filippo;
1457–1504) 123, 192
Lippi, Fra Filippo (c 1406–69) 151, 192,
357
Locatelli, And. (1695–c 1741) 168
Locatelli, Pietro (1634–1710) 133
Lombardelli, G.B. (c 1540–1592) 281
Lombardi, Carlo (c 1554–1620) 113
Longhi, Luca (1507–80) 164
Longhi, Martino (the Elder; fl. 1570–d
1591) 145, 147, 244
Longhi, Martino (the Younger; 1602–60)
156, 166, 195
Longhi, Onorio (c 1569–1619) 156
Longhi, Silla (fl. 1568–1619) 129, 209
Lorenzetti, Pietro (c 1280–after 1345)
357
Lorenzetto Il (Lor. Lotti; 1490–1541) 122,
131, 161, 273, 285
Lorenzo, Bicci di (1373–1452) 75
Lorenzo, Fiorenzo di (1445–1522/25)
142
Lorenzo da Viterbo (c 1440–76) 192
Lotto, Lor. (1480–1556) 69, 127,
150–151, 162, 178–179, 188, 192,
290, 292, 345
Lucchetti, Gius. (1823–1907) 215
Ludovisi, Bern. (c 1713–49) 153
Luteri; see Dossi
Luti, Bened. (1666–1724) 163, 168, 214
Luzi, Luzio (da Todi; called Luzio Romano;
fl. 1528–73) 292, 289, 292

Maccari, Ces. (1840–1919) 127
Maccarone, Curzio 400
Macrino, d' Alba (c 1465/70–after 1528)
69
Maderno, Carlo (1556–1629) 122, 127,
132, 140, 141, 144, 146, 147, 153,
154, 158, 188, 189, 190, 191, 195,
206, 208, 211, 233, 241, 302, 311,
312, 316, 317, 385, 386, 391
Maderno, Stef. (1576–1636) 209, 273,
302, 365
Maestro dell'Incoronazione di Urbino 192
Mafai, Mario (1902–65) 180
Maggi, Paolo (d 1613) 141
Magnasco, Aless. (1681–1747) 193
Magnelli, Alberto (1888–1971) 179
Magni, Giulio (d 1930) 297, 307
Maiano, Giul. da (1432–90) 74, 123

Mainardi, Lattanzio 208
Maini, G.B. (1690–1752) 130
Mancini, Ant. (1852–1930) 180
Mancini, Fr. (c 1694–1758) 193, 319
Manenti, Vinc. (1600–74)
Manetti, Rutilio (1571–1639) 177
Manfredi, Bart. (c 1580–1620) 142, 193
Manfredi, Manfredo (1859–1927) 121,
283
Mangionello, Giuseppe 136
Manno, Fr. (1752–1831) 127
Manzù, Giac. (Manzoni Giacomo;
1908–91) 169, 180, 264, 316, 320,
351
Marabitti, Ignazio 76
Maraini, Ant. (1886–1963) 300, 330
Marangoni, Luigi (1875–1950) 75
Maratta, Carlo (1625–1713) 76–77, 123,
125, 145, 159, 162, 167, 190,
193–194, 197–198, 219, 295, 305,
320, 359, 391
Marchetti, G.B. (1730–1800) 177
Marchionni, Carlo (1702–86) 268, 321
Marchis, Tom. de (1693–1759) 250
Marco di Siena; see Pino
Marconi, Rocco (fl. 1504–29)76
Margaritone (d'Arezzo; fl. c 1262–75) 357
Mari, Giov. Ant. (fl. 1635) 129, 160
Mariani, Camillo (1567–1611) 195
Mariani, Cesare (1826–1901) 300
Marini, Marino 351
Marini, Mich. (b 1459) 73, 124
Marini, Nicola 144
Marini, Pasquale (c 1660–1712) 169
Mariotto, di Nardo (c 1373–1424) 357
Martini, Arturo (1889–1947) 180, 265,
351
Martini, Fr. di Giorgio (1439–1502) 192
Martini, Simone (c 1283–1344) 357
Martinucci, Filippo 231
Marucelli, Paolo (1594–1649) 134
Masaccio (Tommaso Guido or Tommaso di
Ser Giovanni; 1401–c 1428) 227
Mascagni, Paolo 295, 305
Mascherino, Ottaviano (1524–1606) 141,
145, 147, 189, 190, 294, 386
Massarotti, Angelo (c 1645–1732) 168
Matteini, Teodoro (1754–1831) 180
Maturino (da Firenze; ?1490–?1528) 188
Mazzola, Fr.; see Parmigianino
Mazzolino, Lud. (c 1480–1528/30) 69, 151
Mazzoni, Giulio (?1525–?1618) 141, 143,
160, 281
Mazzuoli, Gius. (1644–1725) 214

General Index